11.50 S

psychology
of
the
child
and
the
adolescent

fourth edition
Robert I. Watson
University of Florida
Henry Clay Lindgren
San Francisco State University

psychology of the child and the adolescent

Macmillan Publishing Co., Inc.
New York
Collier Macmillan Publishers
London

Copyright © 1979, Robert I. Watson and Henry Clay Lindgren

Printed in the United States of America

All rights reserved. No part of this book may be reproduced or transmitted in any form or by any means, electronic or mechanical, including photocopying, recording, or any information storage and retrieval system, without permission in writing from the Publisher.

Earlier editions Psychology of the Child, copyright © 1959, 1965 and 1973 by John Wiley & Sons, Inc.

Macmillan Publishing Co., Inc.
866 Third Avenue, New York, New York 10022

Collier Macmillan Canada, Ltd.

Library of Congress Cataloging in Publication Data

Watson, Robert Irving,   Date
  Psychology of the child and the adolescent.

  First-3d ed. published under title: Psychology of the child.
  Bibliography: p.
  Includes indexes.
  1. Child psychology. I. Lindgren, Henry Clay, 1914-   joint author. II. Title.
BF721.W33   1979   155.4   78-3423
ISBN 0-02-424600-X

Printing: 1 2 3 4 5 6 7 8   Year: 9 0 1 2 3 4 5

preface

While the fourth edition of *Psychology of the Child and the Adolescent* retains the basic theme and approach of its previous editions, we feel we have strengthened the text in several ways. As the title suggests, we have included in this edition two new chapters on adolescent development, which, we hope, will make the book more complete and useful. To assist the reader, we have added a glossary of terms and sought to simplify the writing. We have also diligently tried to incorporate the results of recent scholarship.

Some textbooks in child psychology emphasize theory and methodology. Others are primarily concerned with talking to students about the students' own experiences. We have chosen to use both of these approaches because we find each of them attractive. Without theory and methodology, psychology may be appealing in an anecdotal way, but it is not a science. We consider the scientific study of human behavior not only attractive but an important enterprise; we have devoted our lives to it. As teachers, we also know that students learn more effectively when they see how the material relates to their own lives and daily experiences. We want psychology to make sense to students; a student who, after taking a psychology course or reading a psychology textbook, does not understand himself and others at least a little better has failed, and so has his teacher or the author. In essence, our goal has been to bridge the gap between psychologists' views of child behavior and development and students' everyday experiences with children, including their memories of what it was like to be a child.

In writing this book, we have also been strongly influenced by our belief that any subject becomes more interesting and more understandable when a number of its aspects or dimensions are presented. For example, we may understand a child biologically, but our understanding is enhanced if we can also see him as a social organism, as a personality, as affecting the behavior and attitudes of others, and as being affected by others. We have tried to show a picture of the whole child in the hope that our readers will see in themselves the children they once were and will also see the children they have encountered and are now encountering.

The writers of a textbook in child psychology have special advantages in trying both to present scientific knowledge and to make it relevant to their readers. First, there is now a large body of research material and theoretical discussion dealing with many phases of child development; indeed, the amount of material is embarrassing in its richness, and the problem is to decide what to select. Second, child development is a part of everyone's experience. We have all been children; we are all likely to be in contact with children. Many students who take courses in child psychology are looking forward to careers as professionals working with children or careers as parents, often both. It is to them that we dedicate our book.

We are pleased to acknowledge the aid of many people: Fredi Lindgren, for her many helpful suggestions in planning and developing both the third and the fourth editions; Frances Knudtson of San Francisco State University, whose in-depth review of the third edition was very useful in preparing the present edition; and the professors who have used the text and sent their thoughtful comments to us.

Robert I. Watson, Gainesville, Florida

Henry Clay Lindgren, San Francisco, California

contents

photo credits/xvi

1 principles of development

one/The Study of Children and Adolescents: Then and Now /3
Ancient and Medieval Attitudes Toward Children /4
   Pioneers Who Led to Change
   The Industrial Revolution and the Nineteenth Century
   The Era of Childhood Education
The Beginnings of Child Psychology /9
   The Baby Biographers
   G. Stanley Hall and the Child Study Movement
   Binet and the Intelligence Test
   Montessori and the Training of the Senses
   Watson and Behaviorism
   Freud and Psychoanalysis
Child Psychology from 1900 to the Second World War /19
   Tests, Norms, and Individual Differences
   Child Guidance and Clinical Psychology
   Education and Educational Psychology
   Cultural Anthropology
The Modern Period in Child Psychology /24
   Child Psychology and Developmental Psychology
   Developmental and Environmental Approaches
     The Genetic/Developmental Approach
     The Environmental/Experimental Approach: Behaviorism and S-R Research
     Which Approach Today?
   Contributions of Personality and Social Psychology
   Recent Trends
   A View of Child Psychology Today
Summary /30

two/Studying Children and Adolescents Scientifically /33
Child Psychology: A Behavioral Science /34
   Looking at Children Objectively
Techniques in Behavioral Study /39
   The S-R Research Scheme
   Correlational or Differential Methods
   What Correlations Mean
Strategies in Child Study /50
   Observations
   Interviews
   La Méthode Clinique
   Unobtrusive Methods
   Projective Tests
   Cross-sectional Versus Longitudinal Research
   Clinical Treatment and Research with Children
Summary /62

three/The Process of Development /64
Growth and Development /64
Genetic Background and Development /66
   From Cell to Organism
   Studies of Twins
Trends in Development /72
   The Whole Child in a Total Environment
   Developmental Direction
   Differentiation and Integration
   Critical Periods
Piaget's Concept of Development /79
   Centration and Decentering
   The Child as an Active Agent
   Stages in Mental Development
      The Sensorimotor Stage
      The Concrete Operations Stage
      The Formal Operations Stage
   Criticisms of Piagetian Concepts
   Discontinuity and Hierarchization
Maturation and Learning /89
Summary /92

four/Socialization and Personality Development /95
Socialization /95
Learning and Socialization /97
   Classical Conditioning
   Instrumental or Operant Conditioning
   Learning Through Observation, Identification, and Imitation
      Modeling and the Learning of Altruistic Behavior
Factors Underlying Socialization /110
   Drives and Needs

    The Need for Arousal
    The Reward Value of Socialization
    Delaying Gratification
    Learning to Avoid Misbehavior
    Parental Warmth/Parental Control
Psychoanalytic Theories of Socialization and Personality Development /118
    Freudian Views of Human Motivation
        Psychoanalytic Views of Personality
        Anxiety and the Defense Mechanisms
    Stages of Psychosexual Development
    The Neo-Freudians
        The Theories of Erik Erikson
Socialization: Inside and Out /129
Summary /130

ii infancy

five/The Beginnings of Human Life /137
From Cell to Organism /137
    Life Begins
        The Biological Mother-Child Relationship
Prenatal Development /140
        From Egg to Embryo
        The Early Fetal Period
        The Later Fetal Period
    Fetal Characteristics
        Fetal Activity
        Maternal Nutrition
        Maternal Drug Use and Fetal Stress
        Medical Problems and Fetal Stress
Pregnancy and the Mother /149
    Maternal Attitudes
        Reducing Fear and Pain in Childbirth
Childbirth /154
    Rating the Health of the Newborn
    Effects of Pain-Relieving Drugs During Delivery
    Problems of Low-Birth-Weight Infants
The Neonate /159
    Physical Appearance and Bodily Proportions
    Physical Needs and Drives: Hunger and Thirst
    Sleep
    Oxygen Needs
    Need for Stimulation
Sensory Responses /165
    Reactions to Visual Stimuli

X Contents

    Reactions to Auditory Stimuli
    Reactions to Other Sensory Stimuli
Motor Responses /168
    Major Classifications
    Reflexes
    Learning in Neonates
Summary /173

six/Sensorimotor and Mental Development /176
Physical Growth /177
    Changes in Height and Weight
    Nutrition
Sensorimotor Development /184
    Learning and Maturation in Sensorimotor Skills
    Manipulation
    Locomotion
    Recent Research in Sensorimotor Development
    Early Indications of Sex Differences
Cognitive Development: A Piagetian View /191
    Interaction Between Infant and Environment
    The "Object Concept"
    Piagetian Infancy Scales
Perceptual-Conceptual Development /194
    Perception and Sensation
    Preferences for Complexity in Stimuli
    Attention to Unusual Stimuli
    Exploratory Behavior
    Depth Perception
Language Development /204
    Perception and Language Development
    Early Linguistic Development
    Developmental Patterns
    Learning Relationships Between Symbols and Objects
    Theories: Reinforcement and Nativistic
    Effects of Stimulation
Intellectual Development /214
    Developmental Scales
    Predicting Later Intellectual Development
Summary /218

seven/Caregivers and Infants /222
The Infant's Social Environment /222
    Parents as Caregivers
    The Home Environment as a Source of Stimulation
Early Stimulation /226
    Animal Research
    Research with Infants
    The Mother as a Source of Love or Attention

    Breast Feeding Versus Bottle Feeding: A Study in Maternal Attitudes
    Maternal Attitudes and Infant Behavior
Attachment and Maternal Deprivation /237
    Research Dealing with Attachment
    Attachment and Basic Trust
    Animal Research with Maternal Deprivation
    Adequate Stimulation as an Antidote to Deprivation
Attachment, Dependence and Independence /245
    Strivings for Independence
    Independence and Self-Concept
On Babysitters and Other Surrogate Mothers /249
    The Kibbutz Experience
    Working Mothers and Day Care Centers
    Animal Research
    Mothers and Mother Substitutes as Motivators
Summary /253

iii early childhood: the preschool years

eight/Physical and Cognitive Aspects of Development /259
Physical Growth and Development /260
    Height and Weight
    Health Problems
Sensorimotor Development /263
    Learning and Maturation in Sensorimotor Skills
    Stages of Motor Development
    Some Changes in Motor Skills
Cognitive Development /268
    Piagetian Concepts of Cognition
    Animism
    Centering and Conservation
    Logical Structure
Perceptual-Conceptual Development /274
    Concept Formation
        Learning Concepts of Space
        Learning About Time
Summary /279

nine/The Learning of Language and the Development of Intelligence /281
Language Development /281
    Language and Learning
    Language and Thinking

Language Development /283
  Generative/Nativistic Theories
  Environmental/Learning Theories
  Language Structure: A Tool for Understanding
  Semantics and Cognitive Development
  Growth of Vocabulary
  Individual, Group, and Sex Differences in Language Development
  Sociolinguistic Theory
  Language Development and Social-Class Differences
Intellectual Development /298
  Facilitating Intellectual Development: The Early Training Project
  Facilitating Intellectual Development: *Sesame Street*
  Longitudinal Studies of Intellectual Development
  Problem-Solving Ability
Summary /307

ten/Emotional and Personality Development /310
Emotional Development /371
  Differentiating Emotional Responses
  Emotional Responses During Infancy
Fear and Anxiety /312
  Research on Children's Fears
  Fear and Anxiety
  Violence and Children's Fantasies
Anger and Aggression /317
  Anger Research
  Cultural Influences on Aggressiveness
  Social Learning and Aggression
Emotions with Positive Affect /324
  Laughter and Arousal
  Laughter and Cognition
Personality Development /327
  Expectations of Caregivers
Independence, Dependence, and Autonomy /330
  Achieving a Balance Between Dependence and Independence
  Dependence and Independence in the Hawaiian Culture
Self-Concept Development in Preschoolers /333
  Evaluation of the Self
  Origins of Self-Concept
  Sex Typing
    Animal Research on Sex Differences in Behavior
    Maternal Views of Sex-Typed Behaviors
    Sex Typing via Social Learning
Summary /341

eleven/The Social Environment: Parents, Siblings, and Peers /344
The Family as a Social Environment /344
  Family Structure
  Ecological Factors
  Child-Rearing Practices

Developmental Influences of Caregivers' Practices and Attitudes /352
    Effects of the Caregiver on Cognitive Development
    Effects of the Caregiver on Social Development
    Influence of Fathers on Child Behavior
    Are Parents Necessary?
Influence of the Family's Social and Economic Status (SES) /362
    SES and Child-Rearing Patterns
    SES and Cognitive Development
    SES and Crowding
    Influence of Ethnicity and Minority Subculture
    SES Versus Ethnicity: Which Has the More Significant Effect?
    Questions About SES Research
Birth Order /375
    The Advantages of Being First-Born
    Parental Behavior Toward First-Borns
Peer Relationships /379
    Social Participation
    Socialization: General Trends
    Modeling and Prosocial Behavior
Summary /384

IV the middle years

twelve/Physical and Mental Development /391
Sensorimotor Development /392
    Motor Skills
    Learning and Sensorimotor Skills
    The Hyperactive-Child Syndrome
Cognitive Development /398
    Concrete Operations
    Formal Operations
    Physical Causality
    Time and Space Perception
Verbal Development /404
    Field Dependence, Brain Hemisphere Dominance, and Verbal Development
    Learning to Read
        Rapid, Silent Reading
Intellectual Development /408
    The Nature of Intelligence
    The Testing of Intelligence
        The Validity of Intelligence Tests
        Controversies over the Use and Misuse of Intelligence Tests
    Controversies over Genetic and Environmental Effects on Intelligence
        Basic Learning Ability and Problem-Solving Ability
        The Effects of a Depressing Environment
Summary /422

thirteen/Personality, Moral Development, and Parental Influence /426

Personality and Cognition /427
  Interest and Relevance in Reading
  Anxiety: Trait and State
    Anxiety, Problem Solving, and Learning
  Problem Solving by Impulsive and Reflective Children
  Locus of Control

Parental Behavior and Children's Traits /434
  Aggressiveness and Parental Models
  Parental Coerciveness, Warmth, and SES
  Parental Maladjustment and Children's Behavior Problems
  Child-Rearing Practices, Independence, and School Achievement
  Curiosity and Child-Rearing Patterns
  Achievement Motivation: The Need to Achieve (n Ach)

The Development of Self-Awareness /442
  Studies in Self-Esteem
  Under- and Overachievers
  The Ideal Self or Ego-Ideal

Moral Development /448
  Theories of Moral Development
  Piaget on Morality
  Kohlberg's Elaboration of Piaget's Stages
  An Experimental Test of Theories of Moral Development

Summary /455

fourteen/The Peer Group and the School /459

The Peer Group /460
  Peer-group Power
  Cross-cultural Variations in Peer-group Norms
  Peer Groups as Disinhibitors

Aggression and Aggressiveness /467
  Sex Differences in Aggressive Behavior
  Aggression, Hostility, and Fantasy
  Televised Violence and Aggression

Social Attraction /474
  Sociometric Studies
  Social Attraction and Similarity
  Empathy and Social Awareness
  Friendship
  The Beginnings of Prejudice
    Ethnic Prejudice

The School /484
  Behavior Modification
  Praise and Criticism
  Teachers' Attitudes Toward Children's Misbehavior
  Children's Reactions to the School Experience

Summary /497

V adolescence

fifteen/Physical, Mental, and Moral Development /503
   Adolescence: Where It Begins, but Where Does It End?
Physical Development /505
   Physiological Changes
   Physical Skills
   Do People Really Mature Earlier These Days?
   Early and Late Maturers
   Health Problems
Cognitive Development /514
   Piagetian Concepts
   Intellectual Development
   Formal Operations and Measured Intelligence
   Learning and School Achievement
   Are Young People Learning Less These Days?
Moral Judgment /524
   The Moral Views of Adolescents and Their Parents
   Educational Experiences and Moral Judgment
   Laws, Regulations, and Moral Judgment
   Cognitive Ability and Moral Judgment
Summary /530

sixteen/Personality and Social Development /533
   The Subculture of the Adolescent
Adolescents and Their Parents /535
   Dependence, Independence, and Responsibility
   Achievement and Relations with Parents
   Family Life of Users and Nonusers of Drugs
   Family Versus Peer Group
The Peer Group /543
   Conflicts Between Affiliation and Achievement
   The Popularity Cult
   What Values Do Adolescents Really Hold?
Personality /549
   Developmental Tasks
   Self-Concept and Identity Diffusion
   Problems Faced by Girls and Young Women
Occupational Choice /557
   Occupation and Identity
   Vocational Aspirations and Reality
   Part-time and Temporary Work Experiences
Sexual Adjustment /561
   Surveys of Sexual Behavior
   The Sexual Revolution
   Is There a Counterrevolution?
   Sex Differences in Sexual Attitudes

Sex and Personal Identity
Learning the Folklore of Sex
Early Experiences as Predictors of Adult Adjustment /568
Summary /569

Glossary /573

References and Author Index /585

Subject Index /611

Photo Credits

Phiz Mezey took the photographs on the following pages:
1, 36, 38 (2), 51 (2), 71 (2), 84 (2), 85 (3), 90, 102, 104, 107, 113, 118, 128, 135, 153, 156, 159, 170 (2), 171, 183, 217, 224 (upper), 225, 228, 238 (2), 257, 266 (2), 267 (2), 277, 288, 289, 300, 315 (upper two), 319, 321, 325, 335 (2), 351, 359 (2), 369 (upper right), 376 (2), 377, 381 (3), 383, 389, 392, 393, 440, 462, 469, 485, 486 (2), 487 (3), 501, 522 (2), 526, 554, 560 (2), 565.

Credits for the remaining photographs are as follows:
Frontispiece Henry Clay Lindgren
page 5, Henry Clay Lindgren (2)   7, New York Public Library (Locke, Rousseau, Pestalozzi); American Museum of Natural History (Darwin)   11, Culver (Binet); Brown Brothers (Hall); Stanford University (Terman); Italian Cultural Institute (Montessori)   18, Culver (Freud); American Museum of Natural History (Mead); Columbia University (Dewey)   22, Culver (Pavlov and Watson); Columbia University (Thorndike)   53, Courtesy of Robert R. Sears   80, Wayne Behling, Ypsilanti Press   98, Henry Clay Lindgren (2)   99, Henry Clay Lindgren (2)   106, Courtesy of Albert Bandura   126, Jon Erikson, courtesy of Erik H. Erikson   142, Landrum B. Shettles (2)   200, Courtesy of Jerome Kagan   204, G. Lewis, courtesy R. D. Walk   205, L. A. Rothblat, courtesy R. D. Walk   209, Conrad Waldinger, courtesy Fordham University   215, Courtesy Nancy Bayley   224, Henry Clay Lindgren (lower)   234, Ted Greiner   235, Ted Greiner   246, University of Wisconsin Primate Laboratory   247, University of Wisconsin Primate Laboratory   248, Courtesy H. Rheingold and H. L. Schaffer   270, George Roos   271, George Roos (2)   284, Courtesy Noam Chomsky and B. F. Skinner   313, Courtesy Arthur T. Jersild   315, Henry Clay Lindgren (lower)   369, Henry Clay Lindgren (upper left, lower left, lower right)   405, Courtesy H. A. Witkin   407, Clemens Kalischer, courtesy David Elkind   412, Courtesy of the Psychological Corporation   451, Courtesy Lawrence Kohlberg   511, Courtesy Mary Cover Jones (3)   542, Henry Clay Lindgren

i

principles of development

one

The Study of Children and Adolescents: Then and Now

> *If a large part of the justification for a child psychology is the inevitability of children, another large part must be their sentimental and strategic value to us.*
> —BAER AND WRIGHT, 1974

The most popular elective course of the psychology curriculum in colleges and univerisities is not, as you might think, abnormal psychology or the psychology of sex, but child psychology. And interest in child psychology is not limited to campuses—you need only look around you to see books, magazine articles, television programs, and newspaper stories on the subject.

Why is child psychology so popular today? One might answer that of course it is popular, as it always has been, because children are so interesting and appealing. However, even a brief review of the history of child study shows that the idea that children are inherently of interest is culture-bound—that is, it appears in some cultures, such as that of late twentieth-century America, but not in others. Our forebears lived and died for hundreds of thousands of years without showing more than a glimmer of interest in children *as children*. The interest we show today springs from a special combination of values, attitudes, and assumptions that characterize adults in our modern culture. You will find these views discussed in greater detail at various points in this book; essentially they hold: (1) children are not miniature adults, but differ from adults in many respects; (2) if we are to help children to become adequate social beings it is desirable for us to understand them; and (3) understanding children enables us to understand ourselves.

4 Principles of Development

Most of us now meet children in our everyday lives. Many of us are, or look forward to being, parents or teachers. All of us once were children.

ancient and medieval attitudes toward children

The Greeks and Romans of antiquity viewed the child as a future citizen and as a member of the family group, with fairly specific rights and responsibilities. In middle- and upper-class families, at least, children were valued for their own sake, as witness the touching memorials to children that have been found in excavations of the burying grounds adjacent to the ruins of Greek and Roman cities.

With the coming of medieval Christianity, however, life became more adult-centered; a different view prevailed, and children (as well as women) lost status. Church fathers held that, because of Adam's fall, mankind is born in sin. Thus, by extension, children bear the mark of original sin and are innately depraved. The idea that original sin could be beaten out of a child came to dominate child care for many centuries.

During the medieval period there was a great deal of vagueness (which persisted into the eighteenth and even the nineteenth centuries) about the differences between adults and children, and it was not at all clear where childhood ended and adulthood began. As Philippe Ariès (1962)[1] pointed out in his review of childhood through the centuries, medieval children from the age of three or four onward took part in adult activities of all kinds, and there was little difference between adult and child modes of dress. When the artists during the Middle Ages depicted a child (the Christ Child, for example), it was portrayed with the face, body build, and garb of an adult, only smaller. Not until 1430 did Luca della Robbia of Florence sculpt a marble choir loft decorated with singing and dancing children who looked like children, thus creating one of the first and most delightful naturalistic representations of children. Not until nearly the end of the nineteenth century did western society take steps to separate the world of children from the world of adults, marking the shift in thinking by giving children a distinctive kind of clothing, a change that came first in middle- and upper-class families and only slowly and incompletely in lower-class ones.

Thus it has taken hundreds of years for children to be generally

---

[1] When a name (or names) and a year are cited, the reference is listed under the author's name in the References and Author Index toward the end of the book.

During the Middle Ages, people seemed unaware of the unique characteristics of children—those qualities that make them "childlike." This tendency was reflected in their art. The eleventh century mosaic at the left depicts the infant Christ with the features of a young man. It was not until the Renaissance that people began to realize and to appreciate the differences between children and adults. The photograph below displays one of the scenes from Luca della Robbia's bas relief of singing children, sculpted in 1430.

regarded as having unique personalities. Today, proud parents keep pictures of their children in their wallets and purses, and every home has its photographic record of children's progress from infancy to adulthood. During the medieval period, no one bothered; "childhood was simply an unimportant phase of which there was no need to keep a record" (Ariès, 1962). For centuries, children were regarded, not as individuals with certain basic rights, but as nuisances and pieces of property. An Italian visitor to England about 1500 reported that children of both sexes were generally bound out as apprentices at the age of seven to nine for a period of from seven to nine years. Even children of the nobility were often sent away to be trained in the homes of others. So common was this placing out of children that parents were publicly criticized when they did not do it (Queen and Habenstein, 1967).

Pioneers Who Led to Change

One of the first and most influential writers to challenge these early views was John Locke (1632-1704), who believed that children were quite different from adults and merited special care. In 1693 he published the treatise *Some Thoughts Concerning Education,* in which he recommended that young children be permitted to express their feelings and be restrained only when necessary. He disagreed with the practice of apprenticing children or farming them out to other families, claiming that parents had a duty to be interested in their children's upbringing and to keep them near by as much as possible. Being a good example was, he believed, the best kind of influence. Unlike the prevailing Calvinist concepts of child rearing, his attitudes toward children seem modern: "The chief art is to make all that they have to do sport and play too."

Although Locke's book was intended for the use of English gentlemen, it received a great deal of attention throughout the British Isles and on the Continent and established its place as a landmark in educational theory.

Another writer who had great influence on attitudes toward children was the French-Swiss Jean-Jacques Rousseau (1712-1778), who, like Locke, rejected the idea of original sin and the natural depravity of childhood. Although Rousseau's recommendations regarding child rearing are full of quirks and contradictions, what comes through as one reads them is a respect for children as individuals. For example, parents should not insist that their child say "Forgive me," because the child is innocent of wrongdoing. "Wholly unmoral in his actions, he can do nothing morally wrong, and he deserves neither punishment nor reproof." In another passage, Rousseau cautions against "overteaching" a child: "Leave childhood to ripen in your children. In a word, beware of giving anything they need today if it can be deferred without danger to tomorrow."

The Study of Children and Adolescents: Then and Now 7

Pioneer figures in child study

John Locke, 1632-1704

Jean-Jacques Rousseau, 1712-1778

Johann Heinrich Pestalozzi, 1746-1827

Charles Darwin, 1809-1882

Rousseau also expressed a strong faith in the innate goodness of the child, who "is naturally disposed to kindly feeling because he sees that every one about him is inclined to help him, and from this experience he gets the habit of kindly feeling toward his species." Somehow, this basic kindliness becomes warped and frustrated as the child is integrated into society. Then he becomes "jealous, deceitful, and vindictive."

Whereas Locke, like Aristotle long before him, thought of the child as an impressionable and passive medium, shaped by his environment, Rousseau saw the child as an *active* agent in the environment. Rousseau's ideas had great influence on a number of child development specialists today, especially Jean Piaget, the Swiss psychologist whose work and ideas we shall refer to often throughout this book.

Still another Swiss, Johann Heinrich Pestalozzi (1746-1827), was a pioneer in recognizing the importance of understanding children's behavior. Pestalozzi proclaimed his faith in the inborn goodness of the child. He viewed the mother as the child's first and most significant educator and urged her to trust her maternal feelings, maintaining that even when a mother is not consciously trying to teach a child, but only to quiet him and keep him occupied, she is opening up the world to him and preparing him to use his senses and powers of observation.

The Industrial Revolution and the Nineteenth Century

Although the ideas of Locke, Rousseau, and Pestalozzi had some influence on prevalent opinions regarding child care, life for most children was still rather grim. The plight of the poor was so desperate that children were, in effect, rented or leased to employers who commonly treated them little better than animals. When the Industrial Revolution got under way in the second half of the eighteenth century, the exploitation of children became organized on a wholesale basis. Conditions were so bad that the British Parliament in 1802 passed legislation limiting a child's work day to twelve hours—it had been sixteen or more—and forbidding the employment of children under the age of nine. Unfortunately there was no provision for enforcing the law, and employers disregarded it for many years (Gaines, 1974).

This was an age when parents thought it their duty to "break the will" of their children, believing that only harsh discipline could train a child to become an acceptable social being. A middle-class American mother, writing in a woman's magazine in 1834, described her husband's procedure when their sixteen-month-old daughter refused to say "Dear Mama" on command. The infant was placed alone in a room, where she screamed wildly for ten minutes; then she was brought out and again commanded to say "Dear Mama." When the child still refused, she was whipped and the demand made again. This went on for four hours, until the child finally obeyed (Sunley, 1955).

The Era of Childhood Education

As the Industrial Revolution gathered momentum, parents as well as employers began to realize that schooling was desirable and even necessary for children. An economic world was developing that demanded employees who could do more than provide nimble fingers and muscle power; and the skills required for many of the new jobs could not be learned by imitation, as in an apprenticeship. A rapidly changing society called for people who had breadth of understanding and a good range of social and intellectual skills, people who could work together as members of organizations, initiate and conduct civic enterprises, and perform a variety of functions in different social settings.

The schooling that the elite had been providing for their children and young people served as a first model for a broader education whose primary goal was literacy, followed by understanding of the world in its customs, traditions, and practices.

Thus the modern school curriculum was born.

The harsh family discipline of the times was at first carried over into the schools virtually unchanged, but wiser schoolmasters soon realized that horses led to water do not necessarily drink, even when beaten. Furthermore, not every child of six or seven could read Cicero or do higher mathematics, and some adjustment had to be made in curricular materials, adapting them to children's levels of maturity. Initially, parents had the option of determining if their children would attend school, but in the latter part of the nineteenth century a significant number of state and provincial governments in North America passed laws making school attendance compulsory.

At first the time occupied by school attendance was minimal; but it expanded until, today, it has come to occupy almost half the waking hours of half the days of a child's life between the ages of six and sixteen and beyond. Keeping children occupied at learning tasks for longer and longer periods called for increasing amounts of skill, which in turn required understanding—and teachers began to look to child psychologists for answers to their problems about instruction and classroom management.

The problems of teachers were further complicated by the fact that the first textbooks reflected the ideas and interests of adults, not those of the children for whom they were written. As a consequence, textbook writers and publishers, as well, were forced to turn to the growing field of psychology for help in selecting materials and communicating concepts in ways that not only made sense to children but also enhanced their motivation.

the beginnings of child psychology

The Baby Biographers

By the latter part of the nineteenth century, data were accumulating that shed some light on the nature of children. Charles Darwin (1809-

1882), who is best known for his theory of evolution, was one of the first to make systematic observations of child behavior. In 1877 he published his diary of his infant son, based on observations he had begun in 1840. This account showed Darwin to be a sympathetic, understanding, affectionate father, in keeping with the new spirit of the times.

The work of Darwin and others on the study of evolution did much to stimulate scholars' interest in the study of the child. Evidence derived from the study of children was utilized to test the hypothesis of man's descent from animals, for the infant was regarded as a link between animals and the human race.

Closely allied to this idea was the theory of recapitulation, which held that each child relived or successively passed through the different stages of the evolution of animal life (described by the phrase "ontogeny recapitulates phylogeny," which a modern advertiser might well be proud to have coined). The crawling of the infant was said to replicate the swimming of fishes; creeping, the locomotion of mammals; and running, the movement of men. Researchers sought indications that specific behaviors had survived from prehuman eras, as in the grasp or "Darwinian" reflex, which, according to this theory, came about because the primate infant clung to its mother or a tall branch for protection.

An even more ambitious study than Darwin's was the "baby biography" of the physiologist William Thierry Preyer (1841-1897), who took careful, detailed notes of his son's behavior during the first four years of life, noting the development of reflexes and the influence of experience and learning. In 1882, he published his observations under the title *The Mind of the Child*, one of the great classics of child psychology.

As scientific documents, these "naturalistic" accounts had many weaknesses. The observers, for all their intent to be dispassionate and objective, were inclined to see what they were looking for. They also tended to note only positive factors—an understandable bias, when they were recording the behavior of their own children. Furthermore, their methods were often not very systematic; observations were often recorded some time after the event, and the children being studied were probably not very typical of children in general. In spite of such weaknesses, these and other baby biographies laid the groundwork for more scientific approaches to child study, in that they raised questions that could later be resolved by the use of improved methods.

G. Stanley Hall and the Child Study Movement

The writings of Darwin and Preyer helped kindle a great deal of enthusiasm in Europe for the naturalistic study of children. The psychologist who did more than anyone else to import this enthusiasm into America was G. Stanley Hall (1844-1924). Hall, who is considered the father of the child study movement, was committed to the idea that

The Study of Children and Adolescents: Then and Now 11

Pioneer educators and psychologists who influenced important trends in child study early in the twentieth century

G. Stanley Hall

Alfred Binet, 1857-1911

Lewis Madison Terman, 1857-1956

Maria Montessori, 1870-1952

"the study of development was at the heart of the problem of understanding man" (Kessen, 1965). He was especially intrigued by the Darwinian theories of evolution and recapitulation, and was convinced that the development of each individual today corresponds more or less to the experiences that our ancestors went through at various stages during the history of the race. In order to secure data supporting his theory, Hall asked teachers to question their pupils about their experiences. The information that the teachers transmitted to Hall enabled him to accumulate a vast amount of information on children's behavior, impressions, feelings, problems, and beliefs. Hall found these data a rich mine for a number of research projects and published reports on children's lies and the contents of their minds, to cite two examples. The data on which these reports were based were essentially introspective, in the sense that they consisted of the observations the children made of their own behavior. Introspection was, however, a legitimate scientific technique in Hall's day, and it was not until John B. Watson and the other behaviorist psychologists questioned it a few years later that it fell out of favor.

Methodologically, Hall's approach was an improvement over both earlier and later studies because he developed and used a standardized report form—the questionnaire. In his first study, for example, he used specially selected teachers, trained them in uniform methods of questioning, and met with them frequently for evaluation and discussion during the collection of data. Later, he and his students began the practice of circulating questionnaires on various topics to teachers and parents throughout the country. A great deal of information was thus collected in a relatively short time over a wide geographical area.

Hall broadened the scope of his research by circulating questionnaires to other adults, who were asked to record their experiences as children. These sources yielded data that Hall published in the form of reports on children's appetites, fears, punishments, dreams, toy preferences, early sense of self, prayers, perceptions of rhythm, and motor abilities.

In analyzing the data from his questionnaires, Hall used only the simplest of statistical devices. His direct questioning of children, unfortunately, allowed them to be evasive and careless in their replies, often giving the answer they thought he wanted. The untrained recorders he employed were also guilty of many sins of omission and commission. Parents and teachers uncritically and enthusiastically mixed into their reports the results of their own unscientific investigations and impressions.

Such excesses proved to be the undoing of the early child study movement. Hall himself lost enthusiasm and turned his energies toward his other manifold interests, especially the psychology of religion and the aging process.

In spite of its shortcomings, the child study movement of the late nineteenth and early twentieth centuries made positive contributions to child psychology in the initial stages of development. It led to recognition of the value of studying children's behavior objectively and scientifically; it promoted awareness of the deficiencies of unsystematic observations; and it caused people to acknowledge the importance of childhood as a worthy subject for investigation. Moreover, Hall's questionnaire approach was the forerunner of modern survey methods and of personality testing.

Binet and the Intelligence Test

In 1904, the French Minister of Education named a commission to consider proposals to provide mentally retarded Paris schoolchildren with the best possible educational training. This commission decided that no child suspected of mental retardation should be transferred from ordinary classes without first taking a special examination. The task of developing and applying such an examination was taken over by Alfred Binet (1857-1911). The Binet-Simon test, patriarch of all later psychological tests, was thus the direct result of an administrative decision.

The first great advance that Binet made in intelligence testing was to abandon the artifically simplified laboratory tasks used in mental testing prior to his efforts. Short, discrete, simple tasks to test such abilities as tonal memory, estimation of distance, and speed of reaction had been used by early researchers and found to have little predictive value in work with children. Whatever they were measuring, it was not intelligence as the term is used today.

After many years of preliminary work, Binet decided to base his test items on the more complex and realistic tasks of everyday life. In his first scale, done in collaboration with Theodore Simon in 1905, there were fifty tests, including those that required verbal knowledge of objects such as parts of the body, naming of common objects, repeating digits, drawing a design from memory, finding the right word to complete a sentence, and defining abstract terms. The tests were arranged in increasing order of difficulty.

Not until the 1908 and 1911 revisions of the scale did Binet make his second great contribution to mental testing: the grouping of tests according to the age at which they are usually passed. Mental age is the degree of intellectual development of an individual, arrived at by comparing his performance with that of other individuals of the same chronological age. Thus, a mental age of ten years is the degree of intellectual development attained by the average child of ten, although a ten-year-old may have a greater or a lesser mental age. By means of this procedure, a frame of reference was established for the interpretation of test results. Of course, crude comparisons using something analogous to this concept had been known before, as exemplified in remarks such as "He has no more sense than a child." But it was Binet's work that firmly established the assessment of intelligence test results in quantitative form.

In the United States, Lewis Madison Terman, a student of G. Stanley Hall, restandardized and extended the original Binet-Simon scale for American use and published it in 1916 as the Stanford-Binet intelligence scale (Terman did his work at Stanford University). This version soon became the standard testing instrument for measuring children's intelligence. In fact, it is no exaggeration to say that for years the principal task of many psychologists working with children was to administer the Stanford-Binet.

The scale had the great merit of being carefully and objectively standardized. It was constructed with attention to the scientific rigor of its day. As a tool it proved its value in predicting the educational status of school children, in aiding the diagnosis of mental deficiency in children, and in revealing many problems of child psychology and making them open to investigation.

The rapidity with which Binet testing was adopted in the United States can be traced to a number of conditions that made the times right for its appearance. Compulsory school attendance was beginning to be vigorously enforced, and the length of the period of schooling was increasing. Backward students in the schools thus became a problem of growing importance. Juvenile delinquency as a social problem was coming into prominence, and emphasis upon social welfare and the prevention of emotional and mental defects was becoming part of the American scene. Such problems called for large-scale assessment by means of a standardized instrument, a function which was admirably filled by the several revisions of the Stanford-Binet scale. The revision in current use appeared in 1960.

Montessori and the Training of the Senses

Maria Montessori (1870–1952) was the first woman to be granted a medical degree by an Italian university. She early interested herself in the education of mentally retarded children, adapting methods devised by the French physician Edouard Seguin emphasizing the training of perceptual and sensorimotor skills. She achieved amazing results, and retarded children trained by her were able to pass the state examinations in reading and writing prescribed for normal children. It occurred to her that the methods might also work with other children, and she opened a number of small schools in the slums of Rome for children aged three to six. As she worked with these children, she found that learning tasks based on simple materials—blocks, beads, rods, and the like—captured their interest to the point where they would work on a problem for an hour at a time.

Montessori stressed the natural development of children in wholesome and regulated surroundings. In her method, the teacher provides each child with appropriate learning materials and leaves him free to handle them himself, but at the same time watches to see whether his reactions are appropriate. If not, the teacher may intervene and substitute another set of materials that seem more appropriate. Special apparatus is used for certain types of learning, which in turn are related to "periods of sensitivity"—stages in a child's biological and mental development when he is presumed to be more responsive to certain experiences.

Although Montessori's methods seem rather formal in contrast to the practices followed in most nursery schools today, they were revolutionary in her era. Her approach was a refreshing change from the practices then prevailing in Italian schools, which required children of all ages to remain in their seats, memorize facts from textbooks, and complete copybooks that were identical one to another.[2] Montessori attacked traditional educational policies, saying that children taught by such methods were not being disciplined, but "annihilated." School authorities retorted that her approach, which permitted movement and encouraged free exploration, was destructive of discipline. Experience with the Montessori method, however, showed that even problem children were interested and quieted by working with the learning materials.

There has been an attempt in recent years to revive the Montessori movement, but it seems out of phase with most current thinking in America; what once was so radical now appears to emphasize a rigid reliance on conformity. Laura E. Berk (1971), who conducted an investigation of the effects of nursery-school environments on children's behavior, has noted that the Montessori method calls for a high degree of order and routine. In contrast to the usual nursery school today, where children are free to do anything they wish with learning materials, the Montessori school provides a prepared environment featuring highly structured materials and ritualized expectations for their use. Montessori teachers find it necessary to intervene to demonstrate the use of materials and to interrupt when children persist in using them improperly. There is little interaction among the children in the classical Montessori school, in contrast to the other nursery schools, because children work in groups under the direct supervision of teachers or on solitary tasks that demand concentration. Berk also noted that the kind of child who succeeded in the Montessori school "was an adaptive, compliant child, since there were many rules and strictures placed upon him and his progress depended on his conformity to these rules."

In recent years some Montessori schools employing variations on the classical model have appeared, where teachers make use of the materials developed by Montessori but modify the methods to suit a more permissive educational philosophy. It is also somewhat ironic that the Montessori schools, which were originally so successful with the mentally retarded and with children from the slums of Rome, now cater

---

[2] Most schools in most countries of the world, unfortunately, are still run more or less along these lines.

almost exclusively to children of better-educated, affluent, middle-class parents.

Watson and Behaviorism

While Montessori was letting fresh air into European educational methodology, and Binet and Simon were experimenting with their mental scale, American psychology was developing a hard-headed, closely reasoned, and highly empirical approach to research: *behaviorism*. The leading figure in this movement was John B. Watson (1878–1958), who insisted that psychologists should forget about studying the mind and mental processes and concentrate on those aspects of behavior that can be directly observed and precisely measured. Watson found it impossible to use introspection, the approved psychological research method of the day, in his work with human infants and laboratory rats; indeed, some psychologists who relied on introspective methods had concluded that it was impossible to study children scientifically because children could not report their conscious experiences accurately. By discrediting introspection, Watson dispelled all doubts as to the legitimacy of infants and children as subjects for research.

In some of his experimentation with children, Watson used the technique of conditioning that had been developed by the Russian physiologist I. P. Pavlov (1849–1936). Pavlov observed that if a bell is sounded just before a dog is given food, the sound of the bell alone will come to evoke the same response—a flow of saliva—that appears when food is placed in a dog's mouth. Hence any response that an animal characteristically makes to a stimulus can become attached or "conditioned" to another stimulus that is presented repeatedly at the same time. (We will discuss Pavlovian conditioning further in Chapter 4.)

Watson applied conditioning techniques to newborn infants to demonstrate how emotional responses are acquired. His most famous subject, Albert, aged elven months, was reared in a hospital. When first tested, Albert showed no reaction of fear to such stimuli as a white rat, a white rabbit, or a mask of white cotton batting. He reached for practically everything brought near him. However, when a steel bar was struck, producing a sharp sound, Albert displayed fear.

In one of his experiments, Watson displayed a white rat to Albert. Just as he was reaching for the rat, the bar was struck, with a loud sound. Albert jumped violently, burying his face in the mattress. When the rat was presented a second time, Albert again reached for it, and again the bar was struck. This time, in addition to jumping violently, Albert began to whimper. A week later the rat was presented without the sound from the bar. Although he eyed the rat he did not reach for it, and when the rat was placed near him he withdrew his hand. Evidently, the joint exposure to the sight of the rat and the sound of the bar had had an effect. Thereafter, joint presentations of the rat and the bar were made several times. After seven simultaneous presentations the rat was presented alone. The instant Albert saw the rat he began to cry and crawl rapidly away from it. After similar experiments, the rabbit and the cotton mask, formerly eliciting no fear, now evoked fear as well. The fear of the rat had *generalized* to these other objects because of their white, furry texture (Watson and Raynor, 1920).

Through experiments of this kind, Watson demonstrated that many of the fears of infants were acquired and not inherited. He also showed that infants tended to generalize from the conditioning experience, in that a response to one stimulus could also be evoked by other stimuli that were similar in one way or another.

What we recognize today as child psychology came into being as a result of the early work of scientists like Hall, Binet, and Watson. Although they worked on different problems and in different countries, they shared a common passion for objectivity and the conviction that through quantitative measurement this goal could be attained. Each of those pioneers turned his back on traditional, common-sense theories of child behavior and developed new explanatory systems based on scientific approaches.

Freud and Psychoanalysis

An important influence upon modern child psychology has been the work of Sigmund Freud, the founder of psychoanalysis, who was more or less a contemporary of Hall, Binet, and Watson (in fact, it was Hall who introduced Freud and his views to American psychologists). Freud's influence is to be found not only in the direct utilization of psychoanalytic concepts and findings in child psychology today but also in subtle, indirect, and sometimes unnoticed effects upon child-rearing practices. Bearing the imprint of his thinking are present-day concepts of children's motives, parent-child relationships, the effect of unconscious influences, and the problems of disturbed children.

Toward the end of the last century, while still practicing as a neurologist in Vienna, Freud became interested in the more psychological aspects of the problems of his patients, and began to search for a method of treatment that would help them with their emotional problems. Ultimately he arrived at what is known as the method of *free association*, in which the patient is asked to say anything that comes to his mind, to relate all of his thoughts as they occur, no matter how trivial, irrelevant, or distasteful they may appear to be.

According to Freud, this "verbal mind wandering," with little or no direction on the part of the psychoanalyst, invariably led to childhood experiences. Gradually Freud was brought to the conclusion that adult personality maladjustments were directly traceable to unfortunate experiences in childhood. Moreover, it seemed to him that these early experiences—feelings of love and hate toward a father or mother,

18 Principles of Development

A psychoanalyst, an anthropologist, and a philosopher, who each influenced important trends in developmental psychology.

Sigmund Freud, 1856-1939

Margaret Mead, 1901-1978

John Dewey, 1859-1952

jealousy of a brother or sister regarded as favored by a parent—all involved sexual motives in one way or another.

Freud became convinced that these early experiences exerted a profound and heretofore unrecognized influence upon subsequent adult behavior and experience. Although the principles and techniques of psychoanalysis developed from work with adult patients, Freud's findings indicated that childhood experiences were crucial. Freud thus forcefully called attention to childhood as a critical period of development. Indeed, it was not until Freud was able to convince researchers that adult neurotic symptoms were the outcome of childhood experiences that childhood experiences were studied intensively in order to explain present behavior.

Freud was also struck by his patients' inability to see the significance of their free associations and dreams. Whereas it would be clear to him what the free associations and dreams signified, patients would deny, often vigorously, Freud's interpretations. The patients thought and lived on one plane, that of consciousness; they treated as nonexistent another level, that of the unconscious, which contained many extremely important determinants of their behavior. Only after many psychoanalytic sessions were the patients enabled to gain insight into the implications of what they were saying and doing—implications which had been concealed from their everyday awareness, and which were, in effect, unconscious.

Thus the extreme importance of unconscious determinants of behavior came to the fore. Freud was not the first to point out the significance of these determinants, but he was the first to advance a method—free association—whereby they could be adequately studied. It is to Freud, then, that child psychology owes its interest in and appreciation of the importance of unconscious experiences in childhood.

Much later, some psychoanalysts, including Anna Freud, daughter of Sigmund, began to work directly with children. The method of free association cannot be used with young children, since it requires a more advanced verbal level than they possess. Instead, analysts observe children's play and thus are able to obtain data that they analyze and interpret, drawing upon the symbolism Freud had found to be significant with adult patients.

child psychology from 1900 to the second world war

From the beginnings of child psychology in the last century, pioneers in the field extended their research during the first part of the twentieth century. During the 1920s and 1930s there were no longer only a few isolated giants as in the past, but rather many capable workers collectively making a considerable contribution.

Tests, Norms, and Individual Differences

The first part of the twentieth century was the time that saw investigators attracted to the study of specific traits and capacities. Emphasis was placed upon the quantitative and the objective. Specialized studies dealing with learning, intelligence, sensory capacity, motor performance, emotion, language, and thinking were carried on. Studies of intelligence and learning loomed the largest.

With the advent of World War I came the need and the opportunity for large-scale testing of the intelligence of army recruits. The tests developed to meet this need could be applied simultaneously to groups of individuals. Based on this experience, tests were extensively developed for peacetime uses in the school systems. From the measurement of intelligence the use of tests spread to other areas of ability and personality.

During the same period there was a great deal of interest in behavioral norms. Some researchers, like Arnold Gesell, were concerned with identifying the behavior that a child might be expected to display at various ages or stages in his development. Gesell's conclusions were based on his extensive observations of the activity of thousands of infants and children. His work produced many valuable insights, but his conclusions were marred by a lack of concern for environmental factors such as cultural influences. Not only did he believe that a child's developmental fate was entirely determined by his biological heritage; he also assumed that normal healthy children are pretty much alike in the behavioral patterns they display at various ages and stages. In spite of these limitations, Gesell's work produced some valuable data, and we shall be referring to his research from time to time when we discuss infancy and childhood.

Other researchers during the pre–World War II period were concerned with measuring more specific aspects of physical development and behavior and produced age and sex norms in the form of height and weight charts, school achievement tests, and motor-development scales. Unfortunately, in their preoccupation with testing, these research workers tended to lose sight of the child who was the object of the measurement.

Child Guidance and Clinical Psychology

The original impetus for the formation of child guidance clinics arose from a desire to find more effective ways of dealing with juvenile delinquency. Before the advent of such clinics, the child or adolescent offender might have had a physical examination by juvenile authorities, but there was generally no further investigation into why he had performed delinquent acts.

The first child guidance clinic was founded in 1909 by William Healy in Chicago. As the child guidance movement spread, its link to delinquency weakened, and most clinicians became convinced that delinquency is a psychosocial problem, which can be treated by psychological methods.

During the 1920s child guidance clinics were organized in Boston, Philadelphia, Chicago, and other major cities of the United States. Maladjustment in school and home, especially that centering upon parent-child relationships, came to the foreground. Psychoanalytic principles and techniques were rapidly adapted to the setting and personnel of the clinic and to the nature and age of the patients. The child, regarded during an earlier period as a passive victim of whatever circumstances impinged upon him, came to be viewed in the dynamic tradition of psychoanalysis as a very active participant who could be helped by psychotherapy.

Some clinics developed primarily as family service agencies and have been directed and staffed largely by social workers, whereas others have focused more on the emotional and psychological problems of children and have been directed by clinical psychologists or psychiatrists. The work in both types of clinics has, almost from their very beginning, been carried on by teams of professionals from all three disciplines. Although the personnel of these clinics are primarily concerned with serving the needs of their patients, they have over the years produced a great deal of research dealing with the causal aspects of personal and social maladjustments. This research has incidentally shed much light on the nature of normal child development. Many of the techniques that have been developed in the context of clinical treatment have also proved to be useful with children in nonclinical settings.

Education and Educational Psychology

The early attitudes toward the child previously sketched are as much the heritage of education and educational psychology as of child psychology. Preyer, Hall, Montessori, and Binet are part of the history of educational psychology as well as child psychology.

In the more modern period, two individuals stand out as having influenced studies of teaching and learning: John Dewey and Edward L. Thorndike. John Dewey—philosopher, psychologist, and educator—probably has had a more profound influence upon education than any other man of this century. His educational philosophy is widely known, although it is not always put into practice. Through his followers, his work led to the progressive education movement, which emphasizes activity, process, and growth through child- or learner-centered approaches, in contrast to more traditional modes of education, which are curriculum-centered or method-centered.

The studies of Edward L. Thorndike on learning and related topics

22 Principles of Development

Three scientists who had a marked effect on the development of experimental psychology and who thus influenced research methodology in the field of child study

Ivan Petrovich Pavlov, 1849–1936

John Broadus Watson, 1878–1958

Edward Lee Thorndike, 1874–1949

have also had a great effect. His research in learning strongly brought out the fact that the child is an individual, and Thorndike did much to document that newly appreciated fact. The existence of individual differences was now established by research instead of being part of the intuitive grasp of the gifted few "born" teachers.

The work of the educational psychologists and that of their colleagues in other disciplines has led to a concern with the growth and development of each child, in spite of the fact that the educator is responsible for large groups of children. Differentiated curricula, the activity program, the advent of elective subjects, concern with each student's interest and motivation, the open classroom, and the presence of psychological services in the schools—all these things attest to the concern of educators with the individual child and his emotional as well as intellectual needs.

Cultural Anthropology

Research findings in cultural anthropology have also influenced child psychology. Workers in this field attempt to understand man as a social being. In general, they study the so-called primitive cultures throughout the world, although some anthropologists have begun to interest themselves in the cultures of urbanized and industrialized societies.

At first, cultural anthropologists used a descriptive-historical approach, relatively uninfluenced by research trends in other scientific disciplines; but with the 1920s came an interest in analyzing child-rearing practices and other areas of developmental psychology. Margaret Mead (1928), for example, became interested in testing the hypothesis that the storm and stress of adolescence, as experienced and observed in western societies, was a result of particular cultural conditions, instead of an inevitable manifestation of maturational factors as it was generally assumed to be. Inasmuch as this hypothesis could not be tested experimentally, she turned to the comparative analysis of cultures. Her careful and intensive study of fifty adolescent Samoan girls supplied evidence that adolescence was not a period of strain in Samoan society.

Mead's findings are an example of the importance of the principle of cultural relativity. Before her study, people assumed that adolescence was universally a storm-and-stress period because that was the typical experience in Europe and America. Mead's findings thus raised questions about the validity of any assumption based on the observation of subjects from a single culture. As a result of her work in Samoa and other areas of the western Pacific, developmental psychologists have learned to place more confidence in research findings that have been cross-validated in more than one culture.

The anthropologists have forced us to realize that we can never observe human beings who have not been subject to cultural influences, and further that cultural factors are especially important during the formative phase of personality development.

the modern period in child psychology

Child Psychology and Developmental Psychology

Child psychology, as an academic discipline, is likely to be included under the larger heading of developmental psychology, a field concerned with theories and empirical evidence as to developmental trends throughout the life span, from conception to old age and death. Developmental psychology is also concerned with similar trends in other animals—monkeys, rats, and mice, for example. Some of the work with these laboratory animals has shed considerable light on developmental tendencies in man. Developmental psychology deals with the behaviors that characteristically occur at various ages and stages of development. A developmental psychologist is likely to be interested in consistencies and differences among the behaviors that occur at various stages.

Child psychology is the largest branch of developmental psychology. In infancy and childhood the greatest number of changes take place in the shortest period of time; hence, there is more to observe, and more data have been accumulated by researchers. Another reason for our greater store of data may be our interest today in children and childhood.

We should also note that children are, by and large, a captive group of subjects. They are highly accessible by reason of their being in hospitals as neonates, in school as pupils, and in child guidance clinics as patients. They are usually quite cooperative and seem to enjoy being interviewed and observed. Unlike adults, they are unlikely to question the motives of the researcher, or are satisfied with such an explanation as, "We are going to play a game, you and I."

More intelligent than the white rat and less suspicious or preoccupied than the average adult, a child is in many ways the ideal research subject for psychology. It is not surprising that we have gathered more data about children than we have about adolescents or adults. The fact that children are more vulnerable than adults and hence more easily exploited does create ethical problems, and psychologists have to be unusually careful about the way in which they design and conduct their research.

Developmental and Environmental Approaches

Most research in child psychology today can be related to two major research styles or orientations, which may be labeled as *genetic* or *developmental* and *environmental* or *experimental*. The terms are not mutually exclusive, for developmentalists generally concede that environmental factors are extremely important, and environmentalists agree that inherited, biologically determined behavioral tendencies are the starting points for everything that follows. The difference between environmentalists and developmentalists lies rather in what is emphasized in their research, the research methods they use, the kind of theories or hypotheses they test, and the kinds of assumptions they make before their research is undertaken.

The genetic/developmental approach. The developmentalist viewpoint is primarily oriented to the *organism*. It seeks to understand the mechanisms and the biological programming that produce consistencies and regularities in behavior. A basic assumption is that the regularities *do* exist, and the task of the psychologist is to find out what they are. This leads to a concern with structure, either in psychological or in physiological terms. For example, the research of Jean Piaget, mentioned earlier, holds to the idea that the newborn child possesses the basic elements for the development of neurophysical structures which set broad limits to his intellectual functioning. According to Piaget, the few automatic reflexes the newborn child possesses are rapidly transformed into structures that incorporate the experiences he has as he interacts with his environment. In addition, the child is born with the capacity to function in terms of some general principles—a kind of "biological intelligence." All species have the capacity to organize their processes, and organization is one general principle for functioning. What interests Piaget particularly are the psychological structures that differ qualitatively at various stages in an individual's life. The infant, for example, interacts with its environment in a direct physical sense, whereas a school-aged child may employ mental operations. Piaget is not, however, as much concerned with the details of the child's behavior as he is with the psychological structure that underlies these activities.

The environmental/experimental approach: behaviorism and S-R research. A major force in the environmentalist camp is experimental psychology, with its behaviorist orientation. In a typical experiment, the effects of variations in the organism's environment are compared, all other factors being controlled. The organism's basic nature—whether it is that of a two- or three-year-old child, a rat, or a monkey—is, of course, taken into consideration, but the chief interest here is the organism's *behavior*: how it *responds* to the *stimuli* in its environment. This focus on stimulus (S) and response (R) has led to the designation "S-R research." S-R research is particularly well adapted to the study of small, precisely thought-out experiments, particularly in the field of learning, and it is a credo of the environmentalist that all behavior either is learned or else is modifiable by means of learning.

In a review of the effect of experimental or S-R psychology on child psychology, Sheldon H. White (1970) observed that child psychologists prior to the 1950s maintained an orientation that was mainly genetic/developmental. They were not particularly interested in conducting experiments and were not much concerned with learning. In the end, this approach led to a kind of sterility or impasse. Roger G. Barker (1951), in the first survey of child psychology published in the *Annual Review of Psychology,* reflected this situation when he complained that there did not seem to be any definitive body of research that could be called "child psychology" and that there was "little evidence of the existence of a professional group of skilled child behavior specialists." In support of this statement, he reported that his survey of the literature had turned up only one paper reporting original observations or experiments for every three papers devoted to programmatic, didactic, or speculative expositions. In light of the "great demand by professional people for scientific information about children," he regretted that "child psychology should be relatively inactive at a time when so much is expected of it."

According to White, the situation was in a state of change even as Barker wrote. Taking its cue from the behaviorism of John B. Watson, American experimental psychology, was developing two strong currents of research. One current derived from the work of Clark L. Hull (1943), who developed a learning theory that served as a starting point for S-R research. The other current, best typified by the work of B. F. Skinner (1938), has dealt with what has been called "the experimental analysis of behavior." The intense activity in these two branches of learning research inevitably infiltrated child psychology. Robert R. Sears (1943), who was initially interested in testing the validity of psychoanalytic theories, was one of the first to undertake the development of an S-R learning theory within the context of child psychology. This attempt did not succeed as well as was hoped, according to White, but Sears and his co-workers did succeed in producing an interesting and valuable body of research dealing with children's socialization.

The infusion of S-R research interests and methods also had a revitalizing effect on the entire field of child psychology and led to research into various subjects: children's learning; a variety of cognitive areas, such as attention, perception, curiosity, stimulation; emotional responses, including anxiety; and the modification of undesirable behavior.

White believes that the influence of S-R learning theories and methods reached its peak during the 1960s and is now on the decline. Although the S-R approach stimulated a great deal of research and enabled child psychologists to get some new and intriguing perspectives on children and their behavior, it failed to provide them with any synthesizing concepts or any central theories. S-R ways of approaching research also have their sterile aspects. Consider this description of a developing child:

The developing child may be adequately regarded, in conceptual terms, as a cluster of interrelated responses interacting with stimuli (Bijou and Baer, 1961).

Such a formulation is undoubtedly useful in conducting small-scale S-R research, but it is singularly unsatisfying to a child psychologist who needs some overall theoretical framework that he can use to organize and sort out all he knows about children and their behavior.

Which Approach Today? The child psychologist who confronts the question of whether to use an S-R environmentalist approach or a genetic-developmental approach in his research is in a quandary. On the one hand, he is attracted by the methods of the tough-minded, empirical S-R experimentalist, who casts a skeptical eye on partially tested theories and unproven speculations about behavior; on the other hand, he is afraid that close adherence to the S-R line will lead him to lose a great deal of important data and leave him with only a fragmented picture of the behavior he is trying to understand.

A major fact about children is that they are continually changing as they grow, develop, and mature. The S-R psychologist is not particularly interested in those changes, except as they can be related to changes in the environment. In the end, the child psychologist, being more interested in the child than in the environment, typically finds himself in the genetics/development camp, but using S-R methods as much as possible to test his hypotheses. As White points out, there is a move toward a cognitive functionalism, in which psychologists conduct experimental studies with cognitive (thinking, problem-solving) functions and, at the same time, try to integrate data from neurological studies. This neurological work has been carried on extensively in Russia, and White sees it as lying somewhat apart from both the genetic and the S-R traditions.

Contributions of Personality and Social Psychology

Another trend that appeared in the 1950s was a strong current of interest in personality and socialization. This interest was caused in large part by the strong psychoanalytic orientation that was prevalent in clinical psychology and in the child guidance movement. The earliest efforts consisted of testing Freudian theories through various kinds of long-range and short-range on-the-spot studies. When the results of these studies proved to be disappointing, the focus of interest was broadened to include other approaches, particularly those influenced by social factors such as social class, child-rearing practices, and the effect of group norms. There was also considerable investigation of personality traits and "constructs": anxiety, hostility, aggression, level of aspiration, and needs for achievement, affiliation, and dependency.

The relative emphasis placed on S-R research and personality studies can be seen by an analysis of the contents of a Children's Bureau bulletin in 1961, which showed that 13 per cent of the studies during a recent period dealt with topics that could be considered more or less in the S-R tradition—physical, motor, perceptual, cognitive-intellectual, and learning process—and 20 per cent with social, familial, cultural, and personality research. Emotional disturbance in children accounted for 24 per cent, and applied research in education, health, and social service accounted for the remaining 43 per cent.

The increased interest in the personality-social dimensions of childhood is also related to the rapid development of humanistic psychology, especially the "psychology of the self." One of the paths to self-understanding lies through child psychology; we believe that we can find some of the keys to the mystery that is ourselves—who we are—through the study of child development. We all realize that we are infinitely more than we were at birth, and our exploration of the events and experiences of infancy and childhood holds the promise of filling in the gap between what we were when we were born and what we are today. We examine the reports of these events and experiences in search of ourselves—in search of explanations for our successes and failures, our inhibitions and capacities, our potentialities for pleasure and sorrow.

Recent Trends

An analysis of the papers published in the 1971 and 1976–1977 issues of *Developmental Psychology* and *Child Development*, the two leading American journals devoted to child psychology, shows that the research interests of child psychologists have stabilized in some respects, but continue to change. In 1976–1977 about two fifths of the articles were concerned with some aspect of personality and social psychology, but about three fifths dealt with cognitive development. (These proportions include articles that cover both types of subject matter.) Only about 36 per cent of the articles in 1976–1977 made use of classic, S-R experimental design, however, in contrast to about 60 per cent in 1971—a finding that seems to support White's point that S-R influence is declining.

New trends are apparent in the articles in recent issues of all child psychology journals. In the personal-social area, there is considerable interest in cross-cultural psychology, especially with respect to child-rearing practices, cognitive styles (ways of thinking and problem solving), and moral judgment. About a fourth of the articles are directly focused on social-class difference or incorporate that consideration as a relevant variable in the research design. Increasing interest in studies of the learning of sex-related roles and sex identities is also evident. Cognitive research studies frequently stress Piagetian concepts—a trend that has been strong since the 1950s—with special attention to conservation, perception, language development, and memory.

In the main, cognitive development has become the main concern of child psychologists, replacing the fading attraction of Freudian theory. This emphasis has evolved because the nature of the subject—the child—lends itself more to a genetic/developmental than to an S-R/experimental treatment. Experimental psychologists, as we have seen, are relatively uninterested in developmental topics and are principally concerned with the study of learning, defined specifically by them as the process or act of acquiring responses. As far as experimentalists are concerned, White points out, there is no learning theory in child psychology; no learning theory has ever been produced by research with children; and learning theories were never designed to accommodate the data of children's learning.

Research activity in the cognitive field has also been stimulated by intervention programs to help children of the disadvantaged poor to develop skills that will enable them to profit from classroom experiences. Although those who conduct research in cognitive development are relatively uninterested in learning as defined by experimentalists, they have in recent years become much more meticulous with respect to research design. As a result, research in child psychology today is better controlled and much more scientific than the data-gathering expeditions

Like other branches of psychology, child development has become an applied as well as a research field. (Al Johns, *APA Monitor*. © 1970 by the American Psychological Association. Reprinted by permission.)

and speculative theorizing that were characteristic of the field before World War II.

A View of Child Psychology Today

If child psychology is compared with the natural and social sciences, it is evident that it is an unusual discipline. Child psychology is young—indeed, in its childhood—and it is in a formative stage that is changing and challenging. The field is full of exciting complexities.

G. Stanley Hall, the father of the child study movement, lived less than a century ago, whereas Sir Isaac Newton, called the father of physics, lived three centuries ago. Any science evolves slowly, progressing by means of the interplay of ideas and experiments. As each part of the body of knowledge both checks and spurs on the other parts, a theoretical framework evolves to serve as the basis for further advances.

Because child psychology is so young, it can be expected to continue its development. It will do so more slowly than other disciplines, because it deals with more complexities and more variables than other disciplines such as the natural sciences. For example, "H_2O" means an identifiable molecule, but "child" has no such specific and recognizable limits. We are studying a class of immature living organisms. Each member of this class responds to two sets of events, those within the organism and those out in the environment, and both of these types of events are slowly changing. Each way of studying a child—such as the developmental or the environmental—is useful; but combined, the ways are more important than they can ever be separately.

This book is only an introduction to child and adolescent psychology; it cannot make you an expert on children or adolescents. We can hope to interest you to go further and perhaps to extend the boundaries of this young science, to become a new Hall or Binet or Piaget. We shall be satisfied if you become a more informed and more competent person than you would have been if you had not studied child psychology, and if, by learning more about what you were, you achieve a better understanding of what and who you are.

summary

Although common sense would tell us that children are intrinsically interesting, our forebears had an entirely different opinion. From the end of the Roman Empire until the rise of the modern middle class, western society did little to discriminate between children and adults. Discipline was severe, and in some countries children were bound as apprentices at an early age.

One of the first and most influential writers to challenge these views was John Locke, who recommended that young children be permitted to give vent to their feelings and disagreed with the practice of apprenticeship. Locke also rejected the notion that ideas and knowledge are innate and thus laid the foundations of modern scientific methodology. During the eighteenth and nineteenth centuries, first Jean-Jacques Rousseau and later Johann Heinrich Pestalozzi also wrote in favor of tolerance, acceptance, and respect of children as individuals, expressing views that contrasted sharply with the prevailing child-rearing practices. The Industrial Revolution created a need for educated citizens, and more and more parents began to send their children to school. Traditional teaching methods and materials quickly proved to be unequal to the new demands being made on them, and teachers turned to the growing field of psychology for assistance in dealing with the complex problems with which they were faced.

Over a century ago, the "baby biographies" set the scene for the development of child psychology. One biography was written by Charles Darwin, who looked to the behavior of his infant son for support for his theories and made the detailed observations that are necessary to a genuinely scientific study of child behavior. William Preyer, too, published a "baby biography" carefully recording his son's mental development. Although reports of this sort were useful, they tended to be biased by atypical samples and a lack of observational reliability.

G. Stanley Hall, the father of the child study movement, introduced the questionnaire technique—a definite methodological improvement, but still not a refined enough instrument to make any but the most superficial study of children. The advance in quantitative method was continued by Alfred Binet, whose Binet-Simon intelligence tests were developed as a tool to diagnose mental retardation. These tests were noteworthy because they made use of realistic tasks from everyday life rather than the simplified laboratory tasks used previously. Binet also grouped and standardized the tests according to the age level at which they were usually passed. In the United States, the Binet-Simon scale was revised by Lewis M. Terman and published as the Stanford-Binet test.

The natural development of children, stressed a century or so earlier by Rousseau and Pestalozzi, was the theme underlying the work of Maria Montessori, whose teaching of slum children made use of methods and materials that encouraged exploration and the development of sensorimotor skills. John B. Watson, the "father of behaviorism," experimented with the conditioning of infants and helped make children's behavior a legitimate object for scientific study.

The theories of Sigmund Freud, the founder of psychoanalysis, have constituted a major force in the development of modern child psychology. Freud maintained that the psychological problems of adults were directly traceable to stressful childhood experiences, the memories of which were buried in the unconscious. In order to help patients gain insight into these unconscious processes, Freud made use of the free-association method. Because children have not developed linguistically to the point where they can use free association, psychoanalysts observe their play activities as a source of data. Much of the clinical work with disturbed children took place in child guidance clinics, which began to be founded in the first decade of the twentieth century as a way of handling juvenile delinquency.

The years before World War II saw the widespread use of psychological tests and the development of observational methods by a number of researchers, including Arnold Gesell, who was concerned with identifying the ages and stages at which certain forms of behavior are likely to appear. Although much concern was expressed about the individual differences of children, it often seemed that the child was lost somewhere in a maze of figures.

Child psychology is now the largest branch of developmental psychology, and in many ways the child is the ideal psychological research subject. The two major research styles today are the genetic or developmental and the environmental or experimental. The genetic/developmental approach is primarily oriented to the organism; it assumes that regularities in behavior exist and seeks to understand the mechanisms and biological programming that produce them. One example of this approach is the work of Piaget, whose principal interest is in the psychological structure underlying the child's behavior. The environmental/experimental approach, on the other hand, seeks to understand how behavior responds to the stimuli in its environment; one facet of this approach, S-R (stimulus-response) research, is particularly well adapted to small, precisely thought-out experiments.

American experimental psychology, taking its cue from the behaviorism of Watson, developed two strong currents of research, one derived from Hall, who developed a learning theory that served as a starting point for S-R research, and the other, best typified by Skinner, dealing with what has been called "the experimental analysis of behavior."

The child psychologist now confronting the question of whether to use in his research an S-R environmentalist approach or a genetic/developmental approach typically finds himself in the genetic/development camp, but using S-R methods as much as possible to test his hypotheses. There is a move toward a cognitive functionalism, in which psychologists conduct experimental studies with cognitive (thinking, problem-solving) functions while they try to integrate data from neurological studies. Another trend that appeared first in the 1950s is a strong interest in personality and socialization.

two

Studying Children and Adolescents Scientifically

Children and fools cannot lye.
Children learne to creepe ere they can learne to goe.
Burnt child fire dredth.
—PROVERBS COLLECTED BY JOHN HEYWOOD (1497-1580)

As people carried on their casual, everyday observation of children over the centuries, folk sayings arose. Who today has not heard "Spare the rod and spoil the child" (Samuel Butler, 1600-1680) or one of the older proverbs collected by John Heywood (1497-1580)? When many people observe similar phenomena and reach similar conclusions about what they have seen, the result becomes "folk wisdom." It is considered "common sense," and is accepted as fact. But is it fact? During the Middle Ages everyone accepted the "fact" that the earth is flat—you could observe its flatness with your own eyes. Then Columbus sailed far enough to make the earth's curvature apparent—and eventually everyone had to realize that casual observation is not always reliable, even if all your neighbors' observations agree with your own. Observation, folk wisdom, common sense—all could be in error. Something else was needed.

The scientific method came out of the physical or natural sciences as scientists sought a way to determine truth. The scientific method follows this procedure: (1) There is curiosity about a natural phenomenon that is not understood. (2) A hypothesis is advanced to explain the natural phenomenon. (3) An observation or experiment is designed to check the truth of the hypothesis. (4) When the observation or experiment is carried out, there must be controls, so that comparison can be made between subjects undergoing the experimental conditions and other subjects not undergoing the experimental conditions. (5) The results of the experiment must be published so that they can be duplicated; other investigators must in other words, be able to get the same results if they conduct the same experiment under the same conditions.

How closely will you follow the scientific method as you study child psychology? As you will soon see, child psychology differs somewhat from the physical sciences; therefore, using the scientific method as a base, it has built its own methods to satisfy its special needs. Of course, you have neither the experience nor the resources to perform advanced scientific work in child psychology. As you learn to study children scientifically, perhaps you may, however, undertake some simple observations or experiments. Certainly and most importantly, you will acquire the ability to make critical judgments concerning everything you hear or read about children. You will become less likely to accept a statement merely because it is "proverbial" or "common sense," or because "everyone says so."

child psychology: a behavioral science

Child psychology had its origins in natural science, which began to develop its method about four hundred years ago, but a behavioral science is not a natural science. Like natural scientists, behavioral scientists measure physical characteristics, such as weight, height, and age, but they must also measure intangible qualities, such as love, hate, and anxiety. We have more variables; we use different tools, such as interviews and questionnaires. For the behavioral scientist, controls are of extreme importance, and because we are dealing with such subjective subjects—human beings—it is necessary to make a greater effort to achieve objectivity.

Looking at Children Objectively

In everyday life, you appraise the behavior of others (as well as your own behavior) in a subjective or impressionistic way, with results that you find more or less satisfying. Others, however, find your appraisals less useful, partly because your appraisals are likely to be personalized—that is, suited to your individual needs and not to those of others—so that they are strongly influenced by bias. We all put something of ourselves—our beliefs, our values, our psychological needs—into every act of observing. The fact that a number of people may come to similar conclusions as a result of observing similar behavior tends to eliminate individual variations in the data, but it does not avoid the cultural effect—the similarity of beliefs held by all the members of a culture. The effect of cultural bias cannot be overestimated.

Scientific methods of observation are highly systematic in order to hold biases of all kinds to the minimum. In child study, these systematized methods take the form of tests, questionnaires, standardized tasks and interviews, videotapes, and rating scales or schedules. Such methods, if properly designed, not only filter out bias; they also make it possible to record data in a form that can be analyzed by accepted statistical methods. Just as a mining geologist takes a sample of ore, the child psychologist takes a sample of behavior by observing children in one of their natural habitats—a schoolyard, a classroom, a doll-play setting, or a party. It was early realized that the samples could not cover everything the children were doing; samples would have to be limited if they were to be relevant to a particular problem. For example, observations might be made of the popularity of children at a party or their attempts to dominate one another on the playground. We might undertake such an investigation in order to study the possible effects of various child-rearing practices.

The investigator must make many decisions. He must decide upon the time sample to be used: he has to select the particular series of short time periods during which observations are to be made in such a way that the time samples are representative of the whole period under study. He must also define the area selected for study and develop a recording scheme for the categories of behavior to be observed. And he must make provision for evaluating the *reliability* of the observations of his observers. Observer reliability, or more precisely interobserver reliability, is the extent to which two or more observers agree in independently recording the behavior they are seeing.

A measure (or measurement) of maternal care developed by Rheingold (1960) will serve as an illustration. The observers prepared a check list of thirty mothering activities and twelve infant activities. The operations of mothers in caring for their infants were then sampled, in the home and in an institution. The mothering-caretaking activities included such common ones as patting, diapering, dressing. Infant activities observed included vocalizing, crying, and playing with toys. Forty observations were made, one every fifteen seconds, over a ten-minute period. After a rest period of five minutes, a new ten-minute sequence was begun. For each infant this was done for four hours one morning (a total of 160 observations), followed the next day by the same schedule in the afternoon, for a total of eight hours of observation. There were three observers in all, but only one observed a particular infant in a four-hour period. Another observed that same infant the second day. Observer agreement was calculated for each item. For all items it was found to be 90 per cent—the observers agreed to a high degree.

The reliability of a measuring device or test, distinguished from the reliability of observers, must also be established. Often reliability is determined by using the same device repeatedly on the same subject

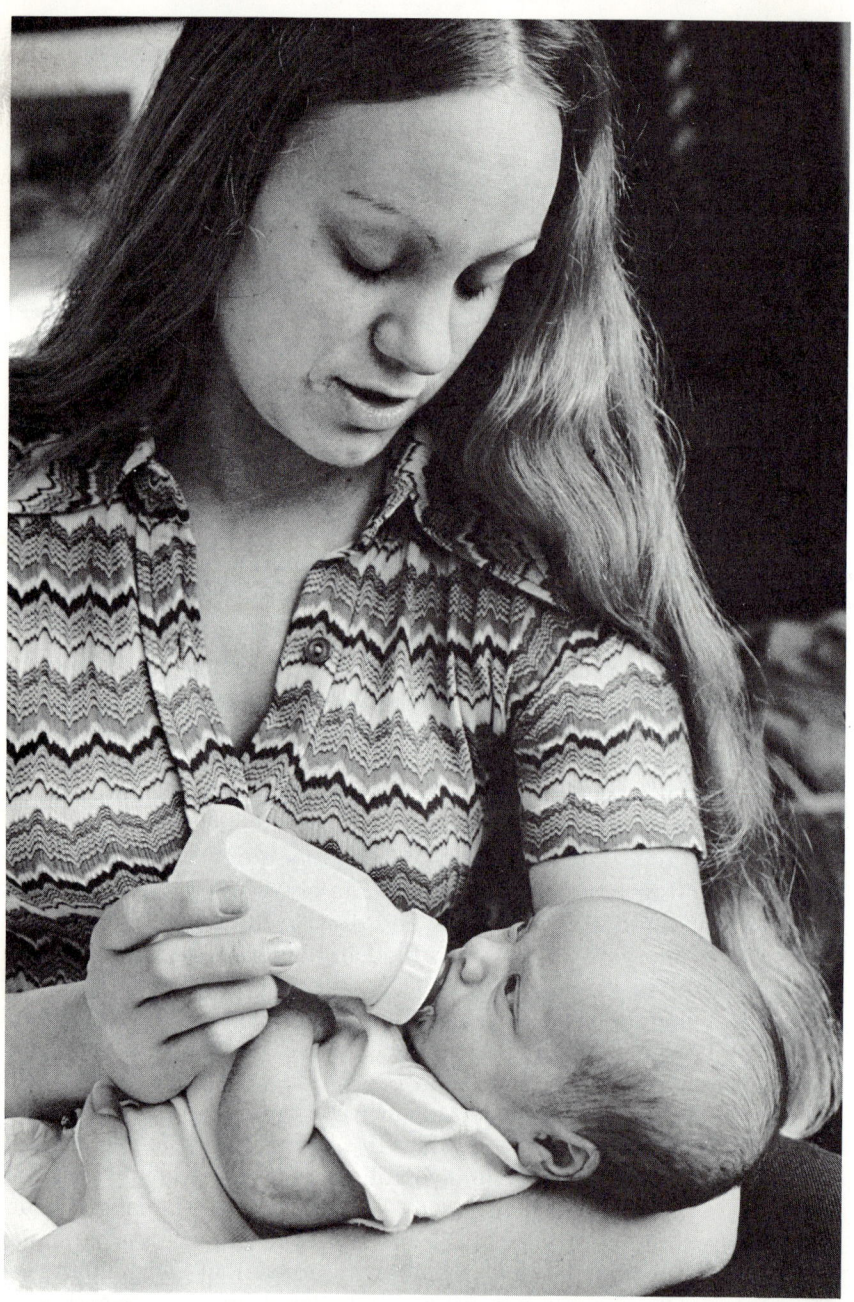

Most people would not think that mothering could be studied scientifically like a chemical or the movement of a planet. Yet carefully designed observation schedules enable psychologists to study both the behavior of mothers and the responses of their infants.

and then comparing the results to determine their consistency. A thermometer that reports a healthy individual's temperature as 90.1 on one occasion and as 99.3 a few minutes later would be considered unreliable. So, too, psychological measuring devices that fluctuate because of imperfections are faulty because they are inconsistent and imprecise—that is, unreliable. A psychological instrument is considered reliable if it yields substantially the same results on the first and second testings when there is no reason to believe the subject has changed in respect to what is being measured.

The investigator must select the techniques he is going to use on his particular problem. Unless he can demonstrate that a technique measures something relevant to that problem, his findings would be ignored by those familiar with the necessity for an investigator to take into consideration the *validity* of his measures—that is, the extent to which an investigator can show that what he is doing actually measures what he is trying to measure.

Sometimes description supplies information that is sufficient to establish validity. In studies of learning, for example, we arrange for the child to be faced with a new problem, and if after practice trials the child makes fewer errors and takes less time, we can say that learning has taken place. Or an investigator asks a child to tell which of two lights is the brighter, and can then say that he has studied visual brightness discrimination. Or he asks a child to press a key as soon as a light flashes, and can then say that he has measured reaction time to a visual stimulus. In these instances there is some direct, unmistakable connection between what he says he is studying and what he is actually studying.

Anything that varies is a *variable*, whether it is visible, like height or weight, or invisible, like love or hate. Height and weight can be measured more or less directly; but love, hostility, and anxiety can be measured only indirectly, by such means as questionnaire responses, behavior, changes in heart rate, and palmar sweating.

As the variables under study increase in complexity, the problem of designing valid measures becomes extremely difficult. The measurement of intelligence is a case in point. Francis Galton, the eminent British amateur of the life sciences, constructed some of the first tests of intelligence, as did James McKeen Cattell, an early American psychologist. Their tests consisted of measures of such variables as tonal memory, estimation of distance, speed of reaction, and rate of tapping. The fact that the researchers claimed to be measuring intelligence added nothing to the validity of the tests, and when the tests were subjected to critical examination, their validity turned out to be nil. When Alfred Binet abandoned this approach and instead attempted a more "global" measure of intelligence, his use of a different approach did not in itself make his method more valid. Evidence had to be accumulated to show that Binet's scale produced results that were

The acid test of the validity of developmental scales, such as measures of intelligence, is the extent to which they reflect observable differences in the competency displayed by children of different ages.

consistent with other indications of intelligence. One such indicator was the change in cognitive ability that occurs with age during childhood—that is, six-year-olds can generally solve problems of greater complexity than three-year-olds can, and ten-year-olds are more competent than six-year-olds. Scores on Binet's scale were consistent with this well-known fact, thus providing one indication of the validity of the scale.

techniques in behavioral study

In a behavioral science some of the work is concerned with testing "tried-and-true" principles. Thus in child psychology there has been considerable testing of such proverbial observations as "spare the rod and spoil the child" and "the burnt child dreads the fire." The scientists turn to objective methods such as measurement. They try to eliminate all factors that might be expected to interfere with the accuracy of their measurement and observation. If they are investigating the validity of a concept that has widespread acceptance, like "spare the rod and spoil the child," they go to unusual lengths to ensure that their data gathering is insulated from possible biases resulting from their belonging to a culture that accepts such concepts as true. The test of the adequacy of their controls is the duplication—or as it is called in psychology, the *replicability*—of their study. Replicability means that any other scientist should be able to replicate or repeat the research and get the same results.

Conducting scientific investigations requires a rigorous self-discipline; a scientist has an iron-clad commitment, for instance, to report whatever findings emerge, irrespective of whether they support or discredit the hypothesis that is being tested.

The investigation is likely to begin with a hypothesis—an educated guess about the relationship between two or more classes of events or variables, for example, the effect that "rod sparing" may have on "child spoiling." Often the hypothesis grows out of theories about human behavior and development. Piaget has theorized that certain ways of interpreting the world appear before other ways in the course of child development. Psychologists have tested Piaget's theories by having children who are at one stage of development participate in experiments that require or tempt them to use interpretative modes appropriate to earlier or later stages.

The S-R Research Scheme

Behavioral scientists are basically concerned with identifying the causal factors that underlie behavior in its various forms. The most straightforward way of determining causes is the scientific experiment.

40 Principles of Development

In psychology, the simplest technique is the stimulus-response or S-R experiment, in which the experimenter decides on a stimulus which he introduces into the environment of his subjects. An S-R experiment is fundamentally the same, whether the subjects are children, rats, or college sophomores. The stimulus may be anything relevant to the hypothesis being tested. It may be the intensity of sound, different modes of instruction, reward, punishment, varying amounts of attention, or air temperature. It may be introduced, varied, or "manipulated" by the investigator. The stimulus is the *independent variable*. The response made by the subjects is the *dependent variable*; its appearance, form, or intensity depends on the independent variable. The experimenter controls all other variables in the experimental situation in order to be sure that the changes he observes in the dependent variable can be due only to the independent variable. Inasmuch as it is difficult to control unwanted sources of variation in natural situations, the ideal setting for the experiment is the psychological laboratory.

An excellent example of an S-R experiment is that carried on by Cynthia Turnure (1971), who was interested in studying the effect of the mother's voice on the infant's behavior, particularly the extent to which an infant could distinguish various versions of his mother's voice, as well as the difference between his mother's voice and that of a stranger. Turnure controlled the stimulus situation by tape-recording the voices of the mother and a strange woman. She could, of course, have used a man's voice or a child's voice for the control stimulus, but then she would not have known whether any observed differences in response were caused by the "motherness" of the stimulus or its "adult-femaleness."

Turnure instituted even more intricate controls. The infants heard three versions of the mother's voice: normal, slightly distorted, and grossly distorted. The different versions made it possible to determine the extent to which infants were using a perceptual-cognitive model of their mothers as a basis for deciding which stimuli could be accepted and which rejected as characteristic of "Mother."

Another type of control was introduced by having several subjects, and having them be of both sexes. The use of only one subject would have raised the question of whether differences in response were caused by the idiosyncratic behavior of a single infant; the use of subjects of the same sex would have left unresolved the question of whether the observed differences were characteristic of only one sex. The more generally applicable the results of an experiment, the more significant they are, because they tell us about human behavior in general and are not limited to the individuals under observation.

Turnure wanted to control another variable: age. Her experiment included three groups of subjects, aged three, six, and nine months, respectively. Her study was cross-sectional, in the sense that it dealt with tiny samples of infanthood at the three ages and not the same infants at three ages over the six-month span from three to nine months. We can nevertheless assume, in the absence of contrary evidence, that differences in the behavior of the infants at each of the three ages are probably typical of all infants of those ages, and hence are the result of developmental processes. The assumption that cross-sectional studies will produce data that permit *longitudinal* interpretations (that is, changes in the same individual noted over an extended period of time) becomes harder to defend for studies of adolescents and adults, but it seems to be reasonable in studies of infants and children.

The dependent variable presented a problem for Turnure. How can one determine whether or not infants are responding differentially to various stimuli? This difficulty was resolved by making motion pictures of each infant and noting all types of movement: smiling, frowning, crying, mouthing, vocalizing, and limb-mouth contact. Controls were also instituted by providing thirty-second neutral "no-stimulus" periods before and after the stimulus-presentation period. This arrangement enabled Turnure to score responses separately for the control and the experimental periods. The scoring of the filmed responses was done by another research worker who did not know the purpose of the experiment—still another type of control.

Turnure's results, incidentally, showed that, with increasing age, infants became quieter during stimulus presentations. Turnure accounted for this in terms of increased attention—the older the infant, the more likely he was to reduce motor activity in order to "concentrate" on the stimuli, presumably to determine their meaning. At three months, furthermore, infants mouthed more when they heard their mother than when they heard the stranger, presumably because of the association of "mother" with "feeding." The six-month-old infants cried more when they heard their mother's voice, particularly her natural voice. Turnure suggested that this may have been caused by the greater attachment that infants of this age have for their mothers, perhaps a kind of "separation protest" initiated by hearing the mother's voice without being able to see her. There were some sex differences. Three-month-old girls were more active than boys of the same age when the mother's voice was distorted, but at nine months the girls were more active than the boys when they heard their mother's normal voice.

In Turnure's experiment another control was provided by the fact that the subjects also served as their own controls—that is, responses made during the stimulus period were compared with responses made by the same infants when there was no stimulus.

From our report of the Turnure experiment (and we mean our statement, not the experiment itself), can you evaluate the scheme or design of this S-R experiment? What was the hypothesis? Were you told enough about the controls? Were you given sufficiently definite information (about number and place, for instance)? Were the results given in full enough detail? Can you name the independent variable? The dependent variable? The controls?

In other studies, particularly with older children, another kind of control is instituted by dividing the subjects into two groups as alike as possible. For example, suppose that in a study of reading ability one wishes to control (equalize) for the effect that individual differences may have on the results. If scores on an intelligence test are available, the top child may be placed in the experimental group, the next highest in the control group, the third highest in the experimental group, and so on, alternating between the groups. Thus, both the average intellectual level and the variability of intelligence of the two groups may be equalized. When this has been done, a test is made to ascertain that the two groups are in fact similar.

The problem of selecting subjects for experimental and control groups becomes more complicated when other possibly significant variables, such as sex, age, socioeconomic status (SES), and race, must also be considered, but basically the way of equalizing remains the same. In general, the accepted practice is to make the experimental and control groups as similar as possible in the independent variables which are not under consideration but which may, nonetheless, cause variation in the dependent variable being studied.

In a typical experiment employing an experimental and a control group, the experimental group is exposed to the independent variable but the control group is not. In the simplest form of this technique, a measure of the dependent variable is administered to *both* groups prior to treatment, in order to determine whether the groups are in fact comparable. Then the experimental group undergoes the experimental procedure and the control group does not. Finally, both groups are observed or tested to determine the effect of the difference in treatment.

Figure 2-1 reports the results of a slightly more complicated version of this basic experimental design, one in which first-grade and fifth-grade boys were given one of three different treatments for their performance in learning a task: they were praised, criticized, or exposed to a neutral stimulus. In this instance, we have two experimental conditions: "praise" and "criticism." The control condition consists of the neutral stimulus. The experimenters' reactions to the boys' performance are therefore the independent variable. The dependent variable consists of the mean (average) number of trials the boys in each of the groups needed in order to learn the task—the more difficulty they experienced, the more trials they required.

As might be expected, the first graders functioned less effectively under all conditions than did the fifth graders, but results show an interesting difference between the two groups. The first graders were more successful when there was some kind of reaction to their performance, either favorable or unfavorable, whereas the fifth graders

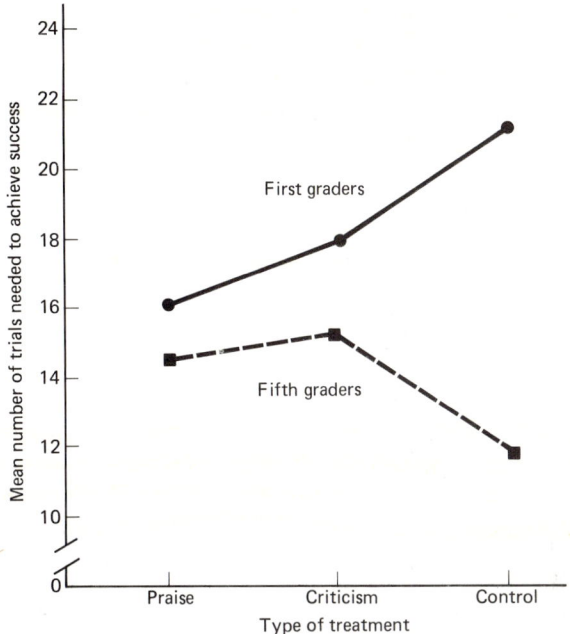

FIGURE 2-1. *Differences in rapidity in learning a perceptual task under three types of conditions experienced by first and fifth grade boys.* (Spear, 1970.)

evidently found praise or criticism distracting and turned in their best performance when neither was given—that is, in the control condition.

We see, therefore, that the independent variable in an experiment is introduced and varied systematically while other variables that might conceivably influence the dependent variable are controlled. Whatever changes occur in the dependent variable are attributed to the differences in the independent variable. This is the S-R research scheme.

Correlational or Differential Methods

In the S-R scheme, the distinguishing operation is the investigator's manipulation of some specific stimulating condition, the independent variable. But there are certain circumstances in which the experimenter cannot arrange conditions and must seek a different way to carry on his research. Indeed, there are some sciences, such as astronomy and geology, in which experiments of the kind we have described are impossible, so far as major problems are concerned. An astronomer cannot vary the orbit of a star to see the effect of the variation; a geologist cannot introduce an ice age in order to observe the resultant changes.

When scientists are unable, for one reason or another, to conduct controlled experiments, they may turn to differential or correlational methods to test their hypotheses. In behavioral science, the use of these methods is also termed R-R (response-response) research, in contrast to S-R (stimulus-response) research, because relationships or differences between *responses*, rather than between *stimuli and responses*, are studied.

In the correlational/differential approach, the investigator studies similarities or differences in two sets of variables. He needs to know, not just the response of children (as Turnure did), but the response of mothers as well. He needs to know how close the response of one group is to the response of the other (correlation) or how different (differentiation).

Margaret and David Steward (1973), for example, used a correlational/differential method when they compared and contrasted the behavior of Anglo-, Mexican-, and Chinese-American mothers who taught their three-year-old sons a beanbag toss game and showed them how to sort objects according to color, size, and shape.

An analysis of the videotaped behavior of the mothers and children from the three subcultures indicated that the Chinese-American mothers did the most praising and encouraging, whereas the Mexican-American mothers did the most scolding and criticizing. The researchers theorized that these differences in maternal behavior patterns may be related to differences in the way that school-aged children from the three subcultures perform in classroom learning tasks.

Experimental (S-R) and correlational/differential methods are often employed in combination. The study whose results were reported in Figure 2-1, for instance, showed not only that manipulating the independent variable had an effect on performance, but also that performance differed according to the ages of the children.

Only a minority of the studies undertaken in developmental psychology are of the S-R or experimental type. The greater proportion are of the R-R or correlational/differential type, because developmental psychologists are generally more interested in finding out what kinds of variables are associated with one another, as well as the ways in which children with varying kinds of experiences and backgrounds differ in their behavior. In studies of child-rearing practices, for example, it is obviously impossible to conduct experiments of the classical, S-R type in order to test the effects of parental attitudes and disciplinary techniques; the only approach is through correlational/differential research.

There is a great deal of interest these days in the effect that economic, social, and emotional forms of deprivation have on children. Psychologists would not of course deliberately create experimental situations in which children would be deprived, but they can and do study the relationship between the degree of deprivation that many children have experienced and their behavior in school and in other social settings. Through correlational/differential studies of this type, we can, if we exercise proper controls, identify those aspects of deprivation that have the most severe effects on children.

The psychologist who employs correlational/differential methods is usually just as concerned about the causes of behavior as is the experimental researcher. When the psychologist uses correlational/differential methods, he does not manipulate independent variables, but identifies them as pre-existing conditions that are likely to bear a causal relationship to consequent or dependent variables. David J. Massari (1975), for example, gave first and third graders a test designed to measure their tendency to make judgments impulsively. He then administered the Children's Embedded-Figures Test (CEFT), which requires subjects to concentrate on certain geometric designs and to ignore the irrelevant lines in which the designs have been embedded.

The results, as indicated in Figure 2-2, showed that children who were more impulsive tended to be distracted by the irrelevant stimuli and

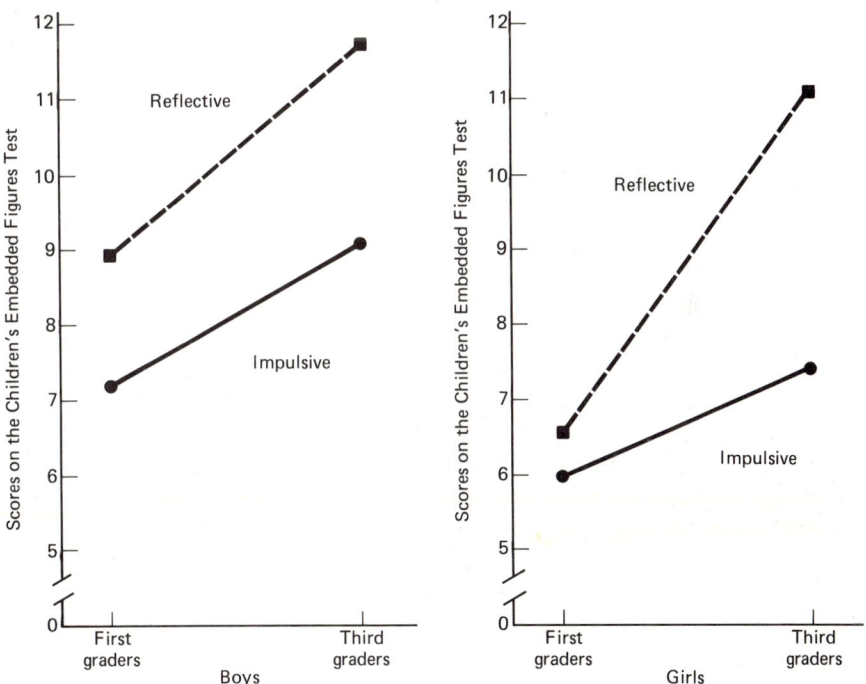

FIGURE 2-2. Results obtained in a correlational/differential study in which impulsivity served as an independent variable, and distractibility, as measured by the Children's Embedded Figures Test (CEFT), served as a dependent variable. (Massari, 1975.)

consequently did not perform as well as the less impulsive or more "reflective" ones. To explain this outcome, it is reasonable to suppose that the degree of impulsivity displayed by the children was not only a pre-existing condition but also had some effect on their performance. Impulsivity, therefore, was an independent variable, and performance on the CEFT was the dependent variable. As Figure 2-2 further indicates, age and sex also functioned as independent variables, as far as performance on the CEFT was concerned.

What Correlations Mean

We have been talking about correlations and differences in very general terms, but if we are to make sense out of psychologists' research it is necessary to have some idea of the statistics in terms of which their findings are reported.

It may seem that trying to apply statistics to something as varied and unpredictable as behavior is impossible. Yet everyone uses statistics in some form or another to describe behavior, usually without being aware of it.

We say that Smith's batting average is .250, a figure that represents his performance in terms of the number of hits he has made divided by the number of times he has been at bat. We hear that the odds are three to one against a certain candidate winning an election. The Weather Bureau says there is a thirty per cent chance of rain. When we are told that the prices of simple cameras range from twenty to thirty dollars, we are able to determine whether we can afford to buy a camera before setting off on a vacation trip.

Psychologists too use such statistics—averages, odds, percentages, and ranges—although they generally use the term "mean" in preference to "average," and "ratio" in preference to "odds." But such statistics are useful only when we are describing a single variable, like batting performance or chances for election. If we are interested in exploring causes of behavior, we are looking for the interaction between at least two variables: the presumed cause, or independent variable, and the resulting behavior, or dependent variable.

The statistic most widely used in developmental psychology is, as we have noted, the correlation. Let us look at a fictitious situation in order to illustrate the usefulness of this statistic. Imagine a teacher—we'll call her Ms. Romero—who has 27 pupils in a combined fifth and sixth grade. Ms. Romero is working for her master's degree in education and is taking a late afternoon seminar, entitled "Research Methods in Developmental Psychology," at a university in a large city located an hour or so away. For her term project she decided to study factors influencing the school performance of the ten fifth graders in her class. She recently gave a standardized reading test to her students and now was wondering about the possible effect that the children's out-of-school activities and their home environment might have on their test scores. In order to gather background data she asked the children to record for one week the amount of time they spent watching television, and also to count the number of books at home. When she had ranked the children according to their reading test scores and had entered the information they reported, she found herself looking at the display of data in Table 2-1.

The first thing she noted was that the children who were the best readers were the ones who reported the greatest number of books and the least hours of television viewing, whereas the poorest readers reported the least number of books and the most hours of viewing. In other words, Ms. Romero observed that there was a *relationship* between reading ability and the number of books in the home, and between reading ability and the hours spent watching television. She tried to put this observation into figures, for purposes of comparison. She noted that the top three readers reported an average of 665 books in their homes and watched television an average of 13 hours a week, whereas the mean number of books in the homes of the three poorest readers was 7, and the mean hours of their television watching were 33.

When she reported her observations to her seminar instructor, he agreed that the means she had computed for the top and bottom trios of students did indicate that reading skill, number of books in the home, and hours spent watching television were interrelated for these children, but he also pointed out that this way of reporting a relationship was awkward. What Ms. Romero ought to do, he said, was to compute a Pearsonian correlation between pairs of the variables. This statistic was

TABLE 2-1. Reading Test Scores, Number of Books in the Home, and Hours Per Week Spent Watching Television for an Imaginary Sample of Fifth Graders.

Students	Reading Test Score	Number of Books in Home	Hours Spent Watching Television in One Week
1. Bill	120	980	15
2. Rosa	115	901	10
3. Kevin	114	114	15
4. Michelle	105	10	25
5. Bob	101	50	26
6. Lori	100	20	28
7. Betty	88	15	31
8. Vicki	85	6	30
9. Carl	72	9	35
10. Brian	70	7	35
Mean or average	97	203	25

much more economical in that it employed a single figure to reflect an entire relationship, thus making it unnecessary to report a series of pairs of means.

Pearsonian correlations, he said, range from +1.00 to −1.00. A correlation of +1.00 indicates that a perfect, positive, one-to-one relationship exists between two sets of variables. Such a correlation represents a situation that may be expressed as "the more of variable X, the more of variable Y." A correlation of −1.00 also represents a perfect one-to-one relationship, but in this instance a negative one, which may be expressed as "the more of variable X, the less of variable Y." A correlation of .00, of course, represents no relationship at all between two variables.

The data that Ms. Romero reported suggested that the relationship between her children's reading test scores and the number of books in their homes was positive: the higher the reading score, the more books, and the lower the reading score, the fewer books. When the instructor put the figures from the first two columns of Table 2-1 into his desk computer, the correlation between the two variables turned out to be positive: +.63.

The correlation between the reading test scores and the hours spent watching television, he predicted, would be negative, for the higher the test score, the fewer the television hours, and the lower the test score, the greater the television hours. The instructor then showed her how to feed the figures from the first and third columns of Table 2-1 into his desk computer. The resulting correlation was −.92. Because it also appeared that the number of books in the home was negatively correlated with the hours spent watching television, Ms. Romero also fed these two sets of figures into the computer and got a correlation of −.75.

Although the correlations in themselves told her nothing about the causal factors underlying the differences in her children's test scores, Ms. Romero felt that they supported her hunch that children from homes in which there was a strong emphasis on intellectual matters were likely to be superior readers, whereas those from homes where this emphasis was lacking were likely to be poorer readers. As far as the negative correlations were concerned, she felt that they suggested that children who watched a great deal of television were not doing much reading on their own, whereas those who were spending much of their time reading had less time for television viewing.

We have used a considerable amount of space discussing correlations because many of the studies conducted by developmental psychologists report their findings in terms of correlations. Hence an understanding of their meaning is helpful in interpreting the research results we shall be presenting from time to time in this book. Examples of correlations that appear in the research literature (plus two from everyday life) are reported in Table 2-2.

TABLE 2-2. Examples of Correlations Between Pairs of Variables

First Variable	Correlation Coefficient	Second Variable
Number of hours worked each month during the school year 1977-1978 by a nursery school teacher earning $10 per hour correlated	+1.00	with amounts the nursery school teacher earned each month. (The more hours she worked, the more she earned, and the fewer hours she worked, the less she earned.)
At the end of each month, the above teacher calculated the number of days she had worked so far during the school year. These end-of-month total correlated	−1.00	with the number of days remaining in the school year. (The more days she worked, the fewer days remained to work.)
IQs earned by children taking Form "L" of the 1937 Stanford-Binet Intelligence Scale correlated	.92[a]	with the IQs earned by the same children taking Form "M" of the same scale (Terman and Merrill, 1937)
The height of children who were measured at age 4 correlated	.81	with the height they attained as adults (Tanner, 1970)
Amount of vocalization observed in girl infants (0-2 years of age) correlated	.56	with their IQs when they reached the age of 13 (Cameron, Livson, and Bayley, 1967)
Height of fathers correlates	.56	with the height of their sons (McNemar, 1955)
Years of education of Brazilian parents correlated	.28	with measures of their children's popularity in elementary school (Lindgren and Guedes, 1963)
Scores obtained by fourth-grade children on a test of attitudes favorable to problem solving correlated	.24	with their scores on an achievement test in arithmetic (Lindgren et al., 1964)
The desirability of fifth-grade boys' first names (as rated by school children) correlated	.00	with their scores on the Iowa Test of Basic Skills (Busse and Seraydarian, 1975)
The IQs of schoolchildren were found to correlate	−.18	with the number of siblings in their respective families (Anastasi, 1956)
The ability of Israeli girls to understand jokes in cartoons correlated	−.23	with the measure of their general level of anxiety (Milgram and Milgram, 1977).
Tendencies of nursery school children to command or order others about correlated	−.31	with their tendencies to comply with others' demands (Berk, 1971)
Ratings sixth-grade boys received from one another on "likability" correlated	−.41	with ratings the same boys received on "depression" (Winder and Rau, 1962)

[a] It is customary to omit the "+" when correlations are positive.

_____strategies in child study

How can the techniques we have described be used? How does the investigator decide, for instance, whether he should employ S-R research design or correlational/differential methods for the investigation he wants to pursue? We now consider the general strategies that form the over-all planning of child study. If the techniques are the bricks and mortar of this behavioral science, the strategies are its architecture.

Observations

There are many ways of observing the behavior of children. They may, for instance, be observed under controlled conditions in the psychological laboratory. The study comparing Chinese-, Anglo-, and Mexican-American mothers interacting with their children that we mentioned earlier in this chapter is an example of a laboratory study, one in which the behavior of the subjects was recorded on videotape and later analyzed (Steward and Steward, 1973).

Observations may also be made in more natural situations—in the classroom, on the playground, or at home. For instance, Sharon Gadberry (1974) observed the behavior of boys 4½ to 5½ years of age who watched television at home with a friend. She noted that their behavior was more passive and that there was much more self-stimulation (scratching, wiggling) when the television was on than during free play before and afterward. When observations and experiments take place in a natural setting, outside the laboratory, they come under the heading of field research, and to the child psychologist there is nothing strange about doing field work in front of a television set.

Because parents' reports of children's behavior have to be interpreted with a great deal of caution, psychologists prefer to use trained observers who are unfamiliar with the children. There are instances, however, in which the data the psychologist requires can be obtained only from parental report. Niem and Collard (1972), for example, were interested in making comparisons between the behaviors of Chinese and American preschool children and finding out how the behavior related to child-rearing patterns in the two cultures. They asked mothers in New England and in Taiwan to record instances of children's aggressiveness over a thirty-day period and to indicate how the mothers dealt with the behavior.

Analysis of the parental reports produced results that were consistent with more impressionistic appraisals of the two cultures, for Chinese children engaged in fewer acts of physical aggression than did American children. Chinese mothers evidently monitored their children's

Psychologists observe the behavior of children in a variety of ways. Here, one psychologist administers an intelligence test, while another observes creative activities in a nursery school.

behavior more than American mothers did, because they reported more incidents of verbal aggression and minor acts of defiance, but they were also more inclined to use love-oriented methods of control. American children, on the other hand, engaged in far more physical aggression and were spanked eleven times more frequently than were Chinese children.

Numerous standardized tests and questionnaires have been devised for use with parents. One of the best known is the Parent Attitudes Research Instrument (PARI), developed by Schaefer and Bell (1958). It consists of 23 scales that measure such dimensions of parent-child interaction as suppression of aggression, strictness, attempts to accelerate or encourage development, and fostering the children's dependency.

Interviews

Questionnaires like the PARI are essentially standardized interview schedules that have been reduced to simple categories and reproduced in printed form. Such questionnaires have advantages over interviews in that they can be more easily administered and analyzed. They also cost less in terms of time and money, for a hundred or so questionnaires can be administered simultaneously to a group of people in less time than it would take to interview a single person.

Questionnaires do, however, have some important disadvantages. A great many people who would not mind describing their experiences and expressing their views in an interview would object to supplying the same information in response to questions posed by a standardized questionnaire. A skilled interviewer, however, is able to put uncooperative parents at ease by saying the right things in the right way to secure their cooperation. The interviewer is also able to sense when parents misunderstand a question and to supply the necessary clarification.

Interviews are often employed to supplement observational methods. Diana Baumrind (1971a), for example, used tape-recorded interviews in combination with observations in study of child-rearing practices we will discuss at the end of this chapter.

Interviews were also the major data-gathering method in a classic study of child-rearing practices conducted by Robert R. Sears and his co-investigators, Eleanor E. Maccoby and Harry Levin (1957), of Harvard University. Interviewers asked almost four hundred mothers living in the Boston area a long series of questions about their experiences with their five-year-old children. They were also queried about their feelings with regard to having children, toilet training, picking up infants when they cry, and so forth. The material collected by the interviewers was analyzed by two raters who operated independently, employing 188 different scales dealing with various dimensions of child-rearing practices.

Sears went on to Stanford, where he conducted an additional study of child-rearing practices, in which he employed interviews with children,

Robert Richardson Sears (1908– has spent his professional career studying the personality and motivational development of children, with special reference to the effect of their parents' attitudes, values, and child-rearing practices.

as well as their fathers and mothers, and also observed them collectively and individually as they dealt with standardized situations in his specially equipped laboratory (Sears, Rau, and Alpert, 1965).

Although Sears' research has not produced any major theories of child development, it has, over the years, generated a great deal of interesting information regarding such aspects of child-parent relations as dependency, the development of conscience, and the effects of maternal warmth. It has also had considerable effect on the work of other investigators.

La Méthode Clinique

Jean Piaget combines interviewing and observational techniques in his méthode clinique. La méthode clinique can be roughly translated as "the clinical method," but it is not quite the same as the methods ordinarily used by clinical psychologists in interviewing and treating patients. The clinical method, as the term is used by most clinicians, refers to a wide variety of techniques, which vary according to the personal orientation and the school of psychology preferred by the individual psychotherapist; these techniques may have as their aim psychodiagnosis or psychotherapy, or both.

Whereas the method used by a clinician is typically employed to gain information about or to help an individual child, Piaget also uses his *méthode clinique* as a means of investigation aimed at learning about the thought processes of children in general. Researchers employing *la méthode clinique* begin by presenting a child with some kind of task or problem. When the child has made an attempt, successful or otherwise, to solve it, the investigator asks him questions about his reasoning and then poses a variation of the problem. With each response the child makes, the investigator asks more questions and then restructures the problem situation in some significant way. The general approach is to try to get inside the child's mind, so to speak, and to see the world as he sees it (Flavell, 1963). Here is an example of how Piaget (1948) used *la méthode clinique* in studying the development of moral judgment of children aged five to seven.

> I (investigator): Do you know what a lie is?
> C (child): It's when you say what isn't true.
> I: Is 2 + 2 = 5 a lie?
> C: Yes, it's a lie.
> I: Why?
> C: Because it isn't right.
> I: Did the boy who said 2 + 2 = 5 know that it wasn't right or did he make a mistake?
> C: He made a mistake.
> I: Then if he made a mistake, did he tell a lie or not?
> C: Yes, he told a lie.
> I: A naughty one?
> C: Not very.
> I: You see this gentleman (a student)?
> C: Yes.
> I: How old do you think he is?
> C: Thirty.
> I: I would say he is 28. (The student says he is 36.) Have we both told lies?
> C: Yes, both lies.
> I: Naughty ones?
> C: Not so very naughty.
> I: Which is the naughtiest, yours or mine, or are they both the same?
> C: Yours is the naughtiest, because the difference is biggest. . . . .
> I: Is it a lie, or did we just make a mistake?
> C: We made a mistake.
> I: Is it a lie all the same, or not?
> C: Yes, it's a lie. (Piaget, 1948)[1]

Piaget concluded, on the basis of interviews like these, that children at this stage of development are aware of the distinction between an intentional misdemeanor and an involuntary mistake, but that they do not stress the distinction and group both together as "lies."

---

[1] Copyright 1948 by the Free Press and published with permission.

Unobtrusive Methods

One of the problems about most tests and questionnaires is that the respondents may have little difficulty in guessing the investigator's motives and hence can slant their responses accordingly. If the questions on the test deal with aggressiveness, the mother who is easily irritated by her son may overstate his misbehavior. On the other hand, she may feel that her reputation as a "good mother" is at stake and may understate the problems she is having with him. Again, a mother may guess what the investigator's hypothesis is and try to "cooperate" by providing him with data that confirm it. This latter tendency is more widespread than is commonly supposed and is one cause underlying the "Rosenthal effect"—so called because of the work of Robert Rosenthal (1966), who noted a persistent tendency for data gathered by research assistants to support their employers' hypotheses. The usual way of guarding against this kind of bias is not to inform observers of the hypotheses being tested; this was the technique of Cynthia Turnure, mentioned earlier in the chapter.

Inasmuch as investigators usually want to observe the normal reactions of children, they usually take pains to see that their research is conducted in a natural and unobtrusive manner and that their goals are completely hidden, or at least skillfully disguised. Indirect approaches generally work best.

One pair of researchers was interested in doing a study on the self-esteem of children—a variable that cannot be measured easily by means of the customary questionnaire, interview, or observational approach. In this investigation, the researchers presented the child with a sheet of paper which bore six circles arranged horizontally. The child was then asked to place symbols representing himself and other members of his family in the circles. On another sheet he was asked to place symbols representing himself and five acquaintances. The test was scored in terms of the rank the child assigned to the symbol that represented himself—the farther to the left (the beginning) of the row, the higher his self-esteem. The investigators used this ingenious test in a number of cross-cultural studies, with interesting results. For instance, in India children who were attending school displayed a considerably higher degree of self-esteem (mean score 28 out of a possible 36) than did those who were unable to attend school (22.1). In Barbados children who were attending select schools had a mean score of 27.6, in contrast to a mean score of 20.8 for those attending ordinary schools (Long and Henderson, 1971).

Projective Tests

The so-called projective tests present the subject with a more or less ambiguous stimulus—a collection of furniture and dolls, for example.

The subject is asked to arrange the items in any way he wishes and then to tell a story about what is going on in the scene he has constructed. Or he is shown an ink blot or a vague picture and asked what he sees in it. In effect, the subject is supposed to "project" something of his thoughts, feelings, and characteristic ways of looking at the world into a relatively unstructured situation and to structure it accordingly. Most of the stimuli that are employed in these projective tests provide the child with no clues to what the test giver is interested in. The child is therefore on his own: whatever accounts he gives represent an unbiased sample of his thoughts and feelings. When projective testing is conducted skillfully, a subject can be led to supply considerable information about his psychological life without being aware that he is doing so, and the tests can be designed to measure an extensive range of variables.

The main problem with projective tests is the difficulty of deriving reliable scores and making valid interpretations. In this respect, they differ from questionnaires, which can be scored easily and accurately and whose results can be analyzed statistically in order to check for reliability and validity. The scoring of projective tests, however, involves judgments that are more or less subjective. Hence it is not unusual for two experienced clinicians who score the same protocol (set of responses) to report scores that are quite different. When there is considerable disagreement about a subject's score, it is difficult to conduct validity studies that enable us to determine what the scores on such tests mean.

There have been a number of attempts to devise projective tests that can be scored in a more reliable way. One such test is the Holtzman Inkblot Technique, or HIT, in which the subject gives one response, or interpretation, to each of forty-five ink blots. The HIT method provides a wider sampling of subject responses that can be scored more precisely than the more conventional Rorschach test, which employs only ten ink blots, to which the subject is permitted to make multiple responses.

The HIT was used successfully in an extensive cross-cultural study in which Mexican and American children at various age levels were followed for five years. Some interesting personality differences emerged. American children tended to be more impulsive, reacting more rapidly to the blots. They also showed greater organizing ability in terms of integrating more elements and larger areas of the blots. The Mexican children were more accurate in their use of visual elements and less likely to respond in ways that were deviant, hostile, and anxious (Holtzman, Diaz-Guerrero, and Swartz, 1975.)

Another projective method that has been used extensively in personality research is the Thematic Apperception Test, or TAT. The children's TAT or CAT, consists of drawings or photographs of animals. The pictures are presented one at a time to the child, who is asked to make up a story for each one. In telling his story he is to imagine what led up to the event shown in the picture, to relate what is happening in the picture, and to state what the outcome will be. Any questions he asks are answered noncommittally, with the nature of the situation and kir of story left entirely to the child.

The fundamental assumption concerning the TAT approach in projective testing is that the child identifies himself with a central figure in the story. The way the figure is described, the problem that is faced, and the means of handling that problem are considered to be reflections of the child's feelings and attitudes.

Although the scoring of the TAT suffers somewhat from reliability problems, it appears to pick up personality variables that cannot be measured easily by other means. The TAT approach has been used extensively in research dealing with certain types of psychological needs, such as the need to achieve (n Ach), the need to affiliate with others (n Aff), and the need to aggress (n Agg). Research of this kind usually makes use of a limited selection of cards that have been found to evoke responses that can be scored for the presence or absence of the need in question. The more "structured" nature of the TAT type of test gives the investigator more control over the stimulus situation than he has with the Rorschach and may account for the greater popularity of the TAT method with researchers.

Play techniques are also used as projective devices in both research and psychotherapy. Such methods are particularly useful in studying younger children, inasmuch as play is a kind of natural medium through which they can communicate feelings more effectively than through words. In play therapy the child is encouraged to play in a spontaneous fashion with the toys and play materials (clay, water, sand, etc.), but in research situations the more usual practice is to present the child with some kind of standard arrangement of materials.

Also popular with students of personality and psychodiagnosticians are test situations in which children produce something of their own—a picture, for example. A picture drawn by a child not only tells us something about his motor (muscle) control but also suggests how he perceives the world. If the picture is that of a person, it may also indicate how he views himself. The draw-a-person test thus may be used as a projective technique, a way of finding out what self-perceptions are being "projected" onto the drawing.

Drawings may thus be used to learn something about a child's view of himself and the world. Figure 2-3 consists of a drawing made by a six-year-old boy who was asked to draw a picture of his family, which consisted of his father and mother, his three-year-old sister, and himself. Although he placed himself third in line, suggesting that he came after his mother in the family's hierarchy, the fact that his little sister was represented as half again taller than he suggests that he had some doubts as to his status. Furthermore, his including what are probably his favorite playthings in the picture implies that they may be important extensions of his self-identity (Grossman and Lindgren, 1959).

58 Principles of Development

FIGURE 2-3. Family portrait, as drawn by a six-year-old boy who has a father, a mother, and a three-year-old sister. (Grossman and Lindgren, 1969.)

Cross-sectional Versus Longitudinal Research

Child psychologists often need information about the changes that take place in children's behavior over an extended period of time. They may be interested in language and want to know the ages at which children use various linguistic forms and the ages at which they use single words, combinations of single words, single sentences, and multiple sentences. They may be interested in the development of another form of learning, such as mathematical ability. They may be interested in the effect that socioeconomic status or culture has as a child grows up in it.

As we indicated earlier in the chapter, there are two ways in which changes can be studied. The most convenient way is to observe groups of children of different ages, record the data obtained from them, and correlate the data with the age. This approach is termed "cross-sectional" because each age sample is considered to be a representative cross section of all children at that state of development. The difficulty, however, is that such research assumes that the children being studied have similar backgrounds. Suppose that the study were made in a number of rural communities, some of which had television and some of which had not. A question might be raised as to whether the language development of children who had been exposed to television would be different from that of those who had not.

The best way to control for varying backgrounds is to carry out a series of observations of the same children over an extended time span. Thus each child's linguistic responses, for instance, serve as a base with which any later new responses can be compared. Such research is termed "longitudinal" because it proceeds in a lengthwise direction in each child's life span and does not include taking behavior samples across the lives of a number of children at only one time. Whereas cross-sectional research studies groups of children at different ages (generally at the same time), longitudinal research studies a single group of children at different ages (and must necessarily wait until the children reach the ages that are being studied).

Longitudinal research gives a more accurate picture of developmental changes. The best example can be found in research on intellectual changes, not in children, but in adults. When intelligence tests were first developed, norms for each age were determined by taking samples of the performance of individuals at different age levels—a cross-sectional approach. Inasmuch as individuals aged thirty or more were observed to make successively lower scores, researchers concluded that intellectual ability declines from the mid-thirties onward (Jones and Conrad, 1933). It was not until sufficient data from longitudinal studies had accumulated that it became clear that verbal intelligence tends to increase, not decline, during the adult years (Owens, 1966). (Nonverbal intelligence does tend to decline slightly during the later adult years, but not as much as the earlier findings suggested [Schaie and Strother, 1968].) The reason for the false reading of the earlier cross-sectional research was that the older individuals in the samples had completed less schooling than the younger samples and the number of years of education has been found to be highly correlated with intelligence test scores (Ginzberg et al., 1959).

There are advantages and disadvantages in both cross-sectional and longitudinal research. We have noted the major disadvantage to cross-sectional research—the misinterpretation of results—but it does have an advantage in that it may be accomplished rapidly and efficiently. Longitudinal research requires the investigator to test or otherwise observe his subjects from time to time over an extended period. It is obviously easier to do one set of observations than to do a series of observations spread over weeks, months, or even years. Not only does it take much longer to do a longitudinal study, but there is also the probability that some subjects will become unavailable. They may move away from the area, for example, or parents may change their minds about permitting further observation. In any event, longitudinal studies are more costly in time and in money.

Sometimes researchers use a short-term longitudinal approach, actually a combination of longitudinal and cross-sectional strategies. This was the strategy employed by Holtzman, Díaz-Guerrero, and Swartz (1975) in the cross-cultural study of Mexican and American children mentioned earlier. The cohorts, or age groupings, of subjects in their research consisted of children who were six, nine, and twelve years old when the study began. Each cohort was followed for five years—in other words, until the children were eleven, fourteen, and seventeen, respectively. This design meant that the age span of the three cohorts overlapped by two years, thus making it possible to determine whether the groups were comparable. For instance, when the youngest group of Mexican children reached the age of nine, their mean vocabulary score was 27.6, which was identical to the score that had been attained by the next older group of Mexican children when they were nine. When scores of two groups the same age are identical or very close on a number of key measures, it is reasonable to assume that the groups are probably comparable in other significant respects.

Clinical Treatment and Research with Children

The clinical treatment of children's psychological problems is closely related to research in child psychology in some respects, although the two fields have somewhat different objectives. Data gathered by the researcher that provide information about children in general can often be helpful to the therapist in diagnosing and treating specific children, and therapists are rich sources of research leads and insights regarding the emotional lives of children in general. The research on self-esteem that we cited earlier, for instance, was to a large extent stimulated by the observation of clinicians that most children with severe problems also have a poor opinion of themselves, and the cross-cultural research we have described is helping to illuminate a great many puzzling aspects of the behavior of some of the children of different ethnic backgrounds who have been referred to clinical and school psychologists for help.

In a sense, every therapist is a researcher, as he tries to find out the dimensions of a child's problem and the causes of the child's distress or failure to cope. And many a clinician has noted recurring themes in the lives of the children he sees and has gathered data to determine whether these themes are associated with common factors. Most of this research has been of an informal nature, with looser controls and smaller numbers of subjects than most of the studies appearing in the research literature. Nonetheless, investigations of this type have scientific value. If they do not always fit the ideal pattern, neither in all cases do the data generated by more elaborately planned studies. A too rigid insistence on greater control would mean the elimination of a considerable amount of interesting material, much of which makes a great deal of sense and suggests paths for future research.

A case in point is a report of Diana Baumrind (1971a) that does not meet the usual scientific criteria, largely because of the small size of her sample. The study dealt with a group of eight families in which the parents and children were unusually harmonious. The data were drawn from a larger study that had a sufficient number of subjects to demonstrate statistically significant relationships among variables, but were described separately in a brief report because of the unusual character of the child-parent relationship. In many ways, the atmosphere of the families seemed ideal: it was marked by a lack of discord and tension and by an emphasis on rationality. Whereas *permissive* parents (in the main study) avoided exercising control over their children but were angry because they had no control, and *authoritarian* parents willingly exercised control, this group of *harmonious* parents did not seem to be either exercising or avoiding control. The parents concentrated, instead, on achieving harmony in the home and on developing principles that could be used as a basis for resolving differences and for what they considered to be the proper approach to life. Many of these families, incidentally, were preparing themselves for living in communes, another factor that makes this small study especially interesting.

Six of the eight children in the study were girls. Their behavior in preschool suggested that they were exceptionally well adjusted: bright, friendly, cooperative, independent, and high-achieving. The two boys, however, though cooperative, were particularly submissive, aimless, dependent, and not achievement-oriented.

Baumrind concluded her brief report by noting that it would be valuable to find more families like these in order to study long-range effects of such families on children's behavior and development.

A study like this stimulates speculation. We wonder, for example, whether the "ideal" family is good for girls but not for boys, or whether "harmonious" families can be achieved more readily if the children are girls.

Research by means of the strategies and techniques we have discussed may answer such questions in ensuing years, or perhaps they may be answered by new methods, in ways not yet known. The psychology of the child is not a finished body of knowledge, it is vital and rapidly changing. Although it has come a long way from the casual observations of folk wisdom, as a science it is young. Its development offers an opportunity not only to behavioral scientists but to the parents and teachers of the future.

summary

Although knowledge begins with observation, the very act of observing influences the event observed. Everyday observations are likely to be uncontrolled, subjective, personalized, and impressionistic. An individual's culture provides a background of "common-sense" knowledge that tends to bias observation.

Behavioral scientists attempt to control for bias by using systematized methods such as standardized tests, scales, schedules, and tasks. They take pains to ensure that observers and measures are *reliable* (precise and dependable) and that measures are *valid*, in the sense that they measure what they mean to measure.

To be truly scientific, an investigation must follow a basic set of rules: it must be *replicable*, and it is likely to begin with a *hypothesis* about the relationship of several *variables*; the variable that is hypothesized as causal is the *independent variable*, and the variable that it influences is the *dependent variable*.

The experimental method is the classic form for S-R research. A stimulus (the independent variable) is systematically introduced in a controlled situation, and the experimenter observes the subject's response (the dependent variable). The experimenter must, however, take steps to ensure that the observed effect is caused by the independent variable, and not by other variables that may appear in association with it. In determining the effect the voice of an infant's mother has on his behavior, for example, the researcher must be sure that the infant is reacting to his mother's voice and not to adult female voices in general. Hence the researcher institutes a control by exposing the infant not only to his mother's voice but to the voice of a strange adult female as well. Age and sex are variables that are usually controlled, and reliability is insured by employing more than one judge or rater of the dependent variable. The experimental group's performance may also be contrasted with that of a comparable control group.

S-R or experimental research is one kind of technique in behavioral study. Another is R-R research, or correlational/differential methods, in which responses are compared or contrasted. This technique is often employed in studies of cross-cultural differences and child-rearing practices, as well as in other types of investigations that do not lend themselves to experimental manipulations of the S-R type. In such studies, pre-existing conditions, attitudes, and values are usually considered to be independent variables, with performance in test situations the dependent variable. Often S-R and R-R methods are used in combination.

Correlation is the statistic most widely used in developmental psychology. Most correlational studies employ the Pearsonian coefficient of correlation, a statistic that ranges between the limits set by +1.00 (the more of one variable, the more of the other, in exact proportion) and −1.00 (the more of one variable, the less of the other, in exact proportion). A correlation of .00 indicates that the relationship between the variables is a random one, brought about by chance.

Children's behavior may be studied in natural surroundings as well as in the laboratory. Some information can be obtained only from parents.

La méthode clinique is an observational method used by Piaget in conducting his inquiries into the way in which children view their world and think. Although the term may be translated as "the clinical method," *la méthode clinique* is really a specialized technique for investigating the thinking of children in general, and does not make use of varied approaches as do the psychodiagnostic and therapeutic methods used by clinicians who treat individual children.

The intent of many tests and measurements is quite obvious to the test taker, thus exposing them to response bias. But researchers who present subjects with disguised or ambiguous situations in the form of projective tests are able to control this source of bias, even though something may be lost in the way of reliability. Some projective tests, like the Holtzman Inkblot Test (HIT), designed to reduce unreliability, have been used successfully in cross-cultural research. Other projective devices include the Thematic Apperception Test (TAT), play techniques, and pictures drawn by children.

Comparisons and contrasts between behavior or characteristics typical or children at various ages and stages of development may be gathered by the *cross-sectional* method, in which samples of children at different ages are observed or tested, or by the *longitudinal* method, which studies the same group of children over an extended period of time. The cross-sectional method is simpler and quicker, but it runs the risk of including unidentified experimental variables. Given sufficient time and resources, the longitudinal method has the advantage that each child serves as his own control, so to speak. Some studies compromise by conducting relatively short-term longitudinal studies of cohorts of subjects whose ages overlap at the ends of the time span being studied.

Psychotherapists and researchers often share common interests with respect to gathering and using data about the psychological dimensions of children's lives, and there is much exchange of data. Clinical research tends to involve smaller numbers and is likely to be less rigorous, in a scientific sense. But such research should be ignored: it often yields interesting leads and produces findings that could not be obtained by conventional strategies.

three

The Process of Development

Whether or not there is a developmental psychology, there certainly is a child psychology. Even if the child is only a small case of the adult organism, he is an extremely common case (indeed, inevitable); the phenomena occurring in the child may not be different in kind from what will occur later, but they may well have major import for what will happen later.
— BAER AND WRIGHT (1974)

The childhood shows the man
As morning shows the day.
— JOHN MILTON

growth and development

Observation of the process of development in young children is a fascinating enterprise, and one that never ceases to delight and amaze parents and other observers. The addition of two ounces to the weight chart, the sudden ability of the baby to hold his head in the midplane rather than turned always to one side, the momentous transfer of a rattle from one hand to the other, the solemn embarking upon the first solo step, or the articulation of the first distinct word—all provide manifestations of this potential of development. Furthermore, within certain rather broad limits the development is orderly and sequential. Just as a plant proceeds from bulb to shoot to leaf to bud to blossom and never, except under certain artificial conditions, modifies this sequence or short-circuits one or another stage, the development of the child proceeds in a lawful manner according to certain rules established by the fact that a child is a living organism and, specifically, a member of the human species.

For example, every parent knows that, in general, a child will sit before he stands, walk before he talks, gain control of his bowel movements before being able to regulate bladder functioning, and so on. On the other hand, it is unlikely that every parent or interested observer has noted important, if subtler, general trends in the developmental process. One of the purposes of this chapter is to call attention to some of these trends.

Basic to all development is growth. In its specific sense, the term *growth* refers to an increase in size or number of parts of an organism, whereas *development* (literally, "unfolding") refers to changes in character or function. Inasmuch as quantitative changes in a young organism are usually accompanied by qualitative changes, the terms *growth* and *development* have taken on overlapping and virtually synonymous meanings in general usage. There are a number of instances, however, where they obviously do not mean the same thing. We think of growth as continuing only to maturity, while development continues throughout the life span, from conception until death. The term *growth*, too, seems somehow to imply physical changes, although we do speak of cognitive growth. *Development* is the more general term, including the concept of change of all kinds, including those associated with maturation and growth, as well as decline.

Development is observable in every phase of life. Whether the field of observation is at the level of the cell, the organ, or the organism, it is still safe to say that some development is always occurring. Although development may be said to begin at the point of conception, we cannot ignore such important pre-existing conditions as the affluence or poverty of the parents, their way of relating to each other, and the kind of society into which the child is born. The birth of a baby and the changes that will manifest themselves in all its future behavior represent in one sense a condensation of the history of life from its most remote beginnings up to the time of the observation. Reflected in every act will be the evolution of the entire biological drama as performed within the confines of a complex physical and social world.

The fact that development is a process rather than a response or a set of responses makes reliable (i.e., repeatable) observation difficult. In other words, development does not sit and wait for repeated measurements of any kind to be made; the organism is constantly changing, and prior conditions can never be exactly duplicated. In actuality no one can claim to have observed the process itself, for development refers to a change detectable from observations made at two or more points on a time continuum. We might take sequential pictures of the metamorphosis from caterpillar to butterfly, project them continuously as motion pictures, and thus apparently compress the development in such a way as to make the *process* itself appear to be the unit of observation. But no matter how much, for purposes of more careful study, we either accelerate or retard representations of development, we can do no more than infer the process from more or less widely separated observations made at different times.

genetic background and development

From Cell to Organism

Although the story of life has infinite dimensions, going back billions of years to the first one-celled organisms and beyond, the scope of this presentation is necessarily limited; hence we will begin our study of the child at some recognizable point—say, the moment of conception, when the sperm has battered its way through seemingly insurmountable obstacles and has united itself with the ovum to form the zygote. At this moment the patterns for the neurophysical development of the person-to-be are set.

Genetic theory generally holds that these patterns are fixed by *genes*: large and complex molecules in the *chromosomes*, the rodlike or threadlike bodies contained in the nuclei of living cells. Each cell normally contains 46 chromosomes, half from each parent. Chromosomes are structures composed of complex double-spiral molecules of deoxyribonucleic acid (DNA). Francis Crick, James D. Watson, and Maurice Wilkins won a Nobel Prize in 1962 for their research showing that DNA molecules provide the biochemical basis for the genetic transmission of characteristics. It is estimated that there are about a million genetic code units, or genes, in a human cell, which averages out to about twenty thousand genes per chromosome. The genes determine the characteristics of another biochemical: ribonucleic acid (RNA). The "master program" of the genes is carried out by RNA molecules, which serve as "messengers" that determine the structure and functioning of body tissue.

Thus the characteristics that any individual displays were set, at least in their initial form, by the DNA molecules in the chromosomes received from the parents. This fact explains the similarities between parents and children, but it does not explain their differences, which come about because of a complex process involving the pairing of chromosomes and the rearranging and trading of genes between chromosomes that take place shortly after conception.

Inasmuch as the number of possible combination of genes is virtually infinite, we can only speculate as to why children actually turn out to be like their parents and siblings in so many ways. These similarities are most obvious in physical traits, such as color of eyes, hair, and skin. They are less obvious in behavioral traits, such as impulsivity, ingenuity, and activity level. The behavior of man is far more modifiable than that of the lesser animals; hence it is far from certain how many individual differences are acquired through biological inheritance and how many through learning. A couple of generations ago, we were certain that the

"*He has my nose and his father's anger.*"

(Drawing by Handelsman © 1975 The New Yorker Magazine, Inc.)

tendency of some families to have an unusual number of, say, artists or athletes among their members was due entirely to the presence of traits that were biologically inherited. Today, we are not at all certain, because it seems to be equally possible that the observed traits may have resulted from social inheritance—that is, from mutual imitation and encouragement, and from the creation of psychological climates favoring the learning of certain skills.

Most of the research on genetic transmission of physical traits has been focused on defects and anomalies, or deviations from the normal. For example, allergy to ragweed pollens has been shown to be genetically transmitted (Blumenthal et al., 1974), as has hemophilia, a disease characterized by excessive bleeding caused by abnormally low levels of blood-clotting agents. Contrary to popular belief, hemophilia is not confined to aristocratic European families, for about twenty thousand persons in the United States are afflicted by moderate to severe forms of the disease (Marx, 1975a). Recent research on right- and left-handedness suggests that it, too, is genetically determined, rather than acquired through learning, as had been previously thought (Hicks and Kinsbourne, 1976).

The effect of genetic abnormalities on violent and antisocial behavior has also been given some attention by researchers. There is the celebrated case of Richard Speck, who murdered eight student nurses and who was reported to have XYY chromosomes. Chromosomes, viewed microscopically, have four branches resembling an X, or lack one branch, resembling a Y. The particular pair of chromosomes that determine an individual's sex are XX in females, but XY in males. A male infant will very occasionally—once in 975 times—inherit an extra male chromosome and thus be classified as XYY. Some experts are convinced that such a combination predisposes an individual to aggression and violence, presumably because the extra Y chromosome makes him "more male."

Ernest B. Hook (1973), a pediatrician who is a member of the Birth Defects Institute of the New York State Department of Health, has reviewed the research evidence and has noted that about 2 per cent of the male inmates in mental and penal institutions possess chromosomes of the XYY type. Although this proportion is 18 times greater than

(Schultz, © 1976, United Feature Syndicate)

would be expected by chance, Hook believes that the over-all probability of an XYY male's being institutionalized is actually very small. Males with the opposite type of anomaly, the XXY type, also have a greater-than-chance likelihood of being institutionalized, but the risk is less than that of males of the XYY type.

If genetic factors, like XYY or XXY chromosomes, predispose individuals to deviant behavior, it is clear that a good many other factors must be present for the behavior to become really abnormal. Inasmuch as impoverished neighborhoods and homes dominated by brutal or irresponsible adults have been found to produce a great deal of psychopathology of all types, it seems likely that environmental stress makes a more important contribution to deviancy than genetic factors. The tendency is therefore for behavioral scientists, especially in America, to weigh environmental factors more heavily than genetic ones in accounting for behavioral trends of all types, abnormal and otherwise.

Support for this view is based on the observation that the human organism is extremely plastic.[1] No other animal can match the human capacity either to produce an endless variety of response patterns or to modify response patterns that are initially biologically determined. The acquisition and the modification of response patterns come about through learning, through the interaction of the human organism with its environment. Theoretically, similar environments should produce similar responses. This does seem to occur to some extent. Individuals growing up in the same social environment speak the same language traits.

Yet there are some doubts. One is tempted to say that the placid temperament of the Hopi and Zuñi Indians and the aggressiveness of the Apaches and Comanches (Benedict, 1934) are the products of their respective cultures, but we cannot be absolutely sure. Clyde Kluckhohn (1949) noted that Zuñi babies who were more than usually active at birth had become placid by the time they were two years old, whereas hyperactive white babies retained their initial hyperactivity. The implication is that the Zuñi culture emphasizes placidity and the white Anglo culture emphasizes activity, and that each culture infuses its children with its own preferred personality style. This seems to confirm the environmentalist's argument, yet we should not overlook another observation made by Kluckhohn: that at birth, the proportion of hyperactive babies was already higher among the whites than among the Zuñis.

And so the question is reopened: Are whites more active than Zuñis because their culture teaches them to be active, or are they more active because more of them were born that way? It is beyond the scope of this book to resolve that question (assuming that it can be resolved), but it is

---

[1] *Plastic* is used here and throughout this book in the accepted meaning of "impressionable, pliable, and malleable," not in its more recently popularized sense of "artificial and synthetic."

important to keep in mind that behind our façade of learned similarities and differences, there may be some genetically acquired tendencies that act on our behavior in ways that usually, for one reason or another, escape our notice.

Studies of Twins

The problem of determining the relative effects of environment and heredity in humans is obviously complex. At present, the problem has been approached largely through the studies of twins.

Twins are of two types: identical twins, products of a single fertilized ovum (hence monozygotic or MZ twins); and unlike twins, products of two different fertilized ova (hence dizygotic or DZ twins). MZ twins are always of the same sex, whereas DZ twins may be of the same sex or of different sexes. Studies of twins have a number of built-in controls and are thus particularly useful for investigators who want to study the interaction of heredity and environment. In the first place, MZ twins have the same genetic elements, whereas nontwin siblings have a similar but not identical genetic background. Siblings—twins or otherwise—differ from individuals coming from assorted families in that they share a similar family environment; any two siblings are exposed to the influence of the same parents, the same cultural environment, the same neighborhood, and so forth. It would seem that they have the same environment, but strictly speaking this is not so. Any child's environment includes the attitudes and expectations that others have for him, and these, in turn, are different for each child in the family, depending on the child's birth order and sex, the extent to which he is wanted or unwanted, and so forth. These variations are fairly well controlled with likesex DZ twins, who in theory differ only genetically from MZ twins.

Twin studies have dealt with three kinds of variables: intelligence, personality traits, and tendencies toward mental disorder. Studies of intelligence report results that seem to show that intelligence is genetically determined for the most part, because the correlation of intelligence test scores for MZ twins raised in different families is .77, whereas that for MZ twins raised together is .76. The correlation for DZ twins raised together is .51 (Shields, 1962).[2] The obvious conclusion could be accepted without question, if it were not for a multitude of studies that show a persistent relationship between environmental quality and intelligence (e.g., Bloom, 1964). We therefore take a second look at the twin research and wonder whether some of the observed similarity was caused by similar environments in the pairs of families in which the separated MZ twins grew up. In another study of MZ twins reared

---

[2] More recent evidence shows that the higher correlations between IQs of MZ twins, in contrast to DZ twins, is in part caused by a statistical quirk—the fact that a greater percentage of MZ twins are mentally retarded (Nichols and Broman, 1974).

Contrary to popular belief, twins are not always identical. The pair seated on their mother's lap are monozygotic (MZ) — that is, alike or identical twins. The other pair are dizygotic (DZ) or unlike twins. Note the differences in skin, hair, and height.

apart, an analysis was made of differences in the educational and social advantages of the pairs of families. Where social differences were small, IQ differences were invariably small, but where social differences were great, IQ differences in seven out of ten cases were also great (Newman, Freeman, and Holzinger, 1937; Johnson, 1963).

With respect to personality traits, Gottesman (1963) compared personality test responses of MZ and DZ adolescents and found that MZ twins were much more similar to one another than were DZ twins on scales measuring such traits as group dependency versus self-sufficiency, confidence versus guilt proneness, and seriousness versus enthusiasm.

Gottesman and Shields (1966) have reviewed a number of studies dealing with the tendency of MZ and DZ twin pairs to develop schizophrenia, a severe mental disorder of psychosis. Their findings were reported in terms of concordance between the pairs—that is, the percentage of times the other twin became schizophrenic if schizophrenia was reported for one twin. What they found was a 58 per cent concordance for MZ twins, in contrast to a 14 per cent concordance for DZ twins.

Taken together, these studies suggest that genetically determined biological factors probably do make a considerable contribution to variations in behavior—not that environmental conditions make a minimal contribution, but rather that a focus on environmental factors is going to tell only part of the story of human behavior. To be sure, the environmental factors are more easily studied and manipulated than are genetic factors, and this in itself is a matter of immense importance.

_____trends in development

The genetic material that makes us different, one from the other, also makes us similar in many ways. One of these ways is the tendency for our development to proceed along predictable lines. This predictability is made possible by the fact that developmental changes take place in an orderly, sequential fashion.

The Whole Child in a Total Environment

The recognition that all developmental phenomena interact with one another is a basic prerequisite to understanding the child. Even though we observe some changes that seem to be unrelated to other trends we have noted, it is most unlikely that this is true, for no child is ever less than *a whole child responding to his total environment.*

Only by accepting this holistic, unitary, integrative view of the entire drama of development can we hope to gain any real understanding of its scope and range. This view does not imply that forces acting on different children are identical in their patterning or in the kind of effect they will have. Not only is each child unique in certain respects, but his environment is also unique. Nevertheless, the main focus of developmental psychology is not the understanding of the *uniqueness* of each human organism, but the *similarities* that organisms share. Unless we can arrive at some generalizations, there can be no science.

The relationship between structure and function, as well, can be viewed holistically. Although it is possible to study an organ, muscle, or nerve in terms of its structure alone, it is best understood with respect to its function, as well as its relationship to other parts of the body. Functions often change during the maturational process. The digestive tract of the infant, for instance, alters its structure with time in order to accommodate foods that are more complex, more varied, and less bland. Because infants vary somewhat in their maturational rates, we put each new food through a test period in order to find out whether or not it "agrees" with a given child. How the infant's digestion fares as he eats the new foods enables us to tell whether his digestive tract has reached the proper point of structural and functional readiness.

In this book we are more concerned with the development of function or behavior rather than with structure. This does not mean that we consider structure unimportant, but instead that function and behavior are of greater interest to psychologists, just as structure is of greater interest to physiologists and anatomists.

Developmental Direction

The general direction of growth moves in fairly steady progression from the head region of the organism downward. This directional gradient has been labeled the cephalocaudal (literally, head-to-tail) sequence. A correlated type of directionality is the proximodistal (near-to-far) pattern—that is, development proceeds from the central area of the body toward the extremities. That growth should so proceed seems determined by the fact that the most rapid development occurs in or near those parts of the cells that are destined to be nervous structure. There appears to be a heightened sensitivity in those areas that facilitates faster growth.

This directionality is characteristic of both structural and functional change: observation of the human embryo and infant reveals that at any given moment, the head is relatively more developed than the legs and feet (see illustrations in Chapter 5). At the functional or behavioral level, therefore, the baby will gain control of his eyes and head before his trunk and legs and will coordinate arm movements before he acquires precise and refined finger manipulation. We shall discuss further examples of this trend in development in subsequent chapters.

Differentiation and Integration

At the moment of conception, the potentiality for everything that eventually appears in the way of structure and function must exist in the fertilized cell, so that development consists of the creation of both differences (or differentiation) and integration—that is, the continuous reorganization into a unified whole of the differences that emerge.

The original cell from which a child eventually develops may thus be thought of as *totipotent*, a term derived from a Latin word meaning "capable of all things." When the cell divides, it abandons its totipotentiality in favor of individuality, giving up its versatility for specialization. As cell division continues, a milestone is eventually reached: the moment when a parent cell gives birth to a particular kind of offspring (nerve, muscle, or gland) and these resulting cells from that point on will reproduce only their own kind. This increasing differentiation is held in check or controlled by integrating forces that enable the organism to act as a coordinated whole at any stage in the developmental process.

A similar process of differentiation and integration can be found at the behavioral level. In some notable experimental and observational work on the development of swimming in the salamander, Coghill (1929) observed that the first movements were gross flexions or bending movements of the entire trunk, beginning in the head region and progressing toward the tail. The flexions may occur either to the right or to the left, and as the reaction becomes more complex, a second contraction in one direction may occur before a contraction in the opposite direction has been completed. When these alternating flexions occur rapidly enough, the animal is swimming: it exerts pressure upon the water and is propelled forward, as shown in Figure 3-1.

Walking on land follows a similar pattern, although of course the salamander cannot develop that skill until it grows legs. There are at first only mass movements of the trunk, succeeded by gradual differentiation or individuation of action of the limbs as they become able to function in relative independence of the movement of the trunk. Myrtle B. McGraw (1946), who studied intensively the development of crawling in infants, commented on the close similarity between this description by Coghill and the behavior that occurs in the human infant.

Another example of this constant interweaving of differentiation and integration can be found in the development of voluntary prehension or clutching in young babies. The newborn infant initially possesses a grasping—sometimes called Darwinian—reflex. Place your finger in a baby's palm and his fingers will close around it with what sometimes appears to be a viselike grip. This reflex—a clear illustration of a specific response to local stimulation—begins to disappear after about six weeks, or else lapses into a relatively static phase during which an object, once grasped, will not be released until the hand makes contact with another surface that relieves the pull on the tendons. When

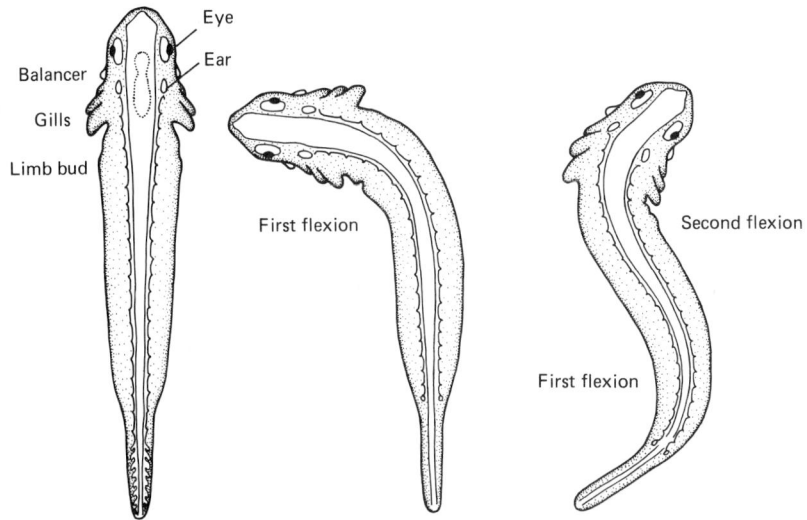

FIGURE 3-1. *The beginnings of aquatic locomotion in the salamander (Amblystoma).* (After Coghill, 1929.)

voluntary attempts at grasping begin sometime later, this reflex is of no value, and a new skill must be developed through a gradual refinement of gross movements of the hand.

There seems to be little doubt that both processes, integration and differentiation, operate simultaneously in the development of behavior. The almost infinite array of behaviors of which an adult is capable cannot, however, be explained merely in terms of a simple process of differentiation from simpler responses. What occurs, instead, is a constant interlacing of differentiation and integration. As soon as a new pattern of behavior emerges, it is woven into the total, everexpanding tapestry of development.

Critical Periods

In the Biblical admonition that there is "a time to be born, and a time to die; a time to plant, and time to pluck up that which has been planted," we find a concise statement of the principle of critical periods.

A life history is characterized by a sequence of important formative events sharply etched against a background of seemingly less significant experience. Furthermore, within any given culture, the critical events will show a high degree of similarity. For example, for the American child there are such memorable occasions as the first day of school, loss of the first baby teeth, being permitted to stay up after midnight, walking to school alone, graduation from high school, paid employment, and many, many more. Most of these events will be retained in the memories of the individual; other significant ones, such as the first solo step or the first use of comprehensible speech, may be remembered only by other family members, but are nonetheless important items on the developmental chart. Another notable fact about such signal events is that deviation from the normal time schedule is almost invariably a conversation piece. The fact that Mary talked before she walked was long a subject of family discussion; that Harold had no girl friends during his entire high school career identified him as deviant from the developmental pattern followed by most of his contemporaries.

The critical-period hypothesis goes far beyond the simple observation that some experiences are more significant than others. It maintains that the young organism is more sensitive to certain kinds of stimuli at some stages of its development than at others. Normal development in later stages can be impeded if the organism has received inadequate nourishment, experienced unusual stress, or lacked appropriate learning experiences during earlier and more sensitive stages.

The critical-period hypothesis also has its positive side: it holds that appropriate treatment experienced during a critical stage may also do more to facilitate positive forms of behavior or desirable developmental changes at later stages than if the same treatment is introduced later.

Some of the evidence favoring the critical-period hypothesis comes from studies with embryos. We can remove from the embryo certain cells that would have developed into the digestive tract and anchor them near the developing heart. If this is done early enough in the life history of the organism, we will find that the cells develop into a type associated with circulatory functioning—liver cells. What the cells become, therefore, would seem to be determined by the situation in which they find themselves. If the operation is done a few days later, however, the cells do not change their character, and the result is merely a closer positioning of heart and intestines.

The animal laboratory, too, provides evidence favoring the critical-period hypothesis. Konrad Lorenz (1935), the famous ethologist, noted that shortly after hatching ducklings will follow the first slowly moving object that is available, be it a painted decoy, a block of wood, or even Professor Lorenz. The acquisition of this response, which Lorenz calls *imprinting*, must occur within 36 hours of hatching for it to become fixed. Thereafter the ducklings will follow no other moving object, not even a mother duck, should one appear belatedly.[2] Harry Harlow (1958, 1962), whose work we will discuss in Chapter 8, found that infant rhesus monkeys who were separated from their mothers and from normal social contacts with other monkeys developed severe problems of social and sexual maladjustment as adults.

---

[2] Lorenz's findings have been questioned by Gilbert Gottlieb (1973), whose experiments show that the quacking sounds made by the mother duck are even more important than her slow, waddling movement in getting ducklings to follow her. In any event, Gottlieb did not challenge the general theory of imprinting.

Evidence favoring the critical-period hypothesis is not as strong for human beings as it is for animals. We cannot experiment on humans as we do on animals, and have to content ourselves with comparing the behavior of children who were deprived or otherwise overstressed when they were very young with that of children whose experiences were more normal. The difficulty with such research, of course, is that of controlling all relevant variables. If, for instance, we find that children who were deprived during preschool years perform less adequately in school than other children do, is this difference caused by the deprivation that occurred during some early, critical period, or was it caused by the fact that they are still being deprived? It is not so much that the research contradicts the critical period hypothesis in human development as that it fails to produce evidence that demonstrates clearly that deprivation or stress has a more significant effect at certain periods than at others.

Nevertheless, the idea that there are periods, especially in early childhood, during which children are more vulnerable is attractive from the standpoints of both common sense and psychological theory. The foundation block of most of the critical-period theory is Freudian. Freud and his interpreters have described several major developmental stages during which the major focus of biological and psychological energy is to be found in one or another bodily zone of development. For example, during the early weeks and months of life, the major source of gratification, and accordingly of potential frustration, resides in those activities associated with nourishment. Calling attention to the importance of these "intake" activities, Freud labeled this the *oral* stage. Later, the focus of energy was presumed to shift to the *anal* and eventually the *genital* zone, at which times the primary source of gratification or satisfaction of important biological and psychological needs was similarly shifted.

Freud maintained that insufficient gratification at any one of these critical periods in effect "freezes" a certain amount of mental energy (his term for this was *fixation of libido*) and hampers subsequent normal development. That is, the child who does not receive sufficient gratification of his oral needs presumably is destined to continue to seek substitute (or direct) gratification of such needs and is unable to effect smooth transition to the next developmental stage. In line with this theory, a child weaned prematurely or too harshly—or, for that matter, indulged too long in sucking activities—might become fixated at the oral level and be unable to move on freely to more mature developmental levels.

A good description of the critical-period hypothesis from the perspective of education is that of Robert J. Havighurst (1953). He used the term *developmental task* to convey the notion of crises in development with which the growing individual must inevitably cope. A developmental task was defined as "a task which arises at or about a certain period in the life of the individual, successful achievement of which leads to his happiness and to success with later tasks, while failure leads to unhappiness in the individual, disapproval by the society, and difficulty with later tasks". In other words, certain developmental tasks must be mastered if the child is to develop normally therafter. These tasks may arise from physical maturation, from cultural pressures, or from the emerging personality that must somehow integrate the forces emanating from the other two sources.

Examples of developmental tasks that must be faced in childhood are learning to walk, to talk, and to comprehend and manipulate letter and numerical symbols. Inadequate achievement in any one of these tasks handicaps the individual to a certain extent in his efforts to cope with later problems; consider, for example, the difficulty faced by a child who has not learned to talk but who attempts to establish rewarding social relationships.

These learning tasks represent an approach toward integration of the demands made on the child by his physical organism and by the society in which he must develop. The manner in which they will be expressed will obviously differ in various social and cultural groups; yet, at the same time, there should be considerable similarity from culture to culture with respect to the tasks themselves, if not to the exact manner in which they are revealed.

We noted earlier that the critical-period hypothesis is an attractive idea. It sounds logical. Indeed, its appeal was so strong during the mid-1960s that it served as the cornerstone of Operation Head Start. This experimental program was instituted in order to provide stimulating and intellectually enriching experiences for socially deprived preschool children from impoverished homes, with the idea that they would be better able to benefit from regular school experiences later on. Socially deprived children characteristically begin school with IQs moderately below normal, on the average. They make slower and less effective progress through the school curriculum. By the time they reach adolescence, their mean IQ has declined even further, and they are likely to be retarded two or more years in basic skills.

The educators of the 1960s took the critical period to be ages three to five and theorized that if deprived children could be given a "head start," by exposing them to an environment calculated to develop school-oriented skills, values, and work habits, they would be able to start school on a more nearly equal footing with children from middle-class homes. Evaluation studies of Head Start's effectiveness have produced mixed results, however. A common finding is that there is an initial IQ gain, but that it does not hold up beyond the first year of school.

Such results can be interpreted in two ways by proponents of the critical-period theory: either the period selected was not as critical as an earlier one would have been, or else the Head Start programs (many of which were put together hastily and administered haphazardly) did not supply what the children lacked (Payne, et al., 1973). It may also be that not one but several critical periods occur during the preschool years, each of which is important for some skill of value.

 Piaget's concept of development

Much of the thinking and planning that went into the development of Operation Head Start borrowed very heavily from the theories of Jean Piaget. Although the Head Start planners were interested in the cognitive (thinking, problem-solving) and social development of children, they based their curricula on the idea that young children learn best from concrete activities—activities in which children can touch and manipulate objects, gain an understanding of the properties of those objects, and apply what they have learned to acquire a comprehension of the world around them. This general concept is "perhaps the most important proposition that the educator can derive from Piaget's work" (Ginsburg and Opper, 1969).

Operation Head Start is only one of the many educational programs which have felt the effect of Piaget's thinking; he is easily the most influential figure in child psychology today. It is for that reason we have set aside this section to examine some of his theories and will consider additional aspects of them at various points throughout this book.

Piaget was born in 1896 at Neuchâtel in the French part of Switzerland. He early demonstrated an interest in science, publishing his first paper at the age of ten. His first scientific field was zoology, and by the age of 21 he had published twenty papers on molluscs. In his early twenties Piaget became interested in psychological problems and worked for a while with Theodore Simon, a collaborator on the Binet scale of intelligence. Piaget was more interested in the responses children gave to the investigator's questions than in the test itself, and was especially fascinated by the incorrect answers and the way children arrived at them. During the same period he also studied at Eugen Bleuler's psychiatric clinic in Zurich, where he became acquainted with the *méthode clinique* that later proved so useful in interviewing children as to their processes of reasoning.[3] In 1921, Piaget published four papers on mental testing and was made director of the Institut Jean-Jacques Rousseau in Geneva, now the Institut des Sciences de L'Education (Institute of Educational Sciences). In the years since he has assumed this position, he has published more than twenty books and

---

[3] Piaget's use of *la méthode clinique* was illustrated by an example we cited in Chapter 2, in which he showed that a six-year-old child is unable to distinguish between a lie and an innocent misstatement.

80 Principles of Development

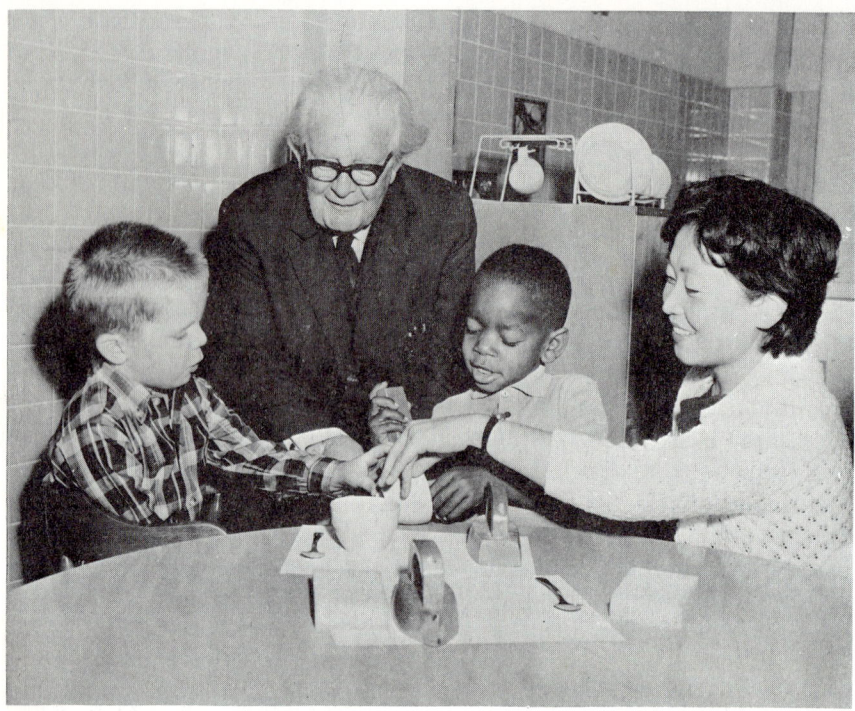

Jean Piaget, Director of the Institute Jean-Jacques Rousseau in Geneva, is the foremost child psychologist of this century.

about two hundred major studies, in addition to becoming involved in a great range of scientific and professional activities (Tuddenham, 1966).

Centration and Decentering

A theme that runs through much of Piaget's work, especially during his earlier years, is that of the relatively inflexible reasoning processes of young children. They have difficulty in dealing with large quantities of sensory data except in ways that are especially conservative and even rigid, by adult standards.

The young child perceives only a part of his environment, "centers" on it, and judges accordingly, ignoring other points of view and available data. Piaget's term for this naïve approach to problem-solving is *centration*. With more maturity, the child is able to *decenter*—to widen his perspective, and to make judgments that embrace a greater complexity and range of the data that are available in his environment. The process of decentration normally continues throughout childhood.

The Child as an Active Agent

We noted earlier in this chapter that in contrast to animals, human beings are more plastic, in the sense that they are more impressionable, flexible, pliable, and malleable. As our environment changes, we readily take on the behavior patterns needed to cope with new demands, and different environments produce different patterns of behavior. This view of human development is essentially *environmentalist*. In its extreme form, it holds that what the individual becomes is the result of his environment, and that genetic contributions from his forebears are of relatively little importance.

This viewpoint stands in contrast to the *genetic* position. In its extreme form, the genetic view holds that individuals turn out the way they do because of inherited traits, and that environment has relatively little effect. The extreme environmentalist view considers the individual as a relatively passive recipient of environmental influences, whereas the extreme genetic view considers the individual as a passive recipient of his inherited characteristics.

Few individuals, behavioral scientists or otherwise, hold the extreme form of either of these views, although there is a tendency for North Americans to be more environmentalist in their orientation and for Europeans to be more geneticist. Piaget is a moderate in this respect. He rejects the extreme environmentalist view that sees the infant and child as essentially passive and instead regards them as active agents who interact vigorously with their physical and social evironment and generate ever-expanding successions of *schemas*[4] that enable them to cope with the world in ways that are increasingly effective.

Stages in Mental Development

In Piaget's system, the environment is important, however; a child must have the opportunity to interact with it in order to construct the schemas required for each stage of cognitive or mental development.

---

[4] Piaget's use of *schema* and *scheme* creates difficulties, even for experts. In a recent statement, intended to clarify what he means by these two terms, Piaget (1970) said, via his translators, that a schema is a simplified mental image, an attempt to represent reality without trying to transform it. The map of a town was suggested as an example of a schema. *Schema* can also refer to an action-object relationship involving a coordination of the neurosensory and neuromuscular systems in order to produce a bit of behavior—an infant's reaching toward a colored object, for instance.

Piaget uses the term *scheme*, however, as a concept that represents what can be repeated and generalized in an action—for example, "what is common in the actions of 'pushing' an object with a stick or any other instrument." Translators of his earlier writings had employed *schema* to refer to both of these concepts, sometimes using the plural *schemas*, and sometimes using the Greek plural, *schemata*. Inasmuch as most child psychologists still use *schema* and *schemas* to apply in both of these senses, we shall follow that practice in this book as well.

An infant who is kept in an exceedingly limited environment will obviously be handicapped. But once he enters a normal environment, in which he can see, touch, and handle common objects, his course of development will proceed in an orderly fashion, according to the sequential stages we shall describe.

Piaget (1970) says that basic to his approach to cognitive development is the idea that each individual's knowledge of the world is the product of his continuous interaction with it. Specifically, it is the individual's acting on and transforming the phenomena he encounters that enable him to know them.

The way in which the child develops his ability to deal with his environment differs at various stages in his life. In his most recent statement, Piaget (1970) has identified three main developmental stages: sensorimotor, concrete operations, and propositional or formal operations. We shall examine each of them briefly to get a glimpse of the kinds of behavior characteristic of each level of development.

The sensorimotor stage. The sensorimotor stage occupies the period from birth to about 18 to 24 months. Piaget has divided it into a number of substages. During the first month or so, the newborn infant exercises his sensorimotor schemas, by sucking, breathing, waving arms and legs, wiggling, gazing, and so forth.

The infant next begins to vary his schemas and then to combine them. He sucks and grasps simultaneously and turns his head to follow a moving object. This substage lasts three or four months and is followed by a third substage in which he takes some initiative in responding to his environment. Until this point he has merely reacted to stimuli; now he begins to initiate involvement. Piaget (1936) described, for example, how his daughter, Lucienne, aged four months and 27 days, kicked at a doll that had been hung from the top of her bassinet hood. The doll swung violently. Lucienne was delighted and kicked at it again. The next day, as soon as she saw the doll, she moved her feet. During the next few days, Piaget hung the doll at different points from the hood, and Lucienne attempted to hit it with her foot.

In the fourth substage, which runs from about eight or nine months of age to eleven or twelve months, the infant coordinates the secondary schemas that he developed in the third period. He plays games—lets objects fall in order to hear their clatter and to have them picked up again by others and given to him, only to let them fall again. Objects are actively explored and used; space, causality, and time begin to have some meaning; curiosity and interest in novelty appear; and the movements of others are imitated. The infant becomes able to locomote during this substage, and during the following two substages he begins to walk, to explore his environment in ever wider circles. Schemas become more and more elaborate, and the infant learns to make use of symbols in a crude or rudimentary way.

The concrete operations stage. The second major stage of development is concrete operations, which begins with a *preoperational* phase, commencing ordinarily at eighteen to twenty-four months and continuing until age seven or eight. One characteristic of a child's thinking during this stage is his lack of *reversibility*, that is, his inability to go back to the beginning of an operation and start over. In order to accomplish reversibility, a child must mentally trace his way back over a sequence of acts until he comes to the point where he made a crucial misjudgment. A basic problem in attaining reversibility is that of dealing with *negation*—that is, canceling the last occurring event and returning to the event that just preceded it. Children cannot deal in a consistent and effective way with negation and reversibility until they have passed through the preoperational stage.

During the preoperational phase, the child acquires language skills and becomes able to deal with the world symbolically instead of merely directly, through motor activity. During this period, space and time are seen by the child as centered on him. As Tuddenham (1966) describes it, time is viewed in terms of "before now," "now," and "not yet," and space is located wherever the child happens to be and moves around with him. "When he is taken for an evening walk, the moon follows him." He is confused when substances change shape and is hence unable to conserve quantity, to use Piaget's terminology—that is, he is unable to grasp the concept that water poured from a broad glass cup into a tall, slender glass cylinder is still the same amount, even though the water level is higher.

In the latter phase of the concrete operations stage, which extends to age eleven or twelve, the child shows the development of reasoning. He is no longer fooled by the conservation problem just described, and is also able to employ two-way classification systems, to order objects in series, and to number them.

The formal operations stage. The third major stage, that of *formal operations*, begins where the concrete operations stage leaves off and is consolidated in adolescence. Individuals in this stage are able to make use of more complicated systems of classification, deal with hypothetical situations, understand and use concepts involving probability, and deal with other complex problems involving logic and reasoning.

A typical Piagetian test of reasoning ability at this stage of development is the pendulum task. A pendulum is constructed by the examiner in the form of a weight hanging from a string, and the child is shown how to vary the length of the string, the amount of weight, the degree of force needed to set the pendulum swinging, and the height from which the pendulum can be released. The child is then asked to solve what is actually a problem in physics, determining which of four variables— length, height, weight, or force—operating alone or in conjunction with others affects the rapidity with which the pendulum swings. The child

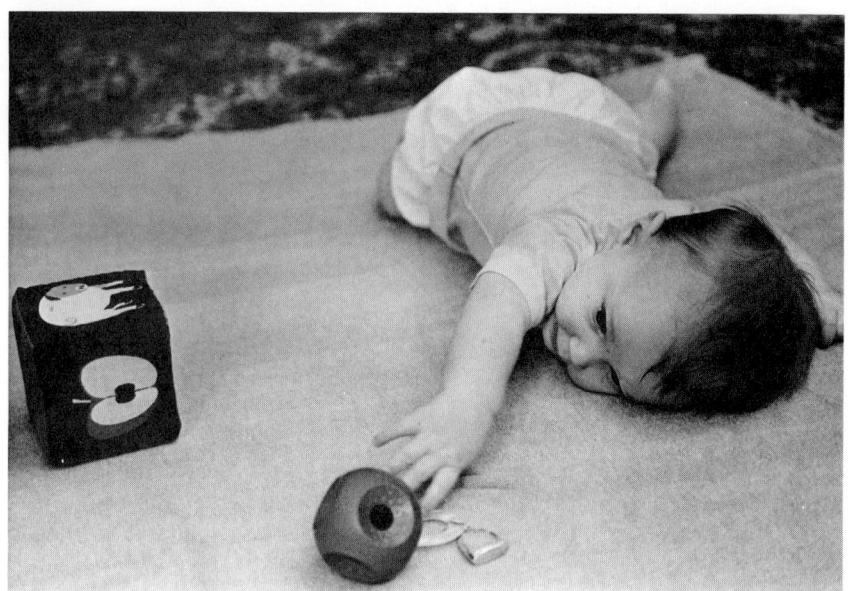

During the sensorimotor stage of development, infants display initiative in responding to and manipulating their environment. In the earlier phases of the stage, they reach for objects that interest them. Later, when they can get around under their own power, they explore their environment more actively. Then, in the concrete operations stage, children deal with tasks that involve complex concepts, such as using the telephone and playing games that require an understanding of elementary physics and hand-eye coordination. Later, in the formal operations stage, they are able to learn tasks that require the use of complicated logical concepts, such as checkers.

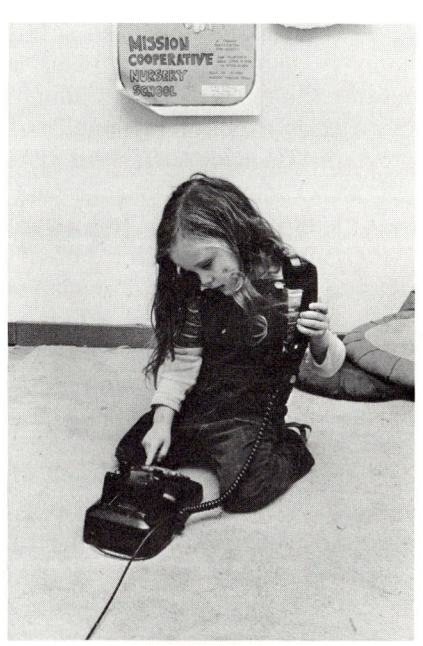
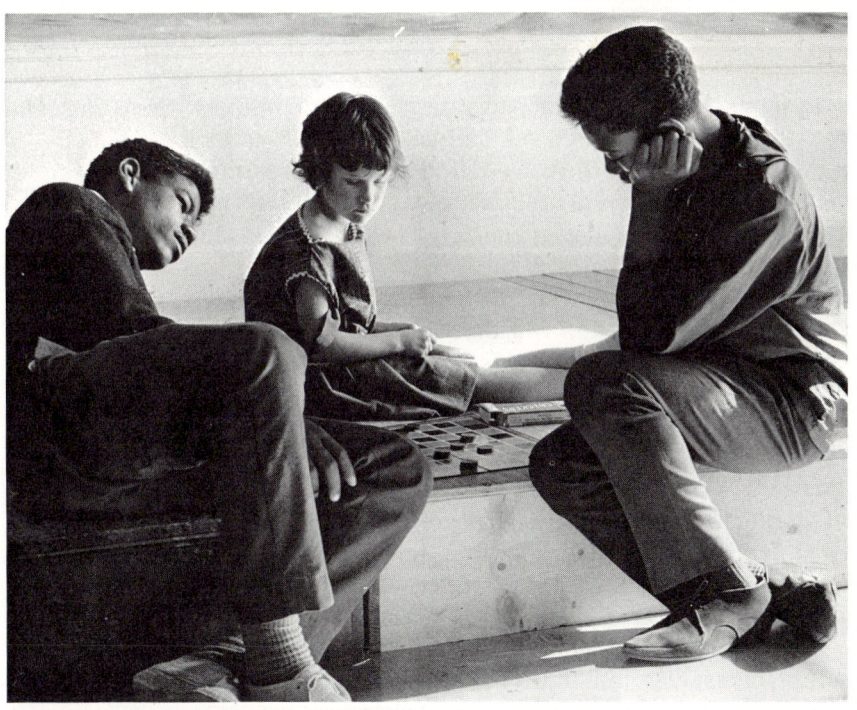

can, for instance, make the string longer or shorter and observe what happens. The examiner plays a limited and noncommital role, recording the child's manipulations and comments, questioning him only when certain points are unclear. The examiner also asks the child to prove his assertions. In short, the child assumes the role of the scientist who seeks an answer to a classical problem in physics, and the examiner tests his understanding and records his behavior.

Preoperational children under age seven approach such a task in a random way, without any plan or pattern. Such tests as they make produce little or no real information. The child who has attained the concrete operational stage may try out a few possibilities and make some accurate observations. He may even hit upon the correct answer, but his reasoning is somewhat unsystematic and illogical. An adolescent who is well into the formal operations stage, however, designs the experiment properly, makes observations that eliminate various possible answers to the question, and uses logic to arrive at the correct answer: the length of the string is the important factor (Piaget and Inhelder, 1958).

Criticisms of Piagetian Concepts

Some critics have taken Piaget to task for tying down these stages to certain age ranges, but Piaget maintains that ages as such are not vital; it is the order in which the stages appear that is important. A child cannot move into the formal operations stage until he has successfully worked through the experiences of the concrete operations stage, whatever his age happens to be.

Ages at which children attain certain stages may, however, vary widely. On the island of Martinique in the Caribbean, children tend to be four years behind children in Montreal, Canada (Laurendeau and Pinard, 1963), and some Brazilian Indians evidently never get to the stage of formal operations (Tuddenham, 1966). Incidentally, some observers have noted that American children apparently attain facility in cognitive processes earlier than the subjects studied by Piaget and his co-worker Barbel Inhelder (Kooistra, 1963; Denney, 1972). One reason for this difference may be the tendency of American parents to encourage active, exploratory, and independent behavior in infants and young children.

Although the idea that the behavioral phenomena of development group themselves into fairly well-defined stages seems to have good empirical support, not all psychologists are convinced. Among the critics of stage theories are Albert Bandura and the late Richard H. Walters (1963a), whose theories on social learning have generated a great deal of experimental research with subjects of all ages. Bandura and Walters maintained that observed similarities in the behavior of children at certain ages can be accounted for primarily by the fact that the children being observed by the researcher are likely to have lived in simliar environments and had similar experiences. Whereas stage theories are concerned largely with similarities among children at various points in their development, social learning theories are more concerned with accounting for differences among individuals and for similarities (or continuities) within the modes of behavior displayed by a given individual.

The debate between stage theorists and social learning theorists is often heated, but the psychologist who listens to them and comes to his own conclusions may decide that both sides have much to offer; that the positions are not as contradictory as they seem at first; and that both camps are, in effect, reacting to different aspects of the same types of behavior. Although Piaget and his followers do relate certain stages of development to certain ages, Piaget does attempt to make it clear that the appearance of a certain mode of cognitive functioning must depend on the child's opportunity to have certain experiences. A child cannot, for example, learn the relationships between quantity and volume unless he has experiences that involve these dimensions of reality. Similarly, even the most committed social learning theorist would agree that children are unable to learn certain forms of behavior before an age when they can make the necessary discriminations and associations.

Jerome Kagan (1971) has raised other objections to Piaget's formulations. He maintains that children do not necessarily have to interact directly with their environment in order to develop an understanding of it. They may gain insight by observing or listening to others. Kagan agrees that touching, feeling, and handling do aid children in developing familiarity with their environment, especially if they are acquiring responses they have never made before. Such direct involvement is, furthermore, more interesting than passive observation and hence increases children's alertness, thus making it more certain that important aspects of the environment will be noted. Kagan also points out that inasmuch as we cannot observe an infant's mental processes as he manipulates toys and other objects, we may jump to the conclusion that it is only through physical interaction that infants attain insights.

Piaget has also been criticized because he uses the clinical method in gathering data, a method that makes it difficult to control for observer bias, as we noted in our discussion of Freud. Piaget (1929) has maintained that he is very much aware of this problem and routinely subjects his findings to the severest criticism. In his defense, it can be said that experimental tests of his findings and conclusions have generally been supportive (with some exceptions, which we shall note in succeeding chapters). Indeed, one of Piaget's great contributions to child psychology has been the large number of studies and experiments that his ideas have generated.

Discontinuity and Hierarchization

Piaget's research makes it clear that development is not merely an additive process; instead, it leads to schemas or structures that could not have been predicted solely from an analysis of the preceding events. In other words, each stage of development is initiated by discontinuities or abrupt changes from the previous one. New, emerging forms of behavior are not merely reorganizations of earlier forms; the infant's locomotion, for instance, shows four stages—lying prone, crawling, creeping, and walking—each involving movements not present at the earlier stage.

This concept of developmental discontinuity is criticized by some psychologists as not being very scientific. Properly understood, there is nothing mystical or strange about it. The concept of discontinuity is present in other sciences, where it is accepted without question. Water, which is formed of two parts of hydrogen and one part of oxygen, has properties that are not found in either of its components; the tulip bulb contains the successive potentialities of leaves, bud, and blossom, without their being evident in the bulb; the visible spectrum of light, which is based on quantitative changes of wave lengths, shows abrupt changes at certain points, when passing from violet to indigo, blue to green, and yellow to orange. Hence there is no special reason why similar discontinuities cannot occur in human behavior and be recognized as scientific facts.

As the structures and functions in a new stage develop, they show an organization that is more elaborate and that includes more elements than do the structures and functions that appeared in earlier stages of the sequence. The previous elements become submerged in the new forms of behavior and lose their separate identities. We observe a three-month-old infant's attempts to grasp an object. He clutches at it and misses; when he is finally successful, he is unable to repeat his action. A few weeks later he is able to clutch and hold an object almost every time, for he has mastered the art of grasping. Some months later, he succeeds, after many tries, in the difficult task of placing one block on top of another. The old skill of grasping is involved, but it has now become submerged in a new and infinitely more complex skill. This process is referred to as *hierarchization* (Werner, 1957). In the developmental theory of Piaget (1950), for example, the various levels or stages of conceptual development show a hierarchy of progressive differentiation. Each new level of thought, of intelligence, uses the material of the lower level or levels, but transforms it by greater differentiation and a new coordination; the new stage draws upon the old, yet is a new stage nonetheless. Each level is an organized totality that is a new entity understandable in terms of itself. A new level is fundamentally an innovation, not derivable from the characteristics of the previous levels.

maturation and learning

As we noted earlier, genetic factors have some influence on intelligence, personality, and susceptibility to certain mental disorders. It is also well known that they determine body shape and size, as well as pigmentation. As we also indicated, there is no certainty as to what the precise limits are to this genetic influence, and they probably vary under different environmental conditions.

During the earlier stages of development, certain gross features of the environment, such as insufficient nutrition or extreme over- or understimulation, may have a negative or retarding effect on development. When the child is able to take an active part in interacting with his social environment, the picture becomes more complicated, and it is often difficult to decide whether a given type of behavior is more genetically or more environmentally determined. A case in point is the restlessness of children during the primary-school years. In North American schools, we provide for recess periods during the primary grades on the assumption that children cannot concentrate on classroom tasks if they have to sit for long hours. In a great many Italian schools, however, there are no recess periods (and no school playgrounds, for that matter); the children sit quietly for long hours working on their assigned tasks. It is difficult to determine which of the two behavior patterns is "normal" and which is learned. Americans who visit Italian schools are likely to view the behavior of the Italian child as "nonnormal" and the result of an unduly constricting environment, whereas Italians are likely to view the restlessness of the American child as resulting from an abnormally overstimulating environment, coupled with an excess of permissiveness.

However much the social environment may affect a child's behavior, there is no evidence that even the most ideal environment—whatever that may be—can speed up the developmental processes and cause a child to progress faster than his genetically determined timetable will allow. Any change in behavior brought about by varying the environment will presumably have to take place within the limits set by that timetable. In other words, learning is limited (or made possible) by maturation. When we use the term *maturation,* we are referring to forms of behavior that appear spontaneously in the developmental sequence; in contrast, the forms of learned behavior are environmentally instigated.

Many definitions have been proposed for the two concepts *learning* and *maturation.* Of the two, learning has been defined with much less ambiguity. Lindgren and Byrne (1975) describe it as "the processes that bring about relatively enduring behavioral changes as the result of experience." "Experience," in this sense, typically includes practice or

Must children be taught how to walk? More fundamentally, is walking a skill that must be learned? Or does it just "come naturally," as a result of maturation?

rehearsal, special training, and observation. Psychologists' definitions of learning also exclude behavioral changes attributable to altered physiological states (such as fatigue, excitement, or hunger), to sensory adaptation, and to maturation (which should not depend on special activity, practice, or training).

Definitions of maturation have not revealed as much uniformity of thinking. In its original scientific usage the term was used by geneticists to denote the development occurring within the immature germ cell prior to the process of fertilization. Arnold Gesell (1933) was one of the first writers to use maturation in a broader sense, applying it to those developmental phenomena that appear in an orderly fashion without the intervention of any known external stimuli. This usage applies the term to *behavior,* as well as to neurophysical changes in the nerves, muscles, and glands that provide the necessary implements for the execution of behavioral activities.

Leonard Carmichael (1951) avoided formulating an explicit definition by proposing three criteria by means of which changes attributable to maturation can be distinguished: (a) the behavior should be demonstrated as developing universally in all or almost all apparently normal organisms of similar physiological endowment; (b) the behavior change must occur in an organism too immature to be able to form stable habit patterns; and (c) the behavior should appear in an organism that has had no opportunity to observe that behavior in another member of the species. Rigid adherence to the criteria, especially the third, would virtually preclude application of the term to any type of human behavior. " 'Maturation' is simply development in which commonly observed differences between individuals are correlated with previous differences in the inner organism rather than in the environment" (Howells, 1945).

The generally unwieldy nature of the concept of maturation and the resistance of the concept to precise definition have led some writers to favor abandoning it altogether, and to encourage instead the adoption of a concept in which outer conditions and inner characteristics merge. As Piaget (1952) has put it, organism and environment form an entity. There is an irreducible interdependence that extends over the subject and object. We can never isolate maturation from learning. Maturation, according to Piaget, is the organism's fundamental tendency to organize experience so that it can be assimilated; learning is the means of introducing new experiences into that organization.

Maturation (nature) interacts with learning (nurture) to form development. It is important to note that they are not additive (+) but interactive (×). The formula is

$$\text{Maturation} \times \text{Learning} = \text{Development}.$$

In the absence of experience of a specified sort, the equation becomes

$$\text{Maturation} \times \text{Zero learning} = \text{Zero achievement}.$$

A case in point would be the absence of reading skills in a primitive society, and the absence of game-stalking skills in a highly urbanized culture.

Another formula applies in the absence of maturation:

$$\text{Zero maturation} \times \text{Learning opportunity} = \text{Zero achievement}.$$

Any fond parent who has tried to teach an infant to talk "before he is ready" is aware of the validity of this formula. To the frustrated parent, it seems as though the infant is "just not trying." He can utter all the sounds that make up spoken words and can say things that are wordlike. Wanting to talk is certainly a factor, of course, but the point is that talking requires the maturation of a great many complexly interrelated muscles and controls, and hence cannot appear until the infant is neurologically and physiologically "ready."

summary

Although growth is basic to all development, the term growth is usually applied to changes in size and complexity, whereas development refers to changes in character or function. Growth ceases with maturity, but development continues throughout the life span. It is difficult to observe the process of development, and our conclusions must be based on data gathered at different points in time.

At the point of conception, the basic patterns for the neurophysical development of the individual are set by genes: large and complex molecules found in chromosomes, which in turn are located in the nuclei of living cells. Half of the 46 chromosomes contained in each cell are contributed by one parent, and half by the other. Deoxyribonucleic acid (DNA) provides the chemical basis for genetic transmission, and ribonucleic acid (RNA) molecules are the "messengers" that determine the structure and function of body tissue. The complex process of rearranging and trading genes between chromosomes which takes place shortly after conception, results in a virtually infinite number of possible genetic combinations. Genetic effects are most obviously detected in physical traits common to families; shared behavioral traits are harder to pin down and may be caused by social inheritance. Research on genetic transmission of physical traits has focused on defects or abnormalities, like hemophilia or allergy to ragweed pollens. The chromosomal abnormality of the type known as, XYY for example, has been thought to predispose males to violent aggressive behavior, but review of research indicates that the risk has been exaggerated. Environmental stresses, such as are experienced by children raised by adults who mistreat them, are more likely causes of deviant behavior in later years.

Human beings are plastic organisms, in the sense that they can acquire an endless variety of behavior patterns. Hence it is difficult to determine whether individual and group differences are brought about by genetic causes or by environmental ones. The relative effects of these two sources have been studied through the observation of identical (monozygotic or MZ) twins and of unlike (dizygotic or DZ) twins. Such studies permit some control of genetic and environmental factors, inasmuch as MZ twins have identical genetic elements, whereas the genetic elements in DZ twins are similar but never identical. Studies show that MZ twins are more similar than DZ twins with respect to IQ, personality traits, and tendencies toward schizophrenia.

Developmental changes occur in an orderly, sequential fashion. Because forces that interact on a child are complex, we must remember that the basic unit of our study is the whole child reacting to a total environment. Structural elements in the developing body are best understood with respect to their function, as well as their relationship to other parts of the body. Growth and development tend to proceed in a downward, head-to-tail or cephalocaudal direction, and simultaneously in an outward or proximodistal direction. The original cell from which the child eventually develops may be thought of as totipotent, as possessing the capacity to become any structure that will later appear in the embryo. As the cell divides and subdivides, it loses its totipotentiality. The new cells are differentiated in terms of structure and function, yet they must all act in interrelated ways in order to form a completely integrated organism—simultaneous processes that are found in the development of the infant's crawling and grasping responses.

The critical-period hypothesis holds that the organism is more sensitive to stress at some periods of development than at other periods. The best evidence comes from studies of embryos and of animals. As far as human development is concerned, critical-period concepts are largely based on Freud's theory that insufficient gratification at certain developmental stages "fixates" the child at that stage and prevents normal development. Havighurst has incorporated the critical-period idea into his theoretical structure of developmental tasks—tasks that must be mastered at earlier stages if social and intellectual development is to proceed normally at later stages. Critical-period concepts also figured largely in the planning of Operation Head Start, a program designed to provide enriched cognitive-social experiences for deprived children during the preschool years. The fact that the program has produced somewhat disappointing results, from the standpoint of cognitive development, may be attributable either to the fact that the age span selected may not be as crucial as earlier periods or to deficiencies in the program or its management.

Piaget's insistence that children need to have direct contact with their environment as a prerequisite to learning has had much effect on Head Start thinking. Piaget, a French Swiss, is easily the best-known child psychologist today. One of his observations is that children initially tend to focus on very specific aspects of their environment, a tendency Piaget calls centering. They then go through stages of decentering, as they become aware of more complex phenomena. Whereas many North American psychologists are inclined to prefer environmental explanations of human behavior, Piaget sees the child as an active agent, whose knowledge of the world and its objects is the product of his operations on and with them. These operations pass through three main stages:

sensorimotor, concrete operations, and formal operations. The sensorimotor stage occupies the period from birth to about two years. During this period, the infant constructs rudimentary schemas of his world. The preoperational phase of the concrete operations stage occupies the preschool and early school years. During this period the child acquires a number of complex skills, including the use of language, but he has problems with reversing or going backward over an action or solution to a problem; he also has not mastered the recognition that quantities are the same, even though they have changed their appearance. In later phases of the concrete operations stage, the child is able to solve more complex problems and is less likely to be misled by conservation manipulations. When a child attains the formal operations stage, he is able to carry out simple experiments systematically and logically.

Piaget answers critics of his age-related stages by saying that it is the order of the stages that is important, not the ages at which they ordinarily appear. Other critics claim that Piaget does not give enough weight to cross-cultural differences in development and point out that skills can be acquired through social learning—imitation—or instruction; they do not necessarily have to be "constructed" through the child's interaction with his environment.

Piaget's work makes it clear that development is not merely additive, but leads to schemas or structures that could not have been predicted solely from preceding events. As the structure and functions of a new stage develop, they show an organization that is more elaborate than are those that appeared in stages earlier in the sequence, and includes more elements than previous stages. This form of *discontinuity* is called *hierarchization*.

It is difficult to ascertain whether observed forms of behavior—the restlessness of North American schoolchildren, for example—are caused by environmental or genetic causes. In any event, whatever environmental forces lead to learning, the changes these forces produce are made possible—and are limited as well—by the maturational level a child has attained. Learning can be fairly precisely defined as behavioral changes resulting from practice or rehearsal, training, and observation, whereas definitions of maturation are more ambiguous, but generally describe some form of behavior that emerges spontaneously because of neurophysical development. Perhaps maturation is best defined by the way in which it affects learning. This relationship is interactive and not additive, for both learning and maturation must occur in an integrated manner if normal development is to take place.

four

Socialization and Personality Development

Children have more need of models than of critics.
—JOSEPH JOUBERT

So far as our personal characteristics are concerned, each of us resembles *all* other, *some* other, and *no* other individuals (Kluckhohn, Murray, and Schneider, 1953). The explanation of how we came to develop these similarities and differences is partly biological and partly environmental, as the previous chapter noted. The biological forces that are set in motion at the point of conception are at first virtually omnipotent, but from birth onward the environment becomes more and more powerful as an influence that shapes behavior and personality. The physical aspects of the environment are likely to be most crucial in early infancy, for it is important that the baby receive nourishment and be protected against possible injury, but within a few weeks, the social environment begins to intrude and to play an ever increasing part in the child's development.

socialization

The process that enables the child to take his place in human society is termed *socialization*. Through socialization, an individual learns modes of experiencing and behaving that enable him to respond in ways that his society considers appropriate. This is an immensely complex process. Society specifies what rewards and restraints are desirable, as well as the conditions under which they will be applied by the child's caregivers. Certain patterns of behavior are considered suitable; they relate not only to the way in which the growing child is expected to interact with others and with his physical environment but also to his inner life—that is, to his feelings, beliefs, attitudes, values, and motives. Society permits some deviation from these general patterns, but a child who develops behavior that differs in significant respects will inevitably experience difficulties in his relations with others and in his ability to find his way in the world.

The process of socialization limits the scope of behavior available to the child, so that it becomes narrower than the range of which he is capable. An example of this narrowing in scope may be found in language learning. An adolescent who has grown up speaking English and who enrolls in high-school German will have difficulty with such sounds as ö and ü. He is likely to find these sounds "unnatural" and will have problems in shaping lips, tongue, and the rest of his speaking apparatus correctly. When he was an infant, however, these sounds were in his repertory, along with English speech sounds that he now has no difficulty in producing. Early in his childhood, the ö and ü dropped out. In learning-theory terms, the English-appropriate sounds were reinforced, whereas the German-appropriate sounds were not reinforced and hence were eliminated.

What happens to curiosity is another example of how the total range of responses becomes restricted. An infant normally begins exploring as soon as he can move about the dwelling area. The usual tendency of parents is to discourage or at least limit this behavior, for the child may get into dangerous situations or make a nuisance of himself, especially in crowded quarters. In some middle-class homes, however, living areas are rendered "childproof," in order to provide infants and young children with adequate space for exploration. There may even be a deliberate attempt on the part of parents to encourage a child to investigate his surroundings. Such parents are, in effect, rewarding him for being curious. Some degree of restriction remains, however. Medicines and cleaning fluids are usually locked up or placed out of reach, and certain hazardous areas, such as the kitchen and the workshop, are blocked off.

When exploratory behavior is discouraged altogether, as it is in some homes and in some cultures, the child learns to react to novel situations in a passive or even an anxious way. When faced by an unfamiliar problem, he shows little initiative, waiting instead for someone to solve it for him or at least show him how to do it. The child whose exploratory behavior has been reinforced, however, is more likely to try different strategies in attempting to solve a problem and may even be irritated if someone takes over and solves it for him.

By way of an example, Caudill and Weinstein (1969) studied the first six years of life of American and Japanese children and reported cultural differences as early as three and four months. They noted that American infants that age, in contrast to Japanese infants, vocalize more and are more active. They also explore their bodies and their physical environment more. The investigators attributed these differences to the tendency of American mothers to have an active and self-assertive baby as a goal, whereas Japanese mothers prefer a passive and contented baby. These goals are clearly reflected in the different ways in which the mothers interact with their children. American mothers talk more to their infants and encourage them to engage in physical activity and exploration. Japanese mothers, on the other hand, carry their infants around with them as much as possible and maintain greater physical, rather than verbal, contact with them. It is naturally harder to manage carrying a baby that is wiggling and exploring; Japanese mothers therefore go to some pains to soothe and quiet their infants. As a result, Japanese infants become more passive toward their environment. It is very likely that some of the differences between the American and Japanese culture, with respect to environmentally oriented responses, can be related to this early interaction between mother and infant.

Presumably physical activity and exploratory behavior are within the initial repertoires of both American and Japanese infants. In one culture, the behavior is encouraged; in the other, it is discouraged. In both instances, the mother's treatment is consistent with her culture's over-all approach to the world and to life in general. Similarly, each culture channels the behavior of its infants in such a way that certain patterns of behavior are discouraged and certain others are encouraged. This shaping of the responses that infants display spontaneously is, however, not the only explanation of the behavior patterns that appear later, as we shall see from the following discussion.

learning and socialization

As far as we know, the differences among newborns from different ethnic or culturally identified groups are minor and in most instances are nonsignificant. All full-term, normal newborns sleep most of the time, have the same reflexes and dietary preferences, and are at the same stage of physical maturation. Comparative studies do show a few minor differences. One study, for instance, shows that Chinese-American newborns tend to be somewhat calmer, more adaptable, and less excitable than American newborns of European stock, but there is also considerable overlap between the two groups, with some Chinese-American infants displaying more excitability than a good portion of the European-American infants (Freedman and Freeman, 1969). There

The culture in which children grow up has a marked effect on their behavior, as well as on their personalities. What is conventional and normal in one culture is considered exotic or unusual in another, as these glimpses of children's experiences and activities in India, Mexico, Rumania, and Spain (during Holy Week) suggest.

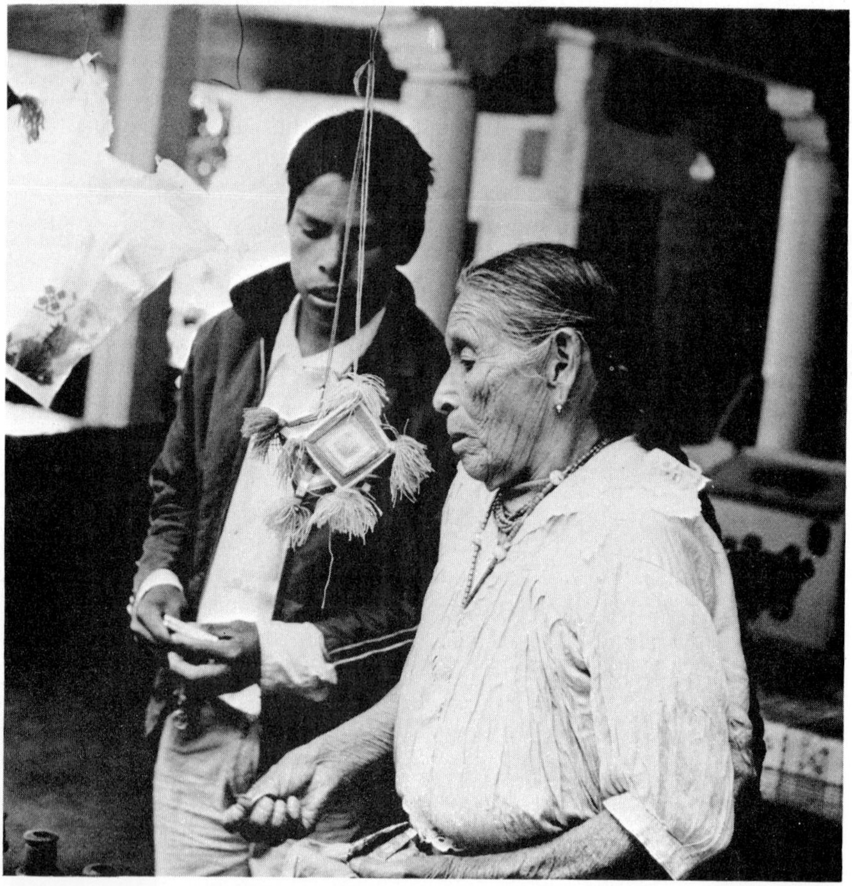

have also been reports that African infants develop more rapidly than European infants, but these findings have been questioned. A carefully controlled study by Warren and Parkin (1974) of African and European newborns shows no behavioral differences between the racial groups, and Warren (1972) has raised questions about the validity and reliability of measures and· the adequacy of scientific controls employed by researchers who had earlier reported racial differences. Warren concluded that the behavioral differences between the races reported in later infancy and childhood were probably caused by differences in child-rearing practices—in other words, to environmental and not to genetic influences.

In sum, then, neonates of different racial and ethnic groups tend to be quite similar. However, cross-cultural research and everyday observation both suggest that behavioral differences are likely to be considerable by the time the neonates have grown to childhood and beyond. Even by the age of two or three, marked cultural differences can be observed in terms of the children's behavior toward familiar and strange adults, other children, and their physical environment. There are also differences in food preference, in language, and in play. These differences in behavior are not inborn; they are all acquired or learned. We now consider the ways in which they are learned.

Classical Conditioning

There are, in theoretical terms, two basic types of learning that can be induced by the experimenter's manipulation of environmental variables. Both types involve conditioning—that is, the modification of responses. Classical conditioning was the first type to be investigated experimentally. As we have already noted, Ivan P. Pavlov (1849–1936), the Russian physiologist, was doing some research on digestive processes, using dogs whose saliva production could be measured by a tube inserted surgically into the jaw. Salivary flow was induced experimentally by placing powdered meat on the dog's tongue. The dogs developed an annoying characteristic, however: they did not wait for the meat, but began to salivate when they heard the experimenter enter the laboratory. After his initial annoyance with this unexpected behavior, Pavlov became interested in the tendency toward this response and began to experiment with it, using the sound of a tuning fork to initiate the salivary flow. Figure 4-1 shows the relationship he observed among the various stimuli and responses in the experimental situation. The meat is the *unconditioned stimulus* (S_1 or US); the salivary flow is the *unconditioned response* (R_1 or UR) to the US. When a new stimulus, like the sound of a tuning fork, is repeatedly paired with the US, it may in some instances become sufficient in itself to produce the salivation response—that is, in the absence of the US. If this occurs, the new stimulus is termed a *conditioned stimulus* (S_2 or CS) and the

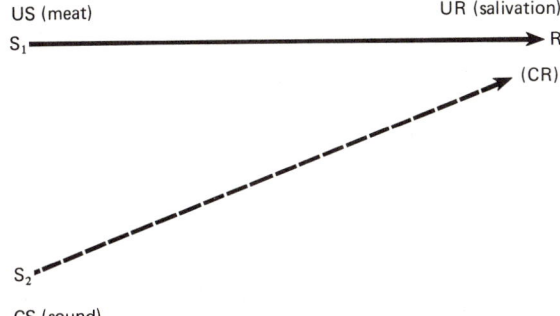

FIGURE 4-1. Classical conditioning: a new stimulus (sound) evokes a response (salivation) initially evoked by another stimulus (meat).

response thus evoked is referred to as the *conditioned response* or CR.

To use an analogous example from infancy, the normal response to the nipple in the mouth is the sucking response. As the infant becomes able to distinguish visual patterns, the appearance of the bottle also stimulates mouth movements, as in sucking. The nipple is the US, and the resulting mouth movements are the UR; the appearance of the bottle is the CS, because it appears in connection with (and hence is "conditioned" to) the nipple. The CR is, of course, the mouth movements that appear when the bottle comes into view.

The classical conditioning response is a relatively rudimentary form of learning and is used to refer to situations in which the experimenter wants to substitute one stimulus for another—that is, he wants the organism to retain a certain response but to produce it in response to a new stimulus, a stimulus other than the one that evoked it in the first place.

Here is another example: When the infant is several weeks old, the mother wants to introduce some solid food into his diet. At feeding time she prepares a little strained banana and puts it into the infant's mouth with a spoon. The infant is puzzled, not knowing what to make of this strange substance. The stimulation of the lips results in the sucking reflex, however, and some of the banana becomes ingested, whereupon the nipple is presented and the usual feeding routine is carried out. For the next few days, the infant is introduced to mashed banana at the start of the feeding period, and in a short time accepts it as a reasonable form of nourishment, making somewhat the same response to it as he makes to milk.

C. Joan Early (1968) conducted a clever experiment in which classical conditioning was used to change fourth and fifth graders' attitudes toward their less popular classmates. Early first conducted a survey in order to identify the less popular children, or "isolates." Then she asked all the children to memorize a list of word pairs. The first half of each word pair consisted of the name of a child in the class and the second half consisted of another word, such as *neat* or *and*. Half of the isolates' names were paired with positive value words like *neat* (the experimen-

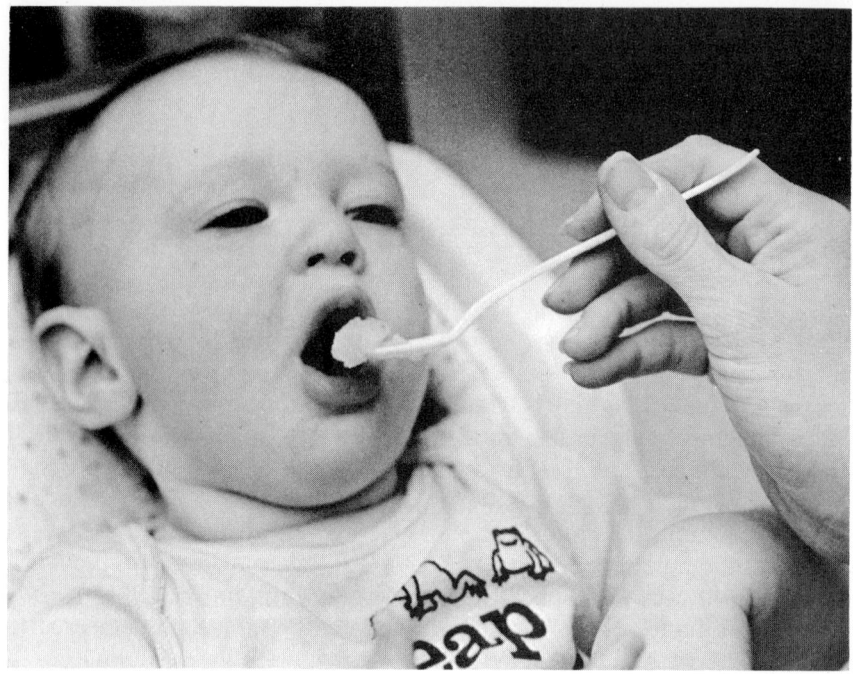
The infant becomes conditioned to the stimulus of approaching food and acquires the response of opening its mouth.

tal group), and the names of the other half (the control group) were paired with neutral-value words like *and*. The names of all the other class members were also paired with neutral-value words.

Early's results showed that the children subsequently gave the experimental isolates more attention and interacted with them more, whereas their behavior toward the control isolates was unchanged. In other words, the task of memorizing and associating positive words with the names of the isolates in the experimental group gave the class members a more favorable attitude toward them. The US in this experiment was the positive word (e.g., *neat*), and the UR was the favorable reaction the children had to the US. The CS was the experimental isolate child and the CR was his classmates' favorable reaction to him.

Instrumental or Operant Conditioning

In most learning situations we are not so concerned with trying to get the organism to give the same response to a new stimulus, but with getting it to give some new responses. A six-year-old may respond to the stimulus *book* by turning the pages and looking for pictures, instead of trying to read. In this instance, we want the child to substitute different responses, and hence we are likely to resort to some form of operant or instrumental conditioning. An initial objective may be getting the child to start figuring out the letters that make up the words, or else of getting him to identify whole words or phrases.

In order to conceptualize what we are trying to do, let us assume that the child has a hierarchy of possible responses to books: looking at the pictures, studying their words, tearing pages out, throwing them at other children, ignoring them. This child looks at the pictures because that response is at the top of the list or hierarchy. The other responses are possible, and we note that occasionally he stops and briefly looks at some of the words and then goes back to the pictures. He may also exchange some shouted words with the child across the table, however, and we can see that it would not take much for them to get into a playful throwing match.

What we want to do, now, is to get the child to attend to the words, at least to the point of asking us some questions about them. In order to accomplish this goal, we use a method termed *reinforcement*. In classical conditioning, reinforcement was accomplished by following the CS by the US—that is, following the appearance of the bottle by placing the nipple in the mouth. In our present problem, we use the technique of *instrumental* or *operant conditioning*, as developed by B. F. Skinner and his followers, and follow the appearance of some desired behavior with something that will reinforce it.

We watch the child, and the next time he stops to look at a printed page, we reinforce that behavior by rewarding him. We could give him a small candy, a stimulus that has been found to be rewarding in working with children, or we might express approval by saying "Good." We decide to do the latter, on the grounds that it is less distracting. We continue to reinforce text-oriented behavior, until we have him spending much more time looking at words.

Now we want him to ask questions. When he talks about the book, we reinforce talking about the text and ignore whatever he says about the pictures. Gradually we reinforce his responses, so that he is spending even more time looking at the textual material and is asking questions about the words. This reinforcing of "successive approximations" of the behavior we want is what Skinner and his followers call "shaping."

We do not mean to imply that this is the way to teach reading, and are using this example only to show how operant conditioning methods can be used to modify behavior, getting a subject to substitute one type of response for another. If motivation and interest in a task are considered important, however, the treatment we have described can be considered as one approach to getting a child involved in a new task.

What we have been describing is the use of reward or positive reinforcement in bringing about learning. Learning can also result from punishment. In some instances, a child's response—for example, emptying the sugarbowl—may be followed by uncomfortable, painful, or otherwise unsatisfying results, and he learns to avoid it. Note that the

Parents use rewards in order to reinforce the behavior they approve of, but most of the reinforcing they do is less obvious and consists of nods, glances, smiles, gestures, approving sounds, or pats.

objective of the reinforcer here is the *elimination* of a response, not the acquisition of a new one. Parents, teachers, and other authority figures often attempt to use punishment in an attempt to get children to try new patterns of behavior, but these attempts usually fail unless there is some positive reinforcing of the desired new pattern. Unfortunately, this second step is overlooked all too often.

Punishment is sometimes referred to as *negative reinforcement*, because the consequences of behavior are unpleasant, rather than satisfying. Strictly speaking, however, negative reinforcement refers to the withdrawal or cessation of an unpleasant stimulus. A rat in a cage, for example, hears the harsh sound of a buzzer, which continues until he presses a lever that the investigator has connected to the switch. He quickly learns, through this negative reinforcement, that whenever the buzzer sounds, he can stop it by pressing the lever. The infant who stops crying when picked up and cuddled similarly uses negative reinforcement to train his parents to produce the desired response.

Learning Through Observation, Identification, and Imitation

We come now to social learning, a type of learning that calls for some initiative on the part of the learner. Albert Bandura (1969) has pointed out that if we were solely dependent on reward and punishment to accomplish socialization, we would never survive the process. Something more is needed to bring novel responses into the repertoire of the individual. Operant conditioning is an improvement over classical conditioning, in that the individual can be guided into more effective modes of behavior, but it does not explain how a child comes to emit a response for the first time. The learning mechanism that enables children to acquire a vast array of responses that are new to them is *imitation*, a process whereby a child matches his behavior to that of another person in a similar situation. The other person thus becomes the *model* for the child, and the imitative process may be termed *modeling*.

Bandura says that fundamental to modeling is *identification*, "a process in which a person patterns his thoughts, feelings, or actions after another person who serves as a model." Bandura describes identification further as a "continuous process in which new responses are acquired and existing repertoires of behavior are modified to some extent," as a result of direct or indirect experiences with models, real or symbolic, whose attitudes, values, beliefs, and motives are revealed by their behavior.

The child who is about to learn a new segment of behavior first *attends* to the person displaying the behavior—the model. In other words, he orients himself to the model's behavior, ignoring other and potentially competing stimuli in the immediate environment. As the

Albert Bandura of Stanford University has played a leading role in directing psychologists' attention to the importance of social learning.

child observes the model's behavior, he recognizes and attends to what is different between his own responses and the model's responses. There has to be some positive motivation, of course; merely observing a model's behavior will not in itself lead to learning unless what the model happens to be doing is relevant to some need of the observer. The observer must also be able to interpret the model's behavior in some symbolic way. In other words, if what the model is doing does not make sense to the observer, it will not be learned. Most, but not all, modeling occurs after the child has acquired a measure of linguistic facility, because explanations enable him to understand the meaning of the model's behavior in terms of both what is being done and why it is important.

The new responses are *acquired* and *retained* by the child by means of his rehearsing them, vicariously (mentally) and in actual behavior.

Imitation is more likely to result in permanent learning when the behaviors lead to satisfying outcomes, and thus are reinforced. Sometimes the model (parent or teacher) reinforces the learning through praise or some kind of behavior or gesture that signifies acceptance. At other times, the child notes that the model's behavior is reinforced by others or merely by the accomplishment of a desired objective. If bicycle riding is the skill being observed, the model's behavior may be considered to be reinforced by his success in not falling off and in guiding the machine successfully. Most of the time, however, the process is one of self-reinforcement, whereby the learner discovers that his own attempts to duplicate the behavior are satisfying or correct.

When clinically oriented psychologists employ the term *identification*, they usually have in mind a related complex of attitudes and behaviors that include modeling but go beyond it. The term used in this sense implies positive regard for, and a desire to affiliate with, the behavior model. Such an attitude makes learning even more probable.

If the learner sees the model as someone he would like to resemble in certain ways, he is more likely to attempt to imitate the model's behavior. Identification, too, leads the learner to imagine himself in the model's place—to *empathize* with him—and to behave the way he believes the model is behaving. "Behaving," in this instance, also includes the less visible aspects of the model's behavior, such as thinking, feeling, and valuing.

Psychoanalytic theorists hold that the child employs his parents as models because they possess the power to express love toward him or to withhold it. Freud (1925) maintained that after an affectionate relation-

Social learning is based on identification, which implies positive regard and a desire to affiliate with the behavior model.

"You, too?"

Imitation and the need for attention are important factors in social learning.
(Reg Hilder in the Christian Science Monitor © 1970 by TCSPS.)

ship has developed between mother and child, the mother may, because of disapproval of the child's misbehavior, threaten to withdraw love, that is, may punish or ignore the child. Such a threat has a powerful effect on a child who has come to expect that the mother's love will be given without conditions or reservations. Experiences in which the mother has indicated to the child that he is not loved when he misbehaves lead him to take on the mother's behavior, attitudes, and values through a process of imitation, identification, or—to use the Freudian term—introjection.

Bandura (1969) grants that a child of warm nurturant (caring) parents is more likely to imitate their behavior, but he prefers to explain this tendency in terms of the fact that such parents interact more frequently with their child than do cold aloof parents, and hence have more opportunities to reinforce his behavior. Bandura's research has led him to conclude that the important independent variable that leads to imitation is the model's power to reward. His research has shown that children are more likely to imitate models who control many rewards than those who are less powerful.

In school situations, children will often go out of their way to perform learning tasks for teachers who will reinforce their behavior with special attention. This is especially true of children from poor homes, where there is a high ratio of children to adults. Children from families that have more advantages are inclined to invest time and energy in school tasks regardless of whether the teacher reinforces them or not. In effect, middle-class children are largely self-reinforcing in school situations, whereas children from impoverished homes are more dependent on the reinforcement supplied by the teacher. Teachers who are willing to give them personal attention are therefore powerful models for them, and it is the attentive teacher's behavior that disadvantaged children will imitate. Colder, rejecting, more socially distant teachers have little reward value for them and hence do not call forth much imitative behavior.

Modeling and the learning of altruistic behavior. An example of an experiment using modeling as a way of inducing more highly socialized behavior in children is the study by Liebert and Poulos (1971), who asked second- and third-grade girls to engage in a judging task in which the reward for accuracy consisted of tokens that could be exchanged for prizes. The more tokens the child earned, the better the prize. Some of the child subjects worked on the task with an adult, and results were rigged so that both earned the same amount of tokens: eight. As the two were about to go into an adjoining room to get their prizes, the experimenter asked them if they would contribute some of their tokens for children in another school, who would not have a chance to earn tokens and exchange them for prizes. The adult then deposited four of her tokens and left. With some of the children, the experimenter also left immediately, so that apparently no one was there to observe whether or not the child contributed anything; with others, the experimenter stayed on and watched the child decide whether or not to share her earnings.

The results, as shown in Figure 4-2, indicate that both the opportunity to observe a model and the presence of a witnessing experimenter facilitated the development of altruism in the form of sharing on the part of the children. Those who had no model to observe, and who were also alone when it came time to share earnings, gave the least, whereas the greatest amount of giving occurred when the children saw the model give and were also watched by the experimenter. Inasmuch as giving was entirely voluntary on the part of the girls, the results show what a powerful effect an adult model has on children's behavior, an effect that is considerably strengthened when another adult is watching.

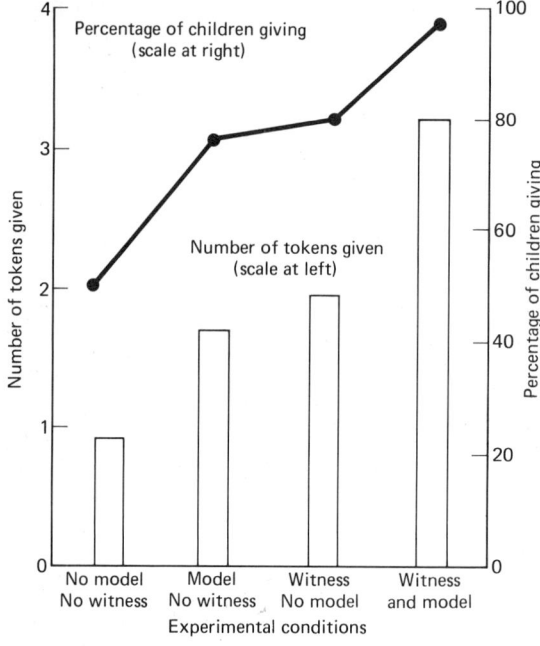

FIGURE 4-2. Effect of watching a model and being observed on the sharing behavior of primary school girls. (After Liebert and Poulos, 1971.)

_____ factors underlying socialization

Drives and Needs

In order for reinforcement to have any effect at all, it must have some relationship to the learner's needs. A food pellet is a reinforcer for a hungry rat, but not for a satiated one. For a school child, a teacher's "That's very good!" may be a reinforcer if bestowed by a loved and admired teacher, but the same comment from a disliked teacher will have little effect.

What we are saying is that organisms, rats and humans alike, are selective in the way they respond to the stimuli in their environment. Some stimuli evoke responses; others do not. The experimentalists call this readiness to respond in appropriate ways to appropriate stimuli a drive.

A drive is a set of internal conditions in an organism that can be aroused by internal or external stimuli and that lead it to seek some goal. Attainment of the goal reduces the drive and reinforces the behavior leading to the goal. Hunger is a drive that leads to food-seeking behavior, and ingestion of food reduces the drive.

Hunger may also be considered as a *need* for food. Used in this sense, the term *need* refers to a deficiency or deficit in some stimulus that is important for the well-being of the organism. *Need* may also refer to the tension that results from the deficit; hence we can speak of a need for nourishment or a need for love. Needs can also be quite complex. Abraham H. Maslow (1954) speaks of a hierarchy of basic needs: needs for maintenance of the organism, needs for love, needs to belong to and have status in a group, and needs for self-actualization and self-expression. Some of these needs, such as the maintenance needs, are deficit needs—needs that depend on deficits. Others are not responses to deficiencies, but go beyond—these are the needs of the individual to become more adequate and effective.

Both needs and drives are *motives*—that is, they describe states that are the wellsprings of behavior, that give the organism a readiness to respond when the proper *cue* or configuration of stimuli appears in the immediate environment.

According to these theories, the earliest learning takes place in connection with drives that can be considered to be maintenance or deficit needs. The infant learns to associate his mother's face and voice with comfort—with being fed, cuddled, and kept warm and dry. A few months later, the appearance of the mother's face leads to a reaching upward, a gesture that demands cuddling. In this way, one learned form of behavior builds on another. Reaching also may be a way of responding to a need to be loved, which many personality theorists consider to be a deficit need, one that must be satisfied if the child is to flourish and develop normal, mature patterns of behavior.

The Need for Arousal

Some forms of goal-directed behavior satisfy the drive-reduction theory very well. This is especially true of physiological drives, like hunger and thirst, as well as of other deficit needs, like the need for love. Other motives do not fit so well. In a drive state, the organism is aroused, and attainment of the goal leads to satisfaction and a reduction in arousal. A great many activities in life, however, are satisfying not because they reduce arousal, but because they increase it. As Berlyne (1970) has pointed out, situations that contain elements that are novel, surprising, ambiguous, or complex are not only arousing, but reinforcing as well. The sudden appearance of a human face over an infant's crib sends him into raptures of delight, and, as soon as he is able, he will initiate peek-a-boo games with adults in order to experience the pleasant shock over and over again. In such instances, it is arousal itself that is rewarding, not its reduction. Indeed, peek-a-boo has been used as a reinforcer in research dealing with infant learning.

As adults we recognize the reward value of arousal when we characterize certain experiences as "interesting," "intriguing," exciting," and the like. Such experiences are likely to be preferable to ones that are quiet, monotonic, uneventful, and dull. True, we may welcome the quiet of the woods after a hectic week in the city, but after a few days most of us look forward to returning to an environment where we will certainly be harassed and frustrated, but seldom bored.

The role that attention plays in human behavior has some puzzling aspects from a theoretical point of view. If we conceive of attention as a satisfaction for a drive to be noticed and attended to, we are overlooking the fact that attention also has an arousal effect and hence is not a drive reducer. To be sure, adults and children alike can work themselves to a frenzy in order to get attention, in which case attention can have a quieting effect, but in the more usual situation, attention adds interest and excitement to an otherwise ordinary experience. If we take a "needs" approach and say that being attended to fills in a deficit caused by a lack of attention, we have a better understanding of the mechanism, but this still disregards the fact that being aroused seems to be a need in itself. The child who unsuccessfully attempts to get his parents' attention may turn to some less preferred, but arousing activity; and if that activity is forbidden, it is all the more exciting. It may also lead to punishment, in which case he gets noticed after all and receives a double reward. Children who are unable to get adult attention for positive, prosocial[1] behavior learn to get it through antisocial behavior. One of the reasons why it is so difficult to unlearn this pattern once it has been established is that both the behavior and the punishment have an arousal effect and hence are reinforcing.

Too much arousal can, of course, lead to satiation and discomfort, so that the relationship between satisfaction and arousal is a curvilinear one. Arousal is rewarding and potentially reinforcing, but only up to a point. In the middle ranges of arousal, we are likely to oscillate, to move up and down on the scale—that is, we reduce the arousal level so we can have the pleasure of increasing it again. The child of nursery school age happily puts his picture puzzle together, dumps it out, and puts it together again. This may be repeated for a dozen times. Then he abandons it to listen to a story. But a few minutes later he returns to the puzzle with renewed interest.

There are several reasons why we learn socialized forms of behavior. One explanation is that we learn to associate "significant others"—our mother, for example—with certain basic physiological drives. The mother's voice, face, and presence become associated with food and comfort. The mother thus takes on primary value and becomes a stimulus that is associated with other important stimuli. This explanation is, in many respects, a classical one.

A second explanation, the operant one, conceives of the parents as taking an active role in socializing their child, in the sense that they reinforce some of his responses and either do not reinforce or negatively reinforce others, in order to get him to display responses that help him to cope with his social environment and to eliminate others that are

---

[1] Positive, friendly, altruistic; the opposite of antisocial.

irrelevant or that actually interfere. Both the classical and the operant explanations explain socializing partly in terms of its survival value.

The Reward Value of Socialization

A third explanation for socialization, one that is related to our recent discussion, is that socializing has a reward value in and of itself. In other words, the child becomes socialized not only because he wishes to survive and is rewarded for socially acceptable responses, but also because interaction with others is perceived as satisfying. Social interaction is likely to be an arousing experience. Of all the activities that are available to the individual, interacting with others has the most potentiality for the novel, the surprising, the ambiguous, and the complex, to use Berlyne's (1967) characterization of experiences that are likely to be arousing. Therefore, being accepted by others and being permitted to associate with them has reward value, and the child learns to seek the company of others and become a member of the group in order to experience this arousal.

An experiment by Irons and Zigler (1969) demonstrates the reward

Socializing has reward value in and of itself.

value of one type of social arousal. The subjects in the experiment were two groups of boys, aged eight and twelve—one group from an institution (a California Youth Authority facility) and one from an elementary school in a suburban residential area.

The boys were asked to play a simple, monotonous game, consisting of dropping marbles in a hole. Each subject was reinforced with approving comments at two-minute intervals as long as he played, and the dependent variable was the length of time the subject continued to play the game.

Because the game was simple and monotonous, the only incentive to continue was the reward value of the reinforcement. Institutionalized children, in contrast to children living with their families, experience less person-to-person interaction with adults. Hence it is not surprising to learn that the institutionalized children in this experiment worked longer at the monotonous task than did the other children.

The Irons-Zigler experiment is one of several that suggest that children who are deprived of normal interaction with adults build up a kind of a "social hunger" that makes them highly responsive to attention, favorable or otherwise (Gallimore, Tharp, and Kemp, 1969; Tizard, 1964; Dowart et al., 1965).

As an infant matures and becomes a child, changing his relationship to society from that of a passive dependent to that of an active participant, he finds that the benefits of membership have their costs. The price exacted by the groups that make up society is conformity to their norms. This demand for conformity requires that a would-be member of a group must modify not only his overt, visible behavior, but his ways of thinking and feeling as well.

To be in a group and not to conform leads to rejection. This may take the form of being ignored, in which case the arousal level is too low, or being criticized or punished, in which case arousal is too high.

None of these explanations of socialization tells the whole story: each describes some of the mechanisms that move the child from an asocial, humanoid organism to a member of society: (1) the association of the mother with certain biological satisfactions; (2) the reinforcement of prosocial behavior; (3) the imitation of the behavior of powerful models; and (4) learning and conforming to social norms as a way of satisfying a need for arousal.

Delaying Gratification

Walter Mischel (1974) maintains that the essence of socialization lies in self-control—specifically, in developing the capacity to pass up small, immediate rewards in the expectation of receiving more substantial ones later. The child (or adult, for that matter) who lacks self-restraint, who is impulsive, who "wants what he wants when he wants it," is not adequately socialized. He is likely to interfere with the rights of others, to be disruptive of social arrangements, and to be asocial—or, when frustrated, antisocial.

The demands of the toddler who demands instant gratification may be annoying, but at least we can understand that his impatience is a product of his immaturity. As he grows older, however, we expect him to become "decentered," to use the Piagetian term, and to recognize that the world cannnot and does not operate solely to meet his demands. In a complexly ordered world, in which rewards are seldom available on a here-and-now basis, successful social adjustment means learning to accept the inevitability of delay and postponement.

The problem is, how can we help children develop the kinds of strategies that will enable them to accept delay of reinforcement? The technique which Mischel developed experimentally was that of asking children to close their eyes and picture the rewards. Specifically, they were told: "Make a color picture of them; put a frame around them." Then they were to open their eyes and repeat the process and were told that from now on they would see a *picture* showing the rewards—that is, they would not see real rewards.

The behavior of children who had been asked to imagine the rewards as pictures was compared with that of children who had been asked to imagine that the rewards were actually in front of them. Results showed that children asked to imagine pictures could postpone gratification two to three times as long as those who thought of the rewards themselves. It made little difference whether the rewards were actually visible to and placed in front of the children or not; what *did* matter was whether they mentally converted the rewards into a picture or whether they thought of the rewards themselves.

In another experiment, children were asked to convert the rewards mentally into symbolic representations. If the reward consisted of marshmallows, the children in the first group were asked to think of them as white, puffy clouds, or round, white moons, whereas the children in the second group concentrated on the chewy, sweet, and soft characteristics of the marshmallows. As might be expected, children in the first group, who thought in more symbolic terms, were able to accept considerably more delay of gratification than those in the second group, who thought of the specific physical properties of the rewards.

Mischel's technique represents an approach to socialization through learning. It does not, however, involve imitation or modeling as Bandura's social learning does, but depends instead on instruction. Mischel's approach is also akin to some ways to Piaget's views of social development, because it recognizes that the child must learn to deal cognitively and symbolically—in mental terms, if you like—with his physical environment. But Piaget looks skeptically at attempts to manipulate the mental processes of children in order to speed up their cognitive or social development and has on occasion taken North

American psychologists and educators to task for seeking short cuts in the name of efficiency.

Learning to Avoid Misbehavior

We have devoted considerable space to explaining the development of prosocial behavior, but have said little about another aspect of socialization: the *avoidance* of antisocial, nonconforming, or asocial behavior. The development of prosocial behavior is the most effective road to socialization. The individual whose attitudes toward others and toward society are positive is likely to find ways of behaving that are consistent with these attitudes.

Much of the literature dealing with socialization, however, is concerned with ways in which behavior that a given social group considers undesirable can be suppressed or eliminated. Part of this concern is caused by the fact that behavior that does not conform to group standards is likely to be highly disturbing to group members and is seen by them as a threat to the cohesiveness and psychological integrity of the group. At the very least, it is distracting and disturbing.

When young children display behavior that is contrary to accepted norms, we are likely to rush to correct them; we see the problem as getting rid of the undesirable behavior, rather than teaching them more socially acceptable patterns. Busy parents and teachers are likely to be preoccupied with many problems, and the first thing that occurs to them when they see a misbehaving child is to get him to stop doing whatever he is doing. As a consequence, the literature on child socialization is concerned to a major degree with ways of getting children to repress impulses, the development of conscience, the effect of punitive methods of control, and the like.

Parental Warmth/Parental Control

Perhaps we worry too much about manipulating children to adapt them to the structural demands of society. The same folk wisdom that tells us that rod-sparing leads to child-spoiling also assures us that "most kids turn out O.K.," implying that child-rearing theories or strategies are irrelevant, and therefore a "hang-loose" approach is best. And many experts on child care, self-styled and otherwise, maintain that "the permissive way is the only way."

Robert Hogan (1973) would reject both extremes, accepting neither the idea that children must be treated as though they were intrinsically antisocial or asocial, nor the belief that the imposition or restrictions is at the best unnecessary, and at the worst undesirable. He writes:

> Most social psychologists assume some sort of natural antagonism between the individual and society. Freud, for example, believed that a

Socialization and Personality Development 117

child becomes able to live in society only after his natural but implacably anarchic tendencies are permanently repressed. One might equally hypothesize, however, that children are not anarchical but social by nature, that they enter the world programmed to be obedient, and that warmth and nurturance are essential in eliciting these tendencies.... Rather than ask what must be done to the child to fit him into society, it may be more important to ask what must be done in order to drive him out.

Hogan then cites research in which the obedience of infants just under a year old was correlated with various aspects of their mothers' behavior toward them. Observations made during a number of visits to homes indicated that the amount of cooperation or noncooperation displayed by the infants was essentially unrelated to (1) the insistence or frequency of their mothers' demands, (2) the number of times their mothers physically manipulated them in order to get them to follow orders or to behave properly, or (3) the extent to which their mothers permitted them to roam around on the floor or restricted them to playpens. The only variables that had any relationship to infant obedience were those related to maternal warmth. Those mothers who were considerate, emotionally supportive, and sensitive to their infants'

"You gotta stop throwing food at Daddy."
Children are likely to disregard suggestions made by mothers whose attitudes and general behavior suggest lack of interest and passivity. (HERMAN, by Unger. © 1978, Universal Press Syndicate.)

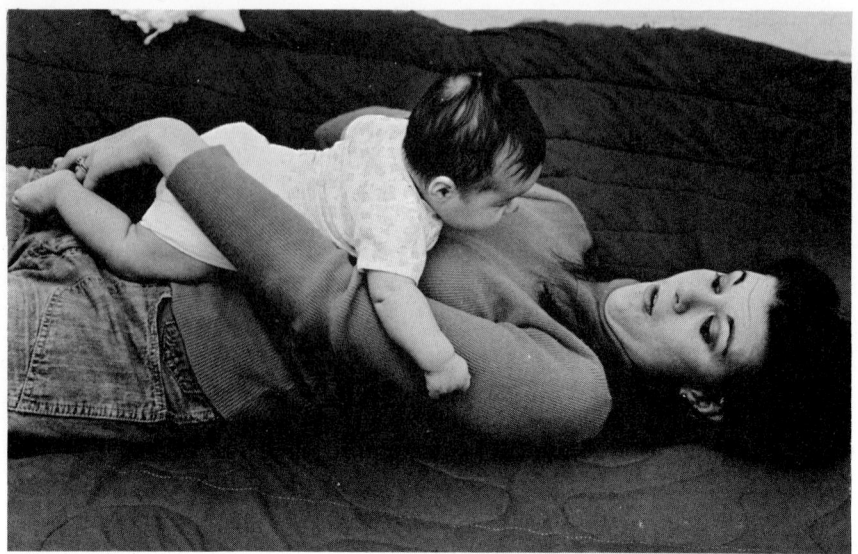

Most people would agree that a mother's expressions of love play an important part in the emotional development of infants, but few are aware that maternal warmth is also fundamental to the willingness of infants to obey their mothers.

needs were likely to be obeyed; those whose behavior suggested attitudes of rejection, displeasure, or disinterest were likely to be ignored or disobeyed (Stayton, Hogan, Ainsworth, 1971).

Hogan notes, however, that a review of the available research evidence

> strongly suggests that while warmth is important, "love is not enough," that as children become more mobile, control factors play a correspondingly larger role in socialization. Thus warm, nurturant, *and* consistently restrictive "authoritative" parents produced the most socialized children.

psychoanalytic theories of socialization and personality development

Personality can be defined as "the relatively enduring and consistent ways of behaving that characterize each individual" (Lindgren and Byrne, 1975). Psychologists employ two basic approaches in the study of personality. They can study it *nomothetically* in terms of those aspects that cause us to resemble all other or some other persons, or they can study it *idiographically,* in terms of the characteristics that make us unique. The nomothetic approach is used by personality/social psychologists, who are seeking bases for making general statements about the human condition; whereas the idiographic approach is used by clinical psychologists or counseling psychologists, who are trying to understand the problems of patients or clients. There is continual interaction between the two modes of research, of course. Freud's idiographic studies of his patients led him to formulate general or nomothetic theories of personality development, and each individual's problems, trait pattern, and view of life are made more understandable when examined in light of what we know about people in general or about the behavior patterns that characterize the social groups in which the individual holds membership.

Freudian Views of Human Motivation

The personality theories that are in vogue among psychologists today owe a great deal to Freud, even though a majority of psychological writers, teachers, and psychotherapists do not consider themselves "Freudians," but instead identify themselves as Gestaltists, existentialists, humanists, transactionalists, Neo-Freudians, or simply eclecticists who choose, cafeteria-style, whatever makes sense to them from the large array of personality theories and their variants that are available. But Freud is the first and foremost of the major theorists, so we shall give him more attention than his successors.

Freud (1924) viewed personality in terms of dynamics—that is, as the interplay of internal forces. These forces interact in reciprocal fashion to urge the individual onward and also to keep him in check from going too far. Freud (1925) specified the dynamics of personality as a theory of instincts and intrinsic motivational factors. Taken together, the instincts are the sum total of psychic energy.

The cardinal assumption of Freudian psychoanalysis is that sexuality is the basic human motive, but Freud and his followers never equated child sexual behavior with adult sexual behavior. Instead, they insisted that there was a direct, continuous connection between the behavior of the child in oral and other pregenital stages and his behavior in the genital (adult heterosexual) stage. Infantile sexuality foreshadows but does not completely define the adult pattern.

Just as the ovum contains the adult potentialities, so infantile sexual behavior foreshadows genital behavior. Sexual factors are accepted as the fundamental motivation, from which nonsexual motivation stems.

The libido is the energy for the sexual drives. Almost any impulse to receive pleasure would be an expression of libido, and hence is nonspecific in that it energizes any activity, but in another sense it is quite specific in that the natural expression is sexual. The libido may be defined as that fixed quantity of sexual energy available to an individual from birth onward. Simple physical needs, such as hunger and thirst, are accepted as having drive energy, but these needs are considered relatively uncomplicated and are of minor importance in Freudian theory.

Freud (1930) also postulated a second class of drives, the self-preservative drives. Later, as psychoanalysis developed, he spoke of life and death instincts; the latter was invested with a self-destructive quality, including the direction of destructive tendencies upon other persons as expressed in aggressive acts toward them. Aggression was considered to be an independent instinctual disposition.

As implied by their accepting the relative independence of aggression as a motive, psychoanalytic theorists have in recent years tended to deemphasize the importance of the sexual motive in accounting for behavior.

Psychoanalytic views of personality. Early in his work with patients, Freud was struck with the ever-recurring phenomenon of their failing to be aware of certain events or aspects of their lives which, he observed, had had a profound effect on them. Because the patients acted as if they were unaware of these significant determinants of their behavior and attitudes, Freud referred to them as "unconscious"; his consequent theoretical formulation stressed the unconscious aspects of mental life. Freud likened the mind to an iceberg, with only its summit of consciousness being above the surface, and with its great unconscious mass lying below the surface.

Originally, Freud adopted a threefold classification of mental life; conscious, foreconscious (capable of becoming conscious but not attended at the moment), and unconscious (actively excluded or repressed from consciousness, or referring to instinctual drives that were never conscious). Although he preserved these distinctions in his later theorizing, he preferred, on the grounds of greater dynamic possibilities, to speak of structural divisions of personality: the *id*, the *ego*, and the *superego*.

In his conception of the structural divisions of personality, the deliberately neutral term *id* (Latin for "it") was given to the source of unconscious energy. The id's aim is the gratification of its impulses, with no sense of morality, logic, or unity of purpose. The major function of the id is to provide free, uninhibited discharge of energy. Its activity is in the service of the pleasure principle: that is, the seeking of pleasure and the avoidance of pain with no other considerations entering the picture—characteristic of a kind of animallike existence based only on satisfaction of bodily desires, without any vestige of "reasonableness" or consideration for the rights of others.

Because the id is unconscious, it has no direct relation to the external world; it can be known only through the ego, which does have the characteristic of being conscious. The ego is partially relaxed in sleep, so that dreams show the intrusion into consciousness of id tendencies. Examination of dreams is one way to gain some dim (and frightening) knowledge of id impulses. The dreams of even the most straitlaced person are said to contain amoral elements that reveal the functioning of the id.

The ego includes the conscious portion of the personality structure. A great portion of the ego exists outside of awareness but can be called into consciousness when needed (that is, it is preconscious), whereas still another part of the ego is unconscious. The unconscious portion of the ego is the result of repression. Materials once conscious, but unacceptable to the ego, are pushed back into the unconscious. Because of its origin this portion of the ego is called "the repressed," and the action of refusing to allow unwelcome impulses to appear in consciousness is known as the mechanism of repression. What is repressed, however, has an "upward driving force," an impulsion or drive to break back into consciousness in one form or another—dreams, for example.

The ego involves both an awareness of self and the carrying on of executive functions. In connection with the latter, as a representative of reality, the ego serves to mediate among the pressures arising from the id (libidinal pressures), the superego (the conscience and "ego-ideal"), and the demands of external reality. An individual's evaluation of an existing situation, whatever it might be, and his anticipation of the future are functions of the ego. Obeying the "reality principle," the ego operates through realistic thinking. Plans are formulated for the satisfaction of needs and carried out (reality testing). In evaluating a situation and in anticipating the future, the ego must reckon with the demands of reality as they exist. In general terms, the ego represents reason, whereas the id represents the untamed passions—although, of course, the latter are represented in consciousness through the ego.

The ego is in control of voluntary movement and is aware of external events. It stores up experiences in memory; it adapts; it learns; it avoids. Thus it stands in relation to both the id and the external world. In following the reality principle, the ego mediates between the imperative pressures from the id, and the demands of external reality.

The ego also takes into consideration the requirements of a third element of personality, the *superego*. In a tentative way, the superego can be said to resemble what in ordinary language is termed "conscience." The superego results from the child's attempts to cope with parental demands that he refrain from behavior that he finds satisfying but that others find disruptive, destructive, or simply "bad." At first the child responds to direct demands, but finds himself unable to refrain from misbehavior when not under parental surveillance. The superego is therefore developed as an entity of internal control; it represents parental values and behaves toward the ego as the parents once did toward the child, making the child feel guilty and reproaching him. Instead of parental criticism there is now self-criticism. The superego has turned aggression against itself.

The prohibitions of the superego must be reckoned with by the ego in expressing id impulses. In this way the superego serves as the vehicle of conscience. When the ego and the superego are in harmony, however, the relationship between the two is felt as pride in accomplishment, and the ego-ideal is manifested. The ego-ideal strives after perfection—and occasionally attains it. There are two major aspects, then, of the superego: the moral prohibitions and restrictions, and the ego-ideal. The former are restricting; the latter is satisfying.

The superego serves an important means of control of those sexual and aggressive impulses which, if not so controlled, would endanger the very foundation of social life.

Anxiety and the defense mechanisms. Anxiety serves as a signal to the ego, alerting it to internal or external danger. Although this emotion is often considered synonymous with fear, Freud preferred the term *anxiety,* because fear is often interpreted as related to something in the external world. Anxiety refers to the perception of internal as well as external dangers and has disturbing and even paralyzing effects. The internal conditions giving rise to anxiety are the product of unacceptable id impulses and/or superego demands.

The so-called ego defense mechanisms need preliminary exposition. Anna Freud (1946), who interpreted and extended her father's theories, maintained that each child uses his ego to defend himself in characteristic fashion against anxiety. Each individual has a typical pattern for the employment of defense mechanisms, and much variety in personality structures is thus made possible.

Repression is one of the major ego defense mechanisms. By preventing the entry of unpleasant thoughts into consciousness, anxiety of a conscious sort is prevented.

Two other illustrative defense mechanisms are *projection,* or attributing to other persons or objects one's own shortcomings, as does the inept workman who blames his tools; and *regression,* or returning to less mature forms of behavior than the individual is capable of, as when a ten-year-old throws a temper tantrum. *Sublimation* is the most successful of the defense mechanism: its discharge of energy brings about a significant cessation of impulses without the continued defensive function of the other mechanisms. Sublimations are the socially approved ways of discharging libido without anxiety; they are desexualized expressions of libido. Forms of social behavior that contain elements of sublimation are social progress, altruism, achievement, and the maintenance of law and order.

Stages of Psychosexual Development

Psychoanalysis posits several stages in psychosexual development. In brief, its view is that the infant shows the capacity to receive pleasure from stimulation of various erogenous zones, which assume successive centrality through the various stages of psychosexual development. An erogenous zone is an area of the body that is sensitive to stimuli and is capable of being stimulated in such a way as to arouse pleasurable libidinal feelings. The lips and oral cavity form one such erogenous zone, the anal region another, and the genital organs still another. Each of these, in sequence, becomes the focus of erotic pleasure in the course of psychosexual development. From birth to adulthood there occur the oral, anal, phallic, and genital psychosexual stages, with the latter two stages separated by the so-called latency period.

During infancy, the obvious source of satisfaction is the mouth. Pleasure comes through taking in nourishment, and displeasure and discomfort come from not receiving it. According to Freudian theory, if the infant is frustrated or dealt with harshly during the oral period, he develops basic fear and anxiety and has problems in dealing with these emotions throughout his life. As a child and an adult, he cannot seem to get enough oral satisfaction and is considered to have been "fixated" at the oral stage of development. If parents overly indulge the infant during the oral period, he may become fixated in a different way—that is, become naïvely trusting and overdependent on others to do things for him.

The next stage, which overlaps the first, is dominated by problems relating to elimination, hence the term the *anal stage*. Defecating becomes a source of pleasure during this period, which extends to about age three, but it may also be a source of difficulty. This is the period during which society, in the form of the parents, begins to make strong demands that the child conform to proper standards of behavior. Toilet training serves as a focus for this contest of wills, and the child learns that he cannot relieve himself where and when he pleases. Not only does he learn to exercise impulse control when it comes to bowel movements; he also learns to please his mother by scheduling his movements so they occur at the proper time and in the proper place.

Fixation at the anal stage of development may occur if toilet training has been initiated too early or is too strict. If the training has been too severe, personality traits like extreme orderliness, stubbornness, and stinginess are said to result, whereas if the child has been able to "defeat" his parents, he is presumed to develop traits of carelessness, extravagance, and unpunctuality.

During the *phallic stage*, which extends through the preschool years, children are thought to discover that the genital area can also be a source of pleasure. For boys, this period is marked by the appearance of the *Oedipus complex*, a constellation of behaviors characterized by strong attachment to the mother, coupled with hostile and jealous feelings toward the father, who is seen as a rival for the mother's affection and attention. (The opposite pattern, sometimes called the *Electra complex*, is said to hold for girls). The complex is normally resolved late in the period when the child comes to accept, like, and admire the like-sex parent and to use him (or her) as a model for behavior. When the Oedipal conflict is not resolved satisfactorily, the child may identify with the parent of the opposite sex, with detrimental results as far as his personality development is concerned.

Following the phallic period, children are thought to enter a period of sexual latency, which ends with the genital stage: puberty, adolescence, and the beginning of adulthood.

Freud and his followers believed that the first five years of life are the most significant in the individual's development, and maintained that the principal structure of personality is formed then, with further development consisting largely of the elaboration of that structure. During these five years children are thought to pass through a number of critical periods, periods in which certain experiences are more likely to affect the course of their later development.

Freud's theories occupy a very significant place in the history of modern concepts of child development today. His ideas regarding anxiety, critical periods, and unconscious processes have a considerable degree of acceptance today, in one form or another, but his ideas about the universality of the Oedipal conflict and fixation at earlier stages of development have not stood up when tested by researchers. Most of Freud's propositions are stated in a form that makes them very difficult to test by experimental or correlational methods, and his followers have been generally disinclined to generate hypotheses that could be tested by suitably controlled studies.

Another problem with psychoanalytic theory, from the viewpoint of developmental psychology, stems from the fact that much of it is derived from the attempt of adults to dredge up childhood memories and hence is not based on direct observations of the behavior of infants and young children. We must also keep in mind that Freud's subjects were all individuals with a considerable degree of emotional disturbance, which leads us to echo Donald T. Campbell's (1975) caution against "basing a normal psychology and recommendations for all child rearing on a psychiatric patient population."

Freud's "perceptual set," or way of looking at things, may also be faulted. He viewed life through the perspective of a middle-class, nineteenth-century Viennese physician and was relatively unaware of the effect that different cultures have on the personality development of children.

Nor did Freud anticipate that styles of parenthood would change. The "ideal" father of the nineteenth century was stereotyped as a stern, unbending, and harsh figure, whereas fathers today are expected to be kind, understanding, and supportive. Calvin S. Hall (1978), one of the foremost authorities on Freud's work, points out that the whole structure of psychoanalytic theory, and not merely the Oedipus complex, was built around the idea of the hostile father. Without the hostile father,

Hall says, the theory collapses, "for Freudian theory consists of interlocking and interdependent parts of which the hostile father is an essential and pervasive element."

In the light of our greater psychological sophistication today, it is easy for us to belittle Freud's contribution. We forget that we are able to see things as clearly as we do because we are, in effect, standing on his shoulders. He is best seen in historical perspective—as a man who, like Darwin, was able to break through the restrictive bonds of the common sense of his day and chart new territory in the study of human behavior.

The Neo-Freudians

Some of Freud's students broke with the great master and set up competing theories of personality. In general, these later theorists tended to place less importance on the sex drive than Freud did and to take a more optimistic view of the individual's struggle to strike a balance between accepting the demands of the social order and finding satisfactory modes of self-expression and self-affirmation.

Carl Jung and Alfred Adler are the best known of these neo-Freudians. Although both had considerable influence in the development of personality theory, Adler made the more significant contributions to child psychology. He held that the child's awareness of his inferiority (small size, helplessness) leads him to develop behavior patterns that enable him to become more competent and thus more mature; each personality, to him, is a unique entity that expresses itself in the form of an individual "life style." Adler was also keenly aware of the conflicts and tensions among siblings: the "dethronement" of the firstborn with the arrival of the second child, the intense competition—sibling rivalry—for status, power, and parental attention.

Jung's influence on child psychology is more indirect than that of Adler. His description of inward-looking and outward-looking modes of living—introversion and extraversion—seem more relevant to the psychology of adolescence and adulthood, but his interest in the lore of other cultures, both present and past, has stimulated research in cross-cultural psychology and the history of childhood.

The theories of Erik Erikson. Among the personality theorists who have followed in Freud's footsteps, none has made a greater contribution than Erik Erikson (1963, 1968), whose concepts of development in childhood and adolescence draw on both psychoanalysis and cultural anthropology. Erikson, like most of the successors of Freud, deemphasizes the sexual theme in personality and is more concerned with the *social* aspect of development. His *psychosocial stages* are shown in Table 4-1, together with those of Freud and of Piaget, whose developmental system we discussed in Chapter 3. We have also supplemented

Erik Homburger Erikson (1902-) studied with the Vienna group of psychoanalysts and was a pioneer in applying psychoanalytic concepts to social anthropology. His many interests include the psychology of art, adolescence and current society, and the development of personal identity.

TABLE 4-1. Schematic Relationship Between Developmental Theories of Freud, Erikson, and Piaget (after Anthony, 1969; and Jersild, 1968)

Stages*	Psychosexual Stages (Freud)	Psychosocial Stages (Erikson)	Cognitive Stages (Piaget)	Emotional Problems
Infancy (0–18 months)	Oral	Trust vs. mistrust	Sensorimotor	Fear of dark, strangers, aloneness, sudden noise, loss of support Feeding and sleeping problems; depression, apathy
Toddler (18 months to 3 years)	Anal	Autonomy vs. doubt, shame	Symbolic	Fear of separation, desertion, sudden movements, strange sounds Negativism, constipation, shyness and withdrawing, night terrors
Preschool (3 to 5 years)	Phallic (Oedipal)	Initiative vs. guilt	Intuitive, preoperational	Fear of animals, imaginary creatures, injury Phobias, nightmares, speech problems, bed-wetting (enuresis)
Elementary school (6 to 11 years)	Latency	Industry vs. inferiority	Concrete operational	Fear of school failure, ridicule, loss of possessions, disfigurement, disease, death School problems, failure to be accepted by peer group
Adolescence (12 to 17 years)	Genital	Identity vs. identity diffusion	Formal operational	Fear of being different physically, socially, intellectually; sexual fears; loss of face Rebelliousness, "acting out," dropping out, destructiveness, apathy, drug-taking

*We should note that Piaget and his followers hold that it is the *sequence of stages* that is significant, not the ages when the stages normally appear. Some children go through the sequence more slowly, and others more rapidly, than the indicated ages would indicate. In any event, the age spans suggested for each of these stages are only suggestive of the developmental periods in which the experiences indicated are likely to occur in the life of the "theoretically normal" child.

According to Erikson, the fundamental psychosocial conflict during infancy is resolved when the infant learns to trust.

the lists with examples of emotional problems drawn from the writings of Arthur T. Jersild (1968) and E. James Anthony (1970).

Erikson analyzes and describes each period of development in terms of the psychosocial crises that must be resolved satisfactorily before the individual can go on to the next stage. In some respects, one can see a similarity here to Havighurst's (1953) developmental tasks, which we mentioned in the foregoing chapter. In addition, Erikson takes into account the significant others or "objects" on which the individual's social behavior is focused, and the outcome that normally results.

During the years of infancy, the psychosocial conflict is one of *trust versus mistrust.* The social object is, of course, the mother, or whoever happens to play the major caregiving role for the infant. The modalities the infant employs are those of receiving and giving in return. The mother gives nourishment, comfort, attention, and love, and the infant responds with warmth, pleasure, and normal growth and development. If all goes well, the infant learns to have confidence in the orderliness and predictability of his environment; if not, he is likely to become fearful, apprehensive, and panicky.

During the toddler stage, crises are likely to occur with respect to *autonomy versus shame and doubt.* Significant relations are with parental figures, and the basic modalities are holding on and letting go. If all goes well, the child should achieve some measure of self-control and will power. He has learned the rudiments of social behavior and has some degree of independence and self-confidence. This does not mean that all is peace and quiet, however. Self-assertion inevitably leads to friction and negativism. If the crises are not surmounted successfully, the child develops a sense of shame, embarrassment, and self-rejection.

The preschool years are concerned with *initiative versus inferiority,* and significant others emerge in the neighborhood play groups and at school. Making and doing things in a group setting are the modalities here. In the North American culture, the world outside the home begins to exert more influence than the family during this period, and social arrangements—rules, regulations, customs, laws and the like—have an increasing amount of importance. If the crises of this period are dealt with adequately, the child develops social competence; otherwise he has a sense of personal and social inferiority and inadequacy.

During adolescence, the crises relate to *identity versus identity diffusion,* and the significant others are groups—both peer groups and out-groups—and models of leadership. The modalities during this stage are concerned with becoming oneself and sharing oneself. The adolescent recognizes the complexities of life and human relations, and learns to empathize and sympathize with others. He experiments with various social roles and, if all goes well, learns to avoid roles that carry a "negative identity"—that is, the antisocial or asocial roles of the chronic rebel, the delinquent, the dropout, or the confirmed "loser."

Erikson's stages number eight in all, the last three covering the adult years and reaching beyond the scope of the present discussion. Like Freud, Erikson's formulations are theoretical and speculative and do not provide many leads for experimental research. All three of the developmental views listed in Table 4-1 are based on clinical research, but it is that of Piaget that has had the strongest influence on child psychology and has generated the most research, as we noted in Chapter 3. However, the psychoanalytic theories of Freud and Erikson have had considerable influence in the applied areas of child psychology—particularly psychotherapy—and they continue to stimulate theories of the broad-gauge, humanistic type in the field of personality.

socialization: inside and out

In this chapter we have discussed two types of explanation for the changes that take place in the behavior of children as they become functioning members of society. The various learning theories described in the first part of the chapter say, in effect, that the major influence is external, that the social environment conditions, reinforces, models, or instructs the child and thus causes him to acquire or learn the skills, strategies, and attitudes that he needs to become accepted by and participate in the society into which he has been born. Such theories generally ignore the reasons *why* these environmental forces have an effect at all, or why children want to become fully functioning members of society.

Whereas learning theories focus on the child's environment, personality theories are primarily concerned with his inner life. Freud, Erikson, and the Neo-Freudians either say overtly or tacitly assure us that there is an inborn mechanism—Erikson (1968) calls it "ground plan"—that determines how children are going to respond to the events in their lives. Such theories do not dismiss environmental effects. On the contrary, they stress the importance of the child's experiences with significant others: experiences that lead him to develop normally socialized patterns of behavior under favorable conditions, and patterns that are inadequate, neurotic, antisocial, or asocial when conditions are unfavorable. In a sense, we are continuing the theme we mentioned in earlier chapters and gave particular attention to in Chapter 3, where we discussed differences between the environmental and the maturational explanations of child development. It is futile to argue which is the more valid. As far as child study is concerned, both approaches have their value. Environmentalist approaches generate more experiments that enable us to test conflicting hypotheses. They may clarify many points about child development, but the concepts examined are seldom broad enough to present a coherent picture. Personality theories of the developmental type, like those of Freud and Erikson, may falter on details and make some incorrect interpretations, but they give us more generally usable concepts of the trends in development.

Both approaches are needed; one complements the other. Learning approaches help by correcting the mistakes of the personality theorists, but broad-scale theories are needed to integrate and interrelate the data from isolated observations of children's behavior.

In the chapters that follow, we shall make use of both social learning theory and personality theory, and in each discussion shall use the approach that makes the best sense in interpreting the available data.

summary

Socialization is the process that enables the child to take on patterns of behavior that permit him to become accepted as a functioning member of the society into which he is born. Each society or culture channels the responses of infants and children so that certain modes of behavior are encouraged and others are discouraged.

Among newborns, there are few ethnic differences of any significance. The behavioral differences that appear later and differentiate members of one culturally defined group from another are probably learned and not genetically determined. Theories of learning propose a number of ways in which acquisition of behavior may occur. Classical or Pavlovian conditioning describes a process in which a response (the unconditioned response or UR), which was initially evoked by a given stimulus (the unconditioned stimulus or US), can be subsequently evoked by a new and unrelated stimulus (the conditioned stimulus or CS), provided the new stimulus has been presented in tandem with the US a sufficient number of times. The response that is then called forth by the CS is termed the conditioned response or CR. This substitution of new stimuli in order to produce prior responses is commonly used by mothers who try to get infants to make the same response to a new food (say, solid food) that they made to previously accepted food (say, milk). Instrumental or operant learning refers to a process whereby the experimenter, parent, or teacher gets a learner to make a new response instead of an older, more familiar one. This may be done if the new response is part of a hierarchy of responses that the child can make to a given stimulus situation. If the response is not part of the hierarchy of responses initially associated with the stimulus, it may be shaped by selective reinforcement of successive approximations to the desired behavior. Although *reinforcement* is generally used in a positive sense, undesirable responses may be eliminated with negative reinforcement. This sort of procedure usually fails unless it is accompanied by positive reinforcement of a substitute behavior.

Bandura suggests that reward and punishment alone cannot account for all social learning. Children acquire new responses through a process of imitation or modeling. Initially, the child attends to the model. If the observed behavior is relevant, can be interpreted symbolically, and is reinforced, it is more likely to be retained. If a child likes or admires a model, he is inclined to identify with him, to empathize with him, and to copy his behavior.

Freudian theory maintains that the parents' ability to express or withhold love causes the child to identify with them and to imitate or introject their attitudes and values, as well as their behavior. Bandura says that children are more likely to imitate authority figures who interact with them more frequently and who have the power to reward them. In general, schoolchildren from impoverished homes are more likely to imitate and comply with the expectations of teachers whose attention is reinforcing, whereas middle-class children, who are more inclined to be self-reinforcing, work at school tasks irrespective of whether the teacher reinforces them or not.

Experimentalists maintain that certain stimuli are reinforcing because they reduce drives, which are internal conditions aroused by internal or external stimuli. Need is a closely related concept that is defined in terms of a deficit in some necessary stimulus. Both drives and needs are motives, and give the organism a readiness to respond to the proper cue.

Although most stimuli are reinforcing because they are linked with the reduction of a drive-induced arousal state, some stimuli are sought because they increase the level of arousal. As the use of words like "interesting" or "exciting" would indicate, we all seek novel stimulation to some degree. This need for arousal may explain why it is so difficult to change the response patterns of children who have had to turn to antisocial behavior for attention. The arousing effect of attention and punishment may actually reinforce the behavior. The relationship between satisfaction and arousal is curvilinear, however, and beyond a certain point arousal becomes unpleasant.

Several reasons have been advanced to explain why we learn to become socialized. One explanation is that significant others become reinforcing through their early association with primary reinforcers. Another is that the parents take an active reinforcing role in the conditioning of the infant's social responses. A third explanation is that socializing is rewarding in itself, as shown by an experiment in which institutionalized children persisted longer on a monotonous task, provided an adult made approving comments, than did children living at home. The adult's comments clearly had more reinforcement value for the institutionalized children, who had relatively fewer contacts with adults than did the other children. The need for the acceptance and reinforcement that can only come from others is what leads the developing child to conform to the norms of the social groups in which he holds membership.

Mischel maintains that the essence of socialization lies in learning self-control—learning to postpone gratification, for example. His experiments show that children can postpone gratification if they are taught to think of rewards in abstract terms, rather than on an immediate, tangible, here-and-now basis. Socialization includes the avoidance of antisocial or asocial behavior, as well as the learning of prosocial forms. Nonstandard forms of behavior are disturbing to groups, and we are likely to intervene in order to suppress the undesirable symptoms. Hogan counsels against too much or too little intervention. He maintains that children are programmed to acquire socialized patterns of behavior, but that they must be treated with warmth and firmness if they are to become adequately socialized.

Personality—which has been defined as the enduring characteristics of individual behavior—may be studied nomothetically, in terms of the traits that cause us to resemble all or some others, or idiographically, in terms of the qualities that make us unique. Freud's concepts of personality development, which are nomothetic statements based on idiographic studies, are also theoretical statements of how socialization takes place. His theories emphasize the interplay between forces that urge individual action and keep it in check as well. The basic urge is the pleasure drive, the libido a motive that is basically sexual. Infant or child sexuality is not, however, the same as adult sexuality. A second class of drives is concerned with self-preservation, but also includes the death instinct and aggression. In the structural view of personality proposed by Freud, most of the determinants of behavior are unconscious. The id is the source of unconscious energy and is concerned only with the seeking of pleasure and the avoidance of pain. The ego, which represents the largely conscious aspect of the personality, plays an executive, mediating role and is in contact with reality. The superego represents conscience—the internalized behavior standards the child takes over from his parents. The conflicts between the drives of the id and the restrictions imposed by the superego generate anxiety. Inasmuch as anxiety is painful and even disabling, the ego makes use of defense mechanisms such as repression, or unconscious forgetting, to protect itself and the id.

Psychoanalysis posits several stages of psychosexual development, each identified with a "pleasure zone" in the body. During infancy, the obvious source of pleasure is the mouth. If the infant is frustrated or dealt with harshly during this oral period, he presumably develops basic fear and anxiety. The anal stage overlaps the oral stage and is dominated by problem relating to elimination. If toilet training has been too severe, personality traits like stinginess and extreme orderliness are said to result; if the child "defeats" his parents, he develops traits like carelessness and extravagance. The phallic stage is marked by the appearance of the Oedipus complex and the discovery that the genital area can be a source of pleasure. Following the phallic stage is a period of sexual latency which ends with the genital stage. Freud's theories have been questioned because they are based on the childhood memories of emotionally disturbed individuals and also reflect his perceptual set—that of a middle-class Viennese physician, who was relatively unaware of cross-cultural differences in personality and child-rearing practices. Nor are his propositions easily tested by experimental and correlational research methods. In spite of this, we must recognize that he made a major contribution to our thinking about personality and its development.

The neo-Freudians, like Jung, Adler, and Erikson, were more optimistic about human development than Freud was and placed less stress on the sex motive. Erikson, whose contributions are the most significant as far as child study is concerned, adapted Freud's psychosexual stages into a system attuned to the social aspects of human development and oriented to the kinds of crises or dilemmas that each individual must successfully resolve if he is to attain psychological maturity.

In sum, the social learning theories emphasize the environmental aspects of socialization but ignore the "why" of learning, whereas the grand-scale personality concepts of theorists like Freud and Erikson are concerned with the inner-life or motivational aspects of the changes that result in social maturity. Freud and Erikson also recognize the importance of the kind of environment a child grows up in, as well as his reaction to it. Social learning theory and personality theory are both important, and happily we do not have to choose one or the other. Social learning theory generates propositions that can be tested more readily through experiments, but personality theory provides conceptual frameworks that enable us to organize and understand data from our observations.

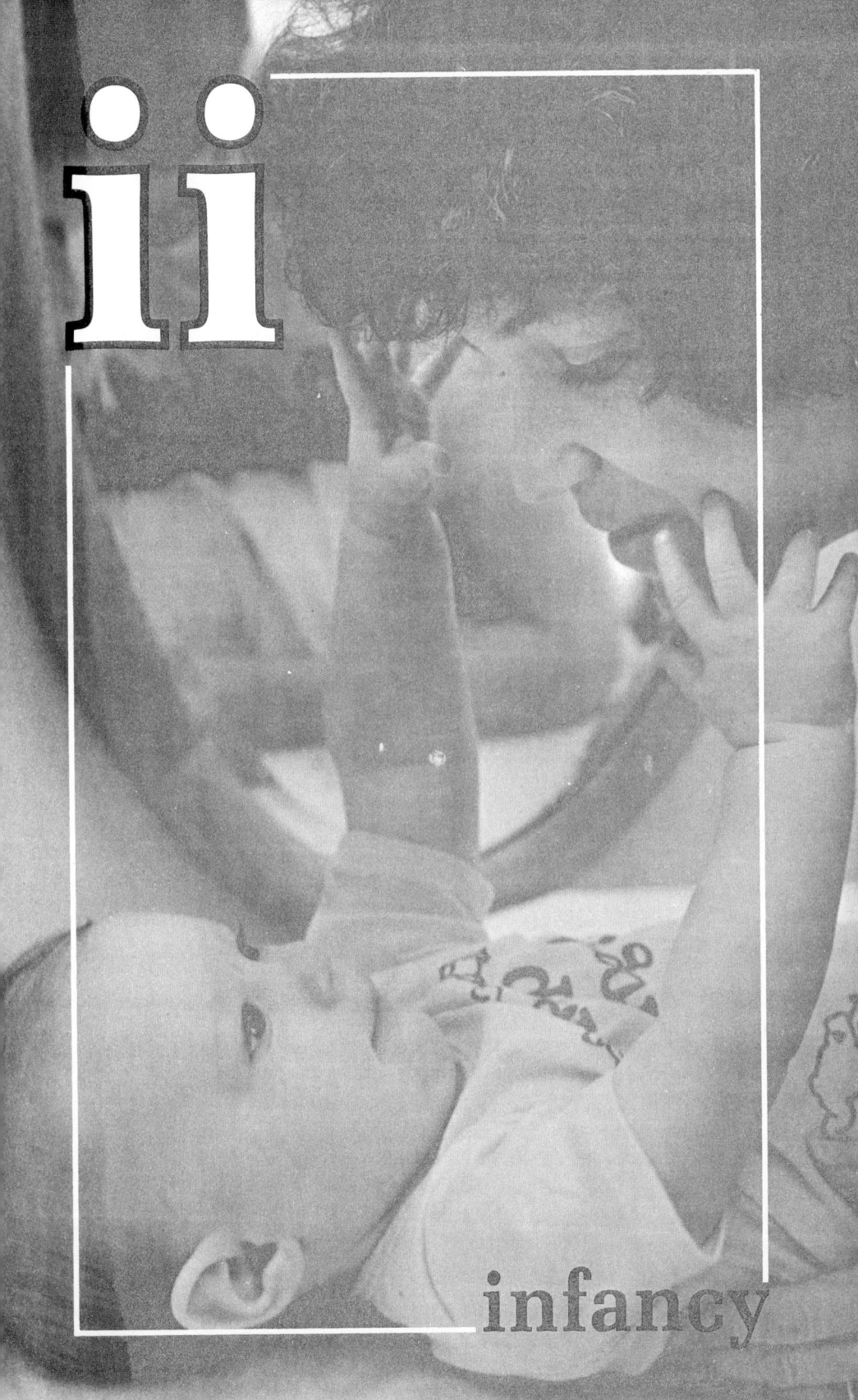

five

The Beginnings of Human Life

Let us call to mind the years before our little child was born. We are now in the same condition as then, except that the time she was with us is to be counted an added blessing.
—PLUTARCH

When does the baby's mental welfare begin? Before birth. And not, of course, because of the effect of maternal impressions upon the unborn child; but, rather because the mother, even during her pregnancy, is developing attitudes, expectancies, and decisions which will inevitably influence the course of the baby's mental growth, particularly in the four fundamental months which follow birth.
—ARNOLD GESELL and FRANCES L. ILG (1943)

It is common practice to date the life of an individual with his birth. Even though we have no recollection of the events of our birth, somehow it seems to mark the point "where we began." It would be more accurate, of course, to date it some nine months before, when we were conceived. Although, in Western cultures an individual's age is calculated from the date of his birth, in other cultures—the Japanese, for example—a year is added to reflect the "true beginning" of the individual's life.

from cell to organism

This backward extension can be carried even further. Although conception and birth are immensely significant milestones in each

138 Infancy

individual's life history, the egg and sperm whose union began it all were formed of cells contributed by each parent, and beyond them there is a continuing biological lifeline that extends into infinity, beyond the vague beginnings of human existence. For the purpose of our present discussion, however, we shall confine ourselves to more immediate events.

Life Begins

Sometime during the middle of the 28-day menstrual cycle[1] of a woman of childbearing age, one of the two ovaries produces an *ovum* or egg, which proceeds down one of the *oviducts* or *Fallopian tubes* toward the *uterus* or womb, as Figure 5-1 shows in schematic form. If coitus takes place, sperm contained in the seminal fluid that has been ejaculated into the vagina start their journey upward toward the egg, a journey that may take several hours.

Once they encounter the ovum in the Fallopian tube, the sperm smash against it in an attempt to penetrate its protective covering. If a sperm is successful in entering the egg, fertilization takes place and a chemical change occurs which prevents other sperm from entering. The resulting cell, termed a *zygote*, immediately begins to divide, splitting first into

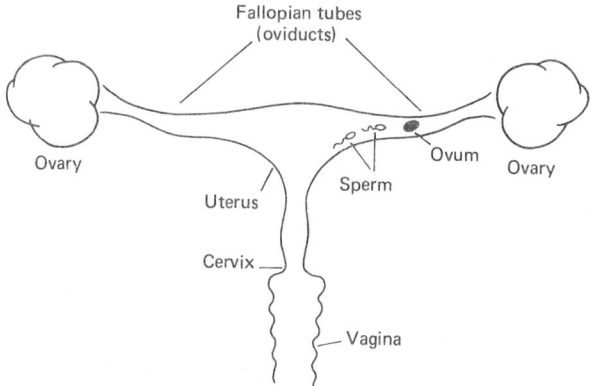

FIGURE 5-1. A schematic representation of the human female reproductive system showing fertilization.

---

[1] Predicting exactly when ovulation will occur is not easy. Wolfgang Jöchle (1970) points out that contrary to popular belief, it is *not* an event "for which a clock is set, and we only have to learn to listen for its strikings." Ovulation may, in fact, be brought by the stimulation and excitement of coitus, "the more so in adolescent girls and preclimacteric (premenopausal) women."

Charles W. Marwick (1970), however, maintains that it is possible to predict five days ahead of time when ovulation will occur, but such a prediction requires daily urinalysis over a month's period, in order to monitor changes in levels of various female sex hormones. Such a procedure, Marwick agrees, is hardly practicable "as a common or garden method of contraception."

two cells, then into four, then eight, and so on. As the cells within the zygote continue to divide, it proceeds down the Fallopian tube and becomes embedded in the wall of the uterus. At this point in its development, the zygote has become a ball of cells, a *blastocyst*. Fluid collects within the blastocyst, pushing certain cells to one side. These cells form the *embryonic disk*, from which the embryo develops. In this clump of cells, a smaller cavity forms, later to be recognized as the *amnion*. The outer layer of cells, called the *trophoblast*, forms the means of attaching the embryo to the uterine wall and also prepares for the subsequent interchange of nutritive and waste products.

The inner mass of cells in this rapidly proliferating system quickly produces a new layer of cells, the *endoderm*, which will line the blastocyst and produce another closed space called the yolk sac. The yolk is an extremely important structure in lower species as it is the chief source of nutritive materials during early developmental periods. In humans, however, its value is transitory and by the end of the fourth week of gestation, it has largely disappeared. Also arising from the endoderm is the *allantois*, a sausage-shaped tube that extends outward toward the periphery of the embryo. The part that remains in contact with the embryonic disk will ultimately constitute the bladder.

Soon a third layer of cells, the *mesoderm*, spreads out into the original blastocyst cavity. These cells become thickened at one end and form the *body stalk*, which will fuse with the allantois to form the *umbilical cord*—the chief avenue over which maternal-fetal interchange will occur. The outer layer of the entire embryo is called the *chorion*. On the outside of the chorion, little spidery filaments, called *villi*, appear and secure themselves in the lining of the uterus. As soon as blood vessels appear, as they do from the allantois and body stalk, they find their way into the openings of the villi and thence into the uterine walls.

The nutritional demands of the rapidly growing embryo cannot for long be satisfied by materials contained within the ovum, and more permanent arrangements must be made. As soon as the zygote is implanted in the uterine wall, the *placenta* begins to develop. This new and temporary organ will handle the interchange of nutrients and waste products until such time as the new organism can sustain independent existence.

The biological mother-child relationship. The relationship between mother and unborn child is essentially that of host and parasite. The mother takes care of all the vital functions, including the provision of nutrients and oxygen and the expulsion of carbon dioxide and other waste products. The nutrients provided the fetus are already carefully "screened"—that is, they are those that have already found their way into the mother's bloodstream. Consequently, the circulatory systems of the two organisms are of crucial importance for future development.

Should the placenta fail to develop properly, or should its function be seriously impaired at any time during the pregnancy, then damage to the fetus is virtually inevitable. The placenta is truly the lifeline of the new organism, and, no matter how excellent the seed that was fertilized and that formed the basis for the new life, normal development cannot occur without adequate placental attachment.

Although the placental villi dip into "pools" or sinuses of maternal blood, there is no direct connection between the bloodstream of mother and child. Indeed, during the early weeks of gestation, the infant does not have anything that could technically be called a bloodstream. Rather he has cells that are developing into blood cells and the beginnings of a circulatory system capable of effecting transfer across the placental barrier. Very early in embryonic life the fetal heart begins to pulse and to force its own blood through its own closed vascular system. Then the outer layer of the embryo begins to form *capillaries* that reach out close to terminals on the maternal side. Actual exchange of chemical materials is accomplished by diffusion through these capillary walls. Thus, although there is no direct connection between the circulatory systems of the two organisms, there is certainly interaction between them.

It is now appropriate to consider the other major circulating and communicating network: the nervous system. Again, there is no direct connection between mother and child in the sense that the nerve fibers of one organism form an open system and become affiliated with fibers from the other system.

Perhaps an accurate way of summarizing the relationship is that the two systems, although separate and distinct, interact nonetheless.

prenatal development

Prenatal development is so orderly a process that it is possible to chart its important features in succint form. The following brief summary of the more significant events in the prenatal calendar will acquaint the reader with the sequence of prenatal growth and give some idea of the patterning and interlocking of growth during this developmental phase. As supplementary material for the following brief synopsis, see Figures 5-2, 5-3, and 5-4, as well as Table 5-1.

From egg to embryo. The first month begins with fertilization and the descent of the ovum from tube to uterus, followed by cell division and formation of the embryonic disc from which a new organism will develop. Early formation of three layers of cells—the *ectoderm*, from which sense organs and nervous system will develop; the *mesoderm*, from which circulatory, skeletal, and muscular systems will develop; and the *endoderm*, from which the digestive and some glandular systems will develop.

TABLE 5-1. Characteristics and Dimensions at Various Stages in Prenatal Development (after Meredith, 1975)

Stage	Age Span in Weeks	Characteristics at End of Period	Average Dimensions* at End of Period
Zygote	0	Single cell	0.14 mm. in diameter
Blastocyst	0–2	Head and trunk differentiated; ovoid disk in shape	maximum dimension 0.2 mm.
Embryo	2–3	Mouth, "gill pouches," upper-limb "buds," small tail; elementary nervous, circulatory, and skeletomuscular systems	3 to 5 mm.
Embryo	5–8	Tail at greatest length; limbs, heels, fingers, toes defined; rudimentary bones; gill pouches become eustachian tubes, glands, windpipe; head and neck constitute almost ½ the total length of embryo	39 mm. in length; 2 g. in weight
Fetus	9–19	Sex organs; finger- and toenails; covering of body hair; tooth buds; tail has disappeared; neck and head constitute ⅓ the length of fetus; upper limbs 30% longer than lower limbs	24.5 cm. in length; 400 g. in weight
Fetus	20–38	Weight increases ⅓ during 9th month (in contrast to 100% increase in 5th month); body hair usually shed; head and neck ¼ of total length of fetus; arms ¼ longer than legs.	50.6 cm. in length; 3330 g. in weight (white fetuses at birth)

* Dimensions are given according to the metric system. Figure about 25 millimeters (mm.) or 2.5 centimeters (cm.) to the inch, and 454 grams (g.) to the pound. In other words, the birth dimensions cited above for the average white infant translate into 20 inches and about 7 pounds 5½ ounces.

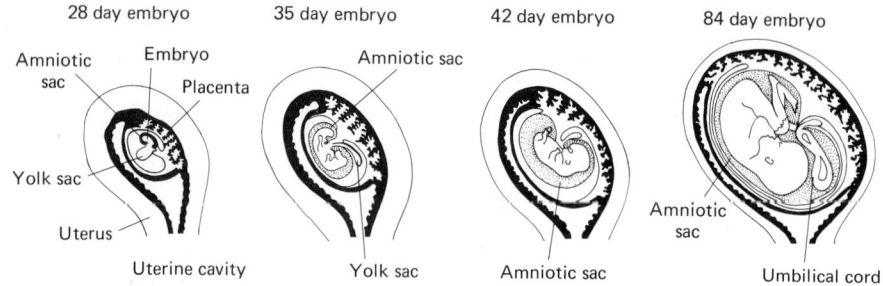

FIGURE 5-2. *The growth of an embryo.* (Nourse et al., 1964, pp. 176–177. Reproduced by permission.)

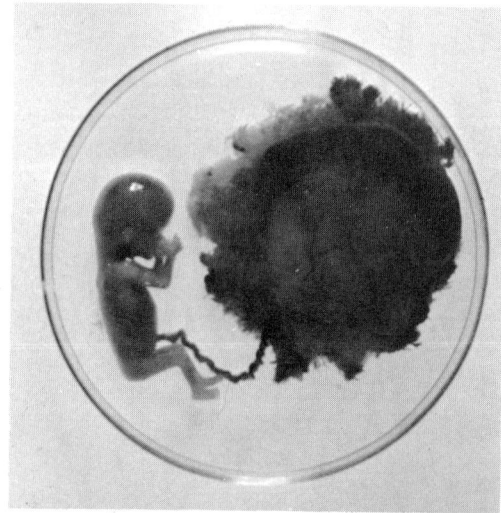

FIGURE 5-3. *Eleven-week old fetus, showing amnion, chorion, yolk, and umbilical cord.*

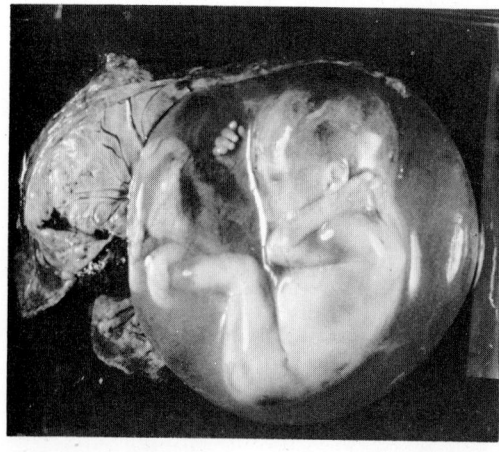

FIGURE 5-4. *Seven-month fetus. By now it is capable of independent life and can survive with special care, if born prematurely.*

Another special layer of cells forms the *amnion* or water-sac, which will surround the developing embryo except at the umbilical cord. The heart tube forms and begins to pulsate and force blood to circulate through blood vessels in the embryonic disk. The nervous system begins to develop, first in the form of a neural groove. The intestinal tract, lungs, liver, and kidneys begin to develop. By the end of one month, the embryo is about ¼" long, curled into a crescent, with small nubbins on the sides of body indicating incipient arms and legs.

During the second month, the embryo increases in size to about 1½ inches. Bones and muscle begin to round out contours of body. The face and neck develop and begin to give features a human appearance. The forehead is very prominent, reflecting the precocious development of the brain in comparison to the rest of the body. The limb buds elongate. The muscles and cartilage develop. Sex organs begin to form.

The early fetal period. The fetal period begins with the third month of pregnancy. Sexual differentiation continues, with male sexual organs showing more rapid development and the female remaining more neutral. Buds for all twenty temporary teeth are laid down. The vocal cords appear; the digestive system shows activity. Stomach cells begin to secrete fluid; the liver pours bile into the intestine. The kidneys begin functioning, with urine gradually seeping into the amniotic fluid. Other waste products are passed through the placenta into the mother's blood. The bones and muscles continue to develop, and by the end of the third month spontaneous movements of arms, legs, shoulders, and fingers are possible.

During the fourth month, the lower parts of the body show a relatively accelerated rate of development, so that head size decreases from one-half to one-fourth of body size. The back straightens; the hands and feet are well formed. The skin appears dark red, owing to the coursing of blood showing through thin skin, and wrinkled, owing to the absence of underlying fat. Finger closure is possible. Reflexes become more active as muscular maturation continues. The fetus begins to stir and to thrust out its arms and legs in movements readily perceived by the mother.

Skin structures begin to attain final form during the fifth month. Sweat and sebaceous glands are formed and function. Skin derivatives also appear—hair, nails on fingers and toes. The bony axis becomes quite straight, and much spontaneous activity occurs. The fetus is lean and wrinkled; it is about one foot long and weighs about one pound. If aborted, it may respire briefly, but will soon die because it seems unable to maintain movements necessary for continued breathing.

In the sixth month, the eyelids, which have been fused shut since the third month, reopen; the eyes are completely formed. Taste buds appear on the tongue and in the mouth and are, in fact, more abundant than in the infant or adult. If born, the six-month fetus will perhaps live a few hours or longer if protected in an incubator. If the fetus is aborted at this point, it remains alive only briefly, but may exhibit "Moro" or startle responses.

The later fetal period. The fetus if prematurely delivered, is capable of independent life from the seventh month onward. The cerebral hemispheres cover almost the entire brain. The seven-month fetus can emit a variety of specialized responses. Generally it is about 16 inches long and weighs about three pounds. If born, it will be able to cry, breathe, and swallow, but is very sensitive to infections and will need a highly sheltered environment for survival.

During the eighth and ninth months, the finishing touches are being put on the various organs and functional capacities. Fat is formed rapidly over the entire body, smoothing out the wrinkled skin and rounding out body contours. The dull red color of the skin fades, so that at birth skin pigmentation is usually very slight in all races. Activity is usually great, and the fetus can change position within the somewhat crowded uterus. Periods of activity will alternate with periods of quiescence. The fetal organs step up their activity and the fetal heart rate becomes quite rapid. The digestive organs continue to expel more waste products, leading to the formation of a fetal stool, called the *meconium*, which is expelled shortly after birth. Violent uterine contractions begin, though milder ones have been tolerated earlier, and the fetus is eventually expelled from the womb into an independent physiological existence.

Fetal Characteristics

Although the fetus has many human characteristics at the beginning of the fetal period, it does not really resemble a human being until about the third month (see Figure 5-2). The head is disproportionately large, with the legs much shorter than they will be eventually, an example of *cephalocaudal,* or head-to-tail direction of development, which we mentioned in Chapter 3. The entire course of prenatal development illustrates the principle of differentiation and integration. Even as early as the eighth week, differentiation is exhibited. It shows, for example, in the heartbeat, and in simple body movements, such as bending of the neck in a prematurely born fetus when stimulated by stroking the cheek with a hair. By about 14 weeks the early predominately generalized responses are less prominent, and less stereotyped forms of activity are being exhibited. After activity on the part of the mother, fetal activity decreases as compared to such activity when the mother is quiet. This decrease in activity after maternal exercise is attributed to the increased oxygen supply that is available to the fetus.

Fetal activity. There has been some interest over the years in the question of whether fetuses can learn through being conditioned. Logic and common sense suggest that learning ought to be possible—after all, organisms at more primitive levels on the evolutionary scale than fetuses are able to learn. But experiments demonstrating the amount and kind of learning that fetuses can accomplish are, as one might imagine, rather difficult to perform, and results are seldom if ever clear-cut. David K. Spelt (1948), for example, attempted to condition fetuses between seven and nine months of age. His unconditioned stimulus, the noise from a loud clapper, produced a jerking movement in the fetus. He apparently was able to get the fetus to give the same response to a conditioned stimulus, a mild vibrator. The question remains, however, as to who was being conditioned: the fetus or the mother? It is possible that the mothers learned to respond to the vibrator and communicated their response in the form of muscle contractions, which led the fetuses to respond in the jerky motions the investigator had been looking for—another possible example of the Rosenthal effect we mentioned in Chapter 2.

Other reactions in fetuses—abrupt changes in fetal heart beat, for instance—may be touched off by sudden maternal emotions. Such responses may be called forth in the fetus by two kinds of signals: changes in the mother's arterial pressure, or by the presence of a glandular secretion in her blood which is associated with strong emotion (Liley, 1972).

The sheer amount of fetal activity appears to be related to the general activity level of the infant and child later on. C. Etta Walters (1965) had 35 women record the movements of their unborn child during the last three months of pregnancy and then subsequently tested the infants at 12, 24, and 36 weeks, using the Gesell Development Schedules, a scale that enables psychologists to judge the rate at which a child is maturing. Walters' observations were consistent with the findings of an earlier study by Richards and Newberry (1938), who reported a very substantial correlation (.62) between fetal activity and scores on the Gesell schedule at six months.

The results of these studies are not too surprising. There is a tendency for the behavior of a given individual to manifest a general consistency. This is, after all, one of the bases on which the science of psychology rests. If people did not behave in consistent ways, it would not be possible to come to any conclusions about them or to make any predictions about their probable future behavior. An active fetus suggests an energetic, healthy organism, one that is likely to develop at an optimum rate after, as well as before, birth.

Maternal nutrition. Other environmental influences are at work during the prenatal period. The nourishment available for the fetus is naturally related to the kind and amount of food ingested by the mother. These differences appear most sharply in comparisons of infants born to poor and to nonpoor mothers. In one survey, autopsies of 252 infants who were stillborn (dead at birth), or who died within 48 hours of birth, showed that the infants of mothers who were "below the poverty level" were 15 per cent smaller than the infants of other mothers. Furthermore, a higher percentage of the infants who were stillborn, had been born to impoverished mothers (Naeye et al., 1969).

Maternal malnutrition may also account for the fact that families from slums and other poverty areas produce a higher percentage of children with birth defects of various kinds than do families where income and nutrition are more adequate (Hepner, 1958; Knobloch and Pasamanick, 1958).

In a special message to Congress, dealing with mental illness and mental retardation, the late President John F. Kennedy (1963) made the following comments, which are as valid today as they were when he uttered them, well over a decade ago:

> Families who are deprived of the basic necessities of life, opportunity, and motivation have a high proportion of the Nation's retarded children. Unfavorable health factors clearly play a major role. Lack of prenatal and postnatal health care, in particular, leads to the birth of brain-damaged children or to an inadequate physical and neurological development. Areas of high infant mortality are often the same areas with high incidence of mental retardation. Studies have shown that women lacking in prenatal care have a much higher likelihood of having mentally retarded children. . . .
>
> Among expectant mothers who do not receive prenatal care, more than 20 percent of all births are premature—two or three times the rate of prematurity among those who do receive adequate care. . . . Premature infants have two or three times as many physical defects and 50 percent more illnesses than full-term infants. The smallest premature babies are 10 times more likely to be mentally retarded.

Insufficient maternal nutrition is a major factor in undersized infants. Surveys show that mortality among infants of subnormal weight is much higher than among those of normal weight, as Figure 5-5 indicates.

Malnutrition, and poor prenatal and postnatal care, are not the only problems that affect the health of infants. Particularly dangerous are syphilis, which may kill the fetus or may result in a crippled or mentally deficient child; rubella (commonly known as German measles), which may lead to deafness and other disabilities; and diabetes, which may cause circulatory and respiratory defects.

Cytomegalovirus (CMV) is the most common infectious cause of birth defects, including mental retardation, blindness, and deafness. Its incidence, like other birth problems, varies with socioeconomic status, ranging from 0.5 per cent in infants born to middle-class parents to 2 per cent in infants born to the very poor. Investigators theorize that CMV may be introduced into the fetus by a primary infection of the mother during pregnancy or that it may already be present but latent. Actually, very little is known about the way CMV operates. The virus and its effects are currently being investigated by several teams of researchers, and means for controlling it may not be far off (Marx, 1975b).

Maternal drug use and fetal stress. In the last decade or so there has been an increase in the number of women of childbearing age who habitually use one or more of the psychoactive drugs—that is, the opiates (heroin, opium), lysergic acid diethylamide (LSD-25), cannabis (marijuana, hashish), cocaine, and the amphetamines (methredine, STP, or "speed"), to name some of those most commonly employed.

It is obviously impossible for legal and moral reasons to conduct experiments on the effect that maternal use of such drugs has on fetal development. There have, however, been some experimental studies of the effects on laboratory animals of some of the more widely used drugs. Birth abnormalities in mice have been produced by LSD (Alexander et al., 1967), and cannabis produces a high percentage of still births, again in mice (Harbison and Mantilla-Plata, 1972). There has also been some correlational research with human subjects. A survey of infants born to narcotic-addicted mothers showed that they, in contrast to other newborns, tended to rate low on the Brazelton Neonatal Behavioral Assessment Scale. Specifically, they were more tremulous, more irritable, less well coordinated, less alert, less stable in mood, and less responsive to cuddling (Strauss et al., 1975).

Other research suggests that those drugs that cause hallucinations (LSD-25, for example), produce birth abnormalities when taken early in the pregnancy (Houston, 1969). This observation would be consistent with other findings: anything that is likely to harm fetuses will have its greatest effects early, when the zygote or embryo has relatively few cells and is most vulnerable. As to preconception effects, one study shows

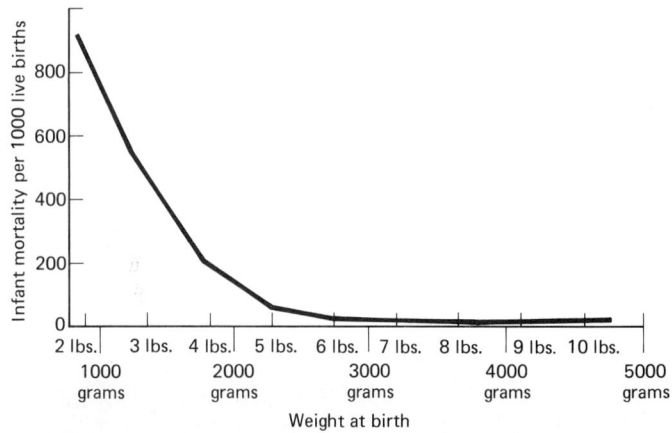

FIGURE 5-5. *Relationship between infant mortality and birth weight.* (White House Conference on Children, 1970.)

that persons taking LSD-25 are far more likely to have chromosome abnormalities than nonusers (Nielsen, Friedrich, and Tsuboi, 1969). Even if there were no research evidence, it could be argued persuasively on common-sense grounds that the use of substances that create an abnormal physical state in the mother are likely to affect the embryo or fetus adversely.

Nicotine has been implicated as a cause of low birth weight in infants (Meredith, 1975). The relationship between maternal smoking and low birth weight has been questioned on the grounds that other factors may be involved, such as the personality traits and general behavior patterns that tend to characterize smokers—higher levels of tension and anxiety, more frequent swings from elation to depression, and the like (Becker et al., 1968). But other evidence indicates that a woman who stops smoking by her fourth month of pregnancy is no more likely than a nonsmoking mother to bear a low-birth-weight infant (Butler et al., 1972). Hence the evidence, on balance, suggests that it is the smoking itself, rather than the psychological traits associated with it, which produces the higher percentage of low-birth-weight infants.

No studies indicate any relationship between average consumption of alcohol and problems in fetuses or neonates, but there is some evidence that women who drink excessively during pregnancy have a greater than normal tendency to bear low-birth-weight infants. There is apparently a "fetal alcohol syndrome" as well, which appears in the form of retarded motor and intellectual development, as well as a higher risk of physical abnormalities (Jones et al., 1973).

Medical problems and fetal stress. Certain forms of medication can also cause fetal problems. A sudden increase in birth defects in Germany during the early 1960s were traced to the mothers' use of a sedative called *thalidomide,* which had been prescribed for the morning sickness of early pregnancy. Exposure to radiation has also been shown to cause birth defects, both in infants born after the atomic bombing of Hiroshima and in infants born to American and British mothers who had received heavy dosages of X rays during pregnancy. Every gynecologist is now well aware of the hazards of X rays, and the general approach followed today is one of caution and conservatism in medication and diagnosis during pregnancy.

Still another problem that may affect the development of the fetus is the incompatibility of Rh blood factors. About 85 per cent of all white persons are Rh positive; that is, a special serum prepared from the blood of rhesus monkeys (hence "Rh"), will cause their blood to clot. The remaining 15 per cent are Rh negative. If an Rh-negative woman is impregnated by an Rh-positive man, their first child is likely to be normal. In subsequent pregnancies, however, there is a fair possibility that there may be a miscarriage or that the child will live only a few hours after birth.

The problem arises from the fact that the fetus inherits an Rh-positive gene from its father, and the Rh-negative blood from the mother carries an antibody that may destroy the red blood corpuscles of the fetus. Although this type of difficulty would theoretically occur about 5 per cent of the time, in actuality it occurs in 0.5 per cent of all pregnancies, probably because antibodies do not pass through the placenta in the majority of instances. In any event, if physicians know of Rh problems beforehand, there are various ways in which the problems of incompatible Rh factors may be averted. For one thing, a special vaccine has been developed which prevents a mother who has delivered an Rh-positive infant from becoming sensitized to any subsequent Rh-positive infants she may bear. Infants who develop Rh disease can also be saved through a series of repeated blood transfusions. If prenatal tests show that a fetus has Rh disease, the blood transfusions can be carried out before birth or immediately thereafter (Zimmerman, 1973).

pregnancy and the mother

A moment's consideration will help to show why it is appropriate to examine the question of the mother's attitudes as they exist prior to the child's birth. Pregnancy is a developmental crisis in a woman's life, a "critical period of adulthood," so to speak. Inescapably she must make some major adjustments in her mode of life, not only because of physiological changes that are taking place within her but also because of the impending arrival of the infant. All aspects of her life are directly or indirectly involved. It is completely natural that she should develop some rather pronounced attitudes toward her role as a mother and toward the child-to-be. She develops some expectations of what motherhood will be like and what the child will be like. These pre-existing attitudes will carry over into her relationships with the child and will affect her behavior as she attempts to cope with him and guide his behavior.

Maternal Attitudes

Before the birth of the child, the mother's attitudes are likely to develop a certain slant or flavor. Are they positive or negative? Resentful or eager? More than likely the prospective mother's feelings are mixed—an over-all sense of fulfillment, coupled with a sense of annoyance at her awkwardness and discomfort as she moves around, heavy with child. A mother who was never irritated with the thought of the coming child would be more (or less) than human.

Zemlick and Watson (1953) were interested in learning whether attitudes of acceptance or rejection had an effect on the prospective mother's psychological and physical adjustment during pregnancy. In other words, they wished to know whether a prospective mother who tended to reject her coming child also showed psychological and physical differences from a mother who adopted a positive, accepting attitude toward her child-to-be. Mothers expecting their first child were their subjects. Each mother was studied by means of: (1) a selection of Thematic Apperception Test (TAT) cards, through which was established her level of anxiety; (2) a psychosomatic inventory (PS), in which she reported her psychological and somatic symptoms; and (3) a Pregnancy Attitude Scale, composed of items which supplied information about her attitudes toward pregnancy, such as the degree to which she wanted the child.

Independently of these data, adjustment to pregnancy, in terms of physical and emotional symptoms, was rated by an obstetrician who saw each mother, on the average, ten times. He also rated the mother's behavior during labor and delivery in terms of her adequacy in meeting this crisis (delivery adjustment rank).

Some of the obtained relationships among these measures are reported in Table 5-2. With the exception of the psychosomatic inventory, the physical symptom rating given by the obstetrician did not correlate significantly with the paper-and-pencil measures. The emotional symptoms noted by the obstetrician were more substantially correlated with the paper-and-pencil measures, however, and the latter also did reasonably well in predicting the mother's behavior at childbirth.

This positive correlation between attitudes of rejection or acceptance verbalized by the mothers on the attitude scale, on the one hand, and emotional symptoms exhibited and delivery adjustment rank, on the other, is particularly noteworthy. Mothers with acceptant attitudes tended to have fewer emotional symptoms and higher delivery adjustment, whereas mothers who exhibited rejecting attitudes tended to have

TABLE 5-2. Relationships[a] Between Paper-and-Pencil Tests of Mothers' Adjustment During Pregnancy and Ratings Given by an Obstetrician During Pregnancy and at Childbirth (data from Zemlick and Watson, 1953)

	Obstetrician's Ratings		
Paper-and-Pencil Measures	Physical Symptoms	Emotional Symptoms	Delivery Adjustment
Anxiety (TAT)	.29 (NS)	.48	.51
Psychosomatic symptoms (PS)	.54	.75	.50
Pregnancy attitude scale	.21 (NS)	.59	.54

[a]Except for figures marked (NS), all correlations are significant at the .10 level of confidence or better.

more emotional symptoms and lower delivery adjustment. The more the mothers rejected their coming child, the stormier pregnancy they seemed to have.

It is important to note that these mothers were not emotionally disturbed or abnormal individuals. None was neurotic, psychotic, or mentally retarded. And yet in these more or less normal, well-meaning mothers varying degrees of acceptance and rejection were found, thus disposing of the allegation sometimes made that only abnormal mothers reject their children.

Barbara A. Doty (1967) made a comparative study of women who were pregnant with their first child (*primiparae* or PP) or pregnant with a child other than their first (*multiparae* or MP). The mothers were also divided into middle and lower socioeconomic groups on the basis of husband's occupation. Doty's results, as shown in Figure 5-6, indicate that lower-class mothers reported more emotional disturbance and rejection of their pregnancy than did middle-class mothers. On the other hand, the lower-class mothers reported fewer physical symptoms.

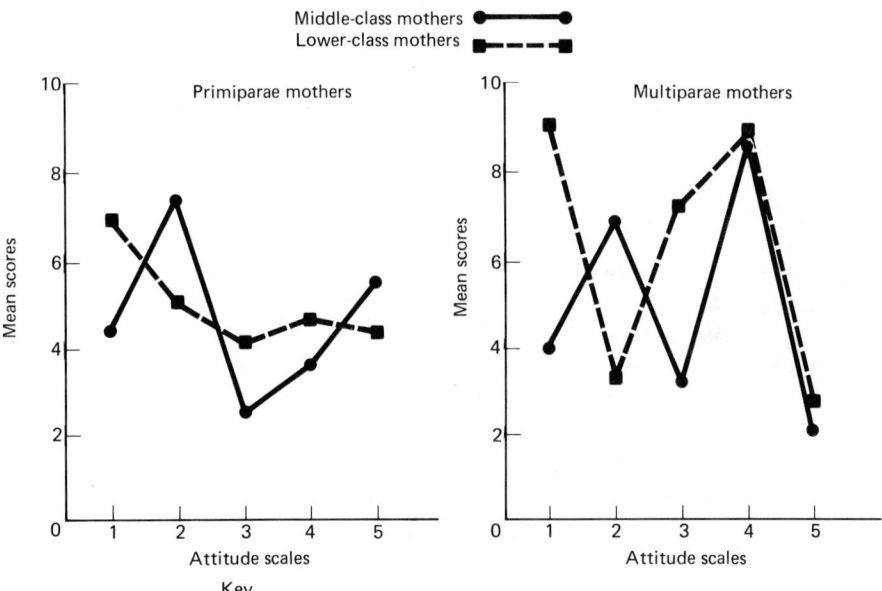

Key
1. Emotional disturbance, including irritability and depression.
2. Physical symptoms of pregnancy.
3. Rejection of pregnancy.
4. Rejection of maternal role.
5. Fear of pregnancy and childbirth.

FIGURE 5-6. Mean scores on scales indicating negative attitudes toward various aspects of childbirth reported by pregnant middle-class and lower-class mothers, both primiparae (PP) and multiparae (MP). The higher the score, the more negative items the mothers checked. (Data from Doty, 1967.)

MP mothers were also more inclined to reject maternal roles than PP mothers, with a slight tendency for attitudes to run stronger with lower-class mothers. Furthermore, MP mothers showed less fear of pregnancy and childbirth than did PP mothers. Having been through it all before, they were less afraid, but did not particularly welcome the responsibility of an additional child.

There are two explanations for the generally more negative attitudes of mothers from lower socioeconomic environments. One is that the arrival of a child into an already difficult economic and social situation makes its problems all the more troublesome. Another and not unrelated point is that lower-class individuals generally report more emotional problems of all types than do middle-class individuals.

Doty administered additional scales to the mothers in her sample and compared the results with other research in the field. She noted that women who express considerable rejection of pregnancy are also likely to report more problems with their infants, suggesting that attitudes toward pregnancy have their aftermath in mother-child relations. Ferreira's (1960) finding that mothers' rejection of pregnancy is related to excessive infant crying is also relevant here, for it shows that the behavior in question can be noticed by outside, objective observers, and not merely by the mothers.

Doty's analysis of her data showed two main patterns. One group consisted largely of lower-class MP mothers, who rejected pregnancy and the maternal role and also scored high on scales measuring (1) hostile attitudes toward one's children and (2) psychopathic (maladjustive) behavior in general. A second group consisted largely of middle-class PP mothers who were very anxious and who expressed fear of childbirth and pregnancy, were inclined to encourage dependency in children, were fearful of harming their baby, and the like.

Reducing fear and pain in childbirth. As pregnancy proceeds, the mother is apt to become increasingly concerned with the coming birth process. Considerable effort in recent years has been directed toward inculcating in her a psychologically healthy, receptive point of view toward the coming experience. The British obstetrician Grantley Dick-Read (1972), the author of *Childbirth Without Fear,* held that if prospective parents and physicians used the proper approach, only a small percentage of deliveries would be traumatic. Perhaps 95 per cent of mothers have no physical abnormalities that would prevent normal childbirth. He maintained that fear is the chief pain-producing agent in what otherwise would be uneventful labor.

Childbirth labor is hard work, to be sure, but it is not intrinsically a fearful experience. The confusion of childbirth with pain is the consequence, Dick-Read maintained, of negative suggestions that lead the mother to view it as a frightening ordeal. The notion that it is the "softness" of modern life that brings on these difficulties was rejected by him as fallacious on the basis of the cogent argument that women's health and longevity are at higher levels than ever before. Fear, Dick-Read said, prevents the balance of effort and relaxation that is an aspect of any hard work. Consequently, teaching the mother correct ways to relax is an important aspect of his methods.

Most mothers who have followed Dick-Read's prescription report that giving birth becomes a profoundly moving, even exhilarating experience. Although Dick-Read produced impressive statistics concerning the value of his method and has won numerous professional supporters and the enthusiastic testimonial of many mothers, it is only fair to add that not all experts accept his methods, especially in their more radically expressed forms.

Dick-Read's methods, which he first proposed in 1914, are similar to those developed by Fernand Lamaze (1970), who has used the psychoprophylactic method with his patients. Lamaze's approach, also termed "prepared childbirth," is based on classical conditioning principles and requires the expectant mother to practice deep breathing and abdominal muscle contractions in preparation for childbirth. Some obstetricians have encouraged prospective parents to become involved in "Lamaze groups," which meet frequently and not only serve as training and discussion sessions, but also provide the advantages of emotional support and even brief therapy.

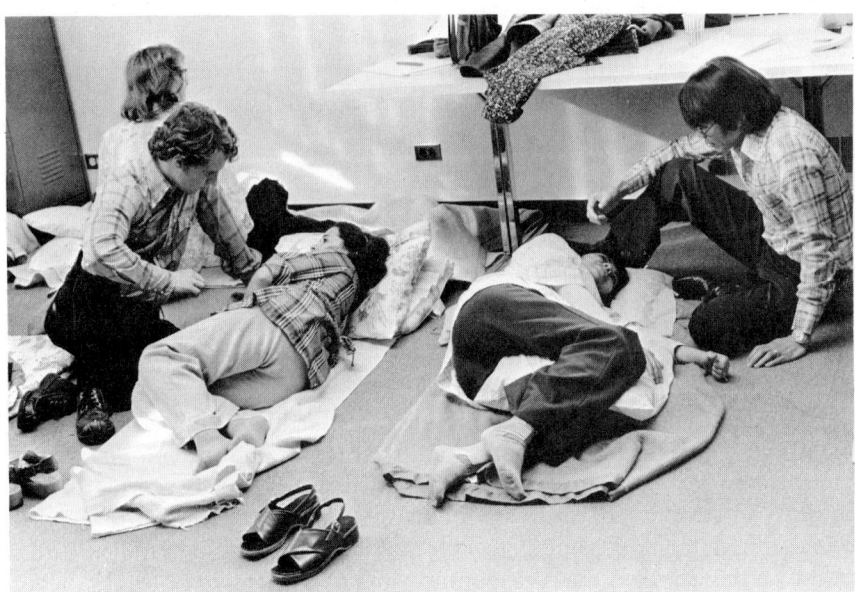

Understanding, acceptance, and emotional support are aided if both prospective parents become involved in "natural childbirth" training and other types of special group activities designed to help them deal with problems preceding and following childbirth.

Another procedure favored in these circles is rooming-in, a hospital arrangement whereby the mother cares for her newborn baby in her hospital room, rather than having the infant lodged in the nursery except for his visits to the mother at feeding time. This procedure signifies more than mere rearrangement of physical facilities. It recognizes the importance of mother and child as a physical and psychological unit both before birth and thereafter.

childbirth

A full-term baby is delivered in about 38 weeks on the average, give or take two or three weeks.[2] If all goes well, the birth process, although work for the mother, and always containing some element of danger for both her and her child, is complete in a very large proportion of cases without harm for either.

During the period between 1915 and 1935, between 6 and 8 per cent of American mothers died in childbirth; the rate today is less than 0.25 per cent. Comparable figures for infant deaths are also indicative of the medical progress that has been made. About 10 per cent of American-born infants died during the first year of life in 1915, whereas less than 2 per cent die during the first year today. The American infant mortality rate compares very favorably with that of most other countries, but is actually a little higher than the Scandinavian countries, Japan, Australia, and the United Kingdom, as Figure 5-7 shows. The infant mortality rate for nonwhites in the United States is about 50 per cent higher than that of whites. (See Figure 5-8.)

Rating the Health of the Newborn

For the last two decades, professionals who work with neonates have been using a scoring system, developed by Virginia Apgar (1953), which consists of the sum of ratings on five three-point scales, covering the newborn infant's breathing effort, muscle tone, heart rate, reflex irritability, and color (from grayish to rosy).

The Apgar test is made immediately after birth, and has a fair degree of predictability as far as infant and child health and development are concerned. Serunian and Broman (1975) obtained Apgar scores for 350 infants and followed them up eight months later, when the Bayley Scales of Motor and Mental Development were administered. Results of the testing showed that those infants who had received normal Apgar

---

[2] The oft-cited figure of 40 weeks is the average time elapsing since the last menstrual period. Inasmuch as conception usually occurs halfway into the menstrual cycle, this means that the actual period of gestation is about two weeks less than the time from the date of the last menstrual period until birth.

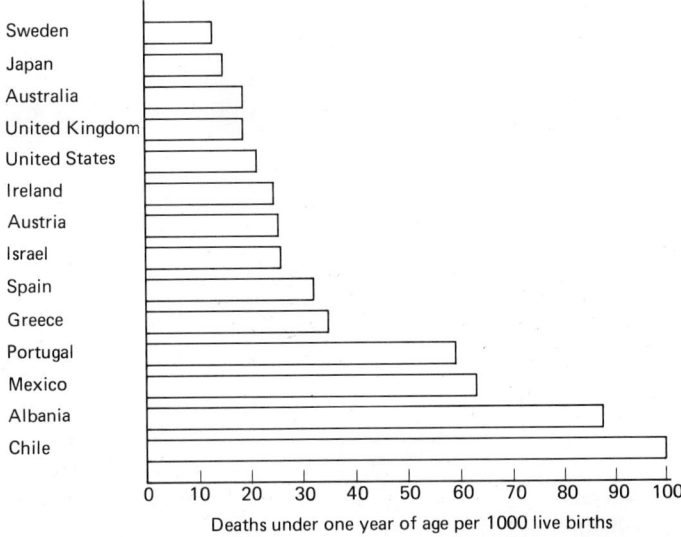

FIGURE 5-7. *Infant mortality rates for a representative sample of countries in various stages of industrialization.* (White House Conference on Children, 1970.)

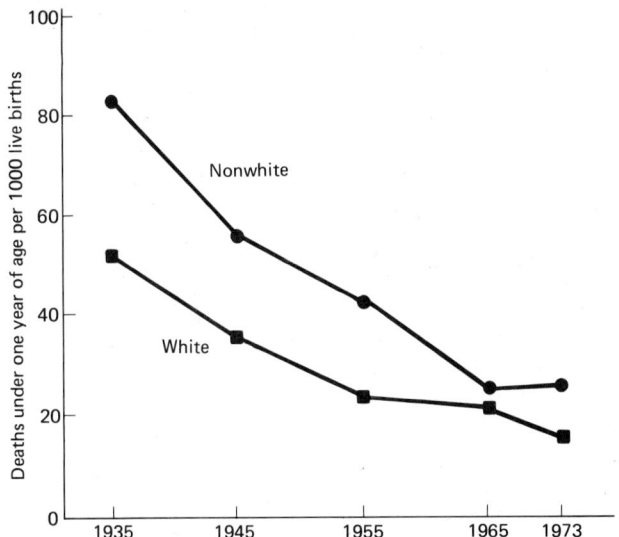

FIGURE 5-8. *Mortality rates for nonwhite and white infants in the United States from 1935 to 1973.* (U.S. Bureau of the Census, 1975.)

scores at birth were rated significantly higher on motor and mental development than those who had received low Apgar scores. There

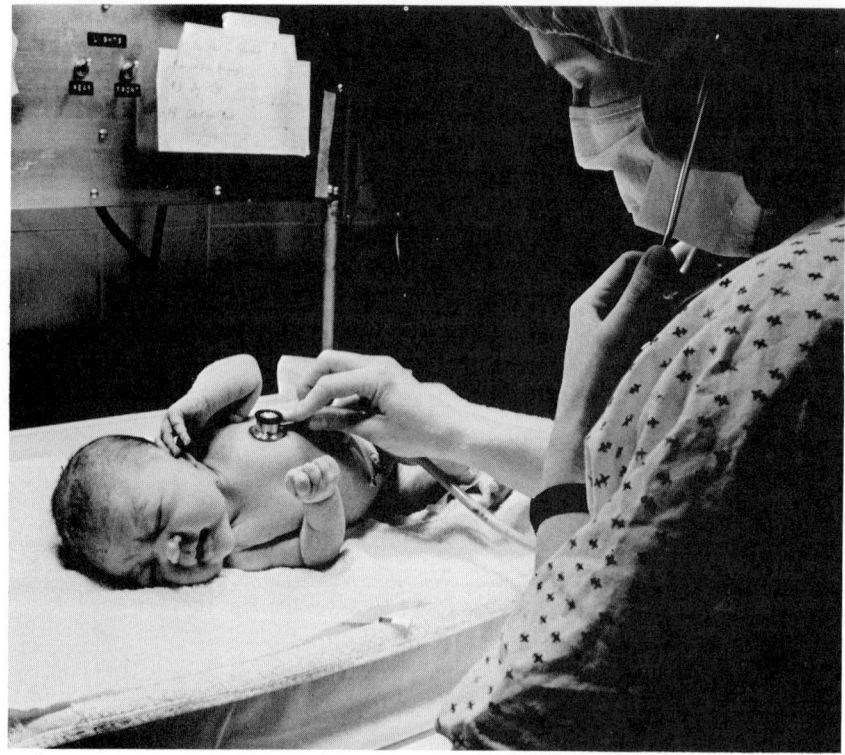

The Apgar test is administered to neonates immediately after birth. In this reenactment, the attendant is examining a neonate four hours old and is taking a reading on its heart rate, one of the five criteria included in the test.

was, furthermore, a significantly higher death rate among infants who had received low Apgar scores.

Other research indicates that Apgar scores have even longer-range predictive power. Nancy Edwards (1970) found that Apgar ratings made one and five minutes after birth correlated .45 with measures of fine motor coordination four years later and even higher, .49, with measures of gross motor coordination. Intelligence tests also administered at age four correlated .26 with Apgar scores, and the correlation of Apgar scores with measures of concept formation was .32, showing a slight but nonetheless significant relationship between physical status at birth and cognitive development in later childhood years.

What these studies suggest is that the general physical condition and energy level that characterize a child, that can be rated immediately after birth, can be used as an index to predict his probable physical and cognitive development in future months and years. Human behavior, as we noted earlier, tends to be generally consistent, and infants who display below average health at birth appear to have poorer than average chances, when it comes to later development.

Effects of Pain-Relieving Drugs During Delivery

Considerable concern has been expressed in recent years regarding the effect on fetuses and neonates of analgesic or pain-relieving drugs administered to mothers at various stages in the birth process. It is difficult to pinpoint the exact relationship between any one of the drugs administered and its effect on neonates, for the amounts and kinds of drugs differ from one delivery to another. Furthermore, those women who have the most difficult delivery are often the ones who receive the heaviest dosages; hence it is difficult to determine whether the behavior patterns that appear in their infants are the result of physical stress—birth trauma—or of drugs.

In spite of these research difficulties, however, evidence is accumulating which implicates drugs in certain kinds of behavioral deficits, at least by association. Infants whose mothers had received heavier doses of drugs have been observed to be more passive and less attentive during feeding (Brown et al., 1975). Aleksandrowicz and Aleksandrowicz (1974) used Brazelton's (1973) Neonatal Assessment Scale to determine the effects of seven drug groups on the behavior of infants who were observed at various stages during their first month of life. The infants were tested on thirteen Brazelton test items, including those listed in Table 5-2. The results, as indicated in Table 5-2, indicate that the infants' habituation to stimulation, orientation, cuddliness, freedom from tremulousness (nervous trembling), and smiling were all adversely related to the amount of drugs that had been administered to their mothers. For two of the variables, freedom from tremulousness and smiling, the effects were evident even as much as a month after birth.

Most of the behavior descriptions in Table 5-2 are self-explanatory, but *habituation* deserves special attention. This behavior is a reaction that students of perception include under the heading of *sensory adaptation*—the tendency of an organism to become less responsive to continued stimulation. An infant whose development is retarded does not habituate to—that is, come to ignore—the repeated sound of a bell, but instead continues to respond to successive bell sounds as he did to the first one. Hence the inclusion of habituation in an inventory that measures competence in newborns.

The fact that the administration of analgesic drugs during childbirth tends to produce neonates that are somewhat passive is a matter of concern for both prospective parents and physicians, of course, but the decision to use or not to use analgesics must take into account a number of other factors, not the least of which is the possible effect on the mother, and possibly on the child as well, of a prolonged and painful birth experience.

TABLE 5-3. Relationships Between the Amount of Mothers' Obstetrical Drug Dosage and Infants' Behaviors, Classified According to the Brazelton Neonatal Assessment Scale (after Aleksandrowicz and Aleksandrowicz, 1974)

Behavior	Strength of Relationship* on Days After Birth as Indicated			
	1st	4th	7th	28th
Failure to habituate to sound of bell	+	+++	?	+
Failure to habituate to pinprick	?	+	++	+
Failure to orientate — to turn toward stimulus	++	+	+	+
Lack of cuddliness (1st, 4th, 7th days only)	++	?	+	0
Tremulousness (4th, 7th, 28th days only)	0	+	+	++
Failure to smile (1st, 7th, 28th days only)	+	0	+	+++

* Key to relationships: 0 essentially none; ? very slight; + slight; ++ moderate; +++ high

Problems of Low-Birth-Weight Infants

A poor start at birth often leads to later complications. Daniel V. Caputo and Wallace Mandell (1970) surveyed the literature on infants having a low birth weight—those that are commonly referred to as "premature." A child's normal birth weight is about 7 pounds (about 3300 grams). Infants weighing 2500 grams (about 5½ pounds) were formerly classified as premature, but more lately pediatricians have used the 2000-gram (4½ pounds) figure as being more accurate, unless there is evidence that the gestation period was less than 37 weeks. As a result of their review, Caputo and Mandell concluded that very low birth weight was likely to be associated with significant neurological and physiological impairment. Children who had very low birth weight are likely (1) to score lower on intelligence tests, (2) to be overrepresented among those who are classified as mentally retarded or who are institutionalized for various disabilities, or (3) to drop out of high school before graduation. Hyperkinetic (overactive, intense, disruptive) and disorganized behavior is also likely to be characteristic of many such children, although as adults they seem to blend into the general population. Language development is frequently retarded, as well as accomplishment in academic subjects. In addition, there are often deficits in physical growth and motor behavior.

If infants that are markedly below normal weight have more than the usual problems, does this mean "The larger, the better"? Some research into this problem suggests that the answer is no. One study showed that children whose birth weight was in the top 5 per cent (that is, over 4250 grams or 9 lbs. 6 oz. for males, or over 4000 grams or 8 lbs. 13 oz. for

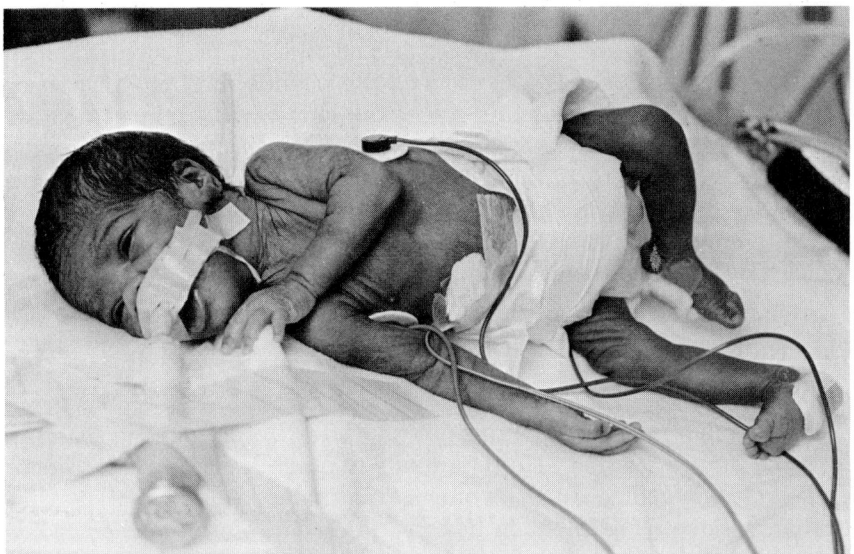

The "premature" or low-birth-weight infant tends to experience more problems than the normal-term infant. The wires attached to this neonate are for the purpose of monitoring its respiration and heart action.

females) tended to have low IQs when they were four years old. One fourth of the children in this special group had IQs below 80, which is about twice the proportion one would expect for normal children. (Babson, Henderson, and Clark, 1969).

the neonate

The term *neonate* means, literally, "newborn," and may be applied to the first five to seven days of life, the interval between birth and infancy. The neonatal period provides the base line of behavior against which to judge the later effects of maturation and learning.

Physical Appearance and Bodily Proportions

Even a fond mother may experience a sense of shock at the first sight of the tiny, wizened, red creature that is her offspring. (The "newborn" babies of the advertisements are apparently about two months of age). The eyes are approximately one half their adult size, and the body as a whole is only one twentieth of its adult dimensions. The head is about one fourth of the body length, as compared to the adult's one seventh. As a consequence of these proportions the neonate appears all head and eyes.

160 Infancy

Figure 5-9 shows something of the neonate's general appearance. At birth, the average newborn weighs 7 or 8 pounds and measures about 20 inches. The range, however, is from 3 to 16 pounds and from 17 to 21 or 22 inches. Males average about 1 per cent longer and 4 ounces heavier than females; white neonates average about 9 ounces heavier than black neonates; twins average about 26 ounces lighter than singletons; and newborns of parents of high socioeconomic status in various parts of the world average from 6 to 9 ounces heavier than the newborns of low socioeconomic status (Meredith, 1975).

Physical Needs and Drives: Hunger and Thirst

The neonate shows his hunger and thirst by crying and moving restlessly until he is fed. He then tends to quiet down and fall asleep. This cycle of feeding and sleeping is the major cycle of activity that neonates show—restless when hungry, quiescent or asleep when fed.

Healthy neonates demand food about every three hours. Gesell and Ilg (1949) reported that, on the average, newborn babies take seven or eight feedings per day. Nevertheless, there is wide individual variation. Some neonates may reach a peak of maximum activity in as short a time as two-and-a-half hours, whereas others may go for as long as five hours between peaks. Moreover, neonates who regularly show a given cycle, say, three hours, may have some intervals shorter or longer than the usual interval.

It should come as no surprise by now that individual differences among infants in the number of feedings should occur both between infants and in the same infant from time to time, making relative and tentative these seemingly precise statements. One neonate was fed on self-demand each day between the second and tenth day of life; it was found that on one of these days he demanded to be fed eleven times but

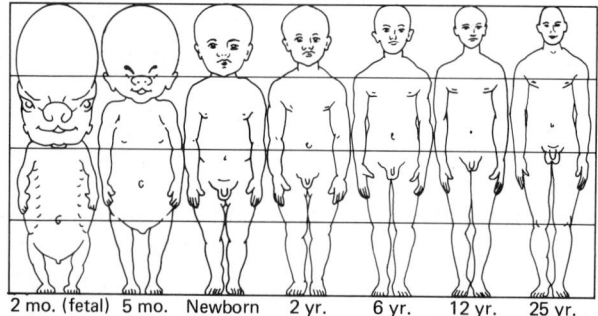

FIGURE 5-9. Changes in body form and proportion before and after birth. (Jackson, 1929. Reproduced by permission.)

on another day only six times. But, nevertheless, there is apt to be a sort of consistency, as shown by the fact that this same neonate five days out of nine demanded nine feedings (Simsarian and McLendon, 1942). Variability, but still with some degree of consistency, seems to characterize the feeding behavior of the neonate.

Pratt (1930) indicated that neonatal feeding involves a series of three activities: (1) head-mouth orientation—contact stimulation of the neonate's cheek elicits a turning of the head toward the source of stimulation, followed by opening of the mouth and snapping movements; (2) lip reflexes coordinated with head-mouth orientation—pursing the lips to contact the nipple; and (3) sucking and swallowing movements that form a rhythm. Swallowing imparts its rhythm upon sucking; this combined rhythm is in turn imposed upon respiration so that breathing is not interfered with. General activity is reduced when sucking starts; the neonate becomes relatively quiescent.

When viewed in the perspective of the neonate's day-to-day behavior, hunger and thirst are clearly not automatic reflex activities. Although based on a reflex pattern, sucking is influenced by repeated reinforcement in securing nourishment. If the infant's hunger and thirst are not reduced, and reduced quite quickly, tensions mount and provoke a considerable amount of bodily activity. Consequently, they are important in his learning activities.

Sleep

Sleep is a form of behavior that occurs in response to body tissue needs. In everyday life we tend to think of sleep as absence of behavior, but in a psychobiological sense it is merely a form of behavior that differs in significant respects from waking behavior.

Observations of neonates show that they spend about 20 hours of their time sleeping and that they reduce this amount gradually to about 16 hours in a week or so. Each sleep period is about three hours in length, and there are some seven or eight sleep periods per 24 hours (Gesell and Ilg, 1949). During this period of development, the young infant is, of course, unaware of any distinction between day or night, as any parent of an infant can ruefully report.

Although we tend to believe that we are relatively quiet and relaxed during normal sleep, observations show that there is much activity taking place and that it can be classified into various levels, ranging from a kind of twilight zone between waking and sleep and a very deep, almost comatose sleep. In one of the intermediate stages, our eyes move rapidly from side to side, under our closed lids, a phenomenon that can be picked up by sensitive electrical devices. This rapid eye movement or REM sleep is the stage at which dreaming takes place and seems to play an important part in rehabilitation and physical restoration processes that take place within the body. One researcher maintains that there is even a "need to dream"; for when adult subjects were prevented (by being awakened) from engaging in REM sleep on certain nights, they engaged in more REM sleep on other nights (Dement, 1960).

Infants spend proportionately more time in REM sleep than do children, who in turn spend more time than adults. Neonates spend more time in REM sleep than do infants, and observations have shown that the amount of time drops day by day after birth. Figure 5-10 displays in graphic form how the amount of time spent in sleep decreases over the life span. The proportion of sleep spent in the REM stage is initially about 50 per cent. This proportion rapidly drops, then gradually levels off to about 20 per cent after the third year of life, according to Roffwarg, Muzio, and Dement (1966). The researchers attributed the high percentage of time spent initially in REM sleep to the need for the centers of neural activity "to handle the enormous rush of stimulations" experienced during and after birth.

Oxygen Needs

An adequate oxygen supply is absolutely necessary to the preservation of life. In neonates, the need for oxygen is intensified by the fact that although breathing is a reflex activity, its rhythm and efficiency are not necessarily stabilized at the time of birth. But within a few days, its level of efficiency is adequate for ordinary needs.

In relative terms, the neonate's respiration mechanisms operate quite

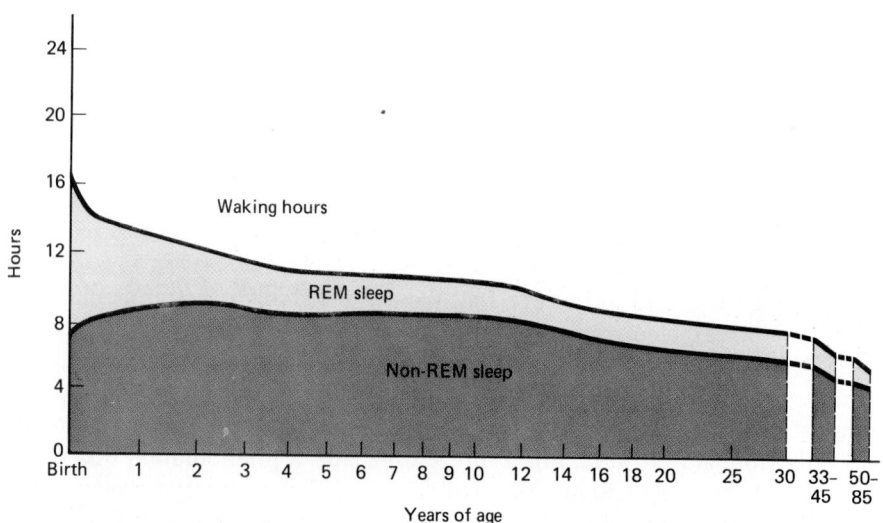

FIGURE 5-10. Changes in the average daily amounts of REM and non-REM sleep over the life span. (Data from Roffwarg, Muzio, and Dement, 1966.)

well. He is less likely to fall victim to *sudden infant death syndrome*, or SIDS. Cessation of breathing, or *apnea*, is apparently the basic problem in SIDS. Not only do ten thousand infants die of SIDS every year in the United States, but the syndrome is the leading cause of death for infants aged one month to a year. At the present moment of writing, no one has any definite ideas why apparently healthy infants stop breathing for twenty seconds or more, but a number of possible leads are being followed up through research. For example, the fact that most of such deaths occur when infants begin to sleep through the night without feeding suggests that there may be a dietary involvement (Marx, 1975c). In any event, SIDS is not a significant problem for neonates, whose breathing reflexes are apparently fairly reliable.

Need for Stimulation

A characteristic that humans share with other animals is what might be termed a "need to be stimulated." We commented on one aspect of this "need for arousal" in Chapter 4, and also mentioned studies showing that newborns show a preference for somewhat more complex visual stimuli, rather than bland ones. Evidence for a need for arousal or stimulation is also provided by a study in which five low-birth-weight (premature) infants were stroked five minutes each hour of the day for ten days, beginning in the first day after birth. The stroking was administered by a nurse or an aide, who rubbed each neonate's neck, back, and arms. A control group of five premature neonates received only the ordinary hospital care. Results showed that the specially handled infants were more active than those in the control group. They also regained their initial birth weights more rapidly. Furthermore, a pediatrician (who had not been informed as to the nature of the experiment) described the infants who had been specially treated as being healthier in terms of growth and motor development when he examined both groups of infants at seven and eight months of age (Solkoff et al., 1969).

The fact that the infants in the experimental group responded favorably to tactile stimulation suggests that the stimulation may have met an important need. One study worthy of mention is that of Salk (1960, 1961), who theorized that neonates missed the sound of their mothers' heartbeat and hence broadcast the sound of a human heart beating at the normal rate to 102 neonates for a four-day period. In contrast to a control group of 112 neonates who did not get this special treatment, the experimental neonates gained weight slightly, whereas the controls lost weight. The experimental group also cried more and were more restless, probably because of a higher level of activity and arousal.

Salk's research was followed up by Yvonne Brackbill and others (1966), who found that there was essentially no difference between the effect of heartbeat sounds and other types of sounds. She did note, however, that infants cried more when there was *no* sound of any kind. She therefore conducted an experiment in which infants were exposed to 1, 2, 3, and 4 modes of stimuli simultaneously. Stimuli where loud sound, bright light, swaddling clothes, and increase in temperature. Results showed that the more the stimulation, the more the infants slept and the less they cried. Under the maximum stimulation, motor activity, breathing irregularities, and heart rate were also reduced (Brackbill, 1973).

In a further experiment, Brackbill (1975) subjected neonates to various levels of sound in order to determine the effect on their sleeping and waking behavior. The newborns were first observed for a half hour in a typical ward setting, in which the average noise level was about 55 decibels. Then the infants were placed in a special cubicle, in which they then heard a continuous recording of "white noise" (a hissing sound produced by electronic sound apparatus) at an intensity of sixty, seventy, or eighty decibels. As Figure 5-11 indicates, higher levels of sound had the more relaxing effect. At eighty decibels, the heart rate was slowest, and the most time was spent in sleep. What is most significant, however, is that with higher levels of sound, the amount of time spent in quiet or non-REM sleep increased, whereas time spent in active or REM sleep decreased.

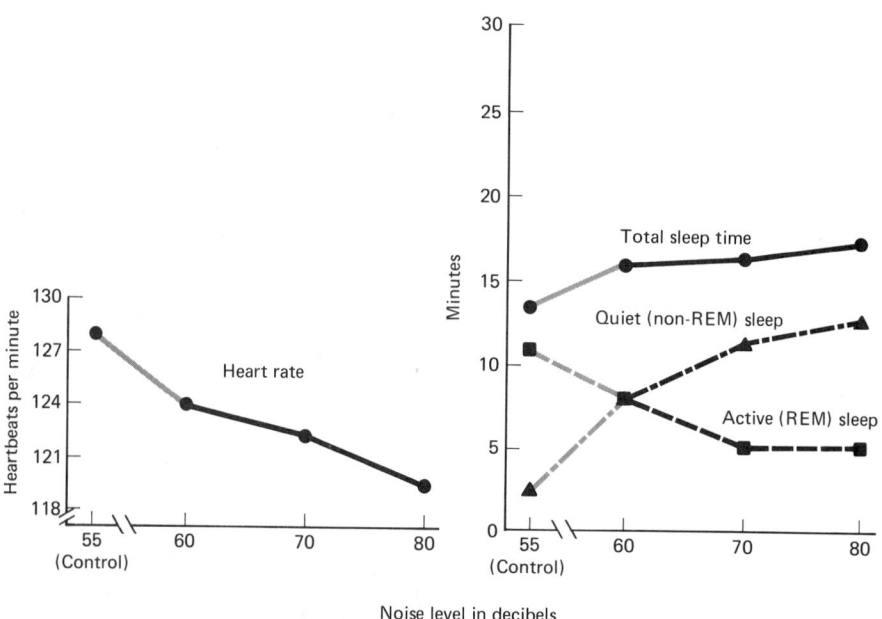

FIGURE 5-11. Relationships between sound level, as measured in decibels, and activity levels in neonates, as measured by heart rate and the amounts of time spent in active (REM) sleep and quiet (non-REM) sleep. (Data from Brackbill, 1975.)

Although common sense would dictate that the more the stimulation, the more the disturbance, these studies—particularly the ones by Brackbill—suggest that the opposite is true. That is, increases in stimulation facilitate healthy development—within reasonable limits, of course, for there obviously is a point at which stimulation becomes disturbing, rather than relaxing. It is reasonable to conclude, however, that stimulation up to a certain level is satisfying, and that it satisfies because it meets some basic need.

Investigators have also determined that very young infants are responsive to stimulation in the genital area. If an infant is having a crying spell, such stimulation tends to quiet him. Lustman (1956), found that newborn infants were quite sensitive to both manual and air-pressure stimulation of the genital region, as shown by temperature increase in this area. In another much early study, nine male infants were observed for eight and a half consecutive hours per day for ten days. Tumescence (erection of the penis) occurred at least once every day in seven newborn infants, and the other two showed such behavior on the eighth and ninth day, respectively. These responses were primarily to internal stimulation: strong sucking or a full bowel or bladder would set off the reflex response. Great individual differences were noted, with the actual number of instances of tumescence varying from a median of four to a median of 35 per day. Tumescence was, in general, experienced as being unpleasant; it was accompanied by restlessness, crying, fretting, and stiffness of the limbs. When tumescence subsided, infants were more relaxed: crying during this state, for example, was almost nonexistent (Halverson, 1943).

It is possible that tumescence is a nonspecific response to arousal, for it seems to be brought on by the stimulation of other sensitive parts of the body—the palms, the soles of the feet, and the lips, for example. It also appears to be brought on by the over-all arousal that occurs in REM sleep. It is now apparent that the penile erection that men and boys commonly experience on awakening is not a reaction to a full bladder, as is popularly supposed, but to the arousal that accompanies REMs (Williams, Holloway, and Griffiths, 1973).

sensory responses

Reactions to Visual Stimuli

Virtually all parts of the eye are present at birth, but the neonate's vision takes place only on a fairly rudimentary level. The eyeball is short, the lens large and spherical; coordination is poor, and the optic nerves have only part of the white fatty sheath or *myelin* that is necessary for adequate neural transmission. It is hardly surprising, then, that the neonate's pupils respond sluggishly to bright light, although there is considerable improvement even within the first 24 hours of life. The focus of the eye tends to be fixed at about seven and a half inches, so that closer or more distant objects are probably seen as blurred (Haynes, White, and Held, 1965). It is possible that the neonate cannot distinguish among various colors, although Fantz (1963) found that neonates looked longer at black-and-white figures that at plain color areas. Not only can newborns distinguish between plain and figured stimuli but they also appear to have preferences. Nelson and Kessen (1969) found that neonates tended to look at the angles and corners in figures, rather than at straight lines. Inasmuch as angles are more complex, this may be the first indication of the preference for greater complexity that appears in many research studies of infants and children.

Neonates also respond to different degrees of brightness. It has been noted that they close the eyes spontaneously to a flash of light and to objects moving toward the eyes. Within a day or two after birth the pupillary reflex (widening or narrowing of the pupil in response to light) has been observed. Eye movements of various sorts have also been found. These include pursuit (following a visual stimulus with movement of the eyes); saccadic (quick, jerky fixations as in adult reading); coordinate (eyes moving together); and coordinate compensatory (head quickly moving in one direction, with eye movements in opposite direction).

The eye movement responses just described are either reflex in character or, at least, of a circumscribed nature. Muscular patterns and general mass behavior of a broader nature have also been elicited. Practically any visual stimuli, if sufficiently intense, will release circulatory and respiratory (for example, "catching" the breath) responses in the neonate. The startle response involving coordination of many parts of the body is also elicited by intense visual stimulation. Thus, both reflex and mass activitiy are reactions to visual stimuli.

Reactions to Auditory Stimuli

Earlier researchers questioned whether a newborn infant is able to hear during the 24 hours following birth, but the use of sophisticated equipment and methodology, such as the analysis of electroencephalograms or EEGs (recordings of "brain waves") have now shown that sound does have some effect on the neural apparatus of the neonate (Kessen, Haith, and Salapatek, 1970). Neonates can apparently also distinguish pitch differences from two days of age onward (Hutt et al., 1968).

Condon and Sander (1974) carried out an interesting series of experiments in which they took motion pictures of neonates in the presence of adults who were talking. A comparison of the films, frame by frame, with the recorded speech of the adults showed that the newborns tended to coordinate their bodily movements to the cadence of the speech sounds. The same phenomenon was observed when neonates heard tape-recorded speech either in Chinese or in English, but they did not respond to recordings of disconnected vowel and tapping sounds. These findings not only indicate that neonates are able to hear; they suggest that right from the beginning neonates are participating in the social interaction taking place in their environment. Condon and Sander also suggest that this early rhythmic and subverbal participation prepares infants for their eventual debut as speaking members of the family group.

Marvin L. Simmer (1971) found the infants 70 hours old cry when they hear another neonate's cry. Moreover, he was able to demonstrate that this response was specifically to the crying sound: inanimate sounds of the same intensity, including a computer simulation of a newborn cry, evoked significantly less crying. Sagi and Hoffman (1976) followed up Simmer's research by testing infants who were only 35 hours old and got essentially the same results. They concluded that their findings, as well as those of Simmer, pointed either to the possibility that this "sympathetic" response is an inborn empathic distress reaction, or to the possibility that hearing the cues of distress from another infant evokes associations with the listener's own past distress. The first explanation is in terms of instinct, whereas the second is consistent with classical conditioning theory. Further research is needed, of course, to determine which of the two explanations is the more valid.

Both studies found, incidentally, that female neonates were more empathic—more responsive to the cries of others—than were males, a finding related to other research showing that four-year-old girls are more empathic and hence more inclined to cooperate than boys the same age (Levine and Hoffman, 1975).

Reactions to Other Sensory Stimuli

In a review of research on sensory and perceptual responses in infants, Spears and Hohle (1967) concluded that evidence showed that the neonate does respond to olfactory stimuli, but only if they are highly aromatic, such as fumes of ammonia or acetic acid. The responsiveness increases rapidly over the first three or four days of life, with weaker and weaker solutions needed to get some kind of response. Newborns also respond differently to water and milk, as well as to solutions containing acid, glucose, and salt. Sugar solutions tend to elicit the sucking response, which is maintained; acid solutions also evoke sucking, but for a shorter period; salt solutions, after being tried a bit, are not sucked; and bitter solutions, such as quinine, are seldom sucked. There are, however, wide individual differences among neonates. The sucking of fingers, thumb, or hand has been observed shortly after birth and even before the first feeding, and there is even one dramatic photograph of a fetus sucking its thumb (Kessen, Haith, and Salapatek, 1970).

Neonates respond to varying concentrations and kinds of sugar much as adults do. Nowlis and Kessen (1976) gave neonates sucrose and glucose in four different concentrations. Sucrose evoked more intensive sucking than glucose did, and the stronger the solution, the more active the sucking.

Research reviewed by Spears and Hohle points to the conclusion that pressure and touch sensitivity are present in neonates and even in fetuses several months before birth. Attempts to get neonates to respond to pain had mixed results in early studies, partly because of the problem of measuring the amount of stimulus being applied. More recently it has been possible to use extremely mild electric shock, which enables the investigator to measure the stimulus precisely and thus control the amount administered. Results show that thresholds for this type of stimulation apparently diminish with each day following birth—in other words, infants respond more quickly to smaller and smaller shock voltages.

Although infants have differentiated responses to various temperatures and hence can be considered as able to distinguish between them, one study suggests that there is no particular value in warming infants' milk formula. The researchers used premature infants, in order to have a conservative test of their procedure. Milk at body temperature was administered to 17 infants, whereas 16 received milk taken directly from the refrigerator at 45° to 52° F. Observation of the two groups over some two thousand feedings showed no differences, outside of an almost imperceptible drop in body temperature (0.2° F) for those receiving cold milk. There were no differences, in other words, in weight gains, crying, sleep patterns, frequency of vomiting, or activity while feeding (Holt et al., 1962).

Sensitivity to being moved or changed in position, which stimulates the static receptors, is shown in postural or "balance" responses, by which the neonate rights himself when not too far off balance. Reactions to internal (organic) stimuli are present. Although the respiratory and circulatory systems supply some of these, the preponderance of the internal stimuli comes from the digestive and excretory systems, as in regurgitation, hiccuping, urination, and excretion.

motor responses

Major Classifications

The distinctions that we make between motor responses and reactions to sensory stimulation, though clear enough in some respects, are largely a matter of emphasis. Here is a listing of the more readily observed responses of the eye, mouth, trunk, and limbs:

1. Eye Responses—opening and closing eyelids, pupillary, pursuit, saccadic, and coordinate compensatory responses (described in reactions to visual stimuli).
2. Facial and Mouth Responses—opening and closing mouth, lip movement, sucking, pushing objects from mouth, yawning, and grimacing.
3. Throat Responses—crying, swallowing, coughing, gagging, vomiting, hiccoughing, cooing, and holding the breath.
4. Head Movements—upward and downward, side to side, and balancing in response to change of bodily position.
5. Arm Responses—closing hand, arm flexion, rubbing face, grasp reflex, and "random" movements.
6. Trunk Reactions—arching back and twisting.
7. Foot and Leg Responses—knee jerk, flexion, extension, kicking (both legs simultaneously), stepping (when neonate held upright with feet touching surface), and toe flexion.
8. Coordinate Responses of Many Body Parts—resting and sleeping position (legs flexed, fists closed, upper arms out straight from shoulder with forearms flexed at right angles parallel to the head), springing position (infant held upright and inclined forward, the arms extend forward and legs are brought up), stretching, shivering, trembling, unrest with crying, creeping, bodily jerk, Moro reflex (throwing arms apart, spreading of fingers, extension of legs, and throwing head back).

Despite the list's incompleteness, the neonate's behavior repertory may still appear surprisingly diversified. Only to the uninitiated eye is the infant a mass of twists and squirms. The neonate starts life with a rather large number of often complicated responses. Potentialities for both differentiation and integration are present. There are both specific movements and mass activity present in his behavior.

Reflexes

The term *reflex behavior* is applied to a group of physical reactions that are not learned or acquired, but are as much a part of our biological makeup as are our muscles, nerves, and organs. We have already described some of them—the response of the pupil to light and the grasping or Darwinian reflex that occurs when the neonate's palm is stroked. Those reflexes that have attracted the greatest amount of attention from students of child behavior are those that tend to drop out of our repertories after a few weeks or months. We describe them here briefly:

The *rooting or sucking reflex* occurs whenever the neonate's cheek is touched. It appears in waking neonates almost immediately after birth

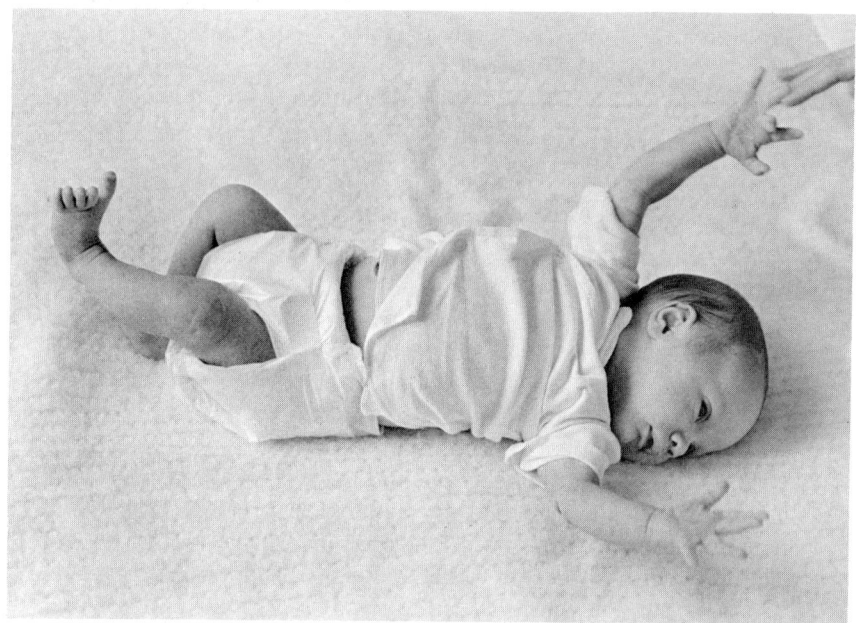

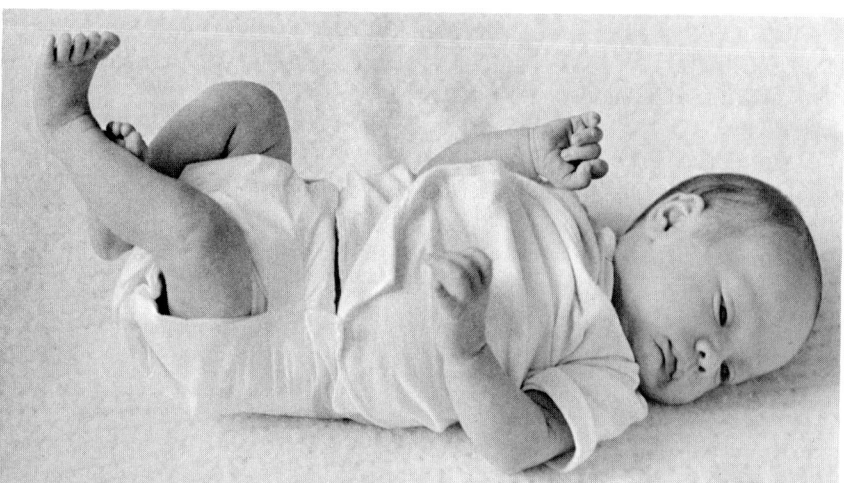

A number of responses that neonates make to sensory stimuli are well-defined and predictable. The Moro reflex, depicted by the first two pictures, is elicited by laying the infant on its back and suddenly hitting the mattress on both sides of its head. The infant will respond to this unexpected shock by flinging its arms open and extending its fingers, a gesture that it immediately follows by bringing its arms close to its body. In the third photograph, the sucking or rooting reflex is elicited by touching the infant near the mouth.

and serves the obvious funciton of connecting the infant with his food supply. Mothers and nurses since the beginning of time have stroked infants' cheeks in order to elicit the rooting reflex and thus encourage their drowsy charges to continue sucking and finish their meals.

The *Babinski reflex* appears in the form of an upward extension of the toes when the sole of a neonate or young infant is stroked. At about six months of age, stroking the sole produces the plantar reflex, in which the toes curl downward. The reflex is not universally observed and is somewhat variable.

The *Babkin reflex* occurs upon pressing the palms of an infant who is lying on his back. The stimulation causes the infant to turn his face to an upward position and open his mouth.

When an infant is lying on his back, a sharp blow to the surface on which he is lying will lead him to react with the *Moro* or *embracing reflex*, also termed the *startle reflex*. His arms and legs will be flung out, his back will arch, and his head will be drawn back. In the second phase of the reaction, he brings his arms to the midline of his body in a grasping or clasping motion. The reflex, which disappears between the third and fifth month, is presumed to have survival value for the young infant.

The *grasping* or *Darwinian reflex* occurs when the neonate's palm is stroked, as we noted in Chapter 3. Myrtle McGraw (1940) found that the infant's ability to support his own weight in this way is relatively high during the first few weeks of life and then declines to a low level after six months. It is not until the child reaches the age of five years that he once again can support himself in a hanging position, an ability he had when he was forty days old.

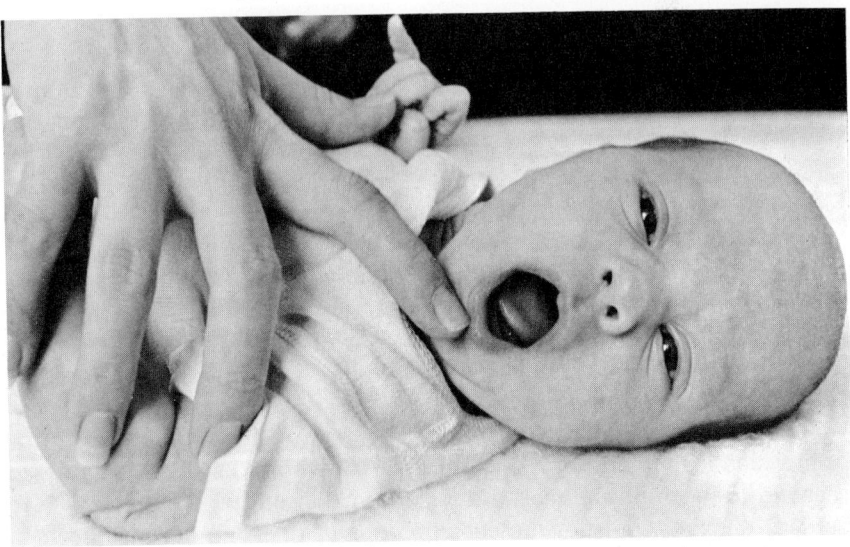

When the infant is held under the arms, with his bare feet touching a flat surface, he will make stepping motions that look very much like walking. This *walking reflex* typically drops out after eight weeks, but can be reinstituted if the head of the infant can be pushed back. Some researchers have reported that young infants who are "walked" regularly—being held by adults, of course—learn to talk without assistance at ages that are earlier than normal (Zelazo, Zelazo, and Kolb, 1972).

Being placed in water in a prone position will elicit the *swimming reflex*. The neonate or young infant swims with his head down and exhales through his mouth. Myrtle McGraw (1943) noted that the reflex is most pronounced at birth and then fades rapidly. Disorganized floundering and struggling begin to appear about 100 days after birth, and by 250 days, the swimming reflex has virtually disappeared. More deliberate, voluntary swimming movements begin to appear at 200 days. Most children do not regain the swimming competence they had as neonates unless they acquire it in the usual way, through instruction or imitation.

Learning in Neonates

The fact that neonates have needs and drives and respond to various stimuli suggests that learning can be induced experimentally. Arnold J. Sameroff (1971) reviewed the research in this area and concluded that operant conditioning experiments can be carried out, but that it is difficult to demonstrate classical conditioning.

An example of successful operant conditioning may be found in a study conducted by Einas R. Siqueland (1968), who was able to get one group of neonates to increase head-turning responses and another group to decrease the same type of response.

Classical conditioning, as we have noted, occurs when a previously neutral conditioned stimulus (CS) is associated with a nonneutral unconditioned stimulus (US)—in the case of the dog, the neutral stimulus of the tuning fork's sound becomes associated with the meat powder so that either will produce the salivation response. The problem with neonates, according to Sameroff, is that there really are no "neutral" stimuli for them. The tuning forks, bells, and buzzers used in operant conditioning experiments are all novel stimuli as far as neonates are concerned, and they respond defensively instead of giving the more neutral *orienting response*—the "Now, what could *that* be?" reaction. The orienting response is basic to a state of awareness that is prerequisite to classical conditioning.

Sameroff suggested two hypotheses to explain the difficulty in instituting classical conditioning: either the newborn infant is unable to respond to stimulus changes, or the newborn infant *is* able to respond to general changes, but not the specific ones of the type that are used in such experiments. In order to respond to the stimulus change required in classical conditioning treatments, the infant must develop the ability to perceive differences in stimuli. The newer studies we cited previously, however, suggest that even neonates are able to make some rudimentary discriminations of stimuli; hence the next few years may see some experimentation with the classical conditioning of infants.

summary

Conception occurs when a sperm cell from male seminal fluid unites with an ovum that has been proceeding down one of the Fallopian tubes leading from an ovary. The fertilized ovum, or zygote, immediately begins to divide and subdivide, becoming a blastocyst that proceeds further into the uterus. Embedded in the uterine wall, the zygote within a few days becomes an embryo and develops a placenta, the indirect connection between the mother and the growing organism, through which nutrients are exchanged for waste products.

By the end of the first month, the embyro is about ¼ inch long, is curled in the form of a crescent, and possesses buds that will become limbs. Development proceeds extremely rapidly during the early weeks and months. By the end of the second month it is about 1½ inches long and has assumed some human features; it is now termed a fetus. By the time the fetus is seven months old, it is about 16 inches long, weighs about three pounds, and can survive in a specially sheltered environment if prematurely born. The fact that fetuses move about, apparently spontaneously, has made it possible to conduct conditioning experiments. Although such experiments yield positive results, they are rather difficult to interpret because of the possibility that it is the mother rather than the fetus who has been conditioned.

Children born to economically deprived mothers tend to be smaller, probably because of substandard maternal nutrition. Low-birth-weight, or premature, infants have a higher mortality rate than normal-sized infants. Mothers who live in poor environments are also more prone to infections, like cytomegalovirus (CTV), which produce birth defects and may cause mental retardation, blindness, and deafness in their infants. The habitual use of narcotics and other psychoactive drugs by pregnant women has an adverse effect on fetuses. Expectant mothers who are confirmed smokers tend to produce a higher than average percentage of low-birth-weight infants. Other medical problems that produce abnormalities in fetuses include the use of thalidomide, excessive X-ray exposure, and incompatibility of Rh blood factors.

Pregnancy is a developmental crisis in a woman's life. Attitudes formed during pregnancy will carry over into the mother's relationship with the child later on. Mothers with attitudes which are generally positive tend to have fewer problems relative to pregnancy and delivery. Doty's study of maternal attitudes indicates that middle-class expectant mothers report more physical symptoms than lower-class mothers, but that their attitudes are generally more positive otherwise. The attitudes of mothers having their first child are also more positive than those of mothers having additional children. Grantley Dick-Read, a British obstetrician, said that childbirth would be less painful, and pain-relieving drugs unnecessary, if women approached it without fear; these are the recommendations that have been echoed in the relaxation training undertaken in groups using the methods of Fernand Lamaze.

Childbirth mortality figures have dropped markedly in the last fifty years. Although the infant mortality rate in the United States is very low, it is even lower in a few other industrialized countries; the mortality rate for nonwhites is higher than that for whites.

The infant's physical condition immediately after birth can be rated by the Apgar test; such ratings tend to be positively correlated with developmental measures made months and even years later. The Brazelton Neonatal Assessment Scale indicates that there is a relationship between the dosage of pain-relieving drugs given to mothers during the childbirth process and some degree of sluggishness or lack of responsiveness in infants during the first days and weeks of life. Premature or low-birth-weight infants have some tendency to have more neurological or physiological problems than the average child, but so do infants who are markedly heavier than the norm.

During the first five to seven days of life, the infant is referred to as a newborn or neonate. The neonate's average weight is seven to eight pounds, his length about 20 inches, and his head is about a fourth of his total body length, a contrast of one seventh as an adult. Neonates on a demand-feeding schedule take nourishment seven or eight times a day, but there are variations in the schedules of individual infants as well as among infants. Neonates spend about five sixths of the day sleeping. About half of their sleep time is what is termed aroused sleep, as indicated by the rapid eye movements (REMs) that take place beneath their closed eyelids. The total amount of time spent in sleep tends to drop rapidly during infancy and childhood and more gradually during the adolescent and adult years. From about three years of age onward, REM sleep occupies about one fifth of the total sleep time. The sudden infant death syndrome (SIDS) that kills about ten thousand infants a year in the United States is rare with neonates. Neonates, like other living organisms, have a "need to be stimulated." Brackbill's research shows that neonates are more relaxed and sleep better with moderate increases in auditory and physical stimulation. Stimulation in the genital area tends to quiet infants. Tumescence or erection of the penis occurs in neonates in response to nonspecific or general arousal, including that of REM sleep.

The neonate's visual apparatus is not fully developed, although he can respond differentially to colors in contrast to black-and-white areas, and to complex as against simple stimuli. Within a few days of birth, the pupillary reflex and some coordinated eye movements occur. Although his auditory apparatus is likewise undeveloped, he can distinguish sounds and even respond physically to the rhythm of adult speech. Taste, smell, pressure, and touch sensitivity are also relatively limited at birth, but responsiveness increases rapidly thereafter. Although neonates can respond to differences in temperature, research shows no preference for warm or cold milk.

Newborns are capable of a large number of motor responses, which become integrated and differentiated in subsequent weeks and months. The rooting or sucking reflex appears at birth. Other reflexes that are present, but drop out after a few weeks or months, include the Babinski reflex, the Babkin reflex, the Moro or startle reflex, the grasping or Darwinian reflex, the walking reflex, and the swimming reflex. Operant conditioning can be accomplished with neonates, but classical conditioning experiments have encountered difficulties because of problems in finding stimuli to condition that are "neutral" to newborns.

six

Sensorimotor and Mental Development

It seems probable, but at present wholly unproven, that optimal size and permanence of an assembly [of nerve cells] is secured by giving it particular stimulation at a particular time. It seems likely, too, that assemblies built early in childhood are under most circumstances more resistant to decay or change than later-built ones. We have no answer to the all-important question of what happens to the cell assemblies if we attempt to teach something too soon, or, conversely, if we delay teaching something too long, so that a new neural organization is starved of exercise.
—J. M. TANNER (1970)

Although we all think we know what an infant is, the term actually has a number of different meanings. In its original Latin, the term *infans* means, literally, a "nonspeaking being," and the common practice of applying the label "infant" to children of 18 months or younger is consistent with that meaning, if we do not count the handful of words and fragments of phrases that the average child can utter at 18 months.

Not being able to speak also implies being unable to care for oneself, and most of us would also think of this latter characteristic in connection with infancy. In legal terms, infancy can include the entire period from birth to the attainment of one's majority, at 18 or even 21 years of age. Until the majority is attained, the individual cannot speak for himself in legal matters and cannot enter into contracts unless an adult takes responsibility.

In this discussion, however, we will hold to the everyday meaning of infancy (which is also the psychological meaning) and limit our discussion to the period from birth to about the middle of the second year of life.

A tremendous amount of biological development takes place within these few months. Once the relatively constant internal environment of the womb has been left behind, external stimulation plays an increasingly significant part in the life of the young organism. From his experiences with the world, the infant is to acquire new ways of behaving. In fact, the scope and intensity of learning during infancy exceeds that of any other period of development. Nevertheless, the influence of maturation remains very evident, as is shown most clearly in physical growth.

physical growth

Changes in Height and Weight

It will be remembered that, on the average, the neonate weighs seven or eight pounds and is about 20 inches long. During the first year of life the infant increases his length by over a third, and his weight almost triples. Owing to the greater gain in weight than in height, the infant at one year appears more thickset. The "top-heaviness" characteristic at birth gradually decreases as legs and trunk increase in length.

Physical development in the second year proceeds rapidly but at a slower rate than in the first year. At age two, the height of the average girl is about 34 inches (87 cm.), whereas that of the average boy is 35 inches (87.5 cm.). Average weights at the same age are: girls, about 31 pounds (14 kg.), and boys, about 32 pounds (14.6 kg.) (U.S. National Center for Health Statistics, 1976). Height and weight are correlated about .60, showing a relatively high degree of relationship between the two indices of physique.

Changes in form and proportion are illustrated in Figure 5-9 in Chapter 5, which shows that parts of the body do not grow equally and at the same rate. As we noted in Chapter 3, the directions of development are from head to tail (cephalocaudal) and from the center outward (proximodistal). This means that head development takes place before neck development, neck development in turn precedes chest growth, and so on. At the same time, upper arm (or leg) growth precedes lower arm (or leg) growth, which in turn precedes hand (or foot) growth. From infancy onward until puberty, the greatest growth takes place at the extremities. Head growth slows down, limb growth is relatively rapid, and trunk growth is intermediate.

Some of the growth changes that take place during these years are illustrated in Figures 6-1 through 6-4. Figure 6-1 presents the growth in

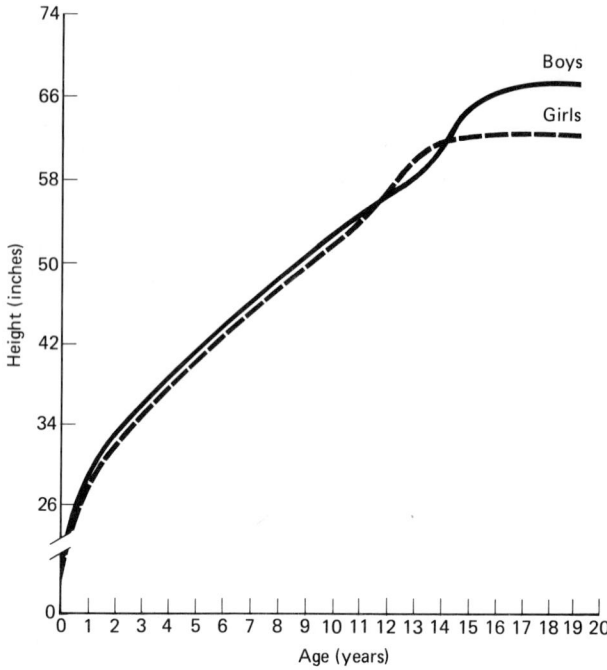

FIGURE 6-1. Typical curves of height attained by boys and girls from birth to age 19. (After Tanner, Whitehouse, and Takaishi, 1966. Reprinted with permission from Mussen (Ed.) Carmichael's Manual of Child Psychology, 3rd ed., Wiley, 1970, p. 82.)

weight (expressed in terms of an annual rate) from the 20th week of fetal age onward. Growth reaches its maximum about the 32nd week of uterine life and then drops off sharply until birth. After birth, there is a sharp rise until about the sixth week, which is followed by a gradual dropping off in growth rate.

Figure 6-2 represents growth curves of attained height for boys and girls through adolescence, and Figure 6-3 includes the same data, but presented in terms of the amount gained per year. Inspection of the two graphs shows that gain is very rapid during the first few years, but settles down to a steady rate until the prepubertal period, when it takes a brief spurt and then slows down markedly.

Figure 6-4 shows the differential growth pattern of various parts of the body. The brain and head grow rapidly at first then slow down. The opposite pattern is displayed by the reproductive organs, whereas the lymphoid glands achieve their greatest growth during the prepuberal period.

These general patterns of growth and maturation are correlated with a number of developmental measures, particularly during the first year of life. Jordan and Spaner (1970) examined the case histories of 353 infants

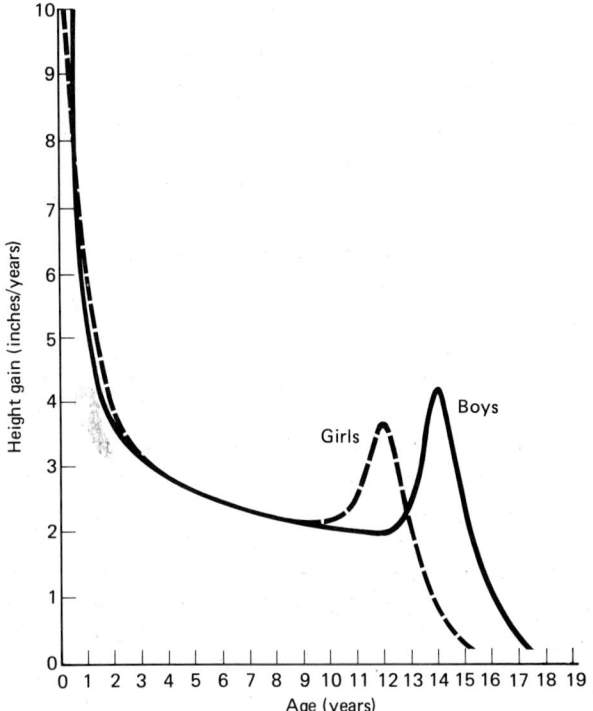

FIGURE 6-2. Typical curves of gains in height, expressed in terms of inches per year, for boys and girls from birth to age 19. (After Tanner, Whitehouse, and Takaishi, 1966. Reprinted with permission from Mussen (Ed.) Carmichael's Manual of Child Psychology, 3rd ed., Wiley, 1970, p. 83.)

with respect to Apgar scores (at five minutes after birth); birth height and weight; and various psychosocial factors relating to the mother's age, socioeconomic status, race, and personality traits. Various combinations of these measures were used in an attempt to predict the weight, height, and general development of infants at 12 months.

Results showed substantial correlations between Apgar scores and other physiological measures, on the one hand, and with height and weight at 12 months, on the other. There was even a modest but significant correlation between the physiological measures and the infants' general development. The correlations between psychosocial variables (mother's age, economic status, etc.) and the infants' status at 12 months were, however, negligible, suggesting that during this period of development, physiological considerations are paramount.

A few years later, Jordan and Spaner (1972) carried out a more extensive version of this study, using one thousand infants and following them for three years. Results confirmed the findings of the earlier study, namely that biological characteristics predicted the children's later

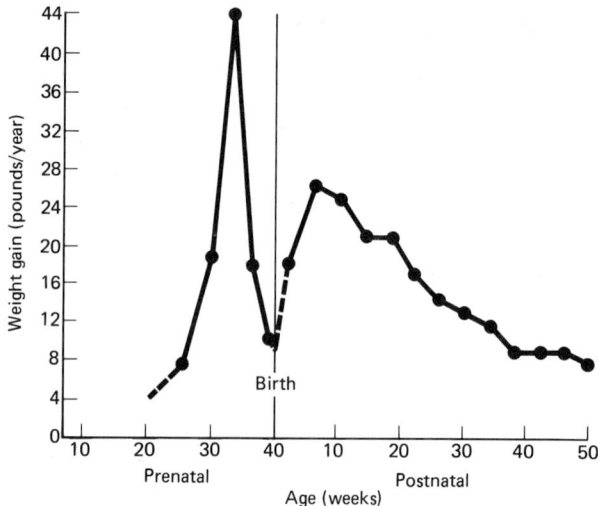

FIGURE 6-3. Chart of weight gain, expressed in terms of pounds per year, from the 20th week of fetal age until the 50th week after birth. (Estimates were indicated by the dash lines.) (After Tanner, 1963, 1970. Reprinted with permission from Mussen (Ed.) Carmichael's Manual of Child Psychology, 3rd ed., Wiley, 1970, p. 91.)

physical growth better than did measures of variables in the children's environment.

Nutrition

The amount and kind of food supplied to infants has a major influence on physical development, as indicated by measures of height and weight; but nutrition influences cognitive development as well. Barry M. Lester (1975) compared the reactions of well-nourished and poorly nourished Guatemalan infants to sound stimuli and found that well-nourished infants showed the usual orienting or attentional response, as indicated by a slight slowing of the heart beat, followed by habituation or recovery to repeated presentations of the sound, but that malnourished infants showed no consistent response. This lack of appropriate responsiveness on the part of poorly nourished infants has been noted by a number of researchers (Eichenwald and Fry, 1969).

As common sense would suggest, it is the children of the very poor who suffer the most from malnutrition. Statistics made available to participants at the most recent White House Conference on Children (1970) show that infants and young children of parents in the lowest income bracket are more than five times as likely to show hemoglobin (red blood cell) deficiencies than children from any other income bracket. In contrast to children from families in the highest income

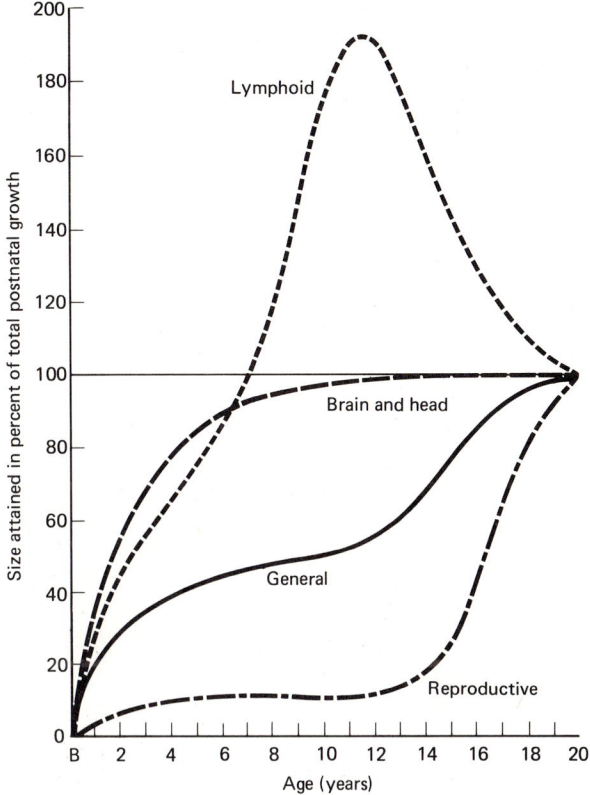

FIGURE 6-4. *Typical growth curves of four different parts or tissues of the body, from birth until age 20. Curves are plotted in terms of total gain and are referred to the size attained at age 20, as represented by 100 on the scale.* (Tanner, 1962 and 1970, after Scammon, 1930. Reprinted with permission from Mussen (Ed.) Carmichael's Manual of Child Psychology, 3rd ed., Wiley, 1970, p. 85.)

bracket, children from poverty homes were also half again more likely to have Vitamin C deficiencies and also four times as likely to suffer from iron deficiencies, as Figure 6-5 indicates.

The question as to whether such infants can recover if placed on an adequate diet has no easy answer. A study by Brockman and Ricciuti (1971) suggest that they cannot. These researchers administered a simple test of the ability to sort eight simple objects to severely malnourished and normally nourished 18- and 34-month-old children from poverty environments in Lima, Peru. The malnourished children scored markedly below the adequately nourished children. Three months later, after the malnourished children had been put on an adequate diet, a retesting on the same tasks showed that they had made

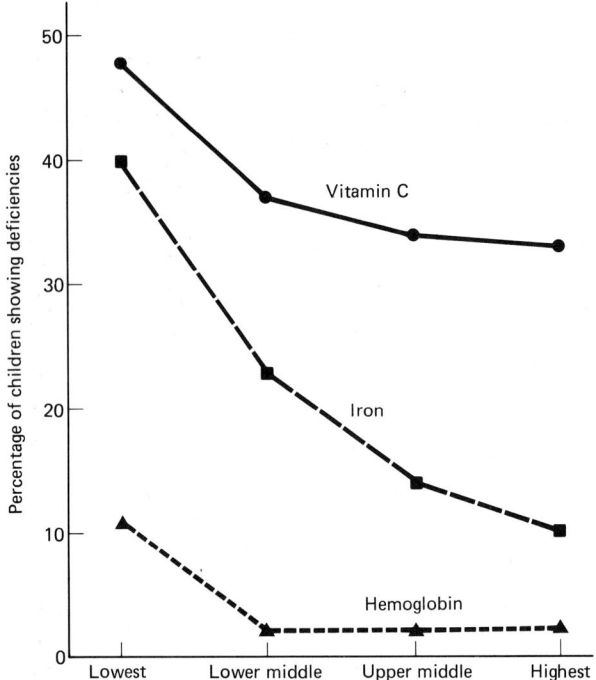

FIGURE 6-5. The effects of malnutrition: percentages of children aged 12 to 23 months, and classified according to family income level, who show the effects of dietary deficiencies. Data are from the first half sample of the Preschool Nutrition Survey conducted by the U.S. Department of Health, Education, and Welfare in 1969. (White House Conference on Children, 1970.)

no progress. Observations during the testing sessions showed that both groups of children were equally motivated by the sorting tasks and showed much interest in them. Hence the differences in the scores can only be caused by the undernourished children's relative inability to discriminate similarities and differences among the objects and to categorize them properly.

Yet other evidence suggests that malnutrition, if corrected, may cause no permanent damage. One team of researchers conducted a follow-up study of Korean orphans who had been adopted during infancy by middle-class American parents. When adopted, one third of the orphans had been markedly malnourished (in the bottom 3 per cent of Korean norms as to height and weight), one third had been subnormally nourished by Korean standards, and one third were within average range. When the children were of school age—some six or seven years on the average after they had arrived in the United States—the researchers gathered data with respect to their height, weight, IQ, and school achievement. Results showed that even those children who had

The physical and mental development of malnourished Korean orphans adopted by American middle-class parents has been found by researchers to be adequate or even better, when compared to norms based on American children in general.

been exceedingly malnourished as infants were not only taller and heavier than Korean children for their age, but that they also had higher IQs and school achievement than the average American youngster. Those children whose nourishment as infants had been more satisfactory rated proportionately higher on all these measures, of course, but the interesting finding is the more than adequate recovery of the severely malnourished children, which the investigators explained as probably resulting from superior diet and enriched environment provided by the adoptive parents, most of whom were upper middle class (Winick, Meyer, and Harris, 1975).

Another research team analyzed the nonverbal mental test scores for 125,000 Dutch military draftees, 20,000 of whom had been born during the winter of 1944–1945, when there was a severe famine in the Netherlands. During this period birth weights were low, and infant mortality was high. They found no evidence, however, that this experience had any effect 19 years later on the mental test scores of the young men who had survived this stressful period (Stein et al., 1972; Stein and Susser, 1973).

Taken together, these two studies provide some basis for a more optimistic view than the findings of Brockman and Ricciuti would suggest, for they suggest that recovery and rehabilitation are possible if initially malnourished children are provided with a satisfactory diet and placed in an environment that is adequate in other respects.

sensorimotor development

As we noted in Chapter 5, the neonate has a larger repertory of sensory responses than is popularly supposed, although it takes sophisticated equipment, such as a heartbeat monitor, to detect some of them. These early responses develop rapidly in variety and intensity during the days and weeks that follow, as bones and muscles strengthen. The cerebral cortex—that barklike "thinking" covering of the brain—is very primitive at birth, but within a month the area controlling the upper limbs and trunk has evolved, and by three months, other primary areas, such as those controlling vision and hearing, are showing signs of development (Tanner, 1970). By six months some of the nerve fibers coming to the cerebral cortex have become *myelinated*—that is, they have become surrounded by *myelin*, the fatty sheath that insulates the fibers and is thought to prevent the energy of the electrochemical messages they carry from leaking into the surrounding body areas.

The over-all result is greater integration of behavior, accompanied by greater specialization and an increase in voluntary control.

Learning and Maturation in Sensorimotor Skills

In spite of the very limited neuromuscular development that occurs during the first few months of life, some learning is nevertheless possible. Robert C. Hulsebus (1973) reviewed well over a hundred studies of operant conditioning of infants. He reported that the movements that were conditioned for infants under twelve months included head turning, sucking, smiling, cessation of crying, vocalizations, eye contact, and manipulations, such as touching a sphere and pulling a string. Reinforcements employed by the researchers included peek-a-boo, taped noises, movement of a mobile, rocking, sucrose, smiles, sucks of milk, touching, tickling, and presentation of colored slides. Some of the more complex studies involved complicated arrangements of equipment, which infants could set in motion by nonnutritive sucking—that is, sucking on a nipple that was connected to an apparatus, rather than to a bottle of milk (Kalnins and Bruner, 1973).

Whereas experimenters today attempt sophisticated experiments in order to test the limits of what infants can learn, earlier investigators were more interested in studying the differential effects of learning and maturation.

A typical illustration is the study of Hopi Indian babies bound to cradleboards, thus experiencing a good deal of movement restraint during their first year of life. They walked independently about as early as did infants who had had much more previous practice (Dennis and Dennis, 1940). Practice missed by being strapped to the cradleboard did not seem to prevent them from walking at the usual age. This finding is interpreted by the investigators as indicative of the clear primacy of maturation over learning in the emergence of walking.

Another classic study compared the behavior of 46-week-old twin girls in stair climbing and cube building. The choice of the age of 46 weeks for initial study was dictated by the fact that this was about the age at which infants were at the threshold of stair-climbing and cube-building responses. Twin T (trained) was given a ten-minute practice session each day for six weeks. Twin C (control) was given no training until the end of the six-week period, at which time she was given *two* weeks of practice. At the end of this practice period, Twin C was performing these activities as well as Twin T, who had the four more weeks of practice but at an earlier age. The investigators concluded that the time of appearance of stair climbing and cube building was not influenced by practice but by the ripening of neural structures (Gesell and Thompson, 1934).

Fowler (1962) took a critical view of such conclusions, saying that the researchers were overemphasizing the influence of maturation. He argued that the roles of perception and experience were ignored and moreover that there was a strong probability that the more complex the skill, the greater the importance of perception and experience. Fowler maintained that there is an initial receptive phase to any motor activity—perceiving the cubes in three-dimensional space or learning to coordinate visual and tactile experiences—which involves learning and is therefore not innate. Moreover, the child is likely to have opportunities to engage in self-initiated practice. In the stair-climbing study, Twin C was not actually allowed to climb stairs or play with the cubes, but the motor skills involved in those tasks could have been acquired in the course of ordinary daily activities. Taking the Gesell and Thompson study together with Fowler's criticisms, we can say that maturation and learning do interact, but that it is difficult or perhaps even futile to try to determine their relative effect precisely.

Manipulation

The classical study of prehension or grasping is that of Halverson (1931), who used a motion picture camera in his intensive study of infants between 16 weeks and a year of age. As Figure 6-6 shows, there are a number of initial stages that precede grasping itself. At first the infants make no contact with the object—a cube, in this instance. At 20 weeks they make contact or squeeze it without grasping. From 24 weeks

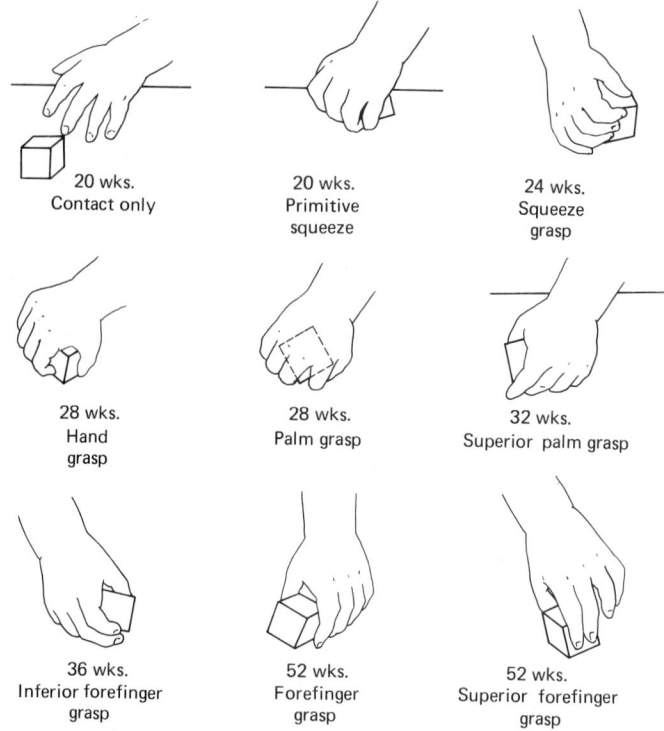

FIGURE 6-6. *The development of prehension or grasping in the first year of life, based on an analysis of cinematographic records.* (Halverson, 1931, Reproduced by permission.)

onward the infant is able to display some form of grasping, first involving much use of the palm in monkeylike fashion and then graduating to the more sophisticated pincerlike grasp similar to that used by older children and adults.

In some instances, a skill learned in one context can present a problem in other contexts. The child who has learned to hold a cube finds that this skill, important as it is, is insufficient and may even interfere with the stacking of cubes. Stacking not only requires grasping, but it also requires the ability to let go, to release the cube that has been so carefully placed on the other one. This is an early instance of reversibility, a frequent source of difficulty. It is hard enough to learn to *do* something—pick up a cube, for instance—but even harder to reverse the process and *undo* it, that is, to let it go.

Locomotion

The neonate may be able to squirm and thus alter its position, but this can hardly be considered locomotion in the sense of moving from place to place. Mary M. Shirley (1931) conducted careful studies of the development in posture and locomotion of a sample of 25 infants, and the representative behaviors she found in the motor sequence are presented in Figure 6-7.

Although Shirley's general sequence has been confirmed, Nancy Bayley (1935) found some reversals of stages. Instead of a regular order of appearance of special abilities, there was a more irregular growth in the ability in question. Moreover, the stages seemed to occur at earlier ages. In Bayley's study, the average age of the onset of walking was found to be 13 instead of 15 months, which is closer to that recorded by other observers, and Bayley's (1969) more recent scale of motor development places the norm at approximately 12 months.

The developmental principles of differentiation and integration, along with cumulative experience, are involved in walking. It is not so obvious that learning to walk also provides examples of the principle of discontinuity and hierarchization in that each stage involves muscular movements not present in earlier stages. Study of Figure 6-7, picture by picture, will show that different muscle groups are being controlled at different stages. First the eyes, head, and neck are involved, then the arms and upper trunk, later the hands and lower trunk, and last the

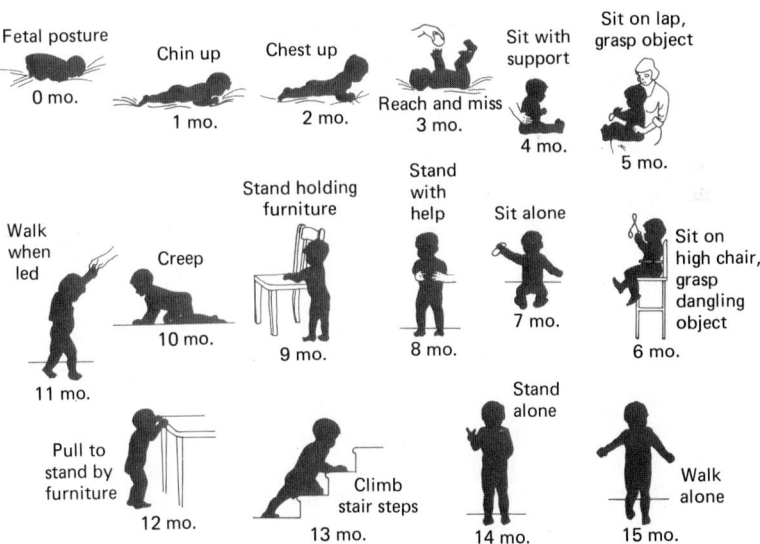

FIGURE 6-7. Sequence of motor development in locomotion. The ages indicated for different behaviors are based on a limited sample of infants. Later research has determined that the average child is able to attain these skills at an earlier age. (Shirley, 1933. Reproduced by permission from Mary M. Shirley, *The First Two Years*, Vol. 11, Intellectual Development. Minneapolis: U. of Minnesota Press, 1933. Copyright renewed, 1961.)

pelvic area and the legs—an example of the cephalocaudal direction of development we mentioned earlier.

Beginning to walk has profound psychological consequences. The infant is more able to bring himself in contact with people, places, and things. This he does because he wants to. Others do not have to come to him. To a much greater degree he now may be independent of adult control. He may walk into areas of which his parents approve, but he may also walk into those of which they emphatically do not. To modify a saying, "Fools, and little children, rush in where angels fear to tread." Thus, beginning at about the age of 15 months and continuing to roughly the age of four, there is a period of great locomotor activity. The period, a strenuous one from the parental point of view, is brought about by the simple factor that the infant is able to walk and run.

Recent Research in Sensorimotor Development

The question of the relative contributions of maturation and learning continues to plague students of child behavior. The usual position is that gestures and other activities that appear during the first few months after birth are largely caused by maturation, inasmuch as the infant's neural apparatus has not matured sufficiently to permit it to respond to its environment in ways that would promote learning.

Some recent research by Meltzoff and Moore (1977) has, however, raised questions about so comfortable an assumption. The subjects employed in their experiments were three girls and three boys, aged approximately two weeks. Each infant saw an experimenter perform four simple movements: protrusion of the lips, opening of the mouth, protrusion of the tongue, and sequential finger movement (opening and closing the hand by moving each finger in order). Each gesture was presented four times in a single fifteen-second response period, during which the experimenter remained motionless, presenting an impassive face to the infant.

The gestures of the experimenter and the behavior of the infant were videotaped. Infant behavior on each of the tapes was judged by six undergraduate students, who were told that the infant had seen one of the four types of gestures, and that it was their task to determine which gesture the infant was imitating. The hand-gesture tapes were rated separately from the others; the judges for these films were asked to indicate which of four possible hand gestures were being imitated. (Paired pictures from the tapes appear in Figure 6-8.)

An analysis of the ratings indicated that the judges were able to make better-than-chance identifications of the infants' imitative attempts. Similar results were obtained when the experiment was replicated with a different sample of babies, and a third set of observations with newborns indicated that imitation may occur in neonates as young as one hour old.

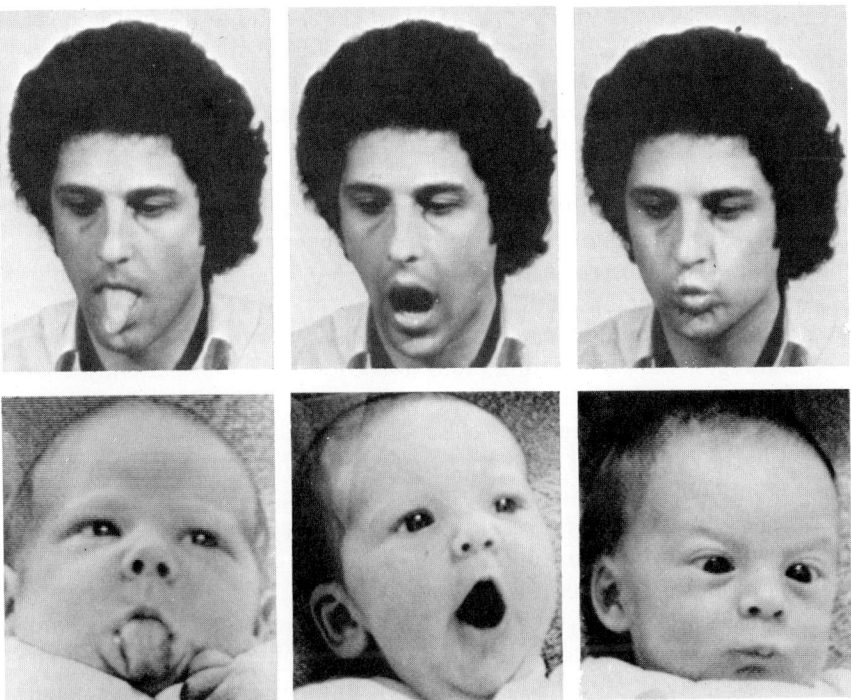

FIGURE 6-8. Photographs from videotape recordings of infants two to three weeks old imitating (a) tongue protrusion, (b) mouth opening, and (c) lip protrusion, as demonstrated by an adult experimenter. (Meltzoff and Moore, 1977. Copyright American Association for the Advancement of Science, 1977.)

This study opens a veritable Pandora's box of controversy and confusion, for it raises the possibility that a vast number of behaviors that psychologists had concluded were maturational or even instinctive in their origin may be environmentally determined—the result of learning.

Early Indications of Sex Differences

In view of the widespread belief that sex differences in personality and behavior during childhood and adulthood are entirely the product of social learning and the expectations of others, it may be well to examine the question of whether differences appear during infancy. Presumably, if such differences do appear, they are likely to be the result of genetic influences and not of social learning. Garai and Scheinfeld (1968) reviewed almost five hundred studies dealing with sex differences throughout the life span. Their conclusions regarding differences appearing during the first year of life may be summarized as follows.

1. Studies are not in agreement as to whether boys are more active than girls at birth, but the evidence is clear that activity differences appear within a few days. For instance, at the age of 23 hours, boys and girls spent approximately the same amount of time in hand-mouth contact and hand sucking, but by 71 hours, boys were clearly ahead of girls (Hendry and Kessen, 1964). The fact that boys' tendency to greater activity is not as evident at birth as later may be related to the fact that there is a greater probability for male infants to be weaker at birth and to have more birth complications.
2. Female neonates are more responsive than males to pain, changes in temperature, and electric shock, a tendency that appears to be related to greater tactile sensitivity and pain reactivity among females of school and college age.
3. By the middle of the first year, boys show more interest in complex geometric stimuli presentations, whereas girls show more interest in representations of faces. (Lewis et al., 1965; Lewis, Kagan, and Kalafat, 1966). Studies of the effectiveness of various types of reinforcement in learning experiments indicate that girls respond more to tonal stimuli, whereas boys respond more to visual stimuli. The reviewers concluded that infant boys tend to show an inherently greater interest in objects and visual patterns, whereas girls are congenitally more responsive to people and faces.

The above differences are the major ones out of a larger number identified by Garai and Scheinfeld in their review of sex differences in infancy. Some years later, however, Maccoby and Jacklin (1974) reviewed approximately 1800 studies of sex differences at all ages, and reported that they could find very few reliable differences between male and female infants. They observed that most of the research is inconclusive, although there are some indications that female infants may be more sensitive to taste, smell, and touch stimuli. They also noted that studies show no sex differences in activity level before one year of age; after twelve months, boys do appear to be more active, although a number of studies show no difference. As to sex differences in perception, they report none.

Thus we have two sets of reviewers, one pair all male reporting in the mid-1960s, and the other all female reporting in the mid-1970s. The male reviewers report many sex differences; the female reviewers report few differences, and meager ones at that. A reading of both reports suggests that each set of reviewers attempted to do a conscientious, objective, and scientific job of evaluating and interpreting the studies they covered. The review of Maccoby and Jacklin is both more recent and more comprehensive. They covered about four times as many studies as Garai and Scheinfeld did, and their book of 634 pages is much more impressive than Garai and Scheinfeld's 131-page monograph. Yet Maccoby and Jacklin's 1800 studies include less than ten per cent of those covered by Garai and Scheinfeld. For instance, the study by Lewis, Kagan, and Kalafat (1966), which demonstrated a male preference for geometric figures and a female preference for faces, was included by Garai and Schoenfeld, but not by Maccoby and Jacklin. Monumental as Maccoby and Jacklin's work obviously is, it appears that we must wait for an even more comprehensive survey of studies before determining exactly what sex differences, if any, are unlearned and hence genetically determined. We shall refer at various points in subsequent chapters to the observations by these reviewers of sex difference research.

cognitive development: a Piagetian view

Cognition has long been used by psychologists to describe aspects of behavior associated with *knowing*—that is, perceiving, imagining, reasoning, thinking, and judging. Traditionally it has been contrasted with the *affective* or emotional aspects of behavior and with *conation*, a term that is little used today and is roughly equivalent to *motivation*.

Interaction Between Infant and Environment

The infant's physical development, especially his sensorimotor development, is intimately tied in with his cognitive development. In Piagetian terms, it is through interacting directly with his environment that the infant develops the schemas that enable him to gain an understanding of the objects and events that make up physical reality. The infant's ability to focus and move his eyes in tandem, and thus to follow a moving object with his gaze, makes it possible for him to look at the point where an object has disappeared. A few weeks later he is able to explore with his eyes a partially hidden object. By the time he is about halfway through his first year, his eyes will return to the starting point, when a slowly moving object disappears. A few weeks later, now able to locomote by crawling, he locates a toy that has been hidden under a screening object such as a piece of furniture. Each of these schemas is based on previously constructed schemas, which are made possible in part by motor development.

Piaget regards cognitive processes as being expressed in thought and intelligence, which he considers to be aspects of the same central cognitive process. He also defines perception as being subordinate to intelligence as a means of individual adaptation or adjustment to the environment (Flavell, 1963). Intellectual functioning is viewed by Piaget as an aspect of the adaptive interaction of child and environment. Adaptation is expressed in two complementary functions—assimilation and accommodation (Piaget, 1957). Assimilation takes place when the organism uses some object in the environment in the course of its activity. It occurs when the new is drawn into the old behavior repertoire and becomes part of the infant's inner organization. For example, when something new is perceived that resembles an old, already familiar object, it is used as would be the old object. Accommodation, on the other hand, occurs when the old repertory is adjusted to account for the new object experienced. Hence, new activities are added to the infant's repertory and the old activities modified to that extent.

In order to aid the reader to "assimilate" and "accommodate" this discussion, the former includes what in old familiar terms we would call generalization and discrimination, whereas accommodation includes differentiation, or the learning of new responses. This adaptational process, embracing assimilation and accommodation as its functions, remains the same as the child grows in age. In each organism-environment interchange, assimilation and accommodation always occur together, although one may at times play a more dominant role than the other.

Piaget's theory of intelligence is primarily a theory of structures or schemas.[1] The term *schema*, when used in this sense, refers to a dynamic network of conceptualized relationships between actions and objects into which the child integrates his ongoing interaction with his environment by means of the nonchanging functions of his intelligence. Schemas are thus progressively organized, reorganized, and thus changed with use, whereas intelligence remains constant.

At birth the only structures available to the infant are the sensorimotor responses we mentioned in the previous chapter. At this stage of development, the infant's actions are not yet internalized in the form of thoughts (Piaget, 1957). As the infant functions at this level, he assimilates the realities of his environment in a fashion that roughly corresponds to the problem-solving abilities of the subhuman animals (Piaget, 1952). He exercises these sensorimotor capacities and gropes about in his environment, for example, showing sucking responses to almost any stimulation of the lips.

The "Object Concept"

Realities are not yet entities; they are only functional elements—something to be sucked, to be handled, or to be moved. Objects do not yet exist as objects. "Out of sight, out of mind" might be said to

---

[1] See the discussion of schemas and schemes on page 81.

characterize the view of the infant. He has not acquired the "object concept" and behaves as if objects that have disappeared from view have ceased to exist (Flavell, 1963). For example, Piaget tells us that an infant of five to eight months of age, already old enough to seize a solid object, will lose interest and turn away if a cloth is thrown over the object before his hand reaches it. At a slightly more advanced age he is capable of seeking an object behind a screen, thus showing the beginnings of the notion of the real exterior permanence of objects. Nevertheless, he is still functioning at the more primitive level.

An infant at the level we are discussing was given the experience of retrieving an object that he saw placed under the left of two pillows. On the next occasion, he sought the object where he had found it before, despite the fact that the examiner, in full view of the infant, had placed it under the *right* pillow. As Piaget indicates, it is as if his action in reaching under the left pillow was decided by the success of the actions by which he had secured the object previously and not by the reality of its external placement under the right pillow on this new occasion.

The infant comes to realize that objects are stable, independent of himself; that they have a shape that remains the same even though as he turns the object its visual appearance varies; that objects retain identity despite varying in apparent size as they approach or recede; and perhaps to him, most surprising of all, that they continue to exist when out of sight. The infant above all has to learn about cause and effect. This lifelong process begins during the first year.

The infant's pushing and pulling make toys move, rattle, and squeak. At first he does not realize that it is necessary for him to touch them to cause these effects. He tries "magic" by waving his hands at them from a distance. It takes a number of weeks or months before he realizes that in order to make an object move he must touch it.

Piagetian Infancy Scales

The most widely used scales based on Piaget's concepts of cognitive development are the Ordinal Scales for Infant Development, by Ina C. Uzgiris and J. McVickers Hunt (1975). The six scales measure the development of visual pursuit and the permanence of objects, the development of means for obtaining desired environmental events, the development of vocal and gestural imitation, the development of operational causality, the construction of object relations in space, and the development of schemas for relating to objects.

Table 6-1 presents a synopsis of the stage sequence of schemas involved in the development of means for obtaining desired environmental events, tasks employed as evidence of the infant's having attained the level of functioning indicated, and the ages at which the behaviors are likely to be observed in infants (but see the table footnote).

perceptual-conceptual development

Perception plays a fundamental role in cognitive development, as we have noted. Although the step sequences in Table 6-1 involve psychomotor activities, they depend heavily on the infant's growing capacity to perceive differences between and relationships among the objects and events in his environment.

Perception and Sensation

Perceptions are more than merely sensing, of course. Although they require the presence of stimuli, they also involve the interpretation of stimuli—the derivation of meaning. In other words, that bright flashing we see as we proceed down the highway is more than a flashing light—it is a neon sign. That clanging we hear is not merely a clanging, it is a church bell. Concepts, in turn, are based on perceptions. We may never have heard a particular church bell before, but we know that it is striking the noon hour because we have observed a relationship between time and church bell sounds. Similarly, an infant who is able to say "Tick-tick" when his mother points to her watch signals the fact that he has constructed an additional schema when he looks at a clock and says "Tick-tick." When he points to a picture of a watch or a clock in a book and says "Tick-tick," he has made further progress in his construction of schemas and has attained a concept that possesses a considerable degree of abstraction.

Everyday observation indicates that sensation plays a large part in helping infants construct schemas of increasing sophistication. During the first year of life and beyond, the infant spends much time getting acquainted with his world—reaching, fondling, poking, hefting, mouthing, staring, rubbing, tasting, and smelling the objects and persons that come his way. Given a toy he will drop it over the edge of his high chair and watch it fall to the floor. He will do this over and over, as long as indulgent family members are willing to cooperate in his discovery and rediscovery of the effects of gravity.

Preferences for Complexity in Stimuli

Even infants, however, can lose interest in events that familiarity has made too simple and devoid of novelty. The tendency to prefer stimuli of increasing complexity appears very early. Robert L. Fantz (1965) conducted a series of interesting experiments to explore the dimensions of his phenomenon. Figure 6-9 shows a schematic cross section of the apparatus he used to present pairs of stimulus cards to infants. Each

TABLE 6-1. Examples of Behavior in Step Sequence of an Infant's Developing Means for Obtaining a Desired Effect on his Environment (after Uzgiris and Hunt, 1975)

Sequence of Steps	Behavior	Month of Age*
1. Rudimentary differentiation of means and ends preparatory to developing hand-eye coordination	Watches hands	2
2. Repetition of schemas that accidentally produce interesting results	Repeats hand or leg movements to keep a toy moving	3
3. More differentiation of means and ends; singling out a schema for more than one end	Grasps toy when both hands and toy are visible	3–4
4. Further progress in use of a schema for grasping	Grasps toy when toy is in view and hand is not	4
5. Anticipatory differentiation of means and ends; execution of one schema preparatory to executing another	Drops object or objects held before reaching for another	8
6. Anticipatory adaptation of means to ends; exploitation of perceived relationships between objects	Pulls an object on which a toy is resting to obtain toy, with or without demonstration	8
7. Use of common behavior patterns as means for multiple ends	Crawls or wriggles to approach and get toy	9
8. Greater discrimination in exploitation of relationships between objects	Resists pulling an object if desired toy is not resting on it	10
9. Construction of alternate means of exploiting perceived characteristics of a situation	Pulls string attached to a desired object	12
10. Further construction of means adapted to an end by using visible extension of a concealed object in order to obtain it	Pulls string attached to hidden object, with or without demonstration	13
11. Exploitation of other objects as extensions of one's own body, showing further progress in anticipatory construction of means adapted to an end	Uses a stick to obtain a toy out of reach, with or without demonstration	15–18

*Uzgiris and Hunt make this statement about the ages indicated below: "These data on age are given only because they are repeatedly requested. They are intended to have no normative value."

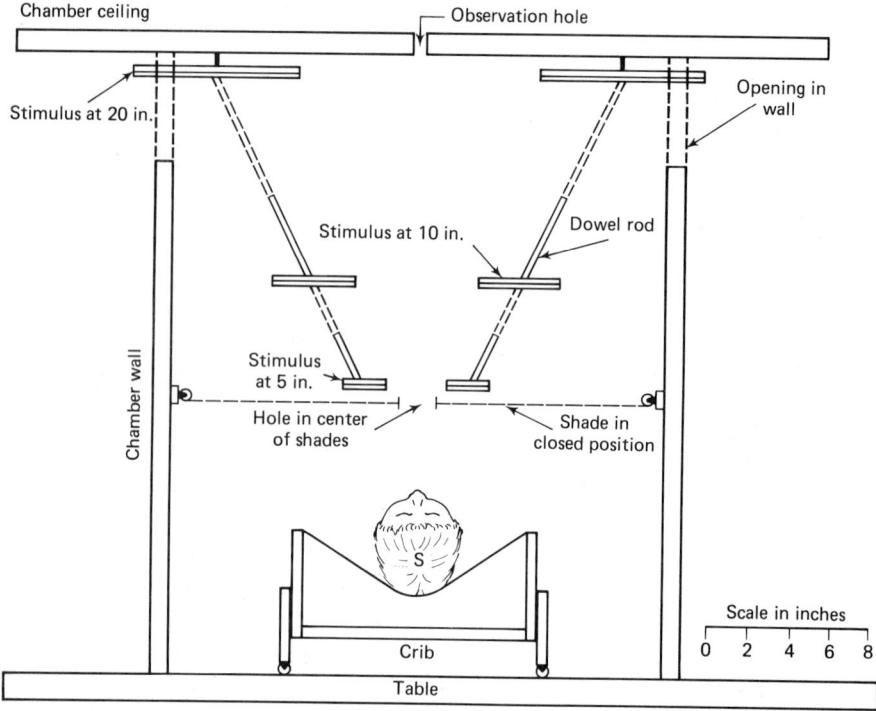

FIGURE 6-9. Schematic cross section of a testing chamber used to observe infants' preferences for stimuli cards. The infant (S) is placed in hammocklike crib, oriented to the observation hole in the ceiling. When the shades are drawn, pairs of stimulus cards are placed at 5, 10, or 20 inches. Shades are then opened and the experimenter watches through the observation hole to see which of the two stimuli are reflected on the pupils of the infant's eyes and also notes the amount of time each stimulus is looked at. (The drawing is to scale, except for the ¼-inch observation hole at the top of the chamber.) (Fantz, Ordy, and Udelf, 1962. Reproduced by permission.)

infant was placed in a hammocklike crib, with its head oriented to the observation hole in the top of the test chamber. The shades were drawn to the position indicated, leaving a two-inch gap that served to attract the infant's gaze to the center. While the shades were in the closed position, the experimenter readied the pair of stimulus cards to be presented. When the shades were opened, the experimenter watched the corneas of the infant's eyes to see which of the two cards was reflected. Figure 6-10 depicts the left eye of an infant who has been presented with a checkerboard stimulus and a plain stimulus. The checkerboard is shown reflected on his pupil, indicating that he is looking at it, in preference to the plain card, which is reflected on the edge of the iris to the right.

Some of Fantz's results are shown in Figure 6-11, which compares the

Sensorimotor and Mental Development 197

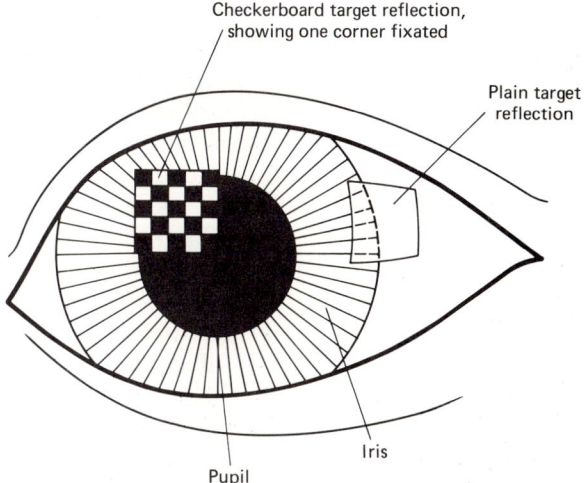

FIGURE 6-10. Schematic drawing of the eye of an infant who is lying in the test chamber and who has been presented with a checkerboard and a plain stimulus. The reflections cast on the eye show that the infant is looking at the more complex stimulus. This diagram depicts a minimal condition for fixation; usually the reflection of the target stimulus would be more centered in the pupil. (Fantz, 1965. Reproduced by permission.)

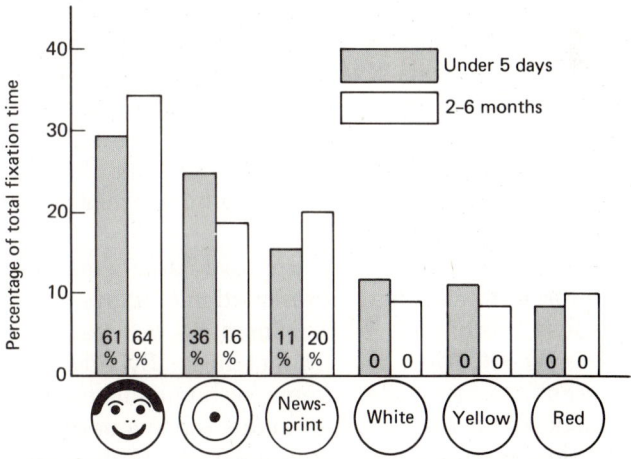

FIGURE 6-11. Visual responses to three black-and-white and three plain discs by newborn and older infants. Percentage of infants in each group looking longer at a particular target is given at the bottom of each bar. (After Fantz, 1965.)

preferences of neonates (less than five days old) with infants two to six months in age. Both groups of subjects displayed preferences for the more complex stimuli, but the older infants' preferences were more pronounced than those of the neonates. Proportionately twice as many of the older infants preferred the newsprint stimulus than did the neonates, and they spent more time in looking at it. Perhaps this is because newsprint may have been seen as being blurred for the neonates, appearing as an all-over gray stimulus, or it may be that the older and more mature infants were attracted to its complexity.

Fantz's findings have been confirmed by other researchers. Brennan, Ames, and Moore (1966) presented infants three, eight, and fourteen weeks old with checkerboard stimuli of increasing complexity, in addition to an all-over gray stimulus. The three-week-old subjects looked longest at the 2 × 2 stimulus; the eight-week subjects, at the 8 × 8 stimulus; and the fourteen-week subjects, at the 24 × 24 stimulus. No group showed any preference for the gray stimulus.

Attention to Unusual Stimuli

Jerome Kagan (1970) and his associates have done a great deal of research on the behavior of infants who are confronted with novel stimuli consisting of photographs and drawings of normal human faces and "scrambled" faces. (See Figure 6-12). Kagan maintains that children, as they encounter the stimuli of their universe, develop schemas[2] or visual concepts that serve as reference points or models which aid in the understanding of each new confrontation with stimuli. At some time during the second month of life, the amount of attention that an infant will bestow on a stimulus configuration will become related to the extent to which the configuration varies or is discrepant from the schemas he has developed. Kagan's discrepancy principle states that stimuli that vary moderately from a schema receive longer periods of attention than do stimuli that either are familiar or are so different that they appear to have no relationship to the schema. The relationship between discrepancy and attention is therefore a curvilinear one, as indicated graphically in Figure 6-13.

An eight-week-old infant gives approximately equal amounts of attention to a three-dimensional representation of a face and an abstract three-dimensional form, but at four months, he spends more time looking at the face than at the abstract form. By now, according to Kagan, the infant has acquired a schema for human faces and rejects the abstraction as being too discrepant from that schema or any other he has developed. When infants this age are shown one of the scrambled faces

---

[2] Kagan employs the Greek form *schemata* as the plural for *schema*, but we will render its plural in the anglicized *schemas*, as being consistent with the usage we employed in our discussion of Piaget, whose translators use *schema* to refer to a concept or construct similar to that of Kagan's.

Sensorimotor and Mental Development 199

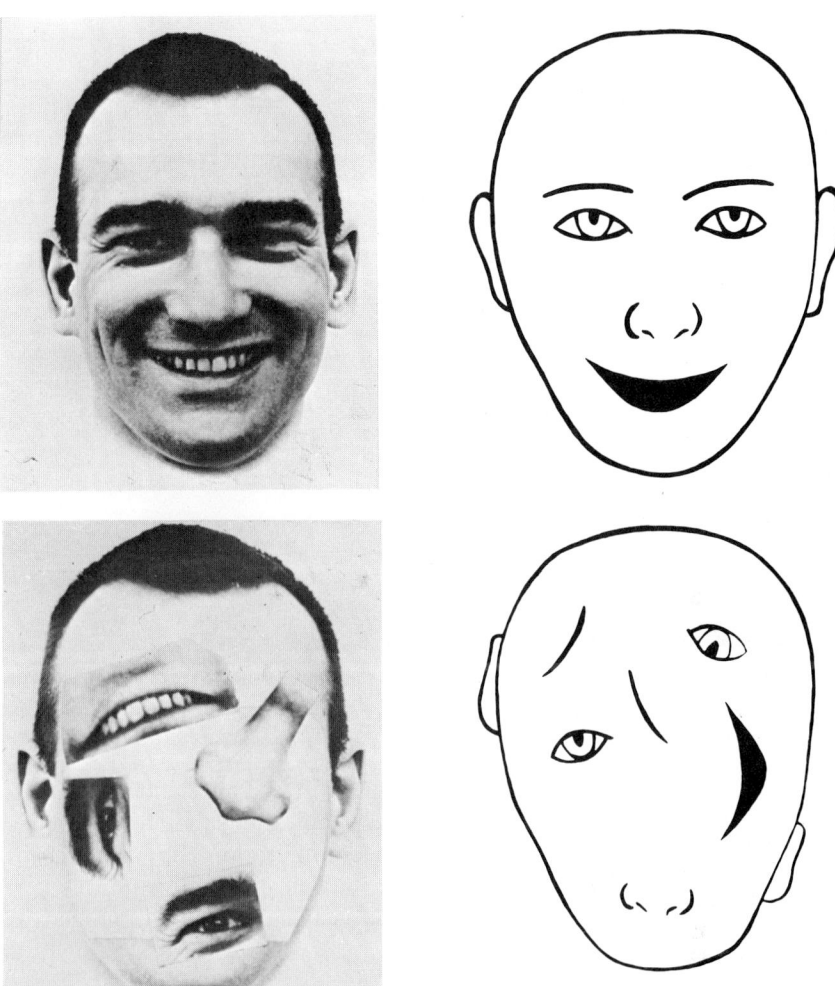

FIGURE 6-12. Representations of normal and "scrambled" faces used in experiments with infant attention. (Kagan, 1970. Copyright 1970 by the American Association for the Advancement of Science.)

in Figure 6-12, the time spent attending is less than for the picture of the normal face, because the scrambled face is too discrepant.

After six months of age, fixation (attention) times for photographic representations of faces drop by over 50 per cent, because such photographs are not discrepant enough to evoke extended gazing. Kagan has also done similar work with masklike representations of human faces. As with the photographic representations, fixation drops markedly during the second half of the first year. From 12 to 36 months, however, the fixation time increases dramatically. Kagan maintains that this change comes about because of the emergence of a new cognitive

Jerome Kagan of Harvard University has been a leading researcher in the cognitive and affective development of children.

structure toward the end of the first year of life. This structure, which Kagan terms a *hypothesis*, is different from the schema. Schemas permit a child to recognize a stimulus configuration, but hypotheses enable him to understand and interpret it. Therefore the stimulus that previously got relatively little attention, because it was recognized as

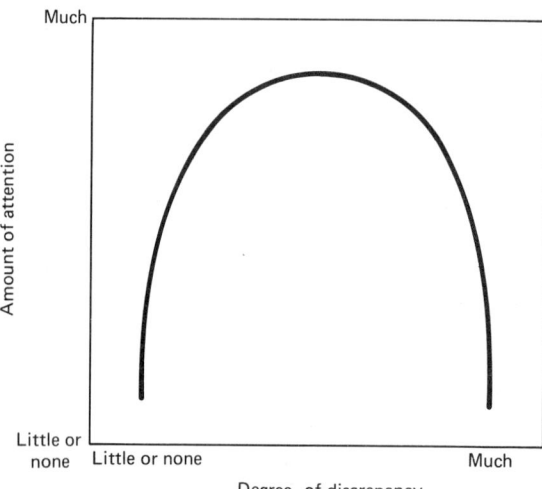

FIGURE 6-13. Schematic representation of the curvilinear relationship between stimuli's discrepancy relative to an infant's schema and the amount of attention they will evoke from an infant.

familiar, now commands more attention because it is identified as a source of new information. As the child matures, he develops an increasingly greater repertory of hypotheses. The more hypotheses in his repertory, the longer he will work at the task of understanding and the more prolonged will be his attention.

The task of assimilating information from a display of stimuli leads to some arousal, which may be expressed in a variety of ways. As the infant looks at the stimuli, he may vocalize, be quiet, thrash about, or smile. These reactions may also be accompanied by changes in the heart rate, respiration, or electrical impulses from the cerebral cortex of the brain. After the information has been assimilated, the infant may react by smiling.

Exploratory Behavior

The attraction of the novel and the complex leads not only to fixation but to exploratory behavior—activities in which the infant engages for their own sake. One cannot explain such behavior in terms of traditional drive-reduction theory, because such behavior, as we have noted, increases arousal: instead of seeking to reduce tension, the infant seeks to increase it. This is also true of the outgoing, exploring, activity-seeking, trying-out behavior that we call play. These behavior tendencies are insatiable; when one play object palls he turns to another. This activity becomes almost all-absorbing. Hunger and the need for elimination are often disregarded unless the infant is reminded by an adult. Of course, this cannot go on indefinitely—he suddenly screams from hunger pangs that have been building up unnoticed, or he has an "accident" and must be changed. He does not get involved in exploratory behavior because of a schedule of reinforcement—he does it because he *enjoys* it.

More systematic observational reports corroborating the presence of exploratory play tendencies are available. Gesell's (1940) normative studies illustrate the appearance of behavior patterns at a given age. Many such patterns are typical of the kinds of behavior under discussion. At one year of age an infant shows gross motor activity, playing with buttons attached to a garment, putting objects in and out of other objects, and participating in reciprocal nursery games, such as "Where is baby?" At 18 months he climbs, moves furniture, and plays with pull toys, teddy bears, dolls, pots and pans. At two years he feeds and toilets a doll or a teddy bear, takes it for a ride, plays with sand and water, filling and emptying dishes, and uses little cars and blocks. However, since these bits of behavior are isolated, with no information provided about their origin, it cannot be said that they arise independent of more primary drives.

Stott (1961) kept a careful behavior diary of his infant son from birth to 18 months, from which he eliminated items bearing a relation to either an organic or a social need. Those individual behaviors remaining, apparently unrelated to any organic or social need, formed the basis of the report. They were classified into five general categories—recognition (looking at the headboard, bending back head to do so); completion (fitting lid on kettle); control (standing in a high chair and shaking until it nearly falls over); exploration (watching movement of adult's feet and hands); and effecting change (studying and hand movement). There seemed to be progressive competence in the child's behavior as the child sought new ways of doing things. The observer could see no connection with either organic (primary) or social needs of these behaviors in his own infant. He could, of course, be mistaken. Nevertheless, in Russia, Federov (1951) independently reached the same conclusions as Stott.

Piaget (1951) interpreted play as the incorporation of experience for the sake of that experience. Its most primitive beginning stages are seen in sucking movements that occur without the presence of a breast or bottle. Perhaps there might be some question as to whether this is really play, but there is no doubt about the next stage, in which prior practice can be distinguished from the activities shown in carrying it on for its own sake. Illustrative is an infant who adopts the habit of throwing back his head to look at objects. At about two months of age he continues to do so "with ever-increasing enjoyment and ever-decreasing interest in the external results."

Piaget observed a seven-month-old infant who had learned to remove an obstacle in order to secure an object. When the barrier continued to be put before him, the infant would push aside the cardboard and burst into laughter, completely forgetting the toy that was the original incentive for his learning. A still older infant was fond of pretending a piece of cloth was a pillow, or of "eating" paper, laughing aloud as she did so. Here symbolization has emerged as a play activity for the infant. Inadequate stimuli were treated as if they were adequate—as if they were something else.

Depth Perception

We come now to another aspect of the infant's relationship to his physical environment, that of depth perception. Although in everyday language we think of depth largely in terms of its vertical dimension—usually of distance between ourselves and objects below us—researchers in the field of perception use the term *depth perception* to apply to the awareness of distance or space between ourselves and objects in our visual field lying in any direction from us—above, below, at the side, or ahead.

A major question, as far as research with infants is concerned, is the extent to which depth perception is learned. There is now some research evidence which suggests that its more elementary forms may be inborn and not acquired through experience. Walk and Gibson (1961) measured depth perception in infants by employing an ingenious piece of laboratory apparatus they termed a "visual cliff," consisting of a center "crawlway" with sheets of glass extending on each side below which a checkerboard pattern was visible. (See Figure 6-14). On one side, the checkerboard was directly beneath the glass; on the other side, it was far below the glass giving what, to an adult, appeared to be a drop off, or cliff side.

When each mother stood at the outside edge of the cliff side of the apparatus and asked her child to crawl toward her, none of the infants would do so. On the "safe" side, however, each infant readily crawled toward his mother. Since even the youngest infants were six months of age—the age at which the essentials of the act of creeping appear—they all had had opportunities for previous experiences from which they might have learned some of the cues to depth perception. Nevertheless, the evidence suggests that at least some aspects of depth perception may be unlearned.

The visual cliff has also been used to measure depth perception in infants two and three months old—long before crawling age. When infants were placed on their stomachs, with eyes oriented to either the deep or the shallow sides of the stimulus box, significant differences in their heart rate appeared, with location on the deep side producing a much slower heartbeat than the shallow side (Campos, Langer, and Krowitz, 1970). As we noted in Chapter 5, a slower heartbeat is associated with the "orienting response," which occurs when infants (as well as other high organisms) are gazing at a stimulus as though in search of its meaning. (The fear response at looking down from heights is one that appears at a later stage in the infant's development.)

A rudimentary form of depth perception was identified in an experimental situation in which infants two to eleven weeks of age were seated in front of a screen on which shadows grew rapidly larger, as though a large object were rapidly approaching either on an impending collision course or a "miss" course. In another version of the experiment, a real object was moved rapidly toward the infant in collision and miss courses.

Videotapes of the behavior of the infants during these confrontations showed that they moved their heads back and brought their arms toward their face when it appeared that the shadow or object would collide with them. Behavior when the stimulus was on a miss course was quite different and consisted of a slow turning of the eyes and head along the path of the shadow or object. When the stimulus retreated, the typical response was one of relaxation (Ball and Tronick, 1971). The results showed rather definitely that even at this early age infants are able to perceive and react to impending collisions and can differentiate between potential collisions and misses, and hence that they possess some elements of depth perception.

language development

Is linguistic behavior properly considered as social or as cognitive behavior? A good argument can be made for either classification. The arguments for social behavior emphasize the social context in which a

FIGURE 6-14. The "visual cliff" as used in experiments to test depth perception in infants.

child develops: the necessity for him to interact with others, especially his caregivers; as well as the role language plays as a social marker, indicating the ethnic identity and status of the language user. The arguments for cognitive behavior remind us that language also develops out of a need to order and to control one's environment, that problem solving is facilitated by language and the symbols it provides, and that a

child's ability to cope with his environment can be measured by his command of language.

We shall resolve the conflict of where linguistic development should be introduced by placing it where most child psychologists put it—within the context of a discussion of cognitive development—even as we recognize that the arguments emphasizing its social functions are very persuasive and cannot be disputed.

Perception and Language Development

Like other forms of cognitive development, the appearance of language and language-related behavior cannot occur until the infant has arrived at a reasonable level of perceptual competence. Before one can reproduce language, one must become aware of it. The interesting study by Condon and Sander (1974) we mentioned in Chapter 5 shows that even neonates have some awareness of speech, in the sense that they attune their bodily movements to its rhythms. It can be argued, of course, that this is not their first experience with the sounds of speech, for even as fetuses they must have experienced some sensation when their mothers spoke.

Infants also appear to possess sufficient sensitivity to make fine discriminations in speech sounds. In a review of research dealing with receptive language development in infancy, Bernard Z. Friedlander (1970) mentioned a number of studies demonstrating that infants one to four months old were able to respond to and hence to distinguish between the consonants /p/ and /t/ and between /b/ and /g/, as well as between the vowels /i/ and /a/. And in Chapter 2 of this text, we described the studies of Cynthia Turnure (1971), who found that infants could distinguish between garbled and normal recordings of the mother's voice and that of a female stranger. Turnure also found that the reactions of her infant subjects to the voices changed over the six-month span covered by her observations. Three-month-old infants tended to mouth more on hearing the mother's voice, suggesting an association between "mother" and "feeding." Six-month-old infants tended to cry more on hearing the mother's voice, especially in its normal presentation. Turnure suggested that this phenomenon could be explained in terms of other studies showing that six-month-old infants characteristically have formed attachments with their mother and hence are disturbed when they can hear but not see her.

Evidence from the research, then, points to the fact that infants are able to distinguish among various speech sounds and that their perception of them changes over time, in keeping with their growing competence as well as their needs.

For children and adults, language competence makes possible the development of systems of classification, which in turn are basic to all forms of problem solving, as we noted above. The studies mentioned so far in this discussion indicate that infants are already able to make some finely tuned discriminations and hence have some of the basic tools needed for classification. A classic study by Bing-Chung Ling (1941) used conditioning methods to establish the fact that infants are able to employ nonlinguistic forms of symbolization in order to indicate discriminations. In her research, infants showed their conceptual discrimination of a correct form by licking it instead of other forms that were also present. The experimenter presented infants six to fifteen months old with blocks differing in form, including circles, crosses, and triangles. Successful selection of one form was rewarded by a coating of saccharine on the correct block's surface. Discrimination shown by licking the correct form was found as early as the sixth month of life. Changing the position of the correct form relative to the others or varying its size had only a slight effect upon accuracy.

Early Linguistic Development

The infant's first attempt to communicate—the cry—is purely self-expressive. Peter H. Wolff (1969) was able to identify three basic crying patterns among neonates: the basic rhythmical hunger cry, the "mad" or angry cry, and the cry in response to physical pain (a reaction to a nurse's drawing a blood sample by heel prick). Wolff also observed the effect of these cries on mothers. There was no fixed pattern of maternal response to the basic or hunger cry—it depended on whether the infant was the first child, the feeding practices of the mother, and so forth. The "mad" cry had a more pronounced effect, for the mothers tended to drop what they were doing and check on their infants. The pain cry got the most prompt response, of course, and elicited a feeling of wanting to soothe and comfort the upset infant.

As to other forms of communication, Wolff noted that in the third week of life smiling responses appear consistently to almost any kind of nonstress stimulation, as long as the baby was alert and inactive. Attention-seeking crying now appeared, as well as noncrying vocalizations. Laughter was likely to appear a week or so later. By the end of the second month, Wolff observed that it was possible to get infants uttering high-pitched squeals to imitate low-pitched "da-da" sounds, and vice versa.

In our discussion of socialization in Chapter 4, we mentioned the fact that the vocabulary of sounds uttered by infants includes all those employed in any language, and that the English-speaking adolescent who is having trouble in learning the German /ö/ and /ü/ undoubtedly had these sounds in his repertory as an infant. When he was an infant, the adolescent was also able to mouth other language sounds that English-speaking people have problems with: the three /h/ sounds of Arabic, the /ich/ and the /ach/ sounds of German, the liquid /ll/ of Welsh, the Parisian glottal /r/, and so on. The richness and breadth of the infant's repertory of sounds of course becomes restricted as infants learn to imitate the speech sounds of their caretakers.

It is possible, too, that some of this selectivity is facilitated by conditioning. Donald K. Routh (1969) was able to get infants aged two to seven months to express certain kinds of sounds in preference to others. He used smiles, a series of three "tsk" sounds, and a light stroking of the infant's abdomen to reinforce consonant sounds for one group of infants, vowel sounds for another group, and any sounds at all for a third group. Figure 6-15 presents some of Routh's findings and shows that infants reinforced for vowels markedly increased their vowel production, whereas their consonant production remained fairly stable. The group reinforced for consonants increased their production of consonants and showed only a slight increase in vowels. Although Routh's findings suggest that reinforcement by adults may play a part in children's language acquisition, it does not necessarily follow that language can be explained entirely in terms of reinforcement. We shall have more to say on this topic at the end of this section.

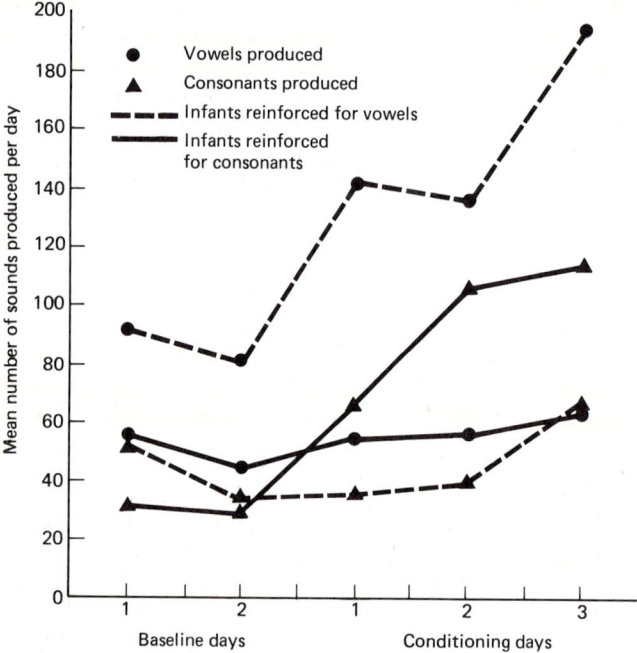

FIGURE 6-15. Mean numbers of consonants and vowels per day uttered by a group of infants who were reinforced for vowels and a group who were reinforced for consonants. Each "day" consisted of nine recording sessions of three minutes each. Recordings were made without reinforcement for baseline days, and reinforcement was instituted during conditioning days. (After Routh, 1969.)

Dorothea Agnes McCarthy (1906-   ), for many years Professor of Psychology at Fordham University, has been one of the pioneer researchers in the language of children.

Developmental Patterns

At what point in their development do infants stop cooing and start babbling? When do they utter their first word? When can they use sentences?

Questions like these are put by parents who anxiously monitor the sounds emitted by their offspring, seeking signs that he is advanced, retarded, or "on schedule." They are also posed by scientists. The answers, however, are more difficult to obtain than one might imagine. The most obvious source of such normative data should be the reports of parents, but parents are hardly the most objective observers. There are, furthermore, problems of classification. Is the "da-da" which the eight-month-old infant utters a glad cry of recognition at seeing his father, or is it merely babbling? Sometimes an infant will learn a verbal response, like "bye-bye", use it for a week, and then either forget it or refuse to use it for months. Has he learned "bye-bye" or not?

In spite of such problems, psychologists have been able to set up norms that indicate or suggest the ages at which children typically are able to engage in various kinds of vocal behavior. Dorothea McCarthy (1954) some years ago collected the reports of a number of researchers and compiled the normative data included in Table 6-2. We have supplemented McCarthy's summary with some of Mary Shirley's (1933) observations of infants whose development she followed longitudinally, over an extended period of time.

The researchers whose observations are summarized in Table 6-2 placed the appearance of the first word at about 40 weeks. Shirley reported that her babies used their first word at about 65 weeks, on the average, although there was considerable variation. Some said their first word as early as eight months, whereas with others it was delayed until as late as two years of age. The mothers themselves credited their infants with a vocabulary of two or three words at 52 weeks, which agrees with the findings reported in Table 6-2. With due allowance for individual variation, it would appear that the average child says his first word before the end of the first year. Gifted children may use words at an even earlier age, whereas other children are retarded to the point of not attempting words until after their second year.

That these findings about the first word seem to vary according to the observer is perhaps because some observers, especially mothers, may be crediting the child with speaking words, basing their reports on utterances which actually are quite far removed from the word in question. Moreover the word or words for which infants are credited by their mothers may be part of a private language wherein a certain sound, perhaps having no resemblance to the word (such as "yo-e" for water), functions as a word in that particular family.

TABLE 6-2. Age in Months at Which Vocalizations Are Likely to Occur According to Samplings of Infant Behavior by Various Observers (McCarthy, 1954)

Age in Months	Vocal Behavior
1.3	Small throaty noises
2–3	Cooing
3	Makes "pleasurable noises"
4	One syllable
4	Self-initiated sound play
6.5	*Ma* or *Mu*
7	Repeats syllables, such as *ma-ma*
8	Vocalizes recognition
8	Vocal interjection
9	Imitates sounds
11	Imitates syllables: *mama, papa, dada*
12	Says two words or more; *jargon*—attempts at conversation in an apparently meaningless language
13	Four words or more
18	*Hello, thank you,* or equivalent
19–24	Names one object or more
21	Repeats things said
21	Joins two words in speech
23–24	Names three objects
24	Simple sentences and phrases

Shirley found that at 66 weeks her infant subjects used seven comprehensive words. There was little improvement until 86 weeks; she believed that probably this lag was caused by the infant's preoccupation with locomotion during this period. By two years of age the average number of words used by her infant subjects was 32. Her observations may be supplemented by returning to those reported in Table 6-2. At two years of age, not only has jargon been discarded but also simple sentences have made their appearance. Considerable development of expressive language ability during the second year has evidently taken place.

Learning Relationships Between Symbols and Objects

The infant's eagerness to speak and to learn names is a major feature of the development of speech. Children have a veritable mania for naming things. Entirely divorced from actual biological needs, this deserves to be called a "hunger for names"; names are learned neither mechanically nor reluctantly, but with enthusiasm.

As most mothers know to their embarrassment, an infant able to use the word "Daddy" may apply it on occasion to any male he sees. Or having learned to use "kitty" for a cat, he is apt to apply it to a dog, a squirrel, or even the fur collar of his mother's coat. Generalization is operating here as it was in other situations we have examined; it is characteristic of the infant to assimilate the new aspect of a situation to what is now old and familiar to him. As he grows older, his cues for discriminatory decisions increase in precision. Illustrative of his growing discrimination is the use by a somewhat older child of an expression such as "funny kitty" for a squirrel. No longer is it a "kitty" alone, but a "funny" one. Some of the cues for "kitty" are present but also something else. The new is seen for what it is, assimilated with the old, and the way prepared for cue discrimination. Attaching distinctive cue-producing responses to heretofore similar stimuli tends to increase their distinctiveness.

The infant applies a word to a wide variety of objects or persons that later will be differentiated by different words. "Dog" means many things according to his total reaction conveyed by the tone of voice, gestures, and bodily movements: "I want that dog, I want to pet and hug him," or "there is an interesting object; you should look at it too," or "I'm scared, hold me, and get me away from here." "Dog" is only one word, to be sure, but it is a word with many meanings. The few words the infant does have are made to stand for many objects and actions.

Theories: Reinforcement and Nativistic

How "dog" loses its excess meanings and becomes attached to the right animal has led to much theorizing and speculation among psychologists and linguists. B. F. Skinner (1957) explained language acquisition in purely operant-conditioning terms, saying that children acquire verbal behavior when their relatively unpatterned vocalizations, which have been selectively reinforced, gradually assume forms that produce appropriate consequences. In other words, a child learns to say "dog" in the first instance because something happens to reinforce that particular syllable when he utters it in appropriate context. Presumably he overgeneralizes at first and applies it to every four-footed animal, but, through being reinforced only for its correct application, he learns to discriminate and apply it more selectively.

This formulation of language learning has been subjected to a great deal of criticism. Noam Chomsky (1959) commented that if we had to learn language by Skinner's rules, we would have to spend a lifetime at the task and still not learn its merest rudiments. The idea of an eager adult waiting in the wings for the right syllable to be produced so that it can be reinforced somehow seems more appropriate for the experimental training of pigeons or rats and does not explain the great variety of behaviors that children acquire in so brief a time span. It seems much simpler to assume that "dog" first emerges in the child's vocabulary through imitation. Experiments like those of Routh (1969), which we cited earlier, show that a certain amount of "shaping" of vocal responses can take place during infancy, but so far no one has been able to demonstrate that infants at, say, six months of age can produce "dog" on cue.

Eric H. Lenneberg (1969) takes a "nativistic" or "biological" approach to linguistic development. He maintains that language forms appear when children are biologically ready to utter them. Indeed, the appearance of various forms is correlated with the appearance of certain motor skills. Sitting and reaching, for instance, are associated with the change from cooing to babbling (about six months). Standing, as well as walking with some assistance, is associated with uttering syllables in repeated sequences, understanding of some words, and application of some sounds regularly to designate persons or objects—in other terms, the appearance of the first words. When the infant has mastered grasping and releasing, is walking with some purpose and without assistance, and is able to creep downstairs backwards, he has come to a point in his language development when he has a repertoire of from three to fifty single words (which he uses as "sentences") and is uttering series of sounds that sound like language but are not "jargon" (to use Gesell's term).

Lenneberg's view, which is also shared by Chomsky (1964, 1967), is that the human organism is biologically "programmed" to generate language. In a study comparing the behavior of infants of normal and deaf parents, Lenneberg found that both groups of infants, through the fourteenth week after birth, were producing about the same amount of vocalization. This finding suggests that such behavior is biologically determined and is not dependent on its being reinforced by adults. A similar finding also appears in a study by Tulkin and Kagan (1970), who observed middle-class and working-class mothers interacting with their ten-month-old baby girls. Although the middle-class mothers initiated more interactions with their infants and talked to them much more, there was no difference in the amount of vocalization emitted by the two groups of infants.

Effects of Stimulation

The studies of Lenneberg and of Tulkin and Kagan were done in a normal home environment in which there was a fairly constant amount of stimulation. In institutional environments, where the amount of stimulation in the form of noise and handling is much less, vocalization is also less. Conversely, an increase in stimulation produces an increase in vocalization for such infants. Rheingold, Gewirtz, and Ross (1959) counted the number of vocalizations made during nine three-minute periods distributed throughout the day for each of 21 institutionalized infants of a median age of three months. The results for the first two days, during which the experimenter merely learned over the crib with an expressionless face, provided a base line. The second two days the experimenter reinforced vocalizations by smiling, clucking, and touching the infant; the last two days were again concerned with nonreinforcement (base line behavior). Conditioning (reinforcement) raised the rate of vocalizing to a statistically significant extent over the base line, and nonreinforcement lowered it to a level approaching the base line.

Environmental restriction, such as occurs with many infants and children living in institutions, presumably has an effect on the learning of language. Characteristically these children do not receive as much individual attention as do children living in the normal family atmosphere. For one thing, the ratio of infants to adults is likely to be much higher in institutions. Babies under six months of age raised in the unstimulating environment of an orphanage have been found to be retarded in frequency of vocalization and kinds of sounds as compared with children raised at home (Brodbeck and Irwin, 1946). Enrichment will, conversely, increase the speech sounds made. Systematic reading of stories to infants from the age of 13 months to that of 30 months leads to a significant difference in the number of vocalizations from this group and another group of infants matched with them for economic status of the father's occupation (Irwin, 1960). After about four months the infants who had been read to showed reliably more speech sounds.

Abrupt changes in the amount of stimulation received by infants can also have an effect on the normal course of development. H. R. Schaffer (1966) studied infants aged 1 to 29 weeks whose parents had to send them to a hospital for various types of ailments. As compared to a control group of infants, who had been in an institution since birth, the newly hospitalized infants showed retardation in the development of psychomotor behavior. When they returned to their homes, their rate of development returned to normal.

intellectual development

Intelligence test scores are, next to age and sex, the most frequently cited variables in research literature dealing with the psychology of childhood. The popularity of such measures with psychologists is based on the fact that intellectual status during the childhood years can be estimated fairly precisely by present-day intelligence tests and that differences in IQ are correlated significantly with a large number of environmental and motivational variables.

The same cannot be said for testing the intelligence of infants. In the first place, their ability to solve problems and derive abstractions is severely limited and in any event is intimately bound up with their sensorimotor and perceptual development. Infants are, furthermore, not very consistent performers. An infant may be able to pick up a pellet skillfully and drop it in a cup on Tuesday, and fail utterly at the same task on Wednesday, Thursday, and Friday. Infants, too, are not very task-oriented and are easily distracted. Textbooks in psychological testing say that intelligence tests for infants are not very reliable, because the scores for a given infant may vary between testings. The fault may not be in the tests, however, and a more probable explanation is that infants themselves are not very reliable.

Developmental Scales

In spite of the difficulty of assessing infant development, there have been some creditable attempts to construct scales that can be used to determine whether an infant is advanced, retarded, or normal with respect to his competence in dealing with his environment. One of these measures is the Uzgiris-Hunt Ordinal Scales for Infant Development, which we mentioned earlier. Uzgiris and Hunt, however, loyal to the Piagetian mandate, maintain that the ages they have attached to the tasks in their scales are not to be construed as normative and are provided by them only in response to numerous requests for such data.

The Cattell Infant Intelligence Scale, developed by Psyche Cattell (1940), was the standard mental measure for many years, but it has largely been supplanted by Nancy Bayley's (1969) Scales of Infant Development. The two Bayley scales, Motor and Mental, intercorrelate between .44 and .78 for most of the first 18 months of life, reflecting the close association between motor and mental development during this

Nancy Bayley is the author of the Bayley Scales of Infant Development. For many years she played an active role as a research at Institute for Human Development of the University of California in Berkeley and at its predecessor, the Institute for Child Welfare.

period. Thereafter the intercorrelation drops to the .24 and .34 range, indicating that the two scales are now measuring skills that can be more readily differentiated.

At the youngest levels, the tasks of the Bayley Mental Scale, as well as those of the Uzgiris-Hunt and Cattell scales, are largely perceptual-motor in nature. Toward the middle of the first year, the scales include a larger number of manipulatory items. In the second year, the scales include an increasing number of tasks requiring the infant to imitate the examiner's behavior and to respond to his verbal requests.

By way of example, at two and one-half months, the average infant will focus on a cube placed on a table directly before him. At four months, he will reach for the cube and may even pick it up. By the time he is five months, he can hold two cubes. At nine months, he can find a cube under an inverted cup and can place it in the cup on command. When he is fourteen months, he can build a tower of two cubes.

In the second year of life, more and more tasks demand verbal ability. The average infant will imitate words at 12.5 months, say two words at 14 months, and name five objects at 25 months. The mental growth curve shown in Figure 6-16 indicates that there is a rapid increase in competence during the first six months and that it levels off somewhat thereafter. This effect is especially pronounced when compared to growth in motor development.

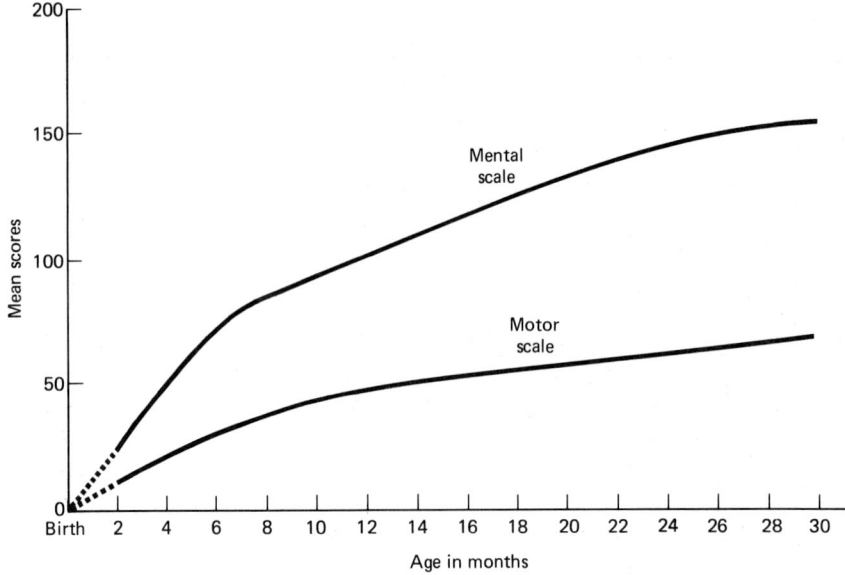

FIGURE 6-16. Growth curves of motor and mental development, as expressed in mean scores of the Bayley Scales of Infant Development at ages 2 to 30 months. (Data from Bayley, 1969.)

Predicting Later Intellectual Development

Although the correlations between mental scales administered during infancy and those taken during the preschool and school years tend to be positive, they are not very high. In a longitudinal study conducted by Elardo, Bradley, and Caldwell (1975), scores on the Bayley mental scale administered at six and twelve months of age correlated only .28 and .32, respectively, with Stanford-Binet IQ at age three, as Table 6-3 shows. It is interesting to note, in Table 6-3, that measures of the amount and kind of stimulation in the infants' homes,[3] made when they were six months old, were better predictors of their mental ability at age three than were either of the Bayley scores. The figures show, furthermore, that mental development as measured by the Bayley scale is not very responsive to environmental stimulation, suggesting that the kind of development it records is largely biologically determined.

This conclusion is supported by some research by Gottfried and Brody (1975), who administered both Bayley scales and several Piagetian measures to 11-month-old infants and compared the results with various physical measures. They found that all the scales were highly intercorrelated and hence measured much the same competencies. The scores were, furthermore, positively correlated with measures of the infants'

[3] The scale employed was the Caldwell Inventory of Home Stimulation.

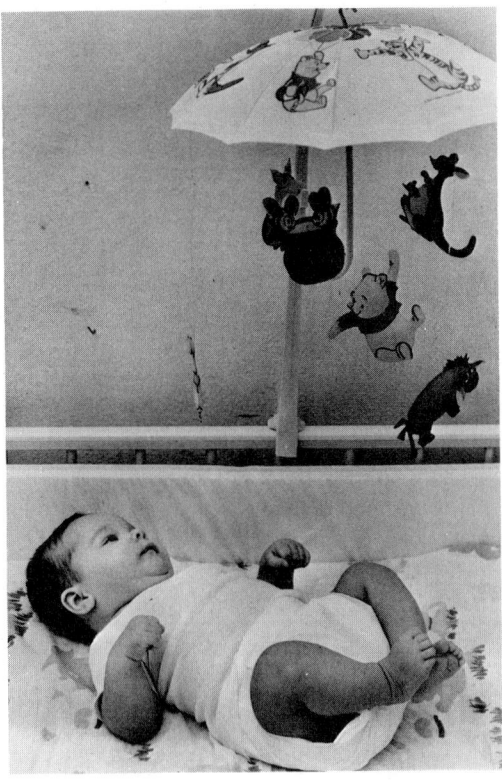

Research has shown that the provision of adequate play materials during infancy makes a significant contribution to the mental development of children.

current weight and head circumference as well as with similar measures taken when they were neonates. The scales were even more highly correlated with the infants' activity, as measured by the amount of space they covered crawling or walking in the laboratory play area. In other words, those infants who scored high on cognitive measures were likely to be those whose physical health was robust and who had a high energy level, whereas low scorers on the tests were likely to be undersized, passive, and essentially uninterested in exploring their environment.

This close relationship between physical and cognitive status during infancy may explain why the Bayley and similar scales are such poor predictors of later intellectual status. Intelligence, as it develops during the preschool years and later, involves problem solving and other abstract operations with the environment. Much depends on the *kind* of environment the child experiences almost from the beginning, as Table 6-3 shows.

This is no reflection upon infant scales of mental ability. Although they measure competencies that are only moderately differentiated from motor ability during the first year of life, they do have considerable value for researchers. As to their practical value, one can say that if an infant scores especially low, something may be amiss. An infant's

TABLE 6-3. Correlations Between the Amount and Kind of Stimulation Available in Infants' Homes and Their Mental Test Scores at Various Ages (data from Elardo, Bradley, and Caldwell, 1975)

Ratings of Potentially Stimulating Variables in the Home Environments of Infants Aged Six Months	Mental Test Scores		
	Bayley at 6 mos.	Bayley at 12 mos.	Stanford-Binet at 36 mos.
Emotional and verbal responsivity of mother	−.01	.09	.25*
Avoidance of restriction and punishment	.00	.04	.24*
Organization of physical and temporal (time) environment	.22	.26	.40**
Provision of adequate play materials	.15	.07	.41**
Mother's involvement with the child	.06	.00	.32**
Opportunities for variety in daily stimulation	.20	.16	.30**
Total score	.14	.16	.50**
Test scores			
Bayley score at 6 months	—	.41**	.28*
Bayley score at 12 months	.41**	—	.32**
Stanford-Binet at 36 months	.28**	.32**	—

* Correlation of moderate significance (p<.05)
** Correlation of considerable significance (p<.01)
(Other correlations are not significantly different from zero)

current mental status is an important source of information, even though his score has only limited predictability for his future status (Bayley, 1970).

summary

Physical development is very rapid during the first year of life, when the infant increases his length by over a third and his weight triples. Biological measures taken early in life are better predictors of later physical development than are the psychosocial variables in the infant's environment. Nutrition is a major factor in physical development, and poorly nourished infants are retarded in their cognitive development. Research with undernourished children in Peru suggests that placing such children on an adequate diet for an extended period does not bring them up to the norm on cognitive measures. But investigators following up severely malnourished infants who had been adopted and brought to the United States by middle-class adoptive parents found that after a few years their physical and intellectual status was above average to superior, the evident result of superior diet and environmental enrichment. Dutch army draftees who had been born during a World War II period of famine also showed no ill effects from their early deprivation.

Although the infant's neural apparatus is very immature at first, he can nevertheless through reinforcement learn simple movements. Both learning and maturation play a part in the acquisition of such skills as locomotion and prehension. The importance of maturation is illustrated by the fact that Hopi Indian babies walk as soon as other infants, even though the Indian cradleboards have prevented an equivalent amount of practice. Studies in which twins are given differential amounts of practice also serve to emphasize the role played by maturation. The performance of the twin who is denied practice rapidly improves to equal that of the trained twin. The development of locomotion reflects an equivalent trend. The principle of discontinuity and hierarchization is also exemplified in that each stage requires muscle movements not present in earlier stages. Learning to walk has profound psychological consequences, and marks the advent of a period of intense locomotor activity, which continues to roughly the age of four. Some recent experiments in which neonates saw and imitated mouth and hand gestures raise a question as to the extent to which certain forms of motor behavior appearing during infancy are learned or appear spontaneously through maturation. Although some studies indicate that sex differences in perceptual style and sensitivity appear in infancy, there are reviewers who maintain that the research is inconclusive and that few sex differences, if any, can be discerned.

Cognitive behavior includes perceiving and other types of behavior associated with thinking; it is contrasted to affective/emotional and motivational aspects. Piaget holds that infants interact with their environment and thus develop cognitive structures that enable them to understand it. His theory of intelligence is primarily a theory of structures or schemas—dynamic networks of conceptualized relationships. An infant's structures are continually modified through use, but his intelligence remains unchanged. To the infant, objects do not exist as such—only in terms of the way in which he interacts with them. Learning to understand the world of reality means learning object permanence; that is, learning that objects have an existence apart from the infant's own experience. Scales have been developed to determine the infant's stage of development according to Piagetian theory.

The infant's ability to perceive is in its earlier stages intimately involved with his psychomotor development. Sensation plays an important role at first; then the infant's ability to abstract enables him to develop concepts. The tendency to prefer stimuli of increasing complexity appears early in life. Fantz found that even neonates prefer to look at complex rather than simple stimuli and that this preference increases with age. Kagan conducted a series of experiments in which infants saw normal and "scrambled" faces and found that stimuli that vary moderately from a schema that the infant has acquired get more attention than those that are very similar or very different. Fixation times for photographs of faces drop after six months, but increase dramatically after twelve months. Kagan attributes this change to the infant's development of hypotheses, cognitive structures that enable him to understand and interpret stimuli. Exploratory behavior and play cannot be explained in terms of classical drive-reduction theory, because they are satisfying in and of themselves. Studies using the "visual cliff" and simulated collisions with objects suggest that infants possess some elements of depth perception at a very early age, a competence which may not have been learned and hence would be inborn.

Language learning cannot begin before the infant has developed sufficient skill to distinguish speech sounds. Research shows that infants respond to the cadences of human speech at a very early age, and quickly learn to identify the mother's voice. Self-expression through various kinds of cries also appears quite early. Smiles also appear toward the end of the first month, followed a few weeks later by rudimentary imitation of simple sounds. Determining when an infant has "learned" a word is not easy, because of problems of classifying sounds, but researchers agree that the first word emerges toward the end of the first year, on the average, although there is much individual variation. The infant's eagerness to speak and learn names is a major feature of the development of speech. Initially, he applies a word to a wide variety of objects or persons that will later be differentiated by different words. How these words lose their excess meanings and become attached to the right object has led to much speculation among psychologists. B. F. Skinner explains language acquisition entirely within an operant-conditioning framework. Chomsky and others are critical of this approach and believe that conditioning cannot explain either the speed with which language is acquired, or the great variety of resultant behaviors. It seems that language forms appear when children are biologically ready to utter them, and their appearance is correlated with the appearance of certain motor skills. This observation suggests that the human organism is biologically "programmed" to produce language. Chomsky's view has been supported by research that shows that the amount of infant vocalization is relatively unaffected by the amount of parental vocalization. However, this does not mean that the amount of infant vocalization is totally independent of environmental factors. Institutionalization and other forms of social and sensory deprivation have a very definite influence.

Intellectual status during the childhood years can be estimated fairly precisely with existing intelligence tests, but measuring intelligence during infancy presents problems, partly because intelligence is merged with sensorimotor development, and partly because infants do not behave very consistently. Nevertheless, some fairly useful scales of mental development have been constructed. The Bayley scale has largely supplanted the Cattell scale. These two tests, like the Piagetian scales, are largely perceptual-motor in nature and are highly correlated with one another. Scores on mental scales administered during infancy are not highly correlated with later development; actually, the best predictors of later intellectual status are those based on assessments of the home environment. In spite of these limitations, infant scales of mental development do have value for researchers, and, in any event, infants who make markedly low scores on such scales deserve special attention.

seven

Caregivers and Infants

> Before she was quite a year old, we began to correct her for crying. This has been a severe but wholesome discipline. It has taught her a command over her feelings, which we trust may be of great service to her in her subsequent life. Now, when she is grieved or displeased, unless she is in a bad humor from bodily suffering, she will suppress the disposition to cry, often with very perceptible struggle and effort. But, even when she is unwell, and bursts into a loud cry, we generally correct her, until she suppresses it. . . . In this discipline, we sometimes used the rod; but more frequently shut her in a room alone, til she became quiet.
> —"Extract from a Mother's Journal,"
> MOTHER'S MAGAZINE, 1834

> It is better to bind your child to you by a feeling of respect, and by gentleness, then fear.
> —TERENCE

the infant's social environment

In the foregoing chapter we noted that infants are much more alert and responsive to their social environment than is popularly supposed. In this chapter, we shall examine the interaction of the infant with his social environment, with particular reference to the adults who play the role of caretakers—or, more preferably, caregivers, to use Michael Lewis' (1974) warmer and more appropriate term. As Lewis also points out, the relations between caregiver and infant do not represent, a one-way street, for the infant's behavior patterns have considerable influence on the way that his caregivers will respond to him.

Parents as Caregivers

In this chapter, the caregiver we shall be most concerned with will be the mother. In every culture and society, it is the mother—biological, adoptive, or foster—who has the most intimate contact with the infant. This is the general rule, although there are notable exceptions, such as the kibbutzim of Israel, as well as instances in which an institution immediately takes charge of a newborn because the mother rejects or abandons the child, or has died, leaving no one else to take over. In a growing number of households, too, a man, for one reason or another, has the entire care of an infant, but such arrangements still constitute only a tiny percentage of all child-care situations. We shall focus our discussion on the mother for another reason: most of the research that deals with infant-caregiver relationships involves the mother.

Our preoccupation with the mother's attitudes and behavior does not imply that the father does not play a significant role in child development at this stage. On the contrary, the research on situations where the father is absent indicates that his contribution is very important. The father's immediate effect on infant development has, however, been little studied. One can speculate that his interaction with the infant has much the same effect as that of the mother, provided that his handling of the infant is consistent with hers. If it is not, the infant may, during the stage when he is differentiating between familiar and strange adults, actually express discomfort and irritation when handled by the father. Perhaps this occurs more often in homes in which mother and father roles are more sharply differentiated.

Today there is a trend in middle-class homes, particularly in urbanized societies, for the roles of fathers and mothers to merge to some degree. Fathers are performing many services for infants that were formerly provided only by mothers: feeding, diapering, bathing, burping, cuddling, and the like. Mothers, too, often leave the home for shopping or employment while fathers take care of the children. Because of the trend toward the merging of caregiver roles, we should make it clear that when we use the term *mother* in general discussions (not research reports) we are referring to the person who happens to be playing the role of mother, be it the father or other adult caregiver.

Older siblings can also play maternal roles. The effects of sibling caregivers on infants have not been researched, partly because variations in the age, sex, and duties of sibling caregivers make it difficult to conduct properly controlled studies, and partly because infant care by siblings is less characteristic of industrialized, Western cultures. Hence we know very little about the differential effects of mother care versus sibling care.

Although we tend to think of the mother when we hear the terms caretaker *and* caregiver, *in actuality the role of caregiver is often played by a number of individuals—grandparents, siblings, and fathers.*

The Home Environment as a Source of Stimulation

We noted in Chapter 4 that all organisms apparently have an inborn need for arousal, that complex stimuli provide more arousal than simple ones, and that attention is not only a rich source of stimuli but a source of reinforcement as well.

It is obvious that caregivers play a vital role in controlling the amount of attention and other kinds of stimuli that infants will experience. They can, for example, expose him to greater varieties and higher levels of stimulation, or they can shelter and insulate him from fluctuations in the amount and kind of stimulation.

Physical stimuli are likely to have more effect on the infant than social stimuli, of course, although we must keep in mind that responsiveness to social stimuli begins very early, as we noted in discussing the experiment by Condon and Sander (1974) on the responsiveness of neonates to adult speech cadences, and the study by Sagi and Hoffman (1976) of empathic distress of neonates in response to crying sounds.

early stimulation

The theory that is currently held by some developmental psychologists is that infancy is a critical period, as far as the need for stimulation and arousal is concerned, and that it makes a great deal of difference, in terms of the later development of the child, whether stimulation is augmented or reduced during these important early months.

Animal Research

A major basis for yoking the critical-period hypothesis with the importance of early stimulation may be found in research with animals. In one of the earlier studies, Seymour Levine (1960) handled (picked up, petted, stroked) certain pups in rat litters but ignored others. At maturity, the handled rats were more relaxed in novel situations, displaying active exploratory behavior, whereas the unhandled rats cowered in corners or crept timidly about, urinating and defecating freely—all signs of stress. The manipulated rats also exhibited a more rapid rate of development: they opened their eyes earlier and achieved motor coordination sooner. They gained weight more rapidly than the unhandled control rats, and continued to gain more rapidly even after the stimulation regimen had been terminated.

Somewhat similar results were reported for kittens that were handled daily from birth until they were 45 days old. Handled kittens approached strange toys and humans more readily. Some of the kittens had also been exposed for five hours a day to a stimulating environment consisting of a large playroom containing kittens from other litters, boys, boxes, a scratching post, and stairs. These kittens also showed superior performance in solving maze problems (Wilson, Warren, and Abbott, 1965).

In another study, young rats were given one of three types of treatment: (1) stimulus enrichment, consisting of playpen experiences; (2) "normal" laboratory environment; or (3) stimulus deprivation, in that they were kept in solitary cages in the dark corners of the animal room. Results showed that the more stimulation the rats had experienced by the end of their treatment period, the more successful they were in solving maze problems.

When the rats were killed and their brain structure analyzed, researchers found a positive relationship between the amount of stimulation received and the amount of *cerebral cortex* they had developed. (The cerebral cortex is the outer layer of the brain—the "thinking area.") The findings therefore suggest that stimulation enrichment promotes the development of cerebral cortex. Analysis also showed that the brain tissues of stimulated rats were richer in *acetylcholine* and *cholinesterase*, biochemicals that facilitate the transmission of neural impulses (Bennett et al., 1964).

Research with somewhat similar results was reported by Norman D. Henderson (1970), who contrasted the brain size of mice raised in standard cages with that of mice raised in a "playpen" type of cage. Not only did the mice receiving the experimental treatment have larger brains; their progeny had still larger brains, especially when they, too, enjoyed a stimulus-enriched environment.

Patricia Wallace (1974) has reviewed the animal research dealing with the effect of complex environments on brain development and has noted that the investigators tend to agree that whereas "environmental enrichment" promotes changes in brain structure and chemistry associated with superior problem-solving ability, the data do not strongly support the critical-period hypothesis that we mentioned earlier. Some of the studies, indeed, show that animals that spent the initial months of their lives isolated in a stimulus-deprived environment can be rehabilitated if moved to enriched environments. Consistent with this are the investigations conducted by Novak and Harlow (1975), who had noted that rhesus monkeys that had experienced complete social isolation during the first twelve months of life were unable to deal adequately with social situations. When, however, these socially deficient monkeys were allowed to interact for 24 weeks with a younger monkey that played the role of "therapist" in gradually educating its "patients," they were able to interact adequately with their agemates. These results led Novak and Harlow to conclude that there may not be a critical period of development for rhesus monkeys.

It is interesting to note that rehabilitational programs for humans are based in similar premises—namely, that it is possible, through psychotherapy or special education, to "make up" for the cognitive and affective deficits suffered by individuals as a result of deprivation or mistreatment during infancy and early childhood.

Research with Infants

It is of course impossible to conduct the kind of controlled studies with humans that can be carried out with animals. Nevertheless, the studies that have been made do indicate that early stimulation is beneficial, even though they do not necessarily confirm the critical-period hypothesis.

A number of experiments demonstrate a relationship between early stimulation or enrichment and cognitive development. Scarr-Salapatek and Williams (1973), for example, studied the effects of a broad-scale stimulus enrichment program on low-birth-weight (that is, premature) infants, most of whom were born to unmarried mothers. The infants in the experimental group received much handling, were rocked while being fed, and were burped over the nurse's shoulder, a position that encourages neonates to explore their environment visually. Mobiles were also hung above their cribs. When their mothers took the infants home, they were given mobiles to take with them, and were encouraged to continue the program of stimulation that had been started at the hospital. During the following year, the mothers were visited weekly by a social worker, who discussed ways of creating a stimulating environ-

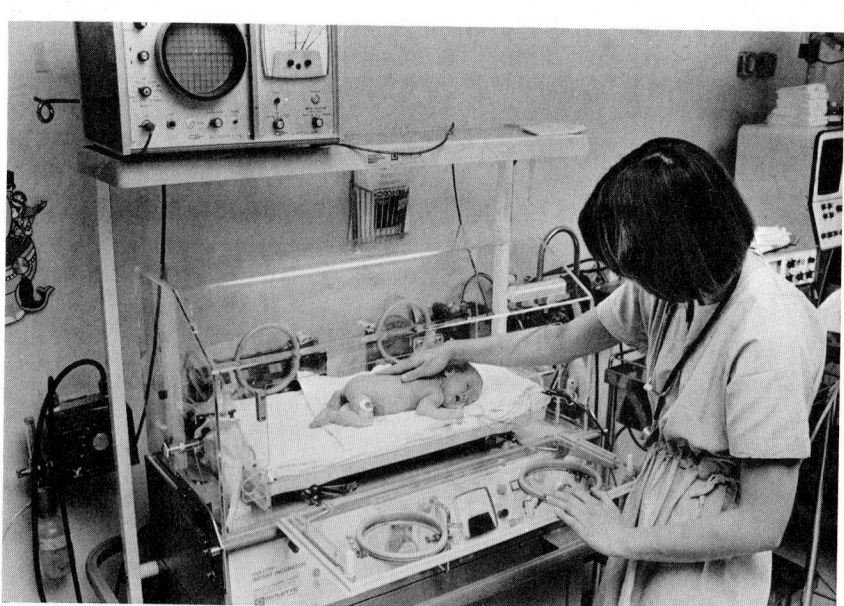

Massaging premature or low-birth-weight infants has been found to facilitate their physical and cognitive development.

ment for the infants and provided them with wall posters, rattles, bellblocks, ring stacks, and picture books.

At the end of the first year, both the experimental and the control groups of infants were tested on the Brazelton scales. Results indicated that the infants in the experimental group had a mean score of 95.3 (100 being normal), whereas those in the control group averaged 85.7. Furthermore, 78 per cent of the experimental group scored above 90, in contrast to only 34 per cent of the control group. These results were especially significant in view of the fact that at one week of age, before the experimental treatment was begun, the infants in the control group had scored higher in physical condition and on various tests of responsiveness.

Similar results were obtained by Ruth Dianne Rice (1977), who trained mothers to massage their premature infants for 15 minutes four times a day for one month after birth. In contrast to a sample of premature infants who did not receive this treatment, the infants who were given the special massage were, at four months of age, heavier and more advanced—both mentally and in terms of their neurological development.

Another group of researchers has been concerned with finding ways to facilitate motor development in infants. This is an area of considerable interest today, inasmuch as motor development in infants is strongly correlated with their cognitive development, so that if we are able to speed up infants' rate of motor development we may at the same time facilitate their intellectual development.

In this study, 26 infants, with an average age of 7 months, were seated in a dark room on a rotating chair, where they were spun slowly (at about 17 revolutions per minute) for one minute. Treatment sessions consisted of two sets of ten spins and were administered twice a week for four weeks. The infants all found the treatment enjoyable; most of them babbled and laughed, and some even fell asleep.

Tests administered a week after treatment had ended indicated that the infants who had been taken on spins were significantly advanced in motor development, as compared to a control group of infants who had not been treated. The advantage produced by the treatment is indicated by the development of a pair of three-month-old fraternal (unlike) twins, who were at the same stage of motor development before the treatment. One was assigned to the experimental group; the other was not. When the twins were tested a month later, the control twin was just beginning to develop control of his head muscles and was unable to sit up. The twin who had been subjected to spinning, however, had mastered head control and was able to sit independently (Clark, Kreutzberg, and Chee, 1977).

The results of this study are consistent with a number of other experiments in "early intervention," which usually find that mild stimulation, given routinely over an extended period of time, speeds up the development of a wide range of skills, both sensorimotor and cognitive.

An even more elaborate longitudinal study is the Milwaukee Project, conducted under the direction of Garber and Heber (1973, 1975) of the University of Wisconsin. Psychologists have long been aware that mental retardation is extremely common among children born in impoverished environments. The economically depressed area of Milwaukee in which the study took place, for example, was occupied by only two per cent of the population of the entire city, but produced 33 per cent of the mentally retarded children in the schools. The University of Wisconsin research team selected a sample of mothers whose IQs were less than 75 and hence were technically classified as mentally retarded. Their infants were randomly assigned to an experimental and a control group before they were three months old. Initially, teachers visited the homes of the infants in the experimental group, established rapport with the mothers, and played with the children. As each mother gained confidence in the teacher, her infant was taken every day to the program's center, where he spent his waking hours being played with, cuddled, and encouraged to engage in games designed to build cognitive skills. Initially, the ratio was one infant to one adult. At fifteen months, the ratio was changed to two infants to one adult and later, to three to one. Mothers were also encouraged to enroll in thirty-week programs which taught them basic academic skills, and featured on-the-job training in laundry work, food service, household work, and practical nursing.

Children in both the experimental and the control group were given cognitive tests from time to time. Results showed the expected drop below the norm for the control group, but an above-normal increase for the experimental group; gradual at first, but then slowly accelerating. By the time the children in the two groups were six-and-a-half years old, those in the experimental group had a mean IQ of 125, whereas the average for the control group was 91.[1]

An IQ of 125 is very high; only about seven per cent of all children reach such a level. The apparent reason for the outstanding success of the Milwaukee Project is the massive amount of stimulation and attention that was given the children over a period of six years, beginning with early infancy. Most other programs of "early intervention" in the lives of children from impoverished environments report only moderate elevations in IQ, but they usually start with children of nursery school age and do not provide as intensive and extensive a regimen of stimulation as did the Milwaukee Project.

---

[1] The fact that the control group children had higher mean IQs than their mothers can be explained in part by the fact that children who participate in a psychological study, even as members of a control group, are exposed to more stimulation and attention than they would receive otherwise.

A series of longitudinal studies by Wayne Dennis (1973, 1975) produced data that are consistent with the findings of the University of Wisconsin group. Dennis and his associates gathered data from 1955 until the early 1970s on the mental development of foundlings housed in a crèche, or orphanage, in Beirut, Lebanon. Children were brought to the crèche about two weeks after birth and ordinarily remained until five or six, when they went to an orphanage for older children. During the period of study, the crèche staff consisted of five nuns, who distributed their attention among about a hundred infants and young children. The adult-to-child ratio was hence very low, much lower than it would be even in a very large family, and lower than it would be in most orphanages in industrialized countries. The mean IQ of the children in the crèche was 53, which is, as Dennis observed, probably the lowest mean IQ reported for otherwise normal children. Follow-up tests of the crèche children who attended a nursery school between the ages of four and six showed that there was also marked behavioral retardation.

During the earlier phases of the study, few children went to adoptive homes. Adoption had not been common in Mediterranean countries, and particularly in the Middle East, but as families became more affluent during the period after World War II, the practice grew. By the late 1960s virtually all the crèche children were being adopted. When Dennis and his associates conducted follow-up testing of those crèche children who had been adopted, they were surprised to find that their average IQ was 81—considerably below the 100 IQ norm of the general population, but almost a 30-point gain over the crèche IQ. Gains were greater when children were adopted younger. Children adopted before one year of age showed normal intellectual growth, whereas those adopted after the age of four and a half developed at a much slower rate.

The Mother as a Source of Love or Attention

The question that naturally arises in connection with Dennis's study of adopted children is whether the increase in IQ is the result of the greater stimulation in the adoptive home, as contrasted to that of the crèche, or whether adopted children are getting something over and beyond stimulation. The term "stimulation" has mechanical and manipulative implications, and it does not seem to reflect very adequately the full range of possibilities in the "tender loving care" that a devoted mother provides for her infant.

The most obvious thing about the behavior of any newborn infant is his complete helplessness. When a need arises, his only means of tension reduction is random motor discharge. Unable to move about, to keep warm, to feed himself, to avoid danger, the infant is entirely dependent on his mother or some other person who takes her place. Because he is unable to cope with his needs, she ministers to him. The infant is a member of a household or an institution that forms his universe. The infant's contact with his universe takes place through the one who fulfills his needs—his mother or his nurse. Other individuals are to be found in his social environment, but they serve as a shadowy background to the mother figure in the foreground.

The average infant is in continuous contact with his mother. *Fed, fondled, talked to, changed, and carried about* express only a few of these forms of contact. This contact is a constant source of stimulation. The infant is encouraged to babble, to form words, to move about, and eventually to sit up, to stand up, and to walk. He is carried about through a house filled with many interesting objects and persons. In this atmosphere of contact between mother and child, the infant learns to reach out to his environment, to make his wants known, and to become a social creature.

It should be apparent by now that what a mother does in caring for an infant is more than simple carrying out of a series of acts. She is also communicating something of herself. Contact between infant and mother is, of course, partly verbal. Sensitivity on the part of both mother and infant to one another's touch, body tensions, and voiced expressions is an important source of communication between them.

Some clinical psychologists distinguish between communication, a purposive attempt to convey information, and contagion, the process by which a feeling state is transmitted from the mother to the infant. An infant who is held by a tense, anxious, or hostile adult often reacts to the experience by crying, only to quiet down when he is shifted to the arms of a more relaxed person. Contagion is not entirely subject to voluntary control. A worried mother trying to convey assurance to her infant may find that he responds to her actual feeling state and not to what she wants him to feel.

Breast Feeding Versus Bottle Feeding: A Study in Maternal Attitudes

The closest contact with the infant occurs during feeding, especially if he is breast-fed. In no other area of infant care has the controversy waxed hotter than it has in the debate over the relative merits of breast feeding and bottle feeding.

There seems to be general agreement that mother's milk is beneficial for infants, although the proponents of substitutes are inclined to argue that properly prepared formulas will do the job about as well in most instances and may even be the method of choice when infants are allergic to mother's milk. In industrialized countries, the nutritional advantages of mother's milk may be offset by the convenience and relatively low cost of substitutes, but in the rest of the world the substitution of cow's milk in either whole or dried form may involve costs that severely tax the fragile economies of poor countries. (See illustrations on pp. 234 and 235.)

Alan Berg (1973), World Bank deputy director for nutrition, says that the waste of human milk probably costs underdeveloped countries more than a billion dollars a year, and Nicholas Wade (1974) points out that a laborer in Uganda may have to spend a third of his income to buy cow's milk for an infant. In Chile, expenditures for cow's milk may run 20 per cent of a laborer's income; in Tanzania, the cost may be 50 percent.

Wade speculates that the trend away from human milk in underdeveloped countries may be the result of an uncritical imitating of the customs of industrialized countries. Bottle feeding has become a status symbol for the women living in the towns and cities of countries that lie below the poverty line, and these women serve as behavior models for mothers who live in villages and rural areas. The trend away from human milk is especially marked in Chile, where the proportion of 13-month-old children being breast-fed dropped from 95 per cent to 5 per cent during the last decade. The trend has been further accelerated by the fact that dried cow's milk has been a major item in food relief shipments sent to impoverished countries.

The increase in bottle feeding of infants has serious long-term implications in that it may contribute to higher birthrates and thus add fuel to the population explosion that threatens the social and economic survival of the entire world. John Knodel (1977), a researcher at the Population Studies Center of the University of Michigan, points out that breast feeding releases hormones in the mother that delay the resumption of the cycle of ovulation. Mothers who do not nurse, however, begin ovulating once more on the average of two months after their infants have been born. Hence the spacing between births is likely to be shorter for mothers who bottle-fed than for those who breast-feed, and the number of children per family may increase.

The usual reasons given for the trend away from breast feeding in industrialized societies are fear of "losing one's figure" (a fear that experts say is unfounded) and the need to maintain a work schedule away from home. A desire to lead a free and unhampered life may be another reason. Wade observes that the trend may have turned the corner, however, and cites evidence from a 1971 survey which showed that 32 per cent of college-educated mothers breast-fed their infants, in contrast to 8 per cent of grade-school-educated women.

Most of the controversy revolves around the sociopsychological costs and benefits of the two modes of feeding. The cost of breast feeding, as far as the mother is concerned, is the relative loss of freedom mentioned above. The rewards for her are a feeling of closeness with the infant, a freedom from monthly periods over a longer interval after childbirth, and a more rapid contraction of the uterus to its prepregnancy size. The breast-fed infant's nutritional status may also be better. Wade points out

The increases in the numbers of women in third-world countries who bottle feed their infants has led their governments to use posters to promote breast-feeding. The Zambian poster tells mothers to supplement breast milk with porridge when infants are six months old. The Ivory Coast poster says that breast feeding is healthy for baby and economical for Mama.

that in developing countries, women often lack the resources and domestic skills necessary to prepare formula food, and sources of water

may be contaminated. In industrialized countries, the long-range effects on children of differences in the two kinds of feeding are likely to be negligible (Schmitt, 1970).

But what about psychological effects on the infant? Psychologists, especially those with a psychoanalytic orientation, have traditionally maintained that the infant who is not breast-fed is the loser and therefore more susceptible to neurotic problems in childhood and even adulthood. The research does not, however, provide any substantiation for this claim.

Martin Heinstein's (1963) longitudinal research with 94 boys and girls yielded results that were consistent with earlier investigations. Although psychoanalytic theorists would predict that oral habits, such as thumb sucking, should be present in children who had been bottle-fed and not breast-fed, Heinstein's data showed that the greatest amount of thumb sucking occurred in girls who had been breast-fed and whose mothers, incidentally, had not only achieved a good marital adjustment but also had a better-than-average degree of emotional stability. Other than this, there were no very consistent patterns of childhood behavior problems that could be related to whether the child had been breast- or bottle-fed.

Heinstein concluded his report by observing that the zeal displayed by some people in urging that children be breast-fed apparently derives from "an oversimplified interpretation of psychoanalytic theory or a long held idyllic picture of mother-infant oneness." He noted, further, that nursing was only "one aspect of the total life space of the infant or child." His data also showed that certain maternal characteristics (such as whether the mother is "cold" or "warm") seem to be more strongly related to children's later adjustment than is the kind of nursing they received as infants.

Maternal Attitudes and Infant Behavior

Inasmuch as the infant's caregivers have maximum control over his environment, it follows that their attitudes and their own general behavior patterns would have a significant effect on his behavior. The work of Marjorie L. Behrens (1954) is consistent with the conclusions of Heinstein. She found that the specific kind of practices followed by mothers with respect to feeding, weaning, and toilet training were not as important as what she called the "total mother person," that is, the mother's general attitudes and conduct. Behrens divided this over-all behavior complex into three components: underlying attitudes; manner of meeting maternal roles; and observed conduct toward the child, as expressed in consistency, permissiveness or overprotection, and adaptation of maternal behavior to the child's needs rather than to specific practices. Her results, stated in general terms, showed high correlations between the various dimensions of the "total mother personality" and the emotional adjustment of the infants.

Results consistent with these general findings were also reported by Waxler and Yarrow (1975), who observed 19-month-old infants and their mothers in a study designed to identify early indications of social learning or imitation. The investigators found that infants were more likely to engage in imitative behavior when mothers reinforced, varied their behavior, and expressed enthusiasm. Mothers who were passive, bland, and relatively uninterested evoked little imitation.

Bonnie R. Seegmiller (1975) worked with black mothers and their first-born sons in a longitudinal study aimed at determining the relationship between maternal behavior patterns and scores on the Bayley infant scales. She, too, found that emotional involvement was an extremely important factor. Infants who scored higher on the mental scale had mothers who were highly involved in their sons' performance—that is, who encouraged their performance both positively, by approval, and negatively, by criticism. The mothers of high-scoring infants were also more empathic and more successful in controlling their children; they derived satisfaction from their sons' achievements and intervened actively. Low-scoring children had mothers who were passive and uninvolved.

attachment and maternal deprivation

Attachment is a term applied primarily to the strong and persistent tendency for an infant to remain near the individuals who are most significant in his life. The mother is usually, but not always, the initial target for this form of behavior, which often carries a strong emotional tone. Attachment is usually strengthened by mutual reinforcement. As the infant seeks out the mother, his approach is often reinforced by her caresses and pleasant words, just as her favorable response is reinforced by the infant's smiles.

Attachment develops out of the mutual interaction between caregiver and infant. In most families, attachment is a two-way relationship. It is not unusual for parents, mothers and fathers alike, to feel relatively neutral at first about their newborn infant, but as they become involved in feeding and cleaning duties, and see him respond to their attention by smiling and cooing or merely by looking up at them, an emotional bond of reciprocated love and affection is forged.

The test of the strength of attachment is separation. The infant breaks into a loud cry at seeing his mother depart, acting as though she had abandoned him for all time. And the mother, during her period of absence, worries about the welfare of the child who has been left with the babysitter.

Research Dealing with Attachment

Most of the studies of attachment have been concerned with infants' attachment to their caregivers. Schaffer and Emerson (1964a) traced the course of social attachment in Scottish infants from early infancy to 18 months of age by observing their reactions to a range of "separation situations"—that is, situations in which the infant was put down after

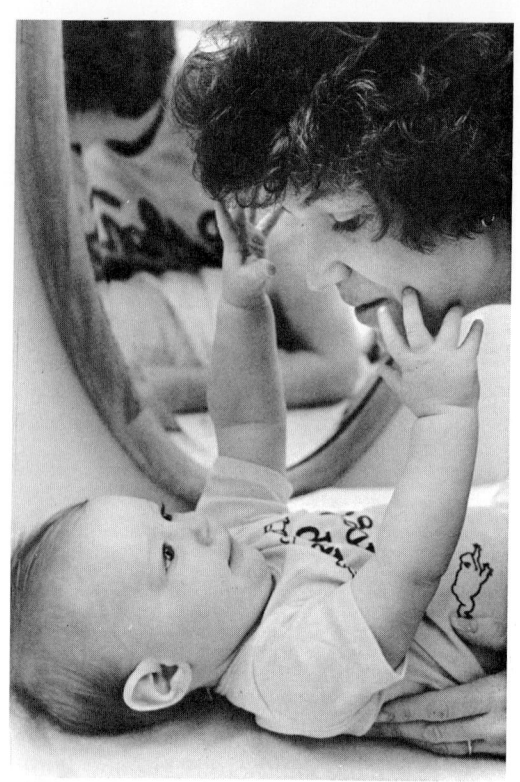

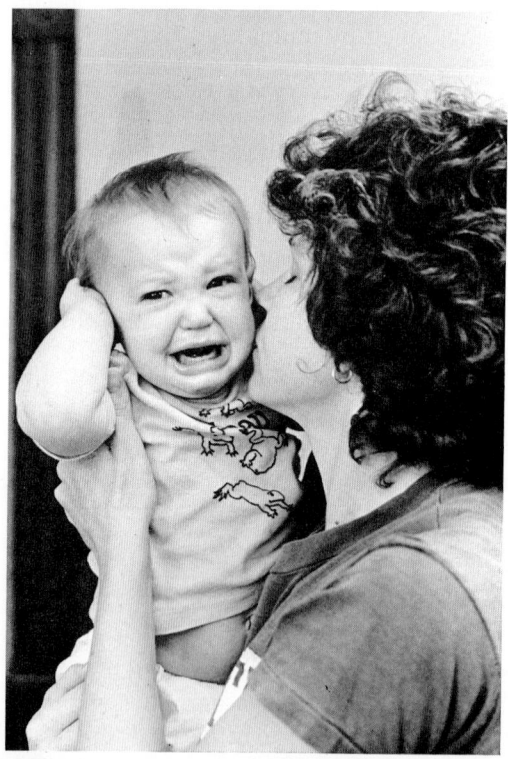

The emotional bonding between mother and infant, which psychologists call "attachment," is strengthened by their interaction. In the first picture, mutual gaze is the reinforcer. In the second picture, the possibility of being held by stranger evokes the threat of separation, with resultant panic and sobs.

being held, in which the mother left the child alone in a room or in a pram, or the like. As Figure 7-1 shows, signs of distress on such occasions tended to appear in some strength about midway through the first year, although there was considerable individual variation, with some infants showing distress at 22 weeks and others not disturbed at being separated until they were over a year old. The greatest distress occurred, on the average, between 41 and 44 weeks, as Figure 7-1 indicates.

In another set of experiments, children as young as five months old were observed once a month in a standardized routine in which a female stranger approached the infant, called him by name, and picked him up. This procedure was followed first in the mother's presence, then in her absence. The reaction of the infants was determined by heart rate measures, coded facial expressions, crying, and postural data (such as stiffening or relaxing). The investigators found no consistent point at which fear could be said to develop, although the onset of some wariness or negative reaction could be placed somewhere in the second half of the first year. Less than 20 per cent of the infants showed such indications at seven months, but almost 60 per cent did so at ten months. There was also much individual variation among infants, with the more wary and apprehensive infants showing considerably greater acceleration in heart rate than the nonwary ones (Waters, Matas, and Sroufe, 1975).

The degree to which infants are attached to their mothers is shown by an experiment by Smith, Zwerg, and Smith (1963), who placed infants in a playpen in such a way that each infant could see his mother, a stranger, or a neutral stimulus on a television screen. The playpen revolved slowly, so that the infant could, by crawling, keep the image in view.

Results showed that infants between 10 and 20 months of age would

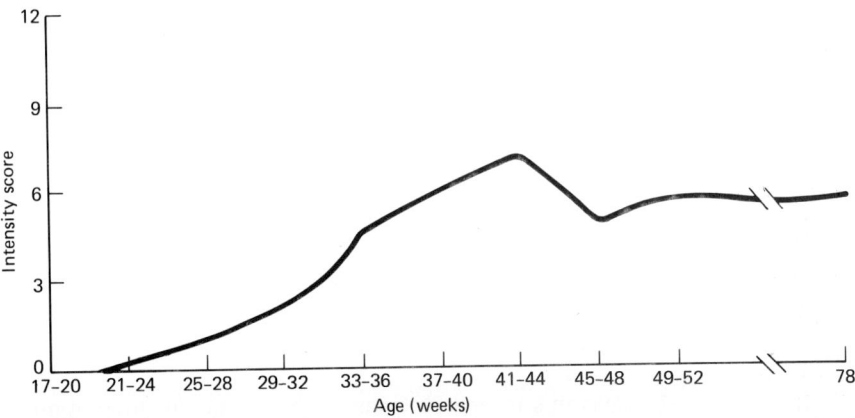

FIGURE 7-1. Development of attachment to the mother, as indicated by intensity of distress in separation situations. (After Schaffer and Emerson, 1964a.)

spend about 35 seconds of a one-minute experimental period crawling to keep in visual contact with the image of the mother, in contrast to about 30 seconds for a stranger, and 15 seconds in a control condition. Infants between 22 and 26 months, however, spent 52 seconds in visual contact with the mother image, 45 seconds with the stranger, 16 seconds with the control contact. With children older than 26 months, the "orienting" behavior toward the mother continued to increase, whereas the interest in the stranger dropped off somewhat. The experimenters also noted that the sharp increase in attempting to keep in contact with the mother, which occurred between 22 and 26 months, coincided with the age at which crying at environmental changes reaches its peak.

Green and Gordon (1964) conducted a somewhat related study that demonstrates the importance of early visual experiences. They separated infant monkeys temporarily from their mothers and placed them in chambers whose single window could be opened by pressing a bar. Previous experience with infant monkeys had shown that they quickly learn how to operate the device and do so repeatedly for the reward of looking briefly through the window into the next room, even when it is empty. In Green and Gordon's experiment, there were two press bars and two windows, each looking out into a different room. This arrangement enabled the researchers to determine the relative preference of the infants for various types of stimuli. Results showed that when anything was placed in one of the rooms, the infants chose that room over the empty room, preferring to look at something rather than nothing. The stimulus that evoked the greatest amount of bar pressing, however, was an adult female monkey. The infants worked harder to see this "mother figure" than they did for views of food, other infants, or plastic forms.

Attachment and Basic Trust

Infancy, as David Elkind (1967) has pointed out, is not only a period in which the child makes social attachments, it is also a period in which he establishes a fundamental feeling tone about the world and the people in it. As we noted in Chapter 4, Erikson (1963) has described this attitude as one of *basic trust*—the expectation that people are reliable and that they will meet one's needs. This expectation develops out of the normal experiences of being cared for on a basis of unconditional acceptance. When needs are not met or acceptance is given only hesitatingly or begrudgingly, the child may get the feeling that the world is unreliable or even a dangerous place. His characteristic attitude becomes one of mistrust, which undermines future attempts to establish healthy relationships with others.

If one accepts Erikson's interpretations of this phase of development, then it becomes obvious that mothering plays a crucial role in infancy, as far as later personality development is concerned.

One dramatic way in which the crucial significance of mothering has been demonstrated may be found in the study of infants deprived of maternal care. Maternal deprivation occurring after an infant has had a satisfactory relationship with his mother for the first six months leads, according to René Spitz (1948), to a condition he termed *anaclitic depression*. One of Spitz's case studies of maternal deprivation is summarized as follows:

> There is first what is described as a "visual search for mother." Such infants cannot be quieted, some cry bitterly, others less vehemently but they cannot be soothed. Nevertheless, at this stage they cling to any adult available.
> The picture changes as the mother continues to be absent. The infant becomes very quiet, does not look up when adults enter the room, does not play, and does not grasp at objects. Along with this passivity and dejection he develops eating difficulties, loses weight and sleeps fitfully. The level of his development generally does not proceed normally and may even decline.

When an infant has no consistent relationship with a caregiver from early infancy onward, a condition termed *marasmus* is said to develop. The following case description is summarized from a longer description by Margaret Ribble (1943):

> The child was normal, weighing over six pounds. The two weeks' stay in the hospital was uneventful. On returning home the mother discovered her husband had deserted her. Thereafter her milk did not agree with the baby. Since the infant refused the breast and began to vomit, he was hospitalized. The mother did not come to see him at this time or later, thus deserting him.
> He was in a crowded ward, and received little attention or handling. He became a finger sucker and spit up whatever he had eaten. At two months of age, he weighed about five pounds and had an appearance of a seven-month fetus, with wasted arms and legs, large head, and large protruding abdomen.
> A thorough physical examination revealed nothing of an organic nature. Concentrated nursing care was given him, and he was fed while being held in a nurse's lap for a half-hour at a time. His position was changed frequently, and he was carried about whenever possible. After some slow improvement, a volunteer "mother" began to come to the hospital twice daily. Her visits were gradually lengthened until she was spending an hour with him on each visit. She had been told the infant needed loving care and physical contact, which she gave him.
> The results were such that by five months of age he weighed nine pounds. He was not alert and vigorous, although some remnants of his difficulties remained, such as retarded motor coordination and finger sucking.

When the writings of Spitz and Ribble appeared over a generation ago, they stimulated some research and a great deal of theorizing. John Bowlby (1951), for instance, wrote an eloquent defense of the thesis that an infant must experience a warm, continuous relationship with a mother or a mother surrogate (substitute) if he is to develop in a mentally healthy way.

Within a few years, however, the studies on which such pronouncements were made came under attack from a number of critics, who cited such weaknesses as inadequate design, uncontrolled factors, imprecise measurements, impressionistic observations, and failure to report crucial data. The clinical pictures of anaclitic depression and marasmus presented by Spitz and Ribble were also challenged by investigators who claimed that infants may display other clinical patterns or even *none at all* as a consequence of institutional life (O'Connor and Franks, 1961; Pinneau, 1955; Yarrow, 1961; Wolins, 1970).

Animal Research with Maternal Deprivation

In more recent years, however, the tide has swung the other way, and psychologists are now more willing to accept the reports of earlier investigators. Their research probably was impressionistic, poorly controlled, and even haphazard, but the fact that more recent studies with maternally deprived infant monkeys yield virtually the same results strongly suggests that the earlier findings were essentially valid, especially in instances in which infants received insufficient stimulation and social contact.

A study by Hinde and Spencer-Booth (1971) yielded outcomes that are typical. They conducted experiments in which infant rhesus monkeys were separated from their mothers at 21 to 32 weeks old—an age at which a rhesus infant still gets milk from its mother but is also capable of feeding itself. The separation period varied between 6 and 13 days. During the first few days of separation, the infants called out a good deal at first and also showed depressed locomotor and play activity, a condition that persisted up to a month after the mother and infant were reunited. Even at the age of 30 months, the behavior of the experimental monkeys was quite different from that of the controls: they engaged in less exploratory behavior, were less actively social, and were more inclined to sit and engage in nonsocial play.

In one test situation, year-old monkeys observed a mirror or a banana placed in an adjoining cage into which a narrow passageway had been opened. In contrast to the control monkeys, those who had experienced the separation some five or six months earlier were more reluctant to enter the strange cage, and once having entered it, spent less time there investigating the object. Not only were they less curious, they also showed a greater degree of apprehensiveness.

Kaufman and Rosenblum (1967) conducted a similar set of experiments with macaque monkeys aged five to six months, who were separated from their mothers for a four-week period and then reunited.

At the start of the separation period, the infants behaved in a very agitated manner. There was much pacing, searching, frequent trips to the door and window, short bursts of erratic play, and frequent movements toward the other members of the cage group. There was also an increased amount of finger sucking, mouthing and handling of various parts of the body, and cooing—the rather plaintive distress call of the young macaque. These reactions continued during most of the first day, during which time the infants did not sleep.

After 24 to 36 hours, the behavior pattern of three of the four infants changed considerably. They sat hunched over, rolled almost into balls, often with their heads between their legs (see Figure 7-2). Such movement as did occur seemed to be in slow motion. They rarely responded to social gestures made by other infants, and play behavior virtually ceased. They appeared disinterested in and alienated from their environment. Occasionally they would look up and coo. Kaufman and Rosenblum observed that the behavior of the infants at this stage of separation was strikingly similar to the "anaclitic depression" that Spitz had observed in human infants deprived of their mothers.

After about a week, the depression gradually lifted, although never completely. Play with peers was still alternated with periods of depression, but in a less severe form. By the end of the month of separation,

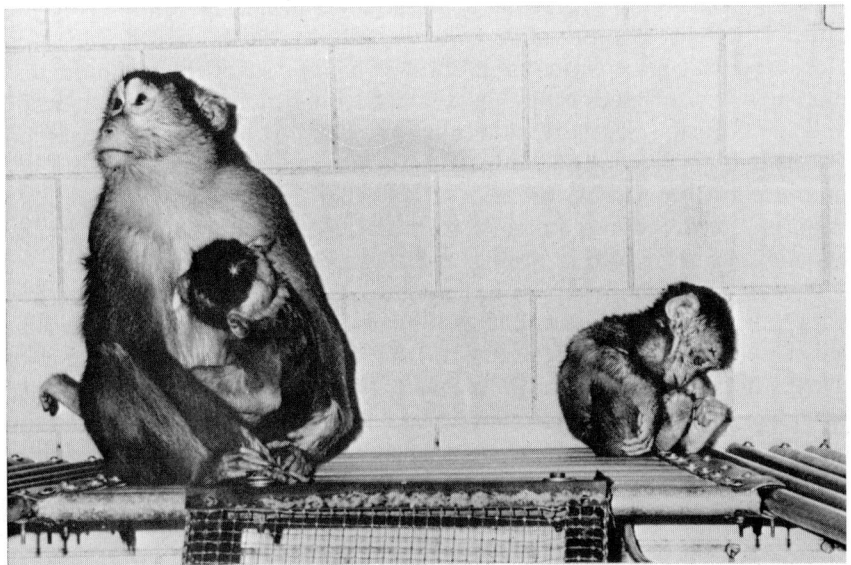

FIGURE 7-2. The effect of maternal deprivation. The depressed posture of the infant at the right is characteristic of infant macaque monkeys after the first day of separation from their mothers. The young monkey at the left is clinging to its mother in a way that is normal for five-month-old monkeys. (Kaufman and Rosenblum, 1967. Copyright 1967 by the American Association for the Advancement of Science.)

the infants appeared alert and active much of the time, yet they still did not behave like typical infants their age.

When the mothers were reintroduced into the cage, another major change occurred in the infants' behavior. Clinging behavior and nipple contact increased dramatically, an effect that continued even until the third month after separation. The persistence of this behavior is significant, because this is a period in which infant monkeys generally reduce close contact with their mothers.

Adequate Stimulation as an Antidote to Deprivation

Humans are not monkeys, of course, and one should not overinterpret the findings of these two experiments, even though they parallel in a number of ways the studies of maternal deprivation of human infants. One difference is that monkey infants can move about and play more readily than human infants; Kaufman and Rosenblum observed that this ability may have made it possible for the monkey infants to recover to some degree from their depression. Another difference is that human adults may take some initiative in providing care and attention to infants that are not their own, whereas monkey adults do not, as Figure 7-2 indicates.

Nevertheless, there may be some general principles underlying the effect of maternal deprivation in both humans and monkeys. Harry F. Harlow (1962), in a series of studies we shall discuss next, found that monkeys reared under mother-deprived conditions became neurotic and maladjusted sexually as adults, but that some of these unwanted effects can be avoided if the infants are not reared in isolation, but are permitted to interact with their peers. What this suggests is that while maternal deprivation may be initially disorganizing for monkeys, it may be compensated for at least in part by other types of stimulation.

It may well be that the clinical signs of marasmus and anaclitic depression reported by Ribble and Spitz were the results of insufficient handling and stimulation. Consider the situation prevailing in some of the institutions studied by Spitz (1945, 1946). The sides of the infants' cribs were covered by blankets, and no toys were available, so that the only visual experiences came from staring at the blank ceiling; certainly these were conditions making for visual deprivation. There was, furthermore, infrequent opportunity for tactile or kinesthetic stimulation.

Harry F. Harlow's (1958) experiments with monkeys lend support to the idea that stimulation in the form of tactile contact is sought by infants. Young monkeys separated from their mothers were "mothered" by the two "surrogate mothers" illustrated in Figure 7-3. One figure was made of a block of wood covered with rubber and cloaked in terry cloth. The second figure, made of wire mesh, differed only in being unable to supply "contact comfort," but in one series of trials it supplied the milk for the infant from a nipple protruding from the figure's front. Light bulbs supplied warmth to both figures. When the infant was allowed free access to either mother, he sought the "lactating," wire mesh mother less and less, whereas he spent more time clinging to the terry-cloth mother, who provided no milk. If the infant was frightened or placed in a strange situation, he rushed to the cloth mother, clung to her, and caressed her. When the terry-cloth mother was present, the infant monkey would venture out to explore a fear-arousing stimulus; when the wire-mesh mother was present, he tended to explore neither the surrounding space nor the strange object. Harlow observed that this "affectional contact" with the cloth mother persisted for many weeks.

Harlow concluded that infant monkeys had an inborn desire for the stimulation obtained from the terry-cloth mother; hence they became emotionally attached to it. Tactile sensory contact with soft, yielding substances or material has been demonstrated to be important in the behavior of infant monkeys, and it is plausible to suppose that it is important for human infants as well.

attachment, dependence, and independence

Dependency may be defined as a condition in which one relies on the help of others in attaining one's goals. This is functional or instrumental dependence. In any society, no matter how primitive, members are functionally dependent on each other for survival, defense, and securing the necessities and comforts of everyday life. We are, furthermore, more functionally dependent at infancy than at any other stage because we are literally quite unable to help ourselves.

Dependency may also be described as a tendency to seeking nurturance—attention, care, and support—from others. This is emotional dependence, a need that we all have to some extent, but it again is stronger during childhood than at other ages.

Functional/instrumental dependence and emotional dependence become merged during infancy. As we noted earlier, the interaction between caregiver and child during the earlier weeks of his life blossoms into attachment, and the emotional rewards of being cared for may become as important as the care itself. The process also works the other way, of course: caregivers come to have a "need to be needed."

Strivings for Independence

Almost as fast as the infant learns to seek help from his caregivers, he learns to get along without it. Independence becomes an end in itself.

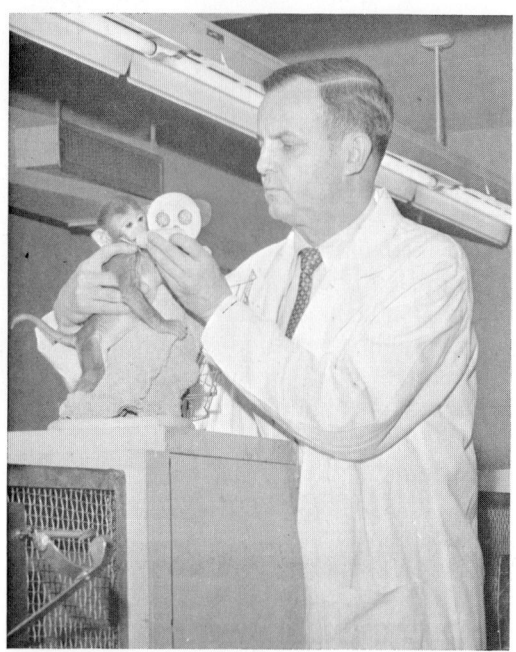

FIGURE 7-3. Harry F. Harlow poses with an infant rhesus monkey that has been separated from its mother and clings to a terry-cloth doll that has been provided by the investigators as a surrogate mother. In the second picture, a mother-deprived infant maintains its grip on its "cloth mother," while it takes nourishment from a nipple in its "wire mother." Monkeys raised in isolation with cloth or wire mothers displayed abnormal behavior as adults unless they, like those in the third photograph, had enjoyed opportunities to engage in daily rough-and-tumble play with other infants.

Rheingold and Eckerman (1970) note that as soon as the infant is able to move, he begins to separate himself from his mother. At first, he does so by inching along on his belly.

> Later he creeps, and then walks away from his mother. He goes out the door and enters another room. In time he walks out of the house, plays in the yard all morning, goes to school, goes still farther away to high school, then to college and to work. He crosses the country, and now he may even go to the moon. Eventually he sets up his own home and produces infants who, in turn, repeat the process.

Rheingold and Eckerman point out that the infant's separation from his mother is of great psychological importance, because it greatly widens his opportunities to interact with the environment. As long as he is in physical contact with his mother, his universe is limited to her person and the adjoining environment. There are limits to what even the most attentive and indulgent mother can bring to an infant. Even when he is carried about, his contacts with the environment are severely limited. Hence the universe can only be explored and understood if the infant becomes separated from his mother.

It makes considerable difference whether the separation is effected voluntarily or not. As we noted previously, human infants who are separated from their mothers after the age of six months or so express or resentment, and infant monkeys go into a stage of restlessness and random hyperactivity, followed by depression. Infants, whether they are human or monkey, can enjoy separation from their mothers only if

Two of the leading investigators of attachment, dependence, and independence are Harriet L. Rheingold of the University of North Carolina and H. L. Schaffer of the University of Strathclyde in Glasgow, Scotland.

they initiate it and are free to return at any moment. When monkey infants leave their mothers, the mothers at first make repeated attempts to retrieve them, but yield after a few weeks. Human mothers make little attempt to retrieve infants, as long as they are not engaging in activities dangerous or injurious.[2]

Rheingold and Eckerman set up a number of experimental situations in which mothers and their ten-month-old infants were placed in one of two adjoining rooms. About two thirds of the infants were in a crawling stage; of the remaining third, half could scoot on their bellies and the other half were already toddling. The experimental manipulations consisted of placing one or more toys in an adjoining room connected to the first room by an open door, through which an infant could see his mother, should he decide to explore the second room. Even when there were no toys in the second room, infants spent about a third of the ten-minute observation period in it. When a toy was placed in the second room, the infants spent a little more time in it, often bringing the toy back to the first room. Infants who visited the second room did not stay there, but instead went back and forth, as though testing the situation and trying their freedom.

---

[2] We must qualify this statement as applying primarily to Western, and particularly to the North American, cultures, in which infants and children are encouraged to behave and act in independent ways. In many Asian and Mediterranean cultures, independence is discouraged, or at least is not encouraged. Sibling caregivers in these cultures often act as extensions of their mothers in encouraging dependence and punishing independence. The underlying motive, however, is not necessarily one of wanting the infant's dependence for its own sake, but is an expression of the prevailing attitude that regards the world as generally hazardous and unconcerned—a view that may be fairly realistic.

In the next phase of the experiment, infants who had participated in the first phase without the toy were now retested with a toy in the adjoining room. The familiarity of the experimental environment was evidently reassuring, because they now spent considerably less time with their mothers and about half of the ten-minute observation period in the second room. Those infants who had experience with the toy in the first observation did not increase their time in the second room on the second trial when one toy was present, but did increase it considerably when three toys were available.

The results were consistent with the idea that infants are attracted by novelty and seek to maximize their stimulation, at least under conditions where they can maintain visual contact with their mothers and feel free to return to them at any time.

Independence and Self-Concept

In his second year, the infant is able to move about. In doing so, he shows the overwhelming importance of independence. He is enthusiastically everywhere and on his own as much as possible. He walks, climbs, jumps, and trots; he pushes his stroller instead of riding in it; he carries things and wants to put on and take off his own clothes. Most of the time he does what he is told, but he may nevertheless show his dawning independence in saying, "no, no" to anything and everything, persistently and vehemently.

We are also aware of this tendency toward independence when we reconsider the evidence about the emergence of self during infancy. The infant has the sense of being a person—a bit fuzzy as to the boundaries of the self, to be sure, but a person for all that, and *he* wants what *he* wants when *he* wants it. One of the factors facilitating the emergence of the self is the oppositional quality of many of the infant's activities. In becoming a person, he wants to be independent. In addition to protesting against help, there is the obvious pride he takes in doing something on his very own, which also reveals tendencies toward independence.

But in all of this pushing out into the world, in his seeking of independence, there is vacillation. The infant takes two steps forward and one step backward, sometimes literally. Off on some gallant adventure, but just out of his mother's sight, he bursts into tears and flees back.

_____on babysitters and other
surrogate mothers

Although the research we have cited regarding both animals and humans suggests that attachment may be a universal phenomenon, other studies raise doubts as to whether an infant must maintain relatively uninterrupted attachment with a single caregiver in order to develop normally.

The Kibbutz Experience

The question of whether changes from one mother figure to another have a disturbing effect has been explored to some extent in the Israeli collective farm settlements, or *kibbutzim*. From early infancy onward, kibbutz children are placed in a nursery, where they are cared for by a substitute or surrogate mother, the *metapalet*. The infants' own mothers do, however, visit them regularly and may even breast-feed them.

The general environment of the kibbutz is warm and supportive. Despite the fact that the kibbutz infant does not see as much of his mother as other infants do of theirs, he does see her frequently and does not experience anything like the maternal deprivation of infants who live in institutions that have an unfavorable caregiver-to-infant ratio.

Rabin (1965) compared kibbutz-reared children with a control group of children from other Israeli villages. In contrast to control infants, kibbutz infants showed some signs of developmental retardation, which Rabin attributed to a level of stimulation which was probably lower than that found in family settings. However, children 9 to 11 years of age who had been reared in kibbutzim appeared to be clearly superior in both intelligence and in social and emotional maturity, when compared to children who lived in villages.

In reviewing research dealing with the communal raising of children, Robert A. LeVine (1970) commented that the evidence regarding the effects of the kibbutz experience on children's psychological characteristics is conflicting. Although it is fairly clear that the children are within the normal ranges of mental health and intelligence, they also seem to be more superficial in their relations with others, more other-directed with respect to their peers, and better suited to army life in adulthood, in contrast to children raised under more usual circumstances. Observers are not, however, in agreement on these latter points.

Working Mothers and Day Care Centers

Popular belief, even in these free-wheeling days, has it that the children of working mothers are neglected and deprived of normal emotional satisfactions and, as a result, are likely to become juvenile delinquents or neurotic misfits.

Research over the years has, however, failed to find evidence to support such conclusions. Hoffman and Nye (1974) have reviewed much of it in their book on working mothers and conclude that maternal employment, as such, does not foster deprivation of the child. It does reduce childbearing, but only among women who have highly satisfying jobs. Rather than increasing dissension and conflict between spouses, it seems to decrease it. Working mothers also have better physical health, although this may be a contributing cause, rather than an effect, of employment.

The research of Anna-Beth Doyle (1975) produced typical findings. She observed infants aged five to thirty months, who were routinely left in a day center that provided one adult staff member for each four children. Their experiences produced at least one positive effect. The children had a mean IQ of 117 on the Cattell Infant Intelligence Scale, in contrast to 109 for a matched control group of children who had remained at home with their mothers. Other comparisons showed minor differences between the groups: in contrast to home-care infants, the day-care infants initiated fewer social contacts, looked at strangers less frequently, and had more respiratory ailments. Outside of the last variable, there seem to have been no negative effects resulting from the day-care experience.

Somewhat similar results were obtained by another team of researchers, who monitored the care mothers and substitute caregivers gave black infants five to six months old. Some of the infants were cared for by their mothers, and the others were cared for either by relatives or by paid babysitters. In contrast to the substitute caregivers, mothers were found to express positive feelings more often, engage in more social play, provide a greater variety of social stimulation, and make available a greater variety of play objects. The length of time the substitute caregiver had been in charge of the infants was an important factor, however; the behavior of those who had been in charge for several months tended to resemble that of the mothers. The obvious explanation is that the greater the length of time, the more the caregiver became emotionally involved with the infant.

The researchers also compared the mental and motor development of the two groups of infants and found virtually no difference between them (Rubenstein, Pedersen, and Yarrow, 1977).

Animal Research

The kind of communal infant rearing that is conducted at nurseries in kibbutzim and elsewhere is rare among subhuman animals, where attachment to a single mother is the general rule. In some species of mice, however, females may combine their young in a communal nest, which they may share for several consecutive litters, even including the litters of their daughters. Pregnant mice housed in the same cage may build one nest, combine their litters after birth, and nurse them simultaneously, often taking turns at feeding all the pups in the commune.

Sayler and Salmon (1969, 1971) conducted a controlled longitudinal study of a number of mice litters, in which single mothers nesting alone raised 7 or 14 pups, groups of two mothers nesting communally raised 14 pups, and groups of three mothers nesting communally raised 14 or 21 pups. Results showed, as might be expected, that fewer pups per mother resulted in faster growth and higher body weights, presumably because of the greater availability of milk. When the pup-to-mother ratio was held constant, however, the communal pups made proportionately greater gains, as compared with those raised in single-mother nests, and three-mother communes produced better results than two-mother communes.

The authors speculated that the superiority of the communal experience could be attributed to more efficient nursing, greater warmth, and more tactile stimulation. It is difficult to say, of course, how much of the advantage in growth can be assigned to each of these variables, but the similarity between the results of this experiment and those of the early stimulation studies is obvious.

As such, Sayler and Salmon's research adds an interesting footnote to the studies of human infants reared by a single mother or mother substitute, or by two or more. In view of the interest during recent years in communal living arrangements among young adults, perhaps we will see additional research on the effects of communal living and infant care on the development of children. Problems of instituting adequate controls are always difficult in such studies, but each one adds something to our understanding of the effects of social stimulation on infants and young children.

Mothers and Mother Substitutes as Motivators

Before we leave the topic of maternal influence during infancy, it may be well to consider one more animal study that has interesting if puzzling implications.

Different breeds of the same or similar animal often behave differently under similar circumstances. Beagles are ordinarily less active than terriers; when terriers have been kept in isolation, they become more active when released, whereas beagles become less so (Fuller, 1967). Wild Norway rats tend to be quite aggressive, but laboratory rats are tame, placid, and docile. Laboratory mice, on the other hand, will characteristically fight when placed in a box together. This is species-specific behavior and is usually thought to be instinctive or innate.

Victor H. Denenberg (1971) conducted an interesting series of experiments in which mouse pups were raised by laboratory rat mothers. Experience has shown that rat mothers treat foster mouse pups appropriately and even tenderly, nursing them, grooming them, and retrieving them when they fall out of the nest. What is of great interest here, however, is that pairs of inbred mice raised by a rat mother do *not* fight when placed in a box. Evidently something happens during their infancy that extinguishes their normal fighting tendencies. That "something" is not the difference in mouse and rat milk, for mouse pups raised by rat "aunts" whose nipples had been surgically removed were also likely to refrain from fighting, even when they had been raised with other mouse "siblings."

This effect apparently applies only to *inbred* laboratory mice and does not obtain with Swiss albino mice, whose fighting tendencies are undiminished by experience with rat foster mothers or aunts. Another mouse tendency, however, was affected by foster care. Mice show a great deal more open-field activity, such as running around and exploring, than do laboratory rats. When the amount of open-field activity was taken as a dependent variable, both inbred and Swiss albino mice who had been reared by rat mothers or aunts showed less activity. The lower activity level was also positively correlated with lower levels of corticosterone in the blood plasma of the experimental animals. Corticosterone is released by the cortex of the adrenal gland its level in the blood may be taken as an index of emotional reactivity. In other words, both the overt behavior and the blood chemistry of the experimental animals were evidently modified by their experience as pups.

Denenberg confessed that he was surprised at the results he had obtained in his research and commented:

> Even though I am a firm believer in motherhood, I must admit that when we started this set of experiments I did not expect to find that the mother's behavior during the nursing period would have such a powerful effect upon so many different biobehavioral systems of the animal. Clearly, if these results have any degree of generality to other mammals, the subtle and not so subtle behavior patterns of the mother during the early stages of the neonate's development have very profound and far-reaching effects.

summary

Infants are influenced by caregivers (mothers, fathers, siblings, parent substitutes) and influence them in return. Although fathers have significant affects on infant development, most research deals with the infant's interaction with his mother. Much of what caregivers provide for infants can be classified as stimulation. Research with animals indicates that early stimulation has generally positive effects on infant development and can promote significant growth of the cerebral cortex—the "thinking area" of the brain. The theory that such stimulation must occur during a critical period in development is not well supported, however, for research suggests that deficiencies resulting from early understimulation can be made up later.

Research with human infants indicates that early stimulation involving a number of different sense modalities is beneficial. In one study of stimulus enrichment, significant results were obtained with low-birth-weight infants. Rotating infants twice a week for brief periods has been found to facilitate their motor development. In another investigation, children of low-IQ mothers from deprived urban areas were placed in a special program during early infancy and were followed for six years. In contrast to a control group, the children in the experimental group had markedly higher IQs. In still another longitudinal study, children in a Lebanese orphanage had mean IQs far below the norm. When the children were adopted, IQs rose, especially for those who had left the orphanage during infancy.

A question that arises with such studies is whether accelerated gains result from increased stimulation or from the "tender loving care" of mothers. The closest contact with the infant occurs during feeding, especially if he is breast-fed. Greater convenience and more personal freedom seem to be the motives in the trend toward bottle feeding of infants in industrialized nations, but mothers in developing countries are imitating this practice as well, in spite of the fact that it strains the economies of these countries. There seem to be some short-range psychological advantages to breast feeding, but in the long run, differences between children who have been breast fed or bottle fed appear to be negligible. What does seem to be important is the general emotional tone of the mother-infant relationship. Mothers who take an active interest in their children's behavior and development seem to elicit more social learning or imitative behavior and to have infants who score higher on scales of mental development than do infants whose mothers are passive and uninvolved.

The infant's tendency to orient himself toward and to remain close to a caregiver, usually the mother, is termed attachment. The test of the attachment bond is separation. Signs of distress at separation, coupled with wariness toward strangers, appear in the second half of the first year of life. Human infants will crawl to maintain visual contact with a televised image of their mothers, and monkey infants will press bars for the chance to look at a female monkey in another room. According to Erikson, the experience of being cared for on an "unconditional acceptance" basis is essential, if the infant is to develop basic trust. Spitz observed that infants separated from their mothers decline into what he termed an anaclitic depression. Total maternal deprivation is said to cause marasmus, a condition in which infants literally waste away, according to Ribble. The research studies of Spitz and Ribble have been questioned on methodological grounds, but recent research with infant monkeys tends to confirm their general conclusions. The effects of maternal deprivation can apparently be reversed by supplementing additional stimulation, both physical and social.

Functional and emotional dependency are both an effect and a cause of attachment. As soon as an infant begins to seek help from others, he begins to assert his independence. One indication is his tendency to roam further from his mother, in order to explore and become involved in interesting and novel activities. In the second year of life, he may express negative reactions toward demands that he conform or cooperate. Such activities aid the formation of his self-concept.

Research with child-care arrangements explores the strength and importance of infant-mother attachment bonds. Children raised in kibbutzim appear to suffer no ill effects from being placed in the charge of different caregivers. They seem socially and mentally very mature, although perhaps more other-directed than other children. Children placed in child-care arrangements because of maternal employment seem to be as well adjusted as other children. Research with species of mice that practice communal raising of litters reveals that having multiple mothers produces faster growth and higher body weights among the pups, even when the pup-to-mother ratio is held constant. Other research with laboratory mice has found that certain behavioral tendencies such as fighting and open-field activity—thought to be innate—are significantly weaker when mice pups are reared by laboratory rat foster mothers. The fact that laboratory rats are much more placid than mice suggests that some of the foster mothers' behavior pattern was transmitted to the mice when they were pups.

iii

early childhood: the preschool years

eight

Physical and Cognitive Aspects of Development

It is thought that the processes of growth are self-stabilizing, or, to take another analogy, "target-seeking." Children, no less than rockets, have their trajectories, governed by the control systems of their genetic constitution and powered by energy absorbed from the natural environment. Deflect the child from its growth trajectory by acute malnutrition or illness, and a restoring force develops so that as soon as the missing food is supplied or the illness terminated the child catches up toward its original curve. When it gets there, it slows down again to adjust its path to the old trajectory once more.
—J. M. TANNER (1970)

The period of early childhood begins with the final stages of infancy, somewhere in the second half of the second year of life, and ends at about age five, when children are ready to embark on their school career and enter kindergarten. Inasmuch as an increasing number of children today, particularly in urban areas, are enrolled in nursery schools or play schools, this period is also referred to as the "nursery school years" or the "preschool years." The first few months of early childhood are also referred to as the "toddler period," for obvious reasons.

These are crucial years. Stanley Bijou (1975) suggests that the preschool period may be the most important one for the individual, for it is then that the foundations are laid for complex behavioral structures. Piaget and Inhelder (1969) point out that it is during these years that the child develops the ability to think and thereby becomes less dependent on sensorimotor actions for the direction of his behavior. This is the period, in other words, in which the child is transformed from someone who depends on action structures to someone who employs thought structures.

physical growth and development

Psychological data on physical growth and development during this period are relatively meager, and we must turn to medical researchers for much of our information. Much of the material that has been gathered is also concerned with sensory and perceptual processes, rather than with hand-eye coordination, large-muscle activity, and other aspects of physical development. There are, nevertheless, some data available that serve to outline physical development during this period, albeit roughly and sketchily.

Height and Weight

The years of early childhood continue the rapid physical growth in height and weight so obvious in infancy, but at a somewhat slower pace. Different parts of the body, however, have different periods of rapid and slow growth so that the proportions are changing throughout childhood, with the skeleton remaining more stable while fat deposits increase and diminish. There are anatomical changes that can be classified as changes in kind, as in prenatal life with the appearance of new types of cells; changes in number, such as the sheer quantity of cells in organs, teeth, and bones; changes of position, such as occur in the heart and the teeth; changes in size, shape, and composition, such as the darkening of eye color or skin.

At five years of age, children average about nine inches taller than they were at age two, and have also gained about four or five pounds per year during the same period. Slow-growing and fast-growing children will of course vary from these averages. At five the average American boy weighs 43 pounds and is 44 inches tall. Girls tend to be slightly shorter and lighter.

By five children's stature tends to be a fairly good predictor of their final mature height, inasmuch as the correlation between height at five and at maturity has been found to be .70 (Watson and Lowry, 1958). It should be noted, however, that this relationship may not apply under some conditions. For example, poorly nourished children do not grow at the same rate as those who are adequately nourished, and children in larger families tend to lag in both height and weight behind children in smaller families (Tanner, 1970).

Health Problems

The preschool period is the time when childhood illnesses are at their peak, particularly colds and other respiratory diseases, which increase during the second year of life and then drop off during the sixth year. Boys seem to be somewhat more vulnerable to respiratory infections during this period; for girls, the vulnerable period seems to be the years from six to eight. Gastrointestinal complaints and other abdominal disorders are most frequent during the first year of life and then drop off sharply to the sixth year, rising somewhat during the middle years of childhood. Allergies follow a somewhat similar course, with the incidence being much lower. Figure 8-1 gives a schematic representation of these trends (Bayer and Snyder, 1950).

Parents characteristically worry a great deal about childhood diseases. They appear very suddenly: a child may be playing vigorously and energetically during the afternoon and then have a considerable fever by bedtime. Fevers can quickly reach dramatic heights: 105° is not unusual. At such times, parents torment themselves with guilt feelings: "Maybe I didn't dress him warmly enough," "Perhaps I shouldn't have let him go into the water so soon after eating," and the like. They are inclined to feel that the illness is their fault, that if they had done their duty and been more protective, the child would not have become ill. The fact of the matter is, however, that a high incidence of illness of various types during childhood is normal. One might even hypothesize that a certain amount of experience with infectious ailments is probably a good thing, enabling the child's body to develop antibodies that help it cope with recurring infections.

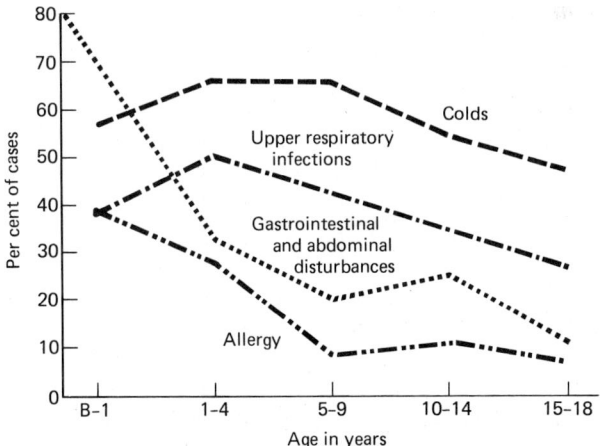

FIGURE 8-1. Relative incidence of various illness categories for a group of normal children. (Bayer and Snyder, 1950. Reproduced by permission.)

262 Early Childhood: The Preschool Years

Childhood diseases also have their psychological aspects. Emotional stress has sometimes been identified as a precipitating factor in infections, and some ailments, such as allergies, are strongly suspected of being caused by stressful relations with parents. Research evidence for these contentions tends to be somewhat sketchy, however, and the usual treatment is medical rather than psychological. Prader, Tanner, and von Harnack (1963), however, report the interesting case of a child who, during early childhood, had two episodes of *anorexia nervosa*, an emotional disorder in which there is a marked loss of appetite for no discernible physical reason. Figure 8-2 consists of a "smoothed curve," representing the average height for normal children, and a more irregular graph representing the height of the young patient. The child's growth was considerably slower than the norm during the episodes of anorexia nervosa, but the termination of each episode was followed by a growth spurt, in which the child seemed to catch up with the norm.

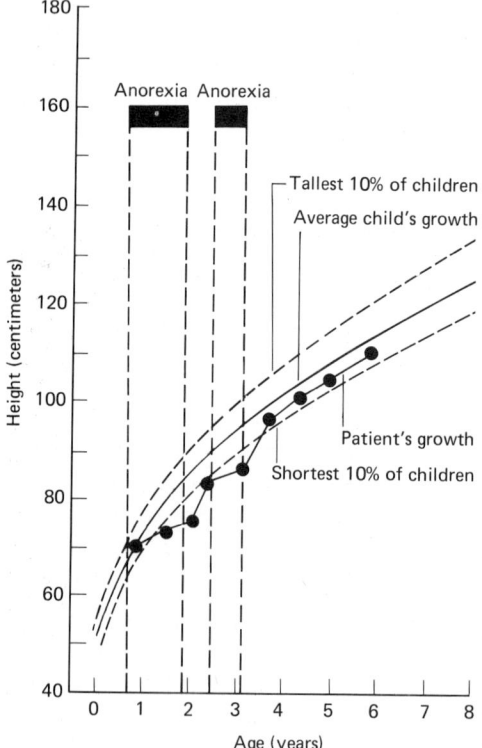

FIGURE 8-2. The effect of poor nutrition on growth. Graph showing height gains of a young girl before, during, and after two episodes of anorexia nervosa, as contrasted with the normal range of height increases for this age span. (After Tanner, 1970, as redrawn from Prader, Tanner, and von Harnack, 1963.)

sensorimotor development

The classical studies of sensorimotor development were conducted during the years before World War II, when there was a great deal of interest in identifying major trends and assigning them to "ages and stages." Gesell and his associates (1940), for example, mentioned as characteristic of the three-year-old his ability to accelerate and decelerate in walking and running, to turn sharp corners, to go upstairs by alternating his feet, even though only for short periods of time. From the child's perspective, being three years old means being ready to abandon the infantile "kiddy car," with its primitive, shoving form of propulsion, for the tricycle, with its complicated means of movement. Jumping, climbing, and riding tricycles occupy a not unconsiderable portion of the preschool child's time. Such activities are derived essentially from the simpler ones of infancy, but carried out with considerably greater ease and efficiency.

Learning and Maturation in Sensorimotor Skills

The influence of learning may be readily seen in such skills as swimming and buttoning clothes. Maturational influences are not confined to infancy; they are also operative during the preschool period. Hicks (1930) observed sixty children between two and a half and six and a half, whom he divided into an experimental and a control group, on the basis of their initial skill at throwing a ball at a moving target. The experimental group practiced ten throws once a week for eight weeks; the control group did not participate in practice sessions. Thereafter, both groups were retested and found to have made gains. The experimental group was not significantly better in performance than was the control group who received no practice. It would appear that the improvement in skill did not result from the specific practice in throwing balls, as the one group had done, but instead from maturation and autogenous (self-initiated) learning.

Autogenous learning refers to the fact that the children, whether or not they were actually throwing balls at a moving target, were, in the course of their daily living, practicing many of the complex and coordinated motions of body, eye, arm, and hand that are utilized in the complex skill of hitting a moving target. As far as clarity of results is concerned, this complicating factor of autogenous learning makes it exceedingly difficult to demonstrate maturational effects with children. Specific practice may be encouraged by the experimenter or parent, but the child continues to live and learn (practice) in ways that probably affect the results obtained. Nevertheless, it is plausible to believe that maturation is still taking place.

Stages of Motor Development

A given motor skill may be considered as passing through stages beginning with nonachievement, or absence of skill through various degrees of proficiency. Mary V. Gutteridge (1939) developed a rating scale defining steps of motor development in terms of specific motor skills. Table 8-1 is adapted from her work.

Gutteridge identified four general stages of major motor development: the first stage, in which no attempt is made to carry out the motor skill in question; the second stage, in which the skill is in the process of formation; the third stage, in which the basic movements have been achieved; and the fourth stage, in which there is skillful execution with variation in its use. Within each stage there are various degrees of skill. The use of initial letters beyond the first ten numbered degrees of skill indicates Gutteridge's recognition that beyond the point in the scale that indicates skilled performances, the child uses his skills in all sorts of variations of the activity executed, even though there is no further increase in proficiency. It is only in the first three stages that there are degrees of increase in skill, in any strict sense. A rating of 8 or better on Gutteridge's scale is considered as indicating that the child is proficient in the particular motor skill. Although another investigator might use another way of formulating the stages and degrees of motor skill, this scale has enough generality to be of significance quite apart from the

TABLE 8-1. Scale of Degrees of Motor Skill Observed in Children's Activities (after Gutteridge, 1939)

Stage or Phase	Degree of Skill
I. No attempt	1. Withdrawal or retreat when opportunity for activity presents itself
	2. No approach or attempt, but no withdrawal or avoidance
II. Process of developing skill	3. Activity attempted, but help or support is sought
	4. Attempts without help or support, but ineptly
	5. Makes progress, but uses unnecessary movements
	6. Practices basic movements
	7. Refines movements
III. Basic movements achieved	8. Coordinates movements
	9. Performs easily and shows satisfaction
	10. Displays accuracy, poise, and grace
IV. Competent execution, with variations	A. Tests skill by taking chances or adding difficulties
	B. Other skills incorporated into activity
	C. Speeds, races, or competes with others or with self
	D. Skills employed in larger projects, such as dramatic play

research in which it has been used. These four major stages and their related, more precisely defined degrees of motor skill may be considered applicable to the motor skills of childhood in general.

Some Changes in Motor Skills

Gutteridge used these ratings in a survey of the activities of nearly two thousand preschool children. The motor activities she studied were climbing; jumping; sliding; tricycling; hopping; galloping; skipping; and throwing, bouncing, and catching balls. Teachers trained as raters made the necessary observations in the natural settings of classroom and playground. Here are some examples of her results:

Climbing was "proficient," as defined for the test, at the end of the third year in nearly 60 per cent of the children. By the end of the sixth year, 97 per cent were proficient. Considerable variability was found; a child or two in the sample was proficient before reaching two years of age, and 3 per cent of them were still not proficient even at the end of the sixth year. The children climbed on every conceivable piece of equipment, whether it was designed for this purpose or not, and most of them climbed as high as opportunity afforded. Some "stunting" occurred even as early as two years.

Jumping had been mastered by 40 per cent of the children by the age of three and a half, whereas about 85 per cent were proficient by the age of six. There was a sharp rise in the percentage of proficiency from the youngest child to that of the four-and-a-half-year-old children, for whom the median rating was nine points. From that age on, there was relatively little increase in proficiency: the median rating for the six-year group was only a little over 9. Variability was considerable at all ages. Among the five-year-olds, the range spanned nine of the ten possible points; even among the six-year-olds, it still spanned six points.

Tricycling was an accomplishment in which 63 per cent of the three-year-olds were proficient; by four years of age, 100 per cent were proficient. Doing tricks on a tricycle was very evident, as most mothers know; riding backwards, turning corners, and navigating narrow spaces were common.

Ball-throwing was a motor skill in which even some of the two- and three-year-old children showed some competence. By the end of the sixth year, about 85 per cent were proficient. The range of achievement at all ages, even the oldest, extended from awkward to excellent.

In general, Gutteridge's survey indicated that a fair proportion of children are proficient in some motor activities before the age of three years, ranging from 1 per cent in tricycling to 50 per cent in sliding. But proficient use in the throwing and catching of balls and control of movements in such activities as hopping, skipping, and galloping did not appear before age four or five.

Preschoolers are at a stage where they can begin to discover the joy and exuberance of gross motor activity, and at the same time may get a thrill of pleasure from the mastery of small-muscle skills, like those needed to fill a bottle or build a creditable tower of blocks.

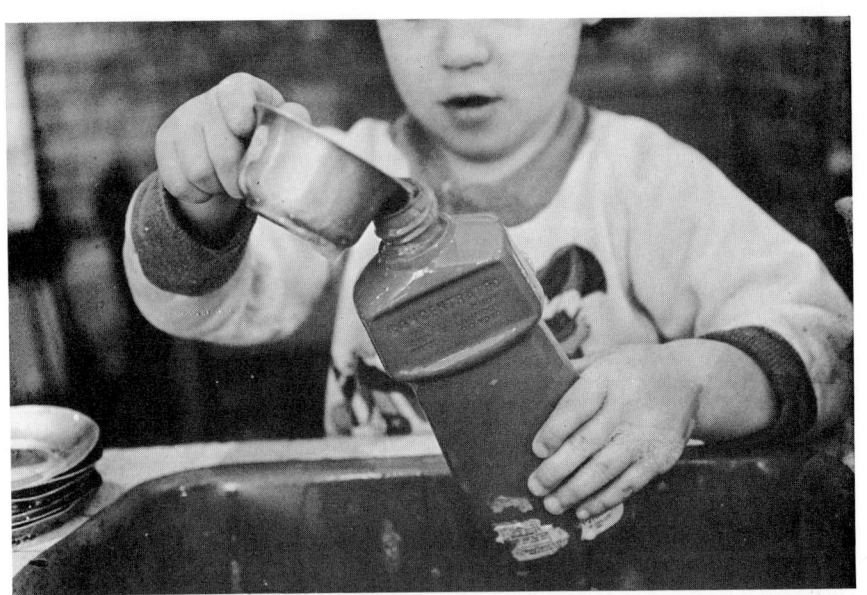

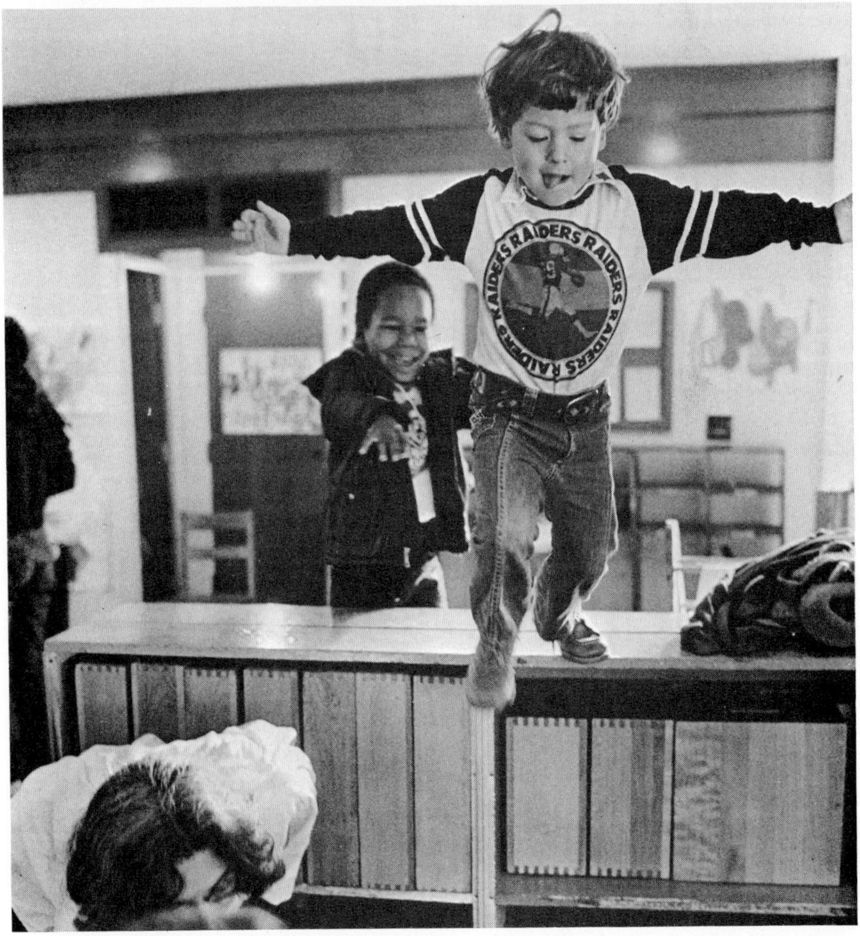
RAIDERS RAIDERS
RAIDERS RAIDERS

Gutteridge noted a number of sex differences. Boys were ahead of girls in climbing, jumping, sliding, skipping, and ball-throwing; girls were more proficient in tricycling, galloping, hopping, and bouncing and catching balls. Variations within each child from one skill to another were also noticeable, although Gutteridge stated there was some evidence of consistency of pattern. This consistency appeared in the form of a tendency for each child to specialize in certain kinds of motor movements and to avoid other types.

cognitive development

As we indicated in Chapter 6, the close association between psychomotor and cognitive skills that is present during the first few months of life starts to dissolve toward the end of the first year. As the infant begins to respond to language and develops some ability to generate and deal with concepts, his cognitive skills become increasingly differentiated from his motor skills.

In about the middle of the second year of life, the infant begins to make internal symbolic representations and to invent solutions to problems, rather than relying entirely on random, trial-and-error approaches. At this stage, he is passing into the early stages of what Piaget calls *preoperational thought*. Thinking cannot occur without symbols; that is, there must be some mentalistic devices that represent objects and behavior and that can be manipulated in abstract fashion. Language is the most obvious symbol system, and preoperational thought develops together with the child's acquisition of this mode of behavior.

Piagetian Concepts of Cognition

According to Piagetian theory, the average child in the early preschool years—say from two to four—is passing through a subperiod preparatory to that of concrete operations. His conceptual operations have not yet taken on the stability and coherence that should occur from about ages seven to eleven.

This subperiod of preparation includes three stages: beginnings of representational thought (ages 2-4); simple representations (4-5½); and articulated representations (5½-7).

The important issue is not these steps in themselves, but the cognitive shift that takes place. The preschool child becomes capable of internally evoking a signifier—a word or image that symbolizes a significant but perceptually absent object or event. He is also able to differentiate between an absent object and the word that represents it.

Although infants possess the ability to use cues, their ability to respond to symbols is much more limited than that of preschoolers. The infant's sensorimotor ability enables him to link one action or perceptual state to another, in a kind of chain; but the representational ability of the preschooler enables him to translate reality into symbols and thus allows him to consider a broad sweep of events and objects simultaneously. The infant's sensorimotor ability permits him to act; but the representational ability the preschooler possesses enables him to contemplate and reflect as well. Representation enables the child to consider the past and future, in addition to the immediate present, and thus makes it possible for him to use his command of language to share his thinking with others.

This ability to manipulate and respond to symbols is a big step, but it is not everything. The preschool child also understands the permanence of concrete objects, even though he has no fully developed concepts of weight, quantity, number, or logic. He is approaching, but has not arrived at, operational thinking.

Animism

Animism—the attribution of life to inanimate objects—occurs in adults as well as children. Boats, guns, and automobiles are some of the objects that adults jokingly or even seriously characterize as being alive—even to the point of giving them names and complaining about their personality traits. Perhaps the practice goes back to our early years of childhood, when it somehow seemed easier to understand things if they were thought to be alive.

> Three-year-old Michael was having difficulty in getting his tricycle up and over a low curb at the edge of a driveway. He pushed and strained, but just did not have the combination of muscle power and weight to get the vehicle over the barrier.
> He was becoming angry, when a playmate, who was watching, said: "I guess it don't want to."
> "It don't want to," Michael agreed, and he wheeled his tricycle around and pedaled off.

Piaget (1926) says that animism occurs in four distinct stages. In the first stage, for children between four and six years of age, everything is alive (unless broken or damaged); in the second stage, at six and seven years, everything that moves is alive; in the third stage, for eight- to ten-year-old children, everything that moves by itself is alive; in the fourth stage when children are eleven or older, life is reserved for animals and plants, or animals alone.

Centering and Conservation

In Chapter 3, we discussed the young child's inclination to "center"—that is, to attend to a single striking feature of an object, disregarding other aspects, and thus, to distort his thinking. For example, on seeing two identical tall, slender containers, he will agree that they both contain identical amounts of liquid. But when the contents of one is poured into a short, broad container, the child will then deny that the remaining tall container and the broad one contain equal amounts. He will argue one way or the other according to whether he "centered" on the tall or the broad container, saying either that B contains more because it is broad or that A contains more because it is tall.

The ability to recognize that transferring liquid from one container to another of a different shape does not result in a change in the amount of liquid is an example of what Piaget terms *conservation*, or, in this specific instance, *conservation of continuous quantities*. Conservation, in Piaget's theoretical framework, refers to the ability of the child to recognize that certain properties of objects—volume, mass, number, and quantity, for instance—do not change, despite the fact that the appearance of the objects has changed. This ability is not fully developed until later in childhood, when the child is no longer misled by appearances and has sharpened his judgment and is willing to trust it. The ability to conserve comes through the child's construction of a system of rules, a result of both maturation and experience with the physical world.

Piaget's ideas on conservation have aroused a great deal of interest, partly because he places a great deal of stress on the importance of the concept as a foundation for all rational activity (see Piaget, 1965), and partly because his research methods for identifying the phenomenon seem rather unorthodox by Anglo-American standards. For one thing, his data have been reported only in an incomplete, anecdotal, and

The Piagetian approach to studying cognitive development in children. Professor Gilbert A. Voyat of the City University of New York presents children with specific tasks and then asks, "What do you think will happen if we do this? Why do you think so? How do you explain that?" Tasks displayed here are conservation of liquid and rotation of landscape.

271

illustrative form: for another, he has not maintained a consistent approach from time to time and from subject to subject (Braine, 1962).

In spite of these imputed deficiencies, experimental work using more conventional research techniques has tended to confirm Piaget's conclusions (Lovell, 1961a; Elkind, 1961; Uzgiris, 1964). These, and other studies, support Piaget's sequence of stages of cognitive development, but they do suggest that English and American children enter the stages at a somewhat younger age than do Piaget's subjects, an observation that has encouraged some researchers to try methods of getting children to accelerate their progress through the various stages. Some of these attempts appear to have succeeded, but Patrick C. Lee (1975) has raised questions about the methods employed and suggests that researchers who claim to have succeeded in accelerating cognitive development may only have taught children how to verbalize more effectively. Lee points out that children are able to *predict* conservation at an earlier age than they are able to *judge* it in a formal test situation. That is, before

The Christian Science Monitor

"Boy! Your wrecking bar works great"

If American children enter stages of cognitive development earlier than children in other countries, it may be because they grow up in a culture in which parents encourage exploration and investigation and also give them access to the tools that make it possible for them to discover the nature of the world they live in. (Bram, The Christian Science Monitor, © 1968 by TCSPS.)

the experimenter has actually poured the water into a differently shaped container, children will say that the quantity will be the same; but after the water has been poured, and they are faced by the apparent change in quantity, their grasp of conservation wavers and slips away from them. The task of determining whether cognitive stages can actually be accelerated is a complex one, and the technical problems of finding acceptable criteria have not yet been resolved.

Rothenburg and Courtney (1969) conducted a study that both confirms Piaget's contentions about the way conservation evolves and shows how the child's ability to use terms like "same" and "more" is related to the concepts he is developing. The task they employed dealt with *conservation of number,* in which a child is asked to say whether one row of blocks has the same or more blocks than a comparison row. The investigators found that only 2 per cent of their sample of children aged two years and five months to four years and four months were able to conserve numbers. They did notice, however, that subjects aged four years and three months to six years had a better grasp of conservation of number, although within this age range their ability was still limited. There were no sex differences in the abilities demonstrated, but children from lower socioeconomic homes scored significantly lower than those from middle-class homes, even among children who were only two and three years old. The investigators concluded that serious cognitive deficits appear among lower-class children at this early age. Their finding would suggest that if there is a "critical period" for cognitive development, it occurs very early in life.

A question sometimes arises as to the role of experience in the development of conservation. Some ingenious researchers administered Piagetian tests of conservation of liquid, number, substance, weight, and volume to two groups of Mexican children, all boys. One group, composed of the children of potters, had considerable experience in making pottery; the control group had no experience of this type. The results, in general, showed that, in contrast to the control group, the potters' children were better able to conserve, particularly with regard to substance. The children were in the six-to-nine age group, when conservation is more likely than in the preschool period, but the point is that interaction with materials in problem-solving situations apparently did facilitate the development of this ability (Price-Williams, Gordon, and Ramirez, 1969).

Logical Structure

It is difficult to separate the child's ability to use logic from other aspects considered in Piaget's research. As Flavell (1963) has noted, the logic employed by children is a factor in virtually all of Piaget's experiments. In this section we shall focus on the origins of children's learning classification, an important aspect of logic.

A typical experiment testing the development of classification consists of giving the child a collection of different objects and asking him to sort them in terms of those that are similar or "go together." In the first stage of the development of logical structures, which occurs between two and a half and five, the child does not organize the objects into classes and subclasses, but rather in terms of what Piaget and Inhelder (1959) call *figural collections*. The child proceeds in a relatively planless, step-by-step manner, frequently shifting his decisions as to what goes with what as new objects catch his eye. The collection of items that finally emerges turns out to be not a logical class, but a complex figure—hence the term *figural collection*. For instance, a three-year-old French-Swiss child who was asked to sort some objects first selected some circles and piled them; then he put some squares next to the circles and added other objects. What he had in mind soon became evident when he looked at this assemblage and said, "Un train, tsch, tsch, tsch!"

Piaget says that there are several difficulties that prevent a child of this age from classifying objects logically: he cannot form classes or wholes that have a certain inner logic and also cannot differentiate or coordinate the qualities that serve as the basis for class membership. Because of these deficiencies, he is highly distractible and keeps shifting his criteria for sorting.

Another difficulty stems from the child's inability to grasp the meaning of "different." In one study researchers asked children to select an object that was different from another. Up to about age three and one-half years they consistently chose objects that were actually similar, but after that age tended to give the appropriate response (Webb, Oliveri, and O'Keeffe, 1974).

In another of Piaget's experiments, the child is shown a display of red squares, blue squares, and blue circles and is asked if all the circles are blue. To this question he gives the interesting answer that they are not, because there are blue squares as well. The problem here is that of confusing the concepts *some* and *all* as applied to different classes and subclasses. The child can use the words *some* and *all*, of course, and sometimes appropriately, but in actuality it seems that his ability to use words has developed more rapidly than his competence in dealing with the reality that the words represent. This disparity was brought out in a study by Donaldson and Balfour (1969), who found that children three and four years old could not distinguish between "more" and "less." "Less" was consistently interpreted by them to mean the same as "more."

perceptual-conceptual development

The principle of differentiation can readily be discerned in the perceptual development among young children. A five-year-old is able to discriminate to some degree among the objects in a classroom—the blackboards, chairs, books, windows, and the rest—whereas the infant sees them as a conglomeration of unfamiliar colored shapes. This is only a relative differentiation on the part of the young child, however. He may perceive a "big" book and a "little" book but not realize that the former is an atlas and the latter the teacher's record book, a discrimination an adult would be able to make at a glance.

A lack of differentiation sometimes extends to the point of fusing the data from the various sense modalities. Some young children experience a response mode termed *synthesia*, when a specific stimulus arouses not only the appropriate sensation but also another sense modality. Color-sounds and color-smells are illustrative: a three-year-old boy said some things "smelled green," and a girl from her third to sixth year had to be corrected often in her oral expression of synesthesias: she persisted in referring to the "gold and silver striking of the hour" and "light- and dark-red whistling." This phenomenon tends to disappear with increasing age, suggesting that it is related to increasing differentiation (Werner, 1940).

Differentiation in perception is also shown by research employing more objective procedures. For example, when children four to six years old were asked to judge the age of adults from photographs, the older children were more accurate than the younger ones (Kogan, Stephens, and Shelton, 1961).

An interesting set of results emerged from a study conducted by Alvin G. Goldstein (1975), who asked subjects whose ages ranged from 3 to 20 years to identify upside-down photos of persons familiar to them. Goldstein found that success improved with age until about 14, but deteriorated thereafter. Subjects 19 and 20 years old were actually no more accurate than three-year-olds. He attributed the poor performance of the young adults to the fact that they are exposed to many more upright faces than children are, and consequently develop a schema-processing mechanism that is less flexible.

Concept Formation

The ability to learn and make use of conceptions facilitates the ease and accuracy of thinking, because concepts (1) reduce the complexity of the environment; (2) provide the means by which the objects of the environment are identified; (3) reduce the necessity of relearning at each new encounter; (4) help in directing, predicting, and planning any activity; and (5) permit ordering and relating classes of objects and events, as in cause and effect. In short, conceptualizing makes reasoning possible (Bruner, 1956).

Granting that the beginnings of conceptualization occur in infancy, what are some of the conceptual tasks the young child emerging from infancy has before him? He enters early childhood with very hazy conceptions of space, time, weight, number, form, color, and size. It is during early and later childhood that he makes his greatest strides in mastering these classes of concepts.

Learning concepts of space. Even at one year of age there is enough appreciation of spatial dimension to perform gestures for up and down and to play "peek-a-boo." By two years of age the child has in his vocabulary such expressions as "up high," "in," "out," and "go away." By the age of three he can tell what street he lives on, but usually not the number. At the age of five he is still very literal and factual, but is capable of taking simple routes in walking through the immediate neighborhood. He is beginning to appreciate the significance of maps and even may make simple maps indicating the way he goes to school.

Piaget maintains that space is not immediately comprehended by the child, but must be constructed through experience. Spatial representations are built up by the child's acting on the object in space. First there are the sensorimotor activities of the infant, but later more efficient and economical internalized activities take over (Piaget and Inhelder, 1956).

In very broad outline, this is the theory that Piaget advances. Suppose we examine it in more detail.

As we stated earlier, Piaget held that during the sensorimotor stage the infant constructed objects from his experiences, learning that objects retain identity even when out of sight and that he, the infant, can influence objects by touching them. Space, then, is not independent of objects.

During the preschool years the child moves on to a cognitive level in which objects in space are apprehended as related to one another, independent of the perceiver. He is now free from the illusion of egocentricity and can take into account movements of objects when they go through positions in which he himself does not participate. For instance, Piaget's daughter Jacqueline had rolled a ball under a sofa. She did not look under the sofa, because she realized the ball had passed under and beyond the sofa to another part of the room. Hence she turned away from where the ball disappeared and went around the sofa to find it. She followed a path different from that taken by the ball, based on an elaborated, independent, and organized spatial conceptualization. The detour she took showed her ability to apprehend space in which bodies other than her own had traveled.

Learning about time. Concepts of time are more abstract than space, partly because of the lack of obvious clues on which to build them. The child of 18 months lives very much in the present. It is characteristic that he finds it difficult to wait, and the only time word he uses is *now*.

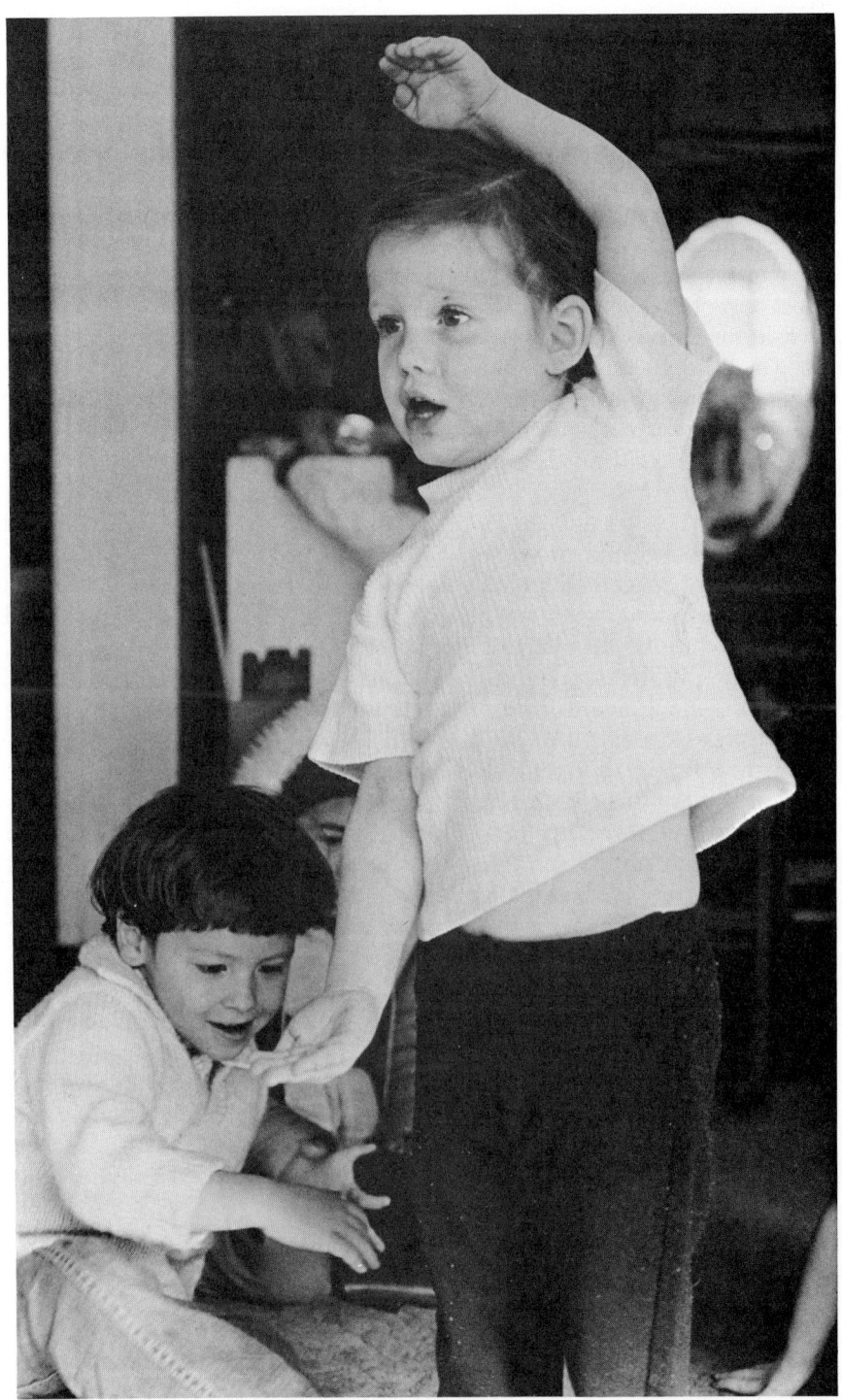
When a child has a good grasp of spatial concepts, he is able, through gestures, to communicate information about space to others.

Only the slightest indications of any sense of timing have yet appeared; for example, the sight of juice and crackers may bring him to the table. At two years of age, he has begun to use words denoting the future, as for example, *gonna* and *in a minute*. He is also beginning to comprehend simple time sequences, as implied in "have dollie after juice."

Parts of the day—morning and afternoon—are understood before the days of the week. By the age of three the child knows his own age, and most basic time words are now in his vocabulary. He can be persuaded to wait for things. Although he shows only a pretense of telling time, the very fact that he does so shows a dawning understanding of the concept of time. During these years he is still living very much in the here and now, as shown by the fact that even at five years it is very difficult for him to conceive of not being alive, of dying, or of anyone having lived before him. At this age, he can name the days of the week and is interested in clocks and calendars.

Hours are learned first, then half-hours, and finally, quarter-hours. Time is first conceived as a sequence in relation to activities, then as divisions of time, such as morning and afternoon; next comes an understanding of the days of the week, and thereafter calendar and clock time. In this sequence, the young child seems to be moving from concrete action toward levels of greater and greater abstraction.

Lorraine Harner (1975) conducted a series of experiments in which two-, three-, and four-year-old children played with a different set of toys on each of three succeeding days. On the second day, the children were shown all three sets of toys and asked to indicate which sets were from yesterday and which for tomorrow. The youngest children understood "yesterday" somewhat better than "tomorrow," but the three-year-olds tended to make errors in choosing "tomorrow's toys" when asked to indicate them. Four-year-olds appeared to have little difficulty in distinguishing between past and future.

Piaget (1969) has expressed theories about children's development of time concepts that are in some ways similar to his ideas about the way concepts of other environmental dimensions are evolved. He says that temporal concepts, like concepts of space, do not merely emerge, but must be *constructed* by the child. For example, the child must learn how to retrace the course of certain events and to coordinate their beginning and end with other events.

The complications involved in such reconstructions often lead to interesting errors. A six-year-old told Piaget that it took him ten minutes to go home, that he would get home more quickly if he ran, but that it would take *longer*. This response demonstrates the child's confusion about time and velocity. Piaget analyzed the child's reasoning along these terms: "(1) if you go quickly you will necessarily cover more space; (2) if you cover more space, you need more time to do so; and (3) if you go more quickly you need more time because you cover more space" (p. 88).

_____summary

The period of early childhood begins with the final stages of infancy, between 18 and 24 months, and ends at about age five. During this period, rapid physical growth continues, although at a somewhat slower pace than in infancy. By five years of age, the average American boy weighs 43 pounds and is 44 inches tall. Girls tend to be slightly smaller. The correlation between height at age five and mature height is .70.

The preschool period is the time when childhood illnesses are at their peak, particularly colds and other respiratory diseases, which increase during the second year and drop off during the sixth year. Allergies and gastrointestinal complaints reach their highest point during the first year of life, and then decline sharply at the sixth year.

During the preschool years, the child shows increasing mastery over the skills acquired during infancy and picks up many new ones as well. Jumping, climbing, and tricycle riding occupy a considerable portion of the preschooler's time. Although some skills are learned, others are the result of maturation. For instance, children who were given supplementary practice in ball-throwing were no more skillful than children who depended purely on maturation and self-initiated practice to acquire the skill. The child passes through four general stages of motor development in learning a skill: (1) when no attempt is made to carry out the motor skill; (2) when the skill is in the process of formation; (3) when the basic movements have been achieved; and (4) when there is skillful execution with variation in use of the skill.

About the middle of the second year, the infant enters the early stages of what Piaget calls preoperational thought. Symbol manipulation, especially in the form of language, now becomes quite important. The ability to allow symbols to represent reality enables the preschooler to consider a broad sweep of events and objects and to think about them. Young children tend to ascribe life to inanimate objects—animism. According to Piaget, animism develops in stages, like other forms of cognitive activity. Piaget also maintains that preschoolers tend to distort their thinking by "centering," or attending to only one feature of an object. This tendency leads to confusions and interferes with conservation. Young children will say that water poured from one container into another container of a different shape will have changed its quantity. Research generally supports Piaget's contentions, although English and American children apparently enter and proceed through cognitive stages more rapidly than Piaget's reports would lead one to expect. There is also some indication that the child's ability to verbalize his observations has an effect on the experimenter's judgments about his cognitive status. Experience, too, is important in the child's ability to develop conservation. A study of Mexican potters' children indicated that their special experience evidently facilitated their ability to conserve substance. Piaget tests classification by asking children to sort objects. Younger children have difficulty because they proceed unsystematically and cannot use concepts associated with "different," "some," "all," "more," and "less."

Some children merge sense modalities and associate smells with colors and colors with sound. Accuracy in judging photographs improves with age, but some skills, like judging upside-down photographs, may actually deteriorate after puberty. Concept formation enables children to reason and to deal more realistically with their environment. Piaget maintains that space is not understood at first, but must be "constructed" through experience. A child must learn that a ball, for instance, exists independently from him and can travel under furniture by a route he cannot follow physically but can determine logically. Concepts of time are more abstract than those of space, partly because there are fewer cues on which to base them. Young children are very present-oriented, but begin to learn words and terms related to the future when they are about two. Confusions are common. Piaget tells of a six-year-old who maintained that it would take him longer to get home if he ran.

nine

The Learning of Language and the Development of Intelligence

Children pick up words as pigeons pease,
And utter them again as God shall please.
　　　　—ENGLISH PROVERBS,
　　　　　COLLECTED BY JOHN RAY (1670)

language development

It is language that most distinguishes human behavior from the behavior of the lower animals, and it is with the acquisition of spoken language that young children claim their place as functioning members of society. As we pointed out in Chapter 6, language also makes it possible for children to learn the symbols that they will employ, with increasing skill, in carrying out the tasks of thinking and problem solving.

Language and Learning

There is an enormous increase in the use of words during the preschool years. This increase is significant not only because knowing more words makes it easier to communicate, but also because gains in vocabulary aid learning of all types. A number of studies have shown that children are more successful in learning to distinguish among various kinds of stimuli if they are taught to name the stimuli they are judging. In other words, knowing verbal "labels" helps learning.

A study by Weir and Stevenson (1959) is an example of this type of research. The experimenters trained children of three, five, seven, and nine years of age to perform a simple task that required them to discriminate between correct and incorrect members of paired pictures of animals. The children in the experimental group were instructed to say the name of the animal before they selected a picture. The children in the control group received the same training, except that they were not requested to mention the animals' names. After the children had attained the same level of success in this task, they were given a similar but more complicated set of problems. Results indicated that those who had been asked to verbalize performed more successfully.

The results of Weir and Stevenson's experiment could be explained by a theory held by some of the early behaviorists, namely, that thinking is really subvocal or covert speech. Such an interpretation presents problems, however, because the speech of young children is fairly limited, and they do not begin to have enough forms to cover all types of problems they are able to solve. Conrad (1971) has pointed out, furthermore, that before the age of five, children do not employ subvocal or covert speech to memorize, reason, or plan. Instead, they use words in socially communicative ways to respond vocally and impulsively to specific situations, including the naming of objects to others. Language is also employed in social contexts in ways that are essentially devoid of conventional meaning, as when a child babbles using real words, but does so apparently because he enjoys their sounds.

Conrad observed a three-year-old child engaged in a task that involved selecting of a card from one group and matching it with an identical card from another group. The child talked to himself as he performed the task, but his words were not consistent with his actions; for example, he would say "Cat goes with cat," while he correctly matched "bat" with "bat." It is clear that the child was not using language labels in a way that would be considered logical or appropriate. It was as though his problem solving and his language usage were proceeding on separate tracks, unrelated to each other.

Language and Thinking

Indeed, the entire concept of verbal functioning as essential to thinking seems suspect. Hans G. Furth (1971), in a review of research relating to the thinking of deaf people, concluded that language plays little part, if any, in their ability to function cognitively. The thinking processes of deaf children and adolescents have been found to be similar to hearing subjects, although individuals deaf from birth, with few exceptions, are severely deficient in linguistic skills. The deaf person who can read lips, for example, is a rarity, and few deaf individuals can read printed material much better than the average fourth-grader, in spite of having spent 10 to 15 years in schools where linguistic skills get maximum stress.

In view of the fact that deaf people attain normal levels of cognitive performance without anything like comparable linguistic ability, it would appear that language competence is probably not a requisite for cognitive development in normal children either. Furth points out that such a conclusion would be consistent with Piaget's position that language is not involved in the development of logical thinking in children (Inhelder and Piaget, 1964).

Still further support for this line of reasoning comes from research by Jerome Kagan (1971), who showed four-year-olds pictures, one at a time. Later, when each picture was shown to the children, together with a picture they had not seen, they were able to pick the one they had seen with 90 per cent accuracy. Language could not have played a part in their thinking, because many of the pictures involved objects they had never seen in their lives (like a slide rule or a lathe); hence their performance could not be explained by the assumption that each picture had been supplied by the child with a language label.

language development

Generative/Nativistic Theories

In Chapter 6 we referred briefly to the controversy between proponents of the operant-conditioning explanation of early language learning, such as B. F. Skinner, and those favoring a biologically based theory, such as Noam Chomsky. Chomsky (1965, 1968) has argued that language development in children can be explained only if one assumes that there is an innate language capacity. The linguistic environment in which children find themselves is, according to Chomsky, deficient in many ways. First, the language that children hear is *degenerate*, because adults talk to children in ways that are different from the way they address each other. Children often hear sentences that are ungrammatical—baby talk, fragments of sentences, and the like—as well as those that are grammatical. For all they know, ungrammatical and grammatical sentences are on a par with one another. The language that children hear is also *limited*, consisting of only a small sample of the statements that are possible in language. Furthermore, their linguistic stimuli are *scattered*, in the sense that they are not organized appropriately for children's learning.

Chomsky pointed out that in spite of the inadequacies of the language that they hear, children all over the world learn to speak at about the same age and also progress at roughly the same rate. He concluded,

Noam Chomsky (above) of the Massachusetts Institute of Technology and B. F. Skinner (below) of Harvard University represent opposing and competing schools of thought in their theories regarding the way in which children develop or acquire language skills.

therefore, that human beings are born with a mechanism that enables them to acquire and develop linguistic competencies. He calls this mechanism a *language acquisition device*, an inherited predisposition that enables young children to process whatever linguistic data come their way and to transform them eventually into a grammatically acceptable competence in their native language.

The position or theory Chomsky developed has been called *generative*, because it holds that each child develops a set of linguistic rules that enable him to *generate* an infinite variety of phrases and sentences, many of which he has never heard anyone utter before and which are original with him.

> Matthew, aged two, was eating a hot dog at the zoo, when a wasp, attracted by the smell of the meat, crawled into the space between his hand and the bun just at the moment when Matthew was closing his hand to get a better grip. Naturally, the outraged wasp stung him. There were tears and loud cries, but no damage other than a somewhat swollen hand.
> When Matthew arrived home, he marched up to his mother and held out his hand.
> "Bee hurt a hand," he said (Fisk, 1976).

Matthew had never heard anyone say a sentence exactly like that. His father, who had bought him the hot dog, had told him "Your hand hurts because the bee stung it," but such an utterance is quite different from "Bee hurt a hand." The point is that Matthew created his sentence out of elements known to him, employing a set of linguistic rules that varied slightly from standard English.

In a review of the various competing theories of language development in children, Harry Osser (1971) noted that there is considerable support for Chomsky's views, for children from various language communities all seem to employ much the same strategies in learning their mother tongue. That is, when children who speak Russian, Japanese, French, or English first learn to talk, they begin by using simplified linguistic constructions that are ungrammatical by usual standards; but these early efforts serve as a bridge between the children's pretalking state and their later competence in speech that is grammatical according to the standards of their society (McNeill, 1968; Slobin, 1970).

The fact that all children literally invent a working set of grammatical rules shows, according to Chomsky, that such skills are not learned, but are generated by processes that are maturational or *nativistic*, to use another term frequently employed to describe Chomsky's position.

The concepts developed by A. R. Luria (1961), a Russian psychologist, are somewhat consistent with the nativistic view of linguistic development. Luria theorized that children's ability to regulate their motor behavior follows an orderly sequence, which is in turn coordinated with their verbal development. As the child matures, he increases his capacity for responding to commands, relating them to signals, and externalizing them. In stage 1 (one year to one and a half years), the infant's speech is inadequate for his self-regulation. Others can direct his action, but their commands cannot arrest or reverse an ongoing motor activity. In stage 2 (two and a half to four and a half years), the child progressively achieves an internalization of speech and partial self-regulation, but it is not until stage 3 (four and a half to five and a half years) that the semantics or "meaning" aspects of words become more important than their activating aspects and permit the child to develop a reasonable degree of self-regulation.

Luria's theories were put to the test by Bates and Katz (1970), who observed children in a day care center. Their conclusions were that the process of interrelating language and action is more complex than conceived by Luria and that the stages were not as well defined as he described them. For instance, even three-year-olds showed the beginnings of behavior that Luria said they should not be developing until they were about five.

Environmental/Learning Theories

As we noted in Chapter 6, the environmentalist/learning theory position taken by Skinner (1957) does seem somewhat narrow, because more seems to be involved in the learning of language than adult reinforcement of proper linguistic forms. Other environmentalist explanations seem to be more valid, however. Imitation appears to be a fairly obvious explanation of the way in which children acquire language. Osser notes that when children and adults interact, adults often repeat what children say, reinforcing and at the same time adding some grammatical niceties. For instance, the child says "Daddy go work," and the mother replies, "Yes, Daddy has gone to work," whereupon the child counters, "Daddy gone work," picking up a new language mode and moving a little closer to standard English. Brown and Bellugi (1964) conducted a longitudinal study of the speech of two children from infancy onward, however, and concluded that the linguistic knowledge they developed could not be accounted for entirely by imitation, reinforcement, and parental expansion of the type we have described. Research has shown that parental approval or disapproval is governed primarily by the validity or truth value of children's utterances and to only a minor degree by the correctness of their grammar (Brown, Cazden, and Bellugi, 1969).

This does not mean that parents have no influence on the grammatical constructions that children learn to use. Keith E. Nelson (1977) conducted an experiment designed to increase the complexity of children's grammatical usage. The children who were to receive the experimental treatment were drawn from a sample who were between

28 and 29 months old and who were using neither complex questions nor complex verbs in their speech. In other words, they asked questions like "Does it hurt?" rather than "Doesn't it hurt?" and made requests like "You help me," instead of ones using a conditional form, such as "You could help me."

The children participated in five one-hour intervention sessions over a two-month period. During these sessions, the women who served as experimenters tried to get the children to talk as much as possible. Whenever a child uttered a statement that could be said in a different way, the experimenter repeated it in a more complex restructured form. For instance, when one child asked "Where it go?" the adult replied "It will go there," in an attempt to introduce the future tense of the verb. When a child said, "I got it. I reached it," the adult said, "You got under the bed and reached it," in order to introduce the idea that a sentence could include two verbs.

Half the children were exposed to complex questions and half to complex verb forms. At the end of the series of intervention sessions, all of the children who had been exposed to complex questions were using them in one way or another, and, with only one exception, were still not using complex verb forms. Of the children who had been exposed to complex verb forms, all were making use of such forms, and, again with one exception, were not using complex questions.

What Nelson's experiment demonstrates is that parents and other adults can lead children to adopt grammatical forms that ordinarily they would not use until they were considerably older. All that seems to be necessary is for the adult to play the role of a model who restates in a more complex form an idea the child has already uttered.

Although the adult model serves as a fountainhead, so to speak, of new speech forms, children do a great deal of improvising on their own. Once a child has learned a principle, such as the formation of plurals for nouns, he applies it to all situations that seem appropriate to him. When he has learned to distinguish between "shoe" and "shoes," he extends the same rule to "boy" and "girl," and so forth. The irregularity of English word forms, however, does set booby traps for the young and innocent, as well as for the foreigner, sometimes with comic effects. The plural rule leads the untutored child to decide that "mans" and "deers" are the plurals of "man" and "deer," for example. Some of the inventions can be quite creative. A boy who took the wrong turn when sent on an errand to the nursery school director's office told his teacher, "I kept wenting and wenting till I got losted."

Braine (1963) observed that an elementary strategy employed by children in the early stages of language learning is that of learning two basic classes of words—what Braine termed *pivot* and *open*. Pivot-class words are those key words that can be used together with open-class words to make two-word sentences. "No" is a pivot-class word in sentences like "No milk," "No ball," and "No, Daddy" (the last statement expressing a preference to be comforted by Mother, rather than Father). The open-class words in these sentences are of course "milk," "ball," and "Daddy." According to Braine, the child learns to use a pivot-class word in a particular situation and then generalizes its use to similar positions or relationships with a wide range of open-class words.

Language Structure: A Tool for Understanding

Bronowski and Bellugi (1970) take a theoretical position that combines elements of both the generative and the environmental points of view. Maintaining that children extract rules of grammar from the sentences they hear and restylize them in speech forms of their own devising, Bronowski and Bellugi claim that children are not taught and do not need to be taught in any direct way what the underlying rules of

Children evidently pick up the rudiments of language through imitating others, and reinforcement also plays a part when adults respond to what children say. But neither imitation nor reinforcement explains how children happen to utter statements they have never heard before.

grammatical structure are; instead, a careful monitoring of their developing speech patterns will indicate that they gradually reconstruct the system employed in their mother tongue. In initial stages of language acquisition, their system is not precisely the same one used by adults, but bit by bit it approaches the adult system in form and complexity.

The way in which children learn these rules is shown by their tendency to pick up a rule and apply it to more instances than is proper. Three- and four-year-olds say things like "He comed yesterday," "It breaked," "Two mans," and the like. These are not phrases that the children have learned, but rather ones that they have generated using the rules they have learned but applying them incorrectly.

The approach used by young children is, according to Bronowski and Bellugi, similar to that which children employ in "reconstructing" (that is, giving structure to) their physical environment. They structure their environment partly by giving objects names, a process that is not merely a matter of learning labels used by adults but is also a way that children use to analyze the environment into distinct parts, which can then be treated as separate objects. The sentences constructed by children imply a view of the world as being separable into things that have an identity and that can be manipulated mentally. This manipulation is made possible by the fact that not only objects, but also actions and properties, can be symbolized by words.

Careful observation of the speech development of young children shows how they use language to structure and cope with the physical and social phenomena of daily experience. Table 9-1 presents a brief synopsis of the linguistic development of Matthew, a child whose parents made special attempts to foster his use of language. Not only does the record demonstrate how infants and toddlers learn to deal with their environment in linguistic terms; it also shows the effect of a language-rich environment, where children are exposed to television programs, like *Sesame Street*, that are specially designed to foster cognitive growth, and where adults encourage and reinforce verbal behavior. As we noted earlier, the norms of language development compiled a generation ago are no longer relevant, and highly verbal toddlers like Matthew, who would have seemed precocious in earlier years, are no longer very unusual.

The language forms listed in Table 9-1 also include examples for a number of trends which characterize the early speech of all children. "Tick-tick" is initially applied to real watches and clocks, and only months later to pictures of clocks, which are abstractions. The first sentences are telegraphic: "Soup hot" stands for "The soup is too hot to eat," for example. Once a word is learned, it can be generalized to other objects which have similar characteristics. Some toddlers apply "dog" to all four-legged animals; for Matthew, softness and texture were the relevant qualities, rather than four-leggedness, and he insisted for a while that every stuffed animal was a "Teddy." Matthew also showed

TABLE 9-1. Highlights of the Language Development of Matthew (Fisk, 1976)

23 weeks	Vocalizes vowels
24 weeks	"Speaks" to toys, using consonants (e.g., "b-b-b")
32 weeks	Combines vowels and consonants (e.g., "dada," "dig-dig-dig," "bubbah")
37 weeks	First word: "tick-tick," produced on request when shown clock or watch.
45 weeks	Calls mother "Mama"; uses "nana" to signify negation, displeasure.
49 weeks	Imitates *Sesame Street* character who said "Mama."
50 weeks	"Dada" and "bye-bye" now meaningful words.
15 months	Says "tick-tick" to picture of clock in book.
16 months	Uses "Teddy," as general term for all soft, stuffed animals; "gaga," for "all gone," "finished."
20 months	Says "bad-bad" to characterize things that hurt him or he has bumped into, also in regard to his own misbehavior. Vocalizes about fifty words. Refers to *Sesame Street* as "Sannan."
21 months	First sentences: "Car go," "Color ball," "Soup hot."
23 months	Three-word sentences: "I get it," "I drop it," "No want it." Says his first and last name correctly. Expresses moral concept: "Mickey bad-bad."
24 months:	Gives age, when asked how old he is. Uses four-word sentences: "Bee hurt a hand."
26 months	Uses past and present tense. On seeing a policeman, says "Policeman." Then, "Policeman walking." Later, when the policeman is out of sight, says "Policeman came." Describes abstract relationships: after hearing adults discuss a friend who has a new job, Matthew observes, "A job—that's working." Notes a cushion on a sofa and says "That's a triangle."

the common tendency for small children to "create" terms which then become recognized and accepted by the rest of the family. Matthew's parents, for example, quickly learned that "Sannan" referred to his favorite television program, *Sesame Street*.

Semantics and Cognitive Development

Theories explaining early language learning which focus on grammar have been criticized by other psycholinguists—Lois Bloom (1975), for example—on the grounds that they are concerned solely with structure and ignore the meaning that the child was attempting to convey by his choice and arrangement of words. Bloom pointed out that the so-called pivot words which appear with great frequency in children's language are employed not because of their usefulness as "pivots," but rather because they refer to what children are learning to talk about. It is the meaning—what is termed the *semantics*—of the child's experience that is ignored by explanations based on pivot grammar. When, at 24 months, Matthew says "Mommy hurt," we have to examine the situation that he is responding to. He may be saying, "I have bumped my head," or he may be looking at the Bandaid on his mother's arm, and recognizing that she has sustained an injury. Matthew makes much use of the word "hurt," not because it is an especially useful word in building two-word sentences, but because painful experiences, his own or those of others, arouse his anxiety.

Bloom concluded that the rules of generative grammar, based on studies of the distribution of certain word forms in children's speech, could not be explained apart from the meaning or semantics of the sentences in which the words occurred. She also pointed out that young children know more about their environment than they can put into words. Their learning of words and short sentences is to a large degree a search for ways in which to express their growing understanding of their environment. The most likely source of explanations for children's linguistic development may therefore be found in their early cognitive development.

Allan Paivio (1971) has reviewed the arguments made by the proponents of generative/nativistic theories, environmental/learning theories, and semantic/cognitive theories. He noted that each type of theory has its advantages, but that no single one is able to offer a completely satisfactory account. Each of the theories describes processes that contribute to the understanding and transmission of meaning by means of language, but it is difficult to untangle them and to determine exactly what it is that each type of process contributes.

Growth of Vocabulary

The figures reported in a number of normative studies on the size of a child's vocabulary at different ages during the preschool years vary considerably, for reasons not hard to identify.

First, there is difficulty in getting agreement on what is meant by "knowing" a word. One investigator may require only that a word be recognized in context, another that it be used in a sentence, and still another that the child be able to define it. Although all of these methods have some claim to legitimacy as indices of the growth of vocabulary, they yield different figures. Second, quite apart from how it is to be measured, there is the ambiguity created by the various meanings, as anyone consulting a dictionary knows. Differing standards toward the variety of meanings to be counted also result in varying estimates of the size of the vocabulary.

Fortunately, there seems to be some agreement that an early study performed by Medorah E. Smith (1926) is, to some extent, more definitive than most of the other studies. Smith standardized a vocabulary test on children one to six years of age. She did so by selecting every twentieth word from a list developed by E. L. Thorndike comprising the ten thousand words most frequently encountered in writing samples. The meanings of these words were elicited by Smith from her subjects by careful use of objects, pictures, and questions. She also took unusual pains to find out whether the child did or did not know the word meanings. The total words correctly known by a child was then multiplied by twenty, because every twentieth word from the list of ten thousand was used. This gave an estimate of the child's oral vocabulary.

The vocabulary sizes that Smith obtained for various ages are reported in Figure 9-1. A logarithmic scale is used in this figure in order to show how each word learned in the earlier stages is, relatively speaking, a major gain, whereas single words learned later only represent minor additions to the vocabulary. When children are around a year old, gains may be measured in terms of single words, but in a few months, gains come in the tens of words, then hundreds. When children are five years old, they are learning to recognize about a hundred new words every three months, but the gain, in proportion to the number they already know, is relatively small.

One fault that may be found in Smith's study is that her estimates may be too low. For one thing, she had no way of determining how many words not on Thorndike's list were known to a child. For another, studies done more recently suggest that children today are familiar with a larger range of words, probably because they are exposed to more media of mass communication, such as television and radio. Furthermore, today's parent has completed more years of education than the typical parent fifty years ago and hence is likely to use a richer

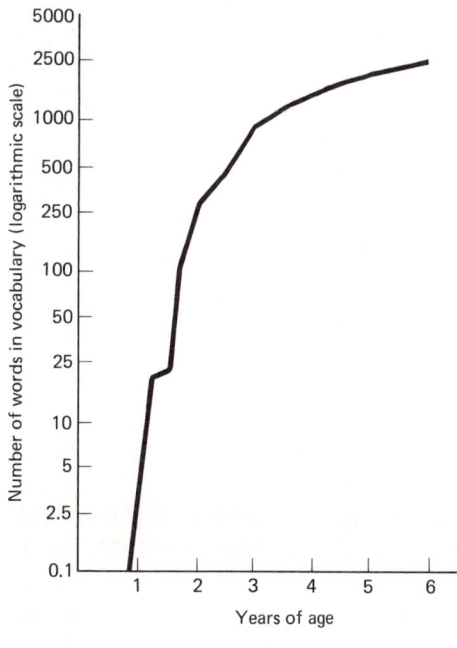

FIGURE 9-1. Logarithmic growth curve of the acquisition of recognition vocabulary by children from infancy to six years of age. (After Smith, 1926.)

vocabulary. With some adjustment for these factors, however, the growth curve resulting from Smith's work seems to be a reasonable representation of the rate at which children pick up new words.

Individual, Group, and Sex Differences in Language Development

Children five years old differ considerably in their facility with oral language. Some are chatterboxes, talking from the moment they wake up in the morning until they fall asleep at night. Others are quiet, almost silent, economical with words, speaking only when spoken to and often using a nod or a shake of the head where a flow of words would be forthcoming from another child. We can also hear variations in articulation, in richness of vocabulary, and in complexity of structure.

Children living in institutions interact with fewer adult models than other children, and are also less likely to have their utterances reinforced. Hence the usual finding is that the speech of institutionalized children is impoverished, in contrast with that of children raised by their own parents, or even in foster homes. Twins tend to be somewhat slower than other children in learning speech, probably because whatever adult attention they receive must be divided between them. As a consequence, an individual member of a set of twins receives less speech-related stimulation and reinforcement than a single child does. On the other hand, firstborn children are more advanced in vocabulary than others. They tend to associate more with adults than do other children and are thus exposed to more opportunities for reinforcement of new language responses.

Sex differences in language skills have often demonstrated that girls show superiority over boys in nearly all aspects of speech development. One aspect of speech development, length of response, will illustrate. McCarthy (1954) summarized 14 major, carefully controlled studies of length of speech responses at preschool ages. Of the 64 comparisons, 43 favored the girls. However, Maccoby and Jacklin (1974), in their monumental survey of research on sex differences, concluded that although studies of verbal development did tend to favor girls, differences were slight, and that boys tend to catch up by age three, except in populations of disadvantaged children.

Sociolinguistic Theory

Sociolinguistic learning theory goes beyond the mere learning of words and sentences and is concerned with how children learn the linguistic styles (whether to say "I is" or "I am," when to talk, when to be silent, and so forth) that prevail in their families. Bernstein (1972) points out that inasmuch as families are extensions of the subculture within the main culture, each child learns the language appropriate to his socioeconomic status and the ideas and values that are appropriate to it. These interlocking speech-and-thought structures constitute his way of reacting to others outside the family and in turn modify their reaction to him. His speech patterns therefore announce who he is, in terms of social class and ethnic group, and also influence the way in which he looks at life and its problems. A five-year-old child with a rich vocabulary and precise grammar identifies himself as a member of an educated family that values ideas and individual differences; a child the same age with minority-group dialect thereby identifies himself as being a member of that group, and as subscribing to their life view, whatever it may be.

Bernstein notes that language serves a different function for a working man and a business executive; the former uses language in here-and-now situations for manipulation and control, whereas the latter uses it for decision making in the immediate environmental context of complex organizations. These two styles of communication carry over to the two men's family relationships and inevitably affect the kind of language forms their children learn. The working-class child will therefore learn to use language in ways that may help him to deal very directly with material objects and people, but will not enable him to deal with complex, abstract phenomena—an approach that will, in turn, give him difficulties at school. Bernstein also believes that if a child from a working-class home were successfully taught the more elaborated linguistic mode of the middle class, this way of using language could alter the relations between him and his family and the other members of the working-class community.

Language Development and Social-Class Differences

Research studies consistently show that middle-class preschoolers use language more effectively than lower-class children. This difference seems to hold irrespective of whether we compare black children who are middle class with those who are lower class, or white middle-class children with white lower-class children. The difference can apparently be accounted for by the greater richness of the middle-class home environment, including the greater willingness of middle-class parents to talk to their children and encourage their verbalization.

Studies also show that middle-class children are better able to use language in problem solving. One experiment compared the performance of two-year-old white boys whose mothers were college graduates with those whose mothers had not graduated from high school. The boys were asked to find cookies located under boxes, each of which was marked by an object unfamiliar to the boys (a valve, a strainer, etc.). In one set of trials, the boys were told merely to find the cookie; in the other set, they were told the names of the objects on the boxes, whereupon the experimenter said, "The cookie will be under the valve," or whatever.

Results showed that the boys of better-educated mothers found that knowing the names of the objects was very helpful, whereas it was of no help to the sons of less educated mothers. The sons of better-educated mothers learned over sixty per cent more objects than did the other boys, and, when the experimenter changed the stimulus object in the middle of the trials, they also were able to make the shift with fewer errors in the verbal trials. Finally, the sons of better-educated mothers took significantly fewer trials to catch on to the location of the cookie during the verbal trials, as Figure 9-2 indicates. In short, this experiment demonstrates that very young children of educated parents not only learn verbal labels more quickly than do children from less educated parents, but also that they are better able to use such labels in solving problems involving their physical environment.

Although the evidence presented by studies like this is largely one-sided, some doubts have been expressed. Hymes (1972), for example, suggests that the efforts of researchers have been too restricted in their scope and that there may be areas of behavior, as yet unexplored, in

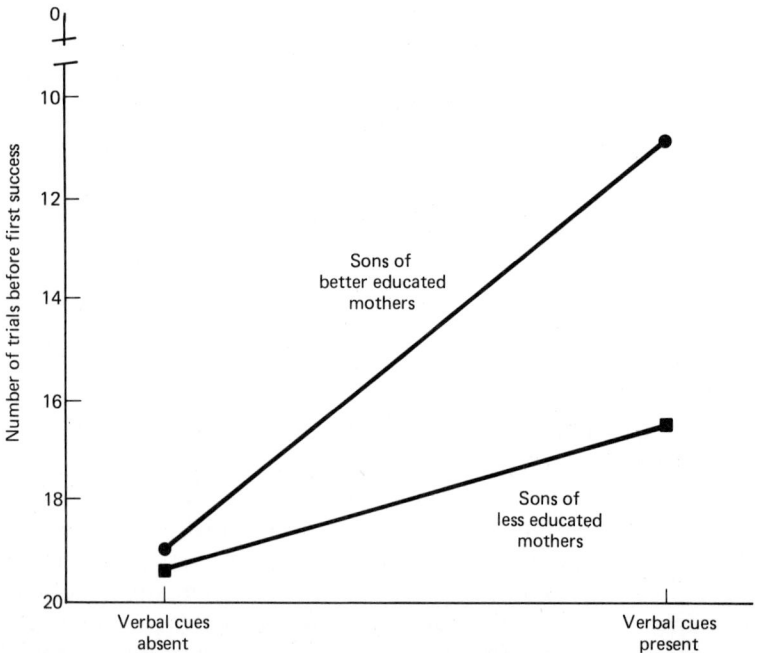

FIGURE 9-2. Differences in the number of trials taken by two-year-old sons of college-educated and grade-school-educated mothers to solve a simple problem when verbal cues were absent or present. (Data from Golden, Bridger, and Montare, 1974.)

which lower-class children may actually excel middle-class children. Osser (1971), too, maintains that the language disparities between children of different social-class groupings may indicate only that the rule systems of their language patterns differ. Lower-class children, for instance, tend to be less explicit and precise in their verbal communication than are middle-class children. This tendency, of course, penalizes them when they encounter the linguistic modes that prevail in a classroom.

Lower-class children also use forms of language that are quite different from those used by middle-class children. A middle-class child is likely to have little difficulty when he encounters the word *something* in his reading, but a lower-class child may puzzle over it in vain until someone tells him that he is looking at the word for *sump'n*.

Osser notes that there are two conflicting points of view with respect to the effect that nonstandard dialects have on children's speech. One is that lower-class dialects do not by themselves interfere with a child's conceptual development. The other point of view is that such dialects (black English, for example) impose serious limitations on the child's ability to develop logical operations (Bereiter and Englemann, 1966).

The view held by most teachers, according to Osser, is that black English and other lower-class dialects render children essentially nonverbal or verbally destitute and hence lead inevitably to academic failure. The argument continues along these lines: irrespective of whether a child remains in lower-class surroundings or whether he moves into the middle class, he must still deal linguistically with a world in which middle-class language, values, and ways of doing things are normal. Furthermore, unless he develops some competency with middle-class language forms (preferably as a *user*, but at least as a *consumer*), he is doomed to a life of alienation and isolation from the mainstream of the social and economic life of the land in which he lives.

The sociolinguistic viewpoint, according to Osser, holds that research showing that lower-class children are cognitively handicapped has not been conducted adequately. Lower-class children are likely to be shy and inarticulate when queried by middle-class interviewers who use middle-class language and middle-class ploys to get them to perform. When the lower-class child is with people he knows and feels comfortable with, he is often as verbal and as articulate as any middle-class child. What is needed, according to Osser, is a school program that will start where the child is linguistically and will go on from there, and he cites some studies to show that the lower-class child will make a good showing when educational programs are presented in the language with which he is familiar.

However, the question is still open. Research by Lorene C. Quay (1971) tested the hypothesis that black children would perform more adequately if tested by friendly, supportive black psychometrists who

TABLE 9-2. Stanford-Binet IQ Means for Four-Year-Old Black Children Who Took the Test Under Standard-English or Black-English Conditions and Were Rewarded for Correct Answers Either with Praise or with Candy (Quay, 1971)

Reward	Black English Version	Standard English Version
Praise	97	96
Candy	95	96

used black dialect, instead of standard "establishment" English. Subjects were one hundred four-year-old black children from Operation Head Start programs, who were given the Stanford-Binet test in either black English or standard English, and who were reinforced either with candy or with praise for correct answers. The results, as presented in Table 9-2, show virtually the same mean IQ under all four conditions. It appears that the children understood standard English as well as the dialect they were used to, and that concrete rewards in the form of candy did not improve their performance.

A number of other studies have also found that dialect differences do not block children's comprehension of standard English (Copple and Suci, 1974). Other tests of the sociolinguistic position will have to be conducted, of course, but the rather definitive results of the studies by Quay and by more recent researchers suggest that we must find reasons other than linguistic ones for the difficulties that the children of less-educated parents experience in school learning.

intellectual development

English and English (1958) noted that there are three concepts basic to *intelligence,* as the term is used by psychologists: the ability to deal with tasks involving *abstractions,* the ability to *learn,* and the ability to deal with *new situations.* Intelligence tests characteristically include all three of these concepts; they confront the child with problems that can be solved abstractly; they measure what he has learned (on the assumption he has been exposed to an environment similar to that of most children); and they present items which themselves are often novel and unlike anything the child will have encountered in his daily life.

An intelligence test, therefore, attempts to tap a number of different areas of cognitive functioning. Children who have been slow to develop cognitive facility for whatever reason will therefore score low on intelligence tests, whereas those who are advanced will score high. The issue of how much of the variation in intelligence test scores can be attributed to genetic factors is, as we indicated earlier, an open question, but the evidence that environmental factors make heavy contributions is impressive. Anything that interferes with normal growth and development is likely to lead to cognitive deficits and a lowering of IQ; malnourishment of the child, serious illness, and birth abnormalities all take their toll. Nonstimulating environments are especially detrimental.

Facilitating Intellectual Development: The Early Training Project

One trend often observed among children of poor and uneducated parents is the tendency for IQs to decline after the first year in school. Characteristically, the child from a poor family starts school with an IQ of about 90, which then declines in eight or nine years into the 80s. In rural areas, the IQ is likely to start in the 80s and then drop to the 70s and even below (Green and Hofmann, 1965). If the preschool years are regarded as a critical period for cognitive development, as some psychologists and many educators believe, we might hypothesize that intervention at this stage could forestall IQ declines of such a magnitude.

One of the more successful intervention programs is the Early Training Project, organized and supervised by Susan W. Gray and Rupert A. Klaus (1970) of George Peabody College for Teachers in Nashville, Tennessee. Gray and Klaus have for some years been developing a number of longitudinal programs for socially and economically deprived black preschool children in Tennessee. Their Early Training Project has been aimed at helping these children develop the kinds of skills and work attitudes that would enable them to maintain normal IQ levels and attain a reasonable level of success in school. Gray and Klaus are particularly interested in encouraging the development of what has been termed *achievement motivation*, especially as it relates to school activities. The term includes such characteristics as persistence, the ability to delay gratification and work for postponed rewards, and an interest in working with typical school materials such as books, crayons, puzzles, and the like.

The Early Training Project has been built around a series of ten-week summer school experiences in which children are exposed to a variety of new stimuli and are reinforced for attempting and persisting with new tasks. The program is also supplemented during the entire year by paraprofessionals—mothers from the black community—who visit the homes of children and encourage parents to behave in supportive and facilitative ways with respect to their children's developing interests and skills.

Achievement motivation is fundamental to school success. Among preschool children it appears in the form of willingness to undertake an assigned or self-selected task and to work at it, ignoring distractions, until the desired goal has been reached.

The Early Training Project has met with some success, as indicated by IQs that run significantly higher than those of a control group of children. After the children have gone through a few years of elementary school, however, most of the initial advantage appears to dwindle. This is not the fault of the experimental program, which takes the children only as far as the first grade: instead, it reflects the deficiencies of a conventional educational program in a racially segregated school system. Incidentally, the few children who attended desegregated schools seem to have been able to maintain their initial advantage better than those who attended segregated schools.

Facilitating Intellectual Development: *Sesame Street*

In the mid-1960s, two programs were initiated with the intention of facilitating or stimulating the cognitive development of preschool children living in impoverished environments: Project Head Start and *Sesame Street*. Evaluation of Head Start results indicated that the project has had only minimal success, as we indicated in Chapter 3, but the story of *Sesame Street* is more encouraging.

Sesame Street consists of a series of televised programs designed for preschool children and produced by the Children's Television Workshop, sponsored jointly by the Carnegie Corporation, the Ford Foundation, the U.S. Office of Economic Opportunity, and the U.S. Office of Education. The programs focus on the development of verbal and quantitative concepts and skills and are presented in an entertaining and lively manner. Assessments of the effect of *Sesame Street* on its viewers have indicated that it is quite effective: the more programs children see, the more concepts they know. Unfortunately, children living in deprived surroundings are less inclined to watch the programs than are middle-class children. In any event, middle-class children are benefitting more from *Sesame Street* than are the children of the poor (Ball and Bogatz, 1970).

An experiment using Spanish-language television programs modeled after *Sesame Street*, entitled *Plaza Sesamo*, found that intervention-via-television works as well in Spanish as in English. The subjects were preschool children from poor homes who were attending day care centers in Mexico. The experimental groups saw daily *Plaza Sesamo* programs, whereas the control groups saw cartoons and other noneducational televised features. Pretesting and posttesting showed that children in the experimental groups scored higher on material taught by *Plaza Sesamo*—namely, general knowledge, understanding of numbers, and recognition of letters and words—than did children in the control groups. What is most interesting, however, is that the children in the experimental groups also scored higher than the control groups on cognitive material *not* specifically taught by *Plaza Sesamo*—namely,

"*It was one of those gratifying days that make teaching worthwhile. I finally taught them something they hadn't already learned on 'Sesame Street.'*"

(Tony Saltzman in the *Phi Delta Kappan*.)

understanding of relationships of parts to wholes, spatial concepts, competence in classifying objects and symbols, and oral comprehension (See Figure 9-3). The experiment showed, in other words, that children exposed to programs designed to encourage the development of specific cognitive skills not only learn the skills in question, but are stimulated to develop other cognitive skills as well (Diaz-Guerrero and Holtzman, 1974).

Longitudinal Studies of Intellectual Development

As we noted previously, intelligence tests administered during infancy have relatively low correlations with later development. The skills that we recognize as being major factors in intellectual functioning are but poorly developed then. Once children learn language skills, however, the scope of their cognitive activities is enlarged, and at the same time we find it easier to test their intelligence. It is not surprising,

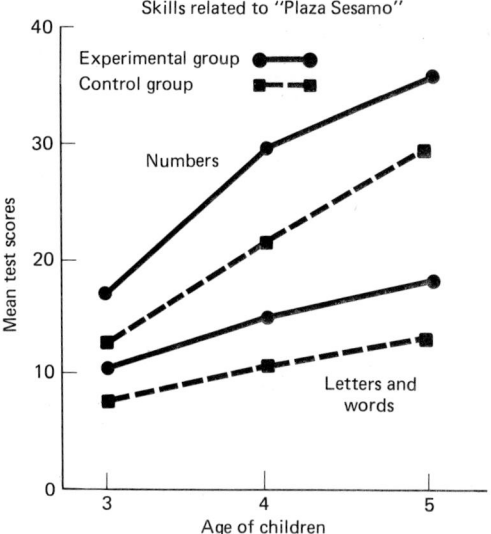

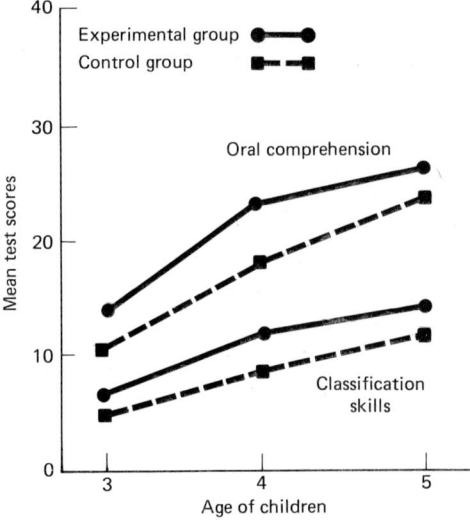

FIGURE 9-3. Scores on cognitive-skill tests made by Mexican preschool children in an experimental group who saw Plaza Sesamo daily for six months and by those in a control group who did not see the program. Subjects were tested on skills and concepts taught by Plaza Sesamo as well as on skills and concepts that were not included in the program. (Data from Diaz-Guerrero and Holtzman, 1974.)

therefore, that tests administered during the preschool years are much better predictors of later intelligence than earlier tests.

As part of the Guidance Study begun in 1928 at the University of California Institute of Child Welfare (now called the Institute of Human Development), 250 children were given periodic intelligence tests, beginning at the age of 21 months. Follow-up research with these children (who are now adults) continues at the present time. Correlations between test performance at 10 and 17 months and measures made during the preschool years are quite substantial, running from .34 to .48

for certain scales or subtests. The ability to make perceptual discriminations seems to have been a key skill that had a significant effect on children's vocal-verbal and manipulatory behavior (Bayley, 1970).

Figure 9-4 shows the correlations between the verbal knowledge subtest of the California Preschool Mental Scale, administered between two and six years of age to children in the California Growth Study (another longitudinal study conducted at the Institute of Child Welfare), and the IQs of the same individuals in later years. This subtest, a measure of what Bayley calls *precocity*, is a particularly good one for this purpose, because verbal skills appear to play a more crucial role than any other factor with respect to school learning, problem solving, and cognitive functioning in general. The graph in Figure 9-4 shows a correlation that is negative during the initial months, but quickly rises to a positive correlation of about .40 and then to .70 about four years of age. After that the relationship between IQ and precocity settles down to .50 to .60 during the school years and then drops to about .40 during the early adult years.

The data reported in Figure 9-4 represent the midpoints of correlations for both male and female subjects. The figures for boys and girls are fairly close during the school years, but at about age 16 the correlation with precocity begins to lower for women than for men. From age 25 onward, the correlation for men actually increased to about .58 at age 36, whereas that for women drops off to about .18. This latter trend may be a reflection of the culturally determined fact that the jobs awarded to men in our culture generally tend to be more intellectually demanding than those available to women.

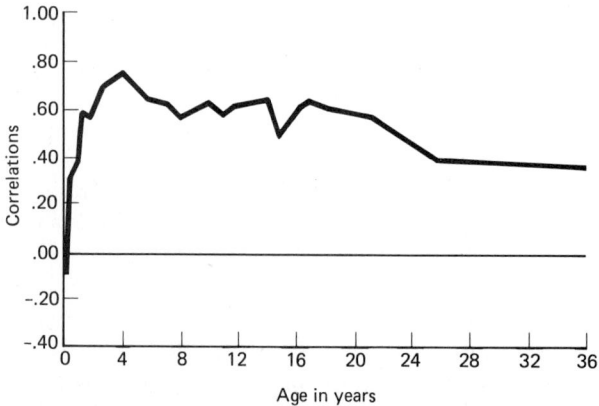

FIGURE 9-4. *Correlations between verbal precocity (as indicated by scores on the Preschool Verbal Knowledge portion of the California Preschool Mental Scale) and IQs of California Growth Study subjects from infancy to adulthood.* (After Bayley, 1966.)

Problem-Solving Ability

During the preschool years, children quickly develop the ability to deal with simple manipulative problems. In fact, there is evidence to show that the approaches used by preschoolers are sometimes more effective with certain types of laboratory problems than are those used by school-age children and adults.

Morton W. Weir (1967), for example, used the device displayed in Figure 9-5 to present subjects with a very simple type of game or problem. The object of the game was to get as many marbles as possible out of the machine. The subject did not know that only one of the three knobs (it was always the same one) was connected to the release mechanism, which was programmed to pay off only one third of the time and at random intervals. In other words, the subject was rewarded only if he pushed the correct knob and then only 33 per cent of the time.

Three-year-olds, in dealing with this problem, quickly found that only one knob paid off and settled down to pushing that one most of the time. Older children and adults, however, were puzzled by the frequent lack of payoff and kept trying to figure out a strategy. They were more likely to believe that the other knobs were involved and kept testing them to be sure. As a consequence, three-year-olds were consistently more successful than older individuals. Figure 9-6 demonstrates the trend very clearly. Three-year-old subjects achieved almost 70 per cent success between the eleventh and the twentieth trial, while adults at

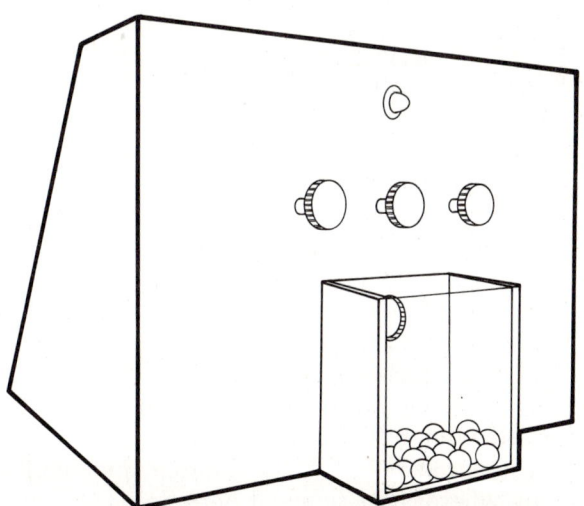

FIGURE 9-5. Line drawing of marble-dispensing device used in research dealing with simple problem-solving strategies. (Weir, 1967. Reproduced by permission.)

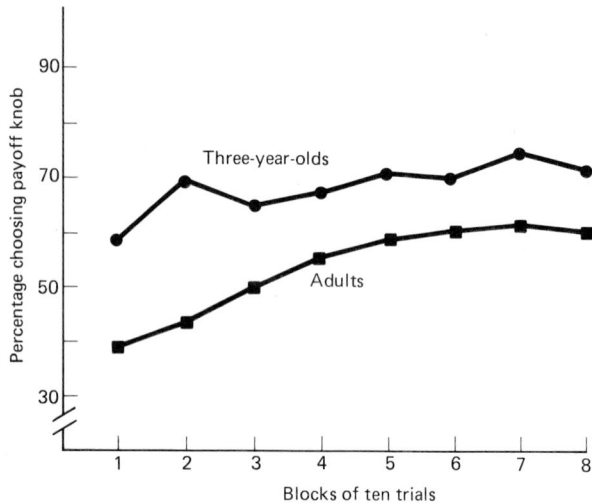

FIGURE 9-6. Performance of three-year-olds and adult subjects in playing a game involving a simple strategy with a 33% payoff. (Weir, 1967. Reproduced by permission.)

that stage were plodding along at about 40 per cent success. Adults made steady improvement during the remainder of the experiment, but never achieved the success of the three-year-olds.

Somewhat similar results were obtained by Tracy and Howard Kendler (1959) with a marble-dispensing device rigged somewhat differently. In their experiments, subjects had to choose between one of two levers that were coded by two different symbolic elements, say, color and shape. After their subject had figured out which symbolic element paid off, the Kendlers, without warning, changed the basis of the payoff. A change in one of the two elements, say from one color to the other, called for a change in strategy that the Kendlers termed a *reversal shift*; a change in *two* elements, say from a color to shape of a symbol, demanded what they termed a *nonreversal shift*. The reversal shift required a partial alteration of strategy; the nonreversal called for a complete abandonment of the former strategy and the learning of a brand new one. Logically, one might think that adults and older children would figure out both types of shifts more successfully than young children, but the results of the Kendlers show that young children learned nonreversal shifts more readily than did older children and adults (Kendler, Kendler, and Wells, 1960).

The Kendlers theorized that older children and adults attack the problem verbally whereas the younger ones do not. A number of the older children actually talked aloud when faced by the sudden change in the payoff arrangement. Verbalization evidently helps in making reversal shifts, but tends to interfere with nonreversal shifts.

Although neither of these two sets of studies have any direct or obvious connection with the problems that children face in growing up, they do shed a little light on the way their thinking develops. As more of such studies are undertaken, we will gain a better understanding of what steps we can take to facilitate the learning of problem-solving skills, both for children in normal circumstances and for those who are socially and economically deprived.

summary

The attainment of the ability to use language in speech enables the child to take his place as a member of society and provides him with a rich source of symbols, which aid him in both verbal and nonverbal learning. Verbal skills may not be essential for cognitive functioning, however, for people deaf from birth onward reach normal levels of cognitive ability without an equal degree of competence in language. Children are also able to perform tasks involving elements for which they have no words in their vocabularies.

There are several contrasting views as to how language is acquired. In opposition to environmentalist theories, Chomsky maintains that language learning results from an innate capacity—a language acquisition mechanism—which enables children to process linguistic data and to generate an infinite variety of original but understandable statements. The fact that children all over the world tend to employ the same strategies and go through much the same stages in learning to talk seems to support Chomsky's nativistic theories.

Luria has theorized that children's verbal development is coordinated with their motor development, but research suggests that the process may be more complicated. Imitation of adults seems to be involved in the learning of language, but parents seem to be more concerned with the truth or validity of small children's utterances and less interested in their grammatical structure. A study in which adults restructured children's statements in more complex ways showed that two-year-olds can be led fairly easily to introduce complex forms into the language they use. Braine has proposed that children learn key (or pivot-class) words, which can be linked with a variety of other (or open-class) words to make sentences. Children apparently introduce structure into their language in much the same way that they structure their environment. Some psycholinguists object to grammatical or structural explanations of language learning because such explanations ignore the semantics of language—what children are actually trying to communicate.

An early study by Smith showed that children's vocabularies grow very rapidly at first, but that the rate slows down by the age of four. Smith's data regarding the rate of growth seem accurate, but she probably understated the amount of words known by the average child at any given age. Today's children also experience wide exposure to the media of mass communication, which has undoubtedly facilitated vocabulary growth. In general, the greater the contact with adult models, the more extensive the vocabulary. Girls apparently make more rapid progress in language learning than boys do at first, but boys catch up at about age three.

Middle-class children are reported to use language more effectively than do lower-class children, perhaps because their parents encourage verbalization more. Studies reporting this advantage have been questioned by some scholars, who maintain that the difference may merely reflect a difference in rule systems in the language forms used by lower-class and middle-class children. Osser, a sociolinguist, claims that lower-class children could do as well in school as any middle-class child if they were taught in their own language forms; but other research indicates that dialect differences do not interfere with the understanding of standard English by lower-class children.

Psychologists conceive intelligence as consisting of three elements: the ability to solve tasks involving abstractions, the ability to learn, and the ability to deal with new situations. Intelligence tests attempt to tap all three of these cognitive abilities. Anything that interferes with normal growth and development will inhibit cognitive development—poor nutrition and birth abnormalities are examples. Environments that are not stimulating also retard cognitive development.

There is a common tendency for the IQs of the children of poor and uneducated parents to decline after the first year of school. This would seem to indicate that the preschool years are critical for cognitive development, and that intervention at that stage might forestall such decrements in IQ. Gray and Klaus have conducted a long-range experimental program for deprived black preschoolers, attempting to teach cognitive skills and stressing achievement motivation. Although IQs have been raised, the gain tends to be lost after a few years in elementary school. Children who have gone through the Head Start program have had similar experiences. The televised program *Sesame Street* has increased the cognitive ability of preschoolers: the more programs they see, the more gains they make. Evaluation of a similar program in Mexico shows that children learned not only the material and skills taught by the program, but a broad spectrum of other cognitive skills as well.

Intelligence tests administered during the preschool years are better predictors of later intelligence than are scores on tests administered in infancy. The California Preschool Mental Scale reveals that verbal skills play the single most important role with respect to later cognitive functioning.

Preschoolers are sometimes better able to solve some manipulative problems and games than adults, especially under conditions in which the required solution is so simple as to elude sophisticated subjects who search for a subtle strategy. Researchers have theorized that older children and adults attack problems verbally, whereas younger children do not.

ten

Emotional and Personality Development

*The childhood shows the man
As morning shows the day.*
— JOHN MILTON

*Children have neither past nor future;
They enjoy the present, which very few of us do.*
— JEAN DE LA BRUYÈRE

One of the major characteristics of young children is their lability—that is, the instability of their emotions. A mild frustration, such as a firm "no" from a parent, will set them off to crying, but the next minute they can be laughing with unrestrained glee as they are drawn into a stimulating game. The emotions of infants are also unstable, of course, but toddlers and preschoolers may appear more emotional because they are more aware of the frustrating, satisfying, and stimulating aspects of their environment and have a wider repertoire of responses to express their emotional states. They not only have some command of language, but they can kick, push, hit, and bite those who have incurred their displeasure—and can also, of course, hug, kiss, and behave in other pleasant ways toward those who meet with favor in their eyes.

From an affective standpoint, early childhood is a very stirring period, one that is very demanding and also exciting for child and caregiver alike.

_____emotional development

Differentiating Emotional Responses

Like many terms that are frequently used by psychologists and other scientists, *emotion* is a difficult word to define. It may be applied both to an increase in or release from tension, and to sustained high, intermediate, or low levels of tension as well. Inasmuch as our only evidence that an emotional state exists consists of the observable behavior that accompanies or results from such tension states or changes in states, it is probably more accurate to speak of *emotional responses* or *emotional behavior*, rather than *emotion*.

The characteristics of emotional responses may be determined from situations in which they occur, as well as from the general direction of the behavior that is displayed. Positive emotions are characterized by a tendency to *approach*. Enjoyment, satisfaction, and love all involve being attracted to objects or persons—wanting to retain them, remain with them, or stay in their proximity.

Negative emotions are of two main types: fear and rage. Fear or anxiety responses have an *away from* quality to them—that is, we want to remove ourselves from offending objects or persons or want them to depart from us. Rage responses have an *against* quality; when we are irritated or angry we want to destroy, humiliate, or injure the offending objects or persons. In very general terms, fear or anxiety responses are characteristic of us when we feel less than adequate to deal with the situation in question, whereas rage or anger responses are associated with a feeling of strength, power, and competence.

Emotional Responses During Infancy

To get some perspective on the development of emotional responses during early childhood, we must look at the emotional life of the infant, a topic we bypassed in our discussion of infancy a few chapters back. Although infants certainly do have emotions, this aspect of their lives does not command as much attention on the part of researchers as does, say, the study of their cognitive development.

Some psychologists maintain that the only emotional response which can be identified in infants is a state of generalized excitement and that the emotions we recognize as fear, disgust, anger, and delight gradually evolve from this early, undifferentiated phase. This view may be too simplistic, however. In Chapter 6 we noted that neonates' cries could be classified according to their mood or state: hunger, anger, or response to injury. The fact that the infants' mothers reacted in different ways to the quality and intensity of these cries suggests that something more precise than generalized excitement was being communicated.

There does, however, seem to be a universal sequence of emotional response appearing at various stages during infancy. Toward the end of the first month the infant begins to smile at seeing a face, be it a strange or a familiar one, and by five or six months of age he is smiling with maximum frequency (Gewirtz, 1965). Nor is it necessary that the infant actually see a face: infants born blind who are socially stimulated also engage in prolonged smiling at six months (Freedman, 1965). Between the ages of four and six months, infants begin to laugh when bounced on the knee or when surprised by the sudden appearance of a face during a game of peek-a-boo.

Responses associated with anxiety tend to appear about the same time. Seeing a stranger is likely to elicit a "sobering" response, which may indicate curiosity but which may also be the first indication of apprehension and tension. Anxiety at the appearance of a stranger apparently reaches its peak at seven to nine months, whereas, anxiety at being separated from the mother or other caregiver begins to appear at eight months and rises to a peak at ten months, as we noted in Chapter 7 (Schaffer and Emerson, 1964a). There is much variation, however; some infants show very little fear of strangers, while others are quite apprehensive. In any event, the closer the infant is to his mother, the less his fear of strangers (Morgan and Ricciuti, 1968).

fear and anxiety

Research on Children's Fears

The emergence of fear at about the middle of the first year, in response to visual novelty—be it the entrance of a stranger or the appearance of a large and unfamiliar object—appears to have its roots in our biological heritage, according to Gordon W. Bronson (1970). Bronson traced the further development of early fearfulness by examining the difference in response patterns over the first eight and a half years of life of boys and girls who served as subjects in the Berkeley Growth Study.

Bronson began with a measure of early indications of sensitivity on the part of his subjects: the percentage of time they spent in crying while being examined and observed by the Study's investigators on various occasions during the first ten months of life. For the period after ten months, Bronson noted various signs of wariness or apprehensiveness, including crying, and recorded them on a scale indicating the degree of shyness or fearfulness these responses represented.

The measures of shyness during earlier periods were then correlated with observations made in the course of interviews conducted during the following eight years. The comparisons showed that boys were quite consistent in their behavior. About half the boys had not cried during the examinations conducted before they were six months old; this group also cried very little during the examinations made over the next two and a half years. The half of the boys who had engaged in considerable crying before six months of age continued to cry a great deal until they were two years old; after that age, neither group cried very much. During the ensuing six years, however, boys who had not cried in early infancy showed few other signs of shyness, whereas those who had been early criers were consistently shyer and more apprehensive.

The girls included in the study showed no such consistency in their behavior over the period. There was a tendency for early noncriers to engage in less crying than the early criers between the ages of seven to nine months, but thereafter there was no difference between the groups. Indeed, from the age of two onward, there was a slight but nonsignificant tendency for early noncriers to be somewhat shyer than the other group.

Bronson was unable to explain why the males in his study demonstrated "a relatively enduring predisposition toward a particular level of fearfulness" and the females did not, but he did note that female monkeys raised in isolation had lost their fearfulness nine months after they had been released, whereas male monkeys subjected to the same treatment had not. Evidently males who are initially fearful tend to remain so, at least during the early stages of their development.

Arthur T. Jersild, for many years on the faculty of Teachers College, Columbia University, is one of the pioneer students of children's fears.

The classic study of fear responses in children was conducted many years ago by Jersild and Holmes (1935). In one phase of their research, they asked parents to record all instances in which their children (aged one to twelve) displayed fear during a three-week period. The number of fear-provoking incidents, averaged about six per day for two-year-olds, but was less than four per day for three-year-olds, and only two per day for children four and five years old.

The correlation between number of fears and intelligence test scores was relatively high for two-year-olds, suggesting that the more intelligent children of this age were more sensitive to possible hazards in their environment. The correlation between fears and intelligence dropped to virtually zero with the five-year-olds, however, probably because of the generally low number of fears at this age.

Fear and Anxiety

Anxiety is generally less intense than fear, and its causes can be less readily identified. The anxious person either is unsure why he is apprehensive or identifies causes that turn out to be illogical or irrelevant. Future events are a prime source of anxiety, because of their unpredictability and uncertainty. The child is *anxious* about the coming visit to the dentist, but he is *fearful* once he is in the dentists's chair.

Although anxiety is upsetting and disturbing, it does have its positive aspects. For one thing, it prods the child into examining and analyzing potentially harmful events in advance of their occurrence and leads him to take some measures to protect himself or to avoid unnecessary hazards. Anxiety about his relations with others also leads him to anticipate their reaction to his actions. It thus plays an important role in socialization.

The negative aspects of anxiety are well known. In its severe form it may immobilize the child, preventing him from interacting in rewarding or fruitful ways with adults or peers. Furthermore, children who would be normally curious and thus be motivated to explore and investigate their environment may be so inhibited by anxiety that they are unable to learn.

Adults can play reassuring roles and thus cushion some of the anxiety-provoking aspects of strange environments. In one experiment, preschool girls were exposed to two types of situations in the presence of their mothers or a strange female. In one situation, which was calculated to arouse a minimum of anxiety, the child was placed in an observation room that was supplied with toys and decorated by smiling faces. In the situation calculated to arouse a maximum of anxiety, there were few toys; the room was decorated by sad faces, and a phonograph in the next room emitted sounds of a child crying, a loud banging on a metallic object, and a shriek. There was a lighted alcohol lamp in the room near a red door; 12 minutes after the child and the adult had

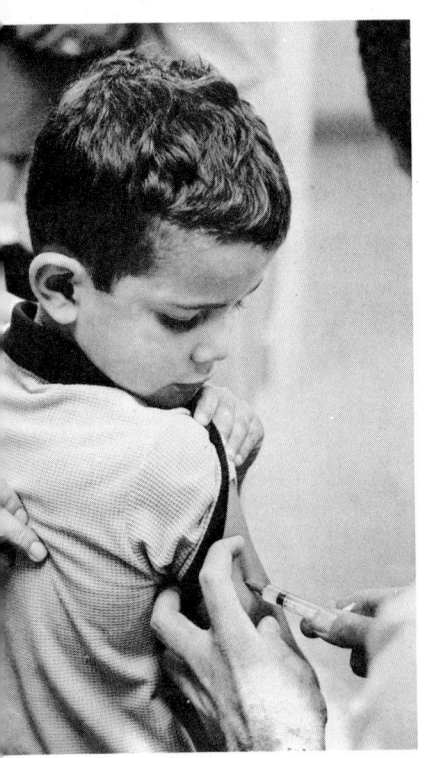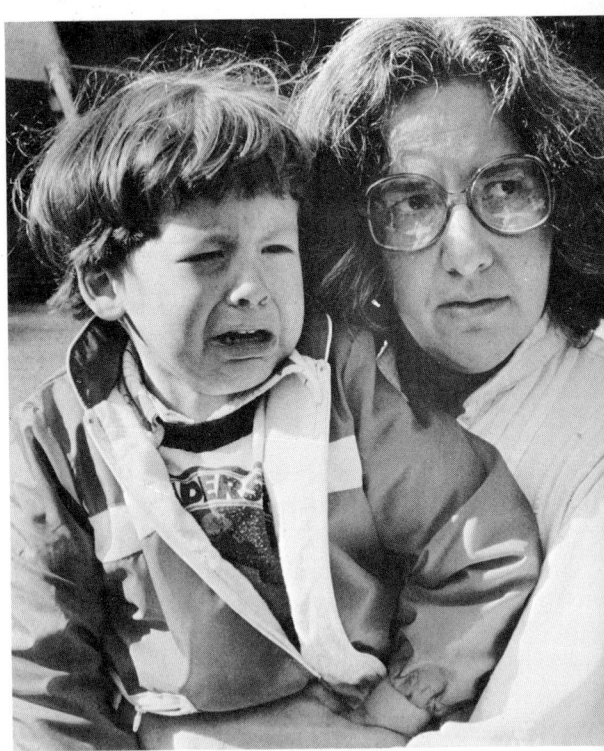

Fear may be triggered by some physical event, such as an injection, or by confronting a new social situation, such as an encounter with a stranger. Anxiety, which is akin to fear, is characterized by a feeling of vague apprehensiveness.

entered, the red door opened, and a hand in an arm-length black glove reached in slowly, extinguishing the lamp.

The behavior of the children was observed in terms of their attempts either to get the adult to pay attention to them or merely to remain in her proximity. As might be expected, the high-anxiety condition led the child to engage in far more proximity-seeking behavior than did the low-anxiety condition. There was no difference, however, in the amount of attention-seeking behavior between the two conditions (Rosenthal, 1965; 1967).

Violence and Children's Fantasies

Television programs are often cited as prime causes of children's fearfulness and aggressiveness. Television is of course fantasy and not reality, and there is a question as to what effects it has on children's behavior. Research has produced ambiguous results, but common sense would strongly support the idea that a diet of televised violence is likely to arouse and stimulate, to encourage modeling or imitation of the behavior portrayed on the screen, and to remove inhibitions against aggressive behavior.

Adults often assume that children have to be taught to enjoy fantasy violence. It may be, however, that human beings are biologically programmed in such a way that they find observing or thinking about violence stimulating, exciting, and interesting—hence attractive. Some research by Louise Bates Ames (1966) suggests that these inclinations appear at a fairly early age. Ames analyzed the stories told by children aged two to five and found that violent themes outnumbered nonviolent ones three to one. The most frequent themes were associated with violent accidents (such as getting killed), with aggression (such as being eaten by a rabbit) a close second. Although boys produced more violent themes than girls, the actual differences were not very large: 76 per cent for boys versus 68 per cent for girls. The highest level of fantasy violence was reached by three-and-a-half-year-old boys, who told stories in which 88 per cent of the themes involved some kind of violence. The lowest point for both sexes was at age 5, when about 67 per cent of the themes were violent.

Ames's method of gathering material was quite simple. She merely took the children aside from their nursery school group and asked them to tell a story. If the child hesitated, the interviewer prompted: "What could your story be about?" This was usually enough to get the child started. Here are a couple of exampled:

> Little bunny rabbit went in the woods and he found a wolf and the wolf ate him all up. But a man heard the bunny rabbit squeaking so he tied the wolf to a railroad track. The train ran right over the wolf (girl, 4½ years).

Pussy cat. . . . He got a crashup from the cars. Then the pussy cat went on the sidewalk and saw another car and he had a crashup. And then a crashup again. Then he had another crashup (boy, 3 years).[1]

Sears, Rau, and Alpert (1965) conducted a series of studies with children of nursery-school age, using fantasy doll play, and found a negative correlation between punishment by parents and aggressive themes expressed by children; those children who expressed the most violent themes in doll play were the ones who experienced the gentlest treatment from their parents. It seems clear that these children had not learned their taste for violence from their parents.

It seems, then, that violence appears in children's fantasy in a spontaneous fashion; it does not have to be stimulated or instigated by outside intervention. The explanation of this phenomenon is quite simple: violence has a high arousal value—it is interesting and exciting. Any child whose life has been relatively sheltered and stress-free might understandably wish to invent crisis material to liven things up.

anger and aggression

There has been relatively little research on the positive emotional responses of childhood—laughter, smiling, and expressing love—and a great deal on the negative responses, especially those associated with *anger* (an emotional state), *aggression* (behavior directed against others, often touched off by anger), and *aggressiveness* (a personality trait characterized by antagonistic and destructive behavior). Fear and anxiety have also attracted some attention on the part of researchers, but not as much as anger and aggression, probably because the latter create more problems that call for prompt intervention on the part of caregivers. Furthermore, the behavioral manifestations of anger and aggressiveness are likely to be highly visible and hence more readily researchable, whereas the withdrawal behavior associated with fear and anxiety are much less obvious and may escape notice.

Anger Research

The classic study of anger in young children was conducted by Florence L. Goodenough (1931), who analyzed records of 45 children, aged 12 months through four years. Every day the mothers of these children recorded the incidents of anger that occurred, noting the time, place, and duration of the outburst, the immediate cause, and the kinds of behavior the children exhibited. From records kept for periods

---

[1] Reprinted by permission.

extending from about one to four months, Goodenough collected over 1800 instances of anger outbursts. Her work is the major study of this aspect of behavior, and subsequent observers generally corroborate her findings.

Goodenough classified expressions of anger under three headings: *undirected energy* (such as kicking randomly, holding the breath, or screaming); *motor or verbal resistance* (such as refusing to cooperate or obey, or resisting being held); and *retaliation* (such as biting, hitting, or shouting at others). An analysis of her findings showed that between the ages of two and five there was a steady decline in the expression of anger in the form of undirected energy; no change in motor or verbal resistance; but an increase in retaliatory behavior. Thus with increasing age, expressions of anger were less random and more likely to take the form of aggression.

Figure 10-1 summarizes Goodenough's findings on age and sex differences in the frequency of anger outbursts. Anger-related responses attain their highest frequency in the middle of the second year and decline thereafter—sharply for girls, but only moderately for boys. This early tendency of boys to be more irritable and aggressive is consistent with later developmental patterns, for school and juvenile authorities universally report that boys are involved in a far greater number of violent and destructive acts than girls are.

Goodenough reported that one of the commonest causes of anger outbursts involved some form of conflict with authority: over adult demands that child go to the toilet, come to meals, or have his face washed; over adult denial of permission to carry out or initiate some

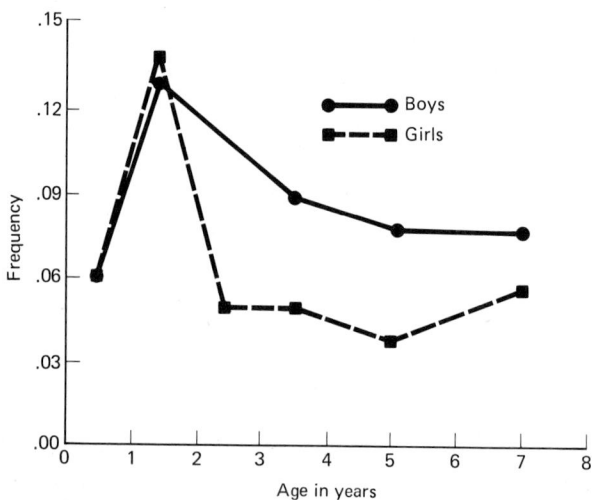

FIGURE 10-1. *Frequency of anger outbursts per hour of observation for a sample of young children. (After Goodenough, 1931.)*

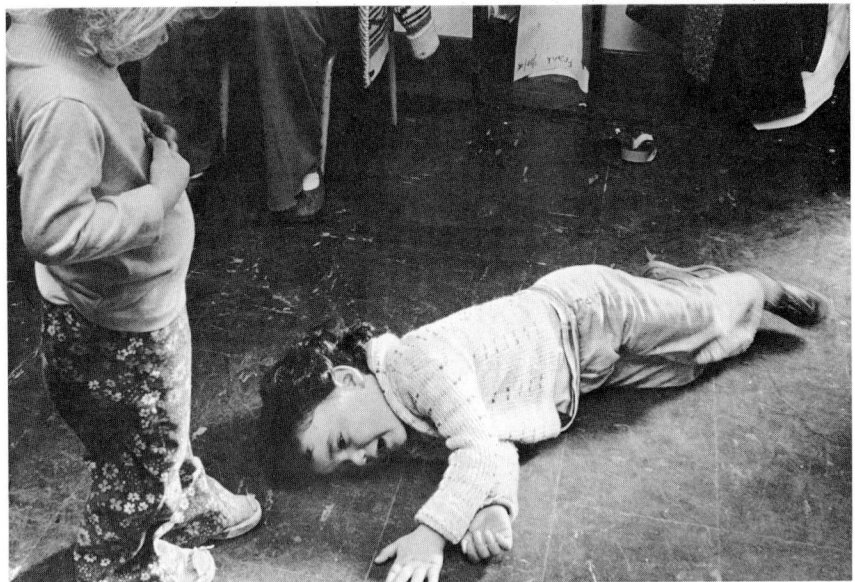

Some children, usually boys, have a very low tolerance for frustration and may react to simple requests and the imposition of reasonable restrictions with outbursts of anger amd tantrums.

activity; or as a reaction to reprimand and punishment. The other major source of outbursts of anger was interpersonal relationships: being denied attention, inability to make desires understood, being denied access to ongoing group activities, resistance to demands that toys or candy be shared, or demands for the possessions of others. The major element in both of these types of situations seems to be frustration. In the first, the child's ongoing activity is interrupted and he is required to do something else, or his freedom to choose is thwarted or limited. In the second, his need or drive to attain something is blocked.

Anger in children ordinarily leads to or is accompanied by aggressive acts: hitting, biting, shouting epithets, and the like. It thus appears to be an intermediate state between frustration and aggression. Goodenough's observations were thus consistent with the prevailing theory of her era—namely that frustration leads to aggression and that aggression is always caused by frustration. The elaborated statement of this theory, published by John Dollard and his colleagues (1939), led to much controversy and a great deal of interesting research, which partly confirmed and partly disconfirmed it. An example of the latter is a classic study by Barker, Dembo, and Lewin (1943). Their experiment, in which young children who were permitted to play with attractive toys which were then taken away from them, showed that frustration under such circumstances led to play patterns that were less mature—regression, rather than aggression or anger. Critics of the frustration-aggression theory also pointed out that as part of the socialization process children learn to deal with frustrations in more mature ways: overlooking them, expressing anger in a harmless manner, solving the problem that is causing the difficulty, negotiating with the frustrator, and so forth.

Cultural Influences on Aggressiveness

In their attempts to socialize their children, parents generally attempt to "extinguish" anger outbursts and aggressive behavior. Nonetheless, we should recognize the fact that free expression of emotions, even in aggressive form, is tolerated by North American society more than by other, more traditional, societies. Just why this is so, as well as the extent to which it is so, is a matter of much debate, but individuals who have observed child-rearing practices in this and in other cultures are struck by the permissiveness of North American adults with regard to children's aggressiveness.

A European or Asiatic adult will quickly intervene in order to quiet a verbal dispute between two preschoolers, whereas a North American is inclinced to "let the children work it out" and to step in only when physical aggression is threatened. Nor do American children lack for aggressive models: the study by Niem and Collard (1972) we cited in Chapter 2 showed that American parents were much more inclined to behave aggressively—to use physical punishment—then were Chinese parents. American boys are also commonly encouraged by parents to learn physical combat skills so that they can "defend their rights," and the violence on television programs that can be viewed by children is a favorite theme of psychological researchers and newspaper feature story writers alike.

Social Learning and Aggression

The proposition that aggressive behavior in children is largely a learned response has been a major focal point in the work of social psychologists since the beginning of the 1960s. The work of Bandura and Walters (1963a, b) on social learning has been especially influential. They proposed that the number or intensity of aggressive responses involves two rather different effects. There is the *modeling* effect, in which the child reproduces the novel response of the model; and there is the *disinhibiting* effect, in which observation of the model results in weakening the inhibition of those aggressive responses already in the repertory of the child.

An investigation demonstrating the generalization of imitative aggressive responses to a setting in which the model was absent was performed by Bandura, Ross, and Ross (1961). In this experiment, a boy or a girl of nursery school age watched an adult model who first spent a minute working with a Tinker-Toy construction set and then punched, tossed, and struck a five-foot inflated clown doll, while making appropriately hostile remarks. A second group of nursery-school children watched a nonaggressive adult spend several minutes working with a Tinker-Toy set. A control group saw no models at all.

Boys who grow up in a culture in which aggressiveness is tolerated and guns are prized as expressions of masculinity and strength are likely to express these elements in fantasy form, through their play.

Each of the children was taken to another room in which he or she was exposed to a situation designed to arouse some degree of frustration: each child was shown attractive toys (a fire engine and a doll set) and allowed to play long enough to get involved. Then the playing was interrupted, and the children were told that these were the very best toys and that a decision had been made to reserve them for other children.

Each child was then taken to a nearby room which contained a variety of toys, some nonaggressive in character (tea set, crayons, cars, and the like), and others of a type which suggested aggressive responses, such as a mallet and a dart gun. There was also a three-foot inflated clown doll. Each child spent twenty minutes alone in the room, his behavior being observed through a one-way mirror.

Behavior that was rated included acts of physical and verbal aggression, and nonimitative physical and verbal aggression, including use of the guns. The subjects previously exposed to the aggressive models expressed a great amount of aggression, differing significantly in this respect from the nonaggressive and control groups. Subjects who had observed the nonaggressive model were less aggressive than the control subjects. Boys showed more aggression than girls, following exposure to the male model.

Rosekrans and Hartup (1967) conducted a social-learning type of experiment that sheds more light on the ways in which children learn to be aggressive. In their experiment, preschool-age children watched an adult female perform such aggressive acts as pounding a doll on the head with a mallet, chopping off the head of a clay figure with a knife, and using a fork to jab the legs of a clay figure. Another adult female praised the model for her behavior (reward), criticized the model (punishment), or alternated between praising and criticizing the model. A fourth group of children who did not see the model constituted a control group. As Figure 10-2 indicates, the extent to which the model was rewarded or punished was reflected in the amount of imitative aggression displayed by the children when they had a chance to play with the same items. An interesting effect occurred, however, when the children were divided into younger (36-58 months) groups and older (60-71 months) groups and their nonimitative responses were tallied.

As Figure 10-2 shows, those younger children who had seen the rewarded model behaved in a decidedly aggressive manner, whereas those who viewed the inconsistent reinforcement of the model were somewhat inhibited. The younger children who saw no model were quite aggressive. This effect could have been predicted from the implements that were available for play purposes: a mallet, a knife, and a fork, to which pounding, cutting, or jabbing are natural responses. The young children who saw the model reprimanded for aggressiveness, however, were totally inhibited.

The older children responded differently. Their nonimitative agres-

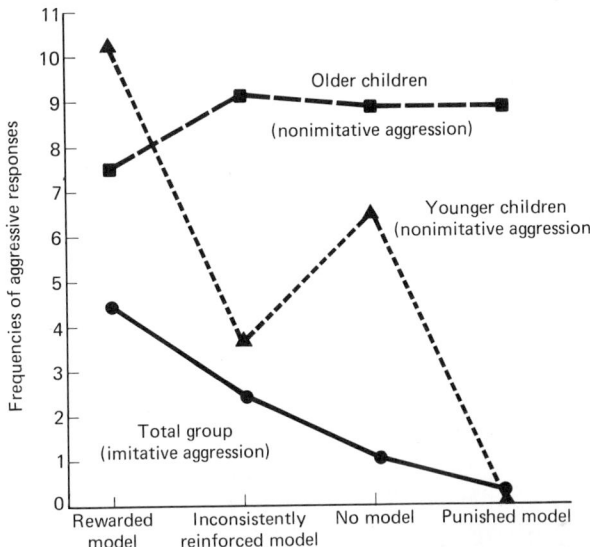

FIGURE 10-2. *Aggressive response frequencies for children who saw (or did not see) the aggression of an adult model who received one of three styles of reinforcement.* (Data from Rosekrans and Hartup, 1967.)

sive responses were generally unrelated to the model's treatment. The authors explain this result in terms of the older children's ability to make finer discrimination among various kinds of aggression and to match their responses only to those categories for which the model was rewarded or punished.

In sum, these and other studies of social learning suggest that aggressiveness in young children can be brought on by observing models who are permitted or encouraged to engage in aggressive acts, or else simply by being in an environment in which there are objects associated with aggression and destruction. Seeing a model restrained from behaving aggressively may have some effect, especially with younger, more impressionable subjects. In the main, these findings are consistent with aggression research conducted with adolescent and adult subjects.

Although the research studies make it fairly clear that aggression in children can be produced by the environment—that is, through the presence of a model or through the availability of instruments of aggression—there are some unanswered problems regarding the sources of aggression. For one thing, they do not explain why boys are consistently more aggressive than girls. We will examine this question in greater detail when we discuss sex differences in personality later in this chapter.

324 Early Childhood: The Preschool Years

"NO, MOM! THAT'S NOT VI'LENCE...
THE GOOD GUYS ARE WINNIN'!"

(Dennis the Menace, courtesy of Hank Ketcham.)

emotions with positive affect

As we noted earlier, there has been relatively little research devoted to positive emotions, most of the research with the emotional development of children being concerned with hostility, aggressiveness, fear, and anxiety. Such research as has been undertaken on the subject of joy and expressions of pleasure was for the most part conducted some forty or fifty years ago. Katherine M. B. Bridges (1931), who conducted a general survey of emotional development in infants, observed that one of the first emotions that could be identified was delight, which appeared before the age of three months. She also noted that indications of elation, affection, and joy were recognizable by two years of age.

Leuba (1941), who studied laughter in his own two infants, found that at about six or seven months smiling and laughter appeared in response to mild, intermittent tickling. Before the end of the first year, the laughter and smiling had been conditioned to the sight of the fingers moving preparatory to tickling.

A very early investigator, Ruth W. Washburn (1929), observed the development of laughter and smiling of 15 infants from eight weeks to one year of age at monthly intervals. She recorded facial responses made in response to a standard set of stimuli presented at monthly observations. Some of the "stimuli" she used were (1) smiling, "chirrup-

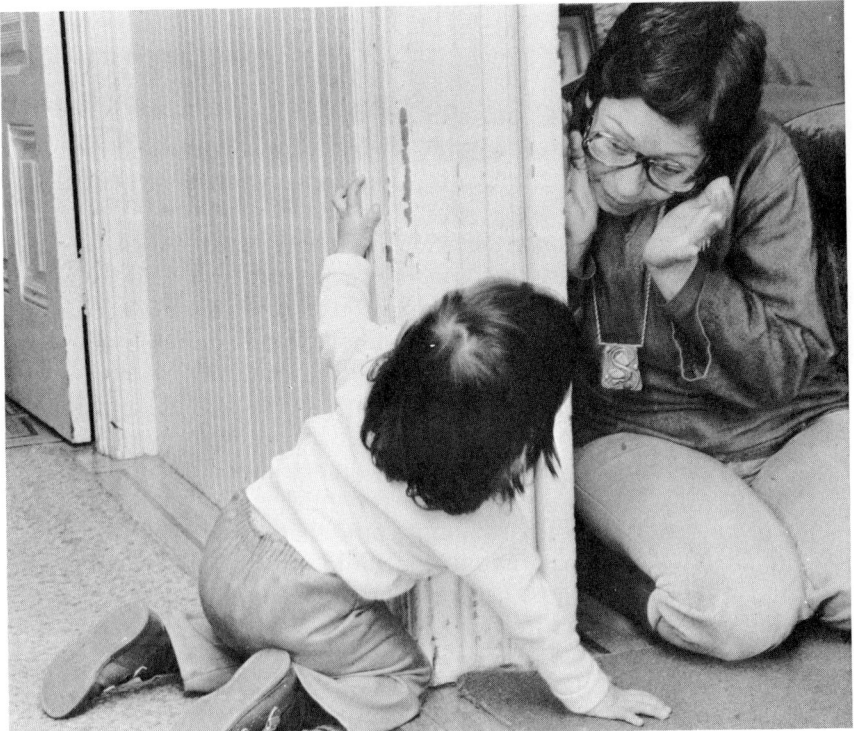

Peek-a-boo is a social game that usually evokes smiles and laughter in infants and young toddlers.

ing," and talking to the infant; (2) peek-a-boo; (3) "threatening head" (lowering of the head toward the infant and saying "ah boo"); (4) hand clapping; (5) sudden reappearance from under table; and (6) tickling. All of the stimuli she used were effective in producing smiles at one or more of the monthly age levels, but some were more effective in producing laughter than others. Laughter in one half or more of the subjects was produced by peek-a-boo, the threatening head, and hand clapping.

Like laughter, smiling is a social response. Hence it is not surprising to learn that it is very highly correlated with vocalizing in infants—another indicator of socializing tendencies (McCall, 1970).

Laughter and Arousal

Social stimulation is a major factor in arousing smiling and laughter. In another early study of positive affect, Catherine W. Brackett (1934) found that laughter occurred most often in social situations—situations in which the children were interacting with one another. Brackett found that almost 85 per cent of the laughter of her groups occurred in social settings. Moreover, laughter in a given child was predominately found when laughter occurred in the other children who were present. Laughter was much less frequent when the children engaged in solitary play.

Ding and Jersild (1932), in addition to noting the social setting of laughter, also collected considerable evidence on laughter and observed that children laughed most frequently when they were engaged in active physical play.

The capacity of the human system to deal with arousal increases with age. Toddlers are obviously better able to cope with arousal than infants are. Furthermore, the enjoyment of arousal appears to increase in proportion to the capacity to deal with it. An experiment by Paul Weisberg (1975) demonstrates the relationship between enjoyment by physical arousal and age. In Weisberg's investigation, male and female college students served as experimenters who tickled or cuddled children aged three, four, five, and six. In the first phase of the experiment, each child was tickled by one experimenter and then cuddled by another experimenter of the sex opposite to that of the first one. In the second phase of the experiment, the child was permitted to choose which of two experimenters he or she preferred to play with. By cross-matching the sexes of children and experimenters and noting the type of stimulation they provided, it was possible to determine the preferences of children at each of the ages. There were few sex differences, except that girls, particularly at age three, were much more likely to avoid male cuddlers. The main finding, however, was a gradual decline in wanting to be cuddled by an adult of either sex and an increase in preference for being tickled. In other words, with increasing age, children preferred an increasing amount of arousal.

Blatz, Allen, and Millichamp (1936) also studied laughter in the nursery-school setting. They were particularly interested in laughter associated with performing certain activities—falling, using the swing, climbing on the jungle gym, going down the slide, and the like. They found that laughter occurred almost always *after* the completion of an event, that is, after the child had reached the bottom of the slide, after he had jumped into the pool, after he had fallen, and after a toy he had thrown actually landed in the water. They considered that their results indicate that laughter comes when a doubt or ambiguity of some sort has been resolved. That is, the activity the child was engaging in had reached a solution and the uncertainty about whether the desired result would occur was resolved by its completion. Children poised at the top of the slide, for example, sense a tiny element of danger. When they arrive at the bottom unhurt, they laugh.

Laughter and Cognition

Although laughter and smiling are affective responses, they appear to depend on cognitive elements as well. Kreitler and Kreitler (1970) showed five-year-old children pictures involving absurd situations and found that they laughed or smiled when they were able to identify absurdity with criticism, mockery, or wonder. Some cognitive strategies did not produce humor responses: describing the details of the pictures, criticizing them in irrelevant ways, stating the theme without noting the absurdity, resolving the absurdity through fantasy, rationalizing the absurdity in terms of reality, and denying the absurdity.

Piddington (1963) took a view that derives from social psychology, suggesting that laughter serves the child in social situations as a way of resolving conflicts or dilemmas and of simultaneously meeting social needs. The validity of this analysis is supported by the fact that the sudden stimuli that produce laughter in young children are the same ones that would produce anger or fear responses under other circumstances. It is quite possible that the child is unable to decide initially whether to be afraid or to be angry and resolves this conflict or dilemma by concluding that he is not really threatened. The qualities of the stimulus situation that enable him to come to that conclusion cannot be specified with any degree of precision. It is plausible, however, to consider that the foreground stimuli (such as the unexpected, sudden ones just mentioned) are pleasant or unpleasant (a trusted adult versus a strange person). In any event, the way in which the child views the situation determines whether he will or will not laugh or smile.

personality development

We are each different, one from the other. Our physical characteristics and general appearance contribute toward this difference, of course, but what gives each of us the stamp of individuality is the way in which the behavior of each of us differs from that of every other person. These behavioral differences are to a large extent the result of the learning that has taken place through a lifetime of experiences, but they are at the same time based on *temperament*—characteristic patterns of responding and reacting that were present at birth and probably determined to a large extent by the assortment of genes that were ours from conception onward. Differences in temperament, in other words, are the products of glandular, neural, and biochemical interactions which vary among individuals and which are genetically determined.

Evidence that temperamental qualities are "built into" the human organism, and not acquired through learning, may be found in the way neonates vary in their reaction to the satisfactions and frustrations of their new life. A number of early researchers observed that infants—even newborns—differ from each other in the degree to which their behavior expresses tension, relaxation, irritability, and general responsivity to both internal and external events.

Not only do infants differ in the way they respond to the world; they also tend to retain the behavioral styles with which they began life. One important investigation that demonstrates this persistence in temperament is a longitudinal study conducted by Thomas, Chess, and Birch (1970), who studied 131 children in 85 families from birth onward, over a 14-year period. They observed that temperamental patterns present at birth were sometimes strengthened, weakened, or otherwise modified by life experiences, but the general tendency was for the basic trends to persist over the years.

The investigators classified these trends under nine headings, which we have listed in Table 10-1, together with brief descriptions. These traits were clearly discernible in about two thirds of the children, the rest displaying a mixture of trends. Most of the children with identifiable trends were described by the researchers as "easy children," children who adapted readily to new situations, were usually in a good mood, and had few problems in sleeping, eating, and elimination. About 10 per cent of the children were described as "difficult," in that they tended to react angrily and impulsively to attempts to manage and

TABLE 10-1. Temperamental Characteristics Identified in a Longitudinal Study of 141 Children (after Thomas, Chess, and Birch, 1970)

Activity

1. *Level of activity.* The ratio of the child's active periods, in contrast to his inactive or passive periods.
2. *Threshold of responsiveness.* The readiness with which the child responds to stimulation, rated in terms of the intensity of the stimulation required to get him to respond.
3. *Intensivity of reaction.* The degree of intensity or energy the child invests in his responses.
4. *Rhythmicity.* The regularity of the child's patterns of sleeping, waking, eating, and elimination.
5. *Distractibility.* The extent to which the child responds to irrelevant or extraneous stimuli and permits them to alter an ongoing sequence of behavior.
6. *Attention span and persistence.* The amount of time the child stays with an activity and resists distraction.

Reaction to Novelty and Change

7. *Approach-withdrawal.* The characteristic way in which the child responds to strangers, new objects, and novel situations.
8. *Adaptability.* The ease with which the child accepts and adjusts to changes in his environment and life style.

Emotional Style

9. *Quality of mood.* The number of episodes in which the child expresses joy, pleasure, or friendliness, in contrast to those in which he expresses unhappiness, displeasure, or unfriendliness.

control them, to be disturbed by new or unexpected situations, and to experience problems in sleeping, eating, and elimination. About a seventh of the subjects were classified as "slow to warm up." These children were relatively inactive, tended to react passively, and reacted to new situations by withdrawing.

Although temperamental trends affect all aspects of behavior, it is in interaction with others that variations are most observable. Parents are especially sensitive to differences in the way their children respond to them.

Rowe and Plomin (1977) have developed a scale of personality dimensions to be used by parents in rating the temperament of children between the ages of one and six. Their scale, which is based on two others employed in earlier research studies, identifies the following factors, each followed by an example:

Sociability
  Child takes a long time to warm up to strangers.
Emotionality
  Child often fusses and cries.
Activity
  Child is always on the go.
Attention-span persistence
  Child gives up easily when difficulties are encountered.
Reaction to food
  Child makes faces at new foods.
Soothability
  When upset by an unexpected situation, child quickly calms down.

Schaffer and Emerson (1964b) conducted a survey among working-class mothers and found that most of them had little difficulty in classifying their infants as "cuddlers" and "noncuddlers." They used these terms to describe the cuddlers:

"Cuddles you back."
"Snuggles into you."
"Laps it up."
"Would let me cuddle him for hours on end."

Noncuddlers were described in these terms:

"Turns face away and begins to struggle."
"Pushes you away."
"Restless and whiny until allowed back in cot."
"Will kick and thrash with his arms, and if you persist will begin to cry."

They reported that the infants behaved the same way with other adults, a tendency that caused the mothers of the noncuddlers some embarrassment.

There were many other differences between the cuddlers and the noncuddlers. For instance, the cuddlers averaged about 11 per cent more sleep per day than the noncuddlers, and were slower in their motor development. The noncuddlers, for example, walked at 52 weeks, on the average, whereas the cuddlers walked at 55 weeks. Thus, cuddling or noncuddling are not isolated traits, but do seem to be indicative of underlying maturational patterns of development.

Expectations of Caregivers

These basic emotional patterns that we call temperament are likely to have an effect on the young child's caregivers. The caregivers are certain to have some expectations of how a child should behave and should respond to them. They also react to the child's demands in their own characteristic way—eagerly, reluctantly, irritably, overprotectingly, or whatever. As a result, certain aspects of the young child's developing behavior patterns will be reinforced; others, if relatively weak, may fade from his repertory. Thus a layer of learned behavior is built around the temperamental core to form the developing personality.

The attitudes and values of the child's caregivers, as expressed in their view of themselves and of the world around them, are also highly relevant, for these motivational factors color much of their behavior toward the infant. It makes a great deal of difference in the way parents behave toward a child if they regard the world as a threatening, dangerous place, against which one should be sheltered and protected at all times, or whether they regard it as safe, secure, and reasonably well ordered. The first stance is likely to lead to overprotection and an insistance on dependent relationships; the second, to permissiveness to explore and encouragement to become self-sufficient and independent. How the child comes to regard himself is therefore determined by the interaction between his temperament and the expectations his caregivers develop regarding him.

independence, dependence, and autonomy

In Chapter 7, we discussed the phenomenon of attachment—the emotional bonding between caregiver and infant, which causes both to want physical closeness. The drive is stronger in infants, of course. The caregiver usually has other roles to play that compete with the desire to remain close to the infant and give him maximum attention, whereas the infant has only one role—that of complete dependency.

About the middle of the second year—sometimes earlier, sometimes later—a fairly marked change takes place, a change that is marked by the beginnings of self-assertion, even negativism. The infant objects to being fed and demands to feed himself, however ineptly. He rejects foods for no apparent reason. He cries if he is whisked away for a diaper change while en route to an attractive toy. This is the period in which Goodenough found the most frequent outbursts of anger.

There are two aspects to self-awareness: identity and definition. Identity is positive and affirmative: it comes from knowing who we are, and grows out of a realization that we are similar to others. The toddler who has been pointing to and naming his eyes, mouth, nose, and ears now points to and names the caregiver's eyes, mouth, nose, and ears. Definition is negative and discriminatory; it comes from knowing who we are not, and grows out of realization that we are different from others. Negativism and the rejection of help from others are its first signs. At this early state in the young child's personality development, the negative stage may seem to be more prominent. He denies dependency ties and attempts to venture forth on his own—not very far, of course, but far enough to give him the first feelings of independence.

Another word for independence is *autonomy*. In Chapter 3, where we presented the psychosocial stages delineated by Erik Erikson (1963, 1968), we noted that the major conflict during the toddler stage is autonomy versus doubt and shame. The next stage, which occurs during the preschool years, is also concerned with independence: initiative versus guilt. Erikson says that in this stage the toddler learns to undertake some self-direction; the danger is that he will become overcontrolled. In this stage, the preschooler comes to enjoy moving about, exploring on his own, and making decisions. Whereas autonomy is largely a defensive stage, concerned with severing bonds with others and with keeping rivals out of one's territory, initiative opens up the possibility of competing successfully with one's rivals. Guilt comes with the thought that one may be too successful and may lead to overconscientiousness.

Achieving a Balance Between Dependence and Independence

E. Kuno Beller (1955, 1957a) conducted a series of studies in which he asked nursery school teachers to rate children on scales measuring behavioral tendencies characterized by dependence and independence. He found that although there was a definite tendency for the more independent children to be less dependent, and for the more dependent children to be less independent, the two traits were not completely the opposite of each other. In other words, the more independent children tended to display some dependent behavior, and some of the more dependent children tended to display some independent behavior.

Beller maintained that dependence and independence should be conceived of as somewhat separate aspects of children's behavior. In other words, it is possible to think of a child learning to depend on others and learning to be independent at the same time. These somewhat incompatible behavior patterns can of course involve the child in considerable emotional conflict and aggravate the emotional storm and stress of early childhood.

Dependence and Independence in the Hawaiian Culture

Some cross-cultural research indicates how dependence-independence conflicts can create problems for children who grow up in complex, industrialized societies like ours, which place a high premium on the ability to function independently, but also require that one know how and when to make use of others' help and advice. Gallimore, Howard, and Jordan (1969) compared the behavior of Hawaiian and Haole (Anglo-American) preschool children, who were given a difficult puzzle to solve. The children were shown the puzzle completely assembled and given directions as to how it could be solved. The puzzle was then taken apart and the children were told: "Go ahead and play with the puzzle and if you want me to help you, just ask and we will play with it together. This is a very hard puzzle."

Most children responded by working with interest and attention for three or four minutes, whereupon activity gradually decreased and then stopped. At this point clear-cut differences between the two groups of children appeared: 93 per cent of the Haole group spontaneously asked for help, in contrast to only 23 per cent of the Hawaiian group. The 77 per cent of the Hawaiians who did not ask for help often appeared to be apprehensive and uncomfortable. In other words, in a situation clearly calling for dependent behavior, the Hawaiian children seemed to want help, but were unable to ask for it.

The background to this behavior pattern may be found in the way in which Hawaiian mothers deal with their children. When children are infants and toddlers, the mother is indulgent to the point of fostering extreme dependency. After a child becomes mobile and verbal, however, she tends to find the dependency burdensome. The child's requests for attention and help are increasingly punished, and he is forced to depend more on his own efforts or the unreliable and often grudging aid of older children. The child initially responds to the mother's withdrawal of nurturance with increasing demands, to which she becomes even more punitive and rejecting.

The child's transition from dependency to self-reliance would be facilitated if the Hawaiian mother would reward independent behavior, but unfortunately she does not: the child is forced to become self-reinforcing before he is ready and never really learns how to respond to reinforcement from adults. When Hawaiian mothers were asked what age children should be able to do such things as eat alone, stay home alone, and the like, they tended to give ages at least a year younger than those given by Haole mothers. In school, Hawaiian children tend to be poor students at all grade levels and seem unaffected by the reinforcements and rewards that teachers typically employ. Other research has shown, incidentally, that poor first-grade achievement is associated with parental pressure for independence during early childhood (Chance, 1961).

As adults, Hawaiians tend to be more peer-oriented and less independent than other ethnic groups. They seem less able to fend for themselves economically and constitute a very high percentage of welfare cases in the state of Hawaii.

What this research shows, then, is that independence in children is not likely to be facilitated when mothers merely discourage dependent behavior. It is as though a child must learn to be properly dependent before he can become independent, and a too early insistence on independence, without accompanying rewards for success along these lines, appears to interfere with achievement later on.

self-concept development in preschoolers

We have described how the child, in the latter stages of infancy, develops some degree of independence and concurrently comes to realize that others are both different from him and at the same time similar. It is difficult to say at what point the I-you/mine-yours relationship emerges. Nor do we know whether it comes gradually or all at once. Probably it is a concept that fades in and out of the young child's perception of self and environment, a concept that is more significant and compelling at some times than at others.

> Mr. Jones sat down at breakfast while Delcy, aged 18 months, was having her cereal and milk. Usually he ate before she did, but this was Saturday, and he had slept in. He arranged his toast, coffee, juice, eggs, and newspaper where he always did, but Delcy, who had been feeding herself cheerfully up to that point, suddenly became upset. She put down her spoon and with both hands gave the newspaper a shove that almost knocked over her father's juice and coffee. Mr. Jones suppressed an angry epithet—after all, Delcy was only a baby—and rearranged his breakfast items, moving everything out of Delcy's reach. Then he realized that she had been clearing an area of "territory" around her plate. This was her mealtime "turf," and she was not going to tolerate any invasion of it.

In this instance, Delcy's self-concept is very active; she is aggressively marking out the boundaries of her personal space. But it was only the mood of the moment. A few minutes later, she was consigned to her playpen and was watching a television program, when Jason, the year-old son of a neighbor who had dropped in for a brief visit, was placed in the playpen beside her. She glanced at him briefly and then turned back to the television screen. Evidently territoriality was not an issue now.

Evaluation of the Self

The self is defined not only by territorial limits but also by a set of values we have with respect to our own person and especially to our behavior. In a general way, we expect desirable things from ourselves and expect to behave in ways that are admirable. We are ever ready to defend our evaluation of our self. We become aggressive or show other defensive maneuvers when something threatens our self-evaluation. If something does not fit these values or we fall short of our view of ourselves, we are apt to explain by saying, "I was not myself." We possess self-esteem to the degree to which we have self-confidence, or satisfaction with our behavior. True, there are varying degrees of self-acceptance. Sometimes we do not value ourselves very highly. We may on occasion dislike or even hate ourselves. By and large, however, our self is something we hold dear.

Parental attitudes contribute to the child's self-evaluation. For example, he may feel at times unwanted, despised, unattractive, or somehow lacking. Fortunately, he also comes in contact with other parental attitudes that are more positive and supportive.

Origins of Self-Concept

There emerges in the child a concept of himself—an awareness of what he thinks he is like. It is his conception of who and what he is. Whence comes this self-concept?

To a highly significant degree, the self is a social product. The self-concept, as Harry Stack Sullivan (1947) once said, is composed of the "reflected appraisals" of others. Through learning the opinions, attitudes, and expectations that others have for him, the child learns "who he is." It is therefore understandable how either exaggerated praise or chronic belittling can have unfortunate effects on the child's self-concept or self-image. Hence if a child's parents regard him as clumsy or bad, it should come as no surprise that the child believes them and acts to some degree in such a way as to correspond to their view. More often than not, however, a child's self-concept is less of a consistent pattern than these illustrations imply. After all, the way he is viewed differs from person to person even in a short space of time. To his

Emotional and Personality Development 335

mother, he may be as a "darling"; to a neighbor boy, a "sissy"; and to his big sister, a "pest"—all within the same hour. How the child integrates all these views of himself and develops a concept of "who he is" is a highly individualized process, based not only on the views of others, but also on his own temperament and experiences, past and present.

By the time children have entered the preschool period of development, they have a fairly well-defined concept of who they are. Many of the attitudes and values that they incorporate into their personality are derived from the models they imitate consciously, in play and fantasy, and unconsciously, in their attempts to deal with their environment.

Sex Typing

Early in the preschool years, perhaps even in the latter months of infancy, a child typically develops an awareness of his or her sexual identity and begins to display behavior appropriate to that identity. Whether the concept of oneself as male or female is biologically determined, or whether it is learned as a result of being taught or imposed by adults, is a matter of some controversy, especially among North American behavioral scientists.

The environmentalist view, which is consistent with the behaviorist tradition, favors a learning explanation of sex-typed differences in behavior and self-concept. As a consequence, there have been a number of research studies designed to determine precisely how sex-related attitudes and behavior are learned. But there is much ready-made, everyday evidence that is often cited. It is often noted, for example, that parents, directly or indirectly, attempt to teach their infant or young child the concepts and views they consider to be appropriate to his or her sex. Sometimes this is done by creating a sex-typed environment. Little girls' bassinets are trimmed with pink ruffles; little boys', with blue or yellow. Little girls usually wear dresses whereas little boys wear short pants or trousers. Toys are also selected along sex-typed lines. Parents of boys frequently voice aspirations: "The build of a football player," "My son the doctor-to-be," or "See that block tower—what an engineer!" Vocational aspirations are less frequently mentioned with respect to girls.

If learning is based on getting children to make associations, such as these, we can say that sex typing begins in infancy. Many parents, however, ignore these traditions. They pay no attention to sex-appropriate colors, give dolls and trucks to girls and boys alike, and dress children of both sexes in easy-to-wash coveralls and zippered play suits. Yet children from such families seem just as likely to display sex-typed behavior as children of more traditionally oriented parents.

It is tempting to explain sex typing in terms of reinforcement, too. But parents with the best intentions in the world of wanting to treat siblings alike find themselves being more restrictive and punitive with energetic, aggressive, resistant, and often destructive sons and being more supportive and indulgent to obedient, affectionate, and charming daughters. This is confusing. Boys are not reinforced for aggressiveness, but are punished for it. Should they not, then, turn out to be as agreeable and cooperative as little girls?

The answer of the learning theorists is that in spite of the negative treatment parents give to little boys' aggressiveness, they probably indicate in other ways that they expect or anticipate aggressiveness and may even occasionally reward it.

Animal research on sex differences in behavior. Are these behavioral differences between girls and boys the result of differences in the way parents treat children of different sex, or are parents responding to differences that are "already there"?

One of the ways of resolving this question is to look at primate research. Presumably the behavior of monkeys is uncontaminated by culturally toned attitudes and values. If young monkeys were found to display sex-related behavior patterns similar to those displayed by young humans, this finding would strengthen the conclusion that such responses are not learned but are biologically predetermined.

One such study that supports this line of reasoning is that of Mitchell and Brandt (1970), who observed the behavior of rhesus monkey mothers toward their infants and noted that they were more punitive toward their male offspring and more protective toward their female infants. The behavior of the monkey infants provided some clues as to the reason for the differential treatment. Male infants tended to be "doers," in that they were more likely to play with other infants, to explore their environment, to run and jump (thus leaving the mother), and to threaten other infants. Female infants, however, were more inclined to be "watchers" and to play passive roles.

Harry F. Harlow (1962) made similar observations regarding sex differences in the behavior of his monkeys. He noted that male infants and adolescents were more likely to make threatening responses, to engage in rough-and-tumble play, and to initiate such play with their own and the opposite sex. Female monkeys, on the other hand, were more likely to engage in grooming other monkeys, a socialized behavior involving stroking and patting. It is hardly surprising that monkey mothers behave differently toward their male and female offspring, in ways that are remarkably similar to those of human parents.

Maternal views of sex-typed behaviors. Some data gathered by the Early School Admissions Project in Baltimore shows that mothers of girls and mothers of boys have different perceptions of the behavior of their children. Table 10-2 lists some of the questions asked by Project researchers and the replies given by over five hundred mothers of children four and five years old.

Although the families were all located in lower-class or inner-city environments, many of the sex differences reported would probably be consistent with those that would be noted if a similar survey had been conducted of mothers living in middle-class areas. There is little doubt, however, of the thrust of their observations: they are telling us that even as preschoolers, girls are more mature, socialized, and cooperative, and that boys are much less so.

Sex typing via social learning. We mentioned earlier the awkward problem of why little boys persist in displaying aggressive, nonconforming behavior when their parents are not reinforcing them for it, but

TABLE 10-2. Differences in Replies Given by Mothers of Four- and Five-Year-Old Children to Questions Posed in Interviews, Classified According to Sex of Child (Galfo, 1971)

	Reply tendencies of mothers of:	
Questions	Girls	Boys
Does the child bring home books from the library?	Yes	Too young
Is there printed matter in the home? (Mothers named books)	More often	Less often
What are child's favorite [television] programs?	Children's shows	Cartoons
Does the child like to listen to the radio?	Yes	No
Does the child have many friends?	Yes	No
Does child carry out chores and errands?	Yes	No
Does child obediently put away clothes and playthings?	Yes	No
Does child obediently wash, bathe, and brush teeth?	Usually	Sometimes, or No
Does child come obediently when called?	Usually	Sometimes, or No
Does child ask to be taken places?	Often	Sometimes
Does child need to be punished?	Rarely	Often, or Sometimes
Does child ever touch himself on privates in public?	No	Yes
Does child stutter or stammer?	No	Yes
Is the child overactive?	No	Yes
Does child ever get wild or uncontrollable when playing, with friends?	No	Yes

indeed are attempting to extinguish it. Social-learning theorists would explain this in terms of boys' imitating male models, girls' imitating female ones. To be sure, adult male models—usually the boys' fathers—do not display much aggressive behavior, unless it is in the punishment of obstreperous young sons, but they do act in ways that are dominant, forceful, and decisive—action that may be enough to convey an image of "machismo" and touch off aggressive, nonconforming behavior patterns

(Schulz, © 1972, United Feature Syndicate.)

in their sons. But this formulation does not explain why boys imitate their fathers in the first place. During infancy they are likely to be closer to their mothers than their fathers, and even during the early childhood years most boys see more of their mothers than their fathers.

In a review of childhood socialization research, Eleanor E. Maccoby (1975) concluded that children *first* develop sex-stereotyped behavior and *then* imitate the same-sex models. The implication is that children already have some idea of what sex they are before they choose their model. The question remains, however, how the children come to display sex-appropriate behavior in the first place. Maccoby rejected the idea that reinforcement is very important, making the point we have touched on—that boys are more likely to be punished for aggressiveness than reinforced for it. Furthermore, there are other sex-linked forms of behavior that emerge independently of reinforcement: the tendency of preschoolers to select playmates of their own sex, for example. It is unlikely that parental reinforcement or modeling, for that matter, plays any part in such behavior patterns.

The only remaining explanation is a biological one. Maccoby conceded that biological factors might lead a child to initiate the kind of behavior appropriate to his or her sex, but maintained that there is more to sex typing than biology. She suggested that children probably develop a set of concepts or rules concerning what behavior is appropriate for each sex, and that the rules are initially oversimplified. These rules are based on all the information available to children: what they are reinforced for, what they see others doing, and the generalizations they hear, such as "Boys don't cry," or "Little girls don't get dirty." And when they see adult models behaving in ways that are different from their rules, they ignore the behavior as odd or embarrassing.

The tendency of children to develop rule systems as guides for their behavior has been noted by us in another context: the learning of language. In Chapter 6 we took note of the idea proposed by Chomsky and Lenneberg that children are biologically organized in such a way that they are bound to generate ways of speaking that are consistent with (but initially not exactly the same as) the language spoken by their family. They do so by developing language rules, which are oversimplified in their initial stages. These rules are of course based on generalizations derived from the spoken language they hear around them.

The development of sex typing seems to proceed along similar lines. Using as a guide their natural inclinations and the promptings of others, children determine their sex and devise crude and simplified sets of rules to serve as a guide: "Since I am a boy, I am going to stay with the other boys outside in the play yard and do what they do," or, "Since I am a girl, I am going to stay with the other girls inside and do what they do."

Both language learning and sex typing are dimensions of socialization; hence it makes sense to assume that each child works his or her way through the process by developing a structure of rules and following it as a guide.

We shall cite only two studies out of the many that have been done in recent years on this interesting phenomenon. The first indicates how early sex typing begins. The second shows how rigid the sex-typing rules are, once children have determined what they are.

In the first investigation, girls and boys twenty months of age, were observed in their homes. Each child was presented with a display of three "masculine" toys (hammer, truck, and gun) and three "feminine" toys (bead bracelet, doll, and iron) and scored for the amount of time he or she played with each item. The experimenter next used each of the toys in an appropriate way in a brief modeling session and then scored the child according to whether he or she imitated the behavior thus displayed.

Results showed that in the free play session, the children tended to prefer sex-appropriate toys. In the modeling sessions, boys displayed more imitation for male toys, while girls more often imitated behavior related to female toys (Fein et al., 1975).

Harper and Sanders (1975) observed the play patterns of nursery-school children over a two-year period and noted that boys spent more time out of doors playing in the sand, on a tractor, and on a climbing structure, whereas girls spent more time indoors at craft tables and in a play kitchen. The same trends were observed for both years, even though during the second year the children were a younger group and the all-female staff held egalitarian views and deliberately encouraged the girls to play outdoors. Nor was clothing a factor: during both years girls who were dressed in jeans spent no more time out of doors than girls wearing dresses.

None of the above discussion should be interpreted to mean that *all* sex differences in behavior are biologically determined and that there are *no* environmental effects. Human beings, as we noted earlier, are the most plastic of all animals and hence can learn an almost infinite variety of behavior patterns. The fact is that sex-typed patterns of behavior differ from culture to culture, especially among the more primitive areas of the world, as Margaret Mead (1935) demonstrated in her anthropological study of the customs and personality of New Guinea tribes. But underneath the great cross-cultural variation in sex-typed patterns, there are some behavioral trends that are probably constitutional (biologically influenced). The most consistent one is the tendency of males to be more aggressive than females. Even Mead found that in tribes where the interpersonal behavior of men was accepting, supporting, and kindly, it was still men who waged war against other tribes. But this persistent behavioral trend does not mean that male infants are fated to grow up to be aggressive. As Maccoby (1973) has pointed out, biological differences between the sexes do not mean that boys "have" more aggression without having to acquire it: rather they have a greater readiness to learn it. It is important that the aggressive behavior of both sexes is subject to modification.

summary

The emotions of young children are very unstable, in that children tend to react strongly to experiences that are frustrating or rewarding. *Emotion* is a difficult word to define. Positive emotions are characterized by "approach" behavior; fear or anxiety, by flight or avoidance; and rage responses by "against" behavior. Neonates' emotions tend to take the form of generalized excitement, although cries indicating hunger, anger, or injury may be identified. Smiling appears toward the end of the first month and reaches a peak at about five or six months of age. Laughter appears when the infant is four to six months old.

Anxiety, in the form of "sobering" when strangers are seen, is evident about the middle of the first year. A few months later, the infant begins to express anxiety when separated from his caregiver. A longitudinal study found that boys who did much crying during the early months of infancy tended to remain apprehensive in strange situations during the early childhood years, whereas those who did not cry tended to be less tense and shy. Girls displayed no such consistency over time. An early study indicated that children's fearfulness was high when they were two, but declined thereafter. In general, children scoring higher on intelligence tests displayed more fear and anxiety during the early toddler years than did those scoring low.

The sources of anxiety are less readily identified than are sources of fear, and anxiety is generally less intense than fear. Anxiety does facilitate concern about the future and stimulates socialization, but in its more severe forms it can have an immobilizing and interfering effect. An experiment with anxiety-arousing situations showed that children tended to stay close to their mothers, or another female adult in situations in which the mother was not available.

Fantasy violence appears to have a natural fascination for young children. A survey by Ames showed that about three fourths of children aged two to five spontaneously tell stories with violent themes. One study reported a negative relationship between parental punishment and aggressive themes in children's doll play, a finding which suggests that violence appears in children's fantasy spontaneously, perhaps because it is exciting and interesting.

Most of the research studies on emotions of preschoolers are concerned with anger and aggressiveness; fewer deal with fear and anxiety and even fewer with the positive emotions.

Goodenough's classic survey shows that anger responses reach their peak during the second year and decline therafter, the decrease being more pronounced for girls. Frustration occurring in interpersonal relationships, especially conflicts with authority, are a prime cause of anger outbursts. Frustration characteristically leads to anger at this stage, and to aggressive acts as well. The theory of Goodenough's day, that frustration always leads to aggression, was partly confirmed by research. One study that disconfirmed it showed that frustration could also lead to less mature behavior or regression. Aggressiveness appears to be tolerated more by North American cultures than by others. Social-learning theorists hold that the aggressive behavior of a child is increased by observing models who aggress. The model's behavior leads him to copy the behavior and also disinhibits him. If the model's aggressive behavior is also rewarded, the child is even more likely to aggress. Aggression is also enhanced if the environment contains objects associated with aggression and destruction.

Affectively pleasant emotions have not stimulated as much research as have fear and anger. Leuba noted that at age six months, his own two infants smiled and laughed when tickled. By the end of the first year they had been conditioned to laugh at the mere sight of fingers moving preparatory to ticking. Other research has revealed a connection between laughter and both social setting and physical activity. The older the child, the more arousal he enjoys, and tickling becomes preferred over cuddling. Laughter may be socially useful because it resolves emotional conflicts and at the same time meets social needs. Most laughter occurs in social situations and is aroused by physical activity in the form of vigorous play or by tickling.

Observation of neonates indicates that some personal qualities or traits are "built into" the human organism and not acquired through learning. These early behavioral styles, called "temperament," tend to persist in one form or another, throughout the life span. Marked temperamental differences can be seen both in neonates and in adolescents in terms of their activity, reactions to novelty and change, and emotional style or mood.

Attachment in infancy gives way in toddlerhood to self-assertion and even negativism. Negativism seems to be a way of expressing awareness of differences from others, whereas recognition of similarities makes it possible to identify with others. Independence or autonomy versus doubt and shame is the major conflict during the toddler stage, according to Erikson. During the preschool years, the major conflict is initiative versus guilt. Beller found that dependence in children is not the direct opposite of independence, that a balance is needed. Research with Hawaiian and Anglo-American children indicates that children must learn to be properly dependent before they can achieve a tent independence.

The self-concept of toddlers may be expressed through territoriality.

Self-evaluation also enhances the young child's sense of self. Harry Stack Sullivan observed that the self is composed of the reflected appraisals of others. Young children develop an awareness of their sexual identity quite early, when they begin to display behavior patterns that are sex-appropriate along traditional lines. The environmentalist view, which is moderately supported by everyday experience, is that these behavioral differences are learned from parents. But children display sex-typed behavior even if parents are nontraditional, and boys tend to be more aggressive than girls even though their aggressive behavior is not reinforced. Research with monkeys suggests that the differential treatment parents give boys and girls may be a result rather than a cause of sex-typed personality traits. Monkey mothers are more punitive toward their male infants and more protective of female infants. Young male monkeys are more aggressive, and females engage in more socially supportive behavior. This idea that boys are inherently more aggressive than girls is also consistent with a survey of inner-city mothers, who reported that their preschool sons were more active, disobedient, and noncooperative than daughters the same age. Maccoby's review of sex typing led her to conclude that children first develop sex-stereotyped behavior and then imitate models of the same sex. Sex-stereotyped behavior is probably biologically determined, at least in its initial stages, but beyond that children tend to develop sets of oversimplified rules as to what kind of sex-typed behavior is appropriate for them; the appearance of these rules parallels the child's development of oversimplified rules that enable him to learn his native language. Studies show that sex typing in behavior appears even during infancy and that rules for sex-typed behavior are extremely rigid during the nursery-school years. Sex stereotypes vary considerably from one culture to another, especially among primitive societies, thus showing that human behavior is malleable and plastic. Maccoby points out that boys are not biologically more aggressive, but that they are readier to learn aggressive behavior than girls are. The behavior of both sexes is, however, subject to modification.

eleven

The Social Environment: Parents, Siblings, and Peers

The value of marriage is not that adults produce children but that children produce adults.
—PETER DE VRIES (1954)

Although the attention that caregivers lavish upon infants or withhold from them may be viewed by us as having social effects, infants, especially in the earlier months, perceive it largely in physical terms—comforting or discomforting, as the case may be. By the time they have become toddlers and can participate in their families' communication network, the social meanings implicit in others' behavior become very important to them and often are more significant than the physical implications of that behavior.

In this chapter we shall examine some of the more prominent aspects of the young child's social environment, with particular attention to his interaction with his caregivers, and shall finish with a passing glance at his relations with other children—his peers.

the family as a social environment

The child's interaction with his caregivers enables him to satisfy his basic needs for survival, safety, and love, but he needs more than these minimal satisfactions to grow and develop normally. The additional ingredient that the family can supply is what might be termed a sense of security, a feeling that one can depend on others. Erikson (1963) felt that this quality, which he termed *trust*, was so important that he placed it in the initial position in his sequence of psychosocial stages.

Family Structure

The characteristic of the family that enables it to satisfy this need for security is its structure. *Structure*, as used in this sense, refers to the predictability and stability of social relationships. In a group that has a relatively high degree of structure, members know what their roles are; therefore they know what to do in different kinds of situations and what to expect of other members. Structure also implies some kind of hierarchy of status and power, with persons at the top able to assign roles and to exact penalties from members who do not perform adequately. The traditional authoritarian family, in which the father is supreme and the mother is the second in command, is an obvious example of a highly structured group. In a society where parental power has been weakened, family structure becomes harder to maintain.

Family structure is, like other social forms, very sensitive to psychosocial trends outside the family. Society at large may be extremely supportive of family structure, or else may undermine parental attempts to impose it. By way of example, it is more difficult for parents to impose a high degree of structure in an urban setting than in a farm setting. The multitude of tasks that must be performed on the farm by all members of the family virtually dictates a highly structured social arrangement. In an urban setting, the family makes relatively fewer demands on the time of family members, whereas society outside the family not only makes more demands but also offers more distractions. As a result, the attention of family members is often directed away from the performance of family-related roles.

Today's families are likely to be less structured than the families of a generation ago. Urbanization is one reason for this change; also, the parents have had more education, a fact that tends to be associated with a greater permissiveness. Moreover, the temper of the times is more in favor of reducing status differences within groups of all kinds, including the family.

Ecological Factors

The physical conditions that prevail in a home are one aspect of its ecology. It makes a difference whether a home is neat and clean or whether it is a cluttered shambles of dirty dishes and soiled clothes. Evidence for this observation may be found in a study of black fifth graders who attended schools in central Harlem, an economically depressed area of New York City. Half the children studied were achieving well above national norms on tests of reading and arithmetic; the other half were achieving far below the norms. A black social worker visited the children's homes and interviewed their parents. She found that the achieving children were more likely than the nonachievers to have homes that were clean and neat. Furthermore, the achieving children were more likely to live a more orderly life; for instance, they were more likely to have assigned home duties, and supper for them was a regular meal and not just haphazard or unscheduled snacking. There was also less crowding—fewer persons per room—in the homes of the achievers (Greenberg and Davidson, 1972).

We have noted that stimulation may have a facilitating effect on children's cognitive development, but the degree of orderliness or structure in a child's life is also important. Some homes are rich in stimuli that have order and focus—stimuli directed at the child in the form of conversation, attention, caressing, fondling, and playing. Ordinarily such stimuli have a facilitating effect on the appearance of more mature forms of behavior. Other homes are also rich in more diffuse stimuli that are not focused on the child's needs: the television may be going full blast 16 or more hours a day, adults may be engaged in loud talk or fighting, and traffic or industrial noises may be intense. Heavy exposure to such stimuli may have an inhibiting or confusing effect on the child's cognitive and affective development.

Child-Rearing Practices

Although an increasing amount of research is being conducted on the ecology of the child's home environment, the aspect of the child's home experience that has received major attention from researchers is his interaction with his caregivers. The work of Diana Baumrind (1967) is one of the many interesting studies that show significant relationships between children's personality and child-rearing practices. In her initial project, she did an intensive study relating the behavior of three groups of middle-class children to the modes of child rearing used by their parents.

Baumrind's subjects consisted of a sample of 32 children drawn from a larger population of 110 three- and four-year-olds enrolled in the nursery school at the Child Study Center of the Institute of Human Development at the University of California at Berkeley. The 110 children were assessed on five personality dimensions: self-control, tendencies to approach or avoid others, self-reliance, subjective mood, and tendencies to relate positively to other children. Children were ranked on these five dimensions by their nursery school teachers and an observer staff of psychologists. Children who received the highest or the lowest ratings were further screened in a test situation designed to assess their responses to success and failure in solving problems.

The 32 children remaining after being screened demonstrated rather clear-cut patterns on the personality dimensions and fell into three well-defined groups: Pattern I children consisted of 13 who ranked high on mood, self-reliance, approach,[1] and self-control; Pattern II children consisted of 11 children who ranked low on peer affiliation and mood[2] and who were not ranked high on "approach"; and Pattern III children consisted of eight who ranked low on self-reliance, as well as on either self-control or approach. Some of the behavioral tendencies that characterized the children in the three groups are listed in Table 11-1.

Measures of parental behavior toward each child were secured by visiting each child's home on two separate occasions. The first period occurred from just before dinner to bedtime, in order to observe the home during a period that was likely to demonstrate the maximum interaction and stress. The second period was chosen by the mother as one in which she thought the situation was the least stressful for herself and the child. Each visit lasted about three hours.

A second set of measures was derived from observing mother-child interaction in two structured situations. In the first, the mother was requested to teach the child some number concepts, using Cuisenaire Rods (rods whose color and length vary according to the numbers they represent). In the second, the child was permitted to engage in a free-play situation, with the mother participating and enhancing his enjoyment or withdrawing to read a magazine if she preferred. Finally, both parents, mother and father, were interviewed separately in two sessions, the first on beliefs and attitudes, and the second on the child's performance.

The material gathered in the course of these various observations was analyzed and scored, and the results were grouped under four headings: parental control, maturity demands, communication, and nurturance. A graphic representation summarizing the relationships between these variables and the three patterns of child behavior may be found in Figure 11-1. The term *parental control,* as used in these graphs, was evidenced by parents' accepting (not retreating from) power conflicts with the child, not giving in to the child's "nuisance value," using incentives and reinforcement, and persisting to obtain positive outcomes. *Parental maturity demands* were evidenced by parents' respecting the child's decisions, granting him independence, and engaging in independence training through control and noncontrol situations. *Parent-child communication* was shown by parents' using reason to get compliance, encouraging verbal give and take, and making it clear that

---

[1] *Approach* refers to tendencies to move toward stimuli that are novel, stressful, exciting, or unexpected in an explorative and curious fashion, in contrast to tendencies to avoid such stimuli or to become anxious when challenged to approach them.

[2] *Mood* refers to tendencies to display zest, pleasure, and buoyancy, and to become happily involved in nursery-school activities.

TABLE 11-1. Behavioral Tendencies Characterizing Three Groups of Nursery-school Children Selected on the Basis of Clear-Cut Personality Differences (see Figure 11-1 for child-rearing emphases associated with each of the personality types) (after Baumrind, 1967)

Pattern I (The self-reliant, self-controlled, approach-oriented, buoyant child)	Pattern II (The anxious, restless, depressed, and disaffiliated child)	Pattern III (The immature child)
Confident	Retreats from situation involving physical risk	Impetuous
Accepts blame	Acts too mature for age	Fatigued at school*
Withstands stress	Does not enjoy self at nursery school	Omnipotent attitude*
Gives his best to play and work	Has difficulty in relating to adults, other than mother	Self-abusive*
Follows standard operating procedure	Does not regret wrongdoing	Apprehensive*
Helps other children to adapt	Tattles or informs on other children	Becomes more childish or hostile when hurt*
Enjoys other children's company	Guileful	Irritable*
	Needlessly disrespectful toward adults	Exploits dependency*
	(Plus traits marked with asterisk [*] in Pattern III)	Cries easily*
		Sets easy goals for self*
		Inconsiderate*
		Boasts*
		Obstructive*

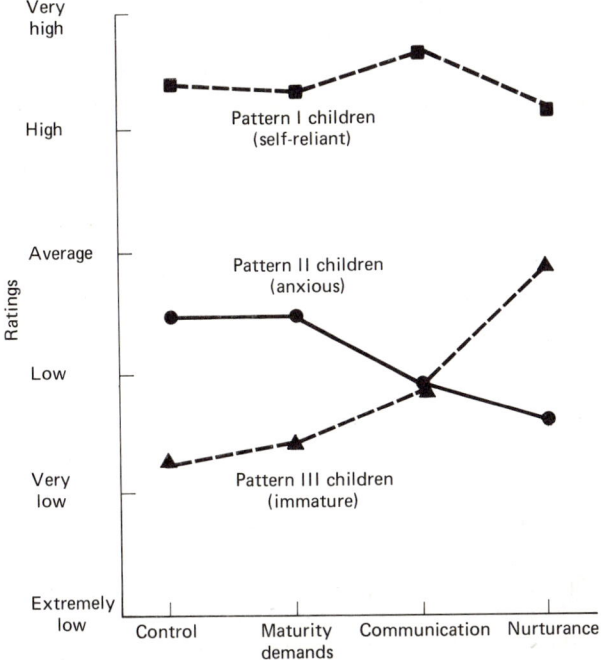

FIGURE 11-1. *Ratings of four dimensions of parental behavior associated with three patterns of child personality: Pattern I (self-reliant, self-controlled, approach-oriented), Pattern II (anxious, restless, depressed, and disaffiliated), and Pattern III (immature). (After Baumrind, 1967.)*

they were the source of power. *Parental nurturance* was indicated by parents' supporting and satisfying the child and using positive incentive and reinforcement.

As Figure 11-1 shows, parents of the most adequate children (Pattern I) tended to rate high on all four variables of behavior. Parents of anxious children (Pattern II) had average to low-average ratings on control and maturity demands, communicated less, and were not very supportive or nurturant. Parents of immature children provided very little control, made few demands for mature behavior, and communicated little, but showed average support and nurturance.

Baumrind's results are, to some extent, in accord with common sense: they show that the best-adjusted children get both firm control and love. Their parents expect mature behavior and engage in considerable communication to make this fact clear. Furthermore, the immature child (who resembles the stereotype of the "spoiled child" in many ways) gets very little control and few demands for mature behavior. Contrary to common sense, however, the Pattern III child gets only an average amount of attention in the form of nurturance and emotional support. The anxious child perhaps fits the common-sense stereotypes least. He gets a moderate degree of control and demand for maturity; his parents interact with him less and are not supportive. In short, the well-adjusted child gets more of everything, and the anxious child and the immature child get less of everything.

Later Baumrind (1971b) conducted a more extended survey of children in the nursery schools of Berkeley, California, studying other aspects of the relationship between parental behavior and the personality traits of children. In general, her findings were consistent with her 1967 study. One dimension she studied was *independence*, the tendency of children to behave in ways that are not stereotyped but are unique to their personality, to make up their own minds on matters, and to question adult authority on occasion. Children scoring high on this dimension were likely to show behavior characterized by dominance, resistance, purposefulness, and orientation toward achievement.

Although psychologists a generation ago tended to believe that firm parental control and demands for maturity prevented the development of independence and led to passivity and overdependence on the part of the children, Baumrind found no data to support these suppositions. "It appears," she commented, "that children are not that easily cowed by parental pressure."

This conclusion did not constitute an endorsement for *authoritarian* methods, which Baumrind distinguished from *authoritative* methods. The *authoritarian* parent attempts to shape, control, and evaluate the child's behavior according to some fixed or absolute standard of behavior. Obedience is regarded as a prime virtue, and forceful measures, including frequent physical punishment, are invoked to suppress deviations. The authoritarian parent does not encourage verbal give and take with the child, insisting that the child not question parental demands but accept them as final. The *authoritative* parent directs the child in a reasonable manner that is oriented to issues, rather than to the formal aspects of behavior. Verbal give and take is encouraged, and the child is shown the reasoning behind parental policies and demands. Although firm control is exercised when parents and children cannot come to an agreement, the child is not hemmed about by restrictions. The parent demonstrates self-respect, but also respects children as individuals with interests and special ways of their own.

A third type, the *permissive* parent, behaves in nonpunitive, accepting, and affirmative ways with respect to children's impulses. Such parents consult with children on family decisions, give explanations for family rules, and make few demands for responsibility for household routines or orderliness. The parents avoid roles as active agents in shaping the child's behavior, but present themselves as resources to be used as he wishes. The child is permitted to regulate his own activities and is not controlled or encouraged to obey externally defined stan-

Parents who exercise firm control and are not afraid to make reasonable demands on their children are more helpful in aiding them to gain maturity than are parents who are overly permissive or authoritarian.

dards. Reason, but not power, is used to accomplish such parental aims as seem necessary.

In Baumrind's research, the children of authoritative parents came off much better than those of either authoritarian parents or permissive ones, tending to be friendlier, more cooperative, more purposive, and more achievement-oriented than the other children. The girls also tended to be more independent. These findings led Baumrind to conclude that socially responsible behavior in children is facilitated by parents who themselves behave in socially responsible ways, who have a strong involvement with their children, and who exercise control over and make use of reinforcement contingencies. Parents can, furthermore, serve as more potent models and reinforcing agents if they do not act in rejecting ways toward their children, as often happens with authoritarian parents.

Baumrind also explored dimensions of nonconforming behavior and attitudes on the part of parents. Her findings showed that authoritative parents who were themselves nonconforming tended to have boys who were more independent, purposive, and dominant. Nor was parental nonconformity associated with a lack of social responsibility. On the other hand, the coupling of nonconformity and authoritative behavior on the part of parents was associated with hostile, resistive behavior on the part of girls.

developmental influences of caregivers' practices and attitudes

The studies that we have just described are particularly interesting because Baumrind made an attempt, through home visitation at supper time, to assess the total atmosphere of the family with respect to its impact on child behavior. The effect of the father as a functioning member of the family group was also observed not only during the supper-time visits, but also by the inclusion of fathers in the interview schedule.

Although a few other studies of parental attitudes and behavior examine the interaction between children and both parents, most of them focus on the mother. This practice can be justified to some extent because it is the mother who has the most intimate contact with the child. Furthermore, looking at the matter from an entirely practical angle, it is the mother who is most available and most eager to cooperate with a researcher.

Effects of the Caregiver on Cognitive Development

Some of the most interesting research regarding the short-term and long-term influence of caregivers on children has been done by investigators participating in the Berkeley Growth Study since its inception in 1928. Their reports, accumulated over the years, form a data bank that has been analyzed and processed many times to yield many intriguing findings regarding the interaction between child-rearing patterns and children's behavioral trends.

One of these analyses was conducted by Bayley and Schaefer (1964), who compared several dimensions of maternal behavior, drawn from observations made when the child was three years old and younger, with measures taken when the child was older. We have presented a sample of their findings in Figure 11-2, which reports the relationships between maternal behavior during this early period and scores of intelligence tests administered when the subjects were 16 to 18 years of age. (We could have included IQs taken at earlier ages, but selected the later scores because they are the most removed, in point of time, from the period of infancy and early childhood, and hence are more meaningful in terms of the kinds of predictions that might be made.) We will have more to say about other personality factors shortly, but have

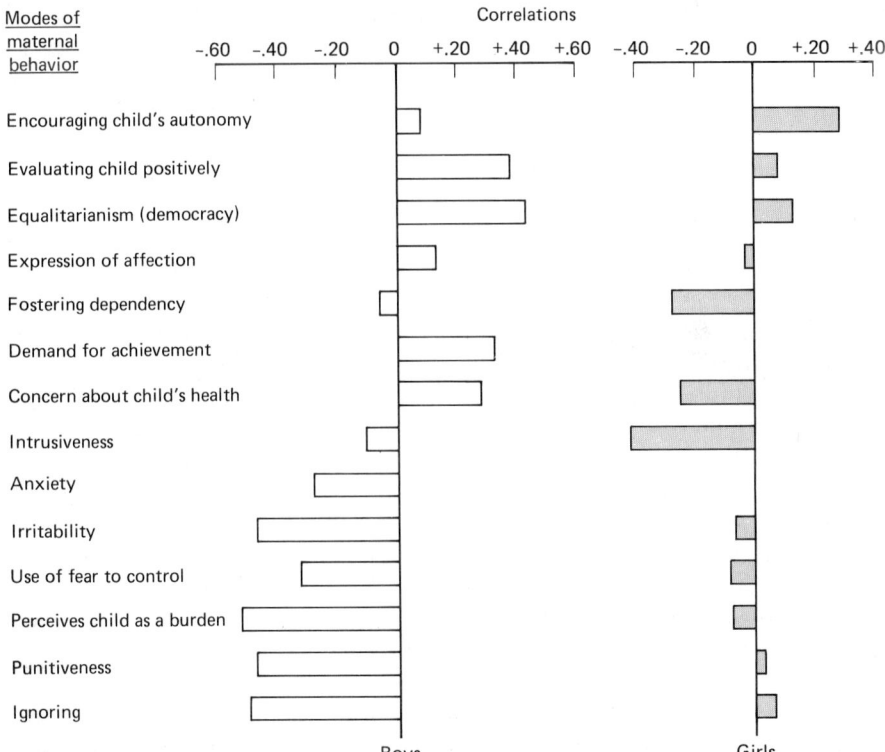

FIGURE 11-2. Relationship between maternal behavior experienced by children from birth to three years of age and their intelligence at ages 16 to 18. (After Bayley and Schaefer, 1964.)

selected intelligence as a relevant variable for Figure 11-2, because it is one that is responsive to many dimensions of mental health and personal adequacy.

Several things can be noted in Figure 11-2. In the first place, if the sizes of correlational coefficients are any indication, maternal behavior has more of a long-range impact on the cognitive growth of boys than it does on girls—particularly the more negative forms of maternal behavior. The data also suggest that girls are, if anything, somewhat tougher and more resilient, psychologically, than boys, although there are a few exceptions to this trend. Girls appear to respond more to maternal encouragement for autonomy or independence than boys do. It seems to be less important, as far as their cognitive development is concerned, whether their mother treats them democratically or not, nor is their IQ much affected by the mother's expression of affection. On the other hand, they appear to be more vulnerable than boys to maternal attempts to foster dependent behavior and to intrude on their life space and privacy. Concern about the child's health appears to facilitate cognitive growth in boys, but has the opposite effect in girls. Maternal expectations and demands for achievement seem important for boys, less so for girls. Negative and rejecting attitudes on the part of mothers seem to have a severe effect on boys and little, if any, on girls. To generalize for a bit, it appears that boys tend to benefit from intense "mothering," but girls respond negatively to it.

In a study that explored a somewhat different aspect of cognitive development, Wulbert and others (1975) identified a group of preschool children whose intelligence, as measured by a nonverbal test, the Leiter International Performance scales, was normal, but whose command of language was below par for their age. The home environment of the language-delayed children was then compared with that of a control group of normal children—so defined because their Leiter IQs were consistent with language development. The home environment of both groups was rated by observers who employed the Inventory of Home Stimulation developed by Bettye M. Caldwell (Caldwell, Heider, and Kaplan, 1973).

The results, as displayed in Figure 11-3, indicate that the language-delayed children, in contrast to the normal children, had mothers who showed less emotional and verbal responsiveness, tended to employ more restriction and punishment, provided fewer adequate play materials, displayed less involvement with their children, and provided fewer opportunities for variety in daily stimulation.

The observers who rated the homes noted that the control-group mothers were more likely to caress their children, speak to them warmly, and praise them to the interviewer. The mothers of language-delayed children, however, tended to talk about their children in critical tones, often scolded and shouted at them, and seldom praised or caressed them.

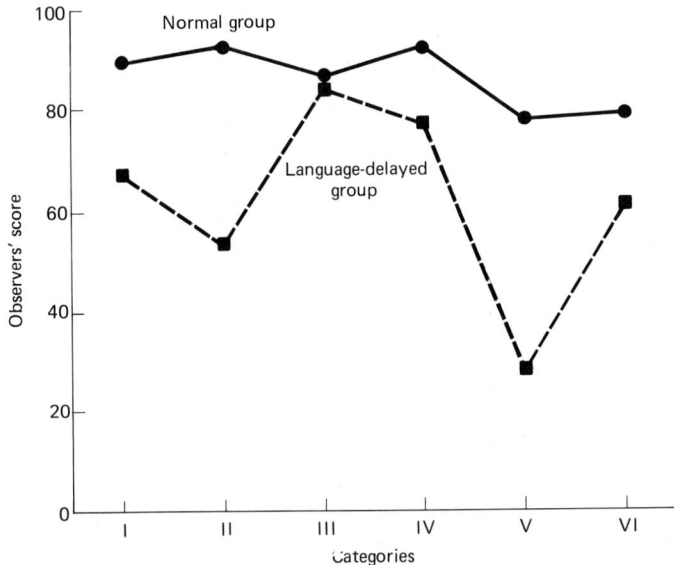

FIGURE 11-3. A comparison of home environments and maternal behavior toward language-delayed and normal preschool children. Scores represent summaries of observers' ratings, based on categories of the Caldwell Inventory of Home Stimulation. (Data from Wulbert et al., 1975.)

The chief difference between the two groups of mothers, however, occurred in Category V: involvement with the child. Although the mothers of the language-delayed children were generally conscientious in meeting their children's physical needs, they otherwise had little interaction with them. It seemed obvious to the observers that the language-delayed children were a source of great frustration to their mothers and that mutual interaction was pleasurable for neither mother nor child. This was not because the children were mentally deficient. Indeed, when the two groups of children were compared with a third group of mentally deficient children, there was essentially no difference between the behavior of the mothers of the normal control group and that of the mothers of the mentally deficient children. Nor was socioeconomic status (SES) much of a factor. The researchers found that low home ratings were related to language delay in children irrespective of the SES of the family, and that the ratings were not related to parental SES either in the normal control group or in the language-delayed group.

Effects of the Caregiver on Social Development

In addition to her research on the relationship between maternal behavior and children's cognitive development, Bayley (1964) also studied the effect of maternal behavior patterns on the personal and social development of the children who were subjects in the Berkeley Growth Study. Some of her results are summarized in Figure 11-4, which consists of a graphic presentation of the correlations between certain forms of maternal behavior experienced by boys during the first three years of life and the amount of friendliness they demonstrated when they were between six and a half and seven years of age. Again, mothers' affectionate, equalitarian (democratic) behavior appears to

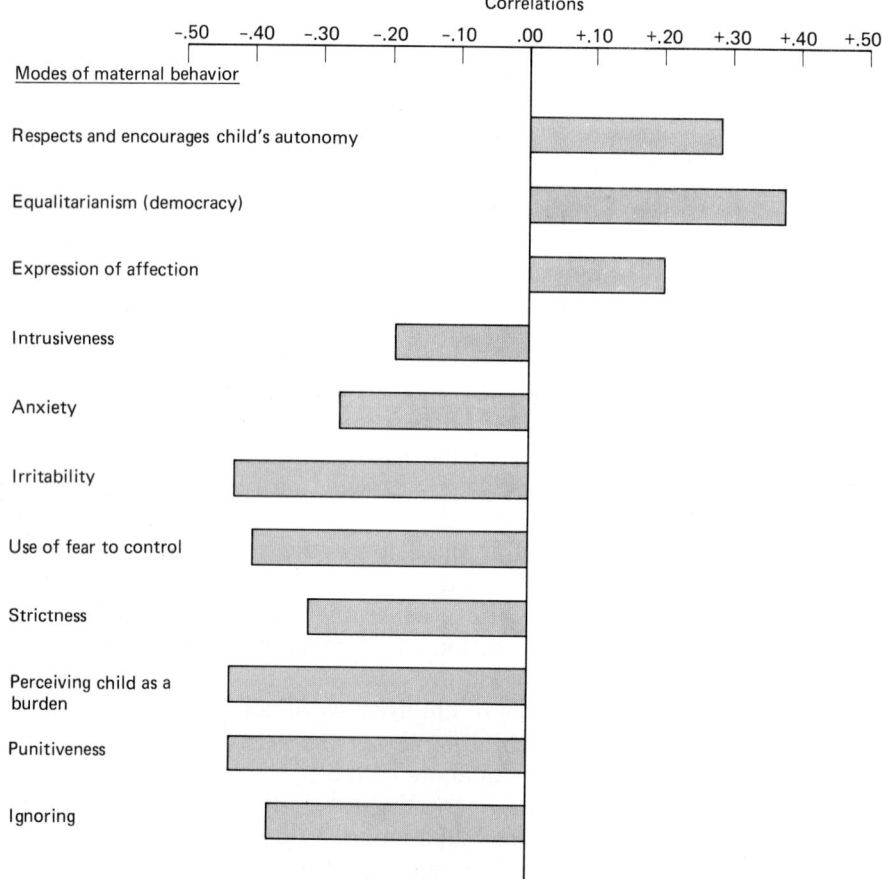

FIGURE 11-4. Correlations between the friendliness of boys aged 6½ to 7 years and modes of maternal behavior they experienced before 3 years of age. (After Bayley, 1964.)

facilitate friendliness, whereas hostile, punitive, and rejecting behavior appears to inhibit it. Similar relationships were also found between mothers' behavior and boys' cooperativeness and attentiveness. Patterns and relationships for girls are also similar, particularly below the age of three, although the correlations diminish somewhat beyond that age. The general impression is that girls are more self-sufficient and somewhat less affected by variations in maternal behavior than boys are.

Influence of Fathers on Child Behavior

The research with respect to the influence of fathers on cognitive and affective development of children can be summed up very simply: fathers are important, especially if they are not there.

There is now a fair amount of research data relating to father absence and its effect on children's behavior. In our discussion of delay of gratification in Chapter 4, we described a series of experiments by Walter Mischel (1974), in which he taught children to deal effectively with delay in gratification by getting them to think of symbolic representations of desired rewards, rather than of the rewards themselves.

Mischel has been conducting research on delay of gratification for two decades. In his earlier studies, he found that a child's willingness to delay gratification was profoundly affected by the presence or absence of a father at home. In these investigations, Mischel (1958) asked West Indian children to do a small task for him. He offered them a choice of rewards: a small candy immediately or a large one a week hence. Children from homes in which fathers were not present tended to prefer the immediate reward. The implication of this finding is, of course, that children from father-absent homes are less able to postpone gratification of needs and wants, and perhaps have less confidence in the reliability of adults.

Lynn and Sawrey (1959) compared Norwegian boys whose fathers were at sea for periods of nine months to two years at a time with those whose fathers were land-based and hence remained at home. Father-absent boys tended to be more infantile and dependent, had poorer relations with their peers, and were less secure in their masculinity than the other boys.

The moral development of 120 preadolescent, mostly lower-class boys attending rural schools was appraised by John W. Santrock (1975). Half the boys were from father-absent homes and the other half from intact homes. Two thirds of the mothers of father-absent boys had been divorced and the rest had been widowed. The teachers of the father-absent boys described them as being less advanced in moral judgment than the other boys, and also said that the sons of divorced mothers showed more "social deviation" (misbehavior) than the sons of widows.

In a similar study of boys living in the Detroit metropolitan area, Martin L. Hoffman (1971) compared moral values and indexes of aggressive behavior for two groups of seventh graders that were matched as to IQ and socioeconomic status. In one group, fathers had been absent from the home for at least six months prior to the study; in the other, families were intact. Boys from father-present homes scored higher than those from father-absent homes on tendency to feel guilty about wrong-doing, internal moral judgment, moral values, and conformity to rules. Teachers also reported a greater tendency toward overt aggression on the part of boys from father-absent homes. Somewhat similar tendencies were also observed for girls, but differences were slight and not as significant statistically. Hoffman concluded that the absence of the father has adverse effects on the conscience development of boys, at least in part because of the lack of an appropriate parental model. There was also some indication that women without husbands express less affection for their sons than do women whose husbands are present.

Blanchard and Biller (1971) used teachers' grades and school achievement measures in studying third-grade boys, who were divided for purposes of comparison into four groups: father absence beginning before the boys were five (early absence); father absence beginning after the boys were five (late absence); father presence in the home less than six waking hours a week (low presence); and father presence in the home more than two waking hours per day (high presence). Results showed that early absence had the most deleterious effect, as Figure 11-5 indicates, but that low presence also interferred with academic performance; in fact, the low-presence group's grades were no better than those for the early-absence group. The researchers concluded that fathers who were highly available provided models of achievement, perseverance, and competence for their sons. The data also suggest that the preschool years are a more critical period, in that father absence then has a more disabling effect.

The reason behind the father's absence appears to be important. Santrock and Wohlford (1970) compared fifth-grade boys, mostly from lower-class homes, whose fathers were present, or were absent because of death, or were absent because of divorce, desertion, or separation. Boys in the last group tended to be more aggressive than the others on a variety of measures and were less tolerant of a delay of gratification, in a test situation like that of Mischel, which we have described. This finding was particularly true of boys whose fathers had left home when the boys were between three and five years of age.

Because of the interest of investigators on the "male-modeling effect" of fathers, most of the research on father absence has been focused on the development of boys. E. Mavis Hetherington (1972), however, studied the personality development of the adolescent daughters of widowed and divorced mothers. In contrast to a control group of girls

It is difficult to determine exactly what effect a father has on the development of boys and girls but investigators are unanimous in reporting that his presence in a home has a psychological influence that is both important and generally positive.

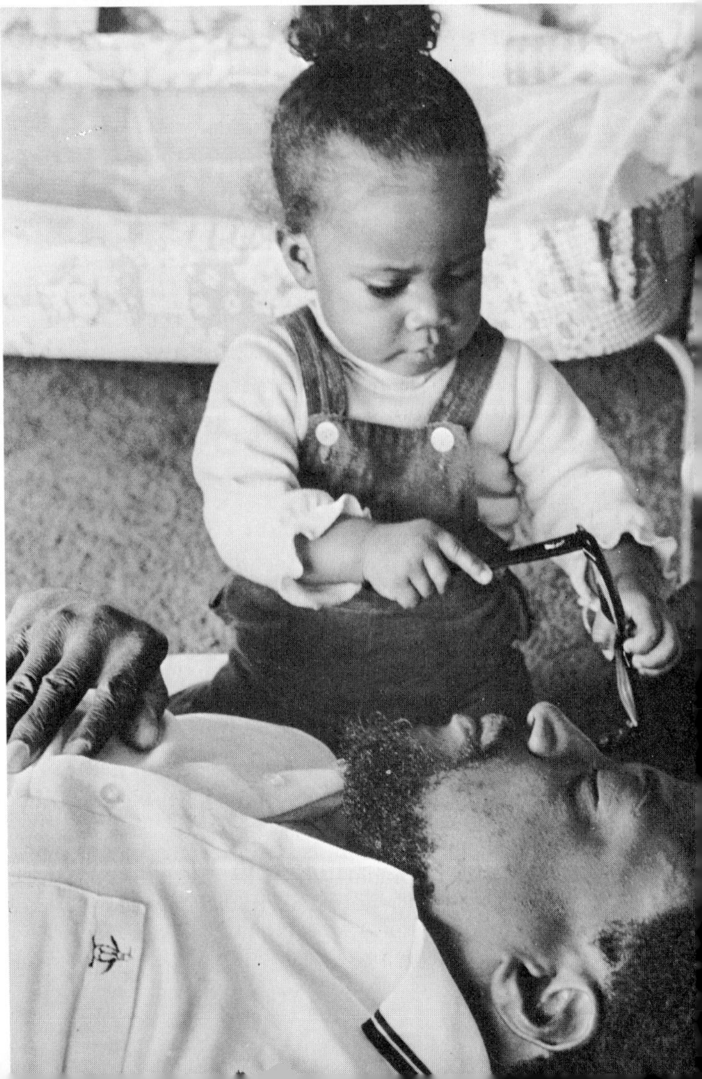

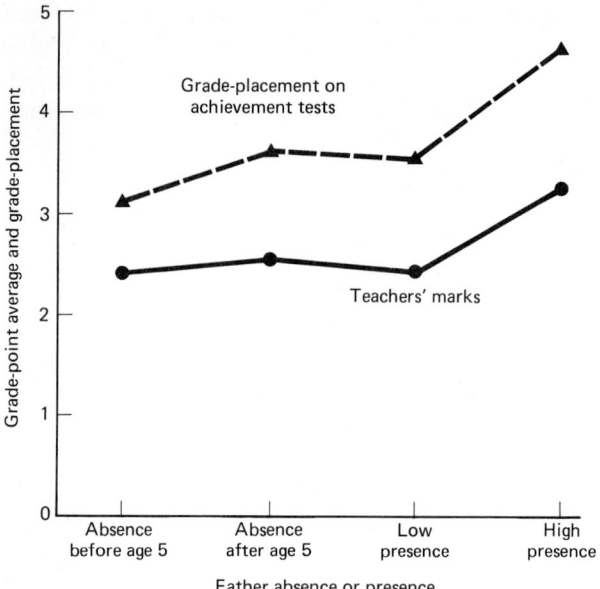

FIGURE 11-5. Relationship between academic performance and the initial point of father absence or the degree of father presence for boys in the third grade. (After Blanchard and Biller, 1971.)

from father-present homes, the daughters of widowed mothers were more inclined to be shy, withdrawn, and socially inhibited with boys their age, whereas the daughters of divorced mothers eagerly sought the company of boys and were more likely to be involved sexually with them.

The following excerpt from an interview with a divorced mother is quite revealing:

> That kid is going to drive me over the hill. I'm at my wit's end. She was so good until the last few years—then Pow! at eleven she really turned on. She went boy crazy. When she was only twelve I came home early from a movie and found her in bed with a young hood and she's been bouncing from bed to bed ever since. She doesn't seem to care who it is, she can't seem to keep her hands off men.

Contrast this report with that made by a widowed mother:

> [Daughter's name] is almost too good. She has lots of girl friends but doesn't date much. When she's with the girls she's gay and bouncy—quite a clown—but she clams up when a man comes in. Even around my brother she never says much. When boys do phone she often puts them off even though she has nothing else to do.

In a follow-up study some years later, Hetherington found that 46 per cent of the daughters of widows had married, in contrast to 67 per cent of the father-present daughters. Of the daughters of divorcees, however, not only had 88 per cent married, but more of them had been pregnant at the time of marriage and a number were already divorced or separated (Hetherington and Parke, 1975). It is clear that the widowed mothers in Hetherington's sample created a psychological home climate that was quite different from that provided by the divorced mothers.

Are Parents Necessary?

It is a routine finding that children from broken homes tend to have more adjustment problems than those from intact homes. K. M. Koller (1971), for example, found that over 61 per cent of delinquent girls in a state training school had suffered some kind of parental loss or deprivation. Over half were deprived of both parents, and an additional third had lost their fathers. By contrast, only 13 per cent of girls in a matched control group, drawn from the general population, had suffered parental deprivation.

There is no doubt that parents play key roles in the upbringing of children, but the question still remains whether parent substitutes can do as well. The common-sense answer to this question is that they cannot, and that individuals providing group care in children's institutions can never make up the psychological deficit suffered by parental loss.

Some contrary evidence to the prevailing view comes from an investigation by Tizard and Rees (1974), who studied preschool-aged children who had been admitted as infants to some rather special British residential nurseries that provided them with an unusual amount of care in the form of much adult attention and generous provision of books, toys, and outings. By the age of four, about 37 per cent of the children had been adopted, mostly by upper-middle-class families; about the same proportion were still in the institutions; and the remainder, about one fourth, had been returned to their own mothers, who for the most part lived in very poor circumstances.

When the Wechsler Pre-Primary Scale of Intelligence was administered to these four-year-olds, the adopted group had the highest mean IQ—115. The next highest mean IQ was that of the children who had remained in the institution—105. The children who had been returned to their mothers averaged 100 IQ.

The very high IQs of the adopted group demonstrate the effect of an enriched environment, whereas the 100 IQ of the children returned to their mothers, although it was the lowest of the three means, is at least average. The 105 IQ of the children remaining in the institution shows, however, that normal cognitive development can be expected when children's surroundings are pleasant and stimulating. The researchers concluded that these findings, together with those of a similar study they conducted, "constitute strong evidence that a good staff-child ratio, together with a generous provision of toys, books, and outings, will promote an average level of cognitive development at 4 years, in the absence of any close and/or continuous relationship with a mother substitute."

Findings that were consistent with the Tizard-Rees study have also been reported by Ruth Goldman (1971), who compared children cared for at home with those reared in institutional settings in Austria, Poland, and Yugoslavia. She found no differences in emotional adjustment between institutional and family-reared children in Austria and Yugoslavia, but family-raised children were better adjusted in Poland, where institutions were generally run along more rigid, impersonal lines.

influence of the family's social and economic status (SES)

During the earlier years of child research, the socioeconomic status (SES) of parents was largely overlooked. It was not until the work of sociologists in the late 1930s that behavioral scientists had firm evidence associating well-defined behavioral trends with various levels of SES. The study of "Yankeetown" by Warner and Lunt (1941) was an important landmark at that time. Warner and his co-workers observed the behavior of all individuals in the small seaport town of Newburyport, Massachusetts, noted who associated with whom, and asked each individual to characterize and describe as many of the other residents as he knew. The researchers analyzed these observations and interpersonal descriptions and classified the townspeople into three major social classes; upper, middle, and lower. Each class was further subdivided into an upper and a lower category, making six subclasses in all.

Sociologists have made extensive use of Warner's methods, with some modifications. The upper class in many communities may be considered to be an extension of the middle class; in any event, it is too small to be of much research interest. The upper-lower class is often termed the *working class,* and the lower-lower class as the *poverty class* or *disadvantaged class.* Although the main basis for determining social class continues to be one of association—who associates with whom— the resulting classifications are so highly correlated with occupational status and educational level that these two variables are usually used by researchers as valid indices of SES—particularly educational level, which is easily quantifiable and readily manipulated statistically.

The upper middle class today may be considered to be composed largely of individuals who have some substantial amount of college education. Most of these individuals have also achieved some degree of occupational status: they are in the professions, or they fill managerial positions, or they are owners of large businesses. The lower middle class is composed of individuals who are clerical or sales workers, highly skilled tradespeople, technicians, or owners of small businesses. They are usually high-school graduates, many of whom have spent additional time in business schools, community colleges, or technical institutes. Members of the working class usually have completed some high school and are employed in skilled, semiskilled, or unskilled occupations of various types. Individuals in the lower lower, or poverty, class generally have little education and are employed sporadically at low-level semiskilled or unskilled jobs. Black people and Latin Americans are heavily represented in this class, but most of its members are white.

According to standards used by the U.S. Department of Health, Education, and Welfare, about 16 per cent of the children in the United States in 1976 were from families below the poverty line. In numbers, this proportion amounted to more than ten million children under 18. Of the total number of children living in poverty homes, six million were white and four million were nonwhite, and 40 per cent are from fatherless families.

Most children from impoverished homes live in rural, rather than urban, settings. Among Indians living on reservations, 80 per cent are in poverty. In 1940, one million children were in families receiving financial aid under the program now known as Aid to Families with Dependent Children. Thirty years later, in 1970, the number was between five and six million, 80 per cent of whom were in families without fathers (White House Conference on Children, 1970). By 1976 the total had reached almost ten million.

SES and Child-Rearing Patterns

The attitudes and values that are associated with various social-class levels generate parental behavior that affects children's development in several ways. Melvin L. Kohn (1963, 1969) has observed that middle-class (MC) parents tend to prepare their children for occupations in which they are likely to make their own decisions and work cooperatively with others, whereas working-class (WC) or lower-class (LC) parents are inclined to prepare their children for occupations in which it is essential to follow explicit rules. For these reasons, MC parents are likely to emphasize independence and social skills. Keeping one's temper plays a key role in social skills, because free expression of anger makes cooperation difficult and jeopardizes one's right to act independently. Hence, child training in MC families is likely to stress reasoning, understanding, discussion of problems, and the like, whereas WC and LC families are likely to emphasize obedience and to punish severely for deviation from the rules. To put this in other terms, MC families are inclined to behave in equalitarian or democratic ways toward their children, and WC and LC families tend to adopt modes that are authoritarian and traditional.

The WC-MC differences reported by Kohn seem to be universal. Leonard I. Pearlin (1971) compared parental values in Washington, D.C., and Turin, and industrial city in Northern Italy, and found that in both cities MC parents gave higher ratings to child-rearing values aimed at forstering dependability, self-control, and consideration for others, whereas WC parents stressed obedience and being neat and clean.

In a cross-cultural study of wider scope, Nancy Frasure Smith (1975) asked MC and WC mothers and fathers in five countries to give their immediate reactions to a six-year-old child's tape-recorded demands for help or aid, as well as his or her displays of temper and insolence. Figure 11-6 indicates that the nationality of the parents had a great deal to do with the severity of their replies, with parents in Belgium and France expressing higher degrees of harshness and less leniency than parents in England, Canada, and the United States. But what is most interesting, for the purposes of the present discussion, is the consistency with which WC parents in each country or language group reveal themselves as being harsher than the MC parents.

SES and Cognitive Development

One interesting study of social-class differences in child-rearing patterns was conducted by Bee and her co-researchers (1969), employing as subjects LC and MC mothers and their four- or five-year-old children. Each mother and her child participated in a ninety-minute session, which began with a ten-minute period in a waiting room, where the two were observed through a one-way mirror. The room was furnished with many toys, and the floor was marked out with quadrants so that observers could plot the child's movements. Observations were coded in such a way that it was possible to score the behavior of both the mother and the child. Results showed that LC mothers made more disapproving statements to their children and made more attempts to get them to modify or stop whatever they were doing.[3]

Both MC mothers and their children made more informational statements. LC children were more inclined to accept their mothers' control and disapproval, but they were more restless, shifting their attention from one toy to another and moving about more.

After the waiting-room session, each mother and her child were brought into another room, where the child was given the task of building a house from blocks. The mother was told that she could give as much help as she wished. Again, there were differences in the two

---

[3] The fact that LC mothers were more disapproving does not mean that their children's behavior was poorer than that of the MC children. Researchers were unable to detect anything about the LC children's behavior that would call for the greater amount of control or disapproval they received.

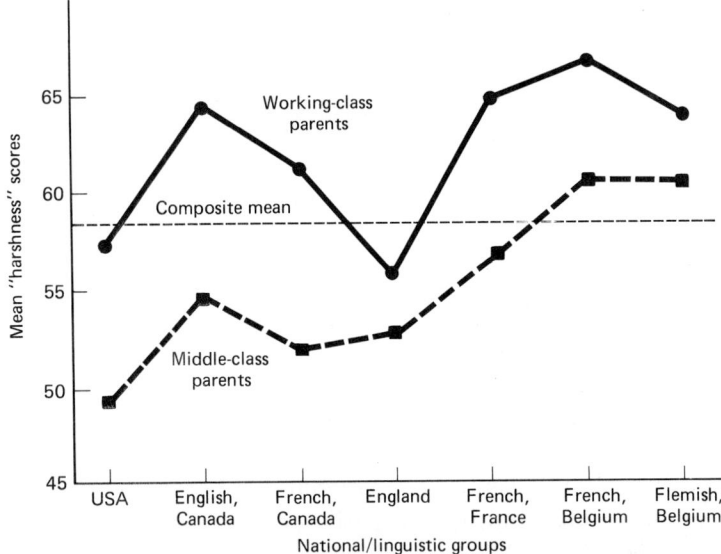

FIGURE 11-6. Differences in harshness* in the reactions of working-class and middle-class parents of seven ethnic/national groups to a six-year-old child's recorded pleas for help or displays of temper and insolence. (Data from Smith, 1975.)

*Points on the graph represent the averaged means for each group, based on their reactions to ten different recorded statements.

groups of mothers. MC mothers made more suggestions over all, and also expressed more approval of the child's performance; LC mothers, on the other hand, expressed more disapproval and were inclined to become more actively involved in the building task in a physical way—that is, handing blocks to the child, putting blocks on the house, and the like.

The researchers concluded that the observations gave them a rather clear picture of social-class differences in maternal behavior, particularly in terms ot helping to explain differences in school performance of LC and MC children. For example, the typical MC mother tended to allow the child to work at his own pace in the problem-solving situation, offering many general structuring suggestions on how to search for a solution to the problem, and spoke approvingly to the child whenever he was doing something correct. She permitted the child to take as much time as he wanted and seldom worked on the problem herself. This approach seemed to encourage the child to explore the problem independently and did not focus his attention on his failures. The typical LC mother, on the other hand, made suggestions that were highly specific and that did not provide any clues to problem-solving strategies. Often she deprived the child of the chance of solving the problem on his own by working on it herself. The researchers concluded that the MC strategy seemed calculated to help children with problems they might have in the future, whereas the LC strategy made it difficult for children to learn concepts that they could generalize to other problem-solving situations.

As we have noted previously, both children and laboratory animals respond favorably to increased inputs of stimulation. A number of research studies show that intellectual stimulation varies with the SES of the home. One of the more recent studies was conducted by Werner, Bierman, and French (1971), who correlated the IQs of almost five hundred children (97 per cent nonwhite or non-Anglo) from different cultural and ethnic backgrounds in rural Hawaii with the intellectual stimulation potential of their homes. Intelligence tests were given twice: at 20 months and at age 10.

Figure 11-7 presents the results for age 10, showing that correlations between children's IQs and family background were all positive. The relationship was quite similar for parental IQs, parental education, and socioeconomic status, but what is particularly interesting is that educational stimulation produced the highest correlation and evidently was the most significant variable. The variable of educational stimulation consisted of a composite rating of the opportunities available in the home for enlarging children's vocabulary; the quality of the language models available for the children; the intellectual activities and interests of the family; the kind of work habits emphasized in the home; the

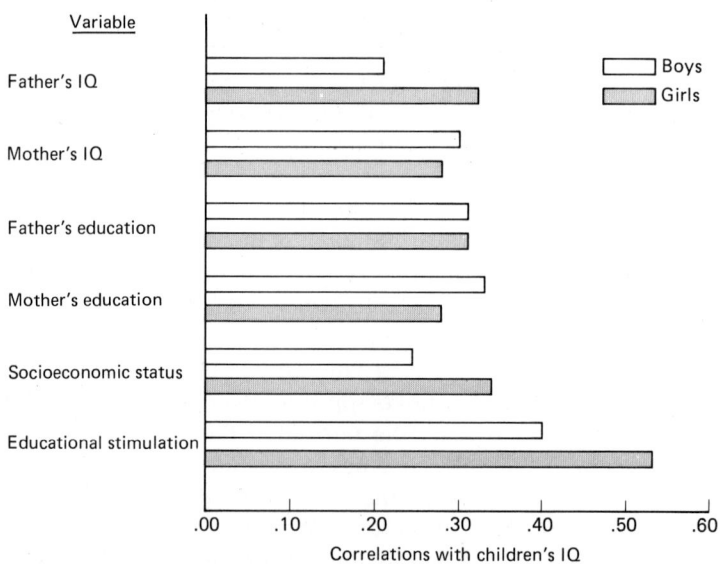

FIGURE 11-7. Correlations between IQs of children aged 10 and (1) measures of parental ability, and (2) environmental ratings. (After Werner, Bierman, and French, 1971.)

availability of learning supplies, books, and periodicals; and the opportunities for children to participate in and explore various aspects of the larger environment through libraries, special lessons, recreational activities, and the like. The intelligence tests given at 20 months also showed positive relationships with parental education, IQ, and SES.

All these variables are interrelated, of course. Parents with more years of education are likely to have higher-status jobs and to be more affluent. They are also more likely to create an environment that is intellectually stimulating for a child. This "hidden curriculum" at home depends partly on economic factors, because it costs money to buy books, subscribe to magazines, pay for music lessons, and participate in a wide range of recreational activities. But educational stimulation is not entirely dependent on economic support, for it also includes such variables as the work habits of the family, the complexity of the language the children are exposed to, and the like. In other words, the parents' attitudes and values are also significant factors. In any event, these variables tend to be correlated with socioeconomic status: the higher the status, the greater the amount of educational stimulation to which the child is exposed; the lower the status, the less the stimulation.

It can be argued, of course, that even children in poor homes receive a great deal of stimulation and reinforcement, and therefore should do as well intellectually as MC children; but it can be answered that life in the inner city tends to be less predictable for children. Bresnahan and Blum (1971) asked the question: What would happen if reinforcement were as chaotic and unpredictable for MC children as it is for lower-class children? They gave first-grade children from MC and LC homes a series of cognitive tasks that were preceded by trial sessions in which they experienced random reinforcement at zero, moderate, or high levels. MC children did better than LC children on the tasks, but when the task was preceded by random reinforcement, the performance of the MC children deteriorated until it was at the same level as that of the LC children. Their findings suggest that one of the reasons why lower-SES children have more problems in the cognitive area may be that the schedules of reinforcement in their homes are not as orderly or as dependable as they are in MC homes.

It now seems clear that sheer stimulation is not enough to promote cognitive development and that it may, if random and unpredictable, be more of a hindrance than a help. In Chapter 6 we mentioned a study by Elardo, Bradley, and Caldwell (1975), in which the Caldwell Inventory of Home Stimulation was found to predict Bayley Mental Development Index scores during infancy and Stanford-Binet IQs at age 3. One of the more important scales on the Inventory is "Organization of physical and temporal environment". Items included on other scales of the Inventory also deal with scheduling and organizing the child's environment: "Structures child's play periods," "Is taken care of by father some time each day," and "Shares at least one meal with mother and father." Organization, structure, and environmental predictability are probably more important in infancy than at any other period in development, but preschoolers and even older children are easily distracted and confused when the events in their lives lack predictability and order.

SES and Crowding

The more individuals who are crowded into a given area of living space, the less orderly and the more unpredictable life becomes. A child cannot easily learn to deal constructively with his environment if he is continually having to cope with the intrusions of others into his personal space or their demands on his time and attention. Some children react defensively—by withdrawing—to this overabundance of stimulation and distraction. This strategy enables them to deal with life on an immediate, short-range basis at home, but prevents their responding appropriately in social situations elsewhere, as at school. Other children, mainly boys, react in overactive ways—by running, shouting, climbing, pushing, fighting, and engaging in destructive acts. This kind of behavior also interferes with cognitive development.

Robert B. Zajonc (1976) has reviewed a number of significant studies that in one way or another deal with a variable that has been termed *population density*—crowdedness—in children's homes. He notes that a large number of studies routinely show that family size is significantly related to children's IQs: the larger the family, the lower the children's IQ is likely to be.

Zajonc also takes notice of the tendency for children born early in the birth-order sequence to have higher IQs than those born later. This advantage evidently stems from three factors: (1) families during their earlier stages are smaller, and homes are thus less crowded; (2) parents can become more involved with their children and give them more attention when families are still small; and (3) older children function as teachers of younger ones, and the act of teaching is particularly stimulating to cognitive development. Early-born children obviously play the teacher more than later-born children do.

Zajonc observes that if the time-spacing between children is extended, however, homes are less crowded, younger children get more attention, and birth order has much less influence on cognitive development. In Scotland and in France, where there is considerably more time between births than in other countries, early-born children have no great advantage. Among French families of four or more children, for example, last-borns have higher mean IQs than firstborns.

But even in Scotland and France, family size has a depressing effect on IQ, with families of four or more scoring below the mean for the general population. We might expect that this effect is entirely caused by poverty, inasmuch as poor parents tend to have larger families than

Poverty takes many forms and has different effects on children. It can mean defeatism and alienation. It can mean getting along with less and sharing resources and tasks. But it can also mean receiving much more friendliness, warmth, and support from family, friends, and neighbors.

"THIS KIND OF BACKGROUND IS OK. IF YOU'RE A SUCCESS LATER BUT IT AIN'T SO HOT NOW"
(Serrano, in *Wall St. Jounal.*)

more affluent ones, but research in France and Holland makes it clear that family size operates somewhat independently of SES as far as children's IQs are concerned. In other words, children from smaller families have the advantage when it comes to cognitive development, irrespective of whether their parents are MC or LC, and large families tend to depress children's IQs, irrespective of whether they are MC or LC.

In any event, the amount and kind of verbal exchange that takes place between parent and child is of crucial importance. This fact was brought out in a study of the interaction between parents and their two-year-old sons, who were either twins or singleton children. The investigators found that the twins experienced fewer verbal interchanges of all types with their parents, and concluded that the lower level of verbal facility commonly observed in twins is the result of each twin having had fewer verbal exchanges with his parents than singleton children do. The researchers also found that the twin situation proved to be a more influential factor than family social status in determining the kind of interaction that took place between parent and child (Lytton, Conway, and Sauvé, 1977).

Economics are not, of course, irrelevant: the data assembled by Zajonc show the usual advantage accruing to MC children. But we should note that family size gives the families of the poor a special handicap, for their smaller apartments and houses mean that there are more persons per room. In other words, a small poor family is likely to be more crowded than a large MC one.

Influence of Ethnicity and Minority Subculture

Living space is not the only factor in cognitive development, of course. The child's view of the world and his relationship to it are important factors. Some ethnic groups value achievement at the cost of group solidarity whereas others value solidarity at the cost of achievement; some cultures permit and encourage interaction with members of other cultures whereas others actively discourage it. Such values play a very significant part in determining the kind of individual the child will become.

The kind of values a culture teaches with respect to the reward systems of society are extremely important. Robert J. Havighurst (1970) notes, for example, that American Indian children respond to praise and blame from members of their families and their peer groups but tend to ignore outsiders. The norm in some Indian groups is that of being quite intolerant of members who show superior knowledge and understanding. Often a teacher will be unable to get Indian children to volunteer an answer, even though several of them may know it. "In oral reading, the whole class tends to read together in audible whispers, so that the child who is supposed to be reciting can simply wait when he comes to a difficult word until he hears it said by his classmates."

Havighurst draws upon Freudian concepts when he makes the point that "an effective reward system in a complex, changing society must be based on a strong ego." Id rewards—that is, rewards oriented toward the satisfaction of primitive, infantile impulses—may have immediate and short-term value in learning situations, but what enables children to develop appropriately mature forms of behavior is a system of rewards based on long-range consequences in the real world. Id rewards must therefore be supplemented by ego and superego rewards, rewards that carry a child "from learning for fun to learning even if it is hard work." Children from cultures that emphasize id rather than ego rewards are likely to have a great deal of difficulty in adapting to life in a "complex, changing society."

Havighurst cites other research showing the effect of the values of an ethnic group on children's behavior. Gross (1967) studied two groups of Jewish boys in Brooklyn, all aged about six, and all middle class. The families of one of the groups were Sephardic (Mediterranean in origin), and the other group's families were Ashkenazic (Northern European). The mothers were all native Americans, and English was the household language. The Ashkenazic boys showed a higher level of cognitive development than did the Sephardic boys, as indicated by the fact that their mean IQ was 17 points higher.

An intensive study of the family training and background of the homes yielded no difference except one: Ashkenazic mothers were more likely to say that their son's future earnings were "unimportant" as compared to other aims in life, whereas the Sephardic mothers were much more likely to say that they wanted their sons to be "wealthy." This difference suggests that the two groups of mothers very likely had different reward systems in dealing with their sons and were also using these systems to reinforce different kinds of behavior. On the surface, it would seem that the Sephardic mothers had the highest level of aspiration for their sons, but in actuality they were not interested in their son's *intellectual* attainments as were the Ashkenazic mothers, and it would appear that although the SES of the two sets of mothers was similar, the Sephardic mothers' outlook was more working class, whereas the Ashkenazic mothers' orientation was more middle class.

Still another characteristic that may have important consequences for cognitive and social development is the attitude a culture teaches with respect to what psychologists term the *locus of control*. Ethnic groups differ with respect to whether their members view themselves as responsible for their successes or failures or whether they attribute such outcomes to fate, luck, or powerful others. The child who holds himself responsible—whose locus of control is internal—is more likely to attempt to solve problems and strive toward distant goals than are children who believes there is little they can do to affect the events in their life. Such children tend to see their locus of control as external.

Toni Falbo (1975) conducted some experiments with children, mostly nonwhite, who were enrolled in Hawaiian kindergartens. The children heard stories in which a five-year-old succeeded or failed at a task and then were asked to explain the outcome. An analysis of their responses indicated that MC children were more likely to explain *success* internally, in terms of the child's having tried hard enough, and *failure* in terms of his not having put forth sufficient effort; on the other hand, children from families whose parents' income came from public welfare were more inclined to give external explanations based on task difficulty and luck.

SES Versus Ethnicity: Which Has the More Significant Effect?

It is not easy to disentangle ethnicity from culture or SES. The findings of Nancy Frasure Smith (1975), which we reported in Figure 11-6, show that in any given ethnic group, working-class (WC) parents are likely to be harsher than MC parents, but a careful analysis shows a great deal of variation between groups. Belgian MC parents were harsher than American WC parents, for instance.

Within the geographical and cultural boundaries of a nation, however, the evidence suggests that SES is likely to be a more significant variable than ethnic identity in the cognitive development of children. Its significance may, however, be obscured by the fact that certain ethnic groups are overrepresented at one social level or another. Tulkin (1968), for instance, found that white schoolchildren tested higher in achievement than black children in the same grade, but when white and black students were matched according to social class and family situation (factors such as broken homes, maternal employment, crowdedness of home), the differences between races disappeared at the middle-class levels. In actuality, even without controlling for family situation, there were no significant differences between white and black middle-class girls, thus suggesting that black boys are more vulnerable to environmental stress than are girls. Differences favored white children at lower SES levels; other research, too, suggests that difficult as the social environment is for white lower-class individuals, it is even more stressful for lower-class black people.

Eleanor Rosch Heider (1971) asked ten-year-old children to describe faces and abstract displays of stimuli from sets of six similar items as accurately as possible, so that another child could pick out items just from hearing a description of them. She found that middle-class children were generally superior both at giving descriptions and at understanding other children's descriptions, irrespective of whether the describers were from the lower class or the middle class, black or white. Lower-class children, however, understood descriptions by other lower-class children better than those of middle-class children. Heider was unable to find any consistent racial differences in the ability to describe or understand, the major difference being attributable to SES. Similar results have since been reported by Quay and Mathews (1977).

Questions About SES Research

We should note that not all behavioral scientists accept the idea that SES makes any important difference in child-rearing practices and in the socialization of children. Edward Zigler (1970) reviewed a large number of research studies and took issue with most of their conclusions. He was inclined to favor a genetic explanation, pointing out that lower-class children tend to perform at a lower Piagetian level than middle-class children. They also have poorer impulse control and are less problem-oriented. Zigler also pointed to inconsistencies in SES research, noting that in the 1940s it was stylish to say that middle-class people were more anxious and more overcontrolling of their children, but that today the conclusions of researchers are the opposite. Whether this criticism of SES research is valid is open to question, however. It can be argued that researchers are more sophisticated now than they were a generation ago, but the possibility that experimenter bias is as much a problem today as it was then is not easily dismissed.

Zigler is not the only psychologist to express misgivings about SES. It is frequently pointed out that differences associated with SES are not caused by SES as such, but by certain attitudes, experiences, and environments that are ordinarily associated with people's SES. Indeed, it often happens that a behavioral difference that seems to be "caused" by SES is actually brought about by some other variable. A survey of French-speaking people in Montreal, for example, showed that the complexity and range of the vocabulary they used varied according to their income, occupational status, and area of residence—all indexes of SES. When the data were analyzed, however, it turned out that the most significant underlying variable was educational level (Sankoff and Lessard, 1975). To be sure, SES levels were correlated with educational attainment, but it was the education that determined the kind of jobs held by the subjects; thus it also determined their income and where they lived.

Because education appears to function as an independent variable that affects not only SES but a whole complex of values, attitudes, behavior patterns, and life styles as well, many psychologists have come to prefer it as an index of social class. Hence in many research reports, SES should be more properly rendered as "educational level." Psychologists have also found that the number of years of education completed is a more reliable measure than more complex scales that take into account occupational level, place of residence, leisure-time acitvities, and the other factors that are used as indicators of SES.

In any event, we should keep in mind that SES as such does not influence behavior; instead, the term is employed as a composite, shorthand label that stands for a cluster of interrelated factors, some of which function as independent variables.

Zigler's genetic explanation of SES differences in cognitive ability leaves unexplained a number of phenomena that could be interpreted environmentally. Here is one. A century ago, most of the people in the United States were lower class; today the majority are middle class. Genetic theory would predict that the proportion of individuals in the two classes either would have remained unchanged over the period, or else that the proportion of lower-class individuals would have increased, because of their higher birth rate. The great increase in the middle class can be explained in environmental terms by a reciprocal interaction between economic and educational development. Expanding industry and commerce demanded educated employees, and such employees were available because of the greater accessibility of education. Each better-educated wave of parents took on the child-rearing patterns characteristic of the educated middle class of their times, and their children and their children's children were raised democratically and in home environments that were intellectually stimulating.

The effects of increased exposure to education are demonstrated by a comparative study of the intelligence of soldiers in World Wars I and II. The median Army Alpha test score of a sample of World War II recruits was 104, which compares to a midpoint score of 62 for enlistees during World War I. The World War II score corresponds to the 83rd percentile on World War I norms. In other words, the "typical" or "average" soldier in World War II scored higher on this intelligence test than 83 per cent of the soliders in World War I (Tuddenham, 1948).

Such a difference cannot be explained in purely genetic terms. The difference can, however, be explained in terms of the greater exposure of the World War II soldiers to education. The average soldier in World War I had a bare eight years of schooling, whereas the typical World War II inductee had completed more than ten years. Furthermore, the number of days in the typical school year was many fewer at the turn of the century than during the 1930s, and school days were shorter as well. Today, the average young adult has completed more than 12 years of education, not counting preschool.

birth order

Developmental psychologists have given considerable attention in the last decade or so to what is termed the *birth-order effect*. Some of this research interest has been brought about by the fact that birth order can be used as a fixed independent variable. In other words, inasmuch as all children of the same parents share the same genetic pool, behavioral differences associated with one birth-order position or another can be attributed to environmental variables peculiar to that position, rather than to genetics.

The Advantages of Being First-born

The greatest degree of consistency is experienced by firstborns. Rosenblatt and Skoogberg (1974) surveyed 39 cultures and found that in all of them first-borns receive more attention than those born later. It is the first-born who enables husband and wife to become father and mother, thus providing them with roles that increase their status and stabilize their marriage. As a consequence, first-borns are the focus for more elaborate birth ceremonies, have more authority over siblings, and receive respect from siblings.

A few pages back we noted the tendency of early-born children to attain higher IQs than later-borns. This effect tends to be most pronounced with first-borns, who get more attention and enjoy proportionately more "living space" during their earliest years than do other early-born children. (In contrast to the average first-born, the average only child tends to score slightly lower on intelligence tests, probably because he gets no opportunity to teach younger siblings, as Zajonc [1976] has pointed out.)

Researchers, like parents, have paid far more attention to the first-born than to later-borns, and there have been literally hundreds of studies detailing the ways in which first-born children differ in personality, social behavior, and cognitive development. Because of the opportunity first-borns have of playing the role of parent substitute, supervising the behavior of their siblings, it is not surprising that research shows them as being more socialized, more responsible, and more favorably disposed to persons in authority than those who were born later (MacDonald, 1969a, b). Laosa and Brophy (1970) conducted a survey of kindergarten children and found that some of the birth-order-related differences that have been noted in adolescents and adults are also present at this early age. Measures of creativity showed first-borns to be more fluent verbally, and they also tended to be slightly more popular with other children.

Not all the characteristics of first-borns are positive. Helen L. Koch (1955) secured teachers' impressions of kindergarten children and then sorted out their ratings according to the children's birth order. Results showed that first-borns were inclined to show more anger, to be more intense emotionally, to make more excuses when things went wrong, and to be less responsive to sympathy and praise from adults. On the other hand, they tended to articulate more clearly in speech than second-borns. First-borns with opposite-sex siblings rated higher on leadership, exhibitionism, and jealousy than those with same-sex siblings.

The opportunities first-born children have of playing the role of parent substitute and of supervising their siblings, enables them to become socialized more rapidly then later-borns and at the same time makes it easy for them to identify with persons in authority.

Parental Behavior Toward First-borns

The behavior of pairs of mothers and four-year-old children drawn from different birth-order positions was observed by Irma Hilton (1967). The mothers of first-born children, in contrast to those of later-borns, were more likely to start the child working on puzzles, to offer suggestions, and generally to interfere with the child's activities. Mothers of other children were more inclined to let them start puzzles on their own. Mothers of first-borns were more likely to make overt gestures of love or emotional support (hugs, kisses, etc.), especially when the child was succeeding on the task assigned by the experimenter. As far as the children themselves were concerned, first-borns tended to be more dependent (more likely, for example, to run to their mother's side during the intermission between testing session) than later-borns and were more likely to ask their mothers for help.

Mary K. Rothbart (1971) conducted a similar study, in which mothers supervised their first- or second-born children, aged five, in a series of tasks. She noted that the mothers put more pressure to achieve on the first-borns and communicated more readily to them. For their part, the first-borns were more compliant than the second-borns.

"Have you lost all interest in your first-born?"

(Drawing by Whitney Darrow, Jr. © 1971, The New Yorker Magazine, Inc.)

Rothbart concluded that the mother of a first-born is more likely to be "intrusive" in the achievement behavior of her child, and speculated that the greater success that the first-born tends to have in school later on may be the result of his willingness to accept performance standards that others have set for him.

Differences in maternal treatment of first- and later-born children appear to apply to monkeys as well as to humans. Rhesus mothers of first-born infants tend to be more tense, anxious, and protective of their offspring than mothers of later-borns. The infants themselves also display birth-order differences. In contrast to later-borns, first-born rhesus infants tend to be more assertive, sociable, and friendly toward their peers. They are also more active and vocalize more (Stevens and Mitchell, 1972).

The fact that first-born children turn out differently from later-borns shows how differences in parental attitudes and treatment can result in personality differences. The over-all impact of differential treatment is not great and probably does not contribute more than a few percentage points to the variance among personality traits. The interesting thing for our purposes is that the first-born serves as a kind of laboratory guinea pig for theories of child development because it is possible to identify the ways in which first-borns differ from other children and to trace the differences back to early childhood experiences that are, for the first-born, systematically different than the experiences of the later-born.

peer relationships

During the preschool years, the young child begins to disengage himself from the home circle and to interact with his peers, sometimes directly and sometimes in a parallel, side-by-side relationship. His relationships in and with groups are inclined to be somewhat tentative, because the child at this age lacks the skills and probably the motivation required for group-oriented behavior. Opportunity has much to do with this, of course. The child who can play with neighbor children has opportunities to learn social skills that are denied the child on a lonely farm, and the child who attends nursery school or spends much time in a well-run day care center is in the most advantageous positon.

Social Participation

A child's social participation with his peers increases in versatility and complexity between the second and the fifth years. These increases with age are shown by the more cooperative nature of the child's participation. Mildred B. Parten (1932, 1933) studied the size of the groups in which children played and the nature of their play activity by a technique of time sampling.

Parten also classified the play behavior of the children into six categories: (1) *unoccupied;* (2) *solitary* (independent) *play;* (3) *onlooker;* (4) *parallel activity* (playing alongside, but not with other children); (5) *associative activity* (common activity, with borrowing, lending, and turns taken); and (6) *cooperative* (working toward some common goal; different roles by various members that supplement one another.

The youngest children tended to engage either in solitary or in parallel play. As their age increased, preschool children engaged more in associative and cooperative play and less in idleness, solitary play, and observing as an onlooker. Parallel play was the only category that did not change materially over the years. It is evident that with increasing age social participation increases.

The proportion of time that preschool children typically spent in various categories of play was recorded by Debra Fatheree (1971), who observed 15 three-year-olds and 20 four-year-olds on a nursery-school playground in Berkeley, California. The observation period for the two groups was 16 minutes, with recordings made at two-minute intervals. The percentage of the observation period that the average child in each group spent in the various Parten play categories is reported in Figure 11-8. Fatheree's results confirm Parten's observations in that the older child spent proportionately more time in parallel, associative, and cooperative play than did the younger ones.

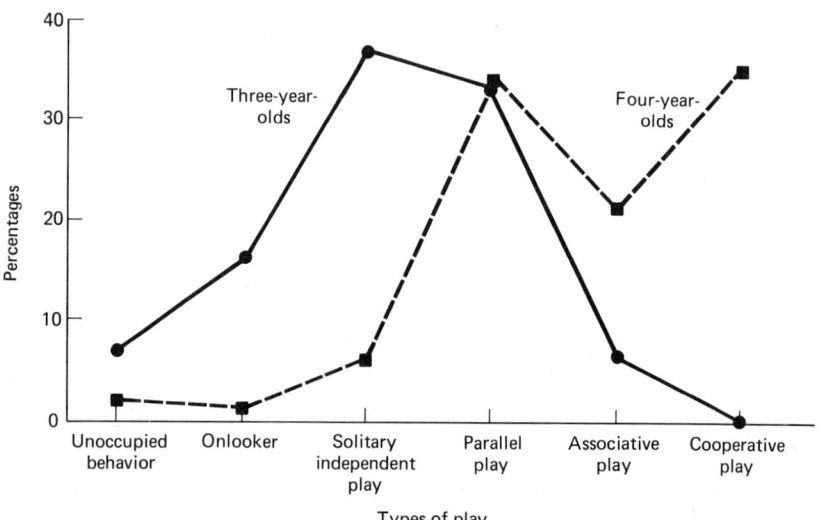

FIGURE 11-8. *Percentages of time spent in various kinds of play by three-year-olds and four-year-olds in a nursery school play yard.* (Data from Fatheree, 1971.)

Play, like other childhood activities, tends to fall into developmental stages. Types of play depicted here are solitary, onlooker, associative, and cooperative.

Socialization: General Trends

The child's increasing tendency to involve others in his play during the preschool years can be explained partly in terms of his attempts to cope with the social dimensions of his environment and to try out new skills, especially those involving the use of language. This increase in social maturity can also be explained in terms of a drive to seek ever more complex stimuli. The introduction of the social element makes any situation more unstable, more unpredictable, more complex, and hence more arousing. Therefore, the child who seeks arousal is likely to seek interaction with others in order to satisfy his need to be stimulated and aroused.

Because association with others satisfies this need for arousal, it is likely to be reinforcing, and any behavior that leads to social interaction is likely to be rewarded. The learning of socialized behavior is also enhanced when children reinforce one another directly through expressions of approval, collaboration on problems, and the like. Charlesworth and Hartup (1967) observed four types of positive social reinforcers in groups of nursery-school children: giving positive attention and approval, giving affection and personal acceptance, submitting to others' demands, and giving things to others. As might be expected, the actions described occurred more frequently in the behavior of four-year-olds than three-year-olds. The researchers also observed that giving social rewards to others was associated with receiving them, and there was a tendency for children who engaged in much positive reinforcement to interact with a relatively large number of children in this way.

In a review of socialization research for this period of development, Willard W. Hartup (1970) noted that even negative social actions may have positive reinforcement value for some children: inasmuch as the attention of others has psychological value, negative attention is better than no attention at all. Hartup also observed that there are wide variations in the extent to which nursery-school groups provide social reinforcement. Much depends on the kind of activity taking place: dramatic play provides more opportunities for reinforcement by peers than does eating.

Hartup noted six categories of social behaviors that change with increasing age during preschool years:

1. Dependency directed toward peers increases; dependency directed toward adults decreases.
2. Sympathy and altruism increase.
3. Ascendancy (tendency to take the lead) increases.
4. Competition increases, particularly under conditions inviting comparative evaluation of performance with others.
5. Quarreling decreases, but quarrels tend to last longer.

6. Aggressive activity increases but tends to decline after the nursery-school years are over (as we noted earlier).

Socialization skills are learned not only as a result of reinforcement but also because other children serve as models. Hartup and Coates (1967) found that "learning to share" could be facilitated by exposing young children to the behavior of a model who shared a great deal. It is important not to make too much of this, however. Preschool children are still very immature when it comes to social skills. In contrast to school-aged children, they are less aware of the "group effect," and group involvement as such does not have the value that it assumes a few years later. For that reason, preschool children are less aware of social norms, which constitute the major factor that binds groups together psychologically and gives them cohesiveness and stability.

Modeling and Prosocial Behavior

In Chapter 4 we described a study by Liebert and Poulos (1971) in which adult models were used to get children to learn one form of altruistic behavior—sharing. Another form of altruistic or prosocial behavior—helping—has been studied by the use of a contrived situation in which a subject is led to believe that he hears someone get into a difficult or dangerous situation and hence provides help. In one experiment, Ervin Staub (1971) preceded the test situation by preparing

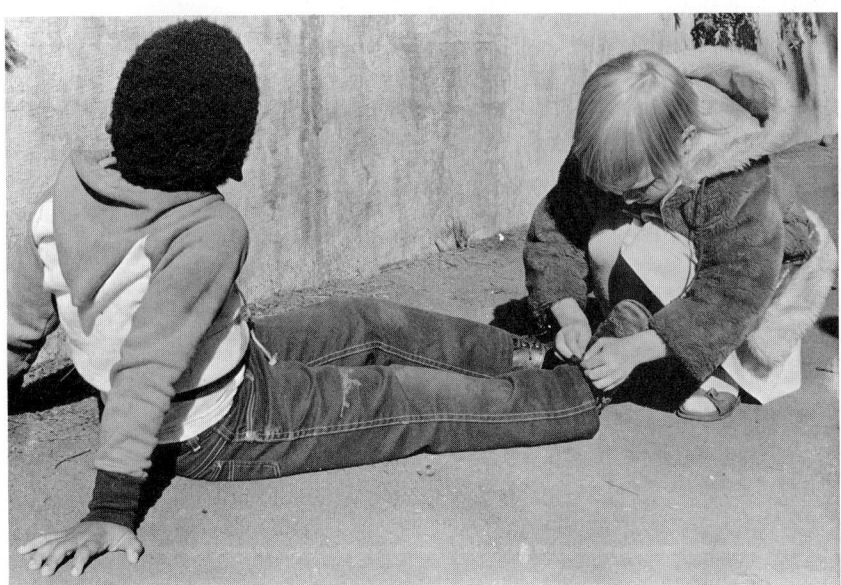

Exposed to the behavior of adults who share and help, children learn similar forms of prosocial behavior.

kindergarten children with one of four treatments: (1) pairs of children enacted situations in which one person needed help, and another one provided it; (2) similar to Condition 1, except that situations were described and not enacted, and children were asked how help could be provided; (3) a combination of role playing and discussion; (4) control—children enacted roles unrelated to helping.

During the testing phase of the experiment an experimenter took each child to a playroom and left him there briefly while she went into an adjoining room to "check on a girl who is playing there." Then she returned and told the child that the girl was playing next door and that he (or she) could play with anything in the playroom. Shortly after she left, the child heard a crash from the adjoining room, followed by sounds of distress and sobbing (actually tape-recorded). While this was going on, the experimenter was watching the child's behavior through a one-way mirror. If the child went to the adjoining room to help, the experimenter appeared and explained the experiment to the child. If not, the experimenter waited for a minute and then entered the room to elicit his reaction to the sounds of distress. Each child who participated also received a bag of candy—his choice out of three kinds available. The child was then told that if he wished, some of the candy could be donated for another child who was ill and whose parents were unable to buy him anything for his birthday.

Results indicated that role playing and discussion of helping behavior had some tendency to facilitate helping of the fictitious child in distress. Although results were not clear-cut, girls were more inclined to offer help than boys.[4] When it came to sharing of candy, however, boys were more inclined to do so than girls, especially if they had engaged in role playing.

summary

As the child passes from infancy into toddlerhood, the social aspects of his environment begin to be important. What families contribute, through their structure, is a sense of security. *Structure* refers to the predictability and stability of social relationships and implies some kind of hierarchy of authority. Today's families are becoming less structured. The ecology of the home is reflected not only by the physical conditions that prevail but also by the degree of orderliness that characterizes the activities that take place there. Much research has focused on child-rearing practices, a major feature of the child's home environment. Baumrind, who investigated the relationship between the behavior of

---

[4] This finding is directly opposite to results obtained in similar experiments with adults, in which men are more likely than women to volunteer to help others in difficult situations. Taking the initiative to extend help to a stranger is, of course, more consistent with the adult male role (Wispé and Freshley, 1971; Schwartz and Clausen, 1970).

parents and the personality patterns of their preschool children, found that self-reliant children tended to have parents who rated high on parental control, parent-child communication, parental nurturance, and parental demands for maturity. The parents of anxious, restless, and depressed children tended to score lower on control and maturity demands, communicated less, and were not very supportive. Parents of immature children showed average support and nurturance, but scored negatively in all other respects. The well-adjusted child gets both firm control and love, and the immature child gets very little control and few demands for mature behavior.

In a second study, Baumrind explored other aspects of the relationship between parental behavior and children's personality traits. One dimension she investigated was *independence*, characterized by dominance, purposefulness, and achievement orientation. Baumrind found that firm parental control and demands for maturity are not detrimental to the development of independence. She differentiated among several types of parents. The *authoritarian* parent evaluates the child's behavior according to some set of absolute standards and demands unquestioning obedience. The *authoritative* parent directs the child in a rational manner that is oriented to issues. Although firm control is exercised, the child is respected as an individual. The *permissive* parent is nonpunitive and accepting with regard to the child's impulses. The children of authoritative parents were found to be friendlier, more cooperative, and more achievement-oriented. Baumrind also observed that authoritative parents who were nonconforming tended to have independent, purposive, and dominant boys, but that their daughters tended to be hostile and resistive.

Much research has focused on the mother-child relationship. Bayley and Schaefer correlated dimensions of earlier maternal behavior with IQs taken when the child was older. Their findings suggest that boys tend to benefit from more intense "mothering," but girls respond better to maternal encouragement for autonomy. A study assessing the home environment of language-delayed children and normal children revealed that the mothers of language-delayed children were more critical, praised seldom, and were less involved with them. Other research by Bayley indicated that preschool boys who experience supportive behavior from their mothers are likely to be better adjusted socially during the school years.

Children from father-absent homes are less willing to accept delay of gratification than other children. Father absence is also somewhat associated with social maladjustment, retarded development in moral judgment, and misbehavior on the part of boys. It makes a difference why the father is absent. Boys whose mothers were widowed are somewhat better adjusted than those whose mothers are divorced, and the earlier the separation occurred, the worse the adjustment. Most of the research on father absence focuses on its effect on boys, but a study by Hetherington indicates that the daughters of widows tended to avoid contact with male peers, whereas the daughters of divorcees displayed the opposite behavior. Although parents make an important contribution to the psychological welfare of young children, some research studies show that institutions that provide a friendly and stimulating atmosphere can also have a positive effect on children's cognitive and emotional development.

Socioeconomic status (SES) is determined by who associates with whom in a community. SES is highly correlated with education. Studies of child-rearing patterns indicate that working-class and other lower-class families emphasize obedience and tend to punish severely, whereas middle-class families are more permissive and stress independence, dependability, self-control, and consideration for others. The tendency of lower-class parents to treat children more harshly than do middle-class parents appears in a number of cultures and countries. In an experiment in which mothers observed their children working on a problem, lower-class mothers were inclined to be more critical and restrictive, whereas middle-class mothers expressed more approval and encouraged independence.

Research by Werner on a largely nonwhite sample of children in Hawaii showed that the single most important determinant of IQ was a variable she called "educational stimulation," a composite rating of work habits at home, family intellectual activities, availability of books, and the like. But another experiment indicates that stimulation alone is not enough, for if it is too random and disorganized, it is not reinforcing. Hence middle-class children exposed to random reinforcement learn no better than lower-class children under similar conditions. Children, especially during their earliest years, encounter difficulties in maintaining normal cognitive development if there is no order or predictibility in the stimuli in their environment. A child growing up in crowded circumstances experiences a great many random and distracting stimuli; such circumstances are likely to prevail in the crowded homes of the poor. This may account for the tendency of early-born children (whose earlier years are spent in less crowded homes) to score higher in intelligence tests than laterborns. As time spacing between children increases, the advantage of early-born children tends to disappear.

Havighurst maintains that children must learn how to respond to systems of ego rather than id rewards, if they are going to find their way in a complex, changing society. Some ethnic groups emphasize id rewards and thus make it difficult for their children to adapt, but the main differences in this respect tend to be SES, rather than ethnic. For example, differences in school achievement between black and white children can be better explained in terms of a higher proportion of the black children coming from lower-SES homes, rather than in ethnic terms.

Not all behavioral scientists accept an SES explanation for achievement differences among children. Some point out that it is the factors associated with SES, and not SES as such, that influence children's behavior the most. Parental education appears to be the most significant of the SES-related variables in this respect. The weight of the research evidence favors an environmental, rather than genetic, explanation of changes in SES and intelligence scores that have taken place over the last fifty to one hundred years in the United States.

The relationship between birth order and children's behavior interests the researcher because of what it reveals about the effect of the family environment. The first-born child has a decided advantage in all cultures because he receives more attention, is born into a less crowded home, and has the added stimulation of teaching his siblings. These experiences tend to make first-borns more socialized, more favorably disposed to authority figures, more verbal, and more popular than later-borns. But first-born children are also inclined to be more emotional, sensitive, and jealous. Observations of mothers of first-borns indicate that they are more inclined to play an active or interfering role than are mothers of later-borns. Similar birth-order–related differences appear in the behavior of rhesus mothers and their infants.

During the preschool years, the child begins to disengage himself from the home circle and to interact more with his peers. His behavior tends to change from solitary and onlooker play to patterns that involve others: parallel, associative, and cooperative play. Part of the child's increasing tendency to involve others in his play may be a response to a need for more complex and arousing stimulus situations. Giving social rewards is associated with receiving them; such action becomes reinforcing in its own right. Social skills are learned not only as a result of reinforcement but also because other children serve as models. Prosocial behavior can also be facilitated by discussion and role-playing.

iv

the middle years

twelve

Physical and Mental Development

The problem for the management of child development is how to find out how to govern the encounters that children have with their environments to foster both an optimally rapid rate of intellectual development and a satisfying life.
—MCVICKERS HUNT (1961)

It seems to me that the whole nature-nurture controversy, centering around the IQ, has become a disaster from the standpoint of trying to find better ways of teaching the young.
—HENRY S. DYER (1971)

The middle and later childhood years span the period from the entry into first grade until junior high school—from the end of the preschool period to adolescence. This is a period in which children begin a major involvement in the world outside the family and the immediate neighborhood. The school plays an important role as a socializing agent, supplanting the parents to a considerable degree.

The sensory and motor development of children during middle and later childhood approaches adult standards. Emotional expressions and the situations that elicit them take on a new direction and subtlety. Cognitive, linguistic, perceptual, and intellectual processes not only continue to develop but also acquire characteristics closer to those of adults than were shown by infants and younger children.

About the end of the third year of life, the growth curve for the average child settles down to a steady rate that continues until the prepuberal growth spurt at about 11½ for girls and 13 or 14 for boys.

392 The Middle Years

Changes in body build are relatively slight during middle and late childhood.

There are, of course, many individual deviations from these general trends. Some girls reach their full adult height at 13, and some boys do not attain it until the early twenties. Although girls reach full maturity about two years earlier than boys, variations of four or five years are still within the normal range.

sensorimotor development

Motor Skills

In the course of the school-age period children refine and extend their sensorimotor skills. Most children keenly enjoy motor activities, and delight in constantly being on the go. "Spectators" among them are still very much in the minority. Although considerable advance in motor abilities has taken place during the infancy and preschool years, the psychological significance of motor development takes on even more importance in this period of later childhood. Much of its psychological

Most school-age children are likely to be "on to go," and spectators tend to be in the minority.

importance rests on the fact that children have reached the age when they become aware of what others think of them, including their status in motor skills.

A high premium is placed on motor skills by older children. No adult who has had any contact with children at play can fail to have noted the exclusion of some child from a play group or else his being grudgingly chosen last in making up a team, because of his lack of strength, speed, or coordination. Having observed situations like these, we cannot but be convinced that such discrimination may contain the possibility of some psychological consequences. Those children fortunate enough to be adept in motor abilities are not only more acceptable to their playmates, but because of these skills are also more apt to be chosen as leaders. Such choices not only may be made in tasks where motor skills are important; they also may be generalized to leadership functions that are essentially independent of motor skills, such as being elected as a class officer.

Speed of response shows a regular increase with age. In a classic study by Goodenough (1935), relevant in this connection, children from age three through eleven were asked to respond to a test whereby each made a voluntary movement on hearing a sound. At three years of age they took about five tenths of a second to respond; at four years of age about four tenths of a second. This increase in speed continued steadily, until at age eleven the children were responding within two tenths of a second.

Similarly, strength increases with age. In both boys and girls there also tends to be a consistent relationship among the indices of strength, height, weight, and health. Thus among measures of motor development there is a tendency for the stronger child to be taller, faster, and healthier than the weaker child. These tendencies are consistent with similar relations between physical and mental ability.

Learning and Sensorimotor Skills

Speed of sensorimotor performance has been studied at different ages and with various activities. In one investigation, Henery and Nelson (1956) assigned several tasks to 10-year-old and 15-year-old boys. One task was quite simple—throwing a celluloid ball downward into a basket and then grasping a suspended tennis ball. The other tasks, although essentially similar, were more complicated—one involved a discrimination between two stimuli; the other required a choice to be made between which of two activities to carry out according to the particular stimulus on a given trial.

In their initial performance on all three tasks, the younger boys were slower, but they learned a greater amount by practice. Correlations of the amount of learning that took place among the different tasks were greater for the younger boys. It would seem that the 10-year-old's final skill depends more on ability to learn. In the older boys, individual differences in initial skill served more to determine final skill.

Smith and Greene (1963) gave boys 9 to 13 years old a writing task in which they were unable to see their hand, which was concealed from them behind a curtain. They could view it, however, on a television screen, which gave them feedback as to their performance. The picture was first normal, then reversed, then upside down, and finally upside down and reversed.

All subjects were able to perform adequately when they viewed the normal picture, but boys under 12 were seldom able to adjust to the reversed or inverted pictures. Older subjects seldom failed to adjust to the task. Results showed that younger subjects were not able to make the complex sensorimotor adaptation necessary to perform adequately when visual feedback was systematically distorted. You may recall the childhood trick of patting one's head and rubbing one's stomach simultaneously; younger children have some difficulty in mastering the activity, but older children and adolescents have little trouble.

The Hyperactive-Child Syndrome

There are some children, mostly boys, who have great difficulty in remaining still. They seem to have a need to be in motion at all times, a need that interferes with many kinds of activities, especially normal classroom learning. This restlessness is often accompanied by aggressiveness and destructiveness; sometimes the frustration caused by having to sit still and work on a demanding task leads the child to rebel and to turn to antisocial forms of behavior.

In recent years, pediatricians and others who work with emotionally disturbed children have come to suspect that some impairment or imbalance in the central nervous system—probably in the brain—is at the basis of the hyperactive-child syndrome and hence use the term *minimal brain dysfunction* (MBD) to describe it.

Mark A. Stewart (1970), a clinical psychologist, points out that hyperactive tendencies appear early, often before the child is two years old. When they occur, they develop into a pattern of symptoms that differ from the behavior of other children in certain systematic ways. Figure 12-1 presents the results of interviews with mothers of hyperactive children and with those of a group of unselected children who were attending the first grade in suburban schools near St. Louis.

Stewart also notes that a high proportion of the hyperactive children have a history of accidental poisoning in early childhood. Furthermore, a high proportion of the children have fathers who are also restless and quick-tempered.

One interesting characeristic of this hyperactivity or *hyperkinesis* is its controllability by drug therapy. Certain drugs apparently have a calming effect on the hyperactive child's behavior, thus enabling him to

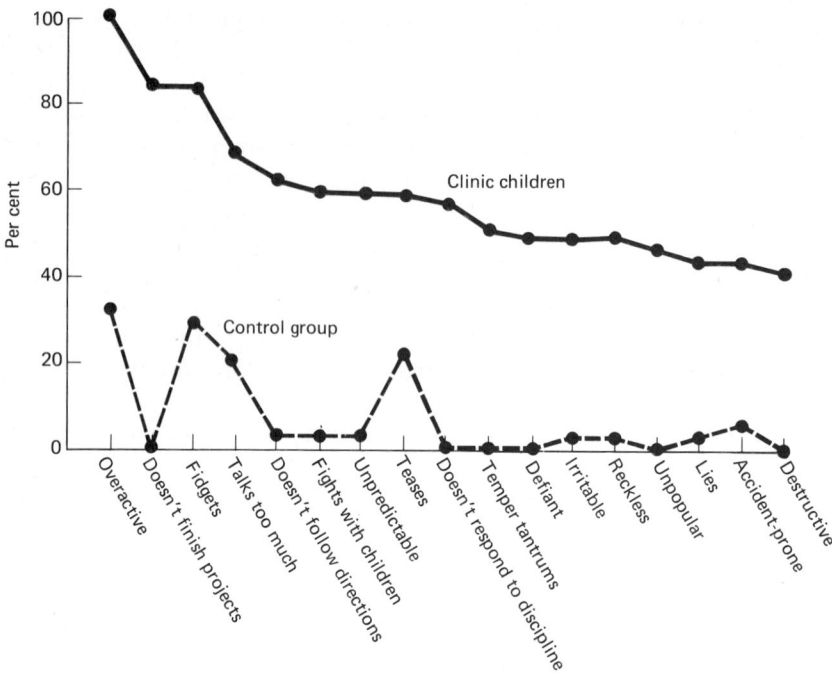

FIGURE 12-1. A comparison of the incidence of behavior symptoms commonly associated with hyperactivity among 37 children (32 boys and 5 girls) who were patients at a psychiatric clinic and a control group of children attending first grade in suburban schools. Percentages refer to the proportion of the children displaying each type of behavior, according to mothers' reports. (After Stewart, 1970.)

persevere longer with assigned tasks and to moderate the intensity of his interaction with others.

The use of these drugs has come under considerable criticism on the part of some psychologists and educators for the following reasons:

1. The drugs being prescribed are *amphetamines* (such as Benzedrine), which have a highly stimulating and energizing effect on adults but, oddly enough, a quieting effect on children thought to have MBD. In adults, continued heavy dosage is likely to have very dangerous results: extreme depression, extreme aggressiveness, and psychotic states. The counterargument is that the drugs have no such effects on hyperkinetic children, and hence that it is safe to use them. We should note, however, that children who take Ritalin, one the drugs most widely used, often complain about headaches, abdominal pain, and general malaise, or "just not feeling very well."
2. Such drugs should be prescribed by physicians only after a careful analysis of all the factors in the case; yet it appears that sometimes prescriptions are written on the suggestion of a

teacher or school official, who has found a certain child "difficult to handle."
3. If one of the tasks of society in general and the school in particular is to help children establish proper emotional controls, the continued use of drugs will teach them only to depend on drugs, without learning proper self-control.

The problem is admittedly a difficult one for the school, the physician, the parents and, of course, the child. School personnel, who have too many problems already and are poorly equipped to deal with hyperactive children, who are often hostile and aggressive, claim that the drugs enable the child to cope with problems that otherwise would go unresolved.

Arnold K. Zukow (1975) cites a typical example, that of E. G., a six-year-old boy who was about to be expelled from school for kicking classmates and his teacher. His parents had difficulty in handling him, his peers avoided him, and he was doing poorly in school, although he had above-average intelligence. After examining the child and going over reports by the boy's parents and teacher, Zukow prescribed a low dosage of Ritalin. Within a week, both teacher and parents reported improvement. After several months of drug treatment, E. G. had made considerable progress, for he was able to concentrate on school work and had been able to make and keep friends.

In spite of many successes like these, a number of questions remain unresolved regarding hyperactivity and its treatment. One study, which compared MBD children on drugs, MBD children off drugs, and normal children, indicated that MBD children are slow to react to stimuli. Paradoxically, when they are taking stimulants, the general effect is that of even slower responses. The fact that the administration of the drugs does improve behavior suggests that the medications produce a general state of arousal, enabling MBD children to perform more effectively on cognitive problems (Zahn, Abate, Little, and Wender, 1975). Powerful stimulants, such as the amphetamines, may not be needed to produce the effect required to control MBD-related behavior. One research team reports some success with caffeine, which is readily available in the form of coffee or tea (Reichard and Elder, 1977).

The confusions and ambiguities implicit in diagnosing and treating hyperactivity are manifold. Thomas E. Twitchell (1971) says that "The whole syndrome has become so nebulous and definitions so blurred that it is becoming another diagnostic wastebasket, and it is no surprise that attempts to determine the incidence of MBD among school children yield estimates ranging from 1 to 20 percent."

Even those who accept MBD as a valid diagnostic category admit that many children, perhaps as many as 60 per cent, are not helped by drug therapy (Wender, 1971). The following comment by Wolff and Hurwitz (1973) is also appropriate:

The indiscriminate use of amphetamines or methylphenidate without benefit of careful medical screening has raised the justified suspicion among parents, particularly in some inner-city communities, that their children are being subdued pharmacologically because drugs are cheaper than providing an adequate learning environment. Others vigorously oppose the use of any psychoactive drug, and continue to depend on prolonged psychotherapy for all such children, despite persuasive evidence that in well-selected populations of hyperkinetic children, for example, specific drug therapy can have dramatic beneficial results.

There is no question that hyperactivity in all its variations poses a difficult problem for the parent, the school, and for the child himself. All we can say at present is that the dimensions of the problem are not clear, that drugs have been of assistance in some instances, and that drug treatment carries potential risks that have not been adequately assessed. In light of our inadequate knowledge, we can do no more than present this brief discussion as one item in our description of children and their developmental progress.

cognitive development

According to Piaget, children generally pass out of the preoperational subperiod when they are around 5 or 6 and are poised on the threshold of the subperiod of concrete operations. This subperiod occurs at about 7 or 8 years of age, and is "characterized by the beginnings of operational groupings in their various concrete forms and with their various types of conservation" (Piaget, 1970). The period of concrete operations is followed by the stage of formal operations, which usually appears between the ages of 11 and 15 (Inhelder and Piaget, 1958).

Concrete Operations

As he does with many of the terms he employs, Piaget uses *operations* in a special sense. To use the definition supplied by Flavell (1963), a leading interpreter of Piagetian theory, an operation is "basically, any representational part of an organized network of related acts." An operation can thus be a way of reacting to a set or class of things that possess some degree of similarity—all wheeled toys, for instance. An operation always presupposes a structured system that includes other and related operations which are inactive at the moment but which have the potentiality to actualize themselves.

Concrete operations generally take on some degree of stability and coherence between the ages of 7 and 11. As the child uses operations on wider ranges of content and materials, the scope of operations becomes broadened, and the structure becomes progressively better integrated and stable.

Consider the problem of differently shaped containers that lead the preschool child to "center" and hence not to understand that the short, broad container and the tall, thin container hold the same amount. By about seven, however, he recognizes that the amount remains constant regardless of the shape of the container. His first crude approximation, "that one is taller, but this one is broader," is an attempt to explain that the height of the one compensates for the width of the other. At a still older age he might say that when the contents were poured from one to the other, the amount would be similar. In so doing he has recognized that the change in quantity is invariant despite change of state. When this and similar examples have been submitted to more precise scrutiny by other investigators, they have verified Piaget's contentions, although they have often found greater age variation from child to child than Piaget's account would suggest (Lovell, 1961b).

In another instance of a concrete operation used by Piaget, the child is first shown two balls of clay equal in size. He is asked to flatten one ball into a pancake; then he is asked about the amount of clay in each ball. Most five- or six-year-olds believe that a change in form produces necessarily a change in amount, saying either that the pancake is larger because it is more spread out or the ball is larger because it is higher. With more mature experience, the child gains the "operation of compensation," and then is able to say that the ball and the pancake have the same amount of clay "because the pancake is thinner, but wider."

Another critical process in finally arriving at "conservation" is awareness of reversibility. This is accomplished when a child acknowledges that he can make the pancake into a ball again. He now understands that the process is reversible—that quantity is "conserved," in Piaget's usage of the term. Piaget uses the term *conservation* with respect to a particular characteristic of a substance, such as weight or volume, which does not vary in spite of changes in its status or appearance." Conservation of matter becomes common at about eight to ten years of age. In short, the child at this age becomes aware that the amount of matter is constant in spite of change in shape. He realizes, then, that this attribute of the object, not merely the object as a whole, is invariant. Similarly, an understanding of conservation of weight is attained at a later age, and that of volume still later.

At this stage the child uses operations, but only for the manipulation of *objects*—that is, *concretely*. For example, eight- and ten-year-olds have no trouble arranging a series of dolls or sticks according to height but fail to solve a similar problem put verbally: "Edith is taller than Susan; Edith is shorter than Lily; who is the tallest of the three?" For this principle to be comprehended, progress to the stage of *formal* operations is necessary.

Formal Operations

Somewhere between the ages of 11 and 15, as we noted earlier, the child begins to use formal operations.

In one experiment demonstrating formal operations, five vessels containing colorless liquids are provided; liquids A, B, and C, turn pink when mixed; when D is added, it removes the color; and E has no effect. These properties can be discovered only when the child systematically examines mixtures of every possible pair, every trio, and so on, in turn. Piaget found that children of this age characteristically hit on two-by-two or three-by-three combinations as the way to solve the problem.

In another experiment, the subject's task is to place two vertical rings of different diameters between a candle and a screen in such manner that their shadows will coincide. The child finally discovers that the problem is solved when the ratio between the distances of the two rings from the candle is the same as the ratio between their diameters. This realization demands an understanding of proportionality.

Formal operations, like conservation, also involve reversibility. An illustration of reversibility in action is the child who is faced with the problem of finding the proper weight to achieve true balance on a scale. He places a weight on the balance pan, finds it to be too heavy, *takes it off*—this is reversibility—and looks for a lighter one.

The young child uses the logical rules implicit in formal operations in an unconscious way; ordinarily he has not been trained in logic. Nevertheless, the application of an implicit logic becomes part of his cognitive abilities. He may not be able to verbalize the rule "If A is greater than B, and B is greater than C, then A is greater than C," but he *can apply* it, and moreover can introduce it into situations with which he is unfamiliar.

To put it another way, the child who uses formal operations at this stage can consider hypotheses that may or may not be true and follow the form of argument, while disregarding the concrete reality in front of him. This ability to be guided by the *form* of argument, ignoring content, gives meaning to the term Piaget employs: formal operations. Competence in using complex, logical operations in different situations is the very essence of thinking involved in formal operations.

Physical Causality

It is appropriate to turn from Piaget's general theory of levels of development to consider a more specific aspect of his views. It was Piaget's work on children's conceptions of physical causality that stimulated widespread interest in the manner in which children develop such conceptions. In studying physical causality, Piaget mentioned or demonstrated various phenomena of nature, and children were then asked to explain them. Thus he would inquire, "What makes the clouds move?" After the child had responded he would further question him until he was satisfied that he had understood the child's conception.

From work along these lines, Piaget arrived at a classification of 17 types of causal thinking. Five of these types, moving from relatively great egocentricity to less egocentricity, and from simple to complex reasoning, have been described by Jean M. Deutsche (1937) in the following ways:

Phenomenistic causality. The fact that two events or stimuli occur together is perceived as the basis of causality. For example, a child explains that a pebble sinks to the bottom of a pail because it is white. There is no comprehension of the true relationship of events.

Animistic causality. Causality is explained in terms of inanimate things being alive and conscious. Clouds move, for example, because they are alive; an engine pulls a train because it is alive and wishes to do so.

Dynamic causality. Events are no longer explained animistically, but the child still sees forces inherent in objects that explain their behavior.

Mechanical causality. Motion is explained by contact and transfer of movement, without the idea of an internal force. Wind pushes the clouds, and pedals make the bicycle go.

Explanation by logical deduction. Causation is explained by the principle of sufficient reason. Such concepts as density and specific weight, are used.

The first three types are definitely precausal (and egocentric); mechanical causality may be considered as transitional; and explanation by logical definition belongs in the category of formal operations. According to Piaget these (and the other 12 levels) are discrete and separate in that children's thinking proceeds in a naturalistic direction during the course of development from one level to the next higher level with relatively little overlap. A child at the level of, say, dynamic causality, would presumably be incapable of logical deduction.

Some support for Piaget's contentions may be seen in Deutsche's (1937) findings, part of which are presented in Figure 12-2. She found that phenomenistic causality declined with age, whereas mechanical and logical causality increased with age. Dynamic causality showed no clear age trend, but this may have been caused by the small number of responses observed. Animistic causality, which does not appear in Figure 12-2, accounted for only one per cent of the responses at ages eight and ten; it clearly was a negligible factor in the reasoning of the children Deutsche surveyed.

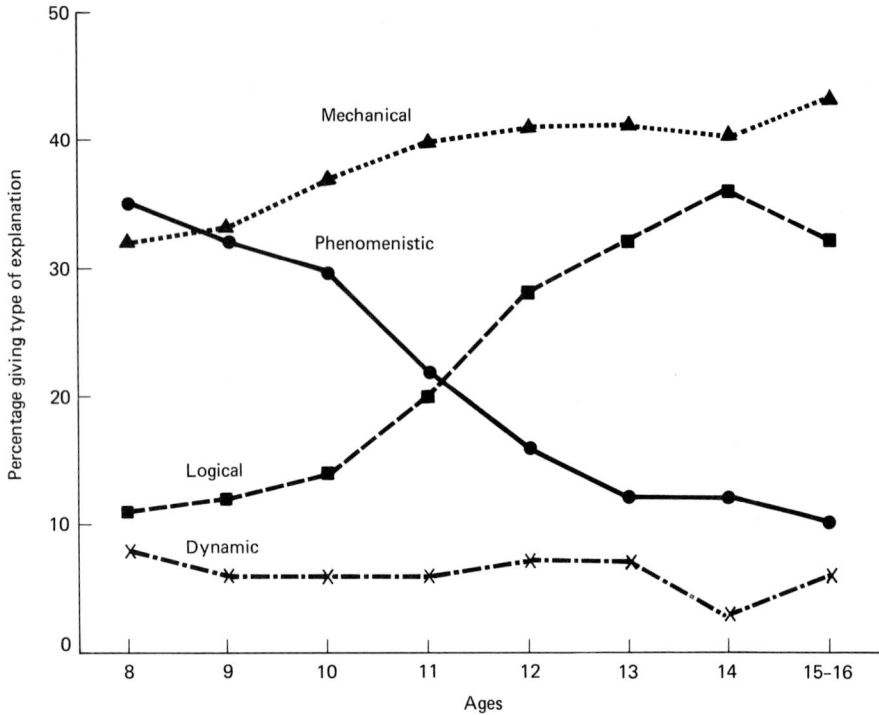

FIGURE 12-2. *Explanations of causality given by children and adolescents aged 8 to 16 and labeled according to Piaget's classifications. (Data from Deutsche, 1937.)*

Using some of the Piagetian problems, Mogar (1960) studied causal reasoning about natural phenomena in children aged five through twelve. Like Deutsche's findings, his results support Piaget's contentions in some respects, but one of Mogar's almost incidental findings is very important. The children in the experimental group were exposed to repeated observation of demonstrations of the phenomena about which they were questioned, whereas the children in the control group did not see them. At the end of the study, the experimental group was much more capable than the control group in working out solutions, and also did so at an earlier age than other investigators had reported. The research we cited in Chapter 11 regarding the children of Mexican potters also suggests that special experiences may facilitate some kinds of cognitive development (Price-Williams, Gordon, and Ramirez, 1969).

Time and Space Perception

Piaget (1955) prefers to use the phrase *time concepts* rather than *time perception* because he considers children's appreciation of time to involve not only perceptual data, but also the logical organization of these data.

Up to about the age of seven, children's constructs of time and speed are closely related. Dolls are moved by an experimenter across a table surface at different speeds, B more rapidly than A, but are stopped by him simultaneously. When children are asked when they stopped, they refuse to say the dolls stopped at the same time. This is not an error in perception: they acknowledge that when B stops, A no longer moves, but they refuse to say they stopped at the same time. They might say B stopped before A because the former is in front of the latter, or they might say that A stopped before B in the sense it is closer to them. In either case they do not understand that the dolls stopped at the same time, because the notion "same time" is meaningless to them when two objects move at different speeds and stopped at different points.

The conservation of relationships of *speed* comes gradually, and then only when children are well into the concrete operations stage, around seven or eight years of age. Then, and only then, is the child ready, says Piaget, to conceive of the construct of time at the concrete level.

Fraisse (1948) made a distinction between time perception and time estimation. He arrived at this differentiation by testing children aged six, eight, and ten for their ability to reproduce time intervals of .5, 1, 5, and 20 seconds. He found only slight age differences for the short intervals, but the two longer intervals were grossly underestimated by the youngest subjects. After eight, the children were much more accurate.

In summarizing the research on time perception for older children, Flickinger and Rehage (1949) concluded that the concept of past versus present was reached at about eight; full understanding of time measurements at about 11; understanding of time-zone lines at about 13; and a mature grasp of time concepts and dates at about 16.

With increasing experience, the child develops a workable understanding of the spatial structure of his world; but he also becomes able to deal with it in symbolic ways. Drozdal and Flavell (1975) conducted an experiment that studied children's ability to deal in abstract terms with large areas of space as that ability related to two other aspects of cognitive development: memory and logic. The children, aged five and ten, were brought individually to the experimenter, who told them a story about Charlie Brown, the cartoon character in *Peanuts*, and his new toy frog. The child was shown "Charlie Brown's house," a row of cardboard boxes covered by soft rubber sheeting in such a way that the child could not see anything in the boxes but could search for objects by feeling.

The experimenter showed the child a Charlie Brown doll whose newly acquired toy frog was attached to his arm by a string. The doll was shown to enter the "house." Pictures of the doll were attached at various points in the row of boxes. The picture posted between the fourth and the fifth box showed the frog attached to the doll's arm, whereas the picture posted between the seventh and the eighth box depicted Charlie Brown without his frog, only a string. When the doll emerged from the end of the row of boxes without his frog, the child was asked where Charlie Brown might look for it. Although the pictures indicated that the most logical area for search—the "critical area"—would be between the fourth and the eighth boxes, only half the five-year-olds suggested that the critical area should be searched; and even they were unable to give adequate explanations as to why. In contrast, all the ten-year-olds said that Charlie Brown should search the critical area and were also able to give explanations that were fully or partially adequate as to the reasons for their choice.

A task of this type clearly demands reversibility—in this case, the ability to retrace one's steps mentally in order to identify the critical area for search. In the five-year-old, the process of decentering, on which reversibility depends, is in only an elementary stage. By the age of ten, the process of decentering is usually well under way, and reversibility is more probable.

verbal development

As we focus on a specific aspect of children's development, it is easy to lose sight of the fact that all aspects are interrelated. It is difficult to study any factor in isolation. In most research, a given developmental variable is examined in relationship to others, as Drozdal and Flavell did in the study just discussed.

This close interrelationship among aspects and dimensions of development is most apparent when we come to language. It seems logical to view language as a social phenomenon; but—as we noted in our discussions of the course of development during infancy and early childhood—language is also important in cognitive functioning. Although we might suppose that language competence and the child's ability to deal with his spatial world would develop independently of each other, some research by Guyer and Friedman (1975) suggests that they may be related.

Field Dependence, Brain Hemisphere Dominance, and Verbal Development

Guyer and Friedman studied a variable that has been extensively researched, especially with adults and adolescents, a variable that is often referred to as field dependence. The standard measure of field dependence is the rod-and-frame test, which is conducted in a darkened room. The subject sees at one end of the room a large, illuminated rectangular frame enclosing an illuminated rod. The rod and its frame are set at various odd angles, and the subject is requested to turn the rod

The rod-and-frame test is used as a measure of field dependence. Here, an investigator adjusts the angle of the rod and its surrounding frame. When she has done this, the subject, who is seated in the tilted chair at the right, will attempt, with the use of a remote control, to bring the rod to a complete vertical position with respect to the earth's surface. This task will be performed in darkness, and the only stimuli visible to the subject will be the rod and its frame whose angled position presents false cues as to how the rod should be adjusted.

at its pivot until it is upright with respect to the ground. The frame, which remains at its odd angle, represents the "field" and serves as a distractor. People who are inclined to be field-dependent—or field-sensitive, to use the term preferred by Guyer and Friedman—tend to be influenced by the angle of the frame and have difficulty in bringing the rod to a true perpendicular, whereas those who are more field-independent are able to ignore the false cues implicit in the frame's position and are better able to position the rod.

Guyer and Friedman were interested in testing the hypothesis that learning disabilities and field sensitivity are both caused by or at least related to the dominance of the right hemisphere of the brain. Considerable research has demonstrated that the left hemisphere of the brain apparently exercises primary control over verbal ability, logical thought, sequential or serial processes of reasoning, and calculation, whereas the right hemisphere appears to dominate memory for forms and faces, perception of human emotion, music and singing, pattern recognition, and various nonverbal abilities (Dewson, 1976; Cohen, 1975). Furthermore, experiments with adults have indicated that right-brain dominance is associated with field sensitivity and left-brain dominance with field independence.

The subjects in the Guyer-Friedman study were boys attending special school for learning-disabled children; they were matched on the basis of age and nonverbal IQ with a control group of boys from a conventional elementary school. The boys were given the rod-and-frame test and a number of verbal and visual measures, together with tests designed to identify the extent to which one or the other brain hemisphere dominates. Results showed that the learning-disabled boys did significantly more poorly than those in the control group on the rod-and-frame test and on verbal tasks as well, but there was no difference between the groups on visual tests. Success in school learning tasks is heavily dependent on verbal competence and other abilities associated with field independence and left-brain dominance. Guyer and Friedman observe that when field-sensitive, visually oriented children interact with a field-independent, highly verbal teacher, the experience can be highly frustrating for both. The students do not understand the teacher's instructions, and the teacher cannot understand why they cannot follow orders. What is needed are teaching methods and instructional materials that capitalize on the visual abilities of so-called learning-disabled children and do not penalize them for right-brain dominance.

Learning to Read

The major step forward in language mastery that children make during the middle years is that of learning to read. Research by David Elkind (1974, 1975) and his associates indicates that reading achievement and logical ability (both left-brain competencies) are highly correlated, and that training children in logical skills can have a significant effect on their achievement in reading.

Elkind has conducted studies with early readers, matched on the basis of age, sex, socioeconomic status of parents, and IQ, with children who were not early readers. His observations indicated that early readers were superior to the control groups on Piagetian measures of conservation, as well as on psycholinguistic measures, such as sound blending.

In a related study, Briggs and Elkind (1973) interviewed the parents of early readers and nonreaders and found that the mothers of early readers had more education and possessed higher occupational status. Fathers of early readers also read to their children more often than did fathers of nonreaders. Furthermore, a number of the early readers had older siblings or friends who spent considerable time reading to them.

Elkind (1974, 1975) also found that a child's motivation to please the significant adults in his life is a necessary, but in itself not sufficient,

David Elkind of the University of Rochester is a leading researcher in the field of cognitive and personality development in children. His views on reading, discussed here, are of particular interest today, when the content and quality of education is being given especially close scrutiny.

factor that makes the sometimes dull and often unrewarding task of learning to read more interesting and worthwhile.

In summary, Elkind saw four requirements for a successful beginning in reading: an environment rich in language, both spoken and in printed form; attachment to adults who read a great deal and who reward children's attempts to read; attainment of the concrete operations stage of cognitive development; and interaction with adults interested in teaching children to read.

Rapid, silent reading. Rapid, silent reading is the skill that schools are expected to develop in the young. Elkind maintains that the development of such skill requires that the visual-verbal system become independent of the sensorimotor system. In such activity, the brain does more work and the eyes do less. This independence of sensorimotor and cognitive systems was shown by an experiment in which readers were required to identify sandpaper letters they could not see, solely on the basis of touch. Success at this task was positively correlated with reading achievement for beginning readers, but was negatively correlated with reading skill for advanced readers. What this means is that sensorimotor discrimination of letters, such as that taught in Montessori schools, is beneficial in the beginning stages of learning to read, but interferes later with the development of skills of rapid reading. Reading aloud and using the finger as a pointer apparently have much the same effect, in that they aid reading in early stages of learning, but impede it in later stages.

Reading is not a passive process but an active one, according to Elkind; meaning does not dwell within written or printed words but must be supplied by the reader from his own storehouse of information. The richness of the meaning the child derives from his reading will therefore depend both on the quality of the material he reads and on the breadth and depth of his own conceptual understanding. Satisfaction in reading is thus contingent on the degree of fit between what is read and the conceptual level of the reader. The construction of meaning from the printed word is also aided by children's experiences in expressing their own experiences in written form. The more children write, the more they will get from their reading, for writing and reading are reciprocal and mutually reinforcing processes whereby meaning is constructed.

Although reading has an active side, Elkind points out that it also has a passive side. He says that many young people are poor readers for the same reason they are poor listeners—that is, they are more concerned about communicating their own thoughts and ideas than they are in understanding the thoughts and ideas of others. They lack what Elkind terms "receptive discipline." Competent readers display receptive discipline when they attend carefully to the representations of others and resist the impulse to let their attention stray off on tangents, in pursuit of their own free associations. Many so-called retarded readers have problems with receptive discipline, rather than with the cognitive skills required for the practice of rapid reading.

intellectual development

Intelligence becomes manifest through the perceiving, choosing, selecting, observing, conceptualizing, and learning that the child carries on. If these activities are generally effective, and involve higher levels of complexity and difficulty—considering the age of the child—we say that he is advanced, bright, or intellectually sharp; if they are the opposite, we say that he is retarded, slow, dull, or mentally deficient. It is only for convenience that we use these polarized terms. Among children, there is no sharp division that separates brightness from dullness. Instead, there is an unbroken continuum from the highest to the lowest degree of competence.

The Nature of Intelligence

David Wechsler (1975), in a Distinguished Professional Contribution Award Address given before an annual convention of the American Psychological Association, observed that there are three major assumptions that are commonly made about the nature of the intelli-

"Read me my report card, Dad."
(Serrano, in *Wall Street Journal*.)

gence. His analysis of the weakness of these assumptions tells us much about the nature of intelligence.

The first is the widespread belief that intelligence is a "quality of the mind," which can be described by such adjectives as *clever, inventive,* or *alert.* In actuality, however, intelligence is an aspect of behavior that is concerned with the appropriateness, effectiveness, and worthwhileness of what individuals do or wish to do.

The second assumption holds that intelligence is a singular and unique trait, independent of other human traits. Actually, it is a complex of many-sided and diverse elements. If we must insist on thinking of it as a capacity or an ability, we must recognize that it is an over-all or global capacity.

A third assumption—that intelligence is concerned solely with the way in which the mind operates or functions logically—is a misstatement of fact. Actually, intelligence also involves drive, persistence, and awareness of goals, traits that have nothing to do with logic but are motivational and noncognitive—affective or emotional, in other words.

In order for behavior to be classified as intelligent, according to Wechsler, the individual performing the behavior must be aware of what he is doing and why. Intelligent behavior must have meaning, intent, direction, significance, and import. It must also be judged worthwhile by others. Wechsler summed up his statement with these words:

> What we measure with tests is not what tests measure—not information, not spatial perception, not reasoning ability. These are only means to an end. What intelligence tests measure, what we hope they measure, is

something more important: the capacity of an individual to understand the world about him and his resourcefulness to cope with its challenges.

Other psychologists through the years have defined intelligence somewhat differently, although there are common threads that tie their definitions together. Woodsworth (1940) thought of intelligence behaviorally, as does Wechsler, and said that it is one of those nouns that should be considered a verb. Spearman (1927) held that there is a general factor or g, which appears in all intelligent behavior, but that there are also many special factors, or s's, which are relatively independent of one another. Some s factors, he theorized, are heavily saturated with g—the ability to deal with numbers, for example. But others are relatively independent of g—for instance, musical or motor ability.

Thurstone's (1946) theory rejected the idea that g was extensively involved in most types of intelligent behavior. He conceived intelligence as composed of factors that functioned more or less independently of one another. Lewis Madison Terman, the author of the Stanford-Binet scale, saw intelligence in rather global terms, as the ability to do abstract thinking.

Spearman, Thurstone, and Terman were inclined to view intelligence as a trait whose eventual parameters are set at birth, but Piaget (1950) tended to disagree. In his theory of development, intelligence is the adaptive aspect of cognition; its function does not vary, but its structures do.

The Testing of Intelligence

Although psychologists in the nineteenth century made some tentative attempts to measure cognitive functioning, the first really effective tests were constructed for use with school children. As we noted in Chapter 1, the scales developed in 1905 by the French psychologists Binet and Simon were adapted for use with American children by Terman in 1916. Both these tests were administered *individually* to children in interview situations. The following year, the United States entered World War I, and the need to classify and train millions of recruits led to the development of the first standardized *group* tests of intelligence: the Army Alpha and the Army Beta. Following the war, a number of standardized group tests made their appearance and found ready use in schools throughout the United States and elsewhere. The testing movement was under way.

Terman had incorporated the mental-age concept employed by Binet and Simon into his scale and, using a suggestion by the German psychologist Wilhelm Stern (1914), reported his scores in terms of a statistic that represented the extent to which a child could be considered above, below, or at age with respect to his intelligence. This statistic, the intelligence quotient or IQ, was computed by dividing the child's mental age by his chronological age and multiplying the result by 100 in order to eliminate decimal points. The IQ became a fixture in mental tests, as well as in everyday language, but it proved to have a number of statistical problems, and today has been replaced by the "deviation IQ," which tells us how a given child's test score compares with the norms for other children his age. With both types of measures, 100 IQ represents the normal or average performance of a child at any age, and IQs higher or lower than 100 tell us the extent to which a child's performance exceeds or falls below this norm.

Table 12-2 gives the percentage of children falling in different IQ categories on the Stanford-Binet test. The IQ levels are also interpreted in terms of the possible learning attainment for individuals falling within various ranges of scores.

Although the Stanford-Binet proved to be a useful test for clinicians and researchers, psychologists felt the need for a test that would give them more information than a single IQ score. David Wechsler developed his Intelligence Scale to meet this need. The initial versions of the scale were for use with adolescents and adults and provided an over-all IQ, a verbal IQ, and a performance (nonverbal) IQ, all based on the subject's performance on 11 subscales.

The Wechsler Intelligence Scale for Children (WISC) appeared in 1949. It is appropriate for use with children aged 5 to 15 and was revised in 1974. Wechsler's Pre-Primary Scale of Intelligence (WPPSI) was published in 1963.

In 1960, a second revision of the Stanford-Binet was published. It

TABLE 12-2. IQ Classifications Commonly Used by Psychologists, Together with Reference Points for Interpretation of IQ Levels (after Merrill, 1938)

IQ	Percentage of Sample	Classification	Interpretation
160 and over	0.03		
160–159	0.2	Very superior	
140–149	1.1		
130–139	3.1	Superior	"PhD material"
120–129	8.2		
110–119	18.1	High average	"College material"
100–109	23.5	Normal or average	High school graduates
90–99	23.0		Can do some high school work
80–89	14.5	Low average	
70–79	5.6	Borderline defective	Can do fifth grade work
60–69	2.0		
50–59	0.4	Mentally defective	Educable mental retardate
40–49	0.2		Trainable mental retardate
39 and below	0.02		

The Wechsler Intelligence Scale for Children (WISC) is one of the most widely used measures of cognitive development.

covers a broader age range than the WISC and is hence used more frequently with younger children. The Stanford-Binet includes more verbal material than the WISC, and it is a better predictor of school performance for that reason. On the other hand, the WISC is more useful in testing children who have learning problems at school or who are verbally handicapped.

Inasmuch as the Stanford-Binet and the WISC take a considerable amount of time to administer, score, and interpret, their use is restricted to special cases, and most of the intelligence testing in the schools is done with standardized paper-and-pencil tests like the California Tests of Mental Maturity, the Kuhlmann-Anderson Intelligence Tests, the Otis-Lennon Mental Ability Tests, and the Lorge-Thorndike Intelligence Tests. Some of these tests correlate a little higher with teachers' marks than the Stanford-Binet, because the problems they present are more similar to those encountered in school.

The validity of intelligence tests. Intelligence tests have come in for a great deal of criticism these days by representatives of various ethnic groups, educators, psychologists, sociologists, politicians, school board members, and students as well. A number of states and cities have even banned their unrestricted use in the public schools. Nevertheless, even in such instances, school psychologists are permitted to employ intelligence tests as psychodiagnostic measures for the children who are referred to them, and a perusal of any journal reporting psychological research with children will show that the use of intelligence tests by investigators continues undiminished. On the one hand, it would appear that the use of intelligence tests and their scores has some built-in problems; on the other hand, it is also clear that the tests must have some validity or they would not enjoy such widespread use by clinicians and researchers.

School psychologists and educational research workers have various reasons for using intelligence tests, but what most people—teachers, school administrators, and parents—look for in a test of a child's ability is what it will tell them about his chances for success. And the kind of success they are almost always interested in is success in school.

As to whether intelligence tests predict school success accurately, the answer is a qualified yes. The qualification applies partly to the numbers of children involved. Let us say that we administer an intelligence test to all the fourth graders in a large school system at the beginning of the school year. We select one group of children who all have an IQ of 90, and a second group who all have an IQ of 110. Let us also say that the two groups take a standardized achievement test in arithmetic skills a year later, when they are starting fifth grade. Figure 12-3 depicts, in schematic terms, the distributions of arithmetic scores we are likely to get for the two groups. Note that the average child in the 90-IQ group makes a mean score which the test's norms tell us is typical of children who are only halfway through the fourth grade, whereas the average child in the 110-IQ group has a score that is typical of children halfway through the fifth grade. And some children in both groups are very advanced in arithmetic, whereas some in both groups are very much retarded, in relationship to what we would expect from fifth graders. Furthermore, some of the children in the 90-IQ group score higher on the arithmetic test than some of those in the 110-IQ groups.

We can see from this example that when we say that intelligence tests predict academic success, we mean that they predict it in a *general* way, and that the predictions hold better for *groups* of children than for *individuals*. In other words, knowledge of the children's intelligence test scores a year ago would have enabled us to predict that the children in the higher-IQ group would perform better in arithmetic than those in the lower-IQ group, but it would not have told us where any single child in either group would score on the arithmetic tests that would be given a year later. We might have said that the *chances are* that, say, four out of the children in the lower-IQ group would score higher on arithmetic than the mean for the higher-IQ group, but the intelligence test scores could not have told us who those four children would be.

Some of the reasons for individual mismatches between IQ and

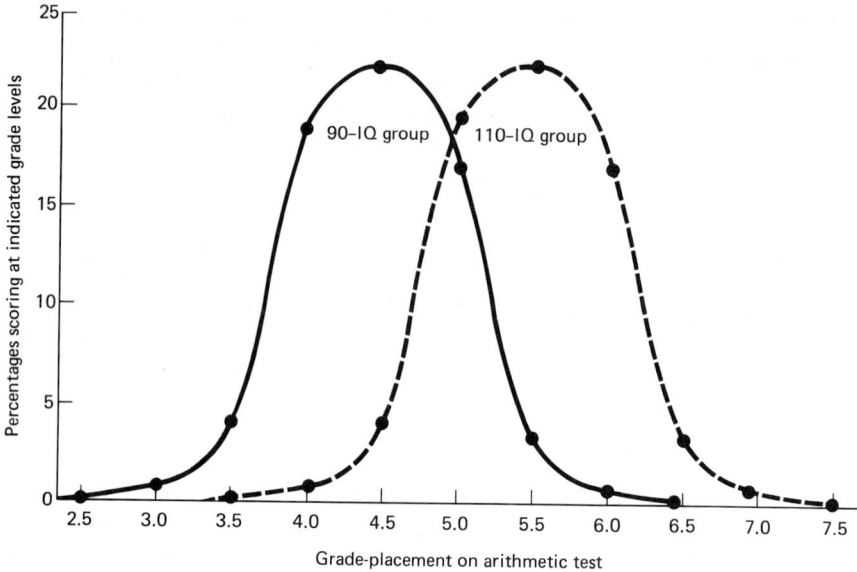

FIGURE 12-3. *Schematic curves representing the theoretical distributions of scores on an arithmetic achievement test taken by a group of fifth graders, all of whom had an IQ of 90 on a test taken a year earlier, and by a second group who all had IQs of 110. Each point on the curve indicates the percentage of children whose arithmetic test score coincides with the mean score for children at that grade level in the samples used by the test's authors.*

measures of school success are motivational. A highly motivated child will diligently complete his assignments, ask the teacher for help when he encounters difficulties, and take school tasks very seriously—what Elkind has called "receptive discipline." Whatever his cognitive capacities are, he will use them to the utmost. Conversely, a bright child may be characteristically apathetic, hostile, or merely distracted. Any of these behavior patterns or traits will interfere with his attainment of success in school. Or he may be a member of a subcultural group that values group solidarity more than personal achievement, in which event he may avoid getting involved in the kind of school activity that would cause him to be more successful than his friends.

There are so many psychological and situational factors that can intervene that the task of the teacher or psychologist who wishes to make predictions for a specific child is indeed a difficult one. This does not mean that we should reject intelligence tests out of hand as invalid, but it does mean that such tests are best used by professionals who understand what tests can and cannot do, who know a great deal about the children who are tested, and who understand the criteria to be used in rating the performance to be predicted, as well as the situation in which the predicted behavior is to be performed. This inevitably means gathering a great deal of background data, including the administration of additional measures on which to base an appraisal.

Research with intelligence tests has produced a vast amount of data confirming their validity in terms of school success. Figure 12-4 presents data that are typical. Although the studies on which the data in Figure 12-4 are based were conducted in Brazilian schools, their findings are consistent with those done in other countries. Indeed, one of the reasons we present them here is to demonstrate that intelligence tests have much the same degree and kind of validity wherever they are used—in developing countries, as well as in highly industrialized ones. The studies reported in Figure 12-4 found that the intelligence tests had a very high positive correlation with school marks in general, with teachers' marks in arithmetic, and with scores on arithmetic achievement tests. These findings suggest that the common factor was the ability to learn in a classroom situation: the greater the ability to learn, the better the school marks and the higher the score on intelligence and achievement tests.

Figure 12-4 also shows that the validity of intelligence tests is not limited to classroom learning, but extends to other life activities as well. The .30 correlation with popularity[1] can be explained in these terms: students who behave in ways that are appropriate, effective, and worthwhile, to use David Wechsler's (1975) terms, are the ones who make the best impressions on teachers and who also eagerly tackle the problems posed by intelligence tests. In addition, it is quite probable that more intelligent children behave in a friendlier way and are more attractive to their peers than less intelligent children.

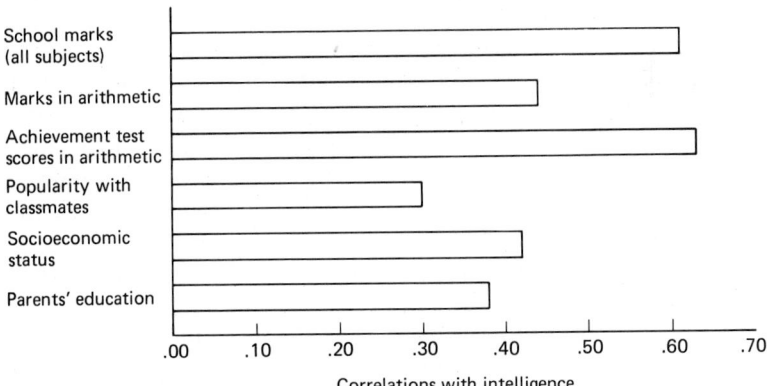

FIGURE 12-4. Correlations between intelligence test scores and school achievement, sociometric ratings (popularity), and indicators of socioeconomic status for two groups of Brazilian elementary school children. (After Lindgren and Guedes, 1963; Lindgren et al., 1964.)

---

[1] Popularity was measured sociometrically, by asking children to indicate which of their classmates they would prefer as companions for study, play, and going to the movies.

Socioeconomic status and parental education are both significantly correlated with intelligence, as Figure 12-4 shows. One possible explanation, which we will discuss shortly, is genetic—namely, that the intellectual potential of the parents is biologically inherited by their children. Another explanation is that better-educated and more affluent parents have smaller families and are able to create a stimulating intellectual environment for their children. Still another finding of one of the studies reported in Figure 12-4 was that the educational level of the parents correlated .28 with their children' popularity. In other words, intelligence test scores, school achievement, popularity, and socioeconomic status all were positively and significantly correlated with one another (Lindgren and Guedes, 1963; Lindgren et al., 1964).

Controversies over the use and misuse of intelligence tests. Although there has been a great deal of criticism directed at the use of intelligence tests with children, the charges boil down to one main issue: the belief that intelligence test results are used in prejudicial ways against students.

There seems to be little doubt that teachers' attitudes do affect their treatment of students and that the kind of treatment students get in turn influences their motivation, self-image, and approach to learning situations. One might add, parenthetically, that teacher attitudes and behavior are not the only psychological forces in students' lives, and probably not even the major ones; peer-group values and parental expectations are usually more influential. But that is not the point at issue. When children are in the classroom, the behavior of their teacher toward them obviously has considerable impact.

The question is whether teachers are influenced by their knowledge of students' intelligence test scores. On this point, the research evidence is unclear. One study, the famous "Pygmalion-effect" study conducted by Rosenthal and Jacobson (1968), reported that when teachers were given fake reports that certain children had unusually high cognitive potentialities, and were in effect "late bloomers," the children so designated were found later to have "blossomed out" with significant increases in IQ. Subsequent research studies have failed to confirm this finding (e.g., Fleming and Anttonen, 1971), one of the difficulties being that most teachers pay little attention to children's IQs (Grosswald, 1970). Many critics consider the Rosenthal-Jacobsen study to have been conducted in an unscientific manner, and Lee J. Cronbach (1975, 1977), a leading specialist in psychological tests, said that it "merits no consideration as research," and that its results are not to be believed. Brophy and Good (1972) reviewed the research on teacher-expectancy effects and conducted a study of their own. They concluded that teachers' expectations can influence the way they react to students and thus affect students' performance, but they found nothing substantial to suggest that students' IQs might be raised or lowered by this experience.

In view of the confusion regarding the possible effect that intelligence test scores have on the fate of children in the classroom, the most defensible policy seems to be that of restricting the use of such tests to research studies and to clinical appraisals of children with special problems. Teachers are, after all, mainly interested in helping children to learn and in diagnosing their learning problems in order to give them the help they need. Intelligence testing would appear to be irrelevant to those goals. Leona E. Tyler (1972), another leading figure in psychological testing, observed that in recent years there has been a general revolt against the IQ technology that has prevailed in the schools for the last half century, and she questioned whether intelligence tests have any place in the educational program.

Controversies over Genetic and Environmental Effects on Intelligence

The question of whether individual differences in intelligence are the result of inherited potentialities or are the effect of environmental differences is one that has more theoretical implications than practical ones, but it is nevertheless another source of heated controversy.

The stand taken by most psychologists for many years has been that the inherited potentiality for intellectual competence varies from individual to individual, but that the extent to which this potentiality is actually developed depends on environmental factors. A child growing up in an intellectually stimulating environment, nurtured by parents who expect him to do the best he can, is likely to develop more of his potential than a child who grows up in a home where nobody cares about books and no one is expected to amount to much. It is therefore quite possible that a child with a relatively low inherited potential living in a stimulating environment might have a higher IQ than one with a high inherited potential living in a severely restricted environment.

In other words, variations in intelligence among individuals and among groups are considered by psychologists to be the result of the *interaction* between inherited potential and the kind of environment in which the child grows and develops, with the relative weight of contributions of heredity and environment varying from individual to individual and group to group, depending on the situation. Most psychologists reject as unproven the notion that some ethnic or racial groups have a higher or lower inherited intellectual potential than other groups. On the other hand, it can be readily demonstrated that the *environments* in which children from different ethnic or racial groups grow up do differ widely.

Skepticism about claims that genetic differences account for virtually all of the variance in IQ is also fostered by such studies as that of Wayne Dennis (1973) and his associates, whose longitudinal research we described in Chapter 8. To review their findings briefly, the investigators noted that the cognitive development of children who remained in the relatively unstimulating atmosphere of a Lebanese orphanage proceeded at an abnormally low rate, as characterized by an IQ of 53. Children who were adopted, however, began to develop at a more normal rate, averaging about 80 IQ. The younger the children were adopted, the more nearly their development approached the normal rate of 100 IQ. Figure 12-5 presents a schematic diagram of the effect of adoption on the intellectual development of orphans of various ages.

Dennis's study is unusual in a number of ways. For one thing, the gain of 50 IQ points attributable to environmental differences is the largest reported by an researcher to date. Most improvements resulting from environmental manipulation are more modest. For instance, Gray and Klaus (1970), in their Early Training Project, noted a maximum difference between their "best" experimental group and their "poorest" control group of only 16 IQ points, and 5 to 10 points is a more usual finding. Most children, however, do not enter experimental treatment programs until they are three or four, whereas Dennis's study dealt with major environmental changes when some of the children were infants.

The fact that the majority of studies in which environment has been "enriched" has resulted in relatively small IQ changes is interpreted by some psychologists—Arthur Jensen (1968, 1969), for example—as evidence that environment has only a minor effect on intelligence. Jensen maintains that 80 per cent of the variance in intelligence can be explained in terms of genetic influences, although he also says that it is nonsense to partition an individual's IQ into hereditary and environ-

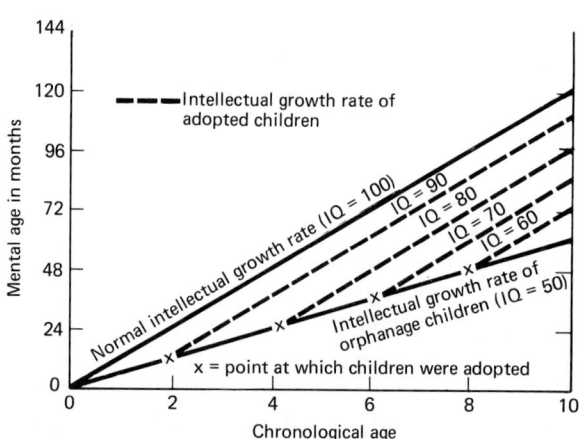

FIGURE 12-5. A schematic representation of the cognitive growth pattern typical of adopted and non-adopted orphans from a Beirut, Lebanon creche. Based on data and conclusions from Dennis, 1973. (From Lindgren, 1973, and reproduced by permission of John Wiley & Sons, Inc.)

mental components. Nevertheless, he disagrees with the position taken by most psychologists on intergroup and interracial differences in IQ and maintains that variations in the "gene pools" lead to observed differences in intelligence among different social and racial groups. Jensen agrees that efforts to improve the education of the disadvantaged child should continue and even be increased, but he cautions against expecting too much. He dismisses as foolish the notion that an individual's intelligence is the product of the interaction of his heredity and his environment.

Jensen's arguments are actually more complex than the foregoing sketchy synopsis would imply, and interested readers are referred to his major statement, which was published by the *Harvard Educational Review* in 1969 under the title "Environment, Heredity, and Intelligence." Comments by other psychologists are also included in the same issue.

Basic learning ability and problem-solving ability. Jensen maintains that only one type of mental ability shows variation among racial and social groups, whereas another type does not. This conclusion is based in part on some earlier research in which Jensen (1961) tested children of two different socioeconomic (SES) levels with tasks that required them to memorize certain word associations. He found no differences between SES levels, with low-SES children doing as well as middle-SES children. He called the ability thus measured *basic learning ability* or *Level I ability*, to use the designation he now prefers (Jensen, 1974). Although Level I ability is necessary for success on intelligence tests, Jensen observes that *Level II ability* is required as well. Level II is what might be described as problem-solving ability—that is, the ability to manipulate symbols, to reason inductively and deductively, and to test hypotheses. Level I does not require the use of these abilities, inasmuch as it involves only straight rote memorization. In view of the fact that (1) Level I ability is an essential element in success on intelligence tests and (2) there are large differences between races and SES levels with respect to intelligence test scores, Jensen reasons that differences in Level II ability are genetically determined, whereas differences in Level I are not.

Barry J. Guinagh (1971) put this proposition of Jensen's to the test by setting up an experiment in which two groups of black children, half scoring high on a measure of Level I and half scoring low, were compared to two groups of white children who were also divided into high and low Level I subgroups. All children were third graders with low-SES backgrounds. IQ was measured by the Raven's Progressive Matrices, a nonverbal test involving the selection of appropriate abstract designs; it is considered by Jensen to be a "culture-fair" measure of Level II.

The experimental treatment consisted of seven half-hour sessions devoted to training the experimental groups of children in the kinds of concepts involved in the Raven test. The Raven test was administered before the experimental session, immediately afterward, and again after a month had elapsed, in order to determine whether the gains, if any, had been retained. Inasmuch as training is, in essence, an environmental manipulation, a finding that training had any effect on Raven test scores would provide evidence in favor of the environmentalist position and against the stand taken by Jensen.

The results, as shown in Figure 12-6, favored the environmentalist argument. Black and white children with high Level I ability who had received the special training made great gains, in contrast to control groups who had no training. Low-Level I black children in the experimental group made some gain, but it was far below that of the high-Level I group. The fact that the results were not a mere coincidence was confirmed by the scores made by the children a month later. The results for the white children also show that training improved Raven Matrices scores, but in their case, there was no relationship with their Level I status. Indeed, it may be that Level I is not as invariant as Jensen maintains.

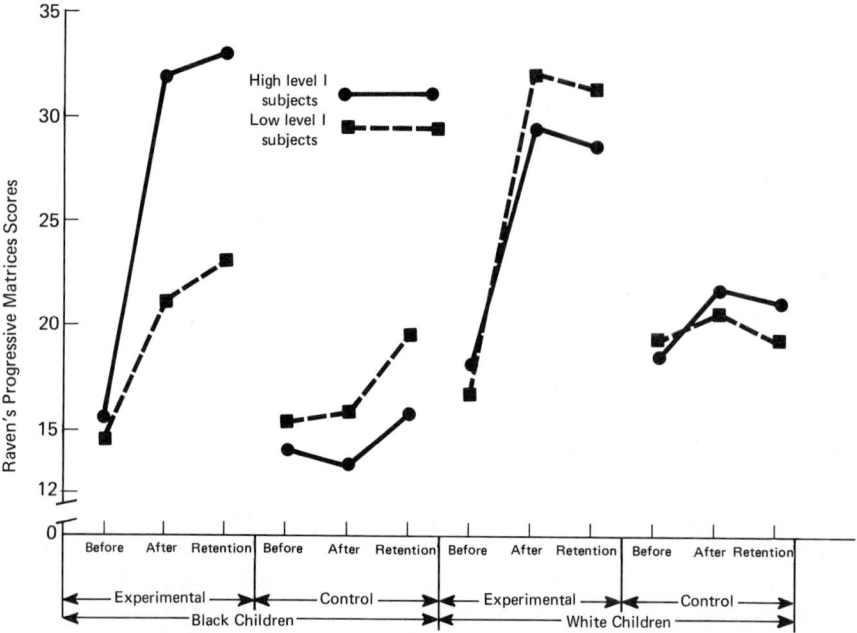

FIGURE 12-6. Results obtained when black and white children rating either high or low on level I ability were given special training in level II tasks. Children in the control groups were given no training. Points on the graphs represent mean scores resulting when Raven's Progressive Matrices (a level II test) was administered before, immediately following, and a month after the special training period. (Data from Guinagh, 1971.)

The fact that the gain of all the white children's groups dropped off slightly when retested a month later, whereas the black children's performance improved after a month, may be accounted for, according to Guinagh, in terms of personality differences between the white and black groups. The black children were more spontaneous and affectionate and tried harder to please the trainers, whereas the white children were more emotionally controlled and more peer-oriented than teacher-oriented.

Results similar to Guinagh's were reported by Bridgeman and Buttram (1975), who taught black and white children to verbalize similarities and differences among geometric figures. Differences appeared between black and white control groups of students who did not receive the special training, but there were no significant differences between black and white students after they had been trained. The investigators concluded that racial differences that appear on Level II-type tasks may be caused by the failure of schools to teach verbal strategies to children who have not learned them outside of the school setting—at home, for example.

The effects of a depressing environment. Other research evidence that raises questions about Jensen's conclusions comes from a study by Sandra Scarr-Salapatek (1971), who conducted a study of IQ and school achievement of black and white children, both twins and nontwins, in Philadelphia schools. She developed two sets of hypotheses for her study. If the genetic model as espoused by Jensen is correct, she reasoned, she should find that the variations among the IQs of the children in her study would be approximately equal in each social class or race, because the environment in which they grew up would have only a moderate effect. On the other hand, if the environmentalist viewpoint is correct, she should find a smaller amount of IQ variation among children from deprived homes, with a larger amount of IQ variance from those from middle-class homes, irrespective of race. The environmentalist reasoning here is that more able children from poor homes would experience a depressing environment that would lead them to perform little better than less able children, whereas the more stimulating environment of middle-class homes would free children to find their own level, so to speak, and hence their IQs would vary more.

What Scarr-Salapatek found was that IQ variance, irrespective of race, was higher among children from the more advantaged homes and lower among those from poorer homes, a finding that tends to support an environmentalist interpretation of intergroup IQ differences, and she observed that "genetic factors cannot be seen as strong determinants of aptitude scores in the disadvantaged groups of either race."

Human beings, as we have noted in our earlier discussions, are very plastic animals. Their ability to learn and adapt their behavior to their environment probably has its limits, but whatever those limits are, they have not been determined as yet. How much human variability is caused by genetic factors that cannot be modified by environmental differences probably never will be known, because we have not attained that Utopia in which every child is adequately loved, nourished, and stimulated. Until such a point is reached, our only way of improving the lot of the individual and of all humankind lies in identifying the environmental elements that produce the most satisfactory results and making needed changes in the environment accordingly.

Although Jensen says that he approves of such continuing research and experimentation, his conclusions unfortunately are more consistent with the idea that children's cognitive levels are predetermined at conception and that there is little point in improving their living conditions in the hope that they will develop their best potential. His findings therefore have been eagerly taken up by individuals who take a more pessimistic and fatalistic view of humanity and who feel that there is little point in wasting time and money on experimental programs like Operation Head Start, child care centers, and other attempts to improve the environment of the children of poverty.

summary

The middle and later childhood years span the period between the end of the preschool period and adolescence. The growth curve settles down to a steady rate throughout most of this period, until the prepuberal growth spurt.

During later childhood, sensorimotor skills are refined and extended. A study by Goodenough showed that speed of response increases steadily throughout these years. Task learning is less specific among younger children, as is indicated by the observation that the correlations between the learning of different motor tasks are higher for that age group.

The hyperactive-child syndrome is believed by some specialists to be caused by a minor neurological impairment or imbalance—minimal brain dysfunction, or MBD. To support this view, they point out that hyperactive tendencies frequently appear before the child is two years old, that such children are likely to have a history of accidental poisoning or fathers who were also restless and quicktempered. Amphetamines seem to have a calming effect on many hyperactive children, just the reverse of the effect these drugs usually have on adults. Critics of drug therapy argue that such drugs are dangerous, that they teach drug dependency, and that they are often prescribed on the mere suggestion of teachers or school officials. Furthermore, there is some question about the validity of MBD as a valid diagnostic category.

As developmental stages are formulated by Piaget, the child enters the period of *concrete operations* at age seven, and begins to use *formal operations* between the ages of 11 and 15. Piaget uses the term *operation* to refer to a representational part of an organized network of related acts. Concrete operations are differentiated from formal operations in that they are limited to the manipulation or arrangement of concrete objects. Formal operations use representational thought and may be thought of as logical rules. One characteristic of formal operations is reversibility, the ability to return to the starting point and begin again.

Piaget was especially interested in the development of conceptions of physical causality. Five of the 17 types of causal thinking he identified are: (1) phenomenistic causality, (2) animistic causality, (3) dynamic causality, (4) mechanical causality, and (5) explanation by logical deduction. The first three types are precausal, the fourth is transitional, and the last belongs in the category of formal operations. Deutsche found a decrease in phenomenistic causality with increasing age, and a corresponding increase in logical deduction. Mogar found that repeated testing of causal reasoning capability improved children's performance on similar tasks.

The child's concepts of space and time also change during middle and late childhood. The conservation of relationships of *speed* does not appear until around seven or eight years of age. Fraisse found that the major age difference was the gross underestimation of large time intervals by younger subjects. With increasing age, children also develop the ability to use memory and logic in dealing in symbolic terms with larger areas of space.

Linguistic development is closely intertwined with other aspects of development, cognitive and other. Research shows that children who are field-dependent (or field-sensitive) are less verbal and are more visually inclined. Their behavior also appears to be dominated by the right half of the brain. Learning-disabled children tend to be field-sensitive and apparently have difficulties in school because they are expected to function in a field-independent way in dealing with material that is largely verbal, and hence more consistent with a left-brain orientation.

Reading is the major step toward language mastery that children make during the middle years. Elkind's research indicates that early reading is facilitated by growing up in a language-rich environment, attachment to adults who value and reward reading, attainment of concrete operations, and contact with adults who want to teach children to read. Rapid, silent reading is a higher level skill, which requires that the visual-verbal system become independent of the sensorimotor system. Verbal self-expression, especially in writing, facilitates the learning of this skill, but so does receptive self-discipline, the ability to put aside one's own thoughts and pay attention to the thoughts of others.

According to David Wechsler, the common assumptions that intelligence is a quality of the mind, that it is a singular, unique, and independent trait, and that it is concerned with the logical operation of the mind are all fallacious. He defines intelligence as the capacity of the individual to understand his environment and cope with it. Some psychologists hold that intelligence is made up of separate factors; others maintain that a general factor is a major determinant.

The first effective test of intelligence was developed by the French psychologists Binet and Simon at the beginning of the century. Terman revised it and published it as the Stanford-Binet, a test whose scores could be converted first into mental ages and thence into IQs, through dividing mental age by chronological age and multiplying the result by 100. Scores on most intelligence tests today are convertible into "deviation IQs," without reference to mental age. Wechsler has developed an individual intelligence test that gives more information regarding the cognitive functioning of the child than the Stanford-Binet test. Because the Stanford-Binet includes more verbal material, it is a better predictor of school performance.

The validity of intelligence tests rests in part on their positive correlation with school success, but for predictive purposes they work best with groups rather than with individuals. Differences in student motivation are important; highly motivated students make the best of their capacities, whereas apathetic, hostile, or distracted students will do more poorly than expected. Intelligence test scores are significantly and positively correlated not only with school success, but with social success and parental SES as well.

The use of intelligence tests has been criticized on the grounds that teachers may base their treatment of children on impressions gained from their IQs. Although research supporting this view is ambiguous, it seems reasonable to restrict the use of intelligence tests in the schools to clinical appraisals by researchers and psychologists of children with special problems.

There is also a rather heated controversy regarding the extent to which differences in intelligence are caused by genetic or environmental causes. Most psychologists hold that intelligence differences are the result of the interaction between the two causal factors, and reject the idea that differences among racial or ethnic groups are likely to be based on genetic differences. Jensen, however, claims that 80 per cent of variance in intelligence is caused by genetic factors and that intelligence-test-score differences among ethnic and racial groups are the product of genetic differences among groups. He says that there is no difference among racial or social groups with respect to Level I ability—the ability to memorize and recall—but that differences in Level II ability—the ability to manipulate symbols and solve problems—are genetically determined. Jensen's belief that the Level II ability for each individual is genetically fixed and invariant has been challenged by experiments in which black and white children were taught strategies that enabled them to attain better scores on tests of Level II ability. A study by Scarr-Salapatek showed that the intelligence test scores of children at lower SES levels vary less than do those at higher levels, irrespective of race, a finding that suggests that environment has a considerable effect on intelligence test scores. The search for environmental variables that facilitate cognitive development continues. Although Jensen favors such research, his conclusions are more supportive of those who would block experiments like Head Start, which attempt to improve the environment and stimulate the cognitive development of the growing child.

thirteen

Personality, Moral Development, and Parental Influence

A child should always say what's true
  And speak when he is spoken to,
And behave manerly at table:
  At least as far as he is able.
                —ROBERT LEWIS STEVENSON

Oh, what a tangled web do parents weave,
When they think their children are naive.
                —OGDEN NASH

There is no such thing as a person who is a good parent all the time, nor a bad parent all the time.
                —ELEANOR E. MACCOBY (1975)

It is only by focusing on a particular variable, such as cognitive development, that we are able to conduct the controlled research that is essential in every scientific undertaking, and that can yield the "hard data" that enable us to make progress in our understanding of the "why" of human behavior. Yet when we try to get a perspective on what our findings really mean, we are continually struck by the fact that any aspect of human behavior is many-sided and can be understood only in terms of a total organism interacting with a total environment. This is not to deny the validity of research on cognitive development, but it is to say that other variables—some of them organismic and some environmental—must always be kept in mind if we are to gain a realistic understanding of children's behavior. And reality-oriented understanding is necessary if we are going to attempt anything with respect to facilitating or suppressing the behavior in question.

personality and cognition

Interest and Relevance in Reading

The teaching of reading is a good example of the many-sidedness of children's behavior. Reading can be viewed as a cognitive process, as we did in Chapter 12, but anyone who wishes to teach reading must be aware of its motivational aspects. It is common knowledge among both teachers and psychologists that children who grow up in homes where adults do a great deal of reading usually have little difficulty in learning to read and may even enter the first grade with some reading skills well established. This advantage may be viewed in purely cognitive terms, in the sense that eager parents taught the children to recognize letters and words and gave them opportunities to practice the techniques on which reading skills are based. The children's advantage may also be viewed in motivational terms: they wanted to please parents who felt reading to be important, and the children themselves were excited enough by books and their contents to initiate the tedious trial-and-error activity that is characteristic of the early stages of learning any complex skill.

But what of other, less fortunate children, who after all represent the vast majority of students who get their first reading experience in the first grade? What teachers find, characteristically, is that girls in this group learn to read more quickly than boys do. In their research on sex differences, furthermore, Maccoby and Jacklin (1974) found that boys are three to ten times more likely than girls to have reading problems, depending on how the disability was defined by the researchers and what population of children was studied. This difference in performance cannot be explained simply in cognitive terms, for differences between boys and girls on cognitive measures are insignificant. There are, however, some sex differences in motivational patterns, and some of these differences appear to be related to reading behavior.

A study of fifth graders by Asher and Markell (1974) illustrates this relationship very well. The researchers asked the children to indicate the degree to which they were interested in each of 25 different topics. A week later, each child was given six paragraphs that had been mutilated by deleting every fifth word. Unbeknownst to the child, three of the passages were on topics in which he or she had indicated a high degree of interest, and three were on topics which he or she had indicated the least interest. Children were asked to fill in words that were missing from the passages, and reading performance was

Most problem readers are boys.

measured in terms of the number of correct words supplied by the student, spelling errors not being counted.[1]

The results, as indicated in Figure 13-1, showed that there was little difference between boys and girls in their ability to read material they rated high in interest value. There was, however, considerable difference between the sexes when it came to low-interest material: girls were just about as competent with low-interest material as they were with high-interest material, whereas boys did poorly with paragraphs in subjects that did not interest them. What this study suggests, in other words, is that the reading problems that boys experience are to a considerable degree motivational. Hence a teacher who works with boys with reading problems may be helped to know that interest value of reading material is of major importance to them.

Anxiety: Trait and State

Interest and perceived relevance are not the only motivational factors that affect cognitive functioning, of course. Anxiety is another. Before we discuss the effects that anxiety may have on cognitive development, however, we should examine the nature of the variable.

The term *anxiety* has two somewhat different meanings in psychological usage: an emotional state and a personality trait. When we use the

---

[1] This method of measuring reading competence is termed the *cloze procedure* (Taylor, 1953).

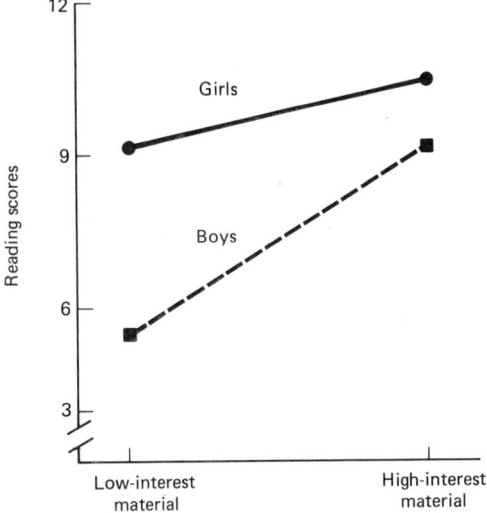

FIGURE 13-1. Differences in the reading performance of fifth-grade boys and girls with respect to their interest in topics of assigned paragraphs. (Data from Asher and Markell, 1974.)

term in the emotional-state sense we are referring to the arousal that occurs when a situation is perceived as being potentially embarrassing, degrading, or guilt-provoking, and in which there is, consequently, a threat to our self-concept or self-image. The kind of pervasive apprehensiveness that we term *anxiety* is likely to occur in our interactions with others or when we are uncertain about the way things will turn out.

Anxiety is a highly socialized emotion that serves as a prime motivator in our attempts to get along with others, to conform to their expectations, and to work with them peacefully and cooperatively. A person who lacks anxiety also lacks concern for the thoughts and feelings of others. Too much anxiety, on the other hand, leads to an intense self-concern and interferes with good social adjustment. Inasmuch as anxiety is an uncomfortable or even painful emotion, we strive to avoid it at all costs and develop defense mechanisms in order to keep situations from provoking further anxiety. *Repression* is one of these mechanisms: it enables us conveniently to forget embarrassing or guilt-laden thoughts, experiences, or perceptions and to go about the business at hand. Another mechanism, *rationalization,* enables us to make explanations of our own behavior that are plausible and reasonable but that conceal some embarrassing reality. The list of mechanisms is endless. Some psychologists hold that virtually any kind of activity can serve as a mechanism to prevent or reduce anxiety.

When psychologists use *anxiety* in reference to a personality trait, they are taking notice of the fact that some people are characteristically more anxious than others—that is, they are quick to perceive psychological threats in their environment, and their general response to threats is more extreme. Such tendencies can be picked up by psychological tests designed for the purpose. These tests enable psychologists to conduct correlational research comparing anxiety test scores to other variables—acceptance by others, or errors in learning, to give two examples. When a psychologist administers such tests, he is usually attempting to measure *trait*, rather than *state*, of anxiety, because he is trying to determine the level of anxiety that is characteristic of an individual or a group of subjects and is not especially concerned with the mood of the moment.

Anxiety, problem solving, and learning. Most of the research studies dealing with measures of anxiety are concerned with the trait, rather than the state. One widely used self-report device is the Children's Form of the Manifest Anxiety Scale (CMAS), developed by Castenada, McCandless, and Palermo (1956). This 42-item questionnaire concerns physiological and psychological indicators of generalized anxiety, worry about such matters as blushing or angering easily, and having sweaty palms. The test has proved to be a useful measure of trait anxiety in grades three to six (Holloway, 1959; 1961).

Investigators using the CMAS often compare children scoring high with those scoring low: "high-anxious" and "low-anxious" children. In contrast to low-anxious children, high-anxious children have been observed to do better on simple tasks, but not as well on more complex ones (Castenada, Palermo, and McCandless, 1956; Palermo, Castenada, and McCandless, 1956).

The idea that moderate levels of anxiety facilitate learning, and that levels too high or too low interfere, was tested by F. N. Cox (1960), who found that the academic performance of fifth-grade boys scoring in the middle ranges of anxiety was superior to that of the other two groups. The poorest performance was in the high-anxious groups. The CMAS was also used by Feldhusen and Klausmeier (1962) to determine the relationship among trait anxiety, intelligence, and school achievement. Results showed that children with the lowest IQs had the highest degree of anxiety. In the middle and low-IQ groups, anxiety scores were negatively correlated with intelligence and achievement, but the relationship for the high-IQ group was approximately zero.

If a moderate degree of anxiety is necessary for good social relations, as we suggested earlier, then we can assume that children's anxiety would increase somewhat with maturity. Some evidence for this proposition is furnished by a study conducted by Amen and Renison (1954), who reported an increase in anxiety with the development of more mature play patterns.

Problem Solving by Impulsive and Reflective Children

Personality and cognition are both involved in another dimension of behavior that has been extensively studied in recent years: reflectiveness versus impulsivity. Kagan and his co-workers (1964) observed two major behavior patterns in children who worked on various types of problems. One pattern was displayed by children who were reflective, took their time, analyzed what was expected or needed, and proceeded carefully to the solution of the problem. Children who followed the other pattern were impulsive; they responded quickly and often randomly, and tended to put down the first answer that came to mind. As might be expected, the reflective children made few errors, whereas the impulsive children made many.

The test that is commonly used in reflection-impulsivity research is the Matching Familiar Figures Test (MFFT), which is composed of items that require the child to match a stimulus figure with one of six alternatives. All the alternative choices resemble the stimulus figure, but five have minor details that vary; only one is an exact replica. (See Figure 13-2).

Children who are identified by the MFFT as "impulsives" are likely to be so classified by other measures. They have difficulty in slowing down when they are asked to walk a six-foot plank or to tap a telegraph key as slowly as possible. In a twenty-questions game, they are likely to ask less mature questions (Ault, 1973). James D. McKinney (1975) found that when children were given a series of problems to solve, those who had been classified as reflective processed relevant information more efficiently than impulsive children and also used strategies that were more systematic and more mature.

Diana Mack Drake (1970) took motion pictures of the eye movements of third graders who were taking the MFFT and found that reflective children examined each picture carefully and solved 78 per cent of the problems successfully, taking about 20 seconds per problem. Impulsive children were much more casual. They merely glanced at the stimulus figures and the alternates and got only 32 per cent of the problems correct, taking about 9 seconds per problem.

When Drake administered the MFFT to adults, she found them less impulsive than the children she had tested, but nevertheless she found the same difference in response style between impulsives and reflectives. A group of investigators who gave the MFFT to children aged four, seven, and nine found that impulsivity declined markedly between ages four and seven, but that there was little change between seven and nine (Costantini, Corsini, and Davis, 1973).

Locus of Control

Reflection-impulsivity research appears to produce results similar to studies that are designed to determine children's locus of control. The first research on this variable was conducted by Julian B. Rotter (1966), who was interested in determining the extent to which people believe that the sources of reinforcement in their lives are *internal* (within themselves) or *external* (fate or powerful others). Rotter measured these beliefs by an Internal-External (I-E) scale, which has been adapted by Nowicki and Strickland (1971) for use with children. Children who are classified as reflective by the MFFT are likely to report, on an I-E scale, that they are personally responsible for their success and failures and hence are identified as "Internals," whereas impulsives give responses that designate them as "Externals" (Montgomery and Finch, 1975).

Throughout the I-E research literature, Internals are shown to be more competent and effective than Externals. For instance, in one experiment which required subjects to work on a verbal ability test, Internals budgeted the time allotted them in a way that was systematically related to the difficulty of each item, whereas Externals did not (Gozali et al., 1973). In a study of white middle-class sixth-grade boys, Externals reported more difficulties with their teacher than Internals did. Externals also were more likely to say that their teacher did not understand them, although they admitted that they did not understand their teacher very well either. Externals, furthermore, expressed more fears, doubts, and confusion than Internals (Bryant, 1974).

Whether a child tends toward internality or externality is related to the way his parents treat him. Roger Content Loeb (1975) studied the interaction between parents and their preadolescent sons as they worked together as teams on a project. The comments of the parents were scored as either *suggestive* (that is, the parent made a suggestion, indicating that the child had a choice) *explained* something, or *directed* (that is, the parent ordered or directed the child to do something). Results, as displayed in Figure 13-3, showed that Internals had parents who permitted and encouraged them to make their own decisions, whereas the Externals' parents were inclined to direct or command. It is

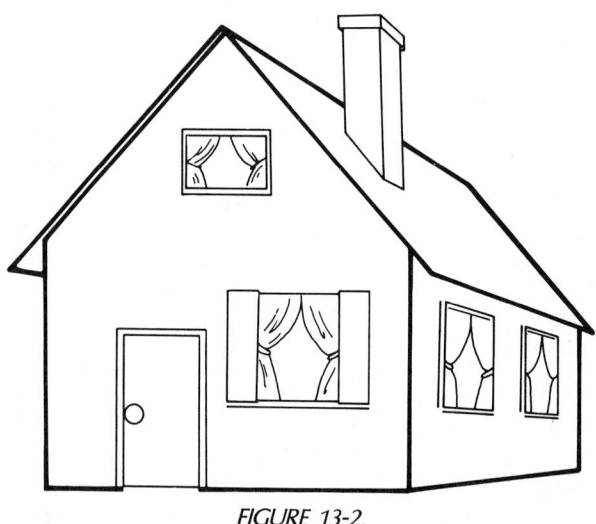

FIGURE 13-2.

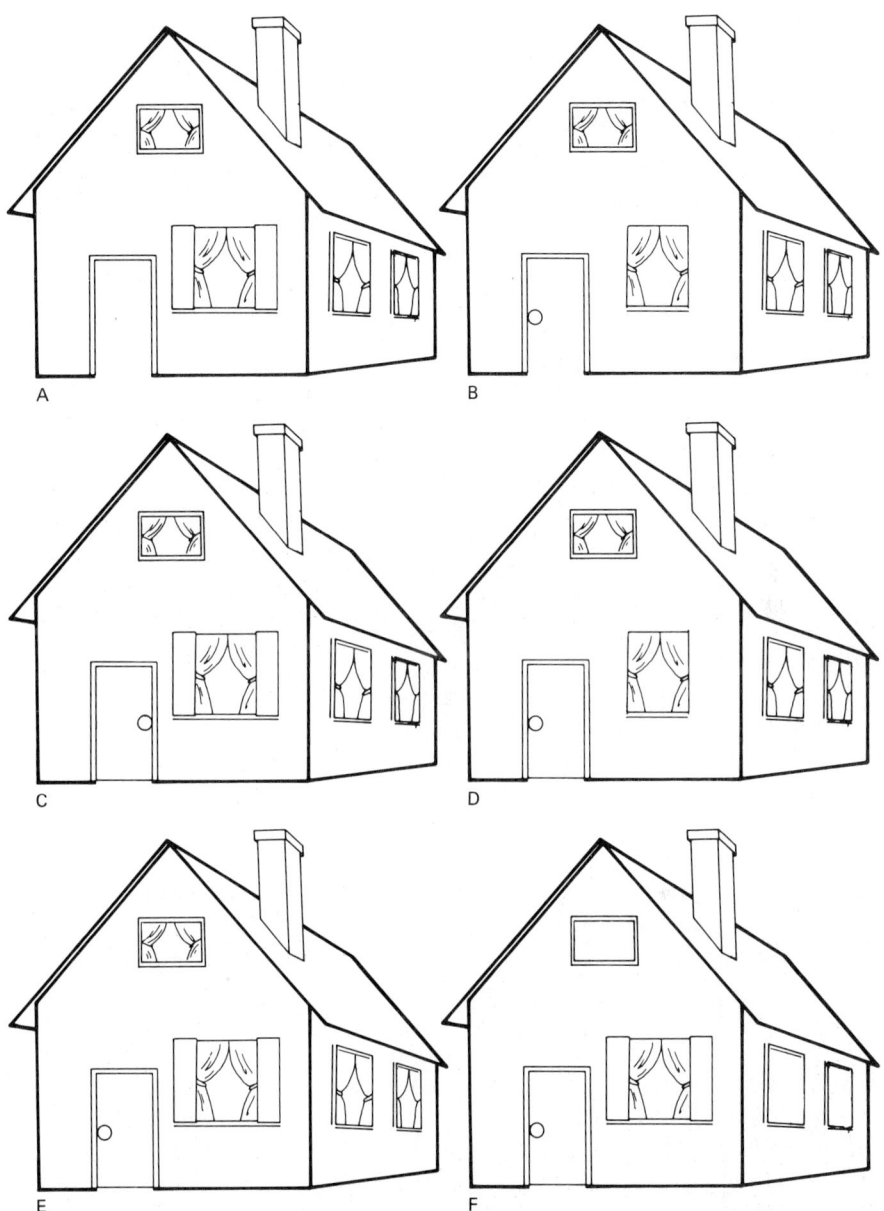

Problem of the type employed in the Matching Familiar Figures Test (MFFT). The child is requested to indicate which one of the six drawings above is exactly the same as the model at the left. Inasmuch as the drawings differ only in minor details, impulsive children are inclined to designate the first drawing that attracts their attention, whereas reflective children are more cautious and make their choice only after considering all alternatives.

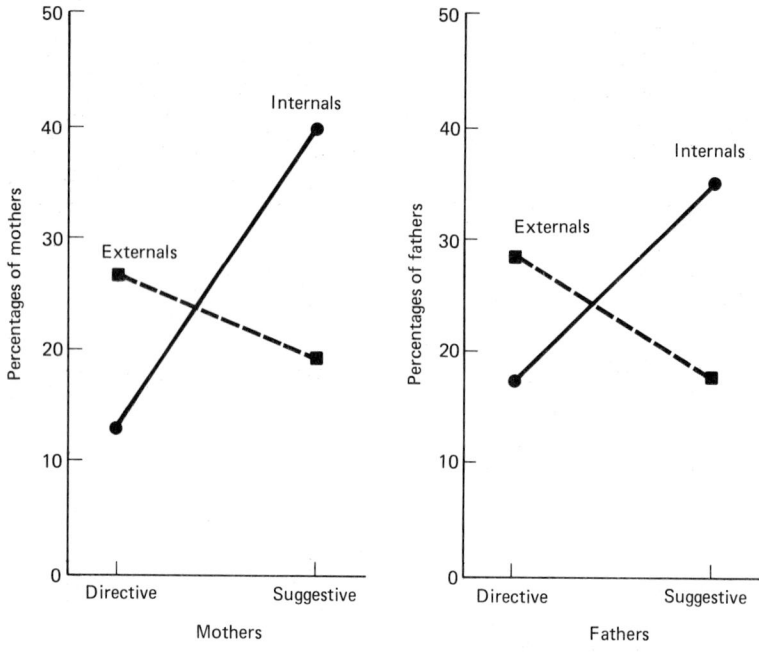

FIGURE 13-3. *Percentages of parents using directive or suggestive modes of behavior, when interacting with sons classified as Internal or External on a Locus of Control measure. (Data from Loeb, 1975.)*

hardly surprising that the Externals reported that the locus of control in their lives resided in others, rather than in themselves.

We should note, however, that the initiative does not always lie with the parents. A child whose view of life is external may avoid making his own decisions and hence actively solicit direction and control from others, just as a child whose orientation is internal, and who is also likely to be reflective, may make such good decisions that his parents are willing to give hime more latitude. In any social arrangement, such as occurs in a family, no one is the complete master of his own fate, and each member tends to adjust his behavior to both the demands and the capabilities of the other members.

parental behavior and children's traits

In our discussion of personality development during infancy, we made the point that the biological makeup of each child provides the initial elements of his personality—his temperament. The kinds of experiences he has during infancy and early childhood shape these early behavioral tendencies and thus influence what kind of person he becomes. A child may be energetic or passive, person-oriented or thing-oriented, but, as we have indicated, the kind of treatment he receives or elicits from this parents has much to do with whether he tends toward the external or the internal end of the locus-of-control scale.

Aggressiveness and Parental Models

Research with children from toddlers onward repeatedly highlights the importance of parents as behavioral models—as focal points in the process termed *social learning* or *imitation*. Indeed, the influence of the parent as model usually seems to loom greater than his influence as a reinforcer. This influence is most pronounced with respect to aggressive behavior.

Here is an example. Leonard D. Eron and others (1963) had 451 children in a semirural school rate each other on a scale of aggressiveness. The parents of the children were then questioned as to their policies on punishment. A comparison of the ratings with ratings of parental discipline showed that the more the punishment at home, the more the aggressiveness toward other children at school. The results held true for boys and girls alike, and it did not matter whether the father or the mother was the punisher.

Another study of more than passing interest was conducted by Cohen and Seghorn (1970), who investigated the background of sexually dangerous persons, men who had been convicted of forceable rape. Inasmuch as this crime rates high on a scale of antisocial aggression, we would expect, from the research findings we have cited at various points in this book, that, as children, these men would have experienced a high degree of parental aggression, and this is, indeed, what the investigators found in a sizable number of cases. In such instances, the offender's father was likely to be a physically cruel person who would often incite, support, and demand physically aggressive behavior from his son. All encounters with the father were characterized by feelings of fear and anger. The mother of the typical rapist was likely to have been a passive woman with intense needs to nurture her son. In a number of instances, her indulgence included giving drugs, excusing her son's immoral and inappropriate behavior, and being self-deceptive about the difficulties experienced by her children in their failures to achieve adequate social adjustment. What such a mother did *not* give was freedom and independence. Instead, she used her passive, dependent behavior to tie her son closely to her. On the one hand, the offender saw his mother as kind, understanding, and giving; but on the other, he had a feeling of being engulfed by or entangled with her.

Parental Coerciveness, Warmth, and SES

One significant variable that often emerges in studies of child rearing is the family's socioeconomic status (SES). Waters and Crandall (1964) found that the SES of a family was essentially unrelated to the amount of care, attention, and affection the mothers expressed, but SES did have a definite relationship with coerciveness. The higher the SES of the mothers they surveyed, the less the likelihood that the mothers would use coercive and threatening suggestions, restrictive regulations, and severe penalties for misbehavior. The survey covered a span of twenty years, from 1940 to 1960, and the evidence showed that during that period there was a tendency for middle-class mothers to become more permissive.

Bayley and Schaefer (1960), in analyzing data from the Berkeley Growth Study, got similar results. The higher the SES of a mother, the more likely she was to be warm, understanding, and accepting, and the less likely to be controlling, irritable, and punitive.

SES differences in families were also found to be associated with the personal adjustment of children. Burchinal, Gardner, and Hawkes

(MEN & WOMEN, © Mel Calman 1977. Distributed by Field Newspaper Syndicate.)

(1958) administered a personality questionnaire to fifth-grade children in midwestern schools. The children of skilled or semiskilled workers were found to have fewer adjustment problems than those of unskilled workers, and the children whose fathers were in business or the professions had still fewer. One interesting finding that emerged was that children whose parents had continued in university beyond the bachelor's degree were somewhat more maladjusted than other middle-class children. Otherwise, maladjustment declined as the family's socioeconomic status increased.

Parental Maladjustment and Children's Behavior Problems

It seems to be a reasonable assumption that neurosis should breed neurosis—that is, parents who have more than the usual number of problems of adjustment would be likely to have poorly adjusted children. This proposition was tested by Wolking, Quast, and Lawton (1966), who administered the Minnesota Multiphasic Personality Inventory (MMPI) to parents of children referred to a clinic for psychiatric treatment. When the parents' scores were analyzed, they were found to reflect a considerably greater degree of personal maladjustment, coupled with many interpersonal problems, in contrast to scores made by the average person. A recurring personality pattern in the "clinic parent" was that of the individual who outwardly conforms, but who expresses hostile and rebellious feelings in indirect ways. Many had established friendships with marginal, highly aggressive adults, thereby gratifying their own antisocial tendencies. The investigators commented that a parent of this type "serves both as a model and a source of vicarious reinforcement for his child's unacceptable behavior, thereby shaping this type of behavior in the child by two of the most powerful methods known."

If we can accept the thesis that there is something in the family situation of an emotionally disturbed child that leads him to be disturbed, it becomes quite interesting to find out why his siblings are not disturbed enough to be referred. In a study which explored this lead, Jarmon and Duhamel (1969) asked boys referred to a child guidance center and their brothers to place two-dimensional figures representing the child, the father, the mother, and the other members of a family on a dark background. The test enabled the researcher to observe the placement of the figures, as well as the distance between them, and to draw conclusions as to the relationship between the child's problems and his perception of family relations. The same test was also given to boys who were neither clinic patients nor members of "clinic families," in order to secure a pool of control-group responses.

The tests showed that, in contrast to the control group boys, both the "clinic children" and their brothers placed the family figures farther apart, thus suggesting a greater degree of psychological distance among the members of the clinic families. The researchers took this to mean the clinic children were the products of disturbed family units, marked by poor marital relationships, rather than products of any specific kind of child-parent relationship. An interesting finding was that the clinic children were more likely to place the child's figure *between* the parents, whereas their brothers were more likely to place the parents *together* and the child *apart*. This placement suggests that the clinic children were less able to avoid involvement in parental disputes and other shared maladjustments.

Child-Rearing Practices, Independence, and School Achievement

Much of the clinical research that has been done with children since the 1920s has focused on negative forms of behavior, such as aggressiveness and neurosis. This has come about because clinical psychologists conducting therapeutic sessions with children and their parents were interested in seeking out the causes of the behavior they were treating. During the post-World War II period of child psychology, however, greater attention has been paid to more positive traits, such as achievement and independence. Such research is more difficult to conduct, partly because behavioral evidence of success is less visible or dramatic than are indications of social failure. It is the old story of our being better able to see what people are doing wrong than what they are doing right. Nevertheless, because of the development of more sophisticated research techniques, psychologists have been able to produce a growing number of studies pointing to the aspects of parental behavior that appear to facilitate or encourage positive aspects of personality and social behavior. The study by Loeb (1975) we mentioned earlier on the relationship between parental behavior and patterns of boys' locus of control is one example of such a study.

School achievement is a ready-made variable for such research, because teachers' marks have a relatively high degree of reliability. Although teachers do vary in their appraisal of specific children, there is nonetheless more consistency than variation in their ratings. A study by Anita Whiting (1971) serves as one example of a study relating school achievement to child-rearing practices. The subjects in Whiting's study were elementary school boys and their parents. The boys were all above average in intelligence, with IQs averaging between 113 and 114. Half of them were performing well, academically speaking: they were getting As and Bs, their achievement test scores were above grade level, and teachers described them as showing initiative, completing assigned work, and functioning independently. The other half were getting Ds and Fs, and their achievement test scores were about six months below the expected grade level; teachers saw these boys as demanding attention, being unconcerned about failure, continually seeking help, and failing to complete assignments.

The parents of both groups of boys were seen together, either in their homes or in the psychologist's office, for interviews and testing. (Incidentally, none of the parents whose sons were nonperformers wanted the psychologist to come to their homes, whereas the other parents preferred to be interviewed in their homes.) The session was taken up with each parent independently filling out a questionnaire, the Age-Independence Scale (AIS), whereupon they participated together in a standardized interview. The AIS is a list of 110 common activities and tasks, pertaining to self-care, cognitive facility, physical skills, social responsibility, autonomy, and wide experience. The parents were asked to indicate the age at which their sons should have attained mastery of each activity or task and also to indicate the ones they thought were most significant.

Whiting's results showed that, in general, parents of successful boys expected independence and mastery of tasks *earlier* than did the parents of the less successful ones. The difference was particularly marked on the Autonomy scale, where the parents of successful boys expected mastery a year earlier, on the average, than did the other parents. When it came to selecting items that were most important to the parent, there was no difference on Cognitive Facility; both groups thought the tasks important. Nor was there much difference on the Physical Skills scale, whose activities were not thought to be very important. There were differences on the other scales, however. Parents of the successful boys were more inclined to stress items from the Autonomy and Social Responsibility scales, whereas the other parents were more likely to emphasize those on the Wide Experience and Self-Care scales.

Another point that emerged from the interview was that the fathers of unsuccessful boys seemed unaware of the school difficulties faced by their sons, either because their wives had not kept them informed or because they felt the problems were typical for boys that age. The fathers of the successful boys, however, enjoyed a closer relationship with their sons and were keenly aware of what was going on at school.

Curiosity and Child-Rearing Patterns

Achievement, independence, and self-esteem are likely to go together. Maw and Maw (1966) noted that a child who scores high on curiosity: (1) reacts positively to new, strange, or incongruous stimuli by moving toward them in order to explore or manipulate them; (2) is strongly motivated to find out more about himself and his environment; (3) seeks new experiences; and (4) shows persistence in examining or exploring stimuli in order to understand them better.

Maw and Maw asked both teachers and classmates to rate fifth graders on their curiosity. The parents of children scoring the highest and the lowest on a composite of these measures were also given the Parental Attitudes Research Instrument (PARI) to complete. Differences between the two groups of parents were in the expected direction, but only in the case of boys. Fathers of high-curiosity boys, in contrast to the other fathers, were less inclined to foster dependence on the part of their sons, or to punish them harshly, and were more egalitarian or democratic in their relations with them. Mothers of high-curiosity boys, in contrast to the other mothers, also did less to foster their sons' dependency. They were, furthermore, less inclined than the other mothers to shelter their sons from outside influences and were less intrusive (meddling) in their sons' lives.

Achievement Motivation: The Need to Achieve (n Ach)

Few motives have received as much attention from personality researchers in recent years as the need to achieve (n Ach). N Ach finds its expression in behavior aimed at mastering, manipulating, and organizing the environment; overcoming obstacles in the solution of problems; completing whatever tasks have been begun; and doing one's best.

Curiosity is important in the child's cognitive development. Unfortunately, some parents discourage it.

The earlier research dealing with children's achievement motivation tended to focus on relations between boys and their parents. The investigators generally found that n Ach was inhibited or suppressed by domineering, authoritarian parents, but was fostered by democratic parents, especially those who encouraged independence and also expected a high level of performance.

Researchers have more recently included girls within the scope of their studies. In one investigation conducted in the Netherlands, investigators identified boys and girls scoring very high or very low on questionnaires measuring n Ach. After securing the cooperation of parents, investigators visited the children's homes, where they gave them a series of fairly complex and demanding tasks, designed to stimulate and encourage child-parent interaction.

The observers noted that parents of children with low n Ach were more inclined to help in ways that suggested solutions to problems, as though they were either protecting them from possible failure or expressing subtle doubts that the child was capable of solving the problem. The help given by the parents of high-n Ach children was of a more nonspecific nature, in that it did not suggest solutions. High-n Ach children also behaved more independently in that they were more likely to refuse help from their parents, expressing a preference to struggle with the problems alone.

Parents of high-n Ach children were inclined to express high expectations and to praise successful moves toward solving the problems; parents of low-n Ach children were less likely to do these things, but were more likely to respond to their children's expressions of insecurity.

When the investigators queried the teachers of these children, they learned that high-n Ach children were viewed as being more interested in striving toward goals, showing a higher degree of personal responsibility for their work, and persisting more in following through on tasks they had begun (Hermans, ter Laak, and Maes, 1972).

The general pattern that emerges from this and other studies of n Ach in childhood is that boys and girls are more inclined to engage in achievement-oriented behavior if their parents encourage it by expressing high expectations and at the same time permitting the freedom and independence which enable children to try out their skills and develop problem-solving strategies.

Kagan and Moss (1960) conducted a longitudinal study of achievement motivation expressed in various ways by children who were being studied by investigators from the Fels Research Institute. Children between the ages of six and ten were rated with respect to their achievement behavior, defined in this phase of the research in terms of the tendency to persist with challenging tasks and to seek involvement in tasks to which a standard of excellence could be applied. Some years later, when the same subjects were between twenty and thirty years of age, an investigator who had no knowledge of the earlier results interviewed them and rated them once again on achievement behavior, as well as on their concern for intellectual competence—that is, the value they placed on intelligence, knowledge, and academic achievement.

A comparison of the ratings made at the two ages indicated a high degree of consistency. Children who had been strongly motivated to achieve tended to be high achievers as adults and also valued intellectual competence. Those who had been low achievers as children tended to be low achievers as adults and to place low value on intellectual competence.

Over all, the Fels investigators considered the period between the ages of six and ten to be crucial for the development of motivation to master intellectual tasks. If the child's experiences during these years are reassuring and give him freedom from too strong dependence on his parents, this motivation develops. Because n Ach proves to be highly correlated with achievement behavior in adulthood, it makes for an effective problem-solving, successfully competitive adult (Sontag and Kagan, 1963).

It is a routine finding that SES differences are related to achievement motivation. Rosen (1962), for example, found a consistent relationship between SES and the amount of achievement and independence training received by boys in both Brazil and the United States, even though the over-all mean for n Ach was lower in Brazil than in the United States. In another study, Rosen (1964) analyzed children's perceptions of their parents and found that middle-class boys saw their parents as more competent, accepting, emotionally secure, and interested in their achievements than did boys from lower-class homes. In the end, it is the parental expectations for achievement that have the most powerful effect on the extent to which children develop n Ach. If their parents do not express confidence in their ability to succeed, it is difficult for children to develop much confidence in themselves.

the development of self-awareness

Each child in his own way, as he moves from infancy through childhood, reaches some sort of understanding of himself and of other persons. He acquires knowledge about and attitudes toward himself and others. With the school years come increased self-awareness, and self-consciousness as well. Entering school exposes each child to the always sharp, often critical, and sometimes unfriendly eyes of his classmates. Every foible, every weakness is open to them, and their comments range from such direct appellations as "Fatso," "Meatball,"

"Skinny," "Dopey," and "Four-eyes" to more individual and subtle, but equally negative, comments. A sharpening of the sense of self could hardly fail to develop under this regimen. The child who is able to stand up to the negative appraisals of others and develop an independent appraisal of his self-worth is one who rates high on self-esteem.

Studies in Self-Esteem

The antecedents of self-esteem have been studied by Stanley Coopersmith (1967, 1968), who administered a fifty-item Self-Esteem Inventory to children in fifth- and sixth-grade classes. Teachers, too, were asked to rate the children on behaviors presumed to be related to self-esteem. Therefore Coopersmith was able to secure two ratings on each child: one subjective and one behavioral. Background data were gathered in the course of a two-and-a-half-hour interview with each child's mother, and each child was also queried as to parental attitudes and practices. In addition, projective tests of personality were administered to each child. In more than 80 per cent of the cases, the children's self-ratings were confirmed by the data from outside sources.

A part of the research dealing with boys showed that those who had a high degree of self-esteem were active, expressive children who were successful both academically and socially. In discussions, they played active roles, eagerly expressed their opinions, did not avoid disagreement, were not especially upset by criticism, showed little destructiveness, and were little troubled by anxiety.

Boys in the middle ranges of self-esteem were quite similar to the high-self-esteem boys, but with more conventional values and behavior patterns. They tended to be somewhat uncertain in their self-ratings and were more dependent on social acceptance than were the high-self-esteem boys.

The low-self-esteem boys tended to be discouraged, depressed, timid, and convinced of their inferiority. In social groups, they were the listeners: they were easily upset by criticism, self-conscious, and preoccupied with emotional problems. Eager for social contact, they were unable to secure it; their bungling attempts at socializing only served to alienate them further from the peer group.

Some glimpse of the differences among the three types of boys is shown by the sketches in Figure 13-4. The instructions were: "Draw a person and complete and drawing in ten minutes." The drawing on the left is by a low-self-esteem boy; it seems to reflect feelings of tentativeness and inadequacy. The second drawing, by a middle-self-esteem boy, is bolder and more definite. When it is compared to the third drawing, done by a high-self-esteem boy, it seems conventional and uninteresting. The third drawing has considerable interest and energy, as well as a touch of humor—all characteristics of the high-self-esteem boys.

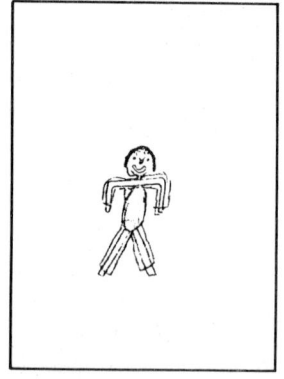  

FIGURE 13-4. *Drawings made by low-, medium-, and high-self-esteem boys as part of a draw-a-person test. (Coopersmith, 1968. Reprinted by permission.)*

Coopersmith noted that his data contradicted a number of popular clichés about child rearing. He found no consistent relationship between children's self-esteem and their height, their physical attractiveness, the size of their family, their early traumatic or upsetting experiences, whether they were breast- or bottle-fed during infancy, or their mother's employment outside the home. The amount of time parents spent with their children was not significant, but what was important was the parents' interest in the children's welfare, concern about their companions, availability for the discussion of problems, and participation in family fun.

Another surprising finding was that the parents of high-self-esteem children were stricter and less permissive than those with medium and low self-esteem. They insisted on high standards of behavior and were firm and consistent in the enforcement of rules. Their discipline was not harsh, however, and they were less punitive than other parents in the survey. The parents of low-self-esteem children tended to be extremely permissive, but inflicted harsh punishment when their children gave them trouble. The latter children considered their parents to be unfair, and they interpreted the absence of definite rules and limits as indicating that their parents were not interested in them.

Although the parents of high-self-esteem children set limits, there was considerable latitude for individual variation. The limits thus established were reasonable, rational, appropriate to the child's age, and not arbitrary and inflexible. At the same time, these parents exerted greater demands than the other parents for academic performance and excellence. The parents themselves were active, poised, self-assured individuals who led active lives outside the context of the home and did not rely on the family for sole and necessary sources of gratification. It seems clear that in these characteristics they served as social learning models for their children.

Under- and Overachievers

The self-concepts of children whose achievement at school is higher than would ordinarily be expected from their IQ (overachievers) have been compared with those whose achievement is lower than that which would be expected (underachievers). In a study by Ann M. Walsh (1956), two such carefully matched groups of elementary school pupils were compared. She found that underachievers showed distinctly more signs of inhibition, insecurity, and defensiveness.

In still another study, this time involving high school boys, the underachievers differed little from the overachievers in self-described emotional and school adjustment, but considerably more underachievers described themselves as restless and undependable, and as belonging to cliques who showed negative attitudes toward school and opposition to authority. The investigators interpreted their findings as supporting a view that underachievers' behavior was "asocialized"; that is, embodying a mild form of delinquency that takes its major focus from the groups with which these particular children associate, the peer clique groups (Morrow and Wilson, 1961).

The usual finding that underachievers tend to have a poorer emotional and social adjustment than children who achieve more adequately does not hold true in all cultures. Lindgren and Mello (1964) administered to fourth-grade overachievers and underachievers in a school in São Paulo, Brazil, a Portuguese version of the Bell Adjustment Inventory and a sentence-completion test measuring adjustment. Unexpectedly, overachievers reported significantly more problems than did underachievers, particularly in emotional adjustment.[2] The extent to which a child is able to meet the demands of the school is likely to be crucial for children's adjustment in the United States and other industrialized countries. The child who succeeds in school is functioning in a way that is more consistent with the values and expectations of his culture than the child who does poorly. Hence the relationship between emotional adjustment and school success is likely to be positive for children in urbanized, industrialized societies. This is less likely to be so in developing countries like Brazil. The authors observed that there seems to be a culturally determined "adjustment norm" in Brazil, probably stronger with lower-class children, that is characterized by such traits as agreeableness and acceptance of others, low levels of hostility and anxiety, and a low drive to achieve and compete academically. The child who deviates from this norm by setting high academic goals for himself is likely to deviate in other ways—that is, he is likely to have

---

[2] Somewhat similar results were reported by Oetting and Dinges (1971), who were perplexed to find that Navajo first graders who were judged by their teachers to have a high degree of adjustment actually scored higher on a scale of anxiety than did other Navajo children judged to have a low degree of adjustment.

more anxiety and to experience poorer relations with his peers than the child who conforms to the cultural norm.

The Ideal Self or Ego-Ideal

The psychological importance of peer group norms to the preadolescent child was shown in a study by Rae Carlson (1963), who compared sixth graders' descriptions of their self-ideal and their parents' description of an "ideal child." An analysis of the responses showed that the self-ideals of the children were closer to those of their classmates than they were to those held by their parents for them. Carlson concluded that parental expectations for their children are likely to be outweighed by the fact that peer and community norms have a greater appeal. In other words, by the time a child is 12 years old, the social world outside the family potentially possesses a greater influence in his personality development than his parents do.

Carlson also observed, as have other researchers, that children rating higher in self-esteem were more likely to be accepted by their peers. An additional and unexpected finding was that the parents were more approving and accepting of boys than of girls and that this tendency was even greater for mothers than for fathers. All mothers overestimated the similarity of their sons to their ideal child, but only two-thirds of the mothers made similar overestimates for their daughters.

A number of studies have focused on differences perceived between an individual's ideal self and what he considers to be his "real self." A common technique in such studies is to have subjects fill out a personality questionnaire once in terms of "the kind of person you really are" and again in terms of "the kind of person you would like to be." The difference between the two sets of ratings thus serves as an index to the disparity between the real and the ideal self. The usual interpretation of the results is that the greater the real self–ideal self disparity, the more the anxiety, guilt, and self-depreciation. Indeed, one of the goals of psychotherapy with adults has traditionally been that of closing the gap between the two self-percepts (Rogers and Dymond, 1954; Turner and Vanderlippe, 1958).

More recent research, however, has raised some questions about such conclusions. A study of the progress of former mental patients, for example, showed that those who were more self-deprecating tended to be more successful in completing a program of rehabilitation (Neff and Koltuv, 1967). It may well be that the individual who is too complacent about himself is the one who is less willing to become involved in self-improvement, and that some degree of self-criticism is necessary for making progress in socialization and self-improvement.

The idea that self-image disparity may be associated with maturity and mental health is supported by a study conducted by Katz, Zigler, and Zalk (1975), in which fifth- and eighth-grade boys were asked to fill out a questionnaire indicating the extent to which they felt that twenty personal descriptions were true about them. Then they checked the statements again, indicating the extent to which they *wished* that the statements were true of them. The first questionnaire yielded a measure of the degree to which each boy's view of his "real self" was positive or negative, and the second, similar data about his "ideal self." Half the boys were drawn from regular classrooms and the other half from classes for emotionally disturbed students. The behavior of half the students in the special classes could be characterized as "acting out"— that is, it was antisocial, aggressive, and hyperactive. The behavior of the other half of the special students displayed characteristics associated with "neurotic problems"—that is, severe anxiety, depression, withdrawal from others, and worries about physical health.

An analysis of the test scores showed some marked differences among the three groups of boys. As the left-hand graph in Figure 13-5 indicates, eighth-grade boys in the regular class had more negative opinions of themselves than did the corresponding group of fifth graders. The two groups of fifth graders in the special classes, by way of contrast, had much more negative self-images than the boys in the regular class. In the eighth grade, there is little difference among the real-self concept of the three groups of boys.

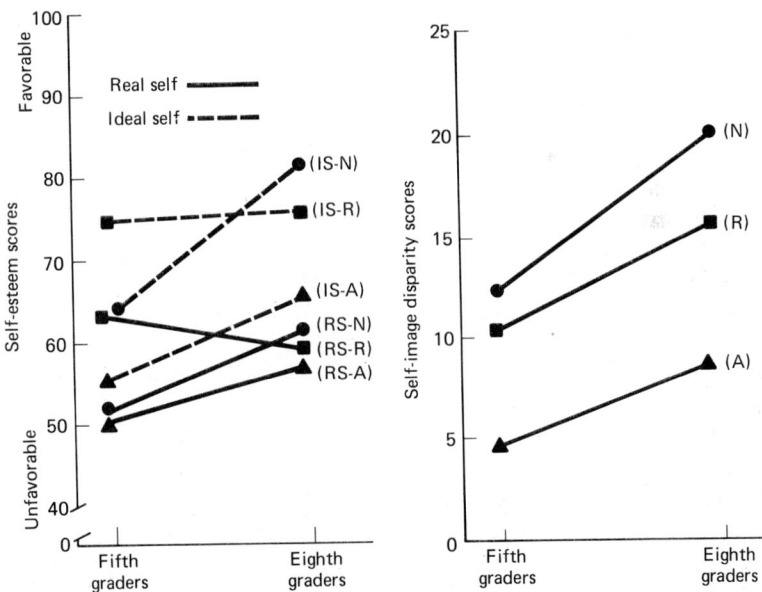

FIGURE 13-5. *Ratings of real self (RS) and ideal self (IS) made by fifth- and eighth-grade boys in regular classes (R) and those placed in special classes because of acting-out (A) or neurotic (N) behavior problems, together with self-image disparity scores for the same groups of subjects. (Data from Katz, Zigler, and Zalk, 1975.)*

The most significant findings, however, are revealed in the right-hand graph of Figure 13-5. We can see here there is a marked increase in the difference or disparity between real- and ideal-self images for boys in the regular classes, but not as much as for the neurotic boys in the special classes. There is some increase in real- and ideal-self disparity for the acting-out boys, but it lags far behind the other two groups.

What these findings suggest is that older boys normally have a poorer image of themselves than do younger boys, and that their behavior is even farther removed from their ideal. This disparity in real- and ideal-self image probably generates enough anxiety and self-doubt for them to keep their antisocial impulses in check. Much the same situation occurs with overly anxious, neurotic boys, but they tend to overdo self-criticism to the point where it interferes with their ability to display socially adequate behavior. The real- and ideal-self gap is much less pronounced with acting-out boys, who have few feelings of guilt, self-doubt, or anxiety and as a consequence are less concerned about their antisocial, aggressive behavior.

These findings are also consistent with the statement we made in connection with our discussion of emotional development in Chapter 10, to the effect that some anxiety is necessary if normal socialization is to take place, but that too much interferes with adequate adjustment.

moral development

So far in this book we have said little about moral development—the emergence of behavior standards that are fundamental to all forms of social behavior. Although the superego or conscience that we mentioned in our discussion of development during early childhood figures significantly in moral development, other personality factors are involved as well. The ability to resist the temptation to engage in self-indulgent or antisocial behavior is one of them.

The earliest research on resistance to temptation was conducted by Hartshorne and May (1928), who found that brighter students were inclined to cheat less than other students, a finding that has also been reported by more recent researchers (Hetherington and Feldman, 1964; Johnson and Gormley, 1972). Hartshorne and May also concluded, after extensive investigation, that there was no evidence for the existence of a general trait that might be termed *honesty*, for whether or not a child yielded to the impulse to cheat seemed to be determined entirely by the situation in which he found himself: the potential rewards to be obtained by cheating, the watchfulness of teachers, the likelihood of being caught, and the like. This conclusion seems to have been based on faulty research techniques, however. When Roger V. Burton (1963) re-examined the procedures employed by Hartshorne and May, and eliminated findings based on measures having low reliability, he found that the data actually demonstrated that the ability to resist the temptation to cheat is an identifiable and relatively stable personality trait, one that can be measured reliably and that characterizes the behavior of some children more than that of others.

Children who tend to resist the temptation to violate rules are likely to score high on internality, as measured by locus-of-control ratings—that is, they are inclined to be self-sufficient and self-reinforcing, in contrast to children who yield easily to temptation, according to P. S. Fry (1975a). Children who resist temptation also rate high on the need for social approval. Fry gathered these data in connection with an experiment designed to determine whether feeling tone or mood has any effect on ability to resist temptation. Children aged seven and eight were taken individually into the experimental room and shown a very attractive toy (a battery-operated mobile with three helicopters) and a less attractive toy (a battery-operated auto). The experimenter told each child that he had to leave them for a few minutes and that during his absence they could play with the auto but were not to touch the mobile. Before the experimenter left, he asked his young subject either to think of something happy or something sad. During the experimenter's absence, each child's behavior was monitored through a one-way mirror. As hypothesized, the children who had been asked to think of something pleasant resisted temptation longer and played with the mobile less than did those who had been told to think of something sad.

What Fry's research shows, then, is that both personality factors and mood are intimately involved in children's ability to resist temptation. This relationship is not confined to children, of course. Many an adult has committed an antisocial act because he felt vindictive, jealous, or depressed.

Theories of Moral Development

Moral standards, especially in their more mature form, are based on more than mood, self-esteem, and the superego's "Thou shalt nots"; they also include prosocial acts as well. Broadly conceived, moral standards cover not only the control of antisocial impulses but also the imperative to be concerned about the welfare and feelings of others and to exercise sound judgment in matters involving conflicts of interest between oneself and others.

In a review of the research relating to this topic, Martin L. Hoffman (1970) noted that there are three major theories bearing on the moral development of children: (1) the "original sin" doctrine, which assumes that each child has inborn antisocial impulses that adults must teach him to curb; (2) the "innate purity" doctrine, which assumes that children are innately good and that adult society exerts corrupting influences from which children should be protected, particularly during their early years; and (3) the *tabula rasa* or "clean slate" doctrine, which assumes that children are born neither good nor bad, but become what their environment causes them to become.

Hoffman characterized Freudian theory as basically an original sin doctrine, in the sense that the young child is held to be possessed by a bundle of drives (the id) that is a potential source of trouble, drives that adults must help him master and control if he is to become a functioning member of society.

The theories of Piaget and his followers are consistent with the innate purity doctrine. Piaget holds that adults play roles that are essentially external and intrusive, as far as the child's development of moral judgment is concerned. This means, according to Hoffman, that "it is only the natural give-and-take that occurs in social interactions among peers that can provide the impetus to moral maturity, by which Piaget means morality guided in the main by higher cognitive processes." It should be noted, however, that Piaget is principally interested in the way in which children use logic in moral judgment, and less concerned with their relationship to adult society, or to society in general.

The *tabula rasa* doctrine is represented by the various learning theory schools—the classical learning theorists, the operant conditioners, and the social-learning theorists—all of which view moral development as a product of the child's social environment.

The original-sin/Freudian doctrine is probably most congruent with everyday practice and is essentially derived from what might be called common sense. Child-rearing practices in the majority of families throughout the world—certainly in the Western world—usually operate on principles consistent with this formulation. Moral development, according to psychoanalytic theory, takes place through the development of the superego, a process we described in Chapter 4. The child identifies with his parents, takes on their values, and suffers guilt when he transgresses. Guilt feelings emanating from the superego enable him to behave in a socially acceptable way, even when his parents are neither visible nor likely to discover his transgressions.

Research evaluating this theory has been concerned with comparative studies of families that to some degree conform to or deviate from conventional child-rearing norms, and with experiments that test the relative efficacy of other theories, especially those of the *tabula rasa* type. There has also been a considerable amount of research attempting to relate child-rearing practices to the development in children of guilt feelings and other mechanisms of self-restraint, but it has been difficult to identify any kind of precise relationship. It is to the credit of this basically common-sense doctrine that as adults we have turned out as well as we have; it is to the discredit of the doctrine that we have turned out as badly as we have. And it is largely because of the failures of common-sense doctrine that the other two competing doctrines have been developed.

Piaget on Morality

Piaget (1948) holds that there are basically two stages in moral development. Before age three[3] and preceding these two stages, there is also an early period in which the child resolves problems of conduct in a ritualistic fashion, without any understanding of the moral issues. The child at this age is unable to do any thinking about what is involved.

From about age three or four until eight or so, the child uses what Piaget terms *objective morality* in his dealing with others. This period is marked by (1) *objective responsibility*, the literal evaluation of an act in terms of its exact conformity to rule, rather than the intent of the rule; (2) *unchangeability of rules*; (3) *absolutism of value*, the child's belief that everyone shares the same ideas of right and wrong; (4) *definition of moral wrongness by sanctions*, whereby a child defines the wrongness of an act by the fact that he is punished; (5) *definition of duty as obedience to authority*; and (6) *immanent justice*, the belief that violations of social norms are followed by accidents or misfortunes inflicted by nature or God (Kohlberg, 1963a).

This earlier stage of morality is also called the stage of *moral realism, morality of constraint,* or *heteronomous morality*.

The second stage is variously termed *subjective morality, autonomous morality, morality of cooperation,* or *reciprocity*, and is marked by giving up the earlier fixed ideas of morality in exchange for a system of beliefs that takes into account the intentions of the individual and the possibility of human error. This appreciation of the feelings, attitudes,

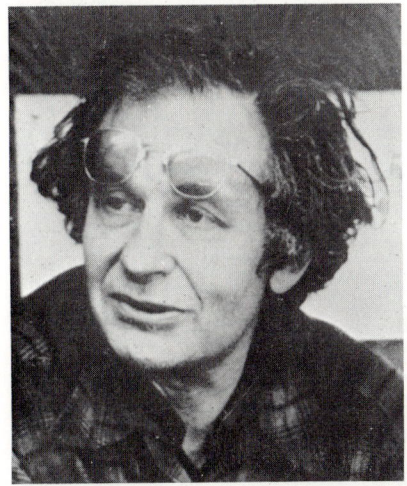

Lawrence Kohlberg of Harvard University is a leading researcher in moral development of children and youth.

---

[3] As in his writings on other aspects of development, Piaget is reluctant to pin down any specific age span as representative of a stage of development. Nevertheless, it is convenient to mention the ages at which children characteristically move from one stage to another, if only to provide some kind of perspective.

needs, and values of others is developed in the context of playing and interacting with others, especially in children's games. In fact, much of Piaget's research into morality was conducted in the course of playing marbles. The rules for such games and the children's attitudes toward the rules provided the raw material from which Piaget shaped his theories of the development of moral judgment.

Kohlberg's Elaboration of Piaget's Stages

Lawrence Kohlberg (1963b) has extended Piaget's sequence into a six-stage system, divided into three levels (see Table 13-1). Kohlberg's first level is an expansion of Piaget's moral-realism stage, and his latter two expand Piaget's autonomous stage. Kohlberg maintains that at age seven most of the statements made by children are at Level I (premoral), with a few statements at Level II (conventional morality), and none at Level III (self-accepted moral principles).

Figure 13-6 shows how Stage 1 (the lower stage in the premoral level) statements decline sharply from the middle years of childhood until adolescence for three groups of boys: American urban, Mexican urban, and Mexican rural (an isolated village on the Yucatan peninsula). Note how children's concepts in the rural setting lag behind those developed in urban areas, where social relationships are more complex and abstract, and Stage 1 concepts are less appropriate. Conversely, devel-

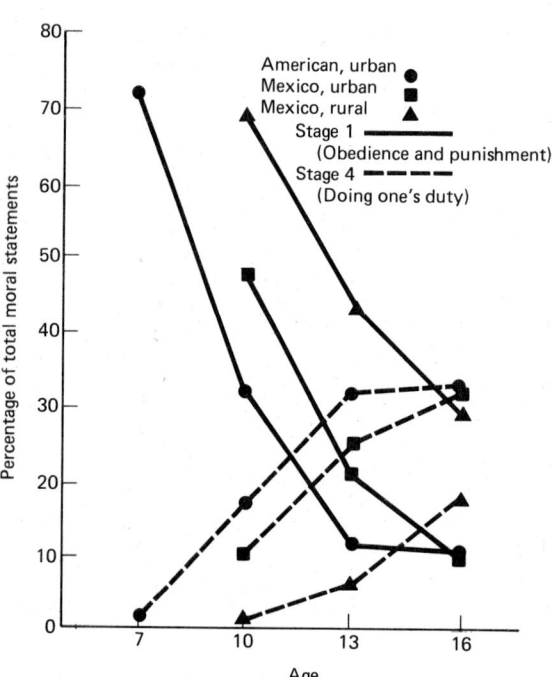

FIGURE 13-6. Changes in moral concepts between middle childhood and adolescence, as reflected by statements made by three groups of boys: American urban, Mexican urban, Mexican rural (Yucatan village). Two types of statements are contrasted: (1) those at the most elementary level, as characterized by an orientation toward obedience and punishment, and (2) those at a more mature level, as characterized by a willingness to "do one's duty" with respect to those in authority and to the social order in general. (After Kohlberg, 1963b, and Kohlberg and Kramer, 1969.)

TABLE 13-1. Stages in Children's Moral Development (after Kohlberg, 1963b)

Level I. Premoral level
   Stage 1. *Obedience and punishment orientation*
               Defers to a superior power because of dislike of punishment
   Stage 2. *Naive hedonistic and instrumental orientation*
               Rightness of conduct determined by extent to which action satisfies self and, occasionally, others; some give-and-take reciprocity.

Level II. Morality of conventional role-conformity
   Stage 3. *"Good-boy"/"nice-girl" morality of maintaining good relations*
               Oriented toward seeking approval and to pleasing and helping others; some consideration of intentions.
   Stage 4. *Authority and social-order-maintaining morality*
               Oriented toward "doing one's duty," respect for authority, and maintaining the social order for its own sake; takes perspective of those who have legitimate rights; believes that virtue must be rewarded.

Level III. Morality of self-accepted moral principles
   Stage 5. *Morality of contract, individual rights, and democratically accepted law*
               Right and wrong defined in terms of laws and regulations, which are seen as having rational bases; duties and obligations seen in terms of abstract concept of contract, which take precedence over individual needs.
   Stage 6. *Morality of individual principles of conscience*
               Orientation that considers laws and regulations, but also bases decisions on mutual respect and trust, internalized ideals, and broader moral principles.

opment of Stage 4 concepts (doing one's duty, showing respect for authority, and maintaining the social order) increases during the years between 10 and 13, and levels off thereafter. Once again, the development of moral concepts on the part of rural boys lags behind that of boys in the urban centers.

An Experimental Test of Theories of Moral Development

Some question regarding the validity of stage theories of moral development has been raised as a result of other experiments, in which children were placed under various kinds of pressures to modify their thinking regarding proper moral behavior. The classic experiment of this type was conducted by Bandura and McDonald (1963), who used two groups of children aged 5 to 11 years, half of whom were making moral judgments characteristic of Piaget's less mature or "objective" stage and the other half who were making more mature judgments of the "subjective" type. The children were presented with pairs of descriptions of incidents. Each pair consisted of one incident in which material damage was great, but there was little intent to be injurious or destructive, and one incident in which the amount of destruction was small, but the individual concerned was guilty of some kind of wrongdoing. Children were asked to determine which incident in each pair was the more serious crime. Children in the "objective" stage tended to judge the wrongdoing in terms of the amount of damage caused, whereas those in the "subjective" stage tended to judge in terms of the intentions of the individual concerned.

The subjects were divided into three groups and in each instance were exposed to a treatment designed to change their style of moral judgment. In one treatment, they watched adult models making judgments counter to the children's orientation, and the children themselves were then reinforced for adopting the model's style of evaluation. In a second treatment, the children watched the models, but were not themselves reinforced by expressions of approval and praise for matching their behavior. In a third treatment, the children had no exposure to models, but were merely reinforced for expressing judgments that ran counter to their dominant tendencies.

Results showed that watching the model was the most effective way of getting children to change their orientation. Reinforcement alone produced little change. Furthermore, when reinforcement was combined with modeling, it added little to the effect of the model on the children's behavior.

The researchers concluded that their results were strong evidence in favor of a social-learning explanation of the development of moral behavior. When these findings are examined in terms of their relevance to everyday life, they suggest that the example set by a parent is a more powerful teacher of moral judgment than is anything he might do *to* a child by way of encouraging him directly or even rewarding him for adopting this or that judgmental style. The fact that the experimental treatment could so readily cause children to progress or regress in the maturity of their moral judgment also raises some doubts as to whether Piaget's moral stages are as well defined as his cognitive stages.

As impressive as Bandura and McDonald's study is, it must be considered in the context of the child's developmental experiences. The fact that the researchers so readily manipulated moral judgments (at least in their verbal form) shows that it can be done, but that does not mean that children in middle and late childhood actually acquire most of their moral values by watching adult models. It seems more reasonable to assume that a number of modes are involved: interacting with peers, copying the behavior of adults and older children, resolving conflicts with authority, becoming the target of criticism and rejection, being punished or praised, and learning when to feel anxious or guilty.[4]

---

[4] Readers interested in examining a more detailed account of the criticisms of the Bandura-McDonald experiment should read Philip A. Cowan, et al., "Social learning and Piaget's cognitive theory of moral development," *Journal of Personality and Social Psychology*, 1969, *11*, 261–274, as well as Albert Bandura's reply, "Social learning of moral judgments," in the same issue, pages 275–279.

Taking all evidence together, it does seem that social learning plays some part in the development of moral judgment, perhaps more in the initial stages than the later ones. Hoffman (1970) suggests that as the child develops his cognitive abilities and interacts with his peers, he reevaluates and shifts his view of authority and regulations, so that they are no longer arbitrary and external, but internalized and rational. During this period, too, children are learning to control antisocial impulses—learning, in effect, to feel anxious and guilty when social norms are violated, even when authority figures are absent.

But something else appears to be needed, over and beyond give-and-take with one's peers, if a child is to develop an adequate degree of moral sensitivity. Hoffman (1975) suggests that this "something else" is parental discipline—not discipline in the narrow sense of punishment, but discipline in the broader sense whereby the parent intervenes, admonishes, insists, interprets, restrains, reprimands, makes statements about what is good and what is bad, exacts penalties, encourages, praises—in other words, does all the things that parents do to get their children to conform to the behavior standards they believe are appropriate. Hoffman says that parental discipline is important because it gives children the experience they need in order to achieve a balance between expressing and controlling their desires—experience they must have in order to "internalize" the necessary controls. A quotation from a presentation by Eleanor E. Maccoby (1975) is relevant here:

> An effective parent must adjust himself to the child's rhythm and be quick to recognize the signs when the input to the child is too much or too little. This does not mean that the parent must allow the child to take complete control of their interactions nor let the child rule the household omnipotently. The firm boundary conditions that a parent sets for the child's actions, and the parent's own needs and reactions, are part of the environmental conditions the child needs to learn about; but the parent's rules can be made more or less learnable.

In its mature form, morality is more than self-control and knowing when to inhibit and when to express one's feelings; it also includes prosocial feelings, especially a sensitivity to the needs of others. Empathy plays a key role here, because it is through becoming aware of others' views and feelings that a child is enabled to grow up to be a truly socialized—and civilized—adult.

summary

Reading, which is largely a cognitive process, has its motivational aspects, as is demonstrated by an experiment in which girls displayed approximately the same level of reading competency irrespective of whether the material was personally interesting to them, whereas boys did as well as girls did on interesting material, but poorly on uninteresting material. Anxiety may be viewed as a state—the pervasive apprehensiveness we feel when we are uncertain about our relations with others or about the way things will turn out. It may also be considered to be a trait—the tendency to be characteristically more anxious than most people. In contrast to children rating low in trait anxiety, those rating high do better on simple tasks but more poorly on complex ones. A moderate amount of anxiety facilitates school performance and social adjustment.

Children can be classified as reflective or impulsive by the Matching Familiar Figures Test. Impulsive children are more likely to respond to questions without thinking and are generally less mature than reflective children. Locus-of-control measures also indicate that impulsive children are likely to be "Externals"—individuals who say that the decisive forces in their life are environmental or external. Those who take personal responsibility for their successes and failures are classified as "Internal" in locus of control and are more likely to be reflective than impulsive. Internal children tend to have parents who permit or encourage independent thinking, whereas External children's parents are more directive.

Punitive parents are likely to have aggressive children. A study of the background of sexually dangerous persons indicated that their fathers were likely to be physically cruel, and their mothers passive and indulgent. SES is apparently unrelated to maternal affection, but mothers in families with low SES employ more coercive and restrictive forms of punishment. The higher the SES of a mother, the more likely she is to be warm and accepting. Higher-SES children also tend to be better adjusted, with the exception of children whose parents continued their education past the bachelor's degree. Children who have been referred to a clinic for psychiatric treatment often have parents who conform outwardly, but express hostile and rebellious feelings in indirect ways. Such children also perceive greater psychological distance between members of their families, as indicated by their placing the two-dimensional representations of family figures used in projective tests farther apart.

Earlier research by clinicians focused on the probable causes of negative behavior in children, but in recent decades there has been more interest in positive behavior, such as achievement and independence. Whiting investigated the relationship of child-rearing practices to school achievement. Her findings showed that the parents of successful boys expected independence and mastery of tasks earlier than did the parents of unsuccessful boys. Achievement, independence, and self-esteem are likely to go together. Studies have indicated that the parents of high-curiosity boys are more democratic in their relations with them and less likely to foster dependence.

Independence training is also related to the need to achieve (n Ach). Generally speaking, earlier independence training by mothers engenders stronger n Ach in their children. Children with high n Ach tend to try harder and take more pleasure in success; they are more popular than those with low n Ach. The desire to complete tasks is another aspect of achievement motivation. Parents of boys with high n Ach tend to hold high aspirations for their sons' performances. During childhood and the early adolescent years, the proportion of achievement themes in fantasy materials increases. Early maternal interest in daughters' achievement tends to be followed by increases in achievement fantasy and in IQ. The amount of achievement fantasy is positively correlated with IQ for both sexes. Need for achievement as expressed between the ages of six and ten has proven to be highly predictive of similar adult tendencies. This period is thought to be crucial for the development of motivation to master intellectual tasks. It is a routine finding that SES differences are related to achievement motivation.

The antecedents of self-esteem were investigated by Coopersmith, who found that children with high self-esteem were little troubled by anxiety, showed little destructiveness, actively expressed their opinions, and were not upset by criticism. Low-self-esteem boys tended to be discouraged, timid, and convinced of their inferiority. Children with high self-esteem were also more likely to have strict parents who administered discipline consistently but not harshly. The parents of high-self-esteem children were also active and self-assured, suggesting that they serve as social learning models for their children. The usual finding that underachievers tend to have poorer emotional and social adjustment does not hold true in all cultures. The norms of developing countries like Brazil tend evidently to deemphasize achievement, and children in such countries who set high academic goals for themselves very likely deviate from prevailing cultural norms in other ways as well.

By the time the child reaches the sixth grade, his "ideal self" probably conforms more closely to the ideals of his peers than to those of his parents. The reduction of the discrepancy between the individual's ideal self and what he considers to be his "real self" has traditionally been one of the goals of psychotherapy. Recent research, however, has indicated that the disparity increases with age and that some disparity is indicative of mental health. The least disparity between real and ideal self is to be found in emotionally disturbed, "acting-out," aggressive boys, and the most disparity with boys whose problems are more of the neurotic type.

The essence of moral development may be found in the ability to resist temptation, which in turn, has been found to be positively related to intelligence, internality in locus of control, the need for social approval, and self-esteem. Children are better able to resist temptation when their mood is positive and less able when it is negative.

Moral standards in their mature form include prosocial acts as well as "thou shalt nots." Hoffman noted that there are three major theories bearing on the moral development: (1) the *original sin* doctrine; (2) the *innate purity* doctrine; and (3) the *tabula rasa* doctrine. Freudian theory is characterized as representing the first doctrine, and Piaget, the second. The *tabula rasa* doctrine is represented by the learning theory schools. According to Freudian doctrine, moral development is a matter of superego development which, in turn, is the result of the child's identification with his parents.

Piaget holds that development of moral judgment during middle childhood is separated into two basic stages. The first stage, *objective morality*, lasts approximately from age three until age eight, and is characterized by rigid conformity to rules that are thought of by the child as arbitrary and universal. The second stage, *subjective morality*, is marked by a system of beliefs that take into account the intentions of the individual and the possibility of human error. Kohlberg has extended Piaget's sequence into a three-level system: the premoral level, conventional morality, and principled morality.

Bandura and McDonald conducted a study in which children were presented with pairs of descriptions of incidents. In one of these incidents the material damage was great, but there was little malicious intent; in the second incident the damage was slight, but the individual involved was guilty of some wrongdoing. Children in the *objective* stage tended to judge the wrongdoing in terms of the extent of damage. In the *subjective* stage, children judged in terms of intentions. The investigators found that reinforcement had little influence on the style of children's moral judgment but that exposure to adult models was effective. The fact that the children's moral judgments could be so easily changed in experiments raises some question as to whether Piaget's moral stages are as well defined as his cognitive stages. All evidence considered, it seems that social learning plays some role in moral development, especially in the early stages. Firm but sympathetic parental discipline is also essential, if children are to "internalize" the necessary controls.

fourteen

The Peer Group and the School

> TV programs give children counterfeit feelings about surrogate experiences that are supposed to be bad for their thinking. School programs make children feel bad about actual experiences that are supposed to be good for their thinking.
> —BERNARD Z. FRIEDLANDER (1976)

> You send your child to the schoolmaster, but 'tis the schoolboys who educate him.
> —RALPH WALDO EMERSON

The major influences during middle and late childhood come from the child's peer group and the school in the North American culture.[1] These two sources of influence do not operate independently, because the school plays a part in bringing the child and the peer group together. Most children, to be sure, have had some interaction with peer groups before entering school, but school provides maximum exposure to peer-group social stimulation. The groups that children are involved in during the preschool years are likely to be loose, informal, and less stable. During the elementary school years, groups tend to become more highly structured and, in the classroom at least, highly formalized.

School children can be said to leave home, literally and figuratively, to a much greater degree than younger children. In a social-ecological

---

[1] This qualification is added because in more traditional cultures—for example, European or Latin American—family influences are stronger and peer group influences weaker during the childhood years than they are in the United States and Canada.

460 The Middle Years

study of a midwestern town, Herbert F. Wright (1956) studied the average number of hours per day spent by the children and adults in family and community settings. As shown in Figure 14-1, infants and preschoolers spent, on the average, about one hour a day outside the home. An increase to six or seven hours outside the home occurred during the elementary-school years—the period we are considering at present. The children spent most of these hours away from home in the company of their agemates, in school or at play.

_____the peer group

Although the parents are the first socializing agents for the child, many of the more complex social skills are learned when he becomes a member of the peer group. Some of these skills are learned directly from peer group members and some from teachers. We shall begin by discussing the peer group, which at this age exerts a major influence on children's values, standards, and behavior.

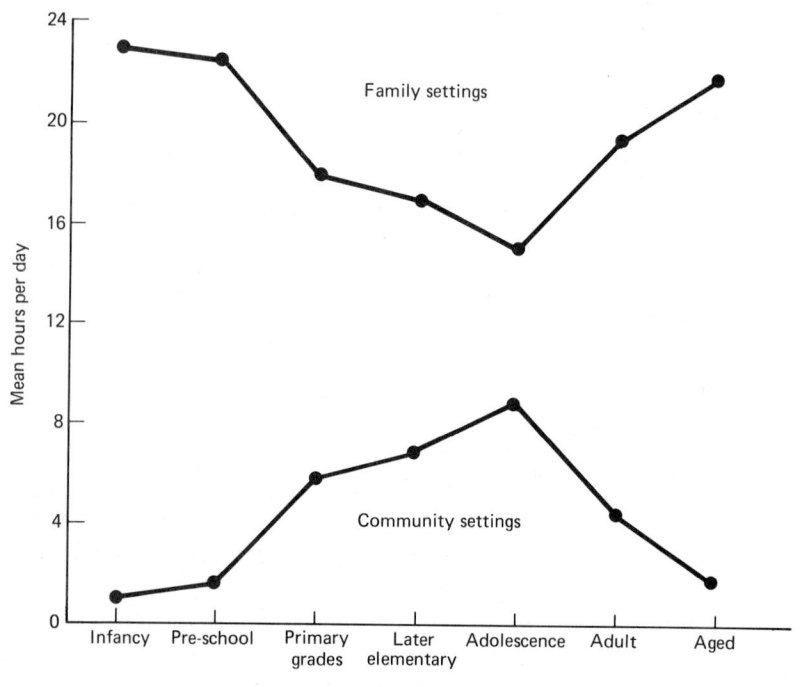

FIGURE 14-1. Average amount of time per day spent by individuals of various ages in home and community settings. (Data from Wright, 1956.)

Peer-group Power

The attractiveness of the peer group has much to do with its power to influence children. As far as most children are concerned, the peer group offers an environment that is generally more exciting and arousing than that provided at home. Part of this excitement comes when the child interacts with individuals who are less familiar to him than are the members of his family, but whose physical and mental powers, as peers and agemates, are likely to be no greater than his own. Part of the excitement also stems from the instability and unpredictability of peer groups. Coping with this unpredictability is a challenge: it offers a set of problems quite different from those encountered at home.

Peer groups are also attractive because they offer status on more equal terms than families do. The status, position, and power of a child at home are relatively fixed—he is an oldest, an only, a second sibling, the youngest, or whatever. Status in a peer group, however, may be created, maintained, and defended by influencing others through intelligence and display of social skills. A child may be assigned a low status by a play group, but he may be free to seek other groups or form his own group of associates. For some children, of course, the struggle for peer-group status and the occasional lapses into anarchy are more than they can cope with, and they cling to a preference for the stability and security of the home, or become involved in solitary activities.

Irrespective of whether the child finds among his agemates the kind of status he seeks or the kind he would prefer to avoid, the peer group experience is inescapable, if only because the adult community has decreed that children and adolescents must attend school. Every child is therefore subject to the social power or influences of his peers. The peer group influences its members, be they willing or unwilling, through the social norms it evolves, the behavioral models it provides, and the rewards and punishments it employs to encourage or to discipline.

Social norms are probably the most significant of these sources of influence. Studies of group behavior have shown that a group member has difficulty in deviating from group norms, even when they require him to utter judgments he knows are incorrect (Asch, 1956) or to engage in behavior he would otherwise consider improper (Milgram, 1964). Social norms that are generated within the context of a group ordinarily influence members' behavior without their being aware of it, and the influence often continues when they are physically away from the group (Sherif, 1936).

The models the peer group provides for a child are likely to have a more significant effect on his behavior than do adult models. For one thing, peer group members are more like him than adults are, and he can "identify" with them, realizing that their actions and ways of thinking are more appropriate for him than are adult behavior and values. In other words, the fact that adults live in a different psycholog-

Social norms affect a wide variety of behaviors: gestures, language, beliefs, attitudes, and, as shown above, clothing. Conforming to peer-group norms gives young people a sense of identity and helps satisfy their need to belong.

ical world and seem so different makes it easy for the child to dismiss their behavior and values as inappropriate for him and to imitate those whose capabilities, interests, and experiences are more like his own. Hence his peers become for him what social psychologists term a "reference group"—a group to which he "refers" in deciding how to behave and how to judge his behavior. To be rejected by a group is a form of punishment; to be accepted is a reward. To be excluded is not only a loss of status; it is a form of loss of identity that leaves the child nowhere to go.

Cross-cultural Variations in Peer-group Norms

Most people would say that peer-group social norms are diametrically opposed to adult behavioral standards. We are tempted to make such assumptions partly because in our interactions with children we often have to act as inhibitors or blockers. Our experiences may, however, be culture-bound and hence not applicable to children in other societies.

A study showing that American children's attitudes toward adult standards are quite different from those of children in other countries was conducted by Urie Bronfenbrenner (1970). Bronfenbrenner asked Russian and American twelve-year-olds how they would behave in a number of imaginary situations involving moral issues, in which peer and adult values were placed in opposition to each other. Here is an example of the kind of test item Bronfenbrenner used in his surveys:

"If you don't mind, Father, this is a private rap group!"

In the earliest stages of social development, children's attention is focused on their parents, but during the middle years of childhood, the peer group becomes important, so much so that at times it takes precedence over parents. (Joseph Farris in the *Saturday Review*.)

The Lost Test

You and your friends accidentally find a sheet of paper which the teacher must have lost. On this sheet are the questions and answers for a quiz that you are going to have tomorrow. Some of the kids suggest that you not say anything to the teacher about it, so that all of you can get better marks. What would you really do? Suppose your friends decide to go ahead. Would you go along with them or refuse?

Children took different versions of the test, each consisting of ten problems, under three different conditions: (1) the *baseline* condition, in which they were told that no one would see their responses except the investigators; (2) the *adult* condition, in which they were told that each child's responses would be posted on a chart and displayed at a parents' meeting to be held the following week; and (3) the *peer* condition, in which the chart would be displayed a week later to the class itself. Responses to the problems were scored on a scale that ranged from −2.5 (going along with peers) to +2.5 (responding to adult-approved standards of behavior). A score of −25 for the ten items would thus represent the ultimate in peer-oriented values, whereas +25 would represent the most extreme adult-oriented outlook.

The results, as shown by Figure 14-2, indicate first of all that there was the usual difference between boys and girls, with both American and Russian boys expressing values that were somewhat more peer-oriented, and girls in both nations being more adult-oriented. Second, and more significant, Russian children were a great deal more accepting of adult standards of behavior than American children were.

Third, although both Russian and American children responded in ways that were slightly more adult-oriented when told that their parents would learn of their responses, knowledge that their peers would hear of them had quite a different effect on the two groups of children: in contrast to their baseline position, American children moved to a more peer-oriented response mode, whereas Russian children became slightly more adult-oriented. In other words, Soviet children wanted their peers to think they were more accepting of adult standards than they really were, whereas American children wanted their peers to think that they *rejected* adult standards more than they actually did. The peer norm for Russian children is apparently much more proadult than it is for American children.

Bronfenbrenner sees this large difference between Russian and American children as an indication that the American family, because of urbanization and of technological changes in the larger society, "has been losing power as a major socializing agent in the lives of children, and the resulting vacuum has been filled by the age-segregated peer group." Ties between Russian children and their parents, on the other hand, have remained strong.

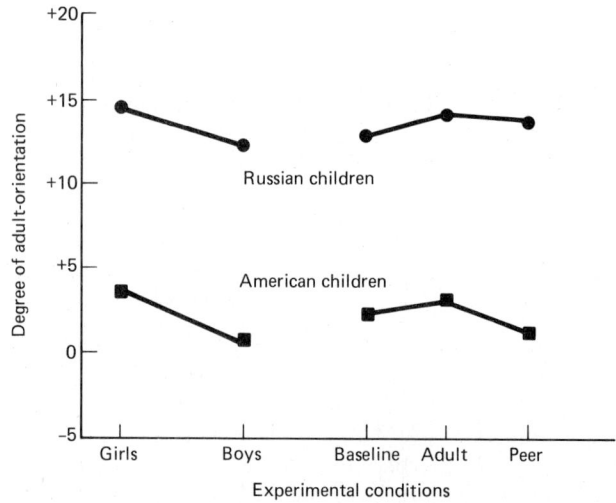

FIGURE 14-2. Differences in degree to which Russian and American children give adult-oriented (in contrast to peer-oriented) responses in conflict situations involving possible misdemeanors. (After Bronfenbrenner, 1970.)

A number of other cross-cultural investigations have yielded results that support Bronfenbrenner's findings. P. S. Fry (1975b), for example, conducted an experiment in which Indian and American boys attending elementary schools in New Delhi served as subjects. As in the experiment by Fry (1975a) that we discussed in Chapter 13, each child was told that he was not to touch a very attractive toy during the experimenter's absence, but could play with a less attractive one. After the experimenter had left the room, and the subject was alone, he saw a brief televised sequence in which a boy his age said that he would or would not observe the injunction not to play with the attractive toy and then proceeded to display behavior consistent with his statement. The model spoke in English or Hindi, according to the nationality of the subject. Children in the control group saw a sequence of a boy combing his hair and brushing his clothes. Each subject was then observed for ten minutes through a one-way mirror.

Fry found that the Indian children were much more resistive to temptation. Some of them obeyed orders strictly, and those who did disobey hesitated longer than the Americans did before yeilding to the urge to play with the attractive toy. Figure 14-3 shows that the differences between the groups and among the three experimental treatments were in some instances quite dramatic. It indicates that both Indian and American boys were more likely to yield to temptation after they had seen a disobedient model, but that the American boys spent three times as much time playing with the forbidden toy as the Indian boys did.

Seeing the televised sequence of the obedient model had an inhibiting effect on both the groups of boys, but the American subjects in this experimental condition still spent seven times more time in disobedient behavior. The behavior of the Indian boys who had seen the obedient model was not significantly different from that of the Indians in the control group, indicating that they were already highly conditioned to obey adult authority. The behavior of the American boys provided a surprise, however: their control group was even *more* obedient than those who had seen the obedient model. Evidently seeing an obedient model led some of the Americans to disobey, perhaps because they found the idea of a boy openly conforming to adult standards somewhat unbelievable!

Peer Groups as Disinhibitors

The studies we have described indicate that a child's willingness to deviate from prescribed social norms is influenced partly by the culture in which he holds membership and partly by the behavior of the models he has observed. In some instances, the group may also have an additional effect in promoting disobedience. What we refer to here is the fact that the presence of others tends to facilitate the individual's performance of well-learned, dominant, or simple responses, and to

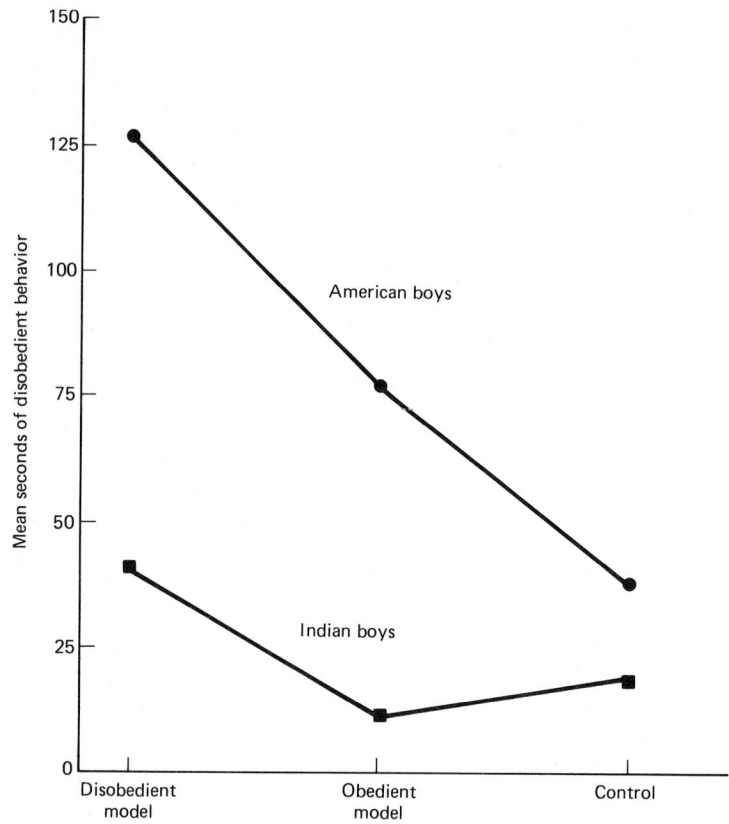

FIGURE 14-3. *Tendencies to yield to temptation on the part of Indian and American boys who had seen a disobedient or obedient model, or a neutral control sequence of televised behavior. Mean differences are reported in terms of the number of seconds out of a ten-minute observation period the subjects spent playing with a forbidden toy. (Data from Fry, 1975b.)*

interfere with or inhibit his performance of less familiar, more difficult, or complex responses (Zajonc, 1966).

Anyone who has much to do with school children knows that they are not easy to deal with when they are excited. When they are keyed up, whatever orderliness they have vanishes, and they surrender to impulses to shout, jump, laugh, cry, strike out at others, or whatever. The social cement that has been holding them together as a group melts away, and anarchy reigns. They become, as is said, "unglued." This is a condition that Philip G. Zimbardo (1969) has termed *deindividuation*—the state in which one forgets that one is an individual and surrenders to impulsive, irrational, and irresponsible behavior. If one is in the context of a group, deindividuation means yielding to whatever the group mood happens to be.

An interesting experiment showing the effect of both the "group effect" and physical arousal on the behavior of children was conducted by a group of researchers from the University of Washington, who prepared a number of experimental conditions for children who traditionally make the rounds of residential areas on Halloween trick-or-treat expeditions. When the trick-or-treaters arrived at the house of the experimenters and made the usual demands for a treat, they were told to approach a bowl containing wrapped pieces of candy and to take only one. In some instances, the children were permitted to go up to the bowl in groups; in other instances the experimenters specified that the children had to approach the bowl one at a time. A concealed observer recorded how many pieces of candy the children actually took.

Before they approached the bowl, some of the children were aroused by having them play a lively game of Simon Says, in which they were told by Simon to jump up and down, clap their hands, and spin around in increasing tempo. Other children were aroused by hearing weird, ghostly sounds as they entered the house preparatory to getting their "treat." Children in the control condition engaged in no activities and heard no noises.

The results, as indicated in Figure 14-4, clearly showed that the three types of experimental conditions all led the children to take more candy over the one-piece limit—that is, "steal"—than they did in the no-arousal condition, alone, in which virtually no stealing took place. The experiment thus demonstrated that under conditions of arousal, children's inhibitions are lowered: they are more likely to yield to temptation. To put it another way, arousal of any kind—social, physical, or sensory—makes children more impulsive.

What is relevant to our present discussion, however, is that the presence of other children was in itself sufficient to bring about a marked increase in stealing. Note that in the control situation, where there was no ghostly noise and no active game, children in groups stole an average of 0.5 candy apiece, but children alone stole virtually none. Furthermore, in the Simon Says condition, the stealing of single children was about one sixth that of those who approached the bowl in groups. There seems to be little doubt that children find the presence of others arousing, and that such social stimulation may at times be sufficient to encourage immature or even antisocial behavior.

aggression and aggressiveness

Sex Differences in Aggressive Behavior

If there is one thing that developmental psychologists and the lay public are agreed upon, it is that boys tend to be more aggressive than

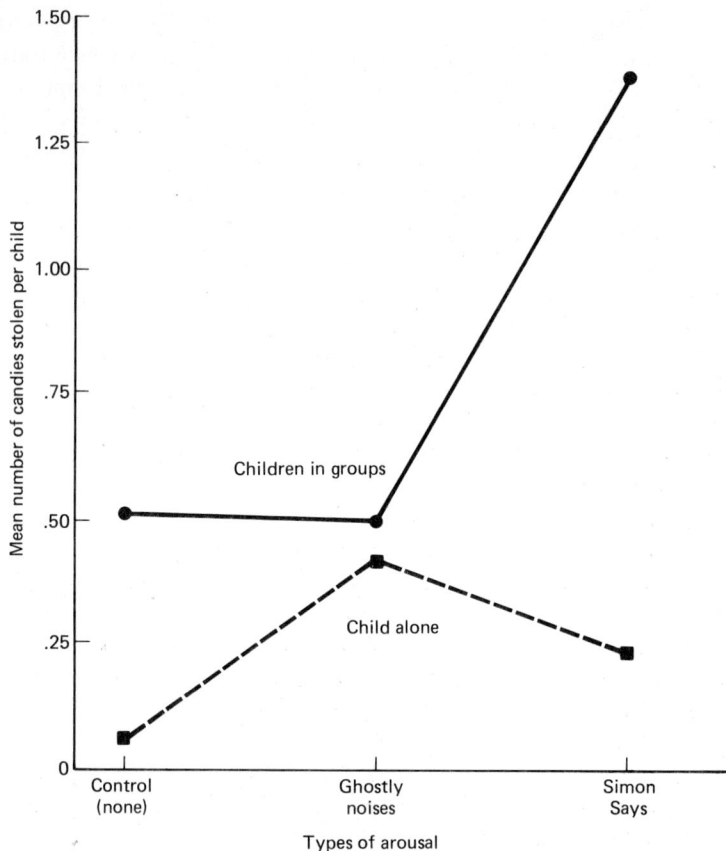

FIGURE 14-4. *Mean number of candies stolen per trick-or-treater when alone or in groups, with or without being aroused by ghostly noises or by participating in a game of Simon Says.* (Data from Diener, et al., 1973.)

girls. Maccoby and Jacklin (1974), in their review of research on sex differences, note that when investigators report significant sex differences, boys are found to be more aggressive than girls in the ratio of about twelve to one. (See Table 14-1).

As we noted in our discussion of aggression during the preschool period of development, psychologists are not in accord as to the extent to which this phenomenon results from constitutional differences or from environmental factors, such as stereotyped expectations on the part of parents and teachers; the weight of evidence, however, seems to be that there is something in the psychological makeup of boys that leads them to learn aggressive patterns of behavior more readily than girls do.

Differences in ways in which boys and girls behave after having experienced a brief period of emotional arousal were studied by Harris and Siebel (1975). The experiment was conducted with third graders,

TABLE 14-1. Number of Research Studies Showing Children of One Sex as More Aggressive Than the Other Sex (data from Maccoby and Jacklin, 1974)

		Number of Studies		
Type of Study	Ages of Children	Males More Aggressive	Females More Aggressive	Nonsignificant Difference
Observational	2–10	10	1	12
Experimental	3–13	17	2	12
Questionnaire (including ratings by parents and teachers)	2–11	9	0	4
Totals		36	3	28

who were brought individually to a testing room and given a box of 25 rubber balloons as a reward for participating in the research. The investigator then showed the child pictures of outdoor scenes and asked him or her to think angry, happy, or sad thoughts. After a half-minute pause, the experimenter pointed out the other equipment in the room: a

Researchers agree that boys are much more aggressive than girls. Their aggressiveness is not necessarily an expression of hostility. Even the best of friends enjoy wrestling and engaging in horseplay.

large, inflated Popeye clown, some toys, and a box labeled "Balloons for other children." The child was told he could play with the clown or the toys, or could, if he wished, put some of his balloons in the box "for the other children." The experimenter then retired from the scene and unobtrusively watched the subject from a distance, pretending to work on some papers.

The responses of the children were scored for aggressiveness (punching or hitting the clown) or for altruism (sharing balloons). The results, as shown in Figure 14-5, indicate that the boys behaved in ways that were virtually opposite to those of the girls. Two thirds of the boys engaged in at least one aggressive act, in contrast to about one fourth of the girls. On the other hand, over half the girls donated some of their balloons, in contrast to less than a third of the boys. Emotional arousal resulting from the induced mood also had the opposite effect on boys and girls, leading to aggressive responses in the case of the boys, and to an inhibition of aggression in case of the girls.

We noted earlier that emotional arousal leads individuals to emit responses that are dominant among those that are available to them. The dominant response evoked by arousal in the Halloween trick-or-treat situation was taking or stealing more candy. In the Harris-Siebel experiment, the emotional arousal that resulted from thinking angry, happy, or sad thoughts apparently elicited a sex-typed response: aggression in the case of the boys, and sharing in the case of the girls.

Aggression, Hostility, and Fantasy

Hostility refers to a group of attitudes characterized by anger, hatred, jealousy, and bitterness toward others. It precedes or accompanies acts of agreession, but it may also be inhibited and concealed in the form of covert hostility, especially when the hostility is directed against authority figures. In such instances, covert hostility appears in the form of stubborness, sulkiness, resistance, and easily hurt feelings.

Covert hostility can express itself in a number of ways. Evelyn Morrison (1969) conducted a study of personality differences in fifth-grade boys who were classified as *overachievers*, in that they were receiving higher marks from their teachers than one would have anticipated from their IQ scores, or as *underachievers*, in that they were receiving lower marks from their teachers than one would have anticipated from their IQ scores. She found that the underachievers showed more hostility toward authority, as revealed by the stories they wrote when viewing pictures on TAT cards. They were also rated as more passive aggressive (that is, stubborn) by their teachers. Incidentally, there was no difference between the underachievers and the overachievers when their achievement was measured by *standardized* tests of achievement: they differed only in the marks they received from their teachers. In other words, the underachievers actually were learning as

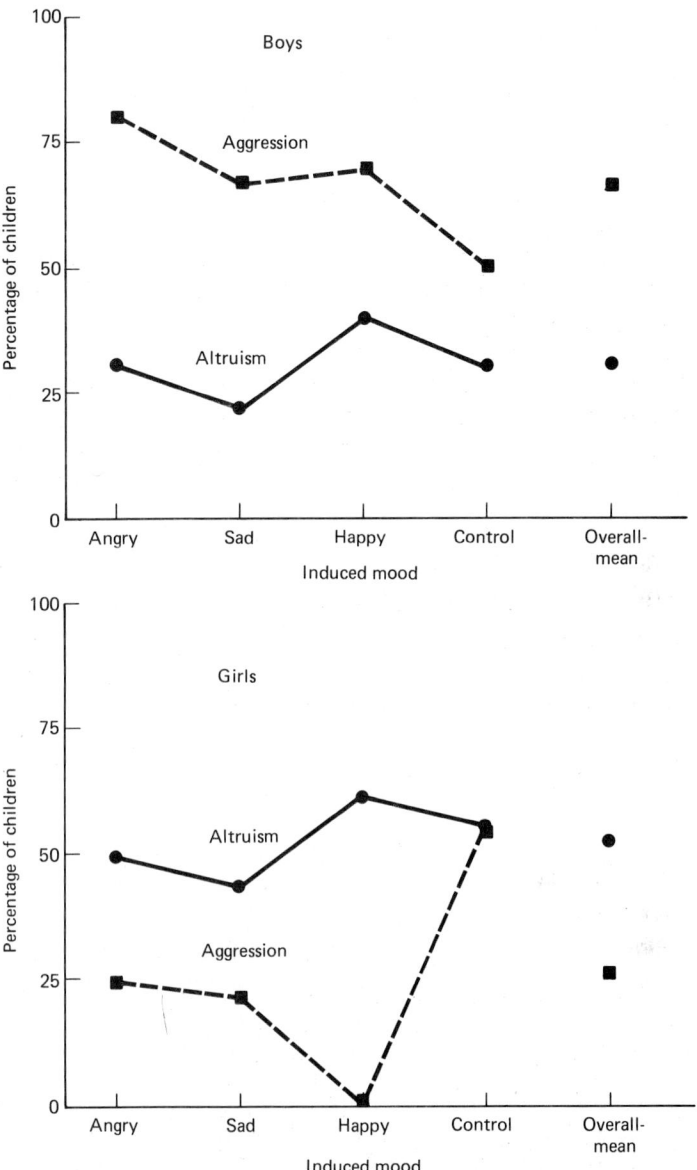

FIGURE 14-5. Tendencies of third-grade boys and girls to act aggressively or altruistically after brief emotional arousal. (Data from Harris and Siebel, 1975.)

much as the overachievers but were unwilling to give their teachers the evidence that would have gained them better grades.

Another dimension of aggression that has attracted much attention throughout the last century is the effect of fantasy materials on behavior. Parents and teachers at about the turn of the century confiscated "penny dreadfuls" and "dime novels," saying such reading matter poisoned the minds of youth and aggravated criminal tendencies. In more recent years, comic books, radio thrillers, and now television crime programs have been similarly accused of corrupting the young. This viewpoint has been supported by some psychiatrists, but a number of psychologists have argued against it, saying that such material may actually have a positive effect on children's emotional and social development by giving them a healthy outlet for normal aggressive tendencies.[2] Research findings are somewhat contradictory. Bandura, Ross, and Ross (1961) showed preschool children films in which two male adults engaged in aggressive play or vigorous nonaggressive play. In one version, aggression was rewarded; in another it was punished. Although the viewing of the rewarded aggressive model was followed by a higher degree of aggressive behavior on the part of the young viewers, there were some confusing results, especially for boys, who also behaved aggressively after seeing the nonaggressive model. Seymour Feshbach (1970) interprets these findings as suggesting that perhaps any kind of vigorous stimulus, aggressive or otherwise, may incite aggressive responses in boys, who are more prone to such behavior than girls are.

Televised Violence and Aggression

The possibility that aggressive fantasy material may actually have the opposite effect on the behavior of boys was explored by Feshbach and Singer (1970), who enlisted the cooperation of parents and private schools and were thus able to control the television viewing behavior of several groups of boys aged 9 to 15 over a period of six weeks. Some groups watched more violent and aggressive programs involving gangsters, outlaws, and the FBI, while others watched nonviolent, nonaggressive programs, such as family situation comedies, variety shows, and *Lassie*. Records were kept of the number of aggressive acts the two groups engaged in. Here are some of the findings.

1. There were no significant differences between the two groups with respect to cursing and swearing, destruction of property, and breaking of rules.
2. The group that watched the nonviolent programs were involved in more than twice as many fistfights as those who watched the violent programs.
3. The nonviolent-program group participated in 859 loud, angry arguments, in constrast to 407 for the other group.
4. The nonviolent-program group engaged in 973 instances of

---

[2] In Chapter 10 we discussed the research of Ames (1966), whose data suggest that even very young children are fascinated by violent and aggressive themes in fantasy material.

criticizing or insulting others, whereas the violent-program group engaged in only 456.
5. With respect to feelings of jealousy, the group watching the nonaggressive films reported 254 instances versus 87 for the other group.

With respect to comic books, objectionable or otherwise, a study by W. Paul Blakely (1958) found that they had no effect on children's behavior, except that seventh graders who read more comic books tended to read more library books as well. As far as cartoon films are concerned, a study of second graders who saw an aggressive cartoon, a nonaggressive cartoon, or no cartoon at all reported no differences in their interpersonal aggressiveness during a group play period that followed the viewing sessions (Hapkiewicz and Roden, 1971).

The relationship between fantasy violence and aggressive behavior is far from clear, however. Common sense would lead to the conclusion that exposure to fantasy violence in the form of television programs and the like would incite aggressive behavior. This view is expressed by Leonard Berkowitz (1970), who cites an impressive array of studies.

Findings typical of much research in fantasy aggression are reported by Cameron and Janky (1971), who asked all parents of kindergarten children in a Michigan school district to cooperate in an experiment in which children were placed on a three-week "diet" of violent television, passive television, or some combination (first period violent, and second period passive, or vice versa). Parents' observations of children's behavior disturbances were the dependent variable.

Results showed that children watching violent programs showed the greatest number of behavior disturbances, and some of the effects still persisted a month later. Findings were not clear-cut, however. Only one third of the children seeing all-violent programs showed any change. Furthermore, the least change was shown by children who were exposed to a diet first of passive films and then of violent ones, a finding that is contrary to what would be expected. The authors also point out that the controls in the study were of necessity quite loose: children were able to watch television at neighbors' homes, where parents were unable to monitor the programs; parents were not 100 per cent vigilant; many television commercials were violent; and so forth. What is more important, however, is that parents who controlled the stimuli were also asked to judge their children's behavior—another opportunity for unconscious bias to slip in. Although the results of the study are consistent with common sense and with Berkowitz's position, they can be accepted as only suggestive. Obviously more research is needed before we can say that we understand the relationship between fantasy violence and the subsequent appearance of aggressiveness.

Another well-known investigation of the effect of television violence consisted of a longitudinal field study, in which information regarding television viewing habits and peer ratings of aggressiveness were gathered for nine-year-old children and again ten years later, when they were nineteen. Statistical analyses of the data indicated that nine-year-old boys who preferred to watch televised violence were also described by their peers as more aggressive than boys who tended to choose other types of programs. Furthermore, watching violent programs at age nine was also correlated with aggressiveness at nineteen, which the investigators interpreted to mean that "there is a probable causative influence of watching violent television programs in formative years on later aggression" (Eron et al., 1972). Although the researchers did not qualify this rather sweeping conclusion, a careful examination of their results indicates that if it is at all valid, it applies only to boys, for the correlations between girls' aggressiveness and their television viewing habits were essentially zero.

As we indicated above, common sense would suggest that watching televised violence *ought* to lead to heightened aggressiveness, but hard research evidence supporting this view continues to elude researchers.

social attraction

We turn now from the more negative side of middle childhood to pleasanter matters: the formation of social bonds among children. As we noted in our discussions of infancy and early childhood, social needs appear very early and quickly assume the status of major motives. In the earliest stages, the child's attention is focused on his parents, but by the middle years, the child's peers get an increasing amount of it.

Sociometric Studies

Jocob L. Moreno (1934) was the pioneer figure in studying patterns of attraction among individuals. His method, which he termed *sociometry*, consists essentially of asking individuals in a group whom they prefer to associate with in work and play activities, and whom they would prefer to avoid. The practice in most sociometric research, however, is to focus on the positive choices, inasmuch as the inclusion of negative choices adds little in the way of precision and reliability.

The basic research on the sociometric method was done some thirty years ago. One of the more important investigations was undertaken by Merl E. Bonney (1943) who conducted a longitudinal study of the stability or constancy of children's sociometric status in the second through the fifth grades in three schools. The bases of choice of acceptability varied from grade to grade, but in each there were from five to six bases of choice, including with whom to have their pictures taken, partner for a party, and to whom to give Christmas presents. The children were also asked the names of their best friends. A composite score was derived for each child. Bonney used a semilongitudinal approach, with most of the subjects tested in successive grades (although there was pupil population turnover). Consequently, correlation between general social acceptance at successive age levels was possible, giving him a measure of social acceptance constancy.

Between the sociometric measure of the second and third grades the correlation was .84; between the third and fourth and fourth and fifth grade it was, respectively, .77 and .67. A high degree of constancy in degree of social acceptability is exhibited from grade to grade. To emphasize this point, the magnitude of the correlations in social acceptability was approximately as large as that between intelligence test scores for the same grades (.75 to .86). In other words, social acceptability ratings are almost as reliable as intelligence test scores.

This constancy of social acceptability was checked by a study of children who transferred from one school to another where, naturally, they were unknown. Although the group was small, in every instance their social acceptance scores at the end of the year in the new school gave them very much the same degree of social acceptability they had had in their previous schools.

Sociometric studies also indicate how patterns of social acceptance shift during the years of middle childhood. Children during the earlier preschool years are not very selective when it comes to the sex of their playmates, although as we noticed in the study by Harper and Sanders (1975), which we mentioned in Chapter 10, there is a tendency even in nursery school for boys to prefer outdoor play and girls to play indoors. This tendency is by no means absolute, however, for little boys often play house with little girls, and girls frequently work out on the jungle gym. As the years go by, however, play activities become more sex-typed, and affiliations become less heterosexual. By the time children are about ten years old, patterns of acceptance have pretty much sorted themselves out along sex lines. Figure 14-6 consists of a sociogram of a typical fourth grade. It shows a strong tendency for boys to choose boys as friends, and girls to choose girls. Although four of the boys—Mort F., Victor, Brian S., and Mort D.—are chosen by girls, only one boy chooses a girl. The boys chosen by girls are also popular with other boys, but Joan, one of the four girls who chooses boys, is an isolate and is not chosen by any child. Joan is a tomboy and the teacher reports that she is very quiet. But when the teacher urges her, she can talk very intelligently.

Social Attraction and Similarity

It is a routine finding in social attraction studies that birds of a feather *do* flock together, and that like *does* attract like. To put this into more technical language, social attraction is strongly influenced by the perceived similarity between persons. And the factor that appears to

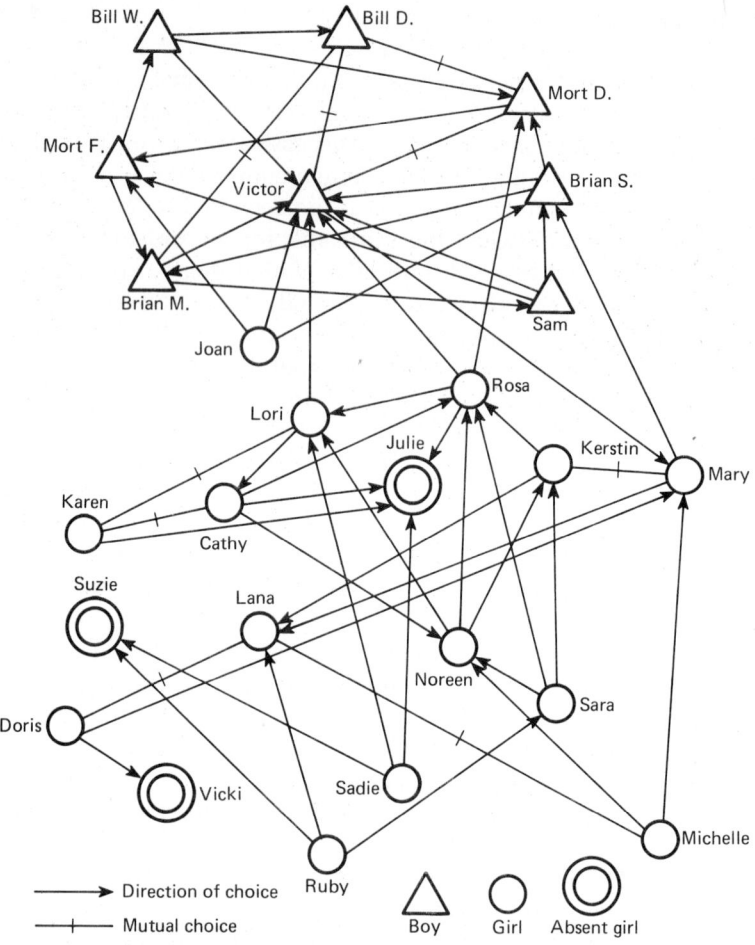

FIGURE 14-6. *Sociogram of a fourth grade, showing preference for own sex typical of this age.* (After Burke, 1971.)

count the most is perceived similarity in attitudes and values (Byrne, 1971).

Sometimes the similarity can be exaggerated. Davitz (1955) asked ten-year-olds at a summer camp to indicate the extent to which they liked two sports and to guess how well these sports were liked by the children at camp who were their highest and lowest sociometric choices. An analysis of the reports showed that the children tended to overestimate the similarity between their own preferences and those of the children who were their highest choices.

This finding may be interpreted as evidence of a fundamental, underlying wish to be similar to persons who are valued highly—in this instance, the members of the peer group, which at this age begins to assume major importance.

It is often observed that strong desires to be liked by others actually may interfere with social adjustment. Lahaderne and Jackson (1970) found that sixth-grade girls who scored high on a questionnaire measuring wanting-to-be-liked tendencies were inclined to withdraw from classroom activities generally. They tended to be inattentive and had poorer academic achievement than girls scoring low on the questionnaire. Very likely such tendencies go along with general feelings of inferiority and inadequacy, which in turn interfere with one's ability to interact with others.

Empathy and Social Awareness

It is quite likely that children who want desperately to be liked are so self-concerned and anxious that they are insensitive or unaware of the feelings and attitudes of others. What they lack is *empathy*—the ability to be sensitively aware of others' perceptions, values, motives, feelings, and attitudes.

One of the earlier but still valid studies of children's empathy was conducted by Dymond, Hughes and Raabe (1952). Picture-story cards, similar to those used in the TAT but adapted to the children's ages, were given to small groups of second- and sixth-graders. After being told a simple story that accompanied each picture, each child was asked a standard series of questions about the thoughts and feelings of the characters in the story. Potential for empathy was measured by the ease (lack of prodding or of the necessity for asking specific questions) with which the child could voice opinions about a pictured individual's thoughts and feelings. The mean score in empathy was significantly higher in the sixth than in the second grade. These results demonstrated that older children, as compared to younger, had more awareness of others' thoughts and feelings.

Research of social psychologists with empathy and social awareness indicates that development of these qualities can be facilitated by familiarity with the social roles of others (Stephan and Stephan, 1971). In one study, sixth graders were assigned roles to play in impromptu scenes: a friend who is sad and who talks to an adult about not being invited to a party; a peer who is angry with another student; and a mischievous student who is sent to the principal's office for misconduct. Experimenters then rated the performance of the children in terms of their sensitivity and awareness of the type of emotion that would be experienced by individuals in such situations—in other words, on their empathy. These ratings were then correlated with sociometric ratings assigned by the children's classmates. Results indicated that the children who demonstrated the most empathy in the role-playing scenes also were the most popular (Mouton, Bell, and Blake, 1956).

Friendship

Although empathy and social sensitivity play an important part in the social attraction of children for one another, becoming aware of the importance of personal traits as the basis for friendship is a gradual process that takes years. This fact is brought out in a survey conducted by Bigelow and La Gaipa (1975) of children in grades one through eight in Windsor, Ontario. Teachers asked the children to think about their best friends of the same sex and to write an essay about what they expected in these individuals that made them different from the other children they knew. The investigators then listed the dimensions or traits the children mentioned and tallied the number of times they appeared in the essays written at each grade level. Some of the dimensions and the grades at which they first appeared to a significant degree are listed in Table 14-2.

A review of the dimensions or criteria of friendship indicates that younger children are more concerned with simpler and more superficial aspects of personality or behavior. The fact that the children happen to be doing the same things together or living next to each other is crucial in second graders' friendships. Physical appearance and dress are also important at this age. A few years later there comes a concern for underlying and more psychologically significant traits: loyalty, trustworthiness, honesty, and integrity. For seventh graders, sharing the same activities is not enough: friends are also expected to share interests, attitudes, and values. There is also an interesting difference

TABLE 14-2. Grade Levels at Which Children Begin to Mention Important Bases or Dimensions of Friendship (data from Bigelow and La Gaipa, 1975)

Dimension	Grade Level
Friend as a giver of help	2
Sharing common activities	2
Propinquity (living nearby)	3
Stimulation value (e.g., physical attractiveness, dress)	3
Sharing organized play	3
Admiration	4
Loyalty and commitment	5
Genuineness	6
Friend as a receiver of help	6
Potential for intimacy	7
Sharing common interests	7
Sharing common attitudes and values	7

between second and seventh graders in that the younger children look upon friends as sources of help, and the older students find their ability to extend help to others to be important as well.

Another study of personality dimensions and friendship patterns focused on third and fourth graders, whose social skills were assessed by role-playing a situation in which a child was trying to make friends. The investigators also made careful, detailed, observations of the classroom activity of the children, recording the frequency and type of their interaction with one another, their activities while working alone, and so forth. In addition, sociometric scores were computed, based on each child's nominations for best friend, work companions, play companions, and the like.

Analyses of the data indicated that the children with the highest sociometric scores—the ones who were popular—had a much better idea of how to go about making friends than the less popular children did. In the classroom, popular children engaged in more positive reinforcement of others than did unpopular children, and received more in return. Popular children also tended to spend less time daydreaming, suggesting that they were more involved in the here-and-now and less interested in making use of this type of psychological escape (Gottman, Gonso, and Rasmussen, 1975).

The Beginnings of Prejudice

Psychologists and other behavioral scientists are unanimous in concluding that stereotyped, hostile, and rejecting attitudes toward members of other ethnic, racial, or religious groups are not inborn, but are learned or acquired from others, usually from adults and older children. This does not mean, however, that children are "born democratic" and hence automatically treat one another as equals until society tells them which personal characteristics are to be prized and which are to be devalued. The formation of status systems is a natural phenomenon that occurs in any grouping of human beings or infrahuman animals. Sociometric studies, of the type we have been discussing over the last few pages, make it clear that in any group of children some are better liked by others, are "overchosen," and hence are more popular, whereas others are less liked, are "underchosen," and hence are less popular.

Some of the attitudes or value systems underlying children's tendencies to be attracted to or to avoid other children are based partially on realistic considerations, as the research we have been discussing indicates. It is easy to understand how children will be attracted to a child who is outgoing and who has a well-developed set of social skills, and will avoid a child who is apathetic or hostile, or one whose social skills are limited. It is the responsibility of teachers and other adults placed in charge of children's groups to help the latter types of children become involved in ongoing group activities, where they can learn the skills and viewpoints that will gain them acceptance and help them become fully functioning members of groups and of society at large.

The kind of rejecting attitude that is based on superficial characteristics unrelated to interpersonal skills, values, or standards of social behavior is what concerns behavioral scientists the most. Such an attitude is prejudiced, in that the target child is "prejudged," even before he has responded in any way. Prejudices are, furthermore, likely to be stereotyped, in the sense that they are rigid and are insulated from correction and disconfirmation.

An ingenious study demonstrating that prejudicial attitudes are learned early in school years was conducted by Lerner, Karabenick, and Meisels (1975) with children in kindergarten and the primary grades. An experimenter showed each child a feltboard and told him that they were to play a game of "Coming close to things." He then placed a picture of a tree on the left side of the board and a picture of an average child of the appropriate sex on the right side. The child was then permitted to practice moving the child's picture any distance he wished from the tree and a number of other targets.

In the experimental phases of the investigation, the experimenter successively placed pictures of three types of "target" children on the board: *endomorphs,* or plump children; *mesomorphs,* or children of average build; and *ectomorphs,* or children of slender build. Both sexes were represented, making six target pictures in all.

The dependent variable was the *social distance,* measured in centimeters, that the subject placed between the picture representing himself and the picture of the target child.

Figure 14-7 shows that the children placed the most social distance between the picture representing themselves and the pictures representing the plump or endomorphic children. The amount of social distance between the subject's picture and all targets increased with each grade level from the first grade onward, but the avoidance or rejection of the plump child, expressed in terms of social distance, increased even more. Thin children and average-build children were apparently regarded as quite similar, however, for social distances were less. These findings suggest that our culture tends to express more prejudice toward fat people than toward thin ones, that even kindergarten children have learned this type of prejudice, and that the degree of prejudice increases during the middle years of childhood.

The second set of graphs, Figure 14-8, present data on the stereotyped attitudes that boys and girls express toward their own and the opposite sex. The greater prejudice is expressed by boys toward girls, but it is clear that the feeling is to a large degree a mutual one. We noted earlier that sex-role identity appears quite early in life, as does preference for sex-typed activities. The Lerner, Karabenick, and Meisels study indicates that boys and girls fortify these sex stereotypes with prejudiced

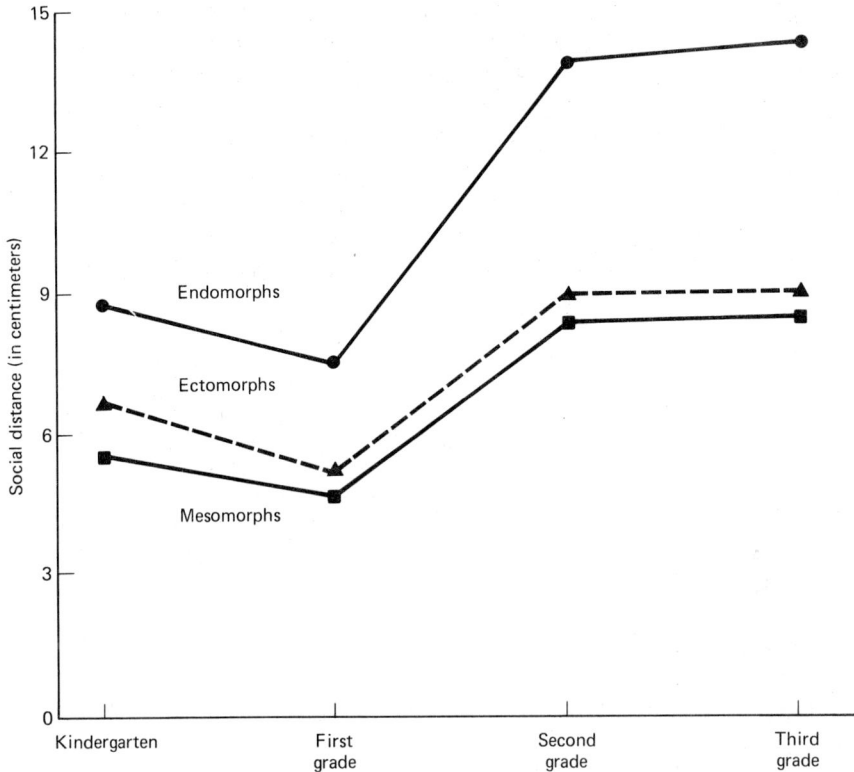

FIGURE 14-7. *Social distance placed by children in kindergarten through grade 3 between figures representing themselves and those representing children who are endomorphic (plump), ectomorphic (thin or slender), or mesomorphic (of average build). (Data from Lerner, Karabenick, and Meisels, 1975.)*

attitudes that make communication and mutual understanding between the sexes difficult.

Like many interpersonal and intergroup attitudes, prejudice is mutually reinforcing. The expression of hostility on the part of one group evokes hostile expressions from the target group—reinforcing, in turn the hostility of the first group, who now feel that they were justified in their initial attitudes toward the target group. Thus are self-fulfilling prophecies maintained.

Ethnic prejudice. Behavioral scientists have been giving prejudice a great deal of attention in recent decades because of its divisiveness. It breaks down the social bonds, sets one group against another, and makes cooperation and collaboration in matters of mutual concern difficult or impossible. Racial prejudice has been a matter of special concern, although other ethnic differences—linguistic ones, for example—have also become the subject of both legal action and research.

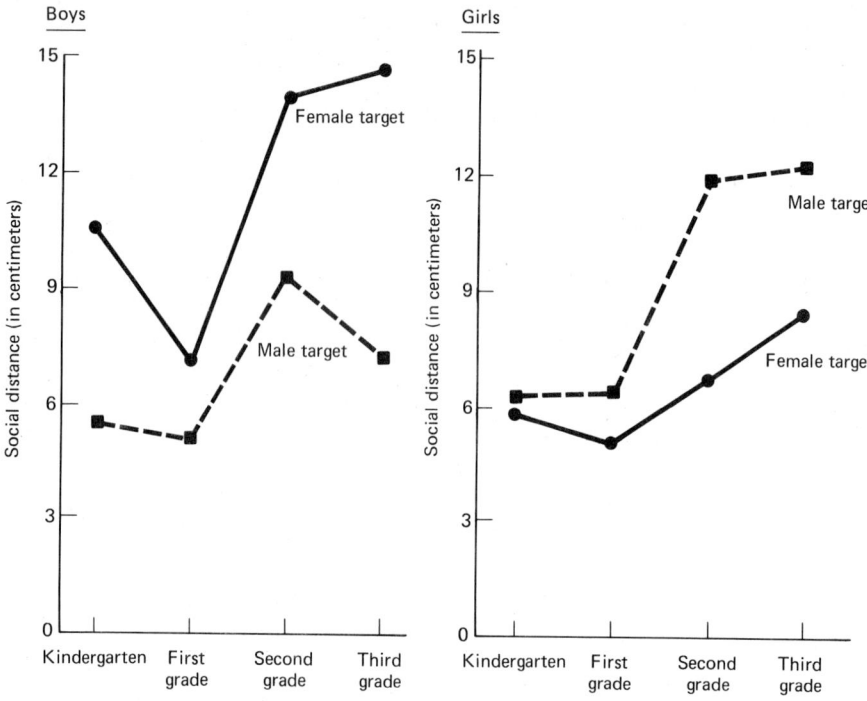

FIGURE 14-8. Social distance placed by boys and girls in kindergarten through grade 3 between figures representing themselves and those representing children of the opposite sex. (Data from Lerner, Karabenick, and Meisels, 1975.)

Children are aware of racial differences quite early, although this does not mean that such awareness is necessarily prejudiced. In one experiment, white and black children aged three to five, from low-income homes, were placed in small play groups. Half the groups were all black or all white; half were evenly divided between the races. The experimenter, who was black, gave each group hand puppets and blocks and told them to go ahead and play. One black and one white observer coded each child's behavior in terms of whether it showed initiation of positive social activity, positive response, or negative response. An examination of the data indicated that children in racially similar groups not only initiated more social acitivity, but also made more negative responses, than did the racially mixed groups. The investigators concluded that children this age are more inhibited in racially mixed groups than in homogeneous ones. The important point is, however, that inasmuch as children responded differently in racially mixed groups, they must have been aware of racial differences and that this awareness had an inhibiting effect on their functioning (Harris and Braun, 1971).

The way in which children who are the targets of prejudice take on a negative self-image was explored by Epstein and Komorita (1966) in a much-discussed study. The investigators asked black children to look at some photographic slides that depicted children who had been labelled as "Piraneans," a fictitious designation. Half the subjects saw slides of white children; the other half were shown slides of black children. The subjects then filled out a social-distance questionnaire that solicited their attitudes toward the fictitious group—whether they would want a Piranean as a friend, whether they would want to marry a Piranean when they grew up, and the like. An analysis of their responses indicated that the black children who had seen slides of white children had favorable attitudes toward "Piraneans," whereas those black children who had seen slides of black children expressed negative attitudes.

The investigators interpreted their findings to mean that black children learn self-rejecting attitudes that reflect the prevailing prejudices of the white majority. These attitudes were apparently picked up from the children's parents, inasmuch as the children reported that their parents' reaction to Piraneans would be similar to their own.

The results of the Epstein-Komorita study are consistent with some earlier studies in which black children were shown a black doll and a white doll and were asked such questions as which one they preferred, which was the good doll, and which was the bad doll. Investigators found that the children tended to value the white doll more highly than the black doll (Clark and Clark, 1947). More recent studies, however, suggest that attitudes may have changed. Harris and Braun (1971) conducted a similar investigation with seven- and eight-year-old black children who were attending interracial schools in a middle-class suburb and in the inner city. The majority of the children of both groups preferred the black doll and rejected the white doll. The children's self-esteem, as measured by a simple questionnaire read aloud to them by a black experimenter, was also positively correlated with their tendency to value the black doll higher than the white one.

Attitudes of white children may be changing as well. Cantor and Paternite (1973) asked second- and third-graders in an Iowa school to choose who "would do a bad thing" and who "would do a good thing" when shown a pair of photographs of boys, one black and one white. There was no tendency for the children to choose a boy of one race or the other in response to either question.

An experiment in which boys had an opportunity to observe models engaging in friendly behavior may point the way whereby ethnic prejudice can be reduced and firmer social bonds be forged. Zimmerman and Brody (1975) observed the interaction between racially mixed pairs of fifth-grade boys and noted the extent to which they faced each other, made eye contact, and talked. The boys then saw a televised sequence in which a black and a white boy played together with some blocks either in a warm and friendly manner or in a very distant, cool, and detached manner. Each pair of boys was then left alone for a five-minute period with a similar assortment of blocks, while the experimenters observed them through a one-way mirror and scored their behavior.

An analysis of the interaction scores indicated that the boys who had seen the warm and friendly sequence were physically closer together in their play and cooperated more than the boys did who had seen the cool version. The investigators concluded that a vicarious experience like watching a televised sequence can influence play patterns and promote prosocial behavior, such as cooperation and physical closeness. They also noted that their results were consistent with the philosophy of televised programs such as *Sesame Street* and *The Electric Company*—programs that feature minority-group members filling important roles, in which they interact cooperatively and supportively with other members of the cast.

the school

The amount of time a North American child spends in school is witness to its importance in our Western, urbanized culture. Between the ages of 6 and 18 a child spends from four to six hours a day, five days a week, 36 weeks a year in the classroom. This amounts to about 180 days a year, and in Northern Europe the school year may run 220 days and more. The number of years students spend in school stands at an all-time high. Although the figures vary from one state to another and are higher in urban areas, the typical adolescent today graduates from high school and also spends some time in college or technical training.[3]

In North America, the school's task has also broadened tremendously during the last hundred years or so. During the last century, schools were concerned largely with imparting certain information and skills. Today, the educator's concern for the "whole child" has permeated the educational program to the point where it is involved in students' personal, social, economic, political, and health development, and programs concerned only with the imparting of information and skills are now considered to be "less than minimal."

The observations made by Robert J. Havighurst (1953) a generation ago regarding the role of the school are as true today as they were then. He noted that Americans use their schools for a wider variety of purposes than any other society. American schools are expected to

---

[3] Current Population Survey data from the U.S. Census Bureau estimate that in 1974 more than three fourths of persons aged 25 to 29 had at least finished high school, and more than a fifth of this age group had completed four years of college or more.

cooperate with the other training institutions of society—the family, the church, industry, and youth-serving organizations—in helping young people learn physical and recreational skills, select and prepare for occupations, prepare for marriage, and learn a scale of values. Basic to all these are the tasks of social development, and American educators consider the teaching of these tasks a major part of the school's responsibility.

Havighurst observed that there is no developmental task of children or adolescents that the school can completely ignore, inasmuch as these tasks are so interrelated that difficulties in classroom tasks often cause difficulties in tasks that are less obviously the responsibility of the school. Failure in academic tasks, for example, may result in failure to achieve a satisfactory vocational adjustment.

It is common knowledge that teachers not only share the views that Havighurst delineated but also that they are actively engaged in implementing them in the classroom. How the teacher serves as an agent of socialization as reflected by a sample of certain relevant research results concerns us here.

The teacher chooses certain activities in preference to others. He or she sets up certain standards and not others and thus gives direction to the group. The teacher, of course, makes choices on the basis of

Whether they like it or not, teachers are the official representatives of adult society and are expected to see that acceptable standards of conduct are maintained in the classroom and on the playground. Sometimes this role interferes with the other roles they must play, especially those that are instructive and emotionally supportive.

Although the school is a highly structured, formalized, and to some extent artificial, environment, it is, for better or worse, society's major attempt to move children out of the family home and into the mainstream of life. The attempts of teachers and school authorities to carry out their tasks in this important undertaking meet with varied success. Some children react with enthusiasm, others with apathy. Some respond with diligence, others with anxiety. Some become interested and involved, and others are merely bored.

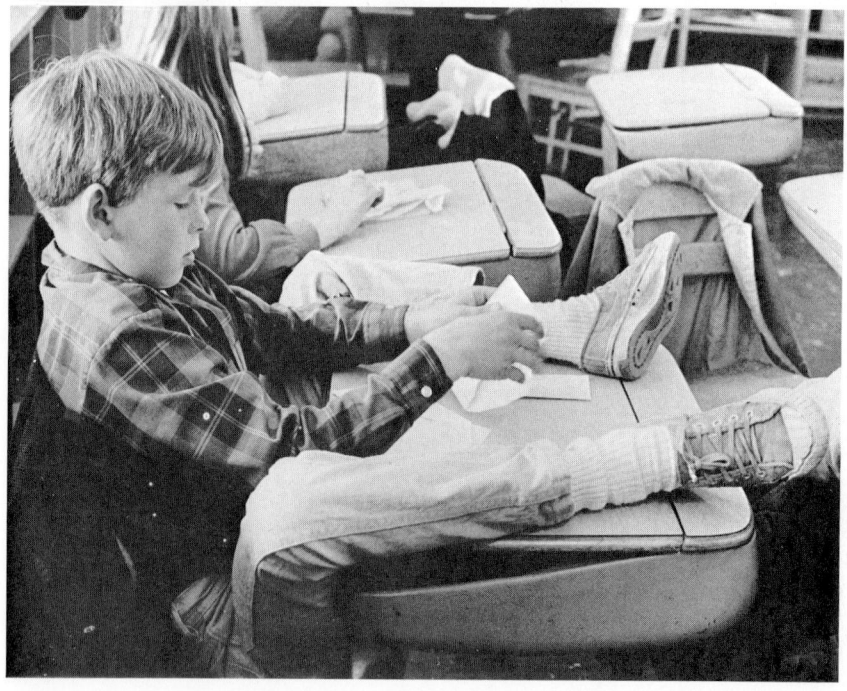

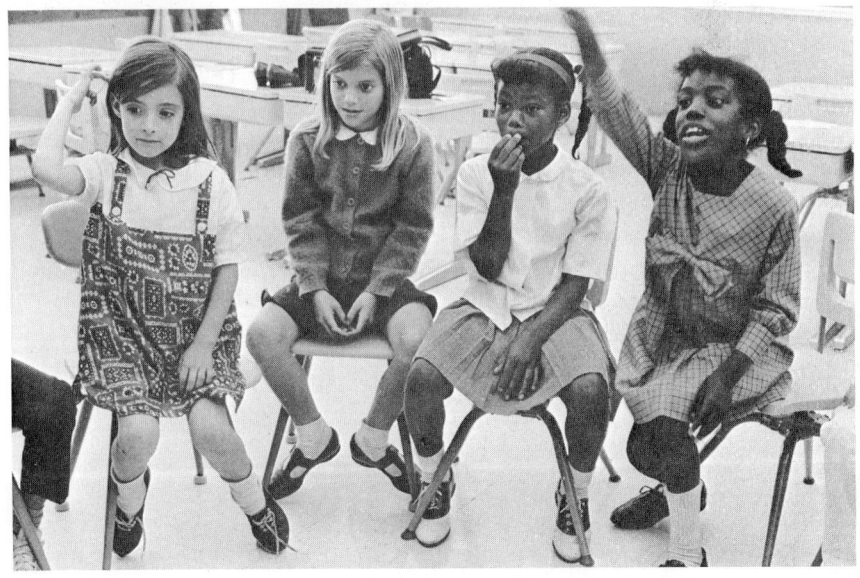

conception of what children are like, how they should behave, and what they should learn; also involved is the teacher's own system of values—most often that of the middle class. The desirability of correct speech, politeness, cleanliness, neatness, and respect for property and thrift are imparted along with more academic information.

The teacher proceeds to socialize the child, using much the same methods as does the mother, and setting up standards of conduct to which the child is expected to conform. In addition to teaching subject matter, the teacher performs a variety of socializing practices. For example, individual children in the school group are helped by a variety of consciously recognized devices—creating situations in which it would be possible to see a previously objectionable child in a new role, getting a child previously ignored to contribute a talent which the other children have not recognized, helping a child to accept the teacher as a person by accepting the child as a person of worth, hoping these will lead to peer acceptance.

The teacher uses rewards and punishments in socialization efforts. Not only are these incentives employed at a formal level, as symbolized by the "gold star" or "staying after school"; they are also used in a variety of more subtle and much broader ways. Any teacher behavior that students regard positively may become a reinforcement that helps socialize children—a nod, a smile, a "that's fine," or merely giving a student full attention by listening. Some teachers, of course, seem unaware that the subtle approach works best and attempt to use more direct methods that hinder more than they help. Consider, for example, the following situation:

> Ms. Mejia looked up from the papers she was grading and said: "James, stop talking to Dick. You're both supposed to be doing Project 7 in your workbook."
> Without stopping to catch her breath, she addressed herself to the entire class:
> "Some of you kids are cooperating, but some aren't at all. Linda is cooperating just fine and doing what she's supposed to be doing, and Robert is, too, but Sheryl is just looking out the window and hasn't even opened her workbook. Now, you kids know this is a classroom and not Disneyland. This is a classroom and we're all supposed to be working. When we're working, we're not wasting time or getting into trouble. Then we're all good citizens. Good citizens do what they're supposed to do and don't make noise or waste time in other silly ways. We can't learn and be good citizens when nobody's paying attention and it gets very noisy."
> And again, without pausing:
> "James, you still haven't got started on the project."

Behavior Modification

Admonitions of the foregoing type help socialize some children, but others ignore it, and a few rebel openly. Some classroom groups, in fact, seem impervious to any attempts at direction and control. Terry Borton (1970) described a class

> in which eighteen children seemed to be devoting all their energies to massacring one another, destroying school equipment and breaking the sound barrier. They were not only oblivious to observers but did not even acknowledge the existence of their teacher. The teacher could not prevent the children from disassembling desks, tearing up classmates' papers, hurling books across the room, and running around the halls at will. I saw no evidence of friendship among the children. In fact, during one half-hour's observation each of the eighteen children was hit or kicked at least once, ten of the children being aggressors. (Reprinted by permission).

The observer who made these comments took over this class and placed it on a "behavior modification" schedule, using principles of operant learning. The regimen she used called for the rewarding of socialized and socializing behaviors and the ignoring of misbehavior. (The rationale for ignoring misbehavior is that any kind of attention, positive or negative, is recognized by misbehaving children as a form of reinforcement that only serves to strengthen it.) Acceptable behavior was reinforced with points that could be traded in at a "store," which stocked a range of tangible rewards, such as candy, puzzles, model planes, comics and outings. The "prices" of rewards at the store were scaled in proportion to their educational relevance, as well as their attractiveness to the children: lollipops and gum were 110 points, and a trip to the zoo was 450 points. Children earned points for doing their assigned work, raising their hands when they wanted to talk, being on time, and following rules. A child typically earned between 20 to 100 points a morning, plus extra "teacher reinforcements" in the form of verbal praise and hugs.

Immediately the room became calmer and began to change, as most of the children busily began to accumulate points.

Some children rebelled, however. One boy strutted up and down, shouting: "I don't want any more points; stop giving them to me!" The other children ignored him completely, and, after a period of engaging in this unreinforced behavior, he sneaked into his seat and began to work furiously in order to accumulate points.

The experience described above is not an isolated incident. Operant conditioning and other behavior-modification methods have been used successfully in many other classrooms to bring order out of chaos and to get children back on the educational track. They have also been employed to eliminate or reduce the severity of a wide range of behavior problems in children and adults.

In one situation, a group of mentally retarded but educable children aged 6 to 15 exhibited unruly behavior on a school bus, getting out of their seats, running up and down the aisle, and leaning out of the bus windows. The problem was not only an exasperating one to the adults in charge, but exposed the children to obvious dangers.

The method employed was one termed *group time-out procedure* by specialists in behavior modification. The children were told that rock music would be played over the sound system as long as all of them were in their seats, but that the music would be stopped for five seconds if anyone left his seat. The result was a marked reduction in out-of-seat behavior (Ritschl, Mongrella, and Presbie, 1972).

Praise and Criticism

Behavior modification is a special skill that can be acquired by teachers and parents who wish to set up the proper controls and follow through with appropriate reinforcements. It is not clear, however, how it can be integrated with a regular school program on a routine basis. A busy teacher who has two or three, or more, activity groups going on simultaneously in the classroom is likely to have enough to do managing and directing the complex situation for which he or she is responsible and reinforcing children done when he or she can. Still another problem is that children react in different ways to rewards (positive reinforcements). Cotler and Palmer (1971) discovered a considerable degree of variability among fourth, fifth, and sixth graders when they used positive reinforcement (Praise), negative reinforcement (Criticism), or no reinforcement in test situations in which the children read printed material aloud. Children were divided into groups in terms of their test-anxiety scores, and were further subdivided in terms of whether their school achievement was higher than would be expected from their IQ (overachievers) or lower than would be expected (underachievers).

Cotler and Palmer found, as might be expected, that girls generally made fewer errors in oral readings than boys, and boys' performances showed the highest degree of variability. Although one might also expect that the poorest performances would occur with children in the Criticism condition, the no reinforcement condition actually produced the most errors for about half the children, and most of the boys in the Criticism condition did better than those in the Praise condition, as Figure 14-9 shows. This suggests that for some children, negative attention actually may stimulate learning better than positive attention or no attention at all.

It is also a routine finding that lower-class children and middle-class children respond differently to symbolic rewards, such as school marks, and to tangible reinforcements, such as money, toys, and candy. An experiment by Cradler and Goodwin (1971) yielded typical results. Their samples consisted of second and sixth graders, who were classified as lower or middle class on the basis of their parents' occupational status. Each child was asked to make up sentences using the past-tense form of common verbs. As the child uttered these sentences, an

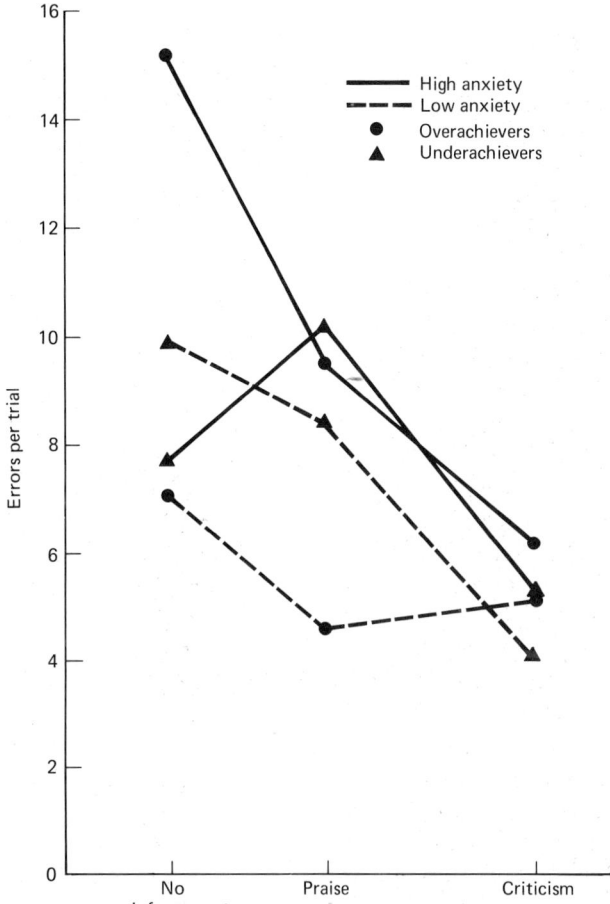

FIGURE 14-9. *Effect of three experimental conditions in eliminating reading errors for elementary school boys, classified according to their test anxiety and their records of school achievement.* (After Cotler and Palmer, 1971.)

experimenter reinforced the use of the pronoun "they" by (1) giving the child a material reward in the form of an M&M candy; (2) praising the child by saying "good"; or (3) rewarding the child symbolically, by writing plus marks on a sheet of paper in full view of the child.

The investigators hypothesized that the middle-class students would utter more "theys" in response to the symbolic rewards of the plus marks or to praise, whereas the lower-class children would respond best to the material reward. Their hypotheses were confirmed, as Figure 14-10 indicates. The most marked effects were for the lower-class second graders and the middle-class sixth graders. The middle-class sixth graders outperformed all groups in response to the symbolic

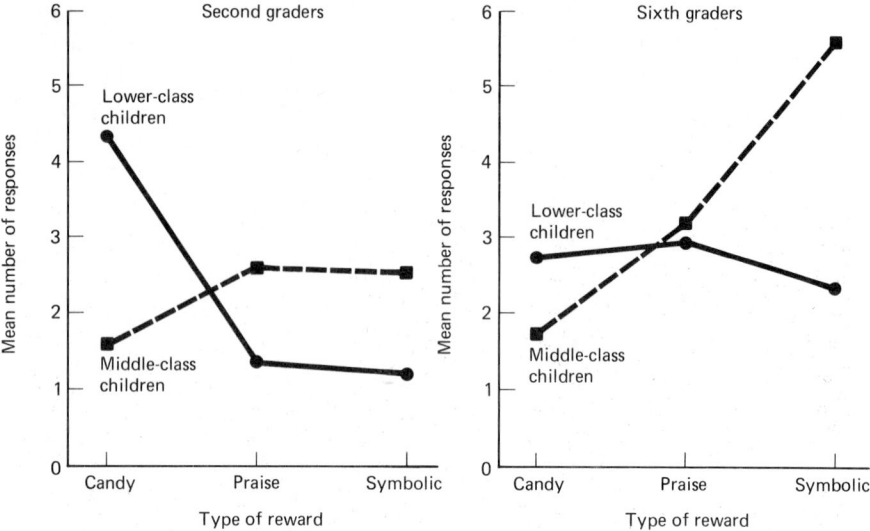

FIGURE 14-10. *Differences in performance of middle-class and lower-class second and sixth graders in response to material rewards, praise, and symbolic rewards.* (Data from Cradler and Goodwin, 1971.)

reward—the plus marks—but were unmoved by the M&Ms. The lower-class second graders were strongly motivated by the M&Ms, but were uninterested in praise or symbolic rewards. On the other hand, neither group of second graders cared much about praise or symbolic rewards, whereas M&Ms had little appeal either to middle-class second graders or to lower-class sixth graders.

The study indicates, in other words, that not only are there differences in the way children from different family backgrounds respond to rewards, but that there are marked differences in their responses at different age levels.

What the Cradler-Goodwin, as well as the Cotler-Palmer, studies clearly show is that there are no hard and fast rules with respect to "the best way to motivate children." A teacher has to develop some kind of sense of the characteristic ways in which the children in his or her class think, feel, and respond, recognizing that what is a reward for one child may be ignored or even resented by another. Such complexities are what make teaching one of the most demanding of the professions.

Teachers' Attitudes Toward Children's Misbehavior

Do teachers really understand the behavior of children? Or are they so preoccupied with making assignments, evaluating achievement, and keeping order that they merely react to it in terms of whether it does or does not fit in with the educational program as scheduled?

Most teachers are, of course, sensitive to the nuances of students' learning-related behavior, but they are also officially or unofficially representatives of adult society, and are usually inclined to react to all aspects of student behavior in keeping with the standards that prevail in the community that employs them. In addition, they must monitor the deportment of twenty, thirty, forty, and even more children at one time. The wish is often expressed, however, that teachers should be more sensitive, more psychologically aware of the meaning of children's behavior, than are most adults. The teacher is considered to be, after all, a professional person who is expected to have a better than average degree of expertise in dealing with children.

Although many have expressed confidence in the perceptiveness of teachers, others have expressed doubts, and these doubts have led to research. A half century ago, E. K. Wickman (1928) conducted an investigation which, initially at least, seemed to give support to the doubters. Wickman's approach was that of securing ratings of mental-hygiene specialists and teachers on the relative seriousness of various specified child behavior symptoms. The specialists and the teachers rated the relative seriousness of the same behavior item quite differently. The results were interpreted as showing that teachers rated as more serious those symptoms associated with noisier, more rebellious, disobedient, outgoing behavior—behavior that threatened the orderliness of the classroom—whereas the specialists rated as more serious the less disruptive symptoms associated with withdrawal, anxiety, and sensitivity, attaching little importance to almost all of those stressed by teachers.

It is evident that teachers were defining seriousness in terms of a moralistic point of view, with stress on aggressiveness against persons and property. Many of the problems the teachers placed as most serious were, in one way or another, challenges to their authority in the classroom. Evidently, seriousness was equated with being a serious threat to the smooth-running functioning of the classroom. But before we become too critical of the attitude expressed by the teachers, it is well to remember that the mental hygienists had a different frame of reference, being much more concerned with behavior that had an ominous implication for the child's future emotional and personal development. The withdrawing type of symptom, unsocialness, as well as depression, suspicion, fearfulness, and sensitiveness, have been demonstrated to be most difficult to overcome in treatment and sometimes to be the early indicators of more serious forms of maladjustment.

The results seemed to reflect discredit on the competence of the teachers, or so the Wickman study was widely interpreted. Actually, it had many serious defects, as Beilin (1959) and Beilin and Werner (1957) have shown, rendering the results much less conclusive than they were interpreted to be. It should be noted that the teacher's job of communicating skills and values can be accomplished only in an orderly environment. The aggressive child disrupts the class; at least the withdrawing child does not do this.

The attitudes and values of teachers in recent years—particularly true of the more experienced teachers (Tolor, Scarpetti, and Lane, 1967—have become more like those of the clinicians. The need to impose structure and order on a classroom group, however, does lead teachers to adopt a no-nonsense approach to their work that is quite different from the nonteacher's view of what the ideal teacher-pupil relationship should be, and that probably varies considerably from views held by students who enroll in teacher-education programs. Supervisors of practice teachers are, of course, highly aware of the personal qualities needed for classroom management. In one study, the supervisors tended to characterize the ideal female elementary teacher as being *dominant, persevering, persistent, serious, opinionated, ambitious, demanding, logical, rigid, clear-thinking, determined,* and *responsible*. This view was in marked contrast to students in introductory education courses, who were more likely to characterize the ideal teacher as being *curious, affectionate, careless, easygoing, unconventional, dreamy, understanding, irresponsible, cheerful, natural, individualistic,* and *thoughtful*. Those students who had some experience in practice teaching, however, had an image of the ideal teacher somewhat closer to that held by their supervisors. This finding suggests that their attitudes had been reoriented by the give and take of the actual classroom situation or that they had been using their supervisors as models. Probably both explanations apply (Uchiyama and Lindgren, 1971).

Children's Reactions to the School Experience

Entrance into school is an experience that is exciting, thrilling, stressful, and anxiety-provoking. For many children, it is the first time that they have had to conform to a group pattern imposed by a single adult who is in charge of too many children to react to each child as an individual. Children are told to listen and not all speak at once. When the time comes for art, each child gets paper and crayons whether he feels like drawing or not. As one child said, "It is awful; all you do is mind all day long," and on another day he commented, "It is really awful. All you do is sit and sit and sit" (Murphy, Murphy, and Newcomb, 1937).

This new pattern of group conformity is moderated somewhat in some schools, but no teacher, no matter how humane and how sympathetic, can respond to or even be aware of each individual child simultaneously. As a consequence, she must make use of teacher-to-group rather than teacher-to-child methods.

The school is a source of frustration as well as of satisfaction. The child must conform or suffer the consequences. If his experiences are too painful, if he is unable to satisfy at least some of his needs, he will reject the school and do everything he can to fight off its influence, awaiting only the day he is of age to leave. In the meantime, he struggles against the teachers, and those children who accept the school become his natural enemies.

How do children react to the demands and pressures of the school? Any school is likely to have things to enjoy and things to complain about. Perhaps the best way to get some perspective on this matter is to look at data comparing American children's experiences with children in another culture. Berk, Rose, and Stewart (1970) replicated a study done in England with nine- and ten-year-old children, who had been asked how they felt about their relationship with their teachers, their class, doing well in school, school work, themselves, conforming or nonconforming behavior in class, and school in general.

Results showed that American children, in general, expressed more positive attitudes about school than British children did. This was true of both middle- and lower-class students, and students at all ability levels. As might be expected, girls in both countries tended to express a more positive attitude toward school than boys, especially with respect to these factors: relationship with the teacher, attitude toward the class, importance of doing well, and conforming behavior in class. These sex differences were more marked with American children.

Differences in social class and ability were more likely to affect the attitudes of British children than American ones. Middle-class or high-IQ British children were more favorable toward school than were working-class children, but there were virtually no SES differences with American children.

Another study comparing the attitudes of children in American schools at various SES levels was conducted by Neale and Proshek (1967). They found a general decline in positive attitudes toward the school during grades four, five, and six, the more significant drop being in favorable attitudes toward *my teacher, my classroom, my school books, following rules, working arithmetic problems, talking in front of class, having to keep quiet, fighting with other children,* and *stealing things.* In fact, the attitudes expressed by the sixth graders were generally more negative than those of fourth graders; even *mother* and *father* were regarded less favorably. It is interesting to note that *reading a book* suffered the least decline of any of the stimulus variables toward which children expressed attitudes. Except for *fighting with other children* and *stealing things,* boys' attitudes toward school were less favorable than those of girls—a routine finding.

There were a number of differences in the reactions of students in the two SES levels that Neale and Proshek tested. As Figure 14-11 shows, there was no over-all difference in attitude toward *mother,* but middle-class children regarded *father* and *college student* more favorably.

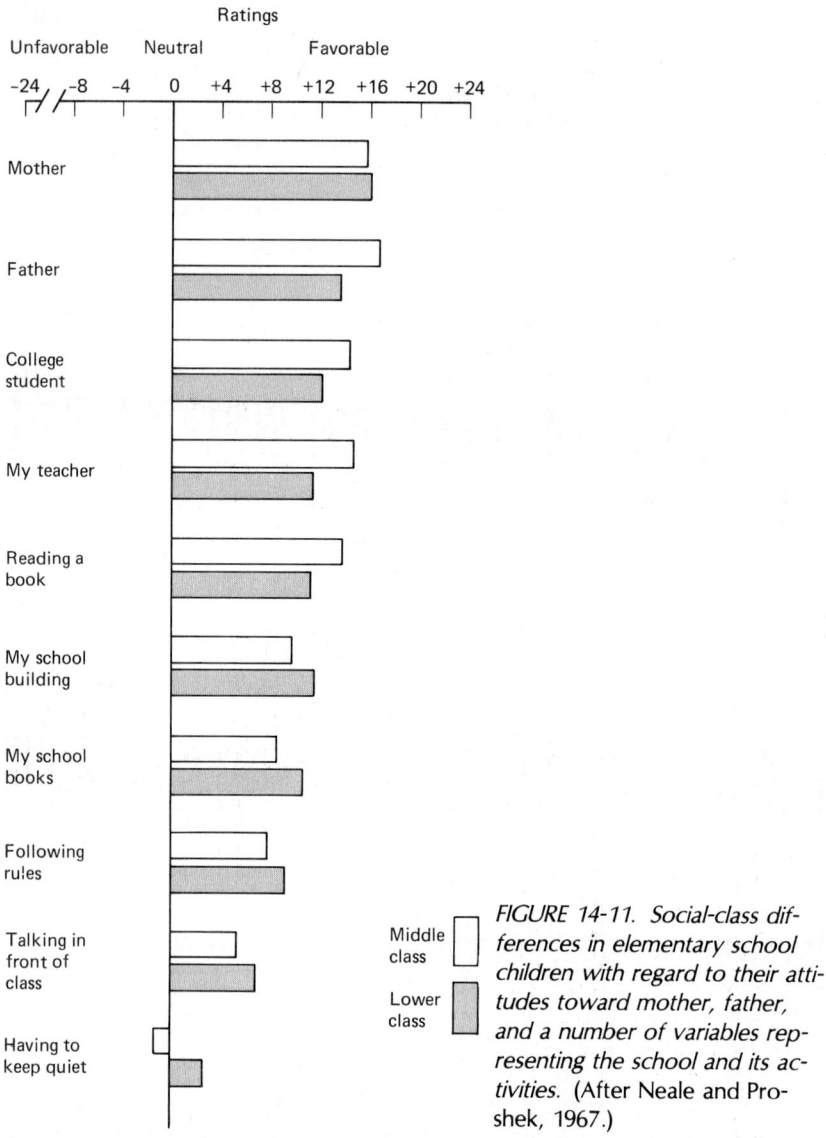

FIGURE 14-11. Social-class differences in elementary school children with regard to their attitudes toward mother, father, and a number of variables representing the school and its activities. (After Neale and Proshek, 1967.)

These differences are in the expected direction: in the more democratic middle-class families, fathers are less of a threat, and the expectation that one go to college is not only accepted but is looked forward to eagerly. Except for *my teacher* and *reading a book*, however, lower-class children regarded school more positively than middle-class children. Some of the differences deserve comment. The visible aspects of education are valued by lower-class children more than some of its activities: *my school books* gets a higher rating than *reading a book*. Conforming to discipline is also more attractive to lower-class children:

following rules and *having to keep quiet* are valued positively. This latter finding makes sense in terms of the fact that the lives of lower-class children are more likely to be chaotic and unpredictable; for many of them, school is the only place where they can count on the security of an orderly, dependable routine.

We should note, however, that although children's evaluations of school decline somewhat with increasing maturity, their reactions are generally positive. Berk, Rose, and Stewart observed that their American subjects, by and large, responded positively to questions about their school and were willing to give it the benefit of the doubt, irrespective of SES and IQ differences. The ratings in Figure 14-11 are also almost entirely positive. Even *following rules* gets a favorable endorsement. Such findings should be heartening and supportive to teachers who find themselves being stricter than they would like to be, who work hard at the task of making their classrooms interesting "laboratories for learning," and who generally try their best to live up to everyone's expectations of them.

summary

In North American culture, the major influence during middle and late childhood comes from the peer group. Children in this age group leave home (literally and figuratively) to a much greater degree than younger children. The time spent at home declines to its lowest level during adolescence. The peer group teaches the child complex social skills he could not acquire at home. It is able to exert influence because it provides the child with an environment that is more exciting and often more attractive than that available at home, an environment in which the child can achieve status and mutual acceptance. The influence of the peer group is expressed through its social norms and behavior models as well as by its power to accept or reject children. American children appear to be more influenced by peer norms than by adult standards of behavior, unlike Russian and Hindu children, for instance. The mere presence of other children has an effect of arousal, which in turn seems to facilitate misbehavior.

Boys are more likely to engage in aggressive behavior than are girls. Emotional arousal appears to facilitate aggressive behavior in boys and prosocial behavior in girls. Hostility, which usually precedes or accompanies acts of aggression, may occur in subsurface or covert forms—stubbornness, for example. An analysis of the fantasy material produced by underachievers suggests that they are covertly hostile. A great deal of current interest has been directed toward the influence of violence and aggression in the mass media. Bandura, Ross, and Ross showed children films of adult aggression and vigorous nonaggressive play. Their results suggest that any kind of vigorous stimulus may incite aggressive responses in boys, who are more prone to such behavior than girls. Feshbach and Singer noted that the opposite effect when they controlled the television viewing behavior of several groups of boys. The boys who saw violent and aggressive programs had fewer fights of all kinds. Berkowitz cites research that comes to conclusions that are opposite to those of Feshbach and Singer and more consistent with common sense. A longitudinal study showed that nine-year-olds who preferred violent television programs were likely to be rated as aggressive by their peers at that age, and also ten years later. The investigators' interpretation that childhood exposure to televised violence leads to adolescent aggressiveness must be qualified, inasmuch as the effect applies to boys but not to girls.

Patterns of social attractiveness in children's groups can be studied by sociometric methods—by asking individual children which of the members of the group they prefer as friends, as co-workers, and the like. Sociometric scores, over time, are about as reliable as intelligence test scores. There is a tendency for children to be attracted to those whom they perceive to be similar to themselves—members of their own sex, for example. Empathy—the ability to be aware of the feelings and attitudes of others—can be measured by projective tests and by role-playing tasks. It plays an important part in popularity and in friendship. Younger children are more likely to base friendship on superficial aspects of behavior; older children realize that friendship rests on deeper, more fundamental factors. Children who are popular are likely to have a better command of social skills than are less popular children. Children's groups have status systems, just as adult groups do. By the time children are in kindergarten they are expressing prejudice against some kinds of children—those who are endomorphic or plump, for example, as well as against members of the opposite sex. Children also exhibit awareness of race differences at a relatively early age. Ethnic prejudices—which tend to be directed against oneself as well as against others—appear to be learned. They can be modified through social-learning procedures—through viewing biracial pairs of models who behave in friendly and cooperative ways, for example.

In North America, the school's task has broadened tremendously during the last century. Schools are expected to help young people learn physical and recreational skills, prepare for marriage, and learn a scale of values. The teacher serves as an agent of socialization, reinforcing certain activities in preference to others. Any teacher behavior that students regard positively, from a smile to a gold star, may become a reinforcement that helps socialize children. Some contemporary methods, notably the "behavior modification" techniques, make use of this fact and attempt to extend control over all such sources of reinforcement. By ignoring misbehavior, rewarding acceptable behavior, and sometimes establishing an "economy" or system of tangible rewards as well, psychologists and teachers can reduce the severity of a wide range of classroom behavior problems. Some research, however, shows considerable variability among children, especially boys, in the way they respond to various reinforcements. In one study, boys tended to make the most errors in reading under No Reinforcement conditions, fewer errors under Praise conditions, and the fewest under Criticism conditions. For one subgroup of boys, Praise produced the greatest number of errors.

Wickman compared the ratings of what teachers and mental-hygiene specialists considered to be serious child behavior symptoms. It seemed that teachers felt that behavior that interferred with the smooth-running functioning of the classroom was serious, whereas the clinicians were most concerned with symptoms of depression or withdrawal. In recent years, however, teacher attitudes have become more like those of the clinicians. The supervisors of practice teachers tend to characterize the ideal female elementary school teacher as being persevering, dominant, ambitious, rigid, and responsible. This is in contrast to the view of students in introductory education courses, who characterize the ideal teacher as curious, affectionate, individualistic, easygoing, and understanding.

The entrance into school is both exciting and anxiety provoking. The child is forced to conform to impersonal group standards, perhaps for the first time. A comparative study of American and British youngsters indicated that American children tend to view school more positively than British children do. Another study shows that the attitudes of American children toward school become more negative with each succeeding grade from grades four to six, but this trend is consistent with their attitudes toward their parents as well. Unexpectedly, lower-class children regard most aspects of school more favorably than middle-class children, perhaps because its structure gives them needed security. In the main, however, the attitudes of the children toward most aspects of their school experience are positive, even regarding such matters as "following rules."

V

adolescence

fifteen

Physical, Mental, and Moral Development

*Just at the age 'twixt boy and youth,
When thought is speech, and speech is truth.*
— WALTER SCOTT

There is no characteristic of adolescence whose germ may not be found in childhood, and whose consequences may not be traced in maturity and old age.
— FREDERICK TRACY (1920)

Adolescence: Where It Begins, but Where Does It End?

Adolescence may be defined—simplistically, perhaps—as the period or stage of development that separates childhood from adulthood.

Few would quarrel with such a definition. It seems obvious that children do not pass directly into adulthood, but instead enter a stage in which they are neither children nor adults, but something else. And describing that "something else" presents difficulties, for it is easier to say what adolescents are not than what they are.

It is also difficult to indicate the limits of adolescence: at what point does it begin, and at what point is it finished? The question is more easily answered with respect to the beginning than the end of the period. The characteristics of adolescence first show themselves about 10, 11, or 12 years of age with the subtle changes in behavior and appearance which we call preadolescence. The onset of adolescence itself becomes most obvious at puberty, with the menarche (the start of the menstrual cycle) in girls, and the first ejaculation of seminal fluid or the pigmentation of pubic hair in boys.

Determining the end of the adolescent period is an elusive matter. In fact, it is when we attempt to specify the point at which adolescence ends and adulthood begins that we come to realize that what we term adolescence is to a large degree a product of our culture, as well as a matter of time and place. The age of 21 was the traditional watershed between adolescence and adulthood for many years, but even when that was so, most states were permitting marriages to take place at ages that ranged below that—in some instances as low as 12. The traditional age barrier of age 21 has also been under some pressure in recent years, for we have seen the voting age dropped to 18, and the drinking age has been set at 18 in almost half the United States and most of the provinces of Canada.

There are other important legal mileposts placed at various points between the mid-teens and the mid-twenties—the age at which contracts can be executed, the age when automobiles may be driven, the age when one may take examinations for certain vocational licenses, and so forth. The point is that until we have finally arrived at the later twenties, there is likely to be some degree of ambiguity about whether we have attained full maturity.

In simpler cultures—that of the Tuaregs of the Sahara, for example—adolescence is brief, and adulthood begins about age 15, the age when young people are ready to take on the basic roles of their society. But in urbanized societies, adult roles are varied and complex. Learning them takes a great deal of practice, experience, and, in some instances, training. This means not only that the terminal point of adolescence is clouded with ambiguity, but also that the period of functional adolescence may be extended even into the thirties.

We should also recognize that adult society is not especially eager to confer adult status on the young. The power struggle between the age groups sometimes breaks out into the open, but more usually it is covert. A report of the Panel on Youth of the President's Science Advisory Committee (1974) has pointed out that society contrives to exclude youth from challenging types of work, both by humanitarian regulations which protect young people from being exploited, and by the increasing professionalization and bureaucratization of jobs. It is hard to argue with the reasonableness of both types of restriction, but their net effect is to make young people "outsiders" in today's society and to prolong the period of training and *de facto* apprenticeship they must serve before finally being accorded adult status.

On the one hand, adults are saying to youth, "It's for your own good and the good of society that we are asking you to wait, be patient, and get the necessary training and experience"; but on the other hand it is clear that keeping youth out enables the members of adult society to keep under control a possible threat to their status and power.

Another ambiguity in defining the terminal points of adolescence arises from the differences in the standards and behavior patterns prevailing in the subcultures which form a part of the larger national culture. Adolescents from working-class families take on adult roles at a fairly early age. In contrast to middle-class youngsters, they are more likely to drop out of school early, seek full-time employment, and start raising families before the age of eighteen.

Young people from middle-class homes or with middle-class aspirations may also leave home at the age of 18, but they are more likely to take on the role of the college student, a role that connotes something less than full-fledged adult status. They may seek part-time or even full-time employment, but usually they do not expect to be doing the same kind of work or to be working at the same level when they are, say, 25. Hence adult status is attained at different ages at different social levels.

There are, of course, many variations on these basic patterns, with some individuals at all social levels attaining full adult status earlier, and others later. These differences, in turn, depend on a variety of factors: family situations, economic conditions, sex, personal characteristics, and the availability of opportunity.

physical development

Physiological Changes

The term *adolescence* means the state of becoming an adult. It is the adolescent years that see the changes in physical appearance and physiological functioning enable each individual to take on the form and functions appropriate to his or her sex. For females this means the enlargement and elevation of the breasts, changes in uterine and pelvic areas, and the initiation of the menstrual cycle. For males, it means the growth of facial hair, the deepening of the voice, and the ability to produce semen. For both sexes, adolescence means increases in height and weight; growth of body hair, especially in the pubic and underarm areas; eruption of new teeth; and marked changes in the contours of the face and body.

Most young people also experience a growth spurt, which usually takes place before puberty but may occur later. The growth spurt often takes the form of a marked increase in height and weight, occurring during the months just before the menarche for girls and before the first ejaculation of semen in boys. Inasmuch as girls generally mature about two years before boys do, there are a few months in which girls are likely to be taller and heavier than boys. (See Figures 6-1 and 6-2 in Chapter 6).

506 Adolescence

The differing rates at which girls and boys attain physical maturity are depicted in Figure 15-1. As we examine Figure 15-1, we note that the differences within each sex are as striking as the differences between the sexes. At 11½ years, a third of the girls have either entered puberty or are already sexually mature; yet two years later a fourth of them still have not attained maturity. In the meantime, two fifths of the boys have not begun the puberty cycle by 13½, and by 15½ ten per cent still have not started.

We can see evidence of these intersex and intrasex variations as we watch junior high school students leaving school. Tall, stringy seventh-grade boys are followed by small, almost childlike ninth graders. Among the seventh graders, we see girls who look, walk, and run like children, as well as girls with womanly curves, who eye the older boys shyly or with a glint of challenge. Within this seeming chaos, however, there is order. The attributes of adulthood may come earlier to some and later to others, but nonetheless they will appear eventually and will emerge in a certain identifiable sequence.

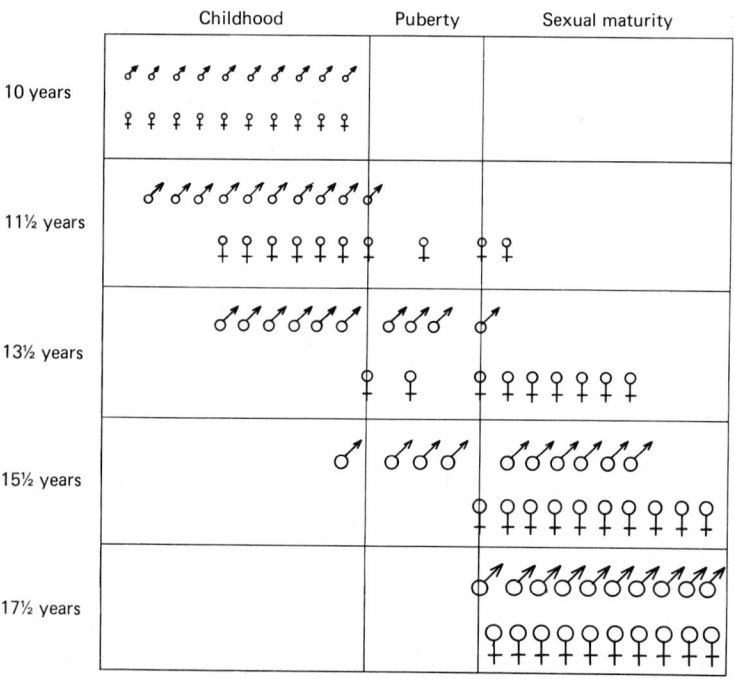

Each ♂ represents 10 per cent of all boys surveyed.
Each ♀ represents 10 per cent of all girls surveyed.

FIGURE 15-1. Differences in ages at which boys and girls enter puberty and attain sexual maturity. (Data from Keliher, 1938, and U.S. Public Health Service, 1973a.)

Physical Skills

Maccoby and Jacklin (1974), in their survey of sex-difference research, list twenty studies comparing the sexes in their performance of perceptual-motor tasks, all involving small-muscle activity. No significant sex differences were found in fifteen of the studies, which covered an age range from 1 to 21 years; the remaining five favored girls.

Comparative data regarding sex differences in large-muscle skills are rather scanty. Theoretically, there should be no difference in childhood, because both sexes are about the same in height, weight, and build, but boys nevertheless commonly excel in sports, perhaps because their desire to conform to masculine sex stereotypes leads them to value success in that area and hence to practice more and compete more energetically. In spite of this motivational advantage, sex differences during the childhood years are not great.

The picture changes markedly during puberty, however, as Figure 15-2 indicates. The data reported here are from an investigation conducted by Anna Espenschade (1971), who administered a number of tests of physical skill to adolescents in the Oakland (California) Growth Study. The graphs representing performance on the fifty-yard dash and the broad jump tell the story very well. Boys and girls are very close together at age 13 on these two skills, but with each succeeding year boys improve, whereas girls do worse. The differences can be explained in terms of boys' developing the kind of muscles that are better suited to such tasks. It may also be that motivation and practice may be involved, with each sex striving to live up to a culturally determined stereotype.

Differences between the sexes on the target throw and distance throw are interesting. Boys at age 13 already have a decided advantage over girls in both these skills. During the next three years, boys increase their ability in the distance throw considerably, but girls remain more or less at the same level. This latter finding suggests that the musculature being developed during adolescence may explain girls' decline in the fifty-yard dash and the broad jump. In other words, if motivation to avoid success in sports were a factor, we would expect that girls' performance in the distance throw would deteriorate as much as it did in the other two skills.

This impression is further supported in the performance on the target throw, a task that involves hand-eye coordination and control, as much as sheer strength. Although girls improve their performance over the three-year period, boys show little improvement and even decline. As in the distance throw, the muscle development of girls does not appear to interfere with performance. If a psychological explanation is preferred, we could say that coordination and control are more acceptable to the self-image of girls than are the vigor and abandon of the fifty-yard dash and the broad jump. But it would nevertheless be

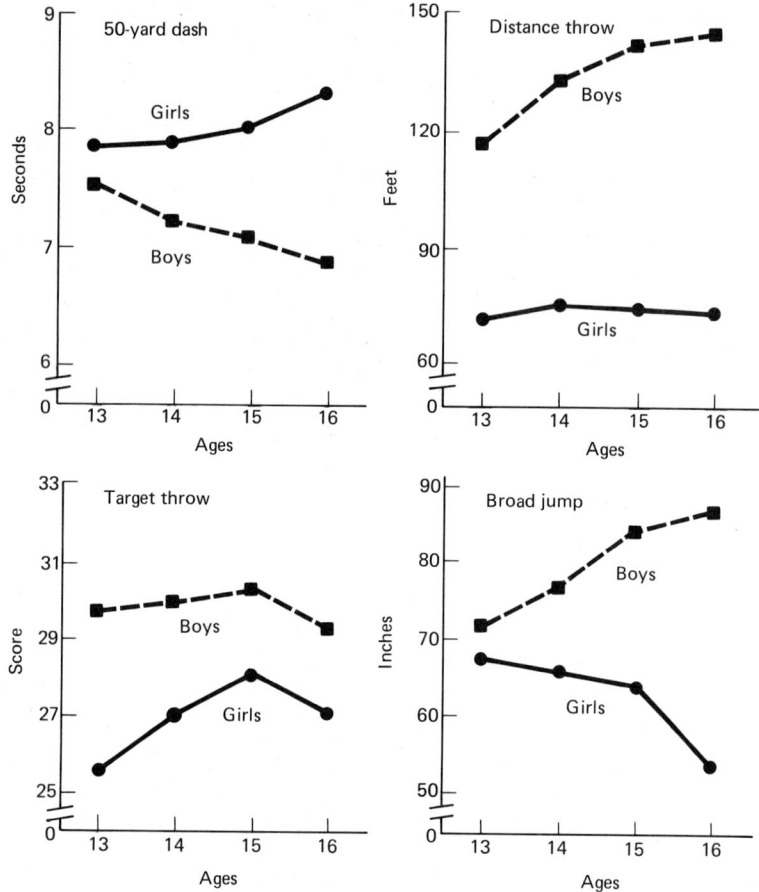

FIGURE 15-2. *Performance of adolescents on motor tests.* (Data from Espenschade, 1971.)

difficult to explain the constant performance that girls maintain over the years in the distance throw.

Do People Really Mature Earlier These Days?

It is common knowledge that young people today are taller than their parents were at the same age. This *secular trend*, as it is termed, has been going on for many years, according to J. M. Tanner (1970), who has collected evidence from a good many growth studies. For example, in 1938 18-year-old Swedish girls averaged two inches taller than girls who were the same age in 1883, whereas the difference for boys the same age and the same two years was closer to three inches. Similarly, twenty-year-old French university students in 1953 were about a half inch taller than students the same age in 1943. Data gathered by the National Center for Health indicate that the height of American youth has increased annually since 1876, when the average 18-year-old male was 65 inches tall, according to military records. The average during the 1960s was 69.2 inches, but the trend may have halted: no increases have been observed since the mid-1950s. The average 18-year-old American female is just short of 65 inches, but there are no comparable figures for the nineteenth century (U.S. Public Health Service, 1976).[1]

The secular trend in height is closely related to a similar trend in onset of puberty. Data for Northern European girls, as reported in Figure 15-3, indicate that over a 120-year period the mean age of menarche has decreased some four years; similar statistics for American girls show a marked decline since 1900. U.S. Department of Public Health (1973a) surveys during the 1960s placed the median age of menarche at 12.76 years.

Tanner (1970), like most experts, explains these secular trends in terms of a general improvement in the nutritional level. This explanation is partially supported by the fact that increases in weight trigger the menarche. Indeed, the critical mean weight seems to be about 105 pounds. At that average weight, the menstrual flow begins for tall and short girls and for early and late maturers alike (Fresch and Revelle, 1970). Better nutrition may, in other words, enable girls to attain the critical weight earlier and hence menstruate earlier. The possibility that better nutrition may be the determining factor is supported by the U.S. Public Health (1973a) survey based on reports from women aged 18 to 79. Women who had attended college had a mean menarcheal age of 12.51 years, in contrast to 13.65 for those who had less than five years of education. Inasmuch as education and economic status tend to be positively correlated, these differences would suggest that the women who had been better nourished as children entered puberty earlier than those who grew up in poverty and whose nourishment was less adequate.

As better nourishment appears to facilitate growth, emotional stress appears to interfere with it, according to Tanner. Recordings of the height of German children show that the secular trend tended to reverse itself during the two world wars, probably because of stress, poor nutrition, or both.

As far as the trend toward increased size in adults is concerned, Tanner suggests that genetic factors, as well as better nutrition, may be

---

[1] When this report appeared, Dr. Peter V. V. Hammill, a medical advisor to the National Center for Health Statistics, was quoted in a newspaper interview as saying: "Probably the most dramatic and significant finding from these data relating to human biology and human growth in general is what may be the end of the trend of constantly increasing size for U.S. children. This could be the result of our having reached the limits of our genetic potential regarding growth. However, all we can say with certainty is that whatever the factors that produced the trend of increasing size, they ceased having effect . . . by 1955 or 1956." (San Francisco *Chronicle*, June 10, 1976.)

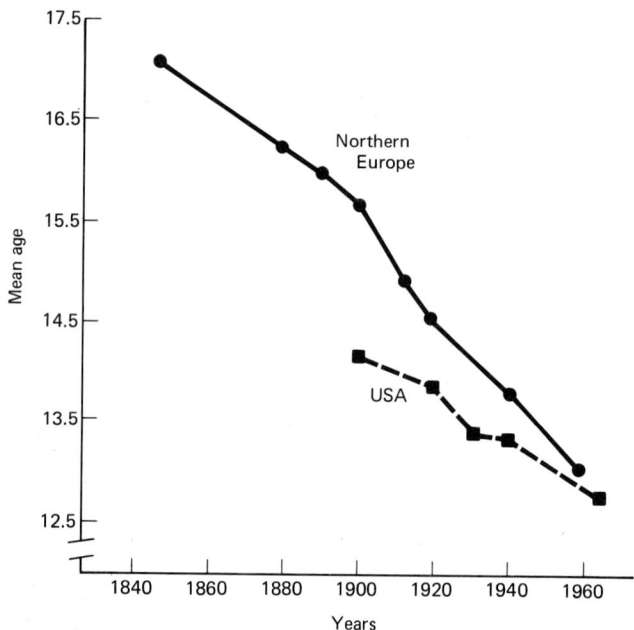

FIGURE 15-3. *Secular trends in age at menarche, 1840 to 1965.* (Based on data from Tanner, 1970, and U.S. Public Health Service, 1973a.)

involved. It is quite possible that tallness may be a dominant trait, genetically speaking, in which case outbreeding, or matings between various social and ethnic segments of the population, could lead to an increase in height. Tanner continues: "There is increasing evidence that such dominance does in fact occur. As for outbreeding, that has been increasing steadily since the invention of the bicycle."

Early and Late Maturers

There seems to be a fairly close relationship between sexual maturity and personality development. Some of the early work in the Berkeley Growth Study, reported by Harold E. Jones (1943), found some interesting differences between boys who mature earlier and those who mature later than their agemates. Jones found that the early-maturing boy has most of the advantages. He is likely to be tall and well developed for his age and, perhaps on that account, is often nominated for positions of leadership and responsibility. This sudden elevation to power may create more problems than he can readily handle, just at a time when his is trying to cope with new bodily dimensions, new interests, and new impulses, but he usually learns that he has more assets than liabilities. He is able, for instance, to learn adult roles earlier than his peers.

Mary Cover Jones (1896–   ) and Harold E. Jones (1894–1960) were both associated for many years with the Institute for Human Development at the University of California in Berkeley and with its predecessor, the Institute for Child Welfare. Their research on early- and late-maturing adolescents is a classic in the field of developmental psychology. Mary Jones is shown below with a grandchild.

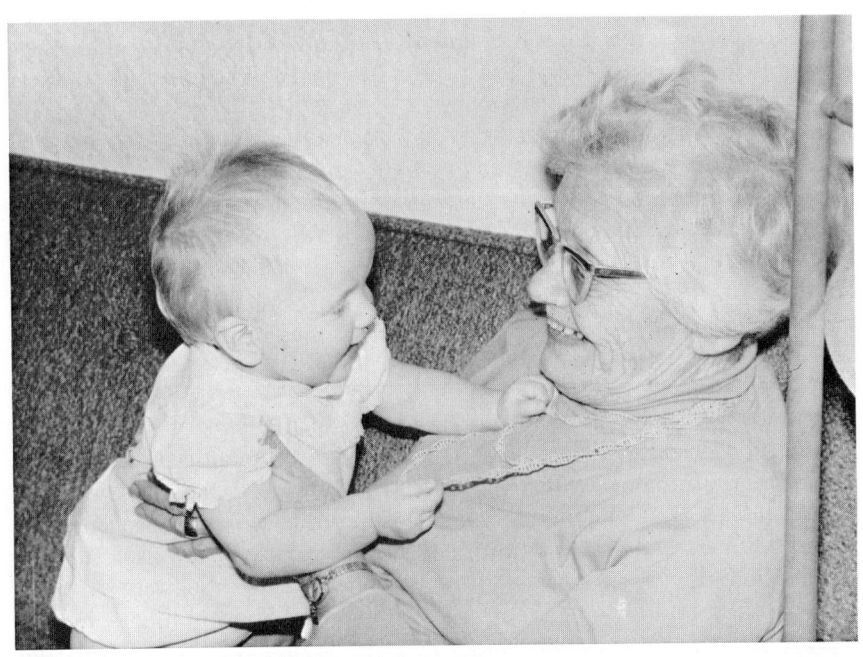

Unlike the early-maturing girl, whose final height is likely to be below average, the height of the early-maturing boy tends to be average.

By way of contrast, the late-maturing boy is likely to be out of phase with his agemates. When he is fifteen or sixteen, he still has not entered puberty, and is likely to be slighted or rejected by his peers. Because of his small size and his physical weakness, he is unable to participate in most sports on an equal basis. If achievement in sports represents a major qualification for acceptance by his peer group, he is inclined to develop feelings of inferiority and inadequacy.

Some early-maturing boys react to their awkward situation by withdrawal and apathy; others become self-effacing and submissive; still others resort to defense mechanisms and "overcompensate" for feelings of inferiority by hyperactivity, aggressiveness, or silliness. As might be expected, such behavior only aggravates their problems and, instead of winning acceptance, it arouses even more hostility on the part of agemates and adults alike. We should note, however, that even this negative attention has some psychological value for such boys: it is better to be attacked and criticized than ignored.

Some of the earlier studies suggested that early-maturing girls may rate low in prestige and status, but subsequent research by Mary Cover Jones and Paul Mussen (1958), and by Margaret S. Faust (1960), shows them to be more popular than late-maturing girls. Faust noted that early-maturing girls did rank low in status in the sixth grade, confirming the earlier research to some extent, but she also found that they recouped their losses when they got to junior high school, where they acquired considerably more prestige.

What the research indicated, then, is that early maturers have a considerable advantage over the average adolescent and especially over late maturers. Not only do they enjoy a high degree of acceptance from their peers, but they are also more self-reliant and independent. Furthermore, they have better relations with their parents than late maturers do (Jones and Mussen, 1958).

Health Problems

In Chapter 8 we noted that the incidence of illnesses of various sorts dropped off sharply during the preschool years and continued to decline well into adolescence. This is, indeed, the general trend, but there are some exceptions. The incidence of communicable diseases (such as measles, chicken pox, and mumps), according to Bayer and Snyder (1950), actually rises during the preschool years, reaching a peak between five and nine years of age, dropping off sharply thereafter.

Gastrointestinal and abdominal disturbances also increase during the middle childhood years, reaching a peak for boys at age 10 and declining to a low point at age 16. The incidence of this type of disorder rises for girls as well, reaching a peak at age 11, then declining somewhat, only to rise to another peak at age 18. As Figure 15-4 shows, girls from mid-childhood onward tend to be more susceptible than boys to gastrointestinal and abdominal disorders. There are probable psychological implications to these differences, inasmuch as emotional upsets and stomach upsets often go together. Boys during this period are more likely to get into fights and accidents, suffering contusions, breaking limbs, and the like. Each sex has its own psychologically appropriate outlet in time of stress.

In a survey of adolescent health problems, the U.S. Public Health Service (1975) reported that about half the young people interviewed made some complaint about acne, sleeplessness, or nervousness. Some of these conditions are either causes or results of other adolescent problems. Most people are concerned about their appearance, but adolescents are often acutely sensitive to blemishes such as acne. Sleeplessness and nervousness are also likely to result from the emotional turbulence of this "storm and stress" period, as adolescence is often termed.

Some 14 per cent of the adolescents in the survey said they were underweight, and 20 per cent said they were overweight. Either health

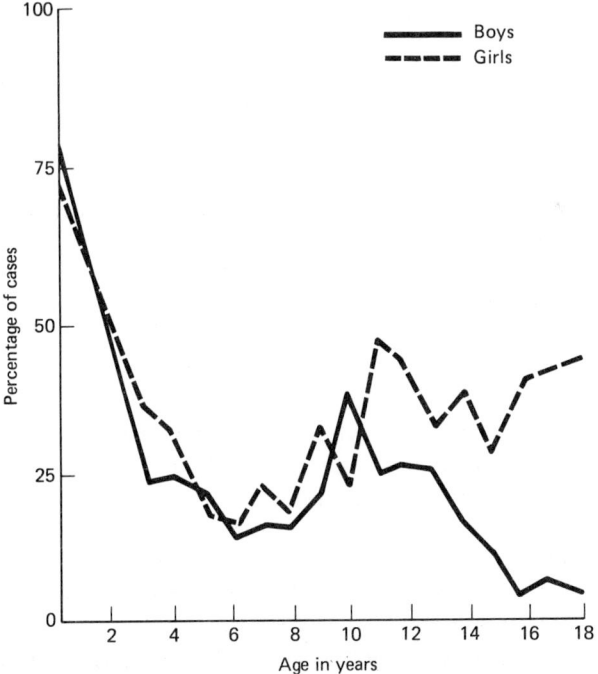

FIGURE 15-4. Incidence of gastrointestinal and abdominal disturbances among children in the Berkeley Guidance Study from birth until age 18. (After Bayer and Snyder, 1950.)

problems are more acute during adolescence than during childhood, or else young people and their parents are inclined to take them more seriously, for 6.5 per cent of the sample in the 12-to-17 age bracket said they were taking medicine, in contrast to only 4 per cent of those between 6 and 11 years of age (U.S. Public Health Service, 1973b).

The Public Health survey also noted that half the adolescents who were interviewed admitted to being fussy about food. This tendency seems to be especially characteristic of young people, many of whom reject out of hand even foods they have never eaten. Lindgren (1962) gave college students a list of thirty foods and asked them to check any they would not eat under any circumstances, even if they were very hungry. Students under 21 rejected significantly more foods than students over that age. The tendency of adolescents to be fussy about food apparently transcends cultural barriers, for when Arab adolescents were given a similar list with the same instructions, the 11-year-olds rejected an average of 12 foods; the 16-year-olds, 10; and the 20-year-olds, only 7 (Babayan, Budayr, and Lindgren, 1966).

Adolescent fussiness appears to be a general trait, not limited to food; Lindgren (1962) found that students under 21 also were more inclined to reject more work situations than those over 21. Furthermore, the subjects under age 21 who rejected many foods also rejected many different kinds of jobs. The adolescent's insecurity about himself and about life in general evidently makes him a person who knows better what he doesn't want than what he does; hence the choosiness.

_____cognitive development

Piagetian Concepts

During the preoperational subperiod of the concrete operations stage of development, the young child characteristically thinks in terms of objects and persons as embedded in the contexts in which he experiences them. Some years later, when he is in elementary school and well into the concrete operations subperiod, he has developed the ability to deal with abstract concepts and generalities, and can also think of the properties of objects, as well as of relations among objects—among individuals as well, of course.

The next and final stage—that of formal operations—characteristically begins in the prepuberal years. There is first a subperiod in which organization takes place, which is followed—perhaps about age 15—with a period of achievement. Edith D. Neimark (1975), in her interpretation of Piaget's theories about adolescent development, mentions eight types of concepts that develop as a result of formal operational thinking:

1. *Combinational.* This concept involves general systematic procedures that can be used to generate such concepts as all possible pairs or other combinations of attributes, such as colors, permutations, and variations in the ordering or grouping of qualities or objects.
2. *Proportions.* Ability to deal with the equality of two ratios, as in conducting a balance experiment, or solving an equation.
3. *Coordination of two systems of reference.*
4. *Mechanical equilibrium.* The principle of equality of action and reaction, a concept closely related to proportion.
5. *Probability.*
6. *Correlation.*
7. *Multiplicative compensations.* A complex type of conservation, involving three dimensions.
8. *Advanced forms of conservation.* Such abstractions as inertia, momentum, and energy—concepts that go beyond immediate observational experience.

A typical experiment that Inhelder and Piaget (1958) use to determine whether an adolescent has attained the stage of formal operations is one in which a subject is shown four vessels of colorless, odorless liquids and a bottle with a dropper. Before the subject's arrival, the experimenter has prepared two glasses: one contains a mixture of the liquids in the first and third vessels; the other contains liquid from the second vessel. The experimenter shows the subjects that when he drops some liquid from the bottle into one of the glasses, its contents will turn yellow; if it is dropped into the other glass, the contents remain colorless. It is the subject's task to reproduce the yellow color, using any of the liquids in the four vessels and the bottle.

The problem can be solved by trial and error, but only if the subject proceeds systematically and remembers what he has done. He must, in effect, work out a rough-and-ready theory that will enable him to reproduce the color a second time. Children in the concrete operations stage can accidentally hit on the solution, but do not understand what they have done, so cannot replicate it, whereas those in the formal operations stage can solve the problem and reproduce the solution when requested. Another formal operations problem, involving adjustments to the rate and speed of a swinging pendulum, has been described in Chapter 3.

It is clear that the kinds of thought processes that are involved in formal operations are fairly complex and abstract. John H. Flavell (1963) says that they are, in effect, the basis of scientific reasoning. Only a fourth of adolescents and a third of all adults ever attain the formal operations stage (Kuhn, Langer, Kohlberg, and Haan, 1977). Piaget (1972) admits the possibility that some individuals are unable to accomplish formal operations, but prefers to believe that people do nevertheless attain that stage in ways that are appropriate to their aptitudes and areas of professional specialization. He also thinks that the tests he employs may be inappropriate for general use and that simpler tasks should be developed. Neimark (1975) concludes that the "stage is not universally attained by all individuals and may not even be stable within an individual over time." In other words, it may be possible for an adolescent to function at a formal operations level, say, when he is enrolled in a well-taught course in physics or chemistry, but after a few years he may "forget" how to use the logical approach he employed in his science course and hence is at a loss as to how to proceed in solving an everyday problem requiring carefully thought-out logical analysis.

Intellectual Development

We noted in Chapter 9 the fact that children are generally able to solve problems of increasing complexity with each year is fundamental to the validity of the Stanford-Binet and the other Binet-type scales that have been developed. Indeed, chronological age is a standard criterion against which all cognitive tests for children are measured. We are able to use chronological age as a satisfactory criterion because mental ability increases in a fairly linear fashion, on the average, throughout the childhood years.

What happens, however, when children reach puberty? Does mental ability continue to increase, or does its development come to a halt?

Terman (1937) concluded that it slowed down considerably, saying that "the yearly gain begins to decrease after the age of thirteen and by the age of sixteen it has become approximately zero." In describing the norms for his test he said that mental ages beyond 15 were artificial and gave instructions that the norms for a mental age of 15 should be used when the test was given to persons 16 or older. This specification led to the assumption—widespread a generation or more ago—that mental growth stops at age 15. It is doubtful whether Terman accepted this rather extreme and literal interpretation, but at the time he was primarily interested in measuring the intelligence of children and was little concerned with subjects in the adolescent years and beyond.

Later research, with more appropriate instruments, indicates that some aspects of mental ability may increase for a good many years, not only throughout puberty, but even well into old age. The scales devised by David Wechsler seem to be more suited than the Stanford-Binet to show mental growth in both adolescents and adults. Two of Wechsler's subtests that have a high degree of reliability and that have been used in developmental research are the Vocabulary Subtest and the Block Design Subtests, both of which were employed in the Health Examination Survey conducted during the 1960s by the U.S. National Center for Health Statistics (U.S. Public Health Service, 1973c) in a study of some 14,000 children and adolescents from 6 to 18.

The Vocabulary Subtest of the Wechsler Intelligence Scale for Children (WISC) consists of a list of 40 words arranged in order of increasing difficulty. The test is administered orally by asking the subject what each of the words mean.

In administering the Block Design Subtest, the investigator shows the subject designs in the test booklet and asks him to reproduce each of them, using small colored wooden cubes. There are ten designs in all, increasing in complexity and requiring either four or nine cubes.

Figure 15-5 presents some of the data from the Health Examination Survey. We note first of all that impressions gained from earlier work with the Stanford-Binet are no longer valid, for there is considerable intellectual growth beyond age 15.[2] There is some confirmation, however, of Terman's observation that mental growth slows down at about age 13. To demonstrate this effect, we have indicated with dotted lines how the mental growth trend for ages 6 to 12 would appear if continued at the same rate to age 18. In other words, the data show that although mental growth continued throughout the age span, the rate of that

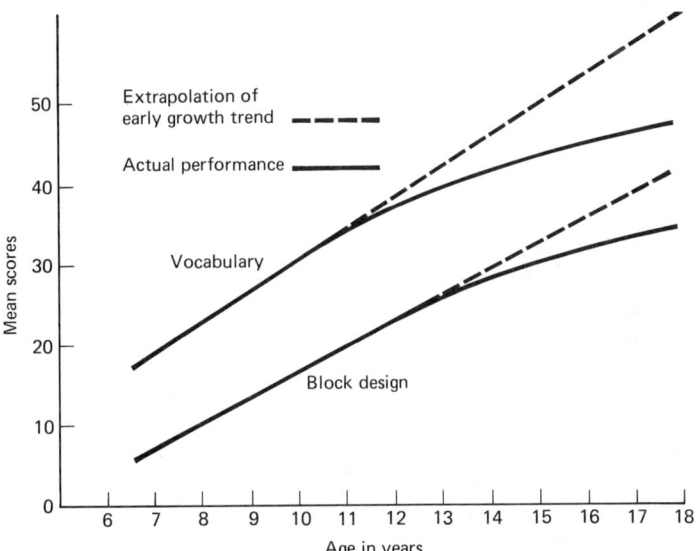

FIGURE 15-5. Mean scores made by national samples of children and youth on the Vocabulary and Block Design subtests of the Wechsler Intelligence Scale for Children (WISC). (After U.S. Public Health Service, 1973c.)

---

[2] The data in Figure 15-5 are from cross-sectional and not longitudinal samples; hence they are not, strictly speaking, growth curves. Because they were gathered over a brief span of years, however, and are based on such a broad sampling of cases, it is reasonable to assume that a longitudinal study of the same children would not have produced markedly different results.

growth began to slow down between 11 and 12 for the Vocabulary Subtest and a year later for Block Design.

We have observed that early maturers have an advantage over late maturers, in that they are more popular, are more self-sufficient, and have better relationships with their parents. A study by Deborah P. Waber (1976) indicates that the cognitive development of these two extreme groups may also differ. She administered a number of verbal and nonverbal tests to early and late maturers of both sexes and found that early maturers performed better on verbal tests, whereas later maturers did better on nonverbal tests. This finding is especially interesting in view of the fact that the kinds of social roles played by early maturers, which we mentioned earlier in this chapter, are of the type that would require more verbal skills than nonverbal ones.

Formal Operations and Measured Intelligence

Piaget is relatively unconcerned about age norms and hence about the relationship between measured intelligence and the pace at which children pass through his operational stages. Psychologists who are interested in the broad spectrum of child development are nevertheless interested in determining whether the two variables are related. The existence of a positive relationship would tell us more about the validity of intelligence tests, as well as something about the variables involved in success on Piagetian tasks. Research correlating the two approaches to assessment is particularly interesting in the study of adolescents. As we have noted, not all adolescents, or even all adults, attain the stage of formal operations, and the question arises as to whether intelligence tests are able to pick up any of the differences between those who attain formal operations and those who do not.

Keating (1975) conducted a study of bright and average fifth and seventh graders. The students, who had been previously classified as bright or average by standardized paper-and-pencil tests, were examined individually on three Piagetian formal operations problems. As Figure 15-6 indicates, a higher percentage of bright students than of average students was able to solve the problems satisfactorily. Using the ability to demonstrate formal operations on any one of the three tasks as a criterion, we find that 31 per cent of the average fifth graders and 62 per cent of the average seventh graders have entered the formal operations stage, but that 93 per cent of the bright fifth graders and 85 per cent of the bright seventh graders have done so. If we use the more rigorous criterion of requiring that all three of the problems be solved, we find that none of the average fifth graders and only 23 per cent of the average seventh graders are able to meet this standard, whereas 47 per cent of the bright fifth graders and 62 per cent of the bright seventh graders are able to do so.

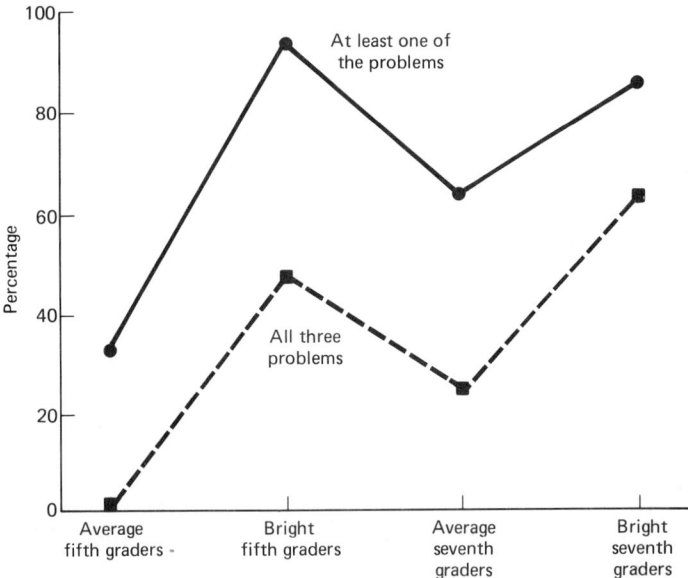

FIGURE 15-6. *Percentage of average and bright fifth and seventh graders demonstrating formal operations on at least one of three Piagetian problems and on all three problems.* (Data from Keating, 1975.)

The great variation in ability that exists in the preadolescent and adolescent stages of development is revealed by the fact that the bright *fifth* graders far outclass average *seventh* graders in their grasp of formal operations, whichever of the two criteria we use, even though the fifth graders were, on the average, two years younger.

One charge that has been leveled against students scoring high on standardized tests is that they are not necessarily superior in intelligence, but are "just good test takers." Keating's research indicates that this allegation has no foundation in fact, and furthermore shows that standardized paper-and-pencil tests and Piagetian problems are to some extent measuring the same variable—namely, cognitive development. As Keating says, the two approaches provide us with two perspectives on what is basically the same intelligence.

Other researchers—Neimark (1975), for example—have also found that standardized test scores translated into mental ages are positively related to the ability of adolescents to demonstrate mastery of formal operations.

Learning and School Achievement

During the middle years of childhood, growth in learning takes place at a very rapid rate; during adolescence, the rate of increase is much slower. Figure 15-7 illustrates differences in reading and arithmetic achievement gains during the two periods of development. The graph is based on data gathered during surveys conducted by the National Center for Health Statistics during the 1960s (U.S. Public Health Service, 1971, 1974). Approximately 14,000 children and adolescents took the Wide Range Achievement test. The data reported in Figure 15-7 consist of cumulative percentage increases in reading and arithmetic scores made by children and adolescents at different ages, as compared with the mean test score made by subjects at the start of the period.

Although the data represent the performance of cross-sectional samples, they do give an approximate idea of what growth curves in the learning of reading and arithmetic would look like, if longitudinal data were available. What the graphs show is that children make rapid gains in reading at first, but that the rate of gain slows down during the elementary school years. Gains in arithmetic are smaller but steadier.

Gains for adolescents in both reading and arithmetic skills, however, are relatively small on a year-to-year basis. There is a slight pick-up in the "growth curve" between the ages of 15 and 16, but it is more apparent than real, and is probably the result of less competent students dropping out of high school. Other data gathered by the survey indicate that those students who do drop out score at about the sixth-grade level on the two tests. Information from another survey shows that the rate of illiteracy among high school dropouts is over 20 per cent, which contrasts with about 1 per cent for adolescents still in high school (U.S. Public Health Service, 1973d).

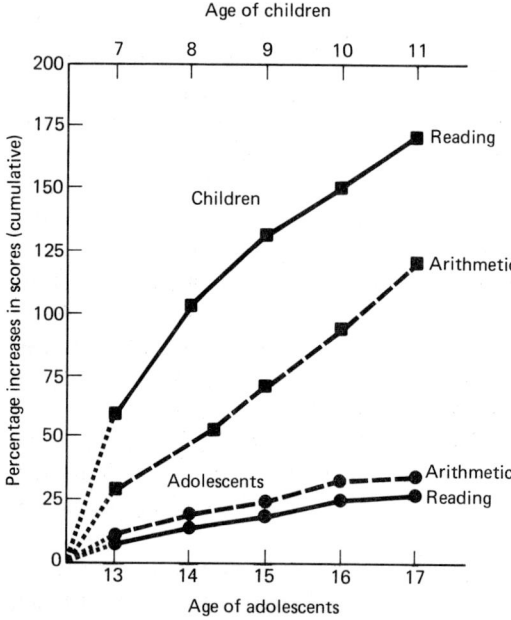

FIGURE 15-7. Cumulative percentage increases in reading and arithmetic achievement test scores during middle childhood and adolescence. (Data from U.S. Public Health Service, 1971, 1974.)

Are Young People Learning Less These Days?

Since the days of ancient Greece, parents and educators have complained about the declining competence of the younger generation, saying that because teachers are less demanding, and because students no longer work as hard as they used to, graduates are unable to read, write, and cipher. The introduction of standardized tests at the end of World War I made it possible to secure hard data to determine whether the accusation had any merit. The results indicated for a number of decades that the popular impression was false and that young people were actually making small but steady gains in the three Rs.

In recent decades, however, the picture has changed, and data from a number of sources make it clear that the average student today achieves at a slightly lower rate each succeeding year and therefore is somewhat less prepared for college than students were ten years ago. For example, L. A. Munday (1976) reports that the mean scores attained by students taking the Iowa Tests of Educational Development increased from 18.1 in 1962 to 18.9 in 1965, when a decline set in. By 1974, the mean score had dropped to 17.6. The mean verbal score on the Scholastic Aptitude Test (SAT), a nationally administered college admissions test, stood at 478 in 1962-1963 and has since declined steadily, until in 1974-1975 it stood at 434. The mean SAT math scores was 502 in 1962-1963, and 472 in 1974-1975.

Munday also points out that between 1965 and 1975 there was a general decline in the achievement test scores of pupils in grades four through eight in the Iowa schools. This loss contrasts with a major increase for the years 1955-1960, and a small increase for 1960-1965. Only third graders made any progress throughout the period, but the gains were negligible.

Taken all together, these findings would suggest that children and adolescents in school are not learning as much as they did in the period before the mid-1960s. This view is further supported by a testing program undertaken by the National Assessment of Educational Progress (NAEP), an agency of the U.S. Office of Education. The NAEP administered a series of writing exercises to national samples of students aged 9, 13, and 17 in the years 1969-1970 and in 1974. The over-all score for the papers was somewhat lower in 1974 than it was at the earlier period. The percentage of poor papers also increased from 20 to 23 for 13-year-olds and from 15 to 22 for 17-year-olds (Larson, 1976).

There is a bright spot in the report, however, for the 1974 results for 9-year-olds were significantly higher than those for 1970. Not only did the over-all mean score increase, but the percentage of poor papers dropped from 23 to 16.

This small ray of hope leads us to explore other explanations for the general decline we have been discussing. We recall the interesting

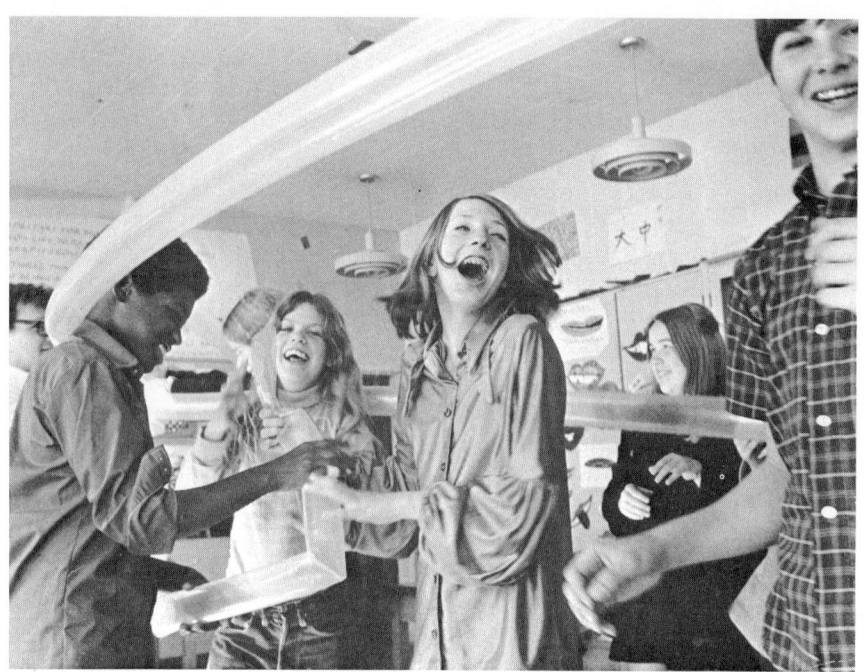

The fact that schools are more open and more permissive these days is said by some to explain the steady decline in college entrance scores. This interpretation has been questioned by others—Zajonc, for example. But the greater degree of openness has also led to closer relations among teenagers, teachers, and parents, who are pooling their views and insights in the solution of common problems.

ideas put forth by Robert B. Zajonc (1976), whose analysis of the relationship between intelligence test scores and family size we discussed in Chapter 11. To recapitulate briefly, Zajonc pointed out that the higher intelligence test scores earned by children with few siblings and by early-born children could be explained in terms of the size of each child's share of his family's intellectual environment. The greater the number of children in a home, the smaller each child's share of attention and intellectual stimulation and the lower his performance on cognitive measures such as intelligence tests. Early-born children have an advantage over their siblings because they spend their early and critical years in a less congested home, where they get relatively more attention from their parents.

Zajonc performed an interesting analysis, which he offered as a possible explanation for the decline in college admission test scores we have discussed. He used the percentage of first-borns in the group taking the SAT each year as an index to the number of children in their families. His rationale was this: as family sizes get larger, the percentage of first-borns automatically drops. In families of two children, 50 per cent are first-born, but in families of five, only 20 per cent are first-born.

Figure 15-8 indicates the relationship between family size and SAT scores. The lower or left-hand line on the graph represents the percentages of first-borns among those taking the SAT during the years 1966 to 1974. The fact that this line drops off sharply indicates that American families were increasing in size during the years the test takers were born. In other words, 37 per cent of the 18-year-olds who took the SAT in 1966 were first-borns, whereas less than 27 per cent of those who took the test in 1974 were first-borns. Inasmuch as children who grow up in larger families and in more crowded homes receive proportionately less attention than children from smaller families, the parallel course of the trend lines in Figure 15-8 suggests that family size crowdedness may have been a causal factor in the phenomenon of the dropping test scores.

Zajonc's analysis goes even further. Because the size of the American family continued to increase through 1962, he predicts that SAT scores will continue to fall, reaching their lowest point in about 1980, when the 18-year-olds born in 1962 take the SAT. Inasmuch as families began to be smaller again after 1962, he also predicted that SAT scores from 1980 onward will rise. The improvement between 1970 and 1974, in 9-year-olds' writing ability, which we mentioned a few paragraphs back, provides some support for Zajonc's prediction, for these were the children born in 1965, after family size had begun to decline.

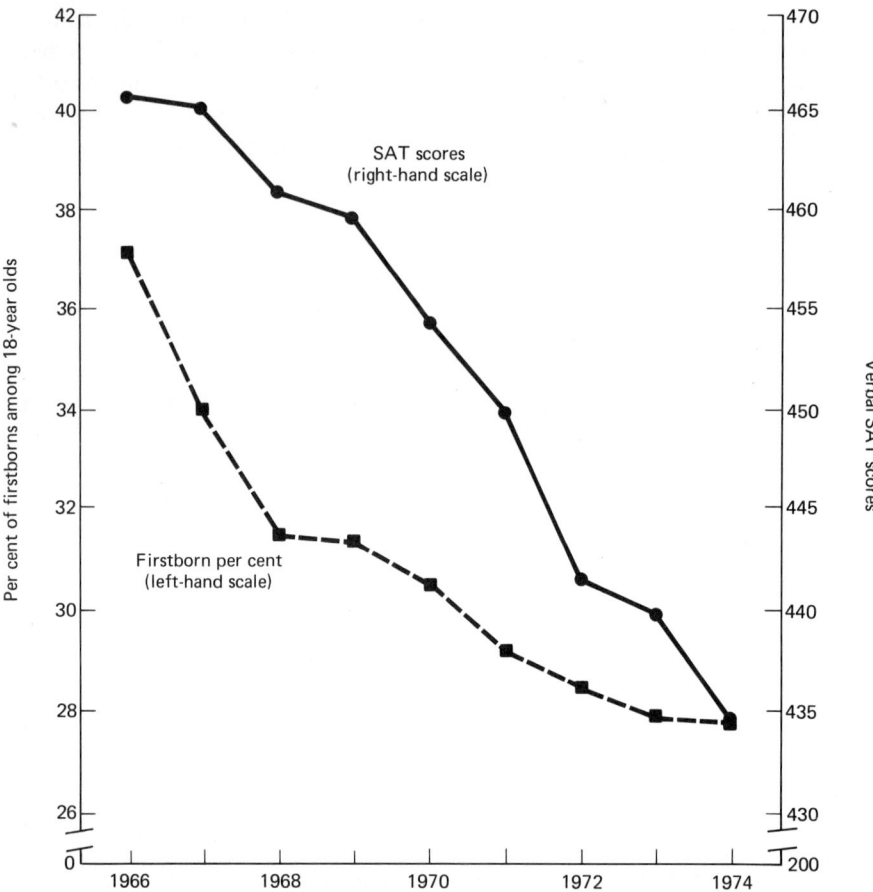

FIGURE 15-8. Mean verbal scores for youths taking the SAT from 1966 to 1974, together with the percentage of 18-year-old firstborns for the same years. (Data from Zajonc, 1976, and Munday, 1976.)

moral judgment

In this section, we shall examine the research on the adolescent's ability to analyze and judge moral issues; discussion of such related topics as norm breaking, nonconformity, and delinquency will be reserved for the next chapter, where we shall deal with personal and social adjustment. In the present discussion we shall focus especially on Kohlberg's (1963b) stages of moral development, which we presented in outline form as Table 13-1 in Chapter 13.

In the earlier years of adolescence, some young people are still at Level I, the Premoral Level of Kohlberg's stages, but the majority are at the Conventional Morality level, Level II; most of their judgments fit either Stage 3, the "good-boy/nice-girl" stage, where getting along with others is paramount, or Stage 4, the "law-and-order" stage. During the late teen years, some young people attain Level III, the postconventional or "principled" level, consisting of Stage 5, the social-contract stage, and Stage 6, the universal ethical principle (or individual principle) stage.

The Moral Views of Adolescents and Their Parents

We noted earlier that many adolescents and adults never really attain the formal operations stage of cognitive development. The same holds true for the moral stages of Level III. Constance E. Holstein (1972) conducted a survey of 14-year-old adolescents and their parents, living in an upper-middle-class suburb near San Francisco. As Table 15-2 indicates, only about a third of the fathers and a fourth of the mothers were functioning at Level III. None of the parents, however, were at Level I, whereas almost two fifths of their children were still at that level. The majority of the sample, adults and adolescents alike, were at Level II, the Conventional level.

Holstein also found some relationship between parents' and children's positions in moral judgment. Most of the children who were at Level I were from families in which both parents were at Level II. In families in which both parents were at Level III, there were no children at Level I, and one child was even at Level III.

TABLE 15-2. Percentages of Upper-middle-class Parents and Their Adolescent Children Classified According to Their Modal Style of Moral Judgment (data from Holstein, 1972)

Moral Judgment Stages	Parents		Children	
	Mothers	Fathers	Girls	Boys
Level I. Preconventional				
Stage 1. Punishment and obedience	0	0	3	4
Stage 2. Instrumental relativity	0	0	34	33
Level II. Conventional				
Stage 3. "Good-boy/good-girl" morality	45	6	41	38
Stage 4. Law and order	32	62	21	21
Level III. Postconventional principles				
Stage 5. Social contract	21	26	0	4
Stage 6. Individual principles	2	6	0	0

Educational Experiences and Moral Judgment

The kinds of changes that take place in moral thinking during adolescence were explored by James R. Rest (1975), who conducted a study in which attitudes of junior-high-school and senior-high-school students living in Minnesota were measured in 1972 and again in 1974. Rest found that 58 per cent of the sample moved up the scale of moral development—from Level II to Level III, for example—and that only 9 per cent moved down the scale. Among the senior-high subjects, those who had gone on to college by 1974 made significantly more judgments at Level III than their peers, although there was no indication in their earlier scores that they were any different from those who were to end their education with high school. College experiences clearly played an important part in their taking positions at Level III.

In the 1974 portion of the survey, the subjects were asked to indicate the experiences they thought had had the greatest effect on their thinking over the past two years. The percentages of the respondents mentioning various types of experiences are listed below. (Inasmuch as some subjects mentioned more than one type of experience, the percentages add up to more than 100).

The person who has arrived at Stage 6 in moral development is able to operate on the basis of individual principles. It is at this stage that we find unconditional, committed altruism, as is demonstrated by this girl, who is helping in the rescue of sea birds caught in an oil spill.

Formal instruction, reading, or study leading to an expanded knowledge of world events, world affairs, and the like. (57%)
New social contacts, the experiences of an expanding social world. (47%)
New "real-world" responsibilities, such as job, marriage, family, and managing money. (40%)
Maturation, age, a sense of "just growing up." (16%)
Direct involvement in community or world affairs—that is, first-hand experiences, in contrast to the secondary, more abstract experiences of the first category. (15%)
Religious experience or instruction. (3%)
No change in thinking over the past two years. (2%)

The relevance of the college experience to changes in moral judgment can be seen in the first category. The experiences mentioned in the second category are also more likely to be encountered by the young person who enters college than by the one who stays at home.

Rest's findings are consistent with those of a number of studies that report that individuals who attend college display significant changes in attitudes and values. Trent and Medsker (1968), for example, conducted a study of ten thousand high-school graduates. Those who went on to college were matched, on the basis of ability and economic background, with those who did not. Over the years, the college group, in contrast to the other subjects, showed greater increases in autonomy, intellectual interests, and enlightened self-awareness. Other longitudinal studies show similar changes taking place in students over the four years they spend in college (Lehmann, 1963; Elton and Rose, 1968).

It is evident, as we analyze the kinds of decisions that have to be made at each level of Kohlberg's scheme of moral development, that each succeeding stage is more demanding intellectually than the preceding one. One would therefore expect that adolescents growing up in households in which intellectual concepts are fostered and modeled would function at higher levels of moral judgment than would adolescents from families whose lives were focused on more tangible and immediate concerns. This possibility was explored by Eugene M. Fodor (1969), who employed Kohlberg's interview schedule to study the moral values of samples of black and white adolescent males who had been matched according to age and IQ. Fodor found no racial differences in the level of moral development, but he did find that boys whose mothers had completed high school or more were functioning at a higher moral level than those whose mothers had not completed high school.

Laws, Regulations, and Moral Judgment

The moral judgments we employ are likely to be closely related to, if not based on, our view of the social order and the way human relations should function. Adelson, Green, and O'Neil (1969) undertook a study of adolescent concepts of this area of experience by interviewing subjects 11, 13, 15, and 18 years old, asking them to imagine that a thousand people were emigrating to an island in the Pacific where they were to set up a new community. The subjects were then queried about the kinds of political and social decisions the imaginary group should make and then were asked to justify the proposed decisions.

The younger subjects had difficulty in dealing with abstract issues. They seemed unconcerned about the social needs that laws and regulations serve, nor did they mention problems of feasibility—that is, they gave no thought to whether the possible gains resulting from a regulation would warrant the cost of enforcing it, or whether a law could be enforced at all. It rarely occurred to the younger adolescents that a law might be absurd, mistaken, or unfair. They assumed that society and its agents were all-knowing and benign and that laws were always enacted for good and sufficient reasons. They also felt that crime detection, arrest, and punishment should be carried out arbitrarily, and they were unconcerned about individual rights and special considerations.

The older adolescents were not much more idealistic than the younger ones, but they were more realistic. They were also more aware of what could or could not be accomplished by laws and regulations and more often saw them as socially valuable. Furthermore, their view of society led them to wonder, when considering a proposal for a law, whether there was more to it than met the eye.

The thinking of the subjects showed a marked shift from narrow moralism to practical logic between the ages of 13 and 15. A sampling of the answers to the question "What is the purpose of laws?" demonstrates the abruptness of that change:

> Age 11. Well, so everybody won't fight and they have certain laws so they won't go around breaking windows and stuff and getting away with it.
> Age 13. To keep people from doing things they're not suppose to like killing people and like . . . if you're in the city, like speeding in the car and things like that.
> Age 15. To help keep us safe and free.
> Age 18. Well, the main purpose would be just to set up a standard of behavior for people, for society living together so that they can live peacefully and in harmony with each other.

The reply of the 11-year-old indicates that he is operating at Level I; the 13- and 15-year-olds are at Level II; whereas the 18-year-old, with his oblique reference to a rational social contract, is clearly at Stage 5 in Level III.

Cognitive Ability and Moral Judgment

Like the other competencies we have discussed in this chapter, judiciousness and concerns about moral problems tend to be related to other aspects of the adolescent's behavior. This relationship is brought out in high-school students' replies to questions asked in the Purdue Opinion Poll. When replies were classified according to the academic performance of the respondents, those who had low grades were more likely to agree with the statement that the police should use whatever means would be necessary to capture and punish criminals, but also that people have the right to take the law into their own hands if they feel they have been unfairly treated. Students with high grades were more likely to disagree with those statements, as Table 15-3 indicates. They were also more likely to be concerned about values—wondering how to tell right from wrong, expressing confusion on moral issues, worrying about not living up to ideals, and the like.

Cognitive ability is undoubtedly involved in the differences between the replies of the two groups, in that students with low grades are less aware of the importance of moral issues and are less likely to see the risks of unbridled police powers or of taking the law into one's own hands, but other factors may be involved as well. Students who get high grades are clearly the successful ones in high school. Not only do they rate higher on tests of cognitive ability, but they also have developed the social sensitivity and skill required to function in a complex, demanding society. Their ego strength and self-esteem enable them not only to succeed academically, but also to be more socially perceptive and more

TABLE 15-3. Percentages of High-School Students with Low or High Course Grades Who Gave Certain Reponses to Statements Involving Human Rights, Social Responsibilities, and Moral Values (after Erlick, 1970a; and Van Horn and Erlick, 1971)

	Students with	
Statements	Low Grades	High Grades
The police should have the right to use whatever means are necessary to capture and punish criminals		
Definitely agree	40	26
Definitely disagree	36	44
When desirable social legislation cannot be secured, persons who are being unfairly treated have the right to use whatever means are necessary to correct conditions.		
Definitely agree	30	14
Definitely disagree	20	49
In the past year, how much have you been bothered by values (wondering how to tell right from wrong; confused on some moral questions, etc.)		
Very much, or quite a bit	21	44
A little, or not very much	41	38

sensitive to the rights and feelings of others. At the same time they express more doubts about their ability to know exactly what to do in any given situation in which they are likely to be involved.

The data from the Purdue Opinion Poll are consistent with the results of studies carried out by Kuhn and others (1977). Kuhn and her co-researchers asked 265 subjects between the ages of ten and fifty to solve three Piagetian problems designed to assess the attainment of the formal operations stage of cognitive development and also asked them to answer questions from Kohlberg's (1963b) moral judgment interview schedule. An analysis of the respondents' replies indicated that reasoning ability, as indicated by the attainment of formal operations, is fundamental to and parallels the development of highly principled moral judgment (Level III in Table 15:2).

_____ summary

Although adolescence is the period separating childhood from adulthood, it is easier to say what adolescents are not than what they are. It is relatively easy to determine where adolescence begins, but where it ends varies greatly among cultures, social classes, and individuals. There is a tendency for our society to prolong adolescence. This has the effect of protecting young people against exploitation and society against inept workers, but it also makes adolescents outsiders in an adult world.

The physical aspects of adolescence involve sexual development, as well as increases in height and weight. At puberty, adolescents also take on the secondary sex characteristics of adults. Girls tend to mature about two years earlier than boys. Although girls and boys are fairly equal in strength and skill during childhood, boys reaching puberty begin to excel in large-muscle activities. Girls maintain their skill in some motor activities, especially those involving control and accuracy, but actually become less competent in others. Sex differences in physical development are causal factors in this loss of skill, but motivation may be involved as well.

For many years there has been a tendency for children to grow up to be taller than their parents. This secular trend, as it is termed, has been going on at least since 1840 in Northern European countries, and in the United States for almost a hundred years. Recent evidence suggests that the trend in the United States may have come to a halt in the mid-1950s. The increases in height may have resulted from improved nutrition, but freedom from extreme stress and cross-matings among different ethnic groups have also been suggested as causes. Increases in weight to an average of 105 pounds appear to trigger the menarche in women. Better-educated (and presumably better-nourished) women tend to report an earlier menarche than women who have less education. Children who attain sexual maturity earlier are likely to be better adjusted socially than late maturers.

Gastrointestinal and abdominal disturbances peak for boys at about age ten and then decline, but their incidence increases for girls and remains high throughout adolescence. About half the adolescents polled in a nationwide survey reported acne, tension-related disturbances, and fussiness about food. Fussiness may be a general trait; adolescents are choosy about work situations as well. Insecurity seems to be a probable cause.

Young people who have been able to function at the concrete operations stage of cognitive development are ready for the formal operations stage, but many adolescents (and many adults as well) never go beyond the level of concrete operations. The formal operations stage requires the ability to deal with permutations, proportions, equations, coordination of systems of reference, probability, correlation, three-dimensional conservation, and highly abstract concepts. These thought processes are basic to scientific thinking.

Intellectual growth tends to slow down during adolescence, but it does not necessarily stop, as was once thought. Late maturers appear to perform better on nonverbal tests, whereas early maturers do better on verbal ones. Students identified as bright by standardized paper-and-pencil tests also tend to be far ahead of their classmates in formal operations. Growth in learning of school subjects like reading and arithmetic tends to be very rapid in elementary school, but proceeds at a much slower pace in adolescence. Since the mid-1960s there has been a decline in the scholastic aptitude and achievement of adolescents. Zajonc explains this phenomenon in terms of the increase in the size of U.S. families: the larger the family, the less attention per child and the less intellectual development. Zajonc predicts that aptitude test scores will continue to drop until 1980 and then begin to rise, as the 18-year-olds who were born into smaller families start to take college entrance examinations.

During the early years of adolescence the majority of children are at Level II, the Conventional Morality Level, of Kohlberg's stages of moral development, but the same can also be said for their parents. Parents who are at Level II are more likely to have children who make judgments at higher levels of morality. Young people who go to college tend to function at higher levels of moral judgment than those who do not. College experiences also promote positive changes in autonomy, intellectualism, and self-awareness. The better the education of parents, the more positive their influence on children's moral judgment. Adolescents' views of the social order are related to the moral judgments they make. When younger adolescents were asked about the kinds of regulations an imaginary community should have, they tended to be unconcerned about the social need for laws and expressed preferences for arbitrary methods in dealing with law breakers. Older adolescents, when queried about the same problem, were more realistic about what laws could and could not do. They were more positive about the advantages of regulations, but were also more skeptical. A poll of high-school students indicated that those who had made better grades, in contrast to those who had low grades, tended to feel that the power of police should be limited and that aggrieved individuals should not have the freedom to take the law into their own hands. They also expressed more concern about moral problems. A survey of subjects between the ages of ten and fifty showed that the development of reasoning ability parallels and is fundamental to the development of principled moral judgment.

sixteen

Personality and Social Development

Don't laugh at a youth for his affectations; he's only trying on one face after another till he finds his own.
—LOGAN PEARSALL SMITH

To me it seems that youth is like spring, an over-praised season—delightful if it happens to be a favoured one, but in practice very rarely favoured and more remarkable, as a general rule, for biting east winds than genial breezes.
—SAMUEL BUTLER

The Subculture of the Adolescent

There is a phenomenon that is known as the "adolescent culture." It is, more precisely, a subculture—a phenomenon that exists largely in Western urbanized societies, where, as we noted in Chapter 15, adolescence is deliberately prolonged.

Urbanized societies of the type that prevail in the western world require a great deal of maintenance. They are, as we say, "labor intensive." Life in such societies is complex and changing, less likely to be predetermined by tradition and religious customs. As a consequence, urbanized societies require continual adjustment, adaptation, tinkering, and repair. They are very demanding of the time and attention of their adult members, who, even when they are relaxing, must be aware of a dozen or so schedules: keep an eye on the clock; don't miss the tax deadline; don't forget appointments; send in this month's time payment now; fourteen minutes for breakfast; remember to call the TV repairman tomorrow; always keep track of what today's bank balance is and what tomorrow's will be; and so on and on.

Young people, who are sheltered or excluded from such an all-embracing involvement with the minutiae of everyday adult life, are left more or less to themselves, to develop a society of their own, hang-loose or frenetic, as the case may be, but with its own structure, norms, regulations, rituals, reference groups, status systems, rewards, and penalties.

The adolescent subculture is hardly a carefree Nirvana—far from it. For one thing, it is even less stable and secure than the fast-moving adult culture. For another, it lacks the controls and defensive structures that adults employ to keep the psychic casualty rate low, or at least manageable. Members of the adolescent subculture are, furthermore, fully aware that they have little status and no prestige in the larger society and are terribly dependent on the significant adults in their lives for whatever freedom and power—read money—they have. This sense of powerlessness and even of alienation expresses itself all too often in the form of excesses in drugs, sex, religion, sensual stimulation, violence, apathy, frenetic activity, idealism, and activism.

Except for the form and the details there is little in today's world that is new about the painful side of adolescence. Goethe celebrated its storm and stress in his *Sorrows of Werther*, which he published in 1774 as the aftermath of a frustrated love affair. The love-blighted sufferings of young Werther and his tragic suicide had a great appeal to the European teenager and young adult of the period and are said to have led to many a suicide among the book's readers. Whereas today's parent worries about his adolescent child's slipping away into a hang-loose common-law marriage or running around with a crowd concerned only with dangerous, illegal pleasures, parents of the eighteenth century worried lest their adolescent son or daughter commit suicide.

The basic concern expressed by parents is the same today as it was two hundred years ago: a fear that one's adolescent children, are committed to a course of self-destruction. The adolescent's side of the story is: fear of being controlled, dominated, and blocked by one's parents, and at the same time of being dismissed as immature and inconsequential.

Most adolescents and their parents do not carry their disagreement to extremes. The majority of them live together more or less amicably, share the joys and sorrows of everyday living, and like each other most of the time. There are quarrels and even angry disagreements, the majority of them over some aspect of the independence-dependence issue or the expectations of the adolescent culture versus the requirements of the world of adults. Such encounters are an inevitable part of the disengagement process, whereby adolescents seek routes to find their own way, and adults reluctantly drift toward old age and the sidelines of life.

"Stephanie wants to know if she can hitch-hike to Seattle, hire out on an iron ore boat, go through the Panama Canal, back up to New York, then work as a Go Go dancer instead of completing her sophomore year of high school. I told her we'd ask you."

(Cochran in the *Wall Street Journal.*)

adolescents and their parents

Dependence, Independence, and Responsibility

The process we have sketchily described is one that was set in motion when the child was conceived. The appearance of the child at birth enables its father and mother to play the roles of parents—a demanding but very self-fulfilling set of roles. Watching a child grow and become more competent is also fulfilling, but it does produce some emotional conflict. The excitement attendant to seeing a child attain a new level of independence is balanced by the parents' realizing that he now has somewhat less need of them, as we noted in Chapter 7.

The basic problem, however, is that children change faster than parents do. The child who last year needed help in zipping his playsuit, and who had to be physically placed on the playground equipment, is now doing his own zipping and racing around the playground with the other children, climbing and sliding with the best of them, while the parent still hovers anxiously and protectively at the edge of the scene.

During the middle childhood years, the parents are often unsure of how much they are really needed—whether to intervene or to let the child learn from mistakes, whether to comfort or to say "You should have known better," whether to guide the choice of playmates or to let matters take their course.

For his part, the child usually becomes increasingly resistant to parental help and particularly to parental direction, guidance, and advice. This resistance reaches a peak during the adolescent years. He initiates many projects, but lacks follow-through; he makes demands for rights and privileges, but objects to being held responsible. Indeed, responsibility becomes a major problem. He is given permission to go out with friends Sunday night if he will spend Monday night doing a school assignment due Tuesday. But he spends Monday night watching a favorite television program and the assignment does not get done. Then he criticizes his mother for not having reminded him on Monday night. She makes a mental note and the next time an assignment is due, she does remind him, whereupon he angrily demands that she stop nagging him and "get off his back."

Responsibility for one's own behavior and conformity to adult demands somehow get confused in such interchanges, a confusion that the peer group makes the most of in its challenge to adult society. But more of that in the following section.

During the adolescent years, the young person is still dependent, both functionally and emotionally, on parents and other adults. Some teenagers view this as a sign of weakness and attempt to overcompensate

"I don't mind my parents forbidding me going out tonight!" Lots of famous people have had unhappy childhoods!"

(Marty Links, © United Feature Syndicate.)

with elaborate gestures at independence, such as running away, getting sexually involved, or becoming a part of the drug scene. Most adolescents are able to deal with their dependency on a more rational basis. They are, in this stage of development, much more able to express and share love than they were as children. They are more capable of empathy and hence have a better understanding of the attitudes and feelings of others, so that they can behave in ways that are considerate and supportive. There are even times when a teenager enjoys being babied a bit, although he may make a show of not wanting such attention and may attempt to be brusque, nonchalant, or tough, in order to prove to himself and others that there is nothing soft about him.

The conflicts that teenagers feel about their relations with their parents are often muted by growing insight into their own behavior. A college freshman wrote:

> I recall one evening when I came home from my part-time job feeling depressed and really wanting to take it out on someone or something. That someone happened to be my mother. Even when I was arguing with her, I realized that I was acting like a child and that she wasn't responsible for my troubles. Because I could account for my actions, I felt ashamed and guilty about the whole thing. At the time, I wished I didn't have to understand my actions because I would have felt justified in fighting with her. (Lindgren and Byrne, 1971. Reprinted by permission.)

Achievement and Relations with Parents

Success in school is the most sensitive barometer of the adolescent's ability to cope with the demands of society. The importance of the contribution that parents make to the success of their adolescent child is indicated by the results of a study conducted by Mary G. Conyers (1977), who surveyed the school records of two groups of ninth graders attending schools in a community of forty thousand inhabitants. The first of these groups consisted of students living at home with both natural parents, a group she described as being from "conventionally structured homes." The other group consisted of all the other ninth graders, who were classified as coming from "unconventionally structured homes." This group constituted about one third of the total number.

As the data reported in Table 16-1 indicate, students from conventionally structured homes had a decided advantage over the others. They were absent from school about one third as often as the other group, and were about one third as likely to be truants, to be expelled, or to drop out of school altogether. Their expulsion rate was only one eighth that of the group from unconventionally structured homes. Finally, the students from conventionally structured homes had grades which were considerably higher than those made by the other group.

TABLE 16-1. Differences in School Records of Ninth Graders from Conventionally Structured Homes and Those from Unconventionally Structured Homes (Conyers, 1977)

Variables	Conventionally Structured Home	Unconventionally Structured Home
Average number of days absent	6.2	13.2
Average percentage of students classified as truants	5.3	15.6
Average percentage of students suspended from school	4.1	12.4
Average number of students expelled from school	0.5	3.8
Average number of students who dropped out of school	4.1	12.4
Median grade-point average	2.35	1.76

School success has been found to be a highly significant predictor of success during the adult years, and Conyers' findings indicate what a significant role parents play in helping or hindering their children's efforts to deal with the challenges and problems they meet outside the home.

There is considerable evidence to show that those adolescents who have the best relations with their parents are those who are most competent and adequate in other ways. Morrow and Wilson (1961) asked two groups of high-school students to fill out a questionnaire dealing with their relations with their parents. One group was making superior grades; the other group had been getting low grades. The two groups had been matched for year in school, intelligence, and family SES. An analysis of the replies of the two groups indicated that the achievers were more likely to report that their parents shared ideas, activities, and confidences with them and that they were more affectionate, approving, and encouraging with respect to school achievement.

The Purdue Opinion Poll produced similar findings in a survey of 12,000 students attending high schools in various parts of the United States. Table 16-2 presents some of the replies made to key questions by students with very low grades and those with excellent grades. It is clear that the high achievers had much better relations with their parents. They felt that their parents understood them, and that, in turn, they understood their parents. They also reported that they had been allowed to have influence on their family and its decisions. Although only 17 per cent believed that parents value independent thinking, this proportion was nevertheless almost three times higher than the 6 per cent of the low achievers who gave this reply. They also were more

TABLE 16-2. Percentages of High-school Students with Very High or Very Low Course Grades Who Gave Certain Replies to Survey Questions Regarding Their Relations with Their Families (data from Erlick, 1970b)

	Low Achievers	High Achievers
How well do you think your parents understand you?		
Very well or moderately well	39	59
Not at all, not very well	30	16
Parents are hard to reach as human beings: it's hard to know what fun they get out of life, what their life goals are.		
Definitely or probably agree	70	31
Definitely or probably disagree	24	68
How much have you been permitted to contribute as a family member?		
Very much	9	34
Not very much	26	9
What do you think parents like most about their children?		
Independent thinking	6	17
Enthusiasm, energy	15	31
Good values, character	12	59
A mother who always tells her children exactly how to do their work is		
Exactly or very much like my mother	53	16
Very little or not at all like my mother	36	59
A mother who asks others what her children do away from home is		
Exactly or very much like my mother	41	9
Very little or not at all like my mother	47	81
A mother who excuses the bad conduct of her children is		
Exactly or very much like my mother	27	6
Very little or not at all like my mother	50	84

likely to believe that parents put emphasis on good values and character, traits that are mentioned by very few of the low achievers.

The reactions of the two groups of students to their mothers' behavior are also very revealing. The mothers of the high achievers did not exercise close control over their children's work; they trusted their children and did not engage in covert detective work to check up on them; but when their children misbehaved they did not indulgently make excuses for them.

An earlier study by Charles Frederick Warnath (1955) also produced results that are consistent with the above studies. Data regarding the family life of ninth-grade boys were gathered by interviewers. Boys whose classmates held them in the greatest of esteem reported that they participated in more family activities; they volunteered more examples of loving, supportive behavior on the part of the family members; they said they were given more freedom to engage in activities outside the home; and they tended to exhibit more characteristics of adult behavior than most of their peers.

What Warnath's study suggests is that teenagers who are driven by family friction and dissension to look for social and emotional satisfactions away from home are likely to be less effective and less likable than are those who find family life to be a pleasant and rewarding experience.

We should note, however, that the relationships are likely to be mutual. It is easy to fault parents for not creating a pleasant home environment, but some of the responsibility lies with individual adolescents as well. The youth who regards every restriction as an infringement of his personal freedom and who is continually "testing the limits" is likely to aggravate, if not actually create, much of the tension he is trying to escape.

We should also recognize that a certain degree of controversy and argument is an inevitable part of "growing away" from the family, and that there are bound to be some hurt feelings, disappointments, and anger on both sides. Where families are sound operating entities, these problems are contained and resolved, at least on a more-or-less basis. Families in which exploitation or self-indulgence is allowed to flourish unchecked are the ones that permit normal disagreements to escalate to destructive heights.

Family Life of Users and Nonusers of Drugs

In a major survey of young drug users and their parents, Richard H. Blum and his associates (1972) compared white, middle-class families whose adolescent and adult children had become involved to some degree in the drug scene with those whose young people had not. The first type of family was termed by the researchers as "high risk" with respect to producing drug users; the second type was termed "low risk." High-risk families were less likely to be church goers; they were more insecure about child rearing and less concerned about self-control as well. High-risk families were less cohesive—that is, family members spent less time in one another's company, did fewer things together, were more permissive, and refrained from setting behavioral norms that applied to all group members. (The norms are important; we often forget, when we extol the warmth and personal support that is to be found in a close-knit, mutually supportive group, that the price its members pay is consensus on and conformity to common patterns of behavior, attitudes, and values.)

In contrast to low-risk families, high-risk families did not come to grips directly with issues and problems, but were inclined to intellectualize about them. Among the parents in high-risk families, the investigators found more alcoholism, more arrests for automobile traffic violations, more indifference toward police and laws, and more time invested in pleasures outside the home.

The investigators concluded that the drug use of young people from high-risk families is in part the result of a constellation of parental beliefs and practices that lead children to express in their behavior the child-rearing goals and personal beliefs of their parents. They wrote:

> In becoming what parents want them to become, some children offered unexpected surprises and problems which parents could not handle equanimously or directly. The low risk families are more satisfied and have far fewer problems than do high risk families. Low risk parents believe they have accomplished their child-rearing goals. Their children, unlike high risk children, sometimes give stronger voice to parental standards than do parents themselves.

The investigators go on to say that parents in both groups did in fact accept the decent and admired values of the American culture, but the high-risk parents emphasized the child's emotional adjustment, individuality, and freedom to explore and change, whereas the low-risk parents gave priority to discipline, family togetherness, love of God and country, respect for authority, and support of the status quo.

Somewhat similar relationships between high and low risk were found with the blue-collar or working-class white families studied by the researchers. Parents in low-risk families at this social level tended to enforce rules rigidly, were less likely to use alcohol, and were more often rated as warm, relaxed, and happy than were high-risk parents. Low-risk families were more traditional: the father's will prevailed when disagreement or uncertainty occurred. Although low-risk parents were stricter, it was the high-risk parents who commented on discipline problems when interviewed, and they also mentioned problem children more frequently. High-risk family members also reported a great deal more problem behavior. They were more likely to have had automobile and other accidents, to have been jailed, to experience trouble with friends or relatives, to have been unconscious at one time or another, to have lost self-control, and to have sexual difficulties.

In rating basic values, the working-class low-risk parents stressed belief in God, love of country, respect for law and order, loving one's parents, and teaching children self-control. High-risk parents stressed getting along with others, self-understanding and maximizing one's potential. High-risk parents saw no value in instilling in children the ideals of great men of the past, and they gave low ranks to the goal of becoming a respected citizen.

Another survey the investigators undertook, interviewing Mexican-Americans, indicated similar differences between low- and high-risk families, except that the differences were even more striking than for the Anglo-American families.

Family Versus Peer Group

One more point in the Blum study is worth noting. The adolescents in all families reported, in one way or another, that their parents' love was important to them. Some of them said this explicitly; others showed it indirectly through resentment and misbehavior when they felt their parents had let them down or abandoned them. The young people made it clear that their parents were the dominant force in their lives—not the peer group, and not the folk heroes of the sports and entertainment world. As far as they were concerned, what their parents taught them was more important and more effective than anything that school teachers, officials and administrators, employers, law enforcement officers, and health experts might tell them.

We stress this point because of the rather widespread belief that teenagers care only about people their own age and are concerned only for what the peer group wants them to do. What the studies we have cited suggest, however, is that the peer group's power is negatively correlated with family cohesiveness, discipline, and warmth—the stronger the family, the less the influence of the peer culture. It seems that the adolescent subculture is to a large degree the creation of adults who encourage the separation and even the alienation of their children.

Blum and his associates report that families whose young people were drug users were singularly uninterested in getting professional help. Some high-risk parents were so strongly committed to permissiveness that they felt it wrong to interfere with a youngster, even if he was using drugs heavily and was involved in selling them. The researchers also suspected that some parents were unconsciously encouraging the delinquency of their child because he was living out the rebelliousness and antisocial values that they could not afford to express openly. Still

Today's teenagers have little cause to feel lonely. The peer group is no farther away than the telephone.

others simply could not bring themselves to discuss problem behavior with their children; they wanted to avoid quarrels, arguments, and unpleasantness. They preferred, instead, to pretend that the problem did not exist.

All three of these behavioral tendencies carry an undertone of parental irresponsibility—of not wanting to get involved. Such strategies only increase the degree of separation between adult and teenager and aggravate their feeling of alienation. But Nature abhors a vacuum, even in behavioral terms. The teenager needs acceptance, identity, and control, and the peer group stands ready to meet these needs.

the peer group

Even competent, involved parents in the best-adjusted families are aware of peer-group power. Here is an example:

> Georgia, a high-school junior, appeared to be headed for a musical career. She had a clear soprano voice and a good dramatic style, and she seemed willing to put in the endless hours of hard work that it takes to be a qualified musician. Thanks to the recommendation of her voice coach, she was offered a summer scholarship with all expenses paid at a well-known conservatory several hundred miles from home. Accepting the scholarship, however, meant that she had to give up plans to teach swimming for the Red Cross, a job she had shared for the previous two years with three close friends. In spite of the entreaties and arguments of her parents and her teacher, she decided to turn down the scholarship. When her mother asked her whether spending a summer teaching swimming was more important than a career in music, she answered: "I know this sounds ridiculous to you, but spending the summer at the pool with Ruthie, Sheryl, and Ann is the most important thing in the world to me right now" (Lindgren and Byrne, 1971).

Conflicts Between Affiliation and Achievement

The issue is affiliation versus achievement. It is the adolescent's need for affiliation—n Aff—that leads him to become involved in the peer group. The need to achieve—n Ach—which we discussed in Chapter 13, is diametrically opposed to n Aff, and has opposite effects on behavior. N Ach causes us to become involved in activities that provide us with feedback as to our own competence: what we can and cannot do, what we must learn in order to perform better, what kind of mistakes we are making, what our strongest and weakest points are, and the like. The person with high n Ach enjoys activities that enable him to evaluate and improve his skills. Competition with others provides him with such opportunities, although he often competes with himself as a way of testing and improving his performance. The person who is high on n Ach is also task-oriented: he likes to complete things he starts, to finish each task so he can get started on the next one, and to look for tasks that are not too easy.

None of this activity is consistent with n Aff, which focuses on such values as being accepted by and getting along with others, conforming to their expectations, and participating in joint activities. A group member who is ambivalent, who wants to "do his own thing" and also be a part of the group, experiences conflict when personal interests and group demands compete for his time and attention. The group member who is preoccupied with self-improvement is likely to be regarded with some distaste by his peers, who believes, rightly or wrongly, that he is aspiring to membership in groups that have higher status than theirs.

Young people who rate high on measures of n Ach are likely to be future-oriented. They feel that the kind of success they aspire to can be attained only in the adult world and that adolescence is only a temporary phase. Hence their tasks and goals are the more substantial ones of the "real world." The activities and values of the adolescent subculture are likely to be viewed by them as irrelevant and distracting. They are likely to take successful adults as their models and their reference group; hence they are viewed by their agemates as selling out to the adult world.

It is popular to think of young people who are high on n Ach and low on n Aff as conformists, and to think that the only nonconformists are the ones who identify themselves with the peer group. In reality, however, neither group has a monopoly on conformity or nonconformity. The dedicated peer-group member seems to be a nonconformist because he openly rejects the values and behavior patterns of the adult world, but in so doing he tacitly conforms to the norms of the peer group. The achiever, of course, tries to conform to adult standards and is a nonconformist as far as peer-group norms are concerned. Almost everyone conforms to the norms of some group or other; the only true nonconformists are those lonely souls who are completely alienated from social contacts of all types and those who are schizophrenic.

Most young people are not completely dominated either by n Ach or by n Aff; most try to satisfy both needs to the best of their ability, and most experience some emotional conflict. This conflict begins in elementary school and becomes acute in the earlier years of secondary school; when adolescents become aware that their eventual adult roles are being determined by their day-by-day decisions even in junior high. Those students who see themselves as going on to college usually make more and more decisions favoring achievement rather than affiliation goals.

Thomas A. Ringness (1967) conducted an investigation into the attitudes of eighth grade boys with IQs of 120 and higher, whom he classified as High, Middle, and Low Achievers. He found that the fundamental ethic of the peer group at that age was academic mediocrity, that the low achievers identified most strongly with this pattern of behavior, and that the high achievers tended to reject it.

Although high achievers tended to accept the goals enunciated for them by teachers, they nevertheless expressed some ambivalence, as did the other boys. The prevailing feeling among the high achievers was that teachers were more concerned with getting students to conform to regulations than with fostering cognitive development or intellectual liveliness. These boys saw schools as places in which to prepare for future occupations, rather than as places to develop talents, pursue interests, or improve social adjustment. The high achievers were, in other words, conforming to teachers' demands because it was in their best interests, but they had few illusions as to the possible contribution of school activities to personal growth.

The Popularity Cult

A somewhat different view of the values of the peer culture can be found in a series of studies by James S. Coleman (1961, 1965). The findings of Coleman's surveys of high-school students' attitudes and values are consistent with a popular stereotype—namely, that the prevailing ethic in high schools is that of having a good time to the exclusion of everything else. What Coleman's students said was that football, popularity, good looks, and having a good time were more important than academic achievement. In other words, his subjects rejected as irrelevant anything that was related to success in the adult world and favored social success in the peer group world instead. N Aff was favored over n Ach.

This rejection of adult values came about, Coleman said, because the world of the school is a compulsory, closed society that coexists but is unrelated to the adolescent world outside the school. In both these societies, in school and out, middle-class adolescents lead lives in which little outside of obedience and conformity is expected of them. Their economic needs are met by others, they do little if any work around the house, and they are not responsible for anyone else.

Coleman's findings that adolescents completely reject adult goals may be no longer relevant. In any event, more recent data appear to contradict it. Donald E. Carter and others (1975) conducted a study of a racially integrated junior high school in Buffalo, New York, in which they correlated social acceptance with a number of other variables. An analysis of the resulting data indicated that grade-point average (GPA) correlated higher with peer acceptance than did any of the other variables. To be sure, the investigators did not have athletics or good looks on their list of variables, but they did include race, sex, age, IQ, years in the school, attendance, and measures of self-concept. The fact that GPA was the most important of these variables suggests that when teachers assign grades, they are responding to much the same personal qualities that students do—probably such qualities as intelligence, verbal fluency, responsibility, cooperativeness, self-esteem, and ego strength.

A study by Callahan and Robin (1969) of high school students' views of leadership produced similar results. The subjects said that academic achievement, maturity, and good citizenship were more important qualities for leaders to have than popularity, good looks, and athletic achievement.

Perhaps times have changed since Coleman's surveys, but it does seem that teenagers, taken as a group, are not as alienated from adult values as many have feared.

What Values Do Adolescents Really Hold?

Nevertheless, one does hear much about adolescents' disenchantment with the success values of the real world, and much of what one hears comes from the lips of young people themselves. How can we rationalize this contradiction, or is it more apparent than real?

Much of it may, of course, be "just talk." The adolescent, like adults at times, may marshall the arguments against work and success merely to evoke counterarguments from others. He may also do so as a way of getting the significant adults in his life to indicate that they do care what he makes of himself. In addition, there may not be just one but several adolescent subcultures, some of them more antiadult than others. The adolescent is likely to be acquainted with all these variations and may try out their lines of reasoning in order to find one that suits him.

It is also possible that adolescents are themselves inconsistent and may vary what they say to suit the circumstances. In Chapter 14 we discussed the powerful influence that groups have on their members, an influence that can make itself felt without the individual member being aware of it. Consequently an adolescent may say one thing when he is filling out a confidential questionnaire for a behavioral scientist and something quite different when he is being observed. For example, Bronfenbrenner (1970) found, in his comparative study of American and Russian youth, that American children were more likely to express an attitude contrary to adult values when they knew that either their parents or their peers would hear of it, than when their position would be known only to the researcher. Such a tendency may be a culturally determined one, but it does suggest that when American teenagers are observed, they feel the need to challenge adults, as though such behavior were expected of them. This view makes some sense, in light of the antiauthority bias that seems to be traditional in the United States and that may be found in the media, in literature, and folklore.

An investigation by Elton E. Snyder (1969) sheds an interesting light on the question of how seriously we can take what adolescents say about their values. Snyder set out to put Coleman's findings and conclusions to the test by conducting a survey of the 1962 graduating class of the only high school in a midwestern community of 38,000. When he asked the students what they would like to be remembered as, over half the males said "most popular," followed by "brilliant student" and "star athlete," in that order. Almost half the females said they wished to be remembered as "leader in activities," followed by "most popular" and "brilliant student." (See Table 16-3.) The students' statements were significantly related to their behavior in high school: about two thirds of those who wanted to be remembered as "brilliant student" were below average in their participation in social activities, whereas those who wanted to be thought of as "most popular" were above average. So far, Snyder's findings were consistent with those of Coleman.

We began to entertain some doubts, however, when we find out how the students actually behaved after they graduated. We are not surprised to learn that those who wanted to be remembered as "brilliant student" went on to college and that most of them secured a bachelor's degree. The surprise comes when we find that almost the same proportion of those students who wanted to be remembered as "most popular," "leader in activities," and "star athlete" *also* went on to college and the bachelor's degree. Indeed, a higher proportion of the "leaders in activities" and "star athletes" actually graduated from college than in the other two groups. If the students were serious about the high value they placed on popularity and athletics, they must have reoriented their thinking markedly when they faced the decisions that had to be made on entering the real world.

TABLE 16-3. Percentages of High School Graduates Subscribing to Certain Values, in Contrast to the Percentages of the Same Group Subscribing to the Same Set of Values Five Years Later (data from Snyder, 1969)

	Responses at Time of Graduation	Responses Five Years Later	
	Would like selves to be remembered as:	Would like sons to be remembered as:	Would like daughters to be remembered as:
Male respondents			
Brilliant student	28	67	54
Most popular	51	7	16
Star athlete	21	26	30
Female respondents			
Brilliant student	21	67	46
Most popular	36	13	17
Leader in activities	43	20	37

Nor was social participation in high school any handicap when it came to college success. Snyder divided the graduates into three groups according to their IQs. Those in the highest group, 111 IQ and over, were half again more likely to have attained the bachelor's degree five years later if they had been socially active in high school. In the middle group, 100-110 IQ, those who had been socially active were four times as likely to graduate from college, whereas in the lowest group, 18 per cent of the socially active students graduated from college and none of the less active ones. (See Figure 16-1.)

Snyder also turned up some interesting findings that are related to our question of what adolescents mean when they say that social success is more important to them than academic success. In his follow-up survey in 1967, Snyder asked the graduates to imagine that they are parents of teenagers who are currently attending high school. How, he asked them, would they like their sons and daughters to be remembered?

Their replies indicate a drastic shift in the values they had expressed five years earlier, as Table 16-3 indicates. Two thirds of the respondents said that they wanted their sons to be remembered as brilliant students. And popularity, which they had rated so high five years earlier, was now at the bottom of the list. The percentages favoring brilliance for daughters were somewhat lower, but the trend was essentially in the same direction. Experience in the real world evidently had a marked effect on values. Perhaps if the students' real-world

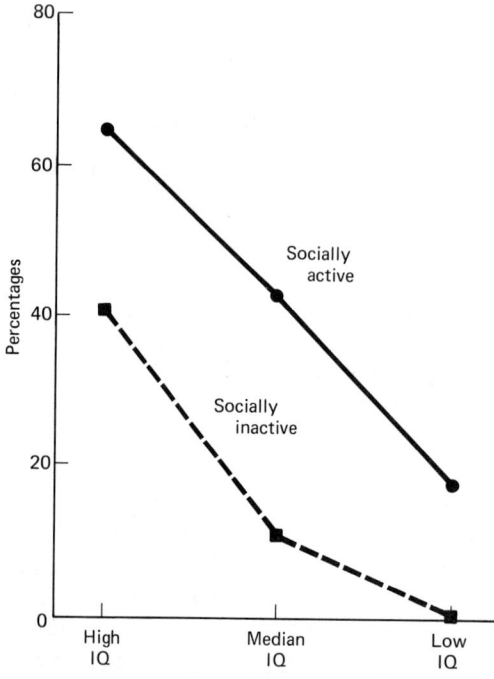

FIGURE 16-1. Percentages of socially active (above-average participation) and socially inactive (below-average participation) high school graduates who received at least a bachelor's degree five years later, classified according to their IQs. (Data from Snyder, 1969.)

contacts had been more extensive in high school, the values they expressed then would have been different.

What this and the other studies we have reviewed suggest is that teenagers may go on record as approving values related to affiliation, but that they are more accepting of achievement values than their replies would lead one to believe. In any event, the apparent priority they give to affiliation values is not a permanent commitment, but one that tends to diminish by early adulthood.

personality

Developmental Tasks

In Chapter 3, when we were discussing various theories of child development, we mentioned Havighurst's (1953) concept of developmental tasks. Havighurst proposed that some of the problems we encounter at various stages of our lives have a special importance, in that solving them prepares us for the next stage of development. The preschooler, for example, prepares himself through play experiences with his peers for the more complex social demands he will encounter at school.

The basic developmental tasks that Havighurst sees as relevant to adolescence are:

1. Accepting one's physique and accepting a masculine or feminine role.
2. Achieving new and more mature relations with agemates of both sexes.
3. Developing emotional independence of parents and other adults.
4. Achieving assurance of economic independence.
5. Selecting and preparing for an occupation.
6. Developing the intellectual skills and concepts necessary for civic competence.
7. Desiring and achieving socially responsible behavior.
8. Preparing for marriage and family life.
9. Building conscious values in harmony with an adequate scientific world picture.

Havighurst and his associates studied the behavior of children and adolescents aged 10, 13, and 16, and found support for his theory, for children who had been successful in coping with the developmental tasks of preadolescence tended to be successful with the developmental tasks of adolescence as well. Contrariwise, those preadolescents who had difficulties with developmental tasks appropriate to that stage were poorly prepared for adolescence and also encountered difficulty with developmental tasks at that stage as well.

The relationship between task accomplishments at successive age levels weakened somewhat over the six years—the span of the study—indicating that initial successes or failures became somewhat less important as time went on. This may have been because of the varying rates at which adolescents mature, or the general effect of peer group influence on individual behavior. Nevertheless, the trends that Havighurst and his associates identified turned out to be relatively stable, confirming the effect of a certain recurring consistency in adjustment patterns: early success promotes further successes, and early failure leads to further failures.

Self-Concept and Identity Diffusion

Havighurst's developmental tasks were sketched out with educators in mind, and hence were concerned with those aspects of life that could be related to curricular goals and to the development of school services, such as counseling. For that reason, the nine tasks listed by Havighurst do not include deeper and more pervasive concerns, such as self-identity.

Erik Erikson (1963) said that when the physical revolution we call puberty takes place in a young person, he becomes acutely concerned with what he appears to be in others' eyes, in contrast to what he feels he is. He continued further:

> In their search for a new sense of continuity and sameness, adolescents have to refight many of the battles of earlier years, even though to do so they must artificially appoint perfectly well-meaning people to play the role of enemies. . . .

What Erikson refers to here, of course, is the tendency for teenagers to maneuver parents and teachers into antagonist roles, in order to have foils against which they may test the limits and learn the parameters of social reality. In the give and take of this struggle, Erikson (1959) says, the adolescent integrates and makes more internally consistent the various identities he has accumulated and is in the process of accumulating. An adolescent, for example, typically identifies with or imitates a number of different key individuals—his parents, usually, but also perhaps a sibling, an adult relative, a close friend, or a teacher.

Because each young person makes a variety of such identifications, some of them inconsistent and contradictory, he runs the risk of experiencing what Erikson calls *identity diffusion*. This problem is surmounted by the adolescent's taking on various roles and "identities," rejecting some, accepting others which seem appropriate, and modifying them in accordance with his unique needs. This sorting, selecting, and blending of roles and identities enables him to put together some self-concepts and behavior patterns that fit his growing sense of "who he is."

The task is not an easy one. The tendency of adults, which we noted earlier, to disengage themselves from the lives of adolescents often means that young people must fend for themselves and do the best they can with the help of the peer group. Kenneth Kenniston (1965) pointed out that identity problems also result from the young person's attempt to span the gulf between childhood and adulthood while immersed in an intervening social environment that is disconnected from both of these periods and is also characterized by internal instability. The task is especially hard on those young people who are college-bound, and hence are oriented to the values of the world of adults, but are at the same time emotionally involved in antiadult (or at least nonadult) activities of the adolescent subculture.

Unresolved problems of identity diffusion can lead to an identity crisis, which Peter Madison (1969) describes as a developmental crisis brought on by an individual's realizing that his personal qualities and capabilities are incompatible with the social roles available to him in his present or anticipated situation. Many identity crises occur in relationship to career choice, as when a student finds that he simply cannot understand higher mathematics and has no hope of getting through the science courses in the premed sequence. As a consequence, he must give up lifelong plans and hopes of becoming a physician.

When the identity crisis comes on unexpectedly and very suddenly, the individual suffers an *identity shock,* in which he is confronted by a fundamental challenge to his self and social roles, which had been successfully integrated up until that moment. Such shocks often occur during the freshman year in college, when a student may experience a sudden drop in self-esteem, accompanied by apathy, depression, discouragement, and a failure to meet commitments.

Madison also identifies another type of identity shock, which is experienced by some students who realize that their background is limited and inadequate, as compared to that of their fellow students.

Still another type of identity crisis noted by Madison is a state he terms *nonbeing,* in which the individual's sense of identity is severely threatened and he fears that the self he knows will not continue to exist. He cites as an example a girl whose identity is closely tied to having a boy as a lover, but who fears that he may not be committed to her as fully as she is to him.

Madison points out that the early college years pose special problems for young people. They arrive on campus with an identity based on high-school success and the knowledge of who they are in their home community. Such identities are of no great value in college, however, and new identities must be formed. The college peer group has values that are usually quite different from those of the one left at home; even the available adult models represent different behavior standards and are, in most colleges, likely to be remote.

Achievement plays a part in the high-school world, as we have noted, although there is always some ambiguity as to whether social success is just as important. But in the college world the achievement orientation is much clearer, and the student's hope of attaining a secure and meaningful identity rests primarily on recognized competence not only in that setting, but also in the real world after college. In the early phases the task seems staggering, as the young person realizes that he is just beginning to get a glimpse of the vast body of knowledge that is required as a background for the competence he must develop.

Still another complication, according to Madison, is that the student is often unsure of what roles he will try to fulfill within the college setting. While the student is paying his dues to enter the adult world, "he must exist within a curious social system dissociated from his previous situation as well as from adult society, a system in which it is difficult to establish a basis for self-esteem and one in which comparatively few supporting roles are available."

The wonder of it all is that so many survive and are successful.

Problems Faced by Girls and Young Women

Identity diffusion poses especially difficult problems for women. Anne P. Constantinople (1969) collected the self-appraisals of almost a thousand undergraduates at the University of Rochester over a period of four years. Her analysis of the data indicated that male students had made fairly steady progress in the various problem areas described by Erikson as crucial to the development of self-esteem and identity, but that female students had not. Constantinople explained the difference in progress by the fact that male students usually enter college with a vocational goal in mind, whereas the goals of female students are likely to be social, using the term in its broadest sense. She continued:

> Much of what occurs in the academic environment of the college helps the male student to make choices and commitments with respect to a future career, thereby helping him to increase his sense of identity. He also has opportunities to try out tentative commitments both in course work and in major fields of study. The same pressures and opportunities, when applied to the female student, in many cases lead to a prolonged sense of identity diffusion. Even if a young woman becomes committed to a particular career field, she still faces a conflict between work and marriage. Young men are not asked to choose between a career and being a father, but many young women feel they must make such a choice. The inability to make this decision or the deferring of having to choose may be reflected in ... identity diffusion among the females.

Fear of success. Constantinople's data were gathered in the mid-1960s, before women were legally recognized as a minority group for purposes of job recruitment and employment. Nevertheless, what she reports has much validity even today with respect to the vocational expectations of college men and women. In spite of the fact that women are no longer excluded from jobs and training opportunities solely on the basis of their sex, the experience of clinicians in college guidance centers is that women clients still outnumber men and that identity problems have not diminished. If anything, women's greater opportunity for vocational self-expression had made the problems of choice, and hence of identity, more difficult for them.

Theoretically, a young woman has as much freedom as a man to select an occupational goal and prepare for it, but the social and psychological realities of life as it is lived pose problems that are not easily resolved. Even in these more enlightened days, according to Rose Laub Coser (1973), it is difficult to determine whether employers really discriminate against women or whether women keep themselves out of jobs because they accept the mandate of society that it is the woman's role to take care of the family, while her husband contributes status and income.

Indeed, it may be that women, adults and adolescents alike, have accepted the mandate of society to the degree that they avoid competing with males on issues that affect later success in a career. There is some evidence that this trend in thinking begins rather early. Girls tend to underestimate their own intellectual abilities more than boys do and have less confidence in their academic ability (Maccoby and Jacklin, 1974). Furthermore, a longitudinal study conducted at the Fels Research Institute reported that a comparison of twelve-year-olds whose IQs had showed marked changes over the years indicated that among children who had gained the most, boys outnumbered girls two to one, whereas girls outnumbered boys two to one among those whose IQs had declined the most. The investigators observed that the girls whose IQs declined tended to rate high on traits traditionally considered to be feminine. In another report on the same children, but covering the ages from 3 to 15, the researchers reported that all the individuals whose IQs had declined by the end of the period were girls. They explained this effect as a "flight into femininity," by which they meant that the girls were more interested in charm and personal attraction than in competing and achieving. The personality characteristics that were prominent in children demonstrating *increases* in IQ were competitiveness, independence from parents, and interest in problem solving—qualities that have been traditionally considered more masculine than feminine (Sontag, Baker, and Nelson, 1958).

The trait that has been identified with avoidance of competition and other success-oriented activity is what Matina S. Horner (1972) has termed *fear of success*. Horner maintains that the possibility of success, especially in competition with males, threatens women's self-esteem and feelings of femininity, and hence arouses anxiety lest one be rejected by others.

Horner measured fear of success by asking subjects to complete stories that began with the description of a fictitious character named Anne, who finds that she had made the highest score during an examination during the first year of medical school. In another story, the character hears that she was at the head of her class in nursing or teacher training.

Story completions can be used as a form of projective test, on the assumption that when subjects describe how Anne feels about her success they are revealing their own reactions. If they say that Anne is elated, we may assume that they feel positive and accepting of success; if they say that Anne is anxious or ill at ease, then we may assume that they, too, experience some emotional discomfort when they think of success for themselves.

When tests of this type were administered by Breedlove and Cicirelli (1974) to women students in college, the students tended to write story

Research by Matina S. Horner and others has shown that girls and women have, because of a "fear of success," avoided fields such as science, where they would be in competition with men. It may be that the new spirit of self-assurance that characterizes many young women today will lead to greater involvement in traditionally "masculine" activities and thus reverse this traditional attitude of defeatism.

completions characterized by fear of success. In completing the medical-school examination story, 70 per cent of the subjects expressed some negative affect—that is, Anne was described as anxious about popularity, marriageability, or loneliness; there was denial of the possibility that a woman would attain such success (perhaps an error had been made in scoring the examination); getting a high mark on an examination meant nothing because talent and competence cannot be measured by exams; and so forth. Only 49 per cent of the story completions relating to the teacher education success showed any negative affect.

Breedlove and Cicirelli interpreted these results as reflecting a prevailing attitude in society of rejecting women who are competitive, and they cited research indicating that the rejection of competitive females begins even during the preschool years. Women who attempt to enter traditionally masculine fields like medicine are generally regarded as aggressive and hence are likely to be rejected. Hence it is not surprising that the great majority of the women subjects expressed some negative feelings about Anne's success. It was not so much Anne's success that they are rejecting, but Anne's unfeminine aggressiveness and forwardness in attempting to compete with men in a man's field.

The fact that almost half the subjects expressed some negative affect even about Anne's success in teacher training was interpreted by the researchers to mean that women are inclined to belittle female success even in a field that is traditionally open to women.

There was also a tendency for women who were further along in college to express greater fear of success. This finding the researchers found consistent with earlier research showing that the closer women are to entering their adult roles, the more they tend to concentrate on their affiliative needs and to deny achievement needs.

In addition to the story-completion tests, the investigators gave the subjects tests designed to measure ascendency (competitiveness, dominance, ambition) and masculinity (rugged individualsim, competitiveness, self-centeredness). There was no relationship between masculinity and the tendency to make fear-of-success responses, but students with low ascendancy scores (reflecting passive-dependent attitudes and more cooperativeness than competitiveness) tended to write more fear-of-success completions for the medical-school story.

In other words, although one would expect that women who were more masculine or more upward-striving would be more accepting of Anne's success in medical school, high scorers on these two scales displayed as much fear of success as low scorers, showing how completely they had taken on the cultural bias against women's success.

Midgley and Abrams (1974), however, did find evidence suggesting that personality traits are involved in fear of success. In addition to administering Horner's test to a sample of female undergraduates, they also asked them to take Rotter's Internal-External Locus of Control (I-E) scale. Their hypothesis that women who saw themselves as internal—that is, as more in control of their own destinies—would be likely to express more approval of Anne's success in the medical-school examination was confirmed. Women with high external scores, as hypothesized, expressed more rejection of Anne in this setting.

After the administration of the tests, the investigators interviewed a sample of the subjects. In contrast to those scoring in the internal direction on the I-E scale, those with high external control scores felt more victimized by circumstances and less able to take positive action to control their environments. They also seemed less sure of themselves and seemed unlikely to be the kind of individuals who would attempt to penetrate the social barriers that obstruct women who attempt to be successful. In short, the data clearly showed that anxiety at the prospect of successful achievement was highest when it was associated with a fatalistic outlook about locuses of control.

The tendency of female subjects to express negative feelings about women's success appears to be widespread. Feather and Simon (1975) used a variation of Horner's test with secondary-school girls in Australia. The girls were asked to react to male or female characters who experienced success or failure in medical school, teacher's college, or nursing school. As Figure 16-2 indicates, the girls, as hypothesized, were very approving of the male character who was successful in medical school, but disapproved of the successful female medical student. They were even approving of the male character who was successful in teacher training and nursing school and somewhat less approving of the

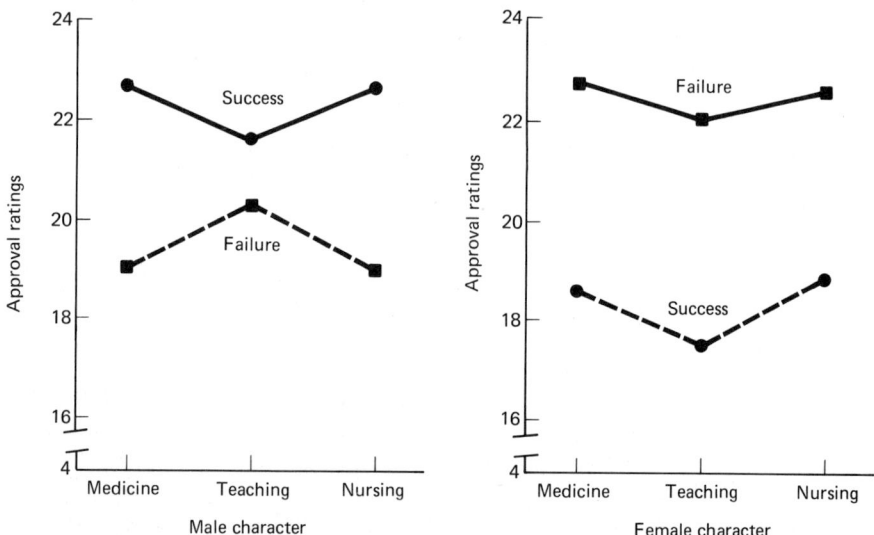

FIGURE 16-2. Ratings by adolescent girls of their acceptance of male and female story characters who succeeded or failed in medical school, teacher training, or nursing school examinations. (Data from Feather and Simon, 1975.)

male character who failed in any of the three situations. Like the women in the Breedlove-Cicirelli study, the Feather-Simon subjects also expressed disapproval of the female character who succeeded in the more traditionally accepted feminine fields. The highest approval of all, however, was reserved for the female character who failed in the three schools.

In short, the girls approved most of females who fail and of males who succeed, but disapproved most of females who succeed, followed by males who fail. It appears as though fear of success in women is likely to be associated with attraction of failure.

occupational choice

As the foregoing discussion suggests, it is difficult to generalize about common problems faced by both boys and girls as they face the need of making a vocational choice, however tentative, and beginning to prepare for it. Differences in SES also complicate matters. Although approximately half of the graduates of American high schools go on to college or some other form of advanced training and presumably prepare for middle-class status, the other half do not, and a great many who start college change their minds after a few weeks or months and seek employment without further training.

Occupation and Identity

Some generalities are valid, nevertheless. One is that occupational status in our culture defines who we are more than any other variable except age and sex. Educational status is important, too, but it is so closely tied in with occupational status that it is difficult to study them separately.

Everyday life abounds in examples of the importance of occupational status. For instance, when we are asked whether so-and-so is successful, we immediately assume that occupational success is meant, and if having an occupation makes success possible, not having one carries the stigmata of failure. Even when the circumstances leading to unemployment are beyond our control, we feel awkward and apologetic. In addition, we feel out of things, inadequate, as though we had let ourselves and everyone else down. The fact that young people today have such difficulty in getting jobs, either part time or full time, adds to their feeling of alienation from the real world.

Here is another example of the important part that occupational status plays in our identity. When two adults meet casually and start to become acquainted, one of the first questions is: "What do you do?" It is not that we compulsively have to compartmentalize everyone we know before we can get to know him or her better, but that knowing the other's occupation tells us much about his or her educational background and daily experiences. In order to get to know another person, it is necessary to have something to talk about and, after the weather and current politics have been exhausted, it is helpful to know something about the other's background in order to find topics of common interest.

When we know what another person's occupation is, we are also likely to know something about his values, tastes, and intersts. Although much of what we know, or think we know, about the traits and personality styles that go with certain occupations is questionable, there is enough validity to the idea that psychologists have been able to construct tests measuring job-related traits and behavioral tendencies. Research with the Strong Vocational Interest Blanks, for example, has shown that the attitudes, values, and interests of scientists and people in business are vastly different, and that librarians and artists are very similar in many respects (Campbell, 1974).

The money that one earns from being employed is important for survival in an economic sense, but it also has psychological implications. There is a crude but fairly consistent relationship between occupational status and income; therefore, unfortunately, self-esteem, status, and income somehow become inextricably tied together. Hence many young people refuse to consider low-status, personal-service occupations in which there is ready employment and instead join the hectic competition for entry into high-status, high-income professions, such as law and medicine. Even if a young person has little hope of actually qualifying for law or medical school, he secures a little vicarious glory for himself by claiming one of these professions as his eventual goal.

Vocational Aspirations and Reality

Mark J. Thomas (1976) conducted a survey of the vocational plans and hopes of black and white adolescents attending a large urban high school in New Jersey. The SES level of the boys was low, as indicated by the fact that all were participating in a federally financed school lunch program.

The boys were asked three job-related questions: A *reality question*—what kind of job they thought they would be able to do when they had finished with school and training; a *preference question*—what kind of job they would choose if they could really get the education and training they needed; and an *aspiration question*—what job they would like if they could get any job they wanted. The realism of the choices made by the boys was calculated in terms of the relationship between their intelligence, as measured by a nonverbal, culture-fair test, and the level of intelligence demanded by the jobs they had mentioned.

Figure 16-3 indicates that the boys were actually quite realistic with respect to the kinds of jobs they thought they would actually get, and also realistic about the kinds of jobs they would like if they could get the right kind of training. The jobs they aspired to were, as we might expect, somewhat unrealistic, but not extravagantly so. Although the graph shows the black youths as being somewhat less realistic than the white boys, the difference between the two racial groups was not statistically significant.

What this study indicates is that young people from lower SES communities actually have expectations that are quite down-to-earth, as far as job and training expectations are concerned, in spite of the fact that they often report aspirations that are unrealistic.

Part-time and Temporary Work Experiences

In Chapter 15, we mentioned some research by Lindgren (1962) that indicated that teenagers tend to be more rejecting of low-status jobs than individuals in their twenties are. This kind of choosiness is best dispelled by actual experiences in the world of work. Once adolescents have had the experience of waiting on tables or washing dishes in a summer resort, they are more willing to consider other low-status jobs. In truth, any job, no matter how glamorous or exciting it is, involves some tedious, monotonous, and repetitive tasks. There is no denying that many of the jobs available to teenagers are little more than

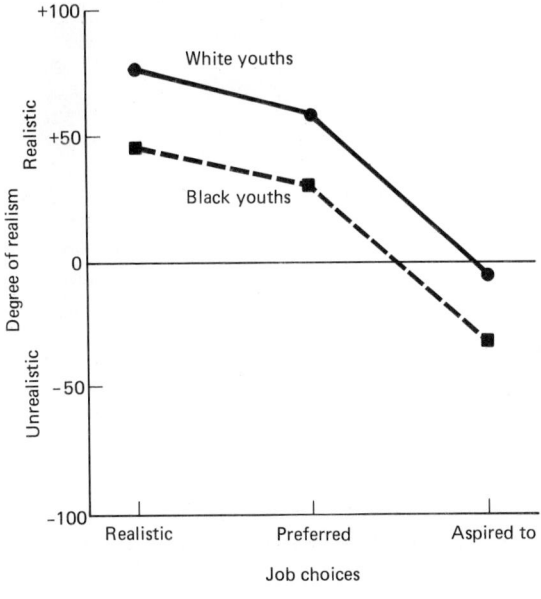

FIGURE 16-3. Degree of realism in the job choices of black and white male high school students asked to indicate a realistic, a preferred, and an aspired-to job choice. (Thomas, 1976.)

Part-time work enables teenagers to bridge the gap between adolescence and adult status and also provides opportunities both to learn new roles and to gain self-assurance.

drudgery. In spite of such shortcomings, the jobs do teach young people some fundamental skills and values, such as how to get along with one's supervisors and fellow employees, how to budget one's time and energy, and the importance of getting the job done that one is paid to do. The rewards of such work lie in the satisfactions that come from participating, albeit temporarily, as a fully functioning member in the real world, standing on one's own feet, receiving money that one has earned and that is not a handout, being valued for one's competence and not on the basis of a family relationships, and so forth.

Temporary and part-time jobs provide important ways of permitting young people to have a trial flight in the world of adults and to achieve some status under their own power. North American adolescents have a special advantage in that their families are usually willing, and even eager, for them to have that kind of experience. An upper-middle-class girl in Canada or the United States has no qualms about filling orders in a hamburger-and-fast-foods outlet; in other parts of the world, her family would be extremely upset and even outraged at the idea. The upper-middle-class North American boy who works part time in a service station has few counterparts in Europe, Latin America, or Asia.

Such jobs are not only valuable learning experiences for young people; they are also openings in the wall that divides the adolescent subculture from the real world.

sexual adjustment

In terms of the amount of time, energy, and anxiety expended, the adolescent's task of finding a way into the world of work is the major problem area of this developmental period, but if one measures in terms of the amount of time and space consumed by the media, sex wins the sweepstakes. The problems of vocational choice and preparation are always present; the adolescent works away at them almost every day; they are so ubiquitous that they are taken for granted. The problems of sexual adjustment are of a quite different nature. It is difficult to deal with them intellectually and rationally, on a day-by-day basis. They are more dramatic and intense; they cut across all phases of interpersonal behavior and self-esteem; and they often emerge at unexpected times.

The ways in which adolescents find their sexual identity and express it are extremely varied. In physiological terms, the sexual urge may have common, even universal elements, but the psychological effects that it has on individual behavior are extremely complex, varied, and often unpredictable. This point was missed by Alfred Kinsey and his co-workers (1948, 1953), who conducted their classic surveys of sexual behavior a generation ago, as well as by Johnson and Masters (1966, 1970) some years later.

Surveys of Sexual Behavior

The Kinsey teams were principally concerned with tallying the frequency of the various forms of sexual behavior and in relating the incidence to various demographic variables, such as age, sex, and educational level. The investigators interviewed several thousand men and women and reported that the male sexual drive appears to be strongest during the late teen years and gradually diminishes after the twenties, whereas the female sex drive is not especially strong during the teen years, reaches its maximum during the twenties, and is maintained at a relatively high level well into middle age. Their findings also confirmed the popular impression that females are, on the average, less readily aroused sexually than males are, and that they do not seem to feel the need for sexual intercourse as often as males do.

Some of these conclusions have been challenged by Masters and Johnson (1966, 1970), who conducted extensive research involving clinical observations of sexual couplings, as well as other forms of sexual activity. Masters and Johnson maintain that there are more similarities than differences in the sexual behavior of men and women.

Determining the relative validity of these two conflicting reports is not easy. The Kinsey team interviewed subjects drawn from a wide range of social groups, whereas the Masters and Johnson research focused on subjects who were either members of the highly educated middle class (members of university and hospital staffs, for example) or paid prostitutes. Although the Kinsey sampling was weighted somewhat with middle-class subjects, it may have been slightly more representative of the general population.

We should keep in mind, however, that both the Kinsey and the Masters-Johnson investigators thought of sexual behavior primarily in physiological terms and were primarily interested in performance.

As far as psychologists are concerned, the contents of the two sets of research reports is probably less interesting than the public's reaction. When the Kinsey reports appeared a generation ago, they evoked a great deal of controversy and even outrage, especially among the uninformed, inasmuch as they reported that masturbation and premarital, extramarital, and homosexual activity were much commoner than had been believed.

The Sexual Revolution

It may well be that the appearance of the Kinsey reports was the first indication that an era of greater sexual permissivness had begun. When the Masters-Johnson studies appeared a decade or so later, they aroused only a minor outcry. By that time, the so-called sexual revolution was well under way, and the lay public was more sophisticated. In fact, the ethics and the methodology of the researchers generated more controversy and criticism than their findings did.

As far as the sexual revolution is concerned, there are two versions of its dimensions. The first is that adolescents are sexually more active than they used to be; the other is that the level of activity is about the same, but that more is known about it, so that it only seems to be higher.

Hard data on social trends are seldom easy to obtain, especially in sensitive areas of behavior like sexual conduct. There are, however, some clues to suggest that for many young people, the times really are more permissive. One indication is the number of babies born to unwed mothers under 19. As Figure 16-4 indicates, the percentage of children born to unwed mothers of all ages has been increasing. In the meantime, the rate for births of all types has been dropping. The rate for illegitimate births had remained fairly stable—just under 5 per cent of all births—until 1960. Since that date, the percentage has risen sharply, until today about one child in seven is born to an unwed mother.

The percentage for unwed mothers 19 and under follows approximately the same course, except that the increase for this age bracket has been somewhat greater: today over half of all illegitimate children are

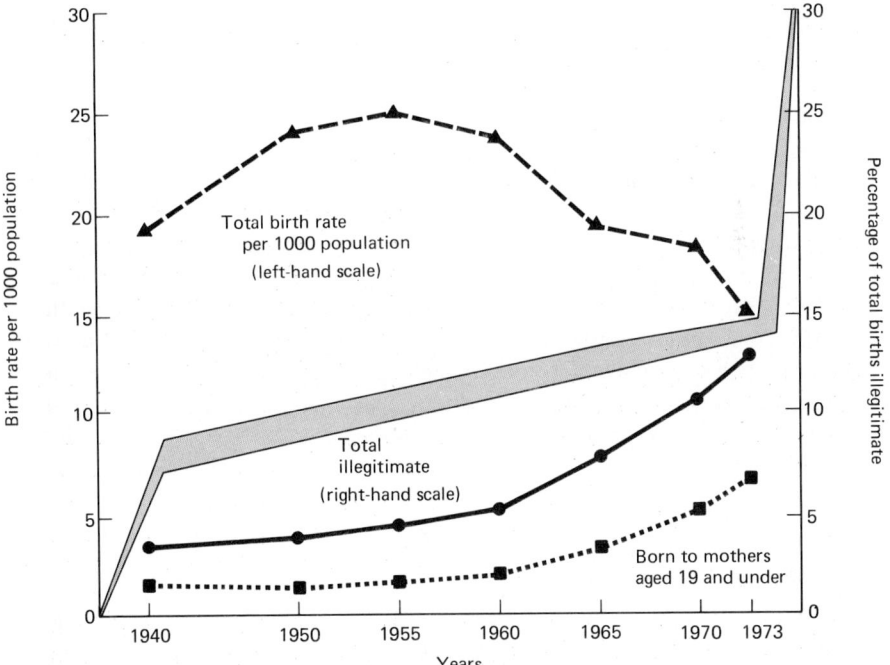

FIGURE 16-4. Birth rate per 1000 in the United States, 1940–1973, together with percentages of children born to unwed mothers of all ages and to unwed mothers aged 19 and under. (Data from U.S. Bureau of the Census, 1976.)

born to teenage mothers. The number of children born to unwed mothers under 15, which does not appear on the graph, has also increased phenomenally. In 1940 it was just over 2,000; in 1960 it was 4,600; and in 1973 it was almost 11,000.

When one keeps in mind that a sizable number of adolescents are using birth-control pills, and that abortions are becoming legal in most states, such figures suggest that teenagers are having sex experiences earlier and oftener than they did even ten years ago. This conclusion is supported by the fact that rates for infectious venereal disease for teenagers have also been increasing steadily during the same period.

Is There a Counterrevolution?

There is some contrary evidence, however. Miller and Simon (1974) conducted a survey of adolescents aged 14 to 17. An analysis of their data produced the unexpected finding that there seems to have been a substantial reduction in the incidence of male premarital sexual intercourse over the years. Other findings reported by Miller and Simon are less surprising. They found that teenagers were more likely to engage in sexual intercourse if (1) their educational aspirations were low, (2) they seldom attended religious services, (3) they were alienated from their parents, and (4) they were involved in delinquent activities.

Surveys of attitudes toward various sexual practices also suggest that a great many young people are not as tolerant as is popularly believed. Edwards and Stinnett (1974) surveyed students at seven universities in various parts of the United States, soliciting their views on "alternate life styles." Table 16-4 presents the percentages of students giving positive, negative, and ambivalent reactions to statements relevant to seven life styles. As the figures indicate, there was no life style that was

TABLE 16-4. Percentages of Students in Seven Universities Expressing Favorable, Unfavorable, or "Uncertain" Reactions to "Alternate Life Styles" (data from Edwards and Stinnett, 1974)

Life-style category	Favorable	Unfavorable	Uncertain
Two-stage or trial marriage	45	29	26
Cohabitation or "living together"	37	44	19
Extramarital sexual relations			
with consent of spouse	14	66	21
without knowledge of spouse	6	82	11
Group marriage	6	74	19
Communal living	30	40	29
Marriage between homosexuals	33	38	29
Total	24	53	22

Teenage pregnancies are more common than they were at one time. A contributing factor may be that young people become sexually mature at a younger age than was true of their parents and grandparents.

approved by a majority of the students, the highest being two-stage or trial marriage, which was acceptable to 45 per cent. The life style that evoked the greatest disfavor was extramarital relations without the knowledge of one's mate. Group marriages and extramarital relations with one's spouse's consent also were regarded with considerable disfavor.

In another question, 65 per cent of the students polled said that none of the alternate life styles was acceptable to them, whereas 25 per cent said that they favored *all* life styles. In reply to the question "Do you believe that traditional monogamous marriage is the most fulfilling type of man-woman relationship?" 70 per cent said "yes," 8 per cent said "no," and 22 per cent were undecided.

We seem to be faced with two sets of seemingly contradictory data: evidence of increased premarital activity on the part of teenagers and evidence indicating that young people are really quite conservative in their views on sex. How can we rationalize these disparities? Because we have no reason to doubt the validity of any of these studies, we can assume either that (1) attitudes are still conservative, but sexual freedom is the prevailing norm, or (2) the sets of data represent different groups of teenagers.

There is little or no evidence for the first interpretation, and studies of the relationship between values and real behavior generally show much more consistency than inconsistency. Furthermore, there are studies suggesting that youngsters who are more strongly identified with peer-group values than with those of the adult world are the ones most likely to engage in premarital sex. The investigation of Miller and Simon (1974), cited above, is only one of a number of studies that make that point. Inasmuch as identification with the peer group tends to be lower among those who attend college than among those who do not, it would appear that the endorsement of conservative values regarding sexual behavior probably is associated with a lower rate of premarital sex. Differences are relative and not absolute, of course. In other words, the college students of today are probably more active sexually than they were ten and twenty years ago, but the degree of involvement is not nearly as great as it is among noncollege youth.

Sex Differences in Sexual Attitudes

Although Masters and Johnson, in their research into the physiology of the sexual response, found no sex differences of any significance, most people believe that women are more conservative, less adventurous, and more inhibited when it comes to sexual behavior. A number of studies support this impression. For example, Edwards and Stinnett, in the research cited above, found that the women were significantly more conservative with respect to alternate life styles than the men were.

A study by Donald L. Mosher (1973) supports the same conclusions. Mosher showed unmarried college students films depicting face-to-face and oral-genital sex, which has been produced by the Institute for Sex Research in Hamburg, Germany, for use in sex clinic training. The films were not "pornographic" by so-called adult-movie standards, but they were quite explicit. In contrast to the male students, female students were more likely to say that the films were disgusting, offensive, and pornographic. They also found the films less enjoyable and the behavior depicted as more abnormal.

Other supporting data come from a study by Izard and Caplan (1974). They asked Vanderbilt University undergraduates to read, in the privacy of their rooms, a chapter from a best-selling book that described the seduction of a virgin by a sexually experienced young man, and to indicate their reactions on a questionnaire. Male students reported more sexual arousal, interest, and pleasure, whereas female students reported more disgust.

Still further data are provided by the Kinsey researchers, who reported that men tended to have more dreams involving sexual arousal and climax. Ehrmann (1959), too, in his survey of premarital dating behavior, found that boys and girls separately agreed that it was the boy who initiated the activity leading to sexual intercourse in about three fourths of the instances in which it occurred.

Sex and Personal Identity

Part of the reason why there are sex differences in response to sexual matters lies in the different meaning that sexual behavior has for males and females. Peter Madison (1969) points out that the ability to initiate and carry out the sex act is deeply involved with male identity in our culture, and that "sexual failure is very damaging to the boy's self-esteem." Self-esteem seems to be less of an issue for girls in such matters. Many boys and young men engage in an aggressive pursuit of sex with girls, which is to a large extent a search for identity through sexual competence. This kind of sexual-competence motivation is what leads boys to treat girls as sex objects. The reverse can also occur, although less often, with girls who entertain doubts about their heterosexuality; under such circumstances, boys can become sex objects to girls.

When each partner regards the other as a sex object, rather than a person, it is because sex is not a mutual interest, but a way of identity formation; the girl is using sex appeal to assure herself that she is able to attract a boy, and the boy is using the girl to establish his masculine identity.

Learning the Folklore of Sex

Madison points out further that sexual learning takes on a special character in our society. Although many if not most parents deliberately attempt to provide some kind of sex education for their children, the most significant teachings are often unconscious ones. The use of "telling silences" is even more important than pointing out specific dangers. The child imaginatively embellishes all these hints and clues, says Madison, "into privately kept sexual feelings that are generally unsocialized and linked in idiosyncratic ways to chance-provided excitement of almost any description."

The entertainment industry and the advertiser also become unintentionally involved as teachers of the young, and inadvertently cause sex to be associated in the youthful mind with an exotic variety of manufactured products, as well as with violence and destructiveness. By the time young people reach late adolescence, these bizarre and totally artificial learnings have led many of them to assume that they are sexually different or even abnormal.

The result of this process, says Madison, is that by the time the final teen years are attained, the young person's sexual motives are shot through with all manner of immature belief and popular folklore. "Fears and misconceptions abound; there are frequent residuals from homosexual play; and sex is largely a solitary, unsocialized motive." Self-centeredness dominates.

early experiences as predictors of adult adjustment

A consideration of the awkward and sometimes calamitous experiences of adolescents as they attempt to grope their way toward vocational and sexual maturity leads one to wonder why so many of them attain a satisfactory adjustment as adults. This further raises the question of whether as psychologists we do not become preoccupied with what is wrong with adolescence rather than what is right about it. There is probably a lesson in all this, a lesson that was detailed by Jean Walker Macfarlane (1971), as she reviewed what she had learned from the Guidance Study, conducted for over thirty years by the Institute of Human Development of the University of California in Berkeley.

Macfarlane noted that the psychologists in the study were inclined to be quite pessimistic about the future mental health of many of the children they observed. Hence it came rather as a shock in later years when they discovered that half the children had become more stable and more effective adults than had been anticipated. A fifth turned out less effective than predicted, and only a third were on target—a poor record by any standard.

The best predictions were for youngsters who were mentally retarded and for those who had overcontrolled, rigid, compulsive personalities and hence were unable or unwilling to reach out and cope with the challenges in their environment. Another group for which predictions were accurate were those whose parents treated them in exceedingly inconsistent ways—overindulgence changing rapidly to devastating harshness. Most of those who were compulsive alcoholics as adults fall into the latter category.

The fifty per cent who turned out better than expected were those who appeared, as children and adolescents, to have "overriding evidences of handicapping personality patterning or disorganization," which led the psychologists to predict "crippled or inadequate adult personalities." These included some who as adolescents seemed dedicated to defying regulations. Others were hard to classify. One was an adolescent who seemed like a listless oddball, who had only average IQ and grades below par. He left the community, made up high-school deficiencies, and became a talented architect. Still another, a self-centered social isolate as an adolescent, grew up to become a responsible business executive.

Macfarlane said that the high percentage of wrong predictions resulted from the tendency of the psychologists to overweigh the negative and seemingly pathological aspects of the personalities of the children and adolescents and to overlook elements that were maturity-producing. They also underrated the capacity of adolescents to unlearn ineffective patterns of behavior and to learn new ones. Still another reason—one that is especially significant for our study of adolescent development—is that "no one becomes mature without living through the pains and confusions of maturing experiences."

Macfarlane's observations should not be taken as a rejection of scientific research in the field of child and adolescent development. She had no quarrel with the data—merely with the interpretations. The predictions probably made sense in terms of the data that had been gathered and the theories of child development that prevailed at the time. With more data and better theories, we will be able to understand children and adolescents more adequately and make more valid predictions. The main task of the scientist is not prediction, however, but gathering the data and making sense of them. Prediction is only a test that enables us to find out whether our observations and interpretations were valid. This is why we need more data and better theories.

summary

Western urbanized societies demand much of adults in the way of attention and maintenance. Young people, left on their own, form adolescent subcultures, which are unstable and do little to protect them from the crises and painful experiences of growing up.

The dependent relationship between children and parents is placed under strain because children change faster than parents do. Parents are left unsure how much love and direction a child needs; children often resist both. This disparity between what children need and what adults want to offer becomes acute during adolescence, and disagreements on that subject become aggravated by adult demands that adolescents conform to acceptable behavior standards and also express responsibility.

Some adolescents deny their residual emotional and functional dependence on adults by flight into some form of delinquency. Most adolescents work through the problems, relying on their growing ability to express and share love and to empathize with others. Those who make the best adjustment in school and also with peers are those who have positive relations with their parents. Even in the best of family situations there is some dissension, however. Studies of the family life of adolescents who were either users or nonusers of drugs confirm these patterns. Middle-class families classified as "high risk" with respect to adolescent drug use tended to be unsure about child-rearing methods, less cohesive, more permissive, less demanding of conformity to norms, more inclined to intellectualize about problems, less concerned about law and order, and more to have problems with respect to alcohol. Similar differences were found with respect to high- and low-risk families who were working class or Mexican-American. In general, low-risk families were stricter and more traditional than high-risk families. Whatever the type of family, however, the adolescents all said that they looked to their parents as sources of love and as teachers of values and behavior standards, and it appears that those parents who were least able to meet these expectations were the ones whose children became more involved in the peer-group culture and hence in drugs.

The adolescent's need for affiliation—n Aff—leads to his involvement in the peer group. N Aff is diametrically opposed to the need to achieve—n Ach. N Ach leads to involvement in activities that improve competence in problem solving and task completion, activities that are solitary and make involvement in the peer group difficult. Achievement is also consistent with adult values, and attempts to express such values arouse resentment on the part of peer-group members. Although the individual who rates high on n Ach is popularly regarded as a conformist, all adolescents conform in one way or another. The question is whether one conforms to adult standards or to peer standards. Peer standards in high school tend to stress academic mediocrity and social success. Coleman's study in the early 1960s found that football, popularity, good looks, and having a good time were more important to high school students than getting good marks. More recent studies suggest that students are probably more responsive to intellectual competence than they are willing to admit. One investigation indicated that high-school students on graduation tended to value social activities higher than academic achievement, but that five years later they said that academic achievement was more important. There was also a disparity between the values they claimed at graduation and their subsequent behavior: most of those who endorsed social values and rejected academic ones actually went on to college and graduated. Involvement in social activities during high school turned out to be a positive factor, however, and was actually predictive of subsequent graduation from college.

Adolescents' developmental tasks include self-acceptance, satisfactory social relations with agemates of both sexes, attaining independence, and preparing for adult status as job holders and as citizens.

Children who successfully deal with the developmental tasks appropriate to their level have fewer problems as adolescents. Erikson says that adolescents accumulate a number of identities, some of them contradictory, which they have to integrate. Failure to achieve integration leads to identity diffusion. Crises occur when the young person realizes that his personal qualities and capabilities are inadequate to the demands that are being made on him. Fundamental challenges to his self and social roles may cause identity shock. The first year of college is especially trying because students find that their precollege identities and models are inappropriate. The achievement norms that prevail in college are clear, but students characteristically are unsure of what kind of adults they want to become.

Identity diffusion poses special problems for young women, many of whom feel that they must choose between a career and being a homemaker. The conflict is experienced by women even today, in spite of the fact that there are fewer barriers to professional goals. Women are also inclined to underrate their abilities, a tendency that appears during the childhood years. Young women's unwillingness to invade job areas that have been traditionally masculine may be caused by fear of success, a trait that is measured by a projective technique, in which subjects complete a one-line story describing a fictitious character, Anne, who discovers that she is at the top of the list in a medical school examination, or in a teacher-training examination. There is a tendency for most young women to say that Anne, the medical student, will experience anxieties about popularity or marriage prospects. Fewer subjects express negative reactions to Anne, the education student, although there is a tendency for female adolescents to feel more positive about "Annes" who are unsuccessful in any field, in contrast to "Annes" who are successful. It is assumed that subjects who are rejecting of the successful Anne, and are more accepting of the unsuccessful one or the one who succeeds in a traditionally feminine field, are expressing their own fear of failure. Young women who feel victimized by circumstances and unable to control their environments—that is, whose locus of control is external—are more likely to experience fear of failure.

Occupational status defines "who we are" in our culture. We feel inadequate when unemployed, and we use a person's occupational status as a means of deducing information about his experiences, interests, and values. The association of occupational status, money, and self-esteem makes it difficult for many young people to be realistic about job choices. A research study suggests that although adolescents may claim glamorous jobs as their objectives, most of them are quite realistic in terms of the kinds of jobs they should prepare for and seek. Part-time and temporary work, even in low-status jobs, provides good learning experiences for adolescents and offers them opportunities for entry into the real world of adult life.

Although problems attendant on occupational choice and adjustment are the major ones in adolescence, those involving sexual adjustment get the most attention and are more emotionally involving. Surveys of sexual behavior by the Kinsey team of researchers some thirty years ago aroused a great deal of controversy and criticism, but probably set the stage for the sexual revolution—the trend toward greater permissiveness. Although some people doubt that young people are more sexually permissive these days, the statistics on unwed teenage mothers and on adolescent venereal disease indicate that young people are engaging in more premarital sex than they did ten and twenty years ago. On the other hand, surveys of college students indicate that their attitudes toward "alternate life styles" of sexual behavior are decidedly conservative. It may be that most of the increase in premarital sex has taken place with adolescents who are closely identified with the peer culture and who reject the values of adult society.

Sexual activity has different meanings for the two sexes. Males are more easily aroused and are more likely to take the initiative in sex activity. Sexual performance is more intimately tied up with identity of males, and they find failure more devaluating of self-esteem. But self-centeredness may dominate when girls employ sex appeal to assure themselves that they can attract boys, and boys exploit girls to establish their masculine identity, each using the other as a sex object. Thanks to parental misinstruction and inaccurate impressions gathered from the media, adolescents develop some rather odd ideas about sex and their own sexuality.

Macfarlane reports, on the basis of her experiences in a longitudinal study covering the years from infancy to adulthood, that most of the pessimistic predictions of the researchers were not validated, and that half the subjects turned out to be better adjusted as adults than had been anticipated. The problems of adolescence were not crippling, but instead prepared them for adulthood. The experience of the psychologists in this study suggests that we need more data and better theories.

Glossary

acetylcholine: One of the biochemicals within the nervous system; the release of acetylcholine facilitates the transmission of nerve impulses.

achievement, need for (n Ach): Motive to work persistently, energetically, and eagerly at the accomplishment of tasks and to seek new tasks to accomplish.

adultomorphism: Views or interpretations of the behavior of children that are characterized by the unwarranted assumption that they think, feel, and perceive as adults do.

affective: Characterized by affect—that is, feeling, emotion, temperament, mood, and attitude—as contrasted with cognition.

affiliation, need for (n Aff): Motive to seek affection and emotional support from others and to become involved in dependency relationships with them.

alienation: The feeling of being estranged from society in general and unable to relate to others.

allantois: A sausage-shaped tube that develops during the early stage of the embryo; a portion of the allantois eventually becomes the bladder.

amnion: The sac or membrane that encloses the fetus. The liquid surrounding the fetus is the amniotic fluid.

amphetamines: Stimulants that act on the nervous system to produce wakefulness, restlessness, irritability, anxiety, and rapid heart rate. Paradoxically, some amphetamines seem to have a quieting effect on hyperactive children.

anaclytic depression: Severe depression encountered in infants whose caregiver is absent for an extended period.

anal stage: According to psychoanalytic theory, the period of development during which bowel control is established and the child's pleasure and conflicts are focused on expelling or retaining feces.

analgesic drugs: Drugs used to relieve pain.

animism: The assumption or belief that important objects are living, or that they have feelings, purposes, and motives.

anorexia nervosa: Loss of appetite for food, caused by severe anxiety.

anxiety: State of uneasiness and tension similar to fear, attributable to some vague source within oneself, occurring with respect to the future, or within the context of interpersonal relations.

Apgar scores: Ratings made immediately after birth of the neonate's breathing, muscle tone, heart rate, reflexes, and color.

apnea: temporary cessation of breathing.
attachment: The state of emotional dependency focused on significant caregivers, characteristic of infants about seven months and older.
authoritarian: Having behavior and attitudes that are highly conventional, judgmental, cynical, and traditional. When applied to parental behavior, the term implies strictness, rigidity, and punitivity, coupled with domineering attitudes and a lack of concern for the rights and feelings of children.
authoritative: Characterized by firmness in parental discipline, based on rational and realistic appraisal of children's capabilities, environmental risks, and the rights and feelings of others who are concerned or involved.

Babinski reflex: A tendency for the toes to extend upward, instead of contracting, when the sole of the foot is stroked; characteristic of young infants.
Babkin reflex: A response elicited from a supine infant, who will raise his head to an upward position and open his mouth when his palms are pressed.
basic learning ability (BLA): As conceptualized by Arthur R. Jensen, rudimentary aspects of human learning, chiefly those involving rote memory.
behaviorism: A school or system of psychology characterized by emphasis on objectivity, empiricism, and the restriction of research data to activities that can be directly observed. Conscious experiences and introspection are specifically excluded.
blastocyst: The ball of cells that develops from the fertilized ovum or zygote and that will become an embryo.

capillaries: Tiny, hairlike blood vessels.
caregiver: Anyone who takes care of an infant or child, usually over an extended period of time.
centration: The tendency for young children to be preoccupied with a specific and sometimes irrelevant feature of an object or situation and hence to overlook other important aspects, thus causing a distortion in reasoning.
cephalocaudal: The developmental trend or direction proceeding from the head to the end of the trunk.
cerebral cortex: The barklike outer layer of the brain hemispheres.
cholinesterase: One of the biochemicals that makes possible the transmission of impulses within the nervous system.
chorion: The outer layer of the embryo.
chromosomes: Pairs of small particles, found in all body cells, which carry genes transmitted from parent to child.
classical conditioning: Conditioning of the type conceptualized by Pavlov, in which a neutral and previously irrelevant stimulus is paired with a stimulus that already evokes a certain response, referred to as an unconditioned stimulus or US. After the pairs of stimuli are presented repeatedly, the neutral stimulus comes to evoke a response similar to that evoked by the second stimulus and is hence referred to as a conditioned stimulus (CS).
cognition: Aspects of behavior associated with knowing—that is, perceiving, imagining, reasoning, thinking, and judging.
cognitive: Characteristic of behavior associated with cognition, usually contrasted with *affective*.
cohort: One of two or more groups of subjects being followed in longitudinal research.

concordance: In genetics, the degree of similarity between pairs of individuals with respect to variables under investigation.

concrete operations period: The stage of cognitive development that usually occurs during the elementary-school years, during which the child typically acquires the ability to conserve, to classify objects, and to arrange them in serial order.

conditioned response (CR): In classical conditioning, the response that the new conditioned stimulus (CS) is able to evoke.

conditioned stimulus (CS): In classical conditioning, the new stimulus that originally did not evoke the desired response, but is now able to do so.

conditioning: The process of acquiring new responses, or learning.

conservation: The ability to recognize that objects' properties (such as quantity, volume, and number) are unchanged in spite of changes in their appearance.

control, scientific: Steps taken by researchers to ensure that their results are not contaminated by the effect of variables other than the ones they are investigating.

correlation, coefficient of: A numerical index reflecting the relationship or correspondence between sets of paired variables.

corticosterone: A biochemical released by the cortex of the adrenal gland; the concentration of corticosterone in the blood may be used as an index of emotional reactivity.

criterion: A standard used as a measure of success in the performance of a task.

critical period: A stage in development during which the availability or absence of key elements, or the experience of unusual stress, will have significant effects on the organism's development during later stages.

cross-cultural research: Research that attempts to identify and measure similarities and differences in psychological traits by comparing people from different cultures and subcultures.

cross-sectional research: The study of a large number of variables in one or more groups at specific points in time, as contrasted with longitudinal research, in which one or more individuals are followed over extended periods of time.

cytomegalovirus (CMV): The most common infectious cause of birth defects.

Darwinian reflex: The grasping reflex that is initiated when a neonate's palm is stroked.

decentering: The process whereby centration gives way to more mature cognitive styles that are based on a greater awareness of the complex characteristics of objects.

decibel: A unit employed in measuring the intensity of sound.

defense mechanism: An unconsciously motivated form of behavior that has the function of preventing or reducing anxiety.

deindividuation: As conceived by Zimbardo, a drop in self-restraint, accompanied by a tendency to yield either to impulse or to group influence.

deoxyribonucleic acid (DNA): Large and complex molecules found in the nuclei of cells or organisms and believed to be the basis for genetic inheritance.

depth perception: The perception of differences in distance, basic to an awareness of the three-dimensionality of space.

development: The sequence of irreversible changes that take place in an organism from its initial state, through maturity, until death.

developmental task: Levels of achievement or competence which, at a given age, are considered to be necessary or desirable for socially acceptable functioning.

differential research: Investigations that compare two or more groups of subjects with respect to significant traits. Often used synonymously with *correlational research*.

disinhibition: The dissolution or dropping of self-restraints.

dizygotic (DZ) twins: Twins who develop from two different fertilized ova or zygotes and who hence are no more similar, genetically speaking, than any two nontwin siblings.

drive: The state of an organism that has been aroused by some internal deficiency (in nourishment or fluids, for example) or by external stimulus, thereby inciting it to take some relevant action.

ecology: The studying of the interaction between the physical and the biological features of the environment.

ectoderm: The outermost layer of cells in the embryo, eventually developing into the skin and nervous system.

ectomorph: An individual whose body structure is characterized by leanness, boniness, and angularity.

ego: In psychoanalytic theory, the regulating and rational aspect of behavior, which restrains the impulses of the id in order to cope with the demands of society and the reality of everyday life. In general terms, the self-concept.

ego-ideal: Our view of the kind of individual we feel we should become, an aspect of the superego.

Electra complex: In psychoanalytic theory, the unconscious, sexually toned attraction of a girl toward her father, coupled with a corresponding rejection of her mother—in other words, the female version of the Oedipus complex.

electroencephalogram (EEG): A recording of the electrical activity in the brain.

embryo: The prenatal organism, during the first six weeks after conception, after the zygote has developed into a blastocyst.

embryonic disc: The cells within the blastocyst that form the embryo.

empathy: The ability to sense the feelings, attitudes, motives, and views of others.

endoderm: The innermost layer of cells in the embryo, eventually developing into the digestive tract and other internal organs.

endomorph: An individual whose body structure is characterized by fatty tissue and plumpness.

ethnic prejudice: Bias and hostile attitudes directed toward the members of other racial and/or religious groups.

existentialists: Psychologists who hold that each individual manifests his identity through the choices he makes in resolving everyday problems and dilemmas.

fallopian tube: Tube leading from an ovary to the uterus.

fear of success: A motivational factor identified by Matina Horner, who found that many adolescent girls and young women are inclined to avoid roles or positions indicative of success and to prefer those characterized by lower or subordinate status.

fetus: The unborn child from about three months onward, when it leaves the embryo stage.

field dependence: A tendency to be distracted by irrelevant visual cues when determining one's position with respect to the physical environment or when trying to locate figures concealed within a complex drawing.

fixation: A form of behavior that persists, either because of repeated reinforcement or because of frustration. Psychoanalytic writers use *fixation* to refer to behavior patterns or personality traits that remain as holdovers from an earlier level of psychosexual development.

formal operations: The stage of cognitive development in which a child acquires the ability to use abstract rules; usually occurs at twelve years of age or later.

full-term: Born at the appropriate stage in development—that is, not prematurely.

gastrointestinal: Involving the digestive tract.

genes: Elements within the chromosomes that carry and transmit hereditary characteristics.

genetics: The study of inherited characteristics.

Gestaltists: Members of the Gestalt school of pscyhology, who studied the tendency to perceive the environment in terms of wholes, patterns, configurations, and forms, rather than specific details.

"global" measures: Tests designed to pick up individual differences with a wide span of behavior—projective tests, for instance.

glucose: A type of sugar that occurs widely in nature; the usual form of sugar consumed by animals.

gynecologist: A physician specializing in the medical problems of women.

habituation: The normal tendency to become less responsive when exposed to repeated stimulation, used as one measure of neonatal competence.

hemoglobin: The iron-containing pigment of the red blood cells.

hierarchization: As conceived by Heinz Werner, the process by which simple skills become "submerged" in complex skills, as more and more of the latter are acquired.

holistic: Unitary, integrated, "global"; based on the idea that the whole is more than the sum of its parts.

hyperactivity: The behavior of children who are assumed to have minimal brain dysfunction, or MBD. The symptoms, which are more often encountered in boys, consist of excessive and essentially random motor behavior, short attention span, distractibility, poor impulse control, and impairment of perceptual accuracy.

hyperkinesis: Hyperactivity.

hypothesis: A tentative and untested explanation of a set of observations.

id: In psychoanalytic theory, unconscious strivings for immediate satisfaction of instinctual drives.

ideal self: *See* ego ideal.

identification: Taking on the values, attitudes, beliefs, and behavior of an admired or respected person. Often employed as a synonym for "modeling."

identity crisis: A state of emotional upset, occurring when an adolescent or young adult feels that his psychological resources fall short of what he needs to deal with the demands of his present or anticipated social situation.

identity diffusion: As conceived by Erik Erickson, the difficulties experienced by adolescents and young adults in achieving mature personality integration.

identity shock: A sudden and unexpected identity crisis.

idiographic: Attempting to study and understand the personality of an individual, rather than traits characteristic of persons in general.

imprinting: A type of learning that may occur during a limited period very early in the life of certain animals; it is relatively unmodifiable thereafter.

independent variable: The variable manipulated by the experimenter in an attempt to produce changes in a dependent variable.

instincts: Responses occurring in most of the members of a given species, even though the opportunities for learning the responses are absent.

instrumental conditioning: *See* operant conditioning.

intelligence: A hypothesized trait, commonly defined in terms of the ability (1) to deal with abstractions, (2) to learn, and (3) to adapt to new situations. Also, the quality or characteristic measured by intelligence tests.

intelligence quotient (IQ): An index to the amount of intellectual development that has been attained by an individual, obtained by dividing the individual's mental age (based on the score he made on a mental test) by his chronological age and multiplying the results by 100.

introjection: Identification.

introspective method: The reporting of one's own experience, a research method used by early psychologists in their study of consciousness.

introversion: A tendency to turn one's interests inward and to avoid interaction with others.

isolate: An individual who, in the course of sociometric survey, is found to be rejected or merely not chosen by other members of his group.

kibbutz (*plural* kibbutzim): Israeli communal societies whose economic activities are centered on farms and small businesses.

language acquisition device: In psycholinguistics, the mechanisms, present in all normal children, that enable them to develop the ability to process linguistic data and thus to achieve grammatically sound competence in their native language.

learning: The processes that produce relatively enduring changes in behavior, resulting from experience. Learning is usually conceived as an effect of the organism's environment and is contrasted with maturation, which is viewed in terms of processes that are primarily initiated and controlled by internal forces.

Level I ability: According to Arthur R. Jensen, the ability to learn by rote, to memorize, and to follow simple directions. Similar to Basic Learning Ability, or BLA.

Level II ability: According to Jensen, the ability to manipulate symbols, to reason, to test hypotheses, and to solve problems.

libido: As conceived by Freud, the energy base of all human strivings—the "life

force." Usually applied in a more narrow sense to the drive for sexual gratification.
locomotion: Moving oneself, through crawling, slithering, walking, jumping, running, etc.
locus of control: The position taken by an individual on a scale that ranges from a belief that the reinforcing agents in his everyday experiences are largely internal (under his own control) to the belief that his reinforcements are largely external in origin (controlled by others or by chance factors). This tendency or trait is measured by Julian B. Rotter's I-E (internal-external) Scale.
longitudinal method: Observation of an individual or a group of individuals over an extended period of time, undertaken for the purpose of identifying and charting changes in characterisitics.
low-birth-weight infant: An infant delivered prematurely, as contrasted with full term.

marasmus: A wasting away of tissues, observed in infants who are poorly nourished and/or understimulated.
maturation: Changes in behavior and structure occurring in all normal members of a species. May be blocked or inhibited if environmental conditions are unfavorable.
meconium: A greenish mass, present in the intestinal tract of a fetus, and excreted shortly after birth.
menarche: The first occurrence of the menstrual cycle, signaling the onset of puberty in adolescent girls.
mesoderm: In the embryo, the middle layer of cells, which develops into bones and muscles.
mesomorph: A person whose body build is characterized by the prominence of muscle and bone, as in the typical athlete.
méthode clinique, la: A method employed by Piagetian interviewers, in which they pose problems to a child and then follow up his replies with probing questions designed to determine the thought processes he is using.
minimal brain dysfunction (MBD): *See* hyperactivity.
modeling: Imitating an admired or otherwise attractive other; the basis of social learning.
monozygotic (MZ) twins: Twins produced from a single fertilized ovum, or zygote; "like twins," as contrasted with "unlike twins."
Moro reflex: A response, consisting of clutching movements of arms and legs, made by a newborn when the surface on which he is lying supine is struck by a sharp, forcible blow. Also termed *startle reflex*.
motor control: The ability to control the muscles that move different parts of the body.
multipara (*plural* multiparae): A woman who has borne more than one child.
myelin: The white, fatty substance that surrounds certain nerve fibers and apparently serves as insulation, thus facilitating neural transmissions.

nativistic theory: A theory of language development holding that human beings are genetically "programmed" to learn language and produce linguistic forms in a developmental sequence that is both identifiable and predictable.
naturalistic observation: Observation of behavior in the organism's normal

environment; as contrasted with observation made under controlled conditions, in the laboratory or elsewhere.

need: A deficiency or lack of an element required by the organism for its minimal or optimal functioning; also, the internal imbalance or tension produced by the deficiency. Sometimes used as synonymous with *drive*.

negation: In Piagetian psychology, the act of "canceling" the last occurring action in a behavior sequence and returning to the action that preceded it.

Neo-Freudians: Those psychologists who have accepted some aspects of psychoanalytic theory but have modified other aspects.

neonate: A newborn infant; the term is rather loosely applied to the period covering the first five to seven days after birth.

neurophysical structures: Elements composing the nervous system—brain, spinal cord, nerves, nerve endings.

nomothetic: Attempting to explain the behavior of people in general, but no one individual in particular, in contrast to idiographic.

nonnutritive sucking: Infantile sucking in the absence of nourishment.

norms: Any set of standards that reflect the usual performance of a comparable group of subjects. Also used loosely as a short form of *social norms*.

nurturant: Helping, caring, protective; emotionally and physically supportive.

object permanence: The awareness that an object that has disappeared from view still exists. The infant's attainment of this stage may be determined by his readiness to search for an object that has been hidden behind one or more screens.

Oedipus complex: In Freudian theory, the unconscious sexually toned attraction a boy comes to feel for his mother, with a parallel feeling of antipathy for his father. The term is often used with respect to children of both sexes, but the corresponding feeling that girls have for their fathers is sometimes termed the *Electra complex*.

olfactory: Related to or involved with the sense of smell.

ontogeny: In genetic terms, the origin and/or development of an individual.

operant conditioning: A procedure whereby an organism is induced to respond in a particular way to a situation by reinforcing or rewarding the response or responses in question.

oral stage: According to Freudian theory, an early stage in development, when pleasure is focused on sucking, biting, and chewing.

orienting reflex: A general state of arousal or attention, following awareness of a change in stimuli.

overachievers: Students whose academic achievement, as measured by course grades or by achievement test scores, surpasses that which would be predicted from their intelligence test scores.

overcompensation: An exaggerated or overeager attempt to make up for some real or fancied lack of a prized ability or trait. The term is often used as a synonym for *compensation*.

oviduct: The tube through which the ovum passes.

ovulation: The release of the ovum by the ovaries.

ovum (plural ova): The germ cell or egg produced by the female.

peer group: Acquaintances of similar age who are also fellow members of the same group.

perception: The process of ordering or making sense out of the stimulation of the sensory organs.

perceptual set: A predisposition to perceive an object or the environment in a certain way. Often referred to merely as "set."

permissiveness: In reference to child-rearing practices, parental attitudes and behavior styles characterized by noninterference with the child's behavior or misbehavior, indulgence, and positive emotional support.

personality: The individual's relatively stable and consistent ways of responding.

phallic stage: In Freudian theory, the stage of psychosexual development following the oral and anal stages; the phallic stage occurs from about age three to age seven, when a boy's interest and feeling are said to be focused on his penis. For girls, the focus is presumably upon whatever is the symbolic equivalent of the penis for them.

phenomenistic causality: The belief that the appearance of two events or stimuli together indicates that one causes the other.

phylogeny: The origin and developmental history of a species.

placenta: The structure within the uterus to which the fetus is attached by its umbilical cord, through which it both receives nourishment and eliminates waste products.

preoperational thought: A stage of cognitive development occurring normally during the second year, when the infant begins to shift away from random, trial-and-error attempts to solve problems and starts to invent solutions requiring the use of symbolic processes.

primapara (*plural* primaparae): A woman who has borne only one child.

projection: The attribution of one's own unconscious motives to others. Also the tendency to "structure" ambiguous stimuli in terms of one's own needs and interests.

projective tests: Standardized tests consisting of more or less unstructured or ambiguous stimuli to which the subject responds with a minimum of restriction or direction.

propinquity: Nearness in time or location.

proximodistal: Proceeding, in the sequence of development as well as the elaboration of control of movements, in an outward direction, beginning with the body axis.

psychoanalysis: The theories developed by Freud and his followers; also, therapeutic practices based on those theories.

psychoanalyst: A psychotherapist whose techniques are based on the theories of Freud or his followers.

puberty: The stage of development at which adolescents become capable of sexual reproduction.

pupillary reflex: Change in the size of the pupil of the eye, in response to changes in the intensity of light.

rapid eye movement (REM): Jerky movement of the eyes taking place beneath the closed eyelids of sleepers, associated with dreaming and with "active" or "aroused" sleep, in contrast to deep sleep.

recapitulation theory: The idea that in the course of the individual's development he passes through stages corresponding to periods in the evolutionary development of his species.

reflective children: Children who "stop and think" when presented with a problem, instead of yielding to the impulse to try the first solution that comes to mind.

reflex: An unlearned response to a specific type of stimulus.

regression: The recurrence of a form of behavior that was appropriate in an earlier stage of development but is now inappropriate and immature.

reinforcement: A stimulus that, when applied following a response, increases the likelihood that the response will reoccur.

reliability: The extent to which a measure gives dependable, consistent, and accurate results.

replicability: The extent to which an investigation that has been repeated yields results similar to the original research.

reversal shifts: A problem-solving strategy that must be mastered by a subject who is first exposed to a series of problems, each containing two elements, and who is then presented with problems in which the meaning of one of the elements has been changed. Problems in which both elements have been changed call for non–reversal-shift strategies.

reversibility: The ability to return to a previous step in a sequence of actions in solving a complex problem.

reward value: The attractiveness of a reinforcement or a goal.

Rh factor: A protein, present in the blood of about 85 per cent of the population (who are designated as Rh-positive), which causes an antibody reaction if introduced into the blood of individuals lacking it (Rh-negatives). If Rh-negative mothers conceive Rh-positive fetuses, severe problems in the form of miscarriages or birth defects may occur with succeeding children, unless proper treatment measures are taken.

ribonucleic acid (RNA): Complex molecules that determine the structure of cells and control their functioning.

Rosenthal effect: Biased results in research, occurring when the investigator either unconsciously overlooks errors in his procedure or in the analysis of results, or else when he unconsciously provides subjects with clues as to his hypothesis. The effect has been studied extensively by Robert Rosenthal. Also termed "experimenter-expectancy effect," or, in classroom teaching, "Pygmalion effect."

schema (*plural* schemas or schemata): In Piagetian theory, a cognitive structure that has been formed by assimilating objects in the environment and accommodating them, and that also serves as a guide to further dealings with such objects.

schizophrenia: A mental disorder in which contact with reality, interpersonal relationships, and thought processes are severely impaired or disturbed.

sebaceous glands: Glands that produce an oily, fatty substance which lubricates the skin.

secular trend: The trend toward earlier sexual maturation and larger bodies, as observed over the centuries.

self-concept: The individual as perceived by himself.

self-esteem: The value attached to oneself. The term is usually employed in a positive sense as synonymous with *good adjustment, ego strength,* and *self-acceptance.*

semen: The male germ cells, carried by the seminal fluid into contact with the ovum during the fertilization process.
sensorimotor skills: Skills that depend on the integrated and coordinated performance of muscles and sensory nerves.
sensory adaptation: Lowered responsiveness in a sense organ resulting from continued stimulation. Also, the heightened sensitivity that occurs in the absence of stimulation.
sex typing: The tendency of small children to become aware of their sex and to display behavior considered appropriate to it.
shaping: Inducing learning through operant conditioning of successive approximations to the final form of the behavior desired.
social distance: A measure of the degree to which another person or group is liked or is perceived as similar to oneself.
social norms: Standards of behavior formulated in terms of the generally accepted expectations of group members with respect to one another's behavior.
socialization: The process whereby a child learns to take his place in human society.
socioeconomic status (SES): Position or prestige level in a society, based on such considerations as wealth, occupation, education, and type and location of residence.
stimulus (plural stimuli): A change in physical energy that activates a sense organ.
stimulus-response (S-R) research: Investigations in which one or more independent variables are manipulated in order to identify causal factors in one or more dependent variables.
structure: A relatively stable organization of environmental or conceptual variables. When the term is used as a verb, it refers to the process of introducing organization and meaning into stimuli, concepts, or social relationships.
sucrose: The sugar that occurs naturally in most land plants and is produced commercially from sugar cane and sugar beets.
sudden infant death syndrome (SIDS): An unexplained illness apparently taking the form of a cessation of breathing, or apnea, during sleep, encountered among infants aged one month to one year.
superego: According to psychoanalytic theory, the moral standards incorporated by the individual, and learned in the initial stages from parents.
synesthesia: Translation of sensations from one sense modality into another, such as the smelling or hearing of colors.

totipotent: Characteristic of a cell at an early stage in the prenatal development of an organism, when it is capable of developing eventually into any type of tissue or organ.
trauma (plural traumata): Injury, wound, shock, or distress.
tumescence: State of being engorged with blood and swollen, applied especially to sex organs after stimulation and arousal.

unconscious: Characteristic of mental processes that lie beyond the limits of awareness and cannot readily be recalled, because of the amount of anxiety they would evoke. As a noun, the body or repository of these mental processes.

validity: The extent to which a test measures what it is expected to measure.
variable: Any quality, characteristic, or trait that can change or that may differ from one individual to another.
visual cliff: A piece of laboratory equipment designed to give young animals and humans the simulated experience of dangerous depths, as would be encountered on a cliff.

zygote: The union of ovum and sperm into a fertilized egg, which forms a new individual.

References and Author Index

Works cited in this book are listed alphabetically by author and year of publication. Numbers in **boldface** type following each citation refer to the text pages on which the works are cited.

Abate, F., see Zahn et al.
Abbott, L., see Wilson et al.
Abrams, M. S., see Midgley & Abrams.
Adams, G., see Brackbill et al.
Adelson J., Green, B., & O'Neil, R., Growth of the idea of law in adolescence. *Develpm. Psychol.*, 1969, **1**, 327–332. **528**
Ainsworth, M. D. S., see Stayton et al.
Alexander, G. J., Miles, B. E., Gold, G. M., & Alexander, R. B., LSD: Injection in early pregnancy produces abnormalities in off-spring of rats. *Science*, 1967, **157**, 459–460. **147**
Aleksandrowicz, M. K., & Aleksandrowicz, D. R., Obstetrical pain-relieving drugs as predictors of infant behavior variability. *Child Develpm.*, 1974, **45**, 935–945. **157–158**
Alexander, R. B., see Alexander, G. J., et al.
Allen, K. D., see Blatz et al.
Alpert, R., see Sears et al.
Amen, E. W., & Renison, N., A study of the relationship between play patterns and anxiety in young children. *Genet. psychol. Monogr.*, 1954, **50**, 3–41. **430**
Ames, E. W., see Brennan et al.
Ames, L. B., Children's stories. *Genet. psychol. Monogr.*, 1966, **73**, 337–396. **316–317, 472**
Anastasi, A., Intelligence and family size. *Psychol. Bull.*, 1956, **53**, 187–209. **49**
Anthony, E. J., The behavior disorders of childhood. In P. H. Mussen, Ed., *Carmichael's manual of child psychology*, 3rd ed. N.Y.: Wiley, 1970. **127–128**
Anttonen, R. G., see Fleming & Antonnen.
Apgar, F., Proposal for new methods of evaluation of newborn infants. *Anesth. Analg.*, 1953, **32**, 260–267. **154–156**
Aries, P., *Centuries of childhood*. N.Y.: Knopf, 1962. **4–5**
Asch, S. E., Studies of independence and conformity. A minority of one against a unanimous majority. *Psychol. Monogr.*, 1956, **70**, No. 9, Whole No. 416. **461**
Asher, S. R., & Markell, R. A., Sex differences in comprehension of high- and low-interest reading material. *J. educ. Psychol.*, 1974, **66**, 680–687. **427–428**
Ault, R. L., Problem-solving strategies of reflective, impulsive, fast-accurate, and slow-inaccurate children. *Develpm. Psychol.*, 1973, **44**, 259–266. **431**

Babayan, S. Y., Budayr, B., & Lindgren, H. C., Age, sex, and culture as variables in food aversion. *J. soc. Psychol.*, 1966, **68**, 15–17. **514**
Babson, S. G., Henderson, N. B., & Clark, W. M., Jr., Preschool intelligence of oversized newborns. *Amer. Psychol. Assn.*

Babson, S. G. (cont.)
Proceedings, 1969, **4**, 267-268. **158-159**

Baer, D. M., see Bijou & Baer.

Baer, D. M., & Wright, J. C., Developmental psychology. Ann. Rev. of Psychol., 1974, **25**, 1-82. **3, 64**

Balfour, G., see Donaldson & Balfour.

Ball, S., & Bogatz, G. A., *The first year of "Sesame Street": An evaluation.* Princeton, N.J.: Educ. Testing Service, 1970. **301**

Ball, W., & Tronick, E., Infant responses to impending collision: Optical and real. Science, 1971, **171**, 818-820. **203**

Bandura, A., Social-learning theory of identificatory processes. In D. A. Goslin, Ed., *Handbook of socialization theory and research.* Chicago: Rand McNally, 1969a. **108-109**

Bandura, A., Social learning of moral judgments. J. pers. soc. Psychol., 1969b, **11**, 275-279. **454**

Bandura, A., & McDonald, F. J., Influence of social reinforcement and the behavior of models in shaping children's moral judgments. J. abnorm. soc. Psychol., 1963, **67**, 274-281. **453-454**

Bandura, A., Ross, D., & Ross, S. A., Transmission of aggression through imitation of aggressive models. J. abnorm. soc. Psychol., 1961, **63**, 575-582. **320-322, 472**

Bandura, A., & Walters, R. H., *Social learning and personality development.* N.Y.: Holt, 1963a. 86, **320-322**

Bandura, A., & Walters, R. H., Aggression. Yearbook Nat. Soc. Stud. Educ., 1963b, **62**, Part I, 384-415. **320-322**

Barker, R. G., Child psychology. Ann. Rev. of Psychol., 1951, **2**, 1-22. **26**

Barker, R. G., Dembo, T., & Lewin, K., Frustration and regression. In R. G. Barker et al., Eds., *Child behavior and development.* N.Y.: McGraw-Hill, 1943. **319**

Bates, H. D., & Katz, M. M., Development of the verbal regulation of behavior. Amer. Psychol. Assn. Proceedings, 1970, **5**, 299-300. **286**

Baumrind, D., Child care practices anteceding three patterns of preschool behavior. Genet. psychol. Monogr., 1967, **75**, 43-88. **346-350**

Baumrind, D., Harmonious parents and their preschool children. Develpm. Psychol., 1971a, **4**, 99-102. **61**

Baumrind D., Current patterns of parental authority. Develpm. Psychol., 1971b, **4**, No. 1, Part 2. **350-352**

Bayer, L. M., & Snyder, M. M., Illness experience of a group of normal children. Child Develpm., 1950, **21**, 93-120. **261, 512-513**

Bayley, N., The development of motor abilities during the first three years. Monogr. Soc. Res. Child Develpm., 1935, No. 1. **187**

Bayley, N., Consistency of maternal and child behaviors in the Berkeley Growth Study. Vita Humana, 1964, **7**, 73-95. **356-357**

Bayley, N., *Manual for the Bayley Scale of Infant Development.* N.Y.: Psychol. Corp. 1969. **187, 214-217**

Bayley, N., Development of mental abilities. In P. H. Mussen, Ed., *Carmichael's manual of child psychology*, 3rd ed., N.Y.: Wiley, 1970. **218, 304**

Bayley, N., & Schaefer, E. S., Relationships between socioeconomic variables and the behavior of mothers toward young children. J. genet. Psychol., 1960, **96**, 61-77. **436**

Bayley, N., & Schaefer, E. S., Correlations of maternal and child behaviors with the development of mental abilities: Data from the Berkeley Growth Study. Monogr. Soc. Res. Child Develpm., 1964, **29**, (6, Whole No. 97). **353-354**

Becker, R. F., King, J. E., & Little, C. R. D., Experimental studies in nicotine absorption during pregnancy, IV. The postmature neonate. Amer. J. Obstet. & Gyn., 1968, **101**, 1109-1119. **148**

Bee, H. L., et al., Social class differences in maternal teaching strategies and speech patterns. Develpm. Psychol., 1969, **1**, 726-734. **364**

Behrens, M. L., Child rearing and the character of structure of the mother. Child. Develpm., 1954, **25**, 225-238. **236**

Beilin, H., Teachers' and clinicians' attitudes toward the behavior problems of children: A reappraisal. Child Develpm., 1959, **30**, 9-26. **493**

Beilin, H., & Werner, E., Sex differences among teachers in the use of criteria of adjustment. J. educ. Psychol., 1957, **48**, 426-436. **493**

Bell, R. L., Jr., see Mouton et al.

Bell, R. Q., see Schaefer & Bell.

Beller, E. K., Dependency and independence in young children. J. genet.

Psychol., 1955, **87**, 25-35. **331-332**

Beller, E. K., Dependency and autonomous achievement striving related to orality and anality in early childhood. *Child Develpm.*, 1957a, **28**, 287-315. **331-332**

Bellugi, U., see Bronowski & Bellugi, and Brown et al.

Benedict, R., *Patterns of culture*. Boston: Houghton Mifflin, 1934. **69**

Bennett, E. L., Diamond, M. C., Krech, D., & Rosenzweig, M. R., Chemical and anatomical plasticity of brain. *Science*, 1964, **146**, 610-619. **222**

Benson, F. W., see Carter et al.

Bereiter, C., & Engelmann, S., *Teaching disadvantaged children in the preschool*. Englewood Cliffs, N.J.: Prentice-Hall, 1966. **297**

Berg, A., *The nutrition factor*. Washington, D.C.: Brookings Institution, 1973. **233**

Berk, L. E., Effects of variations in the nursery school setting on environmental constraints and children's modes of adaptation. *Child Develpm.*, 1971, **42**, 839-869. **15, 49**

Berk, L. E., Rose, M. H., & Stewart, D., Attitudes of English and American children toward their school experience. *J. educ. Psychol.*, 1970, **61**, 33-40. **495, 497**

Berkowitz, L., The contagion of violence: An S-R mediational analysis of some effects of observed aggression. In W. J. Arnold & M. M. Page, Eds., *Nebraska Symposium on Motivation, 1970*. Lincoln: U. of Nebraska Press, 1971. **473**

Berlyne, D. E., Arousal and reinforcement. In D. Levine, Ed., *Nebraska Symposium on Motivation*. Lincoln: U. of Nebraska Press, 1967. **113**

Bernstein, B. A., Sociolinguistic approach to socialization: With some reference to educability. In J. Gumperz & D. Hymes, Eds., *Directions in sociolinguistics*. N.Y.: Holt, 1972. **294**

Bierman, J. M., see Werner et al.

Biglow, B. J., & La Gaipa, J. J., Children's written descriptions of friendship: A multidimensional analysis. *Develpm. Psychol.*, 1975, **11**, 857-858. **478**

Bijou, S. W., Development in the preschool years: A functional analysis. *Amer. Psychologist*, 1975, **30**, 829-837. **259**

Bijou, S. W., & Baer, D. M., *Child development: A systematic and empirical theory*. N.Y.: Appleton-Century-Crofts, 1961. **27**

Biller, H. B., see Blanchard & Buller.

Birch, H. C., see Thomas et al.

Blake, R. R., see Mouton et al.

Blakely, W. P., A study of seventh grade children's reading of comic books as related to certain other variables. *J. genet. Psychol.*, 1958, **93**, 291-301. **473**

Blane, W. A., see Naeye et ai.

Blanchard, R. W., & Biller, H. B., Father availability and academic performance among third-grade boys. *Develpm. Psychol.*, 1971, **4**, 301-305. **358-360**

Blase, B., see Solkoff et al.

Blatz, W. E., Allen, K. D., & Millichamp, D. A., A study of laughter in the nursery school child. *U. of Toronto Stud. Child Develpm. Series*, 1936, No. 7. **326**

Bloom, B., *Stability and change in human characteristics*. N.Y.: Wiley, 1964. **70**

Bloom, L., Language development. In E. M. Hetherington et al., Eds., *Review of research in child development*, Vol. 4. Chicago: U. of Chicago Press, 1975. **291**

Blum, R. H., et al., *Horatio Alger's Children*. San Francisco: Jossey-Bass, 1972. **540-541**

Blum, W. L., see Bresnahan & Blum.

Blumenthal, M. N., et al., Genetic mapping of Ir locus in man: Linkage to second locus of HL-A. *Science*, 1974, **184**, 1301-1303. **68**

Bogatz, G. A., see Ball & Bogatz.

Bonney, M. E., The constancy of sociometric scores and their relationship to teacher judgments of social success, to personality self-ratings. *Sociometry*, 1943, **6**, 409-424. **474**

Borton, T., *Reach, touch, and teach*. N.Y.: McGraw-Hill, 1970. **489**

Bowlby J., *Maternal care and mental health*. Geneva: World Health Organization, 1951. **241**

Brackbill, Y., Continuous stimulation reduces arousal level: Stability of effect over time. *Child Develpm.*, 1973, **44**, 43-46. **164**

Brackbill, Y., Adams, G., Crowell, D. H., & Gray, M. L., Arousal level in neonates and older infants under continuous auditory stimulation. *J. exper. child Psychol.*, 1966, **4**, 178-188. **163**

Brackett, C. W., Laughing and crying of preschool children. *Child develpm. Monogr.*, 1954, No. 14. **325-326**

Bradley, K., see Elardo et al.

Braine, M. D. S., The ontongeny of English

Braine, M. D. S. (cont.) phrase structure: The first phase. *Language*, 1963, **39**, 1-13. **287**

Brandt, E. M., see Mitchell & Brandt.

Braun, J. R., see Harris & Braun.

Brazelton, T. B., *Neonatal Behavioral Assessment Scale*. Philadelphia: Spastics International Medical Publications & Lippincott, 1973. **157**

Breedlove, C. J., & Cicirelli, V. C., Women's fear of success in relation to personal characteristics and type of education. *J. Psychol.*, 1974, **86**, 181-190. **554-557**

Brennan, W. M., Ames, E. W., & Moore, R. W., Age differences in infants' attention to patterns of different complexities. *Science*, 1966, **151**, 354-356. **198**

Bresnahan, J. L., & Blum, W. L., Chaotic reinforcement: A socioeconomic leveler. *Develpm. Psychol.*, 1971, **4**, 89-92. **367**

Bridgeman, B., & Buttram, J., Race differences on nonverbal analogy test performance as a function of verbal strategy learning. *J. educ. Psychol.*, 1975, **67**, 586-590. **421**

Bridger, W. H., see Golden et al.

Bridges, K. M. B., *Social and emotional development of the preschool child*. London: Kegan, Paul, 1931. **324**

Briggs, C., & Elkind, D., Cognitive development in early readers. *Develpm. Psychol.*, 1973, **9**, 278-280. **406**

Brockman, L. B., & Ricciuti, H. N., Severe protein-calorie malnutrition and cognitive development in infancy and early childhood. *Develpm. Psychol.*, 1971, **4**, 312-319. **181, 183-184**

Brodbeck A. J., & Irwin, O. C., The speech behavior of infants without families. *Child Develpm.*, 1946, **17**, 145-156. **213**

Brody, G. H., see Zimmerman & Brody.

Brody, N., see Gottfried & Brody.

Broman, S. H., see Nichols & Broman, and Serunian & Broman.

Bronfenbrenner, U., Reaction to social pressure from adults versus peers among Soviet day school and boarding school pupils in the perspective of an American sample. *J. pers. soc. Psychol.*, 1970, **15**, 178-189. **462-464**

Bronowski, J., & Bellugi, U., Language, name, and concept. *Science*, 1970, **168**, 660-673. **288-290**

Bronson, G. W., Fear of visual novelty. *Develpm. Psychol.*, 1970, **2**, 33-40. **312**

Brophy, J. E., & Good, T. L., Teacher expectancies: beyond the Pygmalion controversy. *Phi Delta Kappan*, 1972, **54**, 276-278. **416**

Brophy, J. E., see Laosa & Brophy.

Brown, J. V., et al., Interactions of black inner-city mothers with their newborn infants. *Child Develpm.*, 1975, **46**, 677-686. **157**

Brown, R., & Bellugi, U., Three processes in the child's acquisition of syntax. *Harvard educ. Rev.*, 1964, **34**, 133-151. **286**

Brown, R., Cazden, C., & Bellugi, U., The child's grammar from I to III. In J. P. Hill, Ed., *Minnesota Symposium on Clinical Psychology*, vol. II. Minneapolis: U. of Minnesota Press, 1969. **286**

Bruner, J. S., et al., *A study of thinking*. N.Y.: Wiley, 1956. **275**

Bruner, J. S., see also Kalnins & Bruner.

Bryant, B. K., Locus of control related to teacher-child interperceptual experiences. *Child Develpm.*, 1974, **45**, 157-164. **432**

Budayr, B., see Babayan et al.

Burchinal, L., Gardner, B., & Hawkes, G. R., Children's personality adjustment and the socio-economic status of their families. *J. genet. Psychol.*, 1958, **92**, 149-159. **437**

Burke E. J., III, Sociogram of a fourth-grade class. Unpublished paper, San Francisco State College, April, 1971. **476**

Burton, R. V., Generality of honesty reconsidered. *Psychol. Rev.*, 1963, **70**, 481-499. **448-449**

Busse, T. V., & Seraydarian, L., Are children's first names related to their achievement, IQ, and school readiness? Unpublished paper, Temple U., 1975. **49**

Butler, R. N. Goldstein, H., & Ross, E. M., Cigarette smoking in pregnancy: Its influence on birthweight and perinatal mortality. *Brit. Med. J.*, 1972, **2**, 127-130. **148**

Buttram, J., see Bridgeman & Buttram.

Byrne, D., *The attraction paradigm*. N.Y.: Academic, 1971. **476**

Byrne, D., see also Lindgren & Byrne.

Caldwell, B. M. Heider, J., & Kaplan, B., The inventory of home stimulation. Unpublished manuscript, Child Development & Mental Retardation Center, U. of Washington, Seattle, 1973. **354-355**

Caldwell, B. M., see also Elardo et al.

Callahan, O. D., & Robin, S. S., A social system analysis of preferred leadership role characteristics in high school. *Sociol. of Educ.*, 1969, **42**, 251–260. **546**

Cameron, J., Livson, N., & Bayley, N., Infant vocalizations and their relationship to mature intelligence. *Science*, 1967, **157**, 331–333. **49**

Cameron, P., & Janky, C., Effects of TV violence on children: A naturalistic experiment. *Amer. Psychol. Assn. Proc.*, 1971, **6**, 233–234. **473**

Campbell D. P., *Manual for the Strong-Campbell Interest Inventory*. Stanford: Stanford U. Press, 1974. **538**

Campbell, D. T., On the conflicts between biological and social evolution and between psychology and moral tradition. *Amer. Psychologist*, 1975, 30, 1103–1126. **124**

Campos, J. J., Langer, A., & Krowitz, A., Cardiac responses on the visual cliff in prelocomotor human infants. *Science*, 1970, **170**, 196–197. **203**

Cantor G. N., & Paternite, C. E., A follow-up study of race awareness using a conflict paradigm. *Child Develpm.*, 1973, **44**, 859–861. **483**

Caplan, S., see Izard & Caplan.

Caputo, D. V., & Mandell, W., Consequences of low birth weight. *Develpm. Psychol.*, 1970, **3**, 363–383. **158**

Carlson, R., Identification and personality structure in preadolescents. *J. abnorm. soc, Psychol.*, 1963, **67**, 566–573. **446**

Carmichael, L., Ontogenetic development. In S. S. Stevens, Ed., *Handbook of experimental psychology*. N.Y.: Wiley, 1951. **91**

Carter, D. E., DeTine, S. L., Spero, J., & Benson, F. W., Peer acceptance and school-related variables in an integrated junior-high school. *J. educ. Psychol.*, 1975, **67**, 267–273. **545–546**

Castenada, A., McCandless, B. R., & Palermo, D. S., The children's form of the Manifest Anxiety Scale. *Child Develpm.*, 1956, **27**, 317–326. **430**

Cattell, P., *The measurement of intelligence of infants*. N.Y.: Psychol. Corp., 1940. **214–215**

Caudill, W., & Weinstein, H., Maternal care and infant behavior in Japan and America. *Psychiatry*, 1969, **32**, 12–45. **97**

Cazden, C., see Brown et al.

Charlesworth, R., & Hartup, W. W., Positive social reinforcement in the nursery school peer group. *Child Develpm.*, 1967, **38**, 993–1002. **382**

Chee, F. K. W., see Clark et al.

Chess, S., see Thomas et al.

Chomsky, N., Review of *Verbal behavior*, by B. F. Skinner. *Language*, 1959, 35, 26–58. **212**

Chomsky, N., Current issues in linguistic theory. In J. A. Fodor and J. J. Kantz, Eds., *The structure of language*. Englewood Cliffs, N. J.: Prentice-Hall, 1964. **212**

Chomsky, N., *Aspects of the theory of syntax*. Cambridge, Mass.: M. I. T. Press, 1965. **283–285**

Chomsky, N., The formal structure of language. In E. H. Lenneberg, Ed., *Biological foundations of language*. N.Y.: Wiley, 1967. **212**

Chomsky, N., *Language and mind*. N.Y.: Harcourt Brace Jovanovich, 1968. **283–285**

Cicirelli, V. G., see Breedlove and Cicirelli.

Clark, D. L. Kreutzberg, J. R., & Chee, F. K. W., Vestibular stimulation influence on motor development. *Science*, 1977, **196**, 1228–1229. **229**

Clark, K. B., & Clark, M. P., Racial identification and preference in Negro children. In E. E. Maccoby et al., Eds., *Readings in social psychology*. N.Y.: Holt, 1947. **483**

Clark, M. P., see Clark & Clark.

Clark, W. M., Jr., see Babson et al.

Clausen, G. T., see Schwartz & Clausen.

Cleary, T. A., see Gozali et al.

Coates, B., see Hartup & Coates.

Coghill, G. E., *Anatomy and the problems of behavior*. N.Y.: Macmillan, 1929. **74–75**

Cohen, G., Left brain, right brain: How strong is the case for cerebral apartheid? *New Behavior*, 1975, Sept., 458–461. **406**

Cohen, M. L., & Seghorn, T., Clinical and research experience with sexually dangerous persons. Unpublished paper, Amer. Psychol. Assn. Convention, Miami, 1970. **435**

Coleman, J. S., *The adolescent society*. N.Y.: Free Press, 1961. **545**

Coleman, J. S., *Adolescents and the schools*. N.Y.: Basic Books, 1965. **545**

Collard, R. R., see Niem & Collard.

Condon, W. S., & Sander, L. W., Neonate movement is synchronized with adult speech: Interactional participation and language acquisition. *Science*, 1974, **183**, 99–101. **166, 206, 226**

Conrad, R., The chronology of the development of covert speech in children. *Develpm. Psychol.*, 1971, **5**, 398–405. **282**

Constantinople, A. P., An Eriksonian measure of personality development in college students. *Develpm. Psychol.*, 1969, **1**, 357–372. **552–553**

Conway, D., see Lytton et al.

Conyers, M. G., Comparing school success of students from conventional and broken homes. *Phi Delta Kappan*, 1977, **58**, 647. **537–538**

Coopersmith, S., *Antecedents of self-esteem*. San Francisco: Freeman, 1967. **443–444**

Coopersmith, S., Studies in self-esteem. *Scient. Amer.*, 1968, 218(2), 96–106. **443–444**

Copple, C. E., & Suci, G. J., The comparative ease of processing Standard English and Black Nonstandard English by lower-class Black children. *Child Develpm.*, 1975, **45**, 1048–1053. **298**

Corsini, D. A., see Costantini et al.

Coser, R. L., Sex roles and economics. *Science*, 1973, **182**, 471–472. **553**

Costantini, A. F., Corsini, D. A., & Davis, J. E., Conceptual tempo, inhibition of movement, and acceleration of movement in 4-, 7-, and 9-year-old children. *Percept. motor Skills.*, 1973, **37**, 779–784. **431**

Cotler, S., & Palmer, R. J., Social reinforcement, individual difference factors, and the reading performance of elementary school children. *J. pers. soc. Psychol.*, 1971, **18**, 97–104. **490–491**

Courtney, R. G., see Rothenburg & Courtney.

Cowan, P. A., Social learning and Piaget's cognitive theory of moral development. *J. pers. soc. Psychol.*, 1969, **11**, 261–274. **454**

Cox, F. N., Corelates of general and test anxiety in children. *Austral. J. Psychol.*, 1960, **12**, 169–177. **430**

Cradler, J. D., & Goodwin, D. L., Conditioning of verbal behavior as a function of age, social class, and type of reinforcement. *J. ed. Psychol.*, 1971, **62**, 279–284. **490–492**

Crandall, V. J., see Waters & Crandall.

Cronbach, L. J., Five decades of public controversy over mental testing. *Amer. Psychologist*, 1975, **30**, 1–14. **416**

Cronbach, L. J., *Educational psychology*, 3rd ed. N.Y.: Harcourt Brace Jovanovich, 1977. **416**

Crowell, D. H., see Brackbill et al.

da Rocha, N. S., see Lindgren et al.

Davidson, H. H., see Greenberg & Davidson.

Davis, J. E., see Costantini et al.

Davitz, J. R., Social perception and sociometric choice of children. *J. abnorm. soc. Psychol.*, 1955, **50**, 173–176. **476**

Day, D., see Kagan et al.

Dellinger, W. S., see Naeye et al.

Dembo, T., see Barker et al.

Dement, W., The effect of dream deprivation. *Science*, 1960, **131**, 1705–1707. **162**

Dement, W. C., see also Raffwarg et al.

Denenberg, V. H., The mother as a motivator. In W. J. Arnold & M. M. Page, Eds., *Nebraska symposium on motivation, 1970*. Lincoln: U. of Nebraska Press, 1971. **252–253**

Denney, N. W., Free classification in preschool children. *Child Develpm.*, 1972, **43**, 1161–1170. **86**

Dennis, M. G., see Dennis & Dennis.

Dennis, W., *Children of the crèche*. Englewood Cliffs, N.J.: Prentice-Hall, 1973. **231, 417–418**

Dennis, W., The mental growth of certain foundlings before and after adoption. In H. C. Lindgren, Ed., *Children's behavior*. Palo Alto, Calif.: Mayfield, 1975. **231**

Dennis, W., & Dennis, M. G., The effects of cradling practices upon the onset of walking in Hopi children. *J. genet. Psychol.*, 1940, **56**, 77–86. **185**

De Tine, S. L., see Carter et al.

Deutsche, J. M., The development of children's concepts of causal relations. *U. Minn. Child Welfare Monogr.*, 1937, No. 13. **401–402**

De Vries, P., *The tunnel of love*. Boston: Little Brown, 1954. **344**

Dewson, J. H., III, Inside every monkey sits a little bit of man. *Stanford Magazine*, 1976, 4(1), 50–54. **406**

Diamond, M. C., see Bennett et al.

Diaz-Guerrero, R., & Holtzman, W. H., Learning by televised "Plaza Sesamo" in

Mexico. *J. educ. Psychol.*, 1974, **66**, 632–643. **301–303**

Diaz-Guerrero, R., see also Holtzman et al.

Dick-Reed, G., *Childbirth without fear*, 4th ed. N.Y.: Harper & Row, 1972. **152–153**

Diener, E., et al., Deindividuating effects of group presence and arousal on stealing by Halloween trick-or-treaters. *Amer. Psychol. Assn. Proceedings*, 1973, **8**, 219–220. **467–468**

Diener, M. M., see Naeye et al.

Ding, G. F., & Jersild, A. T., A study of the laughing and smiling of preschool children. *J. genet. Psychol.*, 1932, **40**, 452–472. **326**

Dinges, N. G., see Oetting & Dinges.

Dollard, J., et al., *Frustration and aggression*. New Haven: Yale U. Press, 1939. **319**

Donaldson, M., & Balfour, G., Less is more: A study of language comprehension in children. *Brit. J. Psychol.*, 1968, **59**, 461–471. **274**

Doty, B. A., Relationships among attitudes in pregnancy and other maternal characteristics. *J. genet. Psychol.*, 1967, **111**, 203–217. **151–152**

Dowart, W., Ezerman, R., Lewis, M., & Rosenhan, D., The effect of brief social deprivation on social and nonsocial reinforcement. *J. pers. soc. Psychol.*, 1965, **2**, 111–115. **114**

Doyle, A-B., Infant development in day care. *Develpm. Psychol.*, 1975, **11**, 655–656. **251**

Drake, D. M., Perceptual correlates of impulsive and reflective behavior. *Develpm. Psychol.*, 1970, **2**, 202–214. **431**

Drozdal, J. G., Jr., & Flavell, J. H., A developmental study of logical search behavior. *Child Develpm.*, 1975, **46**, 389–393. **403–404**

Duhamel, T. R., see Jarmon & Duhamel.

Dyer, H. S., Testing little children—some old problems in new settings. Technical Paper, National Leadership Institute/Early Childhood. U. of Conn., December, 1971. **391**

Dymond, R. F., Hughes, A. S., & Raabe, V. L., Measurable changes in empathy with age. *J. consult. Psychol.*, 1952, **16**, 202–206. **477**

Dymond, R., see Rogers & Dymond.

Early, C. J., Attitude learning in children. *J. educ. Psychol.*, 1968, **59**, 176–180. **101–102**

Eckerman, C. O., see Rheingold & Eckerman.

Edwards, M., & Stinnett, N., Perceptions of college students concerning alternate life styles. *J. Psychol.*, 1974, **87**, 143–156. **564–566**

Edwards, N., The relationship between physical condition immediately after birth and mental and motor performance at age four. *Genet. psychol. Monogr.*, 1970, **78**, 257–289. **156**

Ehrmann, W., *Premarital dating behavior*. N.Y.: Holt, 1959. **567**

Eichenwald, H. F. & Fry, P. C., Nutrition and learning. *Science*, 1969, **163**, 644–648. **180**

Elardo, R., Bradley, R., & Caldwell, B. M., The relation of infants' home environments to mental test performance from six to thirty-six months: A longitudinal study. *Child Develpm.*, 1975, **46**, 71–76. **216–218, 367–368**

Elder, S. T., see Reichard & Elder.

Elkind, D., Children's discovery of the conservation of mass, weight, and volume: Piaget replication study. *J. genet. Psychol.*, 1961, **98**, 219–227. **272**

Elkind, D., Cognition in infancy and early childhood. In Y. Brackbill, Ed., *Infancy and early childhood*. N.Y.: Free Press, 1967. **240**

Elkind, D., Cognitive development and reading. *Claremont Reading Conference*, 38th Yearbook. Claremont (Calif.), Graduate School, 1974. **406–408**

Elkind, D., We can teach reading better. *Today's Education*, 1975, **64**(4), 34–38. **406–408**

Elton, C. F., & Rose, H. A., The face of change. *J. couns. Psychol.*, 1968, **15**, 372–375. **527**

Engelmann, S., see Bereiter & Engelmann.

English, A. C., see English & English.

English, H. B., & English, A. C., *A comprehensive dictionary of psychological and psychoanalytic terms*. N.Y.: McKay, 1958. **298**

Epstein, R., & Komorita, S. S., Prejudice among Negro children as related to parental ethnocentrism and punitiveness. *J. pers. soc. Psychol.*, 1966, **4**, 643–647. **483**

Erikson, E. H., Identity and the life cycle. *Psychol. Issues*, 1959, **1**, No. 1. **550**

Erikson, E. H., *Childhood and society*, 2nd ed. N.Y.: Norton, 1963. **125–128, 331,**

Erikson, E. H. (cont.) **345, 550**

Erikson, E. H., *Identity, youth and crisis.* N.Y.: Norton, 1968. **125–128, 331**

Erlick, A. C., High schools in 1970: A study of the student-school relationship. *Purdue Opinion Panel,* Poll No. 88, April, 1970a. **529–530**

Erlick, A. C., What is wrong and right with today's youth: A study of parent-child relationship. *Purdue Opinion Panel,* Poll No. 87, January, 1970b. **539**

Eron, L. D., Walder, L. D., Toigo, R., & Lefkowitz, M. M., Social class, parental punishment for aggression, and child aggression. *Child Develpm.,* 1963, **34,** 849–867. **435**

Eron, L. D., et al., Does television violence cause aggression? *Amer. Psychologist,* 1972, **27,** 253–263. **474**

Espenschade, A., Motor performance in adolescence. In M. C. Jones et al., Eds., *The course of human development.* Waltham, Mass.: Xerox, 1971. **507–508**

Ezerman, R., see Dowart et al.

Falbo, T., The attributional explanation of academic performance by kindergarteners and their teachers. In H. C. Lindgren, Ed., *Children's behavior.* Palo Alto, Calif.: Mayfield, 1975. **372**

Fantz, R. L., Pattern vision in newborn infants. *Science,* 1963, **140,** 296–297. **166**

Fantz, R. L., Visual perception from birth as shown by pattern selectivity. *Annals of the New York Academy of Science,* 1965, **118,** 793–814. **194–198**

Fantz, R. L., Ordy, J. M., & Udelf, M. S., Maturation of pattern vision in infants during the first six months. *J. compar. physiol. Psychol.,* 1962, **55,** 907–917. **196**

Faraco, I., see Lindgren et al.

Fatheree, D., Play patterns in preschool children. Unpublished student report, San Francisco State College, 1971. **380**

Feather, N. T., & Simon, J. G., Reactions to male and female success and failure in sex-linked occupations: Impressions of personality, causal attributions, and perceived likelihood of different consequences. *J. pers. soc. Psychol.,* 1975, **31,** 20–31. **556–557**

Federov, V. K., cited in H. L. Rheingold and W. C. Stanley, Developmental psychology. *Ann. Rev. Psychol.,* 1963, **14,** 1–8. **202**

Fein, G., et al., Sex stereotypes and preferences in the toy choices of 20-month-old boys and girls. *Develpm. Psychol.,* 1975, **11,** 527–528. **340**

Feldhusen, J. F., & Klausmeier, H. J., Anxiety, intelligence, and achievement in children of low, average, and high intelligence. *Child Develpm.,* 1962, **33,** 403–409. **430**

Feldman, S. E., see Hetherington & Feldman.

Ferreira, A., The pregnant woman's emotional attitude and its reflection on the newborn. *Amer. J. Orthopsychiat.,* 1960, **30,** 553–561. **152**

Feshbach, S., Aggression. In P. H. Mussen, Ed., *Carmichael's manual of child psychology,* 3rd ed. N.Y.: Wiley, 1970. **472**

Feshbach, S., & Singer, R. D., Television and aggression. San Francisco: Jossey-Bass, 1970. **472**

Finch, A. J., Jr., see Montgomery & Finch.

Fisk, L. L. Unpublished report, 1976. **285, 291**

Flavell, J. H., *The developmental psychology of Jean Piaget.* Princeton, N.J.: Van Nostrand, 1963. **54, 192–193, 273, 398, 515**

Flavell, J. H., see also Drozdal & Flavell.

Fleming, E. S., & Anttonin, R. G., Teacher expectancy as related to the academic and personal growth of primary-age children. *Monogr. Soc. Res. Child Develpm.,* 1971, **36**(5), Serial No. 145. **416**

Flickinger, A., & Rechage, K. J., Building time and place concepts. *Improving the reading of world history,* National Council for Social Studies, 20th yearbook, 1949. **403**

Fodor, E. M., Moral judgment in Negro and white adolescents. *J. soc. Psychol.,* 1969, **79,** 289–291. **527**

Fowler, W., Cognitive learning in infancy and early childhood. *Psychol. Bull.,* 1962, **59,** 116–152. **185**

Fraisse, P., *Etude comparée de la perception et de l'estimation de la durée chez les infants et les adultes.* Enfance, 1948, **1,** 199–211. **403**

Franks, C., see O'Connor & Franks.

Freedman, D. G., Hereditary control of early social behavior. In B. M. Foss, Ed., *Determinants of infant behavior,* vol. 3. London: Methuen, 1965. **312**

Freedman, D. G., & Freedman, N. C.,

Behavioral differences between Chinese-American and European-American newborns. *Nature,* 1969, 224–227. **97**

Freedman, N. C., see Freedman & Freedman.

Freeman, F. N., see Newman et al.

French, F. E., see Werner et al.

Fresch, R. E., & Revelle, R., Height and weight at menarche and a hypothesis of critical body weights and adolescent events. *Science,* 1970, **169,** 397–399. **509**

Freshley, H. B., see Wispé & Freshley.

Freud, A., *The ego and mechanisms of defense.* N.Y.: Intl. Universities Press, 1946. **122**

Freud, S., Psychogenic visual disturbances according to psychoanalytic conceptions. *Collected papers,* vol. 2. London: Hogarth, 1924. **119**

Freud, S., Mourning and melancholia. *Collected papers,* vol. 4. London: Hogarth, 1925. **107, 119**

Freud, S., *Civilization and its discontents.* London: Liveright, 1930. **120**

Friedlander, B. Z., Receptive language development in infancy. *Merrill-Palmer Quarterly,* 1970, **16,** 7–51. **206**

Friedlander, B. Z., Effects of television on children's thought and feeling: Some educational implications. Unpublished paper, Amer. Res. Assn. Convention, San Francisco, April 1976. **459**

Friedman, M. P., see Guyer & Friedman.

Friedrich, U., see Nielsen et al.

Fry, P. C., see Eichenwald & Fry.

Fry, P. S., Affect and resistance to temptation. *Develpm. Psychol.,* 1975a, **11,** 466–472. **449**

Fry, P. S., The resistance to temptation: Inhibitory and disinhibitory effects of models on children from India and the United States. *J. cross-cultural Psychol.,* 1975b, **6,** 189–202. **465–466**

Fuller, J. L., Experimental deprivation and later behavior. *Science,* 1967, **158,** 1645–1652. **252**

Furth, H. G., Linguistic deficiency and thinking: Research with deaf subjects. *Psychol. Bull.,* 1971, **76,** 58–72. **282**

Gadberry, S., Television as a baby-sitter: A field comparison of preschoolers' behavior during playtime and during television viewing. *Child Develpm.,* 1974, **45,** 1132–1136. **50**

Gaines, D. I., The story of an English cotton mill lad. *History of Childhood Quarterly,* 1974, **2,** 249–264. **8**

Galfo, A. J., A pilot study of relationships between the sex of culturally disadvantaged children and maternal perceptions of the child and his environment. *Amer. Psychol. Assn. Exper. Publ. System,* April 1971, Ms. No. 405-435. **338–339**

Gallimore, R., Howard, A., & Jordan, C., Independence training among Hawaiians: A cross-cultural study. In H. C. Lindgren, Ed., *Contemporary research in social psychology.* N.Y.: Wiley, 1969. **332–333**

Gallimore, R., Tharp, R. G., & Kemp, B., Positive reinforcing function of "negative attention." *J. exper. child Psychol.,* 1969, **8,** 140–146. **114**

Garai, J. E., & Scheinfeld, A., Sex differences in mental and behavior traits. *Genet. psychol. Monogr.,* 1968, **77,** 160–299. **189–191**

Garber, H., & Heber, R., The Milwaukee Project: Early intervention as a technique to prevent mental retardation. National Leadership Institute—Teacher Education/Early Childhood. U. of Conn. Technical papers, March, 1973. Also in H. C. Lindgren, Ed., *Children's behavior.* Palo Alto, Calif.: Mayfield, 1975. **230**

Gardner, B., see Burchinal et al.

Gesell, A., Maturation and the patterning of behavior. In C. Murchison, Ed., *A handbook of child psychology,* 2nd ed. Worcester, Mass.: Clark U. Press, 1933. **90**

Gesell, A., & Ilg, F. L., *Infant and child in the culture of today.* N.Y.: Harper, 1943. **137**

Gesell, A., & Ilg, F. L., *Child development,* 2nd ed. N.Y.: Harper, 1949. **160–161**

Gesell, A., & Thompson, H., *Infant behavior.* N.Y.: McGraw-Hill, 1934. **185**

Gesell, A., et al., *The first five years of life: A guide to the study of the preschool child.* N.Y.: Harper, 1940. **201, 263**

Gewirtz, J. L., The course of infant smiling in four child-rearing environments in Israel. In B. M. Foss, Ed., *Determinants of infant behavior,* vol. 3. London: Methuen, 1965. **312**

Gibson, E. J., see Walk & Gibson.

Ginsburg, H., & Opper, S., *Piaget's theory of intellectual development: An introduction.* Englewood Cliffs, N.J.: Prentice-Hall, 1969. **79**

Ginzberg, E., et al., The ineffective soldier, vol. 3. Patterns of performance. N.Y.: Columbia U. Press, 1959. **59**

Gold, G. M., see Alexander et al.

Golden, M., Bridger, W. H., & Montare, A., Social class differences in the ability of young children to use verbal information to facilitate learning. Amer. J. Orthopsychiat., 1974, **44**, 86–91. **296**

Goldman, R., Psychosocial development in cross-cultural perspective: A new look at an old issue. Develpm. Psychol., 1971, **5**, 411–419. **362**

Goldstein, A. G., Recognition of inverted photograph of faces by children and adults. J. genet. Psychol., 1975, **127**, 109–123. **275**

Goldstein, H., see Butler et al.

Gonso, J., see Gottman et al.

Good, T. L., see Brophy & Good.

Goodenough, F., The development of the reactive process from early childhood to maturity. J. exper. Psychol., 1935, **18**, 431–450. **394**

Goodenough, F. L., Anger in young children. U. Minn. Inst. Child Welfare Series, 1931, No. 9. **317–318**

Goodwin, D. L., see Cradler & Goodwin.

Gordon, M., see Green & Gordon.

Gordon, W., see Price-Williams et al.

Gormley, J., see Johnson & Gormley.

Gottesman, I. I., Heritability of personality: A demonstration. Psychol. Monogr., 1963, **77**, No. 9 (Whole No. 572). **72**

Gottesman, I. I., & Shields, J., Contributions of twin studies to perspectives on schizophrenia. In B. A. Maher, Ed., Progress in experimental personality research, vol. 3. N.Y.: Academic, 1966. **72**

Gottfried, A. W., & Brody, N., Interrelationships between and correlates of psychometric and Piagetian scales of sensorimotor intelligence. Develpm. Psychol., 1975, **11**, 379–387. **216**

Gottlieb, G., Neglected developmental variables in the study of species identification in birds. Psychol. Bull., 1973, **79**, 362–372. **76**

Gottman, J., Gonso, J., & Rasmussen, B., Social interaction, social competence, and friendship in children. Child Develpm., 1975, **46**, 709–718. **479**

Gozali, H., Cleary, T. A., Walster, G. W., & Gozali, J., Relationship between the internal-external control construct and achievement. J. educ. Psychol., 1973, **64**, 9–14. **432**

Gozali, J., see Gozali et al.

Gray, M. L., see Brackbill et al.

Gray, S. W., & Klaus, R. A., The Early Training Project: A seventh year report. Child Develpm., 1970, **41**, 909–924. **299–301, 418**

Green, B., see Adelson et al.

Green, P. C., & Gordon, M., Maternal deprivation: Its influence on visual exploration in infant monkeys. Science, 1964, **145**, 292–294. **240**

Green, R. L., & Hofmann, L. J., A case study of the effects of educational deprivation on Southern rural Negro children. J. Negro Educ., 1965, **34**, 327–341. **299**

Greenberg, J. W., & Davidson, H. H., Home background and school achievement of black urban ghetto children. Amer. J. Orthopsychiat., 1972, **42**, 803–810. **346**

Greene, P., see Smith & Greene.

Griffiths, W. J., see Williams et al.

Gross, M., Learning readiness in two Jewish groups. N.Y.: Center for Urban Educ., 1967. **371–372**

Grossman, J., & Lindgren, H. C., Workbook in psychology of personal and social adjustment. N.Y.: American Book, 1959. **57–58**

Grosswald, J., Testing perspectives in the large cities. Nat. Council on Measurement in Educ. News, 1970, **13**(3). **416**

Guedes, H. de A., see Lindgren & Guedes.

Guinagh, B. J., An experimental study of basic learning ability and intelligence in low socio-economic status children. Child Develpm., 1971, **42**, 27–36. **419–420**

Gutteridge, M. V., A study of motor achievements of young children. Arch. Psychol., N.Y., 1939, No. 244. **264–268**

Guyer, B. L., & Friedman, M. P., Hemispheric processing and cognitive styles in learning-disabled and normal children. Child Develpm., 1975, **46**, 658–668. **404–416**

Haan, N. S., see Kuhn et al.

Habenstein, R. W., see Queen & Habenstein.

Haith, W. W., see Kessen et al.

Hall, C. S., The incredible Freud. Contemp. Psychol., 1978, **23**, 38–39. **124**

Halverson, H. M., An experimental study of prehension in infants by means of systematic cinema records. Genet. psychol. Monogr., 1931, **10**, 107–286. **185–186**

Halverson, H. M., The development of prehension in infants. In R. G. Barker et al., Eds., *Child behavior and development*. N.Y.: McGraw-Hill, 1943. **165**

Hapiewicz, W. G., & Roden, A. H., The effect of aggressive cartoons on children's interpersonal play. *Child Develpm.*, 1971, **42**, 1583-1585. **473**

Harbison, R. D., & Mantilla-Plata, B., Prenatal toxicity, maternal distribution and placental transfer of tetrahydrocannabinol. *J. pharm. exper. Therapeutics*, 1972, **180**, 446-453. **147**

Harlow, H. F., The nature of love. *Amer. Psychologist*, 1958, **15**, 675-685. **76, 244-247**

Harlow, H. F., The heterosexual affectional system in monkeys. *Amer. Psychologist*, 1962, **17**, 1-9. **244-247, 337**

Harlow, H. F., see also Novak & Harlow.

Harner, L., Yesterday and tomorrow: Development of early understanding of the terms. *Develpm. Psychol.*, 1975, **11**, 864-865. **278**

Harper, L. V., & Sanders, K. M., Preschool children's use of space: Sex differences in outdoor play. *Develpm. Psychol.*, 1975, **11**, 119. **340, 475**

Harris, M. B., & Siebel, C. E., Affect, aggression, and altruism. *Develpm. Psychol.*, 1975, **11**, 623-627. **468-471**

Harris, R. C., see Winick et al.

Harris, S., & Braun, J. R., Self-esteem and racial preference in black children. *Amer. Psychol. Assn. Proceedings*, 1971, **6**, 259-260. **482-483**

Hartshorne, H., & May, M. S., *Studies in deceit*. N.Y.: Macmillan, 1928. **448**

Hartup, W. W., Peer relations. In T. D. Spencer, & N. Kass, Eds., *Perspectives in child psychology*. N.Y.: McGraw-Hill, 1970. **382-383**

Hartup, W. W., & Coates, B., Imitation of a peer as a function of reinforcement from the peer group and rewardingness of the model. *Child Develpm.*, 1967, **38**, 1003-1016. **383**

Hartup, W. W., see also Charlesworth & Hartup, and Rosekrans & Hartup.

Havighurst, R. J., *Human development and education*. N.Y.: Longmans, Green, 1953. **77, 128, 484-485**

Havighurst, R. J., Minority subcultures and the law of effect. *Amer. Psychologist*, 1970, **25**, 313-322. **371**

Hawkes, G. R., see Burchinal et al.

Haynes, H., White, B. L., & Held, R., Visual accommodation in human infants. *Science*, 1965, **148**, 528-530. **166**

Heber, R., see Garber & Heber.

Heider, E. R., Style and accuracy of verbal communications within and between social classes. *J. pers. soc. Psychol.*, 1971, **18**, 33-47. **373**

Heider, J., see Caldwell et al.

Heinstein, M. L., Influence of breast feeding on children's behavior. *Children*, 1963, **10**, 93-97. **236**

Held, R., see Haynes et al.

Henderson, E. H., see Long & Henderson.

Henderson, N. B., see Babson et al.

Henderson, N. D. Brain weight increases resulting from environmental enrichment: A directional dominance in mice. *Science*, 1970, **169**, 776-778. **227**

Hendry, L. S., & Kessen, W., Oral behavior of newborn infants as a function of age and time since feeding. *Child Develpm.*, 1964, **35**, 201-208. **190**

Henery, F. M., & Nelson, G. A., Age differences and interrelationships between skills and learning in gross motor performance of ten- and fifteen-year-old boys. *Res. Quart. Assn. Hlth. Phys. Educ.*, 1956, **27**, 162-175. **394-395**

Hepner, R., Maternal malnutrition and the fetus. *Amer. med. Assn.*, 1958, **169**, 1774-1777. **146**

Hermans, H. J. M., ter Laak, J. J. F., & Maes, P. C. J. M., Achievement motivation and fear of failure in family and school. *Develpm. Psychol.*, 1972, **6**, 520-528. **441**

Hetherington, E. M., Effects of father absence on personality development in adolescent daughters. *Develpm. Psychol.*, 1972, **7**, 313-326. **358-360**

Hetherington, E. M., & Feldman, S. E. College cheating as a function of subject and situational variables. *J. educ. Psychol.*, 1964, **55**, 212-218. **448**

Hetherington, E. M., & Parke, R. D., *Child psychology*. N.Y.: McGraw-Hill, 1975. **361**

Hicks, J. A., The acquisition of motor skill in young children: A study of the effects of practice in throwing at a moving target. *Child Develpm.*, 1930, **1**, 90-105. **263**

Hicks, R. E., & Kinsbourne, M., Human handedness: A partial cross-fostering study. *Science*, 1976, **192**, 908-910. **68**

Hilton, I., Differences in the behavior of mothers toward first- and later-born children. *J. pers. soc. Psychol.*, 1967, **7**, 282-290. **378**

Hinde, R. A., & Spencer-Booth, Y., Effects of brief separation from mother on rhesus monkeys. *Science*, 1971, **173**, 111-118. **242**

Hoffman, L. W., & Nye, F. I., *Working mothers*. San Francisco: Jossey-Bass, 1974. **250**

Hoffman, M. L., Moral development. In P. H. Mussen, Ed., *Carmichael's manual of child psychology*, 3rd ed. N.Y.: Wiley, 1970. **449-450**

Hoffman, M. L., Father absence and conscience development. *Develpm. Psychol.*, 1971, **4**, 400-406. **358**

Hoffman, M. L., Moral internalization, parental power, and the nature of parent-child interaction. *Develpm. Psychol.*, 1975, **11**, 228-239. **455**

Hoffman, M. L., see also Levine & Hoffman, and Sagi & Hoffman.

Hofman, L. J., see Green & Hofman.

Hogan, R., Moral conduct and moral character: A psychological perspective. *Psychol. Bull.*, 1973, **79**, 217-232. **116-118**

Hogan, R., see also Stayton et al.

Hohle, R. H., see Spears & Hohle.

Holloway, F. A., see Williams et al.

Holloway, H. D., Reliability of the Children's Manifest Anxiety Scale at the rural third grade level. *J. educ. Psychol.*, 1959, **49**, 193-196. **430**

Holloway, R. D., Normative data on the Children's Manifest Anxiety Scale at the rural third grade level. *Child Develpm.*, 1961, **32**, 129-134. **430**

Holmes, F. B., see Jersild & Holmes.

Holstein, C. E., The relation of children's moral judgment level to that of their parents and to communication patterns in the family. In M. C. & R. S. Smart, Eds., *Readings in child development and relationships*. N.Y.: Macmillan, 1972. **525**

Holtzman, W. D., Diaz-Guerrero, R., & Swartz, J. D., *Personality development in two cultures*. Austin: U. of Texas Press, 1975. **56, 60**

Holtzman, W. D., see also Diaz-Guerrero & Holtzman.

Holzinger, K. J., see Newman et al.

Hood, E. B., Behavioral implications of the human XYY genotype. *Science*, 1973, **179**, 139-150. **68-69**

Horner, M. S., Toward an understanding of achievement-related conflicts in women. *J. soc. Issues*, 1972, **28**(2), 147-176. **553-557**

Houston, K. B., Review of the evidence and qualifications regarding the effects of hallucinogenic drugs on chromosomes and embryos. *Amer. J. Psychiat.*, 1969, **126**, 251-254. **147**

Howard, A., see Gallimore et al.

Howells, T. H., The obsolete dogmas of heredity. *Psychol. Rev.*, 1945, **52**, 23-34. **91**

Hughes, A. S., see Dymond et al.

Hull, C., *Principles of behavior*. N.Y.: Appleton-Century-Crofts, 1943. **26**

Hulsebus, R. C., Operant conditioning of infant behavior: A review. In H. W. Reese, Ed., *Advances in child development and behavior*, vol. 8. N.Y.: Academic, 1973. **184**

Hunt, J. McV., *Intelligence and experience*. N.Y.: Ronald, 1961. **391**

Hunt, J. McV., see also Uzgiris & Hunt.

Hurwitz, I., see Wolff & Hurwitz.

Hutt, S. J., et al., Auditory sensitivity in the human neonate. *Nature*, 1968, **218**, 888-890. **166**

Hymes, D. H., On communicative competence. In R. Huxley & B. Ingram, Eds., *The mechanism of language development*. London: CIBA Found., 1972. **296-297**

Ilg, F., see Gesell & Ilg.

Inglis, S., see Wulbert et al.

Inhelder, B., & Piaget, J., *The growth of logical thinking: From childhood to adolescence*. N.Y.: Basic Books, 1958. **398, 515**

Inhelder, B., & Piaget, J., *The early growth of logic in the child*. N.Y.: Harper & Row, 1964. **283**

Inhelder, B., see also Piaget & Inhelder.

Irons, N. McC., & Zigler, E., Children's responsiveness to social reinforcement as a function of short-term preliminary social interactions and long-term social deprivation. *Develpm. Psychol.*, 1969, **1**, 402-409. **113-114**

Irwin, O. C., Infant speech: The effect of systematic reading of stories. *J. speech hear. Res.*, 1960, **3**, 187-190. **213**

Irwin, O. C., see also Brodbeck & Irwin.
Izard, C. E., & Caplan, S., Sex differences in emotional responses to erotic literature. *J. consult. clin. Psychol.*, 1974, **42**, 468. **566-567**

Jacklin, C. N., see Maccoby & Jacklin.
Jackson, C. M., Some aspects of growth. In W. J. Robbins, et al., Eds., *Growth*. New Haven: Yale U. Press, 1929. **160**
Jackson, P. W., see Lahaderne & Jackson.
Jacobson, L., see Rosenthal & Jacobson.
Jarmon, H., & Duhamel, T. R., Interpersonal distance in families with emotionally disturbed boys. *Amer. Psychol. Assn. Proceedings*, 1969, **5**, 555-556. **437**
Jensen, A. R., Learning abilities in Mexican-American and Anglo-American children. *Calif. J. educ. Res.*, 1961, **12**, 147-159. **419**
Jensen, A. R., Social class, race, and genetics: Implications for education. *Amer. J. educ. Res.*, 1968, **5**, 1-42. **418-419**
Jensen, A. R., How much can we boost IQ and scholastic achievement? *Harvard educ. Rev.*, 1969, **39**, 1-123. **418-419**
Jensen, A. R., Interaction of Level I and Level II abilities with race and socioeconomic status. *J. educ. Psychol.*, 1974, **66**, 99-111. **419**
Jersild, A. T., *Child psychology*, 6th ed. Englewood Cliffs, N.J.: Prentice-Hall, 1968. **127-128**
Jersild, A. T., & Holmes, F. B., Children's fears. *Child Develpm. Monogr.*, 1935, No. 20. **314**
Jersild, A. T., see also Ding & Jersild.
Jöchle, W., Predicting ovulation—a reply. *Science*, 1970, **169**, 717. **138**
Johnson, C. D., & Gormley, J., Academic cheating: The contribution of sex, personality, and situational variables. *Develpm. Psychol.*, 1972, **6**, 320-325. **448**
Johnson, R. C., Similarity in IQ of separated identical twins as related to length of time spent in same environment. *Child Develpm.*, 1963, **34**, 745-749. **72**
Johnson, V. E., see Masters & Johnson.
Jones, H. E., *Development in adolescence*. N.Y.: Appleton-Century-Crofts, 1943. **510-512**
Jones H. E., & Conrad, H. S., The growth and decline of intelligence: A study of a homogeneous group between the ages of ten and sixty. *Genet. Psychol. Monogr.*, 1933, **13**, 223-298. **59**
Jones, K. L., Smith, D. W., Ulleland, C. N., & Streissguth, A. P., Pattern of malformation in offspring of chronic alcoholic mothers. *Lancet*, 1973, **1**(7815), 1267-1271. **148**
Jones, M. C., & Mussen, P. H., Self-conceptions, motivations, and interpersonal attitudes of early- and late-maturing girls. *Child Develpm.*, 1958, **29**, 491-502. **512**
Jordan, C., see Gallimore et al.
Jordan, T. E., & Spaner, S. D., Biological and ecological influences on development at 24 and 36 months of age. *Psychol. Rep.*, 1972, **31**, 317-332. **178-179**

Kagan, J., Rosman, B., Dady, D., & Phillips, W., Information processing in the child: Significance of analytic and reflective attitudes. *Psychol. Monogr.*, 1964, **78** (1, Whole No. 578). **431**
Kagan, J., Attention and psychological change in the young child. *Science*, 1970, **170**, 826-832. **198-200**
Kagan, J., *Change and continuity in infancy*. N.Y.: Wiley, 1971. **87, 283**
Kagan, J., & Moss, H. A., The stability of passive and dependent behavior from childhood through adulthood. *Child Develpm.*, 1960, **31**, 577-591. **441-442**
Kagan, J., see also Lewis et al., Sontag & Kagan, and Tulkin & Kagan.
Kalnins, I. V., & Bruner, J. S., Infant sucking used to change the clarity of a visual display. In L. J. Stone et al., Eds., *The competent infant*. N.Y.: Basic Books, 1973. **184**
Kaplan, B., see Caldwell et al.
Karabenick, S. A., see Lerner et al.
Katz, M. M., see Bates & Katz.
Katz, P. A., Zigler, E., & Zalk, S. R., Children's self-image disparity: The effects of age, maladjustment, and action-thought orientation. *Develpm. Psychol.*, 1975, **11**, 546-550. **446-447**
Kaufman, I. C., & Rosenblum, L. A., Depression in infant monkeys separated from their mothers. *Science*, 1967, **155**, 1030-1031. **242-244**
Keating, D. P., Precocious cognitive development at the level of formal operations. *Child Develpm.*, 1975, **46**, 276-280. **518-519**
Keliher, A., *Life and growth*. N.Y.: Apple-

Keliher, A. (cont.)
ton-Century-Crofts, 1938. **506**
Kemp, B., see Gallimore et al.
Kendler, H. H., see Kendler & Kendler, and Kendler et al.
Kendler, T. S., & Kendler, H. H., Reversal and nonreversal shifts in kindergarten children. *J. exper. Psychol.*, 1959, **58**, 56–60. **306**
Kendler, T. S., Kendler, H. H., & Wells, D., Reversal and nonreversal shifts in nursery school children. *J. comp. physiol. Psychol.*, 1960, **53**, 83–88. **306**
Kennedy, J. F., Message from the President of the United States relative to mental illness and mental retardation. House of Representatives, 88th Congress, 1st Session, Document No. 58; Feb. 5, 1963. **146**
Kenniston, K., Social change and youth in America. In E. H. Erikson, Ed., *The challenge of youth.* N.Y.: Anchor, 1965. **551**
Kessen, W., *The child.* N.Y.: Wiley, 1965. **11**
Kessen, W., Haith, W. W., & Salapatek, P. H., Human infancy: A bibliography and guide. In P. H. Mussen, Ed., *Carmichael's manual of child psychology*, 3rd ed. N.Y.: Wiley, 1970. **168**
Kessen, W., see also Hendry & Kessen, Nelson & Kessen, and Nelson & Kessen.
King, J. E., see Becker et al.
Kinsbourne, M., see Hicks & Kinsbourne.
Kinsey, A. C., Pomeroy, W. B., & Martin, C. E., *Sexual behavior in the human male.* Philadelphia: Saunders, 1948. **561–562**
Kinsey, A. C., et al., *Sexual behavior in the human female.* Philadelphia: Saunders, 1953. **561–562**
Klaus, R. A., see Gray & Klaus.
Klausmeier, H. J., see Feldhusen & Klausmeier.
Kluckhohn, C., *Mirror for man.* N.Y.: McGraw-Hill, 1949. **69**
Kluckhohn, C., Murray, H. A., & Schneider, D. M., Eds., *Personality in nature, society, and culture.* N.Y.: Knopf, 1953. **95**
Knobloch, H., & Pasamanick, B., Seasonal variations in the birth of the mentally deficient. *Amer. J. publ. Health*, 1958, **48**, 1202–1208. **146**
Knodel, J., Breast-feeding and population growth. *Science*, 1977, **198**, 1111–1115. **233**

Koch, H. L., Some personality correlates of sex, sibling position, and sex of sibling among five- and six-year-old children. *Genet. psychol. Monogr.*, 1955, **52**, 3–50. **376**
Kogan, N., Stephens, J. W., & Shelton, F. C., Age differences: A developmental study of discriminability and affective response. *J. abnorm. soc. Psychol.*, 1961, **62**, 221–230. **275**
Kohlberg, L., Moral development and identification. In H. W. Stevenson et al., Eds., *Child psychology*, 62nd Yearbook, Natl. Soc. Stud. of Educ. Chicago: U. of Chicago Press, 1963a. **451–452**
Kohlberg, L., The development of children's orientations toward a moral order. I. Sequence in the development of moral thought. *Vita Humana*, 1963b, **6**, 11–33. **452–453, 524–525, 530**
Kohlberg, L., & Kramer, R., Continuities and discontinuities in childhood and adult moral development. *Hum. Develpm.*, 1969, **12**, 93–120. **452**
Kohlberg, L., see also Kuhn et al.
Kohn, M. L., Social class and parent-child relationships: An interpretation. *Amer. J. Sociol.*, 1963, **68**, 471–480. **363–364**
Kohn, M. L., *Class and conformity.* Homewood, Ill: Dorsey, 1969. **363–364**
Kolb, S., see Zelazo et al.
Koller, K. M., Parental deprivation, family background, and female delinquency. *Brit J. Psychiat.*, 1971, **118**, 319–327. **361**
Koltuv, M., see Neff & Koltuv.
Komorita, S. S., see Epstein & Komorita.
Kooistra, W. H., Developmental trends in the attainment of conservation, transivity, and relativism in the thinking of children. Unpubl. dissertation, Wayne State U., 1963. **86**
Krech, D., see Bennett et al.
Kreitler, H., & Kreitler, S., Dependence of laughter on cognitive strategies. *Merrill-Palmer Q.*, 1970, **16**, 163–177. **326–327**
Kreitler, S., see Kreitler & Kreitler.
Kreutzberg, J. R., see Clark et al.
Kriegsman, E., see Wulbert et al.
Krowitz, A., see Campos et al.
Kuhn, D., Langer, J., Kohlberg, L., and Haan, N. S., The development of formal operations in logical and moral judgment. *Genet. Psychol. Monogr.*, 1977, **95**, 97–188. **515–516**

La Gaipa, J. J., see Bigelow & La Gaipa.
Lahaderne, H. M., & Jackson, P. W., Withdrawal in the classroom: A note on some educational correlates of social desirability among school children. *J. educ. Psychol.*, 1970, **61**, 97-101. **477**
Lamaze, F., *Painless childbirth: The Lamaze method*. Chicago: Regnery, 1970. **153**
Lane, P. A., see Tolor et al.
Langer, A., see Campos et al.
Langer, J., see Kuhn et al.
Laosa, L. M., & Brophy, J. E., Sex × birth order interaction in measures of sex-typing and affiliation in kindergarten children. *Amer. Psychol. Assn. Proceedings*, 1970, **5**, 363-364. **376**
Larson, R. C., Dissecting changes in writing achievement. *NAEP Newsletter*, 1976, **9**(3), 7. **521**
Laurendeau, M., & Pinard, A., *Causal thinking in the child: A genetic and experimental approach*. N.Y.: Intl. Univ. Press, 1963. **86**
Lawton, J. J., Jr., see Woling et al.
Lee, P. C., Cognitive development in young children. In H. C. Lindgren, Ed., *Children's behavior*. Palo Alto, Calif.: Mayfield, 1975. **272**
Lefkowitz, M. M., see Eron et al.
Lehmann, I. J., The biography of a freshman class. In *Measurement in education*, 20th yearbook, Natl. Council Measmt. in Educ., 1963. **527**
Lenneberg, E. H., On explaining language. *Science*, 1969, **164**, 635-643. **212-213**
Lerner, R. M., Karabenick, S. A., & Meisels, M., Effects of age and sex on the development of personal space schemata toward body build. *J. genet. Psychol.*, 1975, **127**, 91-101. **480-482**
Lessard, R., see Sankoff & Lessard.
Lester, B. M., Cardiac habituation of the orienting response to an auditory signal in infants of varying nutritional status. *Develpm. Psychol.*, 1975, **11**, 432-442. **180**
Leuba, C., Tickling and laughter: Two genetic studies. *J. genet. Psychol.*, 1941, **58**, 201-209. **324**
Lewin, K., see Barker et al.
Levin, H., see Sears et al., 1957.
Levine, L. E., & Hoffman, M. L., Empathy and cooperation in 4-year-olds. *Develpm. Psychol.*, 1975, **11**, 533-534. **167**

LeVine, R. A., Cross-cultural study in child psychology. In P. H. Mussen, Ed., *Carmichael's manual of child psychology*, 3rd ed. N.Y.: Wiley, 1970. **250**
Levine, S., Stimulation in infancy. *Scient. Amer.*, 1960, **202**, 81-87. **226**
Lewis, M., Kagan, J., & Kalafat, J., Patterns of fixation in the young infant. *Child Develpm.*, 1966, **37**, 331-341. **190, 191**
Lewis, M., & Rosenblum, L. A., Eds., *The effect of the infant on its caregiver*. N.Y.: Wiley-Interscience, 1974. **222**
Lewis, M., et al., Infants' responses to facial stimuli during the first year of life. Unpubl. paper, Amer. Psychol. Assn, Convention, Chicago, 1965. **190**
Liebert, R. M., & Poulos, R. W., Eliciting the "norm of giving": Effects of modeling and presence of witness on children's sharing behavior, *Amer. Psychol. Assn. Proceedings*, 1971, **6**, 345-346. **109-110, 383**
Liley, A. W., The foetus as a personality. *Austral. & N.Z. J. Psychiat.*, 1972, **6**, 99-105. **145**
Lindgren, H. C., Age as a variable in aversion toward food and occupation. *J. consult. Psychol.*, 1962, **26**, 101-102. **514, 559**
Lindgren, H. C., *An introduction to social psychology*, 2nd ed. N.Y.: Wiley, 1973. **418**
Lindgren, H. C., & Byrne, D., *Psychology*, 3rd ed. N.Y.: Wiley, 1971. **537, 543**
Lindgren, H. C., & Byrne, D., *Psychology*, 4th ed. N.Y.: Wiley, 1975. **89, 118**
Lindgren, H. C., & Guedes, H. de A., Social status, intelligence, and educational achievement among elementary and secondary students in São Paulo, Brazil. *J. soc. Psychol.*, 1963, **60**, 9-14. **49, 415-416**
Lindgren, H. C., & Mello, M. J., Emotional problems of over- and underachieving children in a Brazilian elementary school. *J. genet. Psychol.*, 1965, **106**, 59-65. **445**
Lindgren, H. C., Silva, I., Faraco, I, & da Rocha, N. S., Attitudes toward problem solving as a function of success in arithmetic in Brazilian schools. *J. educ. Res.*, 1964, **58**, 44-45. **49, 415-416**
Lindgren, H. C., see also Babayan et al., Grossman & Lindgren, and Uchiyama & Lindgren.
Ling, B. C., Form discrimination as a learn-

Ling, B. C. (cont.)
ing cue in infants. *Compar. psychol. Monogr.*, 1941, **17**, No. 2. **207**

Little, B. C., see Zahn et al.

Little, C. R. D., see Becker et al.

Long, B. H., & Henderson, E. H., Measuring self-esteem across cultures. *Amer. Psychol. Assn. Proceedings*, 1971, **6**, 255-256. **55**

Loeb, R. C., Concommitants of boys' locus of control examined in parent-child interactions. *Develpm. Psychol.*, 1975, **11**, 353-358. **432-434, 438**

Lorenz, K., Der Kumpan in der Umwelt des Vogels. Der Artgenosse als auslösendes Moment sozialer Vethaltungsweisen. *J. Orinth.*, 1935, **83**, 137-213. **76**

Lovell, K., A follow-up study of Inhelder's and Piaget's "The growth of logical thinking." *Brit. J. Psychol.*, 1961a, **52**, 143-153. **272**

Lovell, K., A follow-up study of Inhelder's and Piaget's "The growth of logical thinking." *Brit. J. Psychol.*, 1961b, **52**, 155-193. **399**

Lowry, G. H., see Watson & Lowry.

Lunt, P. S., see Warner & Lunt.

Luria, A. R., *The role of speech in the regulation of normal and abnormal behavior*. N.Y.: Liveright, 1961. **285**

Lustman, S. L., Rudiments of the ego. *Psychoanal. Stud. Child*, 1956, **11**, 89-92. **165**

Lynn, D. G., & Sawrey, W. L., The effects of father-absence on Norwegian boys and girls. *J. abnorm. soc. Psychol.*, 1959, **59**, 258-262. **357**

Lytton, H., Conway, D., & Sauvé, R., The impact of twinship on parent-child interaction. *J. pers. soc. Psychol.*, 1977, **35**, 97-107. **370-371**

McCall, R. B., Addendum. The use of multivariate procedures in developmental psychology. In P. H. Mussen, Ed., *Carmichael's manual of child psychology*, 3rd ed. N.Y.: Wiley, 1970. **325**

McCandless, B. R., see Castenada et al.

McCarthy, D., The language development of the preschool child. *U. Minn. Inst. Child Welf. Monogr.*, 1930, No. 4. **294**

McCarthy, D., Language development in children. In L. Carmichael, Ed., *Manual of child psychology*, 2nd ed. N.Y.: Wiley, 1954. **209-210**

MacDonald, A. P., Jr., Manifestations of differential levels of socialization by birth order. *Develpm. Psychol.*, 1969a, **1**, 485-492. **376**

MacDonald, A. P., Jr., Anxiety affiliation, and social isolation. *Develpm. Psychol.*, 1969b, **3**, 242-254. **376**

McDonald, F. J., see Bandura & McDonald.

Macfarlane, J. W., From infancy to adulthood. In M. C. Jones et al., Eds., *The course of human development*. Waltham, Mass.: Xerox, 1971. **568-569**

McGraw, M. B., Suspension grasp behavior of the human infant. *Amer. J. of the Diseases of Cln.*, 1940, **16**, 799-811. **171**

McGraw, M. B., *The neuromuscular maturation of the human infant*. N.Y.: Columbia U. Press, 1943. **172**

McGraw, M. B., Maturation of behavior. In L. Carmichael, Ed., *Manual of child psychology*. N.Y.: Wiley, 1946. **74**

McKinney, J. D., Problem-solving strategies in reflective and impulsive children. *J. educ. Psychol.*, 1975, **67**, 807-820. **431**

McLandon, P. A., see Simsarian & McLandon.

McNeill, D., On theories of language acquisition. In D. Horton and T. Dixon, Eds., *Verbal behavior and general behavior*. Englewood Cliffs, N.J.: Prentice-Hall, 1968. **285**

McNemar, Q., *Psychological statistics*, 2nd ed. N.Y.: Wiley, 1955. **49**

Maccoby, E. E., Sex in the social order. *Science*, 1973, **182**, 469-471. **340-341**

Maccoby, E. E., Socialization theory: Where do we go from here? Unpublished paper, Western Psychol. Assn., Sacramento, April, 1975. **339, 426, 455**

Maccoby, E. E., & Jacklin, C. N., *The psychology of sex differences*. Stanford: Stanford U. Press, 1974. **190-191, 294, 468-469, 553**

Maccoby, E. E., see also Sears et al.

Madison, P., *Personality development in college*. Reading, Mass.: Addison-Wesley, 1969. **551-552, 567-568**

Maes, P. C. J. M., see Hermans et al.

Mandell, W., see Caputo & Mandell.

Mantilla-Plata, B., see Harbison & Mantilla-Plata.

Markell, R. A., see Asher & Markell.

Marwick, C. S., Predicting ovulation—a reply. *Science*, 1970, **169**, 717. **138**

Marx, J. L., Hemophilia: New information about the "royal disease." *Science*, 1975a, **188**, 41-42. **68**

Marx, J. L., Cytomegalovirus: A major cause of birth defects. *Science*, 1975b, **190**, 1184-1186. **147**

Marx, J. L., Crib death: Some promising leads but no solution yet. *Science*, 1975c, **189**, 367-369. **163**

Maslow, A. H., *Motivation and personality.* N.Y.: Harper, 1954. **111**

Massari, D. J., The relationship of reflection-impulsivity to field dependence-independence and internal-external control in children. *J. genet. Psychol.*, 1975, **126**, 61-67. **45**

Masters, W. H., & Johnson, V. E., *Human sexual response.* Boston: Little, Brown, 1966. **561-562**

Masters, W. H., & Johnson, V. E., *Human sexual inadequacy.* Boston: Little, Brown, 1970. **561-562**

Matas, L., see Waters et al.

Mathews, M., see Quay & Mathews.

Maw, W. H., & Maw, E. W., Children's curiosity and parental attitudes. *J. marriage & Family*, 1966, **28**, 343-345. **439-440**

May, M. S., see Hartshorne & May.

Mead, M., *Coming of age in Samoa.* N.Y.: Morrow, 1928. **23**

Mead, M., *Sex and temperament in three primitive societies*, N.Y.: Morrow, 1935. **340**

Medsker, L. L., see Trent & Medsker.

Meisels, M., see Lerner et al.

Mello, M. J., see Lindgren & Mello.

Meltzoff, A. N., & Moore, M. K., Imitation of facial and manual gestures by human neonates. *Science*, 1977, **198**, 75-78. **188-189**

Meredith, H. V., Somatic changes during human prenatal life. *Child Develpm.*, 1975, **46**, 603-610. **141, 148, 160**

Merrill, M. A., The significance of IQs on the Revised Stanford-Binet Scales. *J. educ. Psychol.*, 1938, **29**, 641-651. **461**

Meyer, K. K., see Winick et al.

Midgley, N., & Abrams, M. S., Fear of success and locus of control in young women. *J. consult. clin. Psychol.*, 1974, **42**, 737. **555-556**

Miles, B. E., see Alexander et al.

Milgram, N. A., see Milgram & Milgram.

Milgram, R. M., & Milgram, N. A., The effect of test content and context on the anxiety-intelligence relationship. *J. genet. Psychol.*, 1977, **130**, 121-127. **49**

Milgram, S., Group pressure and action against a person. *J. abnorm. soc. Psychol.*, 1964, **69**, 137-143. **461**

Miller, P. Y., & Simon, W., Adolescent sexual behavior: Context and change. *Soc. Probl.*, 1974, **22**, 58-76. **564**

Millichamp, D. A., see Blatz et al.

Mills, B., see Wulbert et al.

Mischel, W., Preference for delayed reinforcement: An experimental study of a cultural observation. *J. abnorm. soc. Psychol.*, 1958, **56**, 57-61. **357**

Mischel, W., Cognitive appraisals and transformations in self-control. In B. Weiner, Ed., *Cognitive views of human motivation.* N.Y.: Academic, 1974. **114, 357**

Mitchell, G., & Brandt, E. M., Behavioral experiences related to experience of the mother and sex of the infant in the rhesus monkey. *Develpm. Psychol.*, 1970, **3**, 149. **337**

Mitchell, G., see also Stevens & Mitchell.

Mogar, M., Children's causal reasoning about natural phenomena. *Child Develpm.*, 1960, **31**, 59-65. **402**

Mongrella, J., see Ritschl et al.

Montare, A., see Golden et al.

Montgomery, L. E., & Finch, A., Jr., Relection-impulsivity and locus of conflict in emotionally disturbed children. *J. genet. Psychol.*, 1975, **126**, 89-91. **432**

Moore, M. K., see Meltzoff & Moore.

Moore, R. W., see Brennan et al.

Moreno, J. L., *Who shall survive? A new approach to the problem of human interrelations.* Washington: Nerv. & Mental Disease Publ. Co., 1934. **474**

Morgan, G. A., & Ricciuti, H. N., Infants' responses to strangers during the first year. In B. M. Foss, Ed., *Determinants of infant behavior.* London: Methuen, 1963. **312**

Morrison E., Underachievement among preadolescent boys considered in relationship to passive aggression. *J. educ. Psychol.*, 1969, **60**, 168-173. **470**

Morrow, W. R., & Wilson, R. C., The self-reported personal and social adjustment of bright high-achieving and underachieving high school boys. *J. child*

Morrow, W. R. (cont.)
 psychol. & Psychiat., 1961, **2**, 203-209. **445**
Morrow, W. R., & Wilson, R., Family relations of bright high-achieving and underachieving high school boys. Child Develpm., 1961, **32**, 501-510. **538**
Mosher, D. L., Sex differences, sex experience, sex guilt, and explicitly sexual films. J. soc. Issues, 1973, **29**(3), 95-112. 566-567
Mouton, J. S., Bell, R. L., Jr., & Blake, R. R., Role playing skill and sociometric peer status. Group Psychother., 1956, **9**, 7-17. **477**
Munday, L. A., Declining admissions test scores. ACT Res. Report, Res. & Develpm. Div., Amer. Coll. Testing Program, 1976. **521, 524**
Murphy, G., Murphy, L. B., & Newcomb, T. M., Experimental social psychology. N.Y.: Harper, 1937. **444**
Murphy, L. B., see Murphy et al.
Murray, H. A., see Kluckhohn et al.
Mussen, P. H., see Jones & Mussen.
Muzio, J. N., see Roffwarg et al.

Naeye, R. L., Dienner, M. M., Dellinger, W. S., & Blanc, W. A., Urban poverty: Effects on prenatal nutrition. Science, 1969, **166**, 1026. **146**
National Center for Health Statistics Growth Charts, Monthly Vital Statistics Reports, 1976, 25, No. 3 Supplement. **177**
Neale, D. C., & Proshek, J. M., School-related attitudes of culturally disadvantaged elementary school children. J. educ. Psychol., 1967, **58**, 238-244. **495-496**
Neff, W. S., & Koltuv, M., Toleration of psychiatric rehabilitation as a function of coping style. J. consult. Psychol., 1967, **31**, 364-370. **446**
Neimark, E. D., Intellectual development during adolescence. Rev. Child Develpm. Res., 1975, **4**, 541-594. **514-515, 516, 519**
Nelson, G. A., see Henery & Nelson.
Nelson, K. E., Facilitating children's syntax acquisition. Develpm. Psychol., 1977, **13**, 101-107. **286**
Nelson, K., & Kessen, W., Visual scanning by human newborns: Responses to complete triangle, to sides only, and to corners only. Amer. Psychol. Assn. Proceedings, 1969, **4**, 273-274. **166**
Newberry, H., see Richards & Newberry.
Newcomb, T. M., see Murphy et al.
Newman, H. H., Freeman, F. H., & Holzinger, K. J., Twins. Chicago: U. of Chicago Press, 1937. **72**
Nichols, P. L., & Broman, S. H., Familial resemblance in infant development. Develpm. Psychol., 1974, **10**, 442-446. **70**
Nielsen, J., Friedrich, U., & Tsuboi, T., Chromosome abnormalities in patients treated with chlorpromazine, perphenazine, and lysergide. Brit. med. J., 1969, **3**, 634-636. **148**
Niem, T.-I. C., & Collard, R. R., Parental discipline of aggressive behaviors in four-year-old Chinese and American children. Amer. Psychol. Assn. Proceedings, 1972, **7**, 95-96. **50, 320**
Nourse, A. E., et al., The body. N.Y.: Time-Life, 1964. **142**
Novak, M. A., & Harlow, H. F., Social recovery of monkeys isolated for the first year of life: 1. Rehabilitation and therapy. Develpm. Psychol., 1975, **11**, 453-465. **227**
Nowicki, S., & Strickland, B. R., A locus of control scale for children. Unpubl. paper, Amer. Psychol Assn. Convention, Washington, D.C., 1971. **432**
Nowlis, G. H., & Kessen, W., Human newborns differentiate differing concentrations of sucrose and glucose. Science, 1976, **191**, 865-866. **168**
Nye, F. I., see Hoffman & Nye.

O'Connor, N., & Franks, C., Childhood upbringing and other environmental factors. In H. J. Eysenck, Ed., Handbook of abnormal psychology. N.Y.: Basic Books, 1961. **242**
Oetting, E. R., & Dinges, N. C., An anxiety and mood scale for young Navajo children. Amer. Psychol. Assn. exper. publ. System, June, 1971, **12**, Ms. No. 472-35. **445**
O'Keeffe, L., see Webb et al.
Oliveri, M. A., see Webb et al.
Opper, S., see Ginsberg & Opper.
Ordy, J. M., see Fantz et al.
Osser, H., Language development. In G. S. Lesser, Ed., Psychology and educational practice. Chicago: Scott Foresman, 1971. **285, 297**
Owens, W., Age and mental abilities:

Second adult follow-up. *J. educ. Psychol.*, 1966, **57**, 311-325. **59**

Paivio, A., *Imagery and verbal processes.* N.Y.: Holt, 1971. **292**

Palermo, D. S., Castenada, A., & McCandless, B. R., The relationship of anxiety in children to performance in a complex learning task. *Child Develpm.*, 1956, **27**, 333-338. **430**

Palermo, D. S., see also Castenada et al.

Palmer, R. J., see Cotler & Palmer.

Panel on Youth of the President's Science Advisory Committee, *Youth: Transition to adulthood.* Chicago: U. Chicago Press, 1974. **504**

Parke, R. D., see Hetherington & Parke.

Parkin, J. M., see Warren & Parkin.

Parten, M. B., Leadership among preschool children. *J. abnorm. soc. Psychol.*, 1932-33, **27**, 430-440. **379-380**

Pasamanick, B., see Knobloch & Pasamanick.

Paternite, C. E., see Cantor & Paternite.

Payne, J. S., et al., *Head Start: A tragicomedy with epilogue.* N.Y.: Behavioral Publications, 1973. **79**

Pearlin, L. I., *Class context and family relations: A cross-national study.* Boston: Little, Brown, 1971. **364**

Pedersen, F. A., see Rubenstein et al.

Phillips, W., see Kagan et al.

Piaget, J., *The language and thought of the child.* N.Y.: Humanities Press, 1926. **269**

Piaget, J., *The child's conception of the world.* N.Y.: Harcourt Brace, 1929. **87**

Piaget, J., *The moral judgment of children.* Glencoe, Ill.: Free Press, 1948. **54**

Piaget, J., *Psychology of intelligence.* N.Y.: Harcourt Brace, 1950. **88, 410**

Piaget, J., *Play, dreams, and imitation in childhood.* N.Y.: Norton, 1951. **192, 202**

Piaget, J., *The origins of intelligence in children.* N.Y.: Intl. Universities Press, 1952. (Trans. by M. Cook; original, 1936.) **82, 91**

Piaget, J., The development of time concepts in the child. In P. H. Hoch & J. Zubin, Eds., *Psychopathology of childhood.* N.Y.: Grune & Stratton, 1955. **402**

Piaget, J., *Logic and psychology.* N.Y.: Basic Books, 1957. **192**

Piaget, J., *The child's conception of number.* N.Y.: Norton, 1965. **270**

Piaget, J., *The child's conception of time.* N.Y.: Basic Books, 1969. (Trans. by A. J. Pomerans; original, 1946.) **278**

Piaget, J., Piaget's theory. In P. H. Mussen, Ed., *Carmichael's manual of child psychology*, 3rd ed., vol. 1. N.Y.: Wiley, 1970. **82, 398**

Piaget, J., Intellectual development from adolescence to adulthood. *Human Develpm.*, 1972, **15**, 1-12. **515-516**

Piaget, J., & Inhelder, B., *The child's conception of space.* London: Routledge & Kegan Paul, 1956. **276**

Piaget, J., & Inhelder, B., *The growth of logical thinking from childhood to adolescence.* (Trans. A. Parsons & S. Seagrin.) N.Y.: Basic Books, 1958. **86**

Piaget, J., & Inhelder, B., *Le genèse des structures logiques élémentaires: Classifications et sériations.* Neuchâtel, Switzerland: Delachaux & Niestlé, 1959. **274**

Piaget, J., & Inhelder, B., *The psychology of the child.* N.Y.: Basic Books, 1969. **259-260**

Piddington, R., *The psychology of laughter: A study of social adaptation.* N.Y.: Gamut Press, 1963. **327**

Pinard, A., see Laurendeau & Pinard.

Pinneau, S. R., The infantile disorders of hospitalism and anaclitic depression. *Psychol. Bull.*, 1955, **52**, 429-452. **242**

Plomin, R., see Rowe & Plomin.

Poulos, R. W., see Liebert & Poulos.

Prader, A., Tanner, J. M., & von Harnack, G. A., Catchup growth following illness or starvation. *J. Pediat.*, 1963, **62**, 646-659. **262**

Pratt, K. C., et al., *Behavior of the newborn infant.* Columbus: Ohio State U. Press, 1930. **161**

Presbie, R. J., see Ritschl et al.

Price-Williams, D., Gordon, W., & Ramirez, M., III, Skills and conservation: A study of pottery-making children. *Develpm. Psychol.*, 1969, **1**, 769. **273, 402**

Proshek, J. M., see Neale & Proshek.

Quast, W., see Wolking et al.

Quay, L. C., Language dialect, reinforcement, and the intelligence-test performance of Negro children. *Child Develpm.*, 1971, **42**, 5-15. **297-298**

Quay, L. C., & Mathews, M., Social class and intellectual influences on communication encoding. Unpublished paper, Amer.

Quay, L. C. (cont.)
Psychol. Assn. Convention, 1977. **373**
Queen, S. A., & Habenstein, R. W., *The family in various cultures*, 3rd ed. Philadelphia: Lippincott, 1967. **6**

Raabe, V. L., see Dymond et al.
Rabin, A. I., *Growing up in the kibbutz.* N.Y.: Springer, 1965. **250**
Ramirez, M., III, see Price-Williams et al.
Rassmussen, B., see Gottman et al.
Rau, L., see Sears et al.
Rau, L., see Winder & Rau.
Raynor, R., see Watson & Raynor.
Rees, J., see Tizard & Rees.
Rehage, K. J., see Flickinger & Rehage.
Reichard, C. C., & Elder, S. T., The effects of caffeine on reaction time in hyperkinetic and normal children. *Amer. J. Psychiat.*, 1977, **134**, 144-148. **397**
Rest, J. R., Longitudinal study of the defining issues test of moral judgment: A strategy for analyzing developmental change. *Develpm. Psychol.*, 1975, **11**, 738-748. **526-527**
Revelle, R., see Fresch & Revelle.
Rheingold, H. L., The measurement of maternal care. *Child Develpm.*, 1960, **31**, 565-575. **35**
Rheingold, H. L., & Eckerman, C. O., The infant separates himself from his mother. *Science*, 1970, **168**, 78-83. **247-249**
Rheingold, H. L., Gewirtz, J. L., & Ross, H. W., Social conditioning. *J. comp. physiol. Psychol.*, 1959, **57**, 68-73. **213**
Ribble, M. A., *The rights of infants.* N.Y.: Columbia U. Press, 1943. **241**
Ricciuti, H. N., see Brockman & Ricciuti, and Morgan & Ricciuti.
Rice, R. D., Neurophysiological development in premature infants following stimulation. *Develpm. Psychol.*, 1977, **13**, 69-76. **229**
Richards, T. W., & Newberry, H., Studies in fetal behavior: III. Can performance test items at six months postnatally be predicted on the basis of fetal activity? *Child Develpm.*, 1938, **9**, 79-86. **145**
Ringness, T. A., Identification patterns, motivation, and school achievement of bright junior high school boys. *J. educ. Psychol.*, 1967, **58**, 93-102. **544**
Ritschl, C., Mongrella, J., & Presbie, R. J., Group time-out from rock and roll music and out-of-seat behavior of handicapped children while riding a school bus. *Psychol. Rep.*, 1972, **31**, 967-973. **490**
Robin, S. S., see Callahan & Robin.
Roden, A. H., see Hapkiewicz & Rodan.
Roffwarg, H. P., Muzio, J. N., & Dement, W. C., Ontogenetic development of the human sleep-dream cycle. *Science*, 1966, **152**, 604-619. **162**
Rogers, C. R., & Dymond, R., *Psychotherapy and personality change.* Chicago: U. of Chicago Press, 1954. **446**
Rose, H. A., see Elton & Rose.
Rose, M. H., see Burk et al.
Rosekrans, M. A., & Hartup, W. W., Imitation influences of consistent and inconsistent response consequences to a model on aggressive behavior in children. *J. pers. soc. Psychol.*, 1967, **7**, 429-434. **322-323**
Rosen, B. C., Socialization and achievement motivation in Brazil. *Amer. sociol. Rev.*, 1962, **27**, 612-624. **442**
Rosen, B. C., Social class and the child's perception of the parent. *Child Develpm.*, 1964, **35**, 1147-1153. **442**
Rosenblatt, P. C., & Skoogberg, E. L., Birth-order in cross-cultural perspective. *Develpm. Psychol.*, 1974, **10**, 48-54. **375**
Rosenblum, L. A., see Kaufman & Rosenblum, and Lewis & Rosenblum.
Rosenhan, D., see Dowart et al.
Rosenthal, M. K., The generalization of dependency behaviors from mother to stranger. Unpublished doctoral dissertation, Stanford U., 1965. **316**
Rosenthal, M. K., The generalization of dependency behavior from mother to stranger. *J. child psychol. Psychiat.*, 1967, **8**, 117-133. **316**
Rosenthal, R., *Experimenter effects in behavioral research.* N.Y.: Academic., 1966. **55, 145**
Rosenthal, R., & Jacobson, L., *Pygmalion in the classroom.* N.Y.: Holt, 1968. **416**
Rosenzweig, M. R., see Bennett et al.
Rosman, B., see Kagan et al.
Ross, D., see Bandura et al.
Ross, E. N., see Butler et al.
Ross, S. A., see Bandura et al.
Rothbart, M. K., Birth order and mother-child interaction in an achievement situation. *J. pers. soc. Psychol.*, 1971, **17**, 113-119. **378-379**
Rothenburg, B. B., & Courtney, R. G., Conservation of number in very young

children. *Develpm. Psychol.*, 1969, **1**, 493-502. **273**

Rotter, J. B., Generalized expectancies for internal versus external control of reinforcement. *Psychol. Monogr.*, 1966, **80** (1, Whole No. 609). **431**

Routh, D. K., Conditioning of vocal response differentiation in infants. *Develpm. Psychol.*, 1969, **1**, 219-226. **208, 212**

Rowe, D., & Plomin, R., Temperament in early childhood. *J. pers. Assess.*, 1977, **41**, 150-156. **329**

Rubenstein, J. L., Pedersen, F. A., & Yarrow, L. J., What happens when Mother is away?: A comparison of mothers and substitute caregivers. *Develpm. Psychol.*, 1977, **13**, 529-530. **251**

Sagi, A., & Hoffman, M. L., Empathic distress in the newborn. *Develpm. Psychol.*, 1976, **12**, 175-176. **167, 226**

Salapatek, P. H., see Kessen et al.

Salk, L., The effects of normal heartbeat sound on the behavior of the newborn infant: Implications for mental health. *World ment. Health*, 1960, **12**, 168-175. **163**

Salk, L., The importance of the heartbeat rhythm to human nature: Theoretical, clinical, and experimental observations. *Proceedings, 3rd World Cong. Psychiat.*, vol. 1. Montreal: McGill U. Press, 1961. **163**

Salmon, M., see Sayler & Salmon.

Sameroff, A. J., Can conditioned responses be established in the newborn infant: 1971? *Develpm. Psychol.*, 1971, **5**, 1-12. **172**

Sander, L. W., see Condon and Sander.

Sanders, K. M., see Harper and Sanders.

Sankoff, D., & Lessard, R., Vocabulary richness: A sociolinguistic analysis. *Science*, 1975, **190**, 689. **374**

Santrock, J. W., Father absence, perceived maternal behavior, and moral development in boys. *Child Develpm.*, 1975, **46**, 753-757. **357**

Santrock, J. W., & Wohlford, P., Effects of father absence: Influence of the reason for and the onset of the absence. *Amer. Psychol. Assn. Proceedings*, 1970, **5**, 265-266. **358**

Sauvé, R., see Lytton et al.

Sawrey, W. L., see Lynn & Sawrey.

Sayler, A., & Salmon, M., Communal nursing in mice: Influence of multiple mothers on the growth of the young. *Science*, 1969, **164**, 1309-1310. **251-252**

Sayler, A., & Salmon, M., An ethological analysis of communal nursing by the house mouse (*mus musculus*). *Behaviour*, 1971, **40**, 62-85. **252-253**

Scammon, R. E., The measurement of the body in childhood. In J. A. Harris et al., *The measurement of man*. Minneapolis: U. of Minn. Press, 1930. **181**

Scarpetti, W. L., see Tolor et al.

Scarr-Salapatek, S., Race, social class, and IQ. *Science*, 1971, **174**, 1285-1295. **421**

Scarr-Salapatek, S., & Williams, M. L., The effects of early stimulation on low-birth-weight infants. *Child Develpm.*, 1973, **44**, 94-101. **228-229**

Schaefer, E. S., & Bell, R. Q., Development of a parental attitude research instrument. *Child Develpm.*, 1958, **29**, 339-361. **52**

Schaefer, E. S., see Bayley & Schaefer.

Schaffer, H. R., Activity level as a constitutional determinant of infantile reaction to deprivation. *Child Develpm.*, 1966, **37**, 595-602. **213-214**

Schaffer, H. R., & Emerson, P. E., The development of social attachments in infancy. *Monogr. Soc. Res. Child Develpm.*, 1964a, **29**, No. 3. **237-239, 312**

Schaffer, H. R., & Emerson, P. E., Patterns of response to physical contact in early human development. *J. child psychiat. Psychol.*, 1964b, **5**, 1-13. **329-330**

Schaie, C. W., & Strother, C. R., A cross-cultural study of age changes in cognitive behavior. *Psychol. Bull.*, 1968, **70**, 671-680. **59**

Scheinfeld, A., see Garai & Scheinfeld.

Schmitt, M. H., Superiority of breast-feeding: Fact or fancy? *Amer. J. Nursing*, 1970, **70**, 1488-1493. **235**

Schneider, D. M., see Kluckhohn et al.

Schwartz, S. H., & Clausen G. T., Responsibility, norms, and helping in an emergency. *J. pers. soc. Psychol.*, 1970, **16**, 299-310. **384**

Sears, R. R., Maccoby, E. E., & Levin, H. *Patterns of child rearing*. Evanston: Row, Peterson, 1957. **52**

Sears, R. R., Rau, L., & Alpert, R., *Identification and child rearing*. Stanford: Stanford U. Press, 1965. **53, 317**

Seegmiller, B. R., Relations between behavioral characteristics of infants, their mothers' behaviors, and performance on the Bayley mental and motor scales. *J. Psychol.*, 1975, **90**, 99–111. **237**

Seghorn, T., see Cohen & Seghorn.

Seraydarian, L., see Busse & Seraydarian.

Serunian, S. A., & Broman, S. H., Relationship of Apgar scores and Bayley mental and motor scores. *Child Develpm.*, 1975, **46**, 696–700. **154**

Shelton, F. C., see Kogan et al.

Sherif, M., *The psychology of social norms*. N.Y.: Harper, 1936. **461**

Shields, J., *Monozygotic twins*. London: Oxford U. Press, 1962. **70**

Shields, J., see also Gottesman & Shields.

Shirley, M. M., *The first two years: A study of twenty-five babies, vol 1. Postural and locomotor development*. Minneapolis: U. of Minn. Press, 1931. **187**

Shirley, M. M., *The first two years, vol. 2. Intellectual development*. Minneapolis: U. of Minn. Press, 1933. **187, 209–211**

Siebel, C. E., see Harris & Siebel.

Silva, I., see Lindgren et al.

Simner, M. L., Newborn's response to the cry of another infant. *Develpm. Psychol.*, 1971, **5**, 136–150. **167**

Simon, J. G., see Feather & Simon.

Simon, W., see Miller & Simon.

Simsarian, F. P., & McLendon, P. A., Feeding behavior of an infant during the first twelve weeks of life on a self-demand schedule. *J. Pediat.*, 1942, **20**, 93–103. **161**

Singer, R. D., see Feshbach & Singer.

Siqueland, E. R., Reinforcement patterns and extinction in human newborns. *J. exp. child. Psychol.*, 1968, **6**, 431–442. **172**

Skinner, B. F., *The behavior of organisms*. N.Y.: Appleton-Century-Crofts, 1938. **26**

Skinner, B. F., *Verbal behavior*. N.Y.: Appleton-Century-Crofts, 1957. **212, 286**

Skoogberg, E. L., see Rosenblatt & Skoogberg.

Slobin, D. I. Universals of grammatical development in children. In G. B. Flores d'Arcais & J. M. Levelt, Eds., *Advances in psycholinguistics*. N.Y.: American Elsevier, 1970. **285**

Smith, D. W., see Jones, K. L. et al.

Smith, K. U., & Greene, P., A critical period in maturation of performance with space-displaced vision. *Percept. & motor Skills*, 1963, **17**, 627–639. **395**

Smith, K. U. Zwerg, C., & Smith, N. J., Sensory-feedback analysis of infant control of the behavioral environment. *Percept. & motor Skills*, 1963, **16**, 725–732. **239–240**

Smith, M. E., An investigation of the development of the sentence and the extent of the vocabulary in young children. *U. Iowa Stud. Child. Welf.*, 1926, **3**, No. 5. **292–294**

Smith, N. F., The influence of social class and ethnicity: A multi-national study of parental child training values. Unpubl. ᵤₑ, 'r Intl. Soc. for the Study of Behav. Develpm., U. of Surry, Guildford, England, July 1975. **364–365, 372**

Smith, N. J., see Smith, K. U. et al.

Snyder, E. E., A longitudinal analysis of the relationship between high school student values, social participation, and educational-occupational achievement. *Sociol. Educ.*, 1969, **42**, 261–270. **546–548**

Snyder, M. M., see Bayer & Snyder.

Solkoff, N., Yaffe, S., Weintraub, D., & Blase, B., Effects of handling on the subsequent developments of premature infants. *Develpm. Psychol.*, 1969, **1**, 765–768. **163**

Sontag, L. W., Baker, C. T., & Nelson, V. L., Mental growth and personality development: A longitudinal study. *Soc. Res. Child Develpm. Monogr.*, 1958, **23**, No. 68. **553**

Sontag, L. W., & Kagan, J., The emergence of intellectual achievement motives. *Amer. J. Orthopsychiat.*, 1963, **33**, 532–535. **442**

Spaner, S. D., see Jordan & Spaner.

Spear, P. S., Motivational effects of praise and criticism on children's learning. *Develpm. Psychol.*, 1970, **3**, 124–132. **42–43**

Spearman, C. E., *The abilities of man*. N.Y.: Macmillan, 1927. **410**

Spears, W. C., & Hohle, R. H., Sensory and perceptual processes in infants. In Y. Brackbill, Ed., *Infancy and early childhood*. N.Y.: Free Press, 1967. **167**

Spelt, D. K., The conditioning of the human fetus in utero. *J. exper. Psychol.*, 1948, **38**, 338–346. **145**

Spencer-Booth, Y., see Hinde & Spencer-

Booth.
Spero, J., see Carter et al.
Spitz, R. A., Hospitalism. *Psychoanal. Stud. Child*, 1945, **1**, 54-74. **244**
Spitz, R. A., Hospitalism: A follow-up report. *Psychoanal. stud. Child*, 1946, **2**, 113-117. **244**
Spitz, R. A., The importance of the mother-child relationship during the first year of life: A synopsis in five sketches. *Ment. health Today*, **1948**, 7, 7-13. **241**
Sroufe, L. A., see Waters et al.
Staub, E., The use of role playing and induction in children's learning of helping and sharing behavior. *Child Develpm.*, 1971, **42**, 805-816. **383**
Stayton, D., Hogan, R., & Ainsworth, M. D. S., Infant obedience and maternal behavior: The origins of socialization reconsidered. *Child Develpm.*, 1971, **42**, 1057-1069. **118**
Stein, Z., et al., Nutrition and mental performance. *Science*, 1972, **178**, 708-713. **183**
Stein, Z., & Susser, M., Pregnancy and famine. *Science*, 1973, **180**, 133-136. **183**
Stephan, C., see Stephan & Stephan.
Stephan, W. C., & Stephan, C., Role differentiation, empathy, and neurosis in urban migrants and lower-class residents of Santiago, Chile. *J. pers. soc. Psychol.*, 1971, **19**, 1-6. **477**
Stephens, J. W., see Kogan et al.
Stern W., *The psychological methods of testing intelligence*. (Trans. by G. M. Whipple.) Baltimore: Warwick & York, 1914. **410-411**
Stevens, C. W., & Mitchell, G., Birth order effects, sex differences, and sex preferences in the peer-directed behaviors of rhesus monkeys. *Internatl. J. Psychobiol.*, 1972, **2**, 117-128. **379**
Stevenson, H. W., see Weir & Stevenson.
Steward, D., see Steward & Steward.
Steward, M., & Steward, D., The observation of Anglo-, Mexican-, and Chinese-American mothers teaching their young sons. *Child Develpm.*, 1973, **44**, 329-337. **44, 50**
Stewart, D., see Berk et al.
Stewart, M. A., Hyperactive children. *Sci. Amer.*, 1970, **222**(4), 94-99. **395-396**
Stinnett, N., see Edwards & Stinnett.
Stott, D. H., An empirical approach to motivation based on the behavior of the young child. *J. child psychol. Psychiat.*, 1961, **2**, 97-117. **201-202**
Strauss, M. E., et al., Behavior of narcotics-addicted newborns. *Child Develpm.*, 1975, **46**, 887-893. **147**
Streissguth, A. P., see Jones, K. L. et al.
Strickland, B. R., see Nowicki & Strickland.
Strother, C. R., see Schaie & Strother.
Suci, G. J., see Copple & Suci.
Sullivan, H. S., *Conceptions of modern psychiatry*. Washington: Wm. Allanson White Psychiat. Found., 1947. **334**
Sunley, R., Early nineteeth century literature on child rearing. In. M. Mead & M. Wolfenstein, Eds., *Childhood in contemporary cultures*. Chicago: U. of Chicago Press, 1955. **8**
Susser, M., see Stein & Susser.
Swartz, J. D., see Holtzman et al.

Takaishi, M., see Tanner et al.
Tanner, J. M., *Growth at adolescence*, 2nd ed., Philadelphia: Davis, 1962. **181**
Tanner, J. M., The regulation of human growth. *Child Develpm.*, 1963, **34**, 817-848. **180**
Tanner, J. M., Physical growth. In P. H. Mussen, Ed., *Carmichael's manual of child psychology*, 3rd ed. N.Y.: Wiley, 1970. **176, 180-181, 184, 508-510**
Tanner, J. M., Whitehouse, R. H., & Takaishi, M., Standards from birth to maturity for height, weight, height velocity, and weight velocity: British children, 1965. *Arch. dis. Childhood*, 1966, **41**, 613-635. **178-179**
Tanner, J. M., see also Prader et al.
Taylor, W. L., "Cloze procedures": A new tool for measuring readability. *Journalism Quart.*, 1953, **30**, 415-433. **428**
ter Laak, J. J. F., see Hermans et al.
Terman, L. M., & Merrill, M. A., *Measuring intelligence*. Boston: Houghton, Mifflin, 1937. **49, 516**
Tharp, R. G., see Gallimore et al.
Thomas, A., Chess, S., & Birch, H, C., The origin of personality. *Scientific American*, 1970, **223**(2), 102-109. **328-329.**
Thomas, M. J., Realism and socioeconomic status (SES) of occupational plans of low SES black and white male adolescents. *J. couns. Psychol.*, 1976, **23**, 46-49. **558-559**

Thompson, H., see Gesell & Thompson.
Thurstone, L. L., Theories of intelligence. *Scientific Monthly*, 1946, **62,** 101–112. **410**
Tizard, B., & Rees, J., A comparison of effects of adoption, restoration to the natural mother, and continued institutionalization on the cognitive development of four-year-old children. *Child Develpm.*, 1974, **45,** 92–99. **361–362**
Tizard. J., *Community services for the mentally handicapped.* London: Oxford U. Press, 1964. **114**
Toigo, R., see Eron et al.
Tolor, A., Scarpetti, W. L., & Lane, P. A., Teachers' attitudes toward children's behavior revisited. *J. educ. Psychol.*, 1967, **58,** 175–180. **494**
Tracy, F., *The psychology of adolescence.* N. Y.: Macmillan, 1920. **503**
Trent, J. W., & Medsker, L. L., *Beyond high school.* San Francisco: Jossey-Bass, 1968. **527**
Tronick, E., see Ball & Tronick.
Tsuboi, T., see Nielsen et al.
Tuddenham, R. D., Soldier intelligence in World Wars I and II. *Amer. Psychologist*, 1948, **3,** 54–56. **375**
Tuddenham, R. D., Jean Piaget and the world of the child. *Amer. Psychologist*, 1966, **21,** 207–217. **80, 83, 86**
Tulkin, S. R., Race, class, family, and school achievement. *J. pers. soc. Psychol.*, 1968, **9,** 31–37. **373**
Tulkin, S. R., & Kagan, J., Mother-child interaction: Social class differences in the first year of life. *Amer. Psychol. Assn. Proceedings*, 1970, **5,** 261–262. **213**
Turner, R. H., & Vanderlippe, R. H., Self-ideal congruence as an index of adjustment. *J. abnorm. soc. Psychol.*, 1958, **57,** 202–206. **446**
Turnure, C., Response to voice of mother and stranger by babies in the first year. *Develpm. Psychol.*, 1971, **4,** 182–190. **40–41, 55, 206**
Twitchell, T. E., A behavioral syndrome. *Science*, 1971, **174,** 135–136. **397**
Tyler, L. E., Human abilities. *Ann. Rev. Psychol.*, 1972, **23,** 177–206. **417**

Uchiyama, A., & Lindgren, H. C., Ideal teacher concepts: Attitude shift after practice teaching. *Psychol. Rep.*, 1971, **28,** 470. **494**
Udelf, M. S., see Frantz et al.
Ulleland, C. N., see Jones et al.
U.S. Bureau of the Census, *Statistical abstract of the United States; 1975.* Washington: General Printing Office, 1975. **155**
U.S. Public Health Service, *School achievement of children by demographic and socioeconomic factors,* U.S. DHEW Publication (HSM), 72–1011, November, 1971. **520**
U.S. Public Health Service, *Age at menarche.* DHEW Publication (HRA), 74–1615, November, 1973a. **506, 509–510**
U.S. Public Health Service. *Intellectual development of youths as measured by a short form of the Wechsler Intelligence Scale.* DHEW Publication (HRA), 74–1610, September, 1973c. **516–518**
U.S. Public Health Service, *Literacy among youths 12–17 years,* U.S. DHEW Publication (HRA), 74–1613, December, 1973d. **520**
U.S. Public Health Service, *Reading and arithmetic achievement among youths 12–17 years as measured by the Wide Range Achievement Test,* U.S. DHEW Publication (HRA), 74–1618, February, 1974. **520**
U.S. Public Health Service, *Self-reported health behavior and attitudes of youths 12–17 years.* DHEW Publication (HRA), 75–1629, April, 1975. **513–514**
Uzgiris, I. C., Situational generality of conservation. *Child Develpm.*, 1964, **35,** 831–841. **272**
Uzgiris, I. C., & Hunt, J. McV., *Assessment in infancy.* Urbana: U. of Illinois Press, 1975. **193–194, 214–215**

Vanderlippe, R. H., see Turner & Vanderlippe.
VanHorn, C., & Erlick, A. C., The American way of life: Politics, patriotism, isolation. *Purdue Opinion Panel,* Poll No. 90, January, 1971. **529–530**
von Harnack, G. A., see Prader et al.

Waber, D. P., Sex difference in cognition: A function of maturation rate? *Science*, 1976, **192,** 572–574. **518**
Wade, N., Bottle-feeding: Adverse effects of a western technology. *Science*, 1974,

184, 45-48. **233**

Walder, L. D., see Eron et al.

Walk, R. D., & Gibson, E. J., A comparative and analytical study of visual depth perception. *Psychol. Monogr.*, 1961, **75**, No. 15. **203-205**

Wallace, P., Complex environments: Effects on brain development. *Science*, 1974, **185**, 1035-1037. **227**

Walsh, A. M., *Self-concepts of bright boys with learning difficulties.* N.Y.: Bureau of Publications, Teachers College, Columbia U., 1956. **445**

Walster, G. W., see Gozali et al.

Walters, C. E., Prediction of postnatal development from fetal activity. *Child Develpm.*, 1965, **36**, 801-808. **145**

Walters, R. H., see Bandura & Walters.

Warnath, C. F., The relationship of family cohesiveness and adolescent independence to social effectiveness. *Marriage & family Living*, 1955, **17**, 346-348. **539**

Warner, W. L., & Lunt, P. S., *The social life of a modern community.* New Haven: Yale U. Press, 1941. **362**

Warren, J. M., see Wilson et al.

Warren, N., African infant precocity. *Psychol. Bull.*, 1972, **78**, 353-367. **100**

Warren, N., & Parkin, J. M., A neurological and behavioral comparison of African and European newborns in Uganda. *Child Develpm.*, 1974, **45**, 966-971. **100**

Washburn, R. W., A study of smiling and laughing of infants in the first year of life. *Genet. psychol. Monogr.*, 1929, **6**, 397-537. **71, 324**

Waters, E., & Crandall, V. J., Social class and observed maternal behavior from 1940 to 1960. *Child Develpm.*, 1964, **35**, 1021-1032. **436**

Waters, E., Matas, L., & Sroufe, L. A., Infants' reaction to an approaching stranger: Description, validation, and functional significant to wariness. *Child Develpm.*, 1975, **46**, 348-356. **239**

Watson, E. H., & Lowrey, G. H., *Growth and development of children.* Chicago: Yearbook Publishers, 1958. **260**

Watson, J. B., & Raynor, R., Conditioned emotional reactions. *J. exper. Psychol.*, 1920, **3**, 1-4. **17**

Watson, R. I., see Zemlick & Watson.

Waxler, C. Z., & Yarrow, M. R., An observational study of maternal models. *Develpm. Psychol.*, 1975, **11**, 485-494. **236**

Webb, R. A., Oliveri, M. A., & O'Keeffe, L. Investigations of the meaning of "different" in the language of young children. *Child Develpm.*, 1974, **45**, 984-991. **274**

Wechsler, D., Intelligence defined and undefined: A relativistic appraisal. *Amer. Psychologist*, 1975, **30**, 135-139. **408-410, 415**

Weinstein, H., see Caudill & Weinstein.

Weintraub, D., see Solkoff et al.

Weir, M. W., Children's behavior in probabilistic tasks. *Young Children*, 1967, **23**, 90-105. **305-306**

Weir, M. W., & Stevenson, H. W., The effects of verbalization in children's learning as a function of chronological age. *Child Develpm.*, 1959, **36**, 173-178. **282**

Weisberg, P., Developmental differences in children's preferences for high- and low-arousing forms of contact stimulation. *Child Develpm.*, 1975, **46**, 975-979. **326**

Wells, D., see Kendler et al.

Wender, P. H., *Minimal brain dysfunction in children.* N.Y.: Wiley-Interscience, 1971. **397**

Wender, P. H., see also Zahn et al.

Werner, E. E., Bierman, J. M., & French, F. E., *The children of Kauai.* Honolulu: U. of Hawaii Press, 1971. **366-367**

Werner, E., see Beilin & Werner.

Werner, H., *Comparative psychology of mental development.* N.Y.: Harper, 1940. **275**

Werner, H., The concept of development from a comparative and organismic point of view. In D. B. Harris, Ed., *The concept of development: An issue in the study of human behavior.* Minneapolis: U. of Minnesota Press, 1957. **88**

White, B. L., see Haynes et al.

White, S. H., The learning theory tradition and child psychology. In P. H. Mussen, Ed., *Carmichael's manual of child psychology*, 3rd ed. N.Y.: Wiley, 1970. **26-28**

Whitehouse, R. H., see Tanner et al.

White House Conference on Children, *Profiles of children.* Washington: Govt. Printing Office, 1970. **147-155, 180-182, 363**

Whiting, A., Parental expectation for independent behavior and achievement of elementary school boys. In H. C. Lindgren & F. Lindgren, Eds., *Current read-*

Whiting, A. (cont.) ings in educational psychology, 2nd ed. N.Y.: Wiley, 1971. **438–439**

Wickman, E. K., Children's behavior and teachers' attitudes. N.Y.: Commonwealth Fund, 1928. **493**

Williams, H. L., Holloway, F. A., & Griffiths, W. J., Physiological psychology: Sleep. Ann. Rev. Psychol., 1973, **24,** 279–316. **165**

Williams, M. L., see Scarr-Salapateck & Williams.

Wilson, M., Warren, J. M., & Abbott, L., Infantile stimulation, activity, and learning by cats. Child Develpm., 1965, **36,** 843–853. **227**

Wilson, R. C., see Morrow & Wilson.

Wilson, R. R., see Morrow & Wilson.

Winder, C. L., & Rau, L., Parental attitudes associated with social deviance in preadolescent boys. J. abnorm. soc. Psychol., 1962, **64,** 418–424. **49**

Winick, M., Meyer, K. K., & Harris, R. C., Malnutrition and environmental enrichment by early adoption. Science, 1975, **190,** 1173–1175. **183**

Wispé, L. B., & Freshley, H. B., Race, sex, and sympathetic helping behavior: The broken bag caper. J. pers. soc. Psychol., 1971, **17,** 59–65. **384**

Wohlford, P., see Santrock & Wohlford.

Wolff, P. H., The natural history of crying and other vocalizations in early infancy. In B. M. Foss, Ed., Determinants of infant behavior. London: Methuen, 1969. **207**

Wolff, P. H., & Hurwitz, I., Functional implications of the minimal brain damage syndrome. Seminars in Psychiatry, 1973, **5,** 105–116. **397–398**

Wolins, M., Young children in institutions: Some additional evidence. Develpm. Psychol., 1970, **2,** 99–109. **242**

Wolking, W. D., Quast, W., & Lawton, J. J., Jr., MMPI profiles of the parents of behaviorally disturbed children and parents from the general population. J. clin. Psychol., 1966, **22,** 39–48. **437**

Woodworth, R. S., Psychology, 4th ed. N.Y.: Holt, 1940. **410**

Wright, H. F., Psychological development in the Midwest. Child Develpm., 1956, **27,** 265–286. **460**

Wulbert, M., Inglis, S., Kriegsmann, E., & Mills, B., Language delay and associated mother-child interactions. Develpm. Psychol., 1975, **11,** 61–70. **354–355**

Yaffe, S., see Solkoff et al.

Yarrow, L. J., Maternal deprivation: Toward an empirical and conceptual reevaluation. Psychol. Bull., 1961, **58,** 459–490. **242**

Yarrow, L. J., see also Rubenstein et al.

Yarrow, M. R., see Waxler & Yarrow.

Zahn, T. P., Abate, F., Little B. C., & Wender, P. H., Minimal brain dysfunction, stimulant drugs, and autonomic nervous system activity. Archives of General Psychiatry, 1975, **32,** 381–387. **397**

Zajonc, R. B., Social psychology: An experimental approach. Belmont, Calif.: Wadsworth, 1966. **466**

Zajonc, R. B., Family configuration and intelligence. Science, 1976, **192,** 227–236. **368–370, 375, 523–524**

Zalk, S. R., see Katz et al.

Zelazo, N. A., see Zelazo et al.

Zelazo, P. R., Zelazo, N. A., & Kolb, S., Walking in the newborn. Science, 1972, **176,** 314–316. **172**

Zemlick, M. R., & Watson, R. I., Maternal attitudes of acceptance and rejection during and after pregnancy. Amer. J. Orthopsychiat., 1953, **23,** 570–584. **149–150**

Zerg, C., see Smith et al.

Zigler, E., Social class and the socialization process. Rev. educ. Res., 1970, **40,** 87–110. **373**

Zigler, E., see also Irons & Zigler, and Katz et al.

Zimbardo, P. G., The human choice: Individuation, reason, and order, versus deindividuation, impulse, and chaos. In W. J. Arnold & D. Levine, Ed., Nebraska symposium on motivation, 1969, **17,** 237–307. **466**

Zimmerman, B. J., & Brody, G. H., Race and modelling influences on the interpersonal play patterns of boys. J. educ. Psychol., 1975, **67,** 591–598. **483–484**

Zimmerman, D. R., Rh: The intimate history of a disease and its conquest. N.Y.: Macmillan, 1973. **149**

Zukow, A. H., Helping the hyperkinetic child. Today's Education, 1975, **64**(3), 39–41. **397**

Subject Index

Words in *italics* are defined in the Glossary.

Achievement, declines since 1962, 521–523
  in high school and college, 552
  and need for affiliation, 477
  in school, and child-rearing practices, 438–439
Achievement need, as conflicting with affiliation needs, 543–546
  and intervention programs, 299
  and parental attitudes, 440–442
Adler, Alfred, 125
Adolescence, changing values during, 546–549
  cognitive development during, 514–524
  dependence during, 535
  developmental tasks of, 549–550
  drug usage during, 540–541
  "food fussiness" during, 514
  formal operation during, 515, 518–519
  health problems during, 512–514
  identity diffusion during, 550–552
  influence of parents on moral development during, 525
  intellectual development during, 516–518
  leadership during, 546
  moral judgment during, 524–530
  parents' role during, 535–543
  part-time employment during, 559–560
  peer-group influence in, 542–549
  personality and social development in, 533–569
  personality development in, 549–557
  physical changes during, 505–510
  physical, mental, and moral development during, 503–530
  and physical skills, 507–508
  popularity during, 545–549
  problems of, 534–535
  problems of occupational choice in, 557–561
  problems experienced, as predictors of adult adjustment, 568–569
  Samoan, 23
  self-concept development in, 550–552
  sexual adjustment in, 561–568
  sexual maturation during, 506, 508–510
  social activity during, 546–549
  the subculture of, 533–534
  "testing the limits" during, 540
  values held during, 546–549
Adoption, effect on children, 231
Adult adjustment, predicting, 568–569
Affiliation need, as conflicting with achievement need, 477, 543–546
African infants, rapid development observed in, 100
Agression, in American and Chinese children, 50–52
  and social learning, 472–474
Aggressive impulses, control of, 122
Aggressiveness, cultural influences on, 320
  and early experiences in rats and mice, 252–253
  as instinctive, 252–253
  longitudinal study of, 474
  in males, 339–341
  during preschool years, 317–323
  in school-age children, 467–471

Aggressiveness, (cont.)
    sex differences in, 467-471
    and social learning, 320-323
    teachers' and mental health specialists' attitudes toward, 493-494
Aid to Families with Dependent Children, 363
Alcoholism, and infant birth weight, 148
Allantois, 139
Altruism, and sublimation, 122
Allergy, 68
    during childhood, 261, 262
Aloofness in parents, and social learning, 108-109
"Alternate life styles," students' attitudes toward, 564-565
Altruistic behavior, in preschool children, 383-384
    and social learning, 109-110
Amnion, or water sac, 142-143
Amphetamines, as prescribed for hyperactivity, 396-397
Anaclitic depression, 241, 244
Anal stage, 123
Analgesic drugs, effects during childbirth, 157-158
Anger, during preschool years, 317-323
Animism, 269, 401
Anorexia nervosa, 262
Anthropology, cultural, 23
Anxiety, described, 311, 314
    and ego defense mechanisms, 429
    first appearance of, 312
    in Freudian theory, 122
    and ideal self, 448
    during pregnancy, 150
    in preschool years, 314-316
    and problem solving, 430
    and reading achievement, 490-491
    and school learning, 430
    and socialization, 314, 430
Apaches, 69
Apgar test, 154-156
    as predictive of physiological development of infants, 179-180
Aristotle, 8
Arousal, and aggressive and altruistic behavior, 470-472
    and laughter, 325-327
    need for, 111-113, 114
Ashkenazic culture, 371-372
Athletics, interest in, during adolescence, 546-548
Attachment, and animal research, 242-245
    and basic trust, 240-242

    and independence, 245-249
    in infants, 235-240
    and institutional care, 242
Attention, mother as source of, 231-232
Attitudes toward children, ancient and medieval, 4-6
    during nineteenth century, 8
Authoritarian parents, 61
Authority, adolescents' attitudes toward, 546
Autonomy, 331

Babinski reflex, 170
Babkin reflex, 170
"Baby biographers," 9-10
Babysitters, 249-252
Barbados children, 55
Basic learning ability (BLA), and problem-solving ability, 419-420
Basic trust, in infants, 240-242
Bayley Scales of Motor and Mental Development, 154-156, 214-216
Behaviorism, 16-17
Behavior modification, 488-492
Belgium, child-rearing patterns in, 364-365
Bell Adjustment Inventory, 445
Bias, in research, 55
Binet, Alfred, 13-14, 37-38, 410
Birth defects, and cytomegalovirus, 146-147
    and maternal drug use, 147-148
    and maternal nutrition, 145-146
Birth order, 125
    influences on personality development, 375-379
    and intelligence test scores, 368, 523-524
    and language development, 294
Birth weight, above normal, 158-159
    subnormal, 146, 158-159
Blastocyst, 139, 141
Bleuler, Eugen, 79
Body stalk, of embryo, 139
Brain hemisphere dominance, 404-406
Brazelton Neonatal Behavioral Assessment Scale, 147, 157-158, 229
Brazilian children, 415, 442, 445
Breast feeding, 232-236
    and children's self-esteem, 444
    and delay of ovulation, 233
    psychological effects of, 236
British children, attitudes toward school, 495
Broken homes, and school adjustment of adolescents, 537-538
Butler, Samuel, 533

Caldwell Inventory of Home Stimulation, 216, 218
Canada, child-rearing patterns in, 364–365
Cannabis use, and fetal stress, 147
Caregivers, influence on infants, 222–253
Cartoons, effect on children's behavior, 473
Cattell Infant Scale, 214–215
Cattell, J. McK., 37
Causality, children's concepts of, 400–402
Centration, 80, 269–270, 399
Cephalocaudal development, 73, 144
Cerebral cortex, of stimulated rats, 227
Childbirth, attitudes regarding, 149–154
  mortality during, 154–156
  without fear, 153–154
Child Development (journal), 28
Child guidance clinics, 20–21
Child-rearing practices, 52–53
  and achievement motivation, 440–442
  and aggressiveness, 435–436
  and behavior problems, 437–438
  and birth order, 375–379
  and cognitive development, 352–357
  and curiosity, 96–97, 439–440
  and ideal self, 446
  and independence, 438–439
  and locus of control, 432–434, 438–439
  and personality development, 346–352, 434–442
  with preschool children, 346–379
Child Study Movement, 10–12, 30
Children's Apperception Test (CAT), 56
Children's Embedded Figures Test (CEFT), 45–46
Children's Television Workshop, 301
Chinese children, 50–52
Chinese-American infants, lack of excitability in, 97
Chinese-American mothers, behavior of, 44
Chorion, 139
Chromsomes, 68–69
Classical conditioning, 100–102
Classification skills, 273–274
Clinical method, 53
Clinical research, 60–61
Clinical treatment, 60–61
Cloze procedure, 427–428
Cognition, and laughter, 326–327
Cognitive development, in adolescence, 514–524
  and child-rearing practices, 352–357
  in elementary school years, 398–422
  during infancy, 191–193

and moral development, 528–530
in preschool children, 268–278
Piagetian concepts of, 268–274
Coitus, 138
Colds, frequency during childhood, 261
Comanches, 69
Communal rearing of infants, among animals, 251–253
  in kibbutzim, 250
Communication, between mother and infant, 232
Competition, and need for achievement, 543–544
Complex stimuli, infants' preference for, 194–198
Conceptual development, in preschool children, 275–278
Concrete operations, 83, 398–399
Conditioned response (CR), 100–102
Conditioned stimulus (CS), 100–102
Conflict, psychosocial, 128–129
Conservation, 83, 399
  of continuous quantities, 270
  of liquid, 270–271, 273
  of number, 273
  in preschool children, 269–273
  of substance, 273
  of volume, 273
Controls, experimental, 33, 40, 42
Cooperation, in infants, 117
Correlational methods, 43–49
Correlations, meaning of, 46–49
Crawling, 74
Crick, F., 66
Critical period hypothesis, 75–79, 227
Criticism, effects on behavior, 42–43
  effect of teachers', 490–492
Cross-cultural psychology, 28
Cross-sectional research, 40–41, 58–60
Crying, of infants, and mothers' previous rejection of pregnancy, 152
  of infants, mothers' responses to, 207
  during preschool years, 312–313
Crying sounds, neonates' reactions to, 167
Cuddling, responses to, 147, 329–330
Cultural bias, in research, 34
"Culture-fair" tests, 419
Curiosity, 96–97
  and child-rearing patterns, 439–440
Cytomegalovirus (CMV), and birth defects, 146–147

Darwin, Charles, 7, 9–10, 125
Darwinian reflex, 74–75, 171–172
Day care centers, 250–251

Daydreaming, 479
Deafness, and language development, 282-283
Decentering, 80, 115
Defense mechanisms, 122
   in late-maturing adolescents, 512
Deindividuation, and peer group, 465-467
Delay of gratification, and father's absence, 357
Delight, in infants, 324
Delivery, effect of pain-relieving drugs during, 157-158
Della Robbia, Luca, 4-5
Deoxyribonucleic acid (DNA), 66
Dependent attitudes, in Hawaiian children, 332-333
Dependent variable, 40-42
Depth perception, during infancy, 202-205
Development, defined, 65
Developmental Psychology (journal), 28
Developmental psychology, scope of, 24-27
Developmental tasks, 77-78
   during adolescence, 549-550
Dewey, John, 18, 21
Differential methods, 43-49
Differentiation, in development, 74-75
Directionality, in development, 73-75
Disadvantaged children, 29
Discipline, and aggressiveness, 435-436
   and children's personality development, 349-352
   and moral development, 455
   in nineteenth century, 8
   parental, 116-118
   as practiced by American and Chinese parents, 50-52
   and punishment, 105, 116, 435, 436-437, 444
   and social-class differences, 364-365
Discontinuity, and development, 88
Divorce, effects on children's personality development, 357-361, 537-538
Dizygotic (DZ) twins, 70-72
Draw-a-Person Test, 57, 443-444
Drug usage, during adolescence, 540-541
Dutch children and youth, effect of malnutrition on, 183

Early intervention, with animals, 226-227
   with infants, 226-240
   with low-birth-weight infants, 228-229
   the Milwaukee project, 230-231
Ego, 120-125
Ego defense mechanisms, 122

Ego rewards, 371
Electra complex, 123
"Electric Company, The," 484
Elementary school years, achievement motivation in, 440-442
   anxiety during, 428-430
   children's behavior problems in, 437-438
   cognitive development during, 398-422, 427-428
   concrete operations in, 398-399
   development of aggressiveness during, 435
   development of curiosity during, 439-440
   development of independence during, 438-440
   development of self-awareness during, 442-448
   formal operations in, 400
   and ideal self, 446-448
   impulsivity during, 430-431
   intellectual development during, 408-422
   and learning of reading, 427-428
   and locus of control, 431-434
   moral development during, 448-455
   and notions of causality, 400-402
   and over- and underachievers, 445-446
   personality development during, 428-448
   physical and mental development during, 391-425
   and school achievement, 438-440
   and self-esteem, 443-444
   sensorimotor development during, 392-398
   social acceptance in, 443
Embedded Figures Test, 45-46
Embracing reflex, 170
Embryo, 140-143, 147
   effects of maternal drug usage on, 147-148
Embryonic disk, 143
Emerson, Ralph Waldo, 459
Emotion, defined, 311
Emotional development, during infancy, 311-313, 317-318, 324-325
   in preschool years, 310-327
Emotional disturbance, during pregnancy, 151-153
Empathy, 477-479
   in mothers, 237
   and mothers' control of infants, 237
   sex differences in, 167

and social learning, 107
Endoderm, 139–140
Endomorphic children, prejudice toward, 480–481
England, child-rearing patterns in, 364–365
Environmental influences, on development, 66–72
Environmental/experimental approach, 25–29
Environmentalist views, 81
Erikson, Erik H., 125–129
Erogenous zones, in psychoanalytic theory, 123
Ethnic prejudice, 481–484
Evolution, theory of, 10
Excitement, need for, 111–112
Existential psychology, 119
Expectations, of caregivers, 330
Experience, and development, 89–92
Experimental research, 25–29
Exploratory behavior, 96–97
  in infancy, 201–202

Fallopian tubes, 138
Family, size of, 368–370
  social class of, 362–375
  as social environment, 344–379
  structure of, 345
Family activities, and adolescent adjustment, 539–540
Family size, and children's IQ, 368–370
  and physical growth of children, 260
Fantasies, during preschool years, 316–317
Fantasy violence, 316–317, 472–474
Father absence, 357–361
Fathers, as caregivers, 223
  changes in role of, 124
Fear, during pregnancy, 151–153
Fear responses, 312–317
  defined, 311
"Fear of success," in young women, 552–557
Feeding, of neonates, 160–161
Feeding practices, and children's personality development, 236
Feltboard technique, 480
Fetal alcohol syndrome, 148
Fetal stress, and maternal drug use, 147–148
  and maternal smoking, 148
Fetus, 141–149
  activity of, 144–145
  conditioning behavior of, 145
  effects of poverty on, 146
  and maternal nutrition, 145–147

sucking response in, 168
Field-dependence, 405–406
Figural collections, 274
Firstborns, cognitive development of, 375–376
  language development in, 294
  parental attitudes toward, 378–379
  personality development of, 376
  and Scholastic Aptitude Test (SAT) scores, 523–524
Fixation, in Freudian theory, 123
"Flight into femininity," during adolescence, 553
Formal operations, 83–86, 400
  in adolescence, 514–516
  and intelligence, 518–519
France, child-rearing patterns in, 364–365
Free association, in psychoanalytic practice, 17
French Canadians, child-rearing practices of, 364–365
  cognitive development of, 374
Freud, Anna, 19
Freud, Sigmund, 17–19, 119–125
Freudian theories, of moral development, 450
Friendship, 478–479
Frustration, as cause of aggression, 319–320
Future, preschoolers' concepts of, 278

Galton, Francis, 37
Gastrointestinal disturbances, 261
  during adolescence, 513
Genes, 66
Genetic/developmental approach, 25–29
Genetic explanations, of social-class differences in intelligence, 373–374
Genetic views, 81
Genetics, and development, 66–72
  and secular trend in height, 509–510
Genital stage, 124
German, learning of, 96
Gesell, Arnold, 20
Gesell Developmental Schedules, 145
Gestalt psychology, 119
Gestation, period of, 154
Goethe, Johann Wolfgang von, 534
Grammatical rules, learning of, 285–291
Grasping reflex, 74–75, 171
Gratification, learning to delay, 114–116
Greeks, ancient, attitudes toward children, 4
Guatemalan infants, malnourishment in, 180

Habituation, of neonates, 157-158
Hall, G. Stanley, 10-13, 30
Hallucinogens, and fetal stress, 147
Hammill, Peter V. V., 509
Harmonious parenting, 61
Hawaiian children, independence and dependence in, 332-333
　intellectual development of, 366
　and locus of control, 372
Head Start Program, 78-79
Healy, William, 20-21
Height, changes in, during adolescence, 509-510
　increases between birth and twenty years, 178-179
　of preschool children, 260
　relationship to weight, 180-182
Helping behavior, in preschool years, 384
Hemoglobin deficiencies, and malnutrition, 180-182
Hemophilia, 68
"Hidden curriculum," in home, 367
Hierarchization, in development, 88
Hierarchy, of responses, 103
Holistic view, of development, 72-73
Holtzman Inkblot Technique (HIT), 56
Hopi Indian infants, 69, 185
Hostility, defined, 470
Humanistic psychology, 119
Hyperactivity, 395-398, 447
　in American Indian and Anglo-American children, 69
Hyperkinesis, 395-398, 447
　in low-birth-weight children, 158
Hypothesis, in research, 33, 39
　in Kagan's theory, 200

Id, 120-125
Id rewards, 371
Identification, and social learning, 105-109
Identity, appearance of, 331
Identity diffusion, 129
　during adolescence, 550-552
　among college women, 552
Idiographic approaches, to study of personality, 119
Illness, and child development, 259, 261
Imitation, and aggression, 320-323
　and language learning, 286-287
　in neonates and infants, 188-189
　and social learning, 105-109
Imprinting, 76
Impulsivity, 430-431
Independence, and achievement motivation, 441
　and child-rearing practices, 438-439
　in Hawaiian children, 332-333
　infant strivings for, 245-249
　during preschool years, 330-333, 350
　and self-concept, 249
Independent variable, 40-42
Indian (American) children, 371
Indian (Hindu) children, 55
　and obedience, 465-466
Industrial Revolution, and behavior toward children, 8-9
Infancy, appearance of anxiety during, 312
　appearance of smiling response in, 312
　attention to unusual stimuli in, 198-201
　changes in height and weight during, 177-181
　classical conditioning in, 207
　cognitive development during, 191-193
　crying and mothers' responses, 207
　definition of, 176-177
　depth perception in, 202-205
　development of locomotion skills during, 186-188
　development of manipulation skills during, 185-186
　development of means for affecting environment in, 195
　development of schemas in, 192-193
　development of symbolization during, 211
　developmental patterns of language learning during, 209-211
　early linguistic development during, 207-208
　effect of institutions during, 213-214
　emotional development during, 311-313, 317-318, 324-325
　exploratory behavior during, 201-202
　habituation in, 180
　hemoglobin deficiencies in, 180-182
　independence strivings during, 331
　intellectual development during, 214-218
　language development in, 204-214
　learning of discrimination during, 207
　learning through imitation in, 188-189
　negativism during, 331
　nutrition and malnutrition during, 180-184
　"object concept" development in, 192-193
　operant conditioning in, 208
　orienting response in, 180, 203
　perception and sensation in, 194
　perceptual-conceptual development in,

Subject Index

194-214
physical growth during, 177-181
play patterns during, 202
relationship between perception and language development in, 206-207
responses to cuddling during, 329-330
sensorimotor development during, 184-191
and sex differences in sensorimotor development, 189-191
smiling response in, 312
weight gain during, 180
Infant mortality, and birth weight, 146-147
rates, of, 155
Instincts, in personality development, 119-125
Institutional care, and personality development, 361-362
Institutional residence, and language development, 294
Instrumental conditioning, 102-105
Integration, in development, 74-75
Intellectual development, during adolescence, 516-518
and birth order, 375-379
of early and late maturers, 518
in the Early Training Project, 299-301
and home environment, 353, 366
longitudinal studies, of, 302-305
in the Milwaukee Project, 230-231
and precocity, 304
and problem-solving ability, 305-307
and "Sesame Street," 301-302
Intelligence, changes in adult years, 59
defined, 409-410
effects of early intervention on, 417-419
effects of stimulation in home on, 216, 218
environmental effects on, 418, 421-422
of infants, scales for measuring, 214-217
and influence of teachers' attitudes, 416
racial differences in, 419-421
as related to fears in preschool years, 314
Intelligence tests, 410-422
controversies regarding, 416-417
and school success, 413
validity of, 412-416
Internal-External (I-E) Scale, 432-434
Intervention programs, 78-79
the Early Training Project, 299-301
the Milwaukee Project, 230-231
Interviews, in research, 52-54
Introjection, and social learning, 108-109
IQ, meaning of, 411

IQ gain, 78
as result of early intervention, 230-231, 299-301
Israeli children, 223, 250
Italian children, 89
Ivory Coast, breast-feeding campaign in, 235

Japanese children, 96-97
Jung, Carl, 125

Kagan, Jerome, 200
Kibbutzim, 223, 250
Korean orphans, as adopted by American parents, 182-184

Lamaze method, 153
Language acquisition device, 285
Language development, 283-291
of deaf children, 282-283
effects of stimulation on, 213-214
environmental theories of, 286-288
in infants, 204-214
in low-birth-weight children, 158
and motor development, 285-286
nativistic theories of, 283-286
in preschool children, 281-298
and problem solving, 295-296
reinforcement and nativistic theories of, 211-213
and semantics, 291-292
sex differences in, 294
and structuring of the environment, 290
Language-delayed children, and maternal behavior, 354-355
Laughter, 324-327
Learning, autogenous, 263
and development, 89-92
and socialization, 97-109
Lebanese orphans, effect of adoption on, 231
Libido, 119-125
Listening ability, and learning to read, 408
Locke, John, 6-8
Locomotion skills, development of, in infants, 186-188
Locus of control, 372, 431-434, 555-556
Logical structure, in preschool children, 273-274
Longitudinal research, 41, 58-60
Love, mother as source of, 231-232
parental, 116-118
Low-birth-weight infants, 146-148
and maternal alcohol use, 148
problems of, 158-159

Low-birth-weight infants, (cont.)
  stimulation of, 163, 228-229
  and wartime famine, 183
Lysergic acid diethylamide (LSD-25), effects on fetus, 147-148

Malnutrition, and child development, 259, 260, 262
  and habituation, 180
  and the orienting response, 180
  and vitamin deficiencies, 180-184
Marasmus, 241
Matching Familiar Figures Test, 431-433
Maternal attitudes, during pregnancy, 149-153
  and infant behavior, 236-237
Maternal care, research on, 35
Maternal deprivation, animal research on, 242-245
Maternal employment, 444
Maternal nutrition, during pregnancy, 145-147
Maternal warmth, 117
  and children's personality development, 236
Maturation, 89-92
  early and late, 510-512, 518
  in preschool children, 263
  relationship to learning in infants, 185
  secular trend in, 508-510
Mechanisms of defense, 122
Meconium, 144
Medieval attitudes, toward children, 4
Menarche, arrival of, 509-510
Menstrual cycle, 138
Mental health specialists, and attitudes toward children's misbehavior, 493-494
Mental retardation, and impoverished environments, 230
  and maternal interaction, 146
  as measured by the Binet scale, 13
Mesoderm, 139-140
Metapalet, in kibbutzim, 250
Méthode clinique, 1a, 53-54, 79
Methylphenidate, as treatment for hyperactivity, 398
Mexican children, cognitive development of, 273, 301-303, 402
  and morality, 452-453
  personality development of, 56, 60
Mexican-American families, and teenager drug usage, 541-542
Mexican-American mothers, 44
Milk temperature, and neonates' reactions, 168
Milwaukee Project, 230-231
Minimal brain dysfunction (MBD), 395-398
Misbehavior, and father absence, 357-361
  learning avoidance of, 116
  teachers' attitudes toward, 493-494
Modeling, and aggression, 320-323
  and helping others, 384
  as social learning, 105-109
Monozygotic (MZ) twins, 70-72
Montessori, Maria, 11, 14-15
Montessori methods, 407
Moral development, in adolescence, 524-530
  in elementary school years, 448-455
  experimental studies of, 453-455
  Freudian views of, 450
  in Mexican and American children, 452-453
  and parental discipline, 455
  Piagetian views of, 451-453
  theories of, 449-452
Moral judgment, 54
  and cognitive ability, 528-530
  and educational experiences, 526-527
  influence of parents on, 525
  and law and order, 528
"More" and "less," learning concepts of, 274
Moro reflex, 170
Mother's voice, child's responses to, 40-42
Mothers, employed outside home, 250-251
  as source of love and attention, 231-232
  substitute or surrogate, 245-246, 249-253
Motivation, to achieve, 299, 440-442, 543-546
  affiliative, 477, 543-546
  Freudian views of, 119-125
Motor development, in infants, stimulation of, 229
  and language development, 285-286
Motor skills, sex differences in, 268
  stages of, 264-268

Narcotics addiction, and fetal stress, 147
National Assessment of Educational Progress (NAEP), 521
Nativistic theories of language development, 212, 283-286
Navajo children, 445
Need for achievement. *See* Achievement need
Need for affiliation. *See* affiliation need

Subject Index 619

Negativism, during infancy, 331
Neonates, conditioning of, 172-173
  effects of analgesic drugs given to mothers, 157-158
  imitation in, 188-189
  learning in, 172-173
  motor responses of, 168-173
  need for stimulation, 163-165
  nourishment of, 160-161
  orientation toward stimuli, 157-158
  orienting response in, 172
  oxygen needs of, 162
  physical needs of, 160-165
  physical proportions of, 159-160
  reflexes of, 169-172
  REM sleep of, 161-162
  sensory responses in, 165-168
  sex differences in empathy, 167
  sleep patterns of, 161-162
  smiling in, 157-158
  sucking of fingers and hands by, 167
  tremulousness of, 157
Neonates' reactions, to auditory stimuli, 166-167
  to color, 166
  to crying sounds, 167
  to flavors, 167-168
  to milk temperature, 168
  to olfactory stimuli, 167
  to sugar solutions, 168
  to visual stimuli, 165-166
Netherlands children, 441
New Guinea cultures, and sex typing of behavior, 340
Newborn, See neonates
Newton, Isaac, 30
Nicotine, effects on birth weight, 148
Nomothetic approaches, to personality study, 119
Nonreversal shift, in problem solving, 306-307

Obedience, in Hindu and American boys, 465-466
Obesity, in adolescence, 513
  and prejudice, in children, 481
Observation, learning through, 105-109
Observations, in research 50-52
Occupational choice, during adolescence, 557-561
Oedipus complex, 123-124
Operant learning, 102-105
  in infants, 208
Operation Head Start, 78-79, 422
Opiates, and fetal stress, 147

Oral stage, 123
Orderliness, in home environments, psychological importance of, 346
Orienting response, in infants, 203
  in neonates, 172-173
Overachievers, 445, 470
Overcompensation, in late-maturing adolescents, 512
Oviducts, 138
Ovulation, 138
  as delayed by breast feeding, 233

Parental Attitudes Research Instrument (PARI), 52, 440
Parental control, and children's personality development, 349-352
Parental discipline, and moral development, 455
Parental harshness, and social-class differences, 364-365
Parental warmth, and social learning, 108-109
Parents, adolescent conflicts with, 535-537
  as authorities, 116-118
  as caregivers, 223
  control by, 116-118
  moral influence of, 525
  as observers of children's behavior, 473
  and their understanding of adolescents, 538-539
  warmth of, 116-118
Past, preschoolers' concepts of, 278
Patience, the learning of, 114-116
Pavlov, I. P., 16, 100-101
Peer acceptance, and grade-point average, 545-546
Peer Groups, as compared with family, 461
  attitudes toward adult standards, 462-464
  as disinhibitors, 465-467
  influence during adolescence, 542-549
  influence during childhood years, 461-467
  as reference groups, 462
  and social norms, 461-462
Peer relationships, and helping others, 384
  in play, 380
  in preschool years, 379-384
Perceptual development, in preschool children, 274-275
Permissiveness, in parents, 61, 116-118, 350-352, 444
Personality, idiographic and nomothetic views of, 119

Personality development, and birth order, 375–379
  dynamic theories of, 118–129
  as influenced by child-rearing patterns, 349–352
  in preschool years, 327–341
  psychoanalytic theories of, 118–129
  and socialization, 95–134
  and temperament, 327–330
Peruvian children, and malnutrition, 181–182
Pestalozzi, Johann Heinrich, 7–8
Phallic stage, 123–124
Physical defects, and prenatal care, 146
Physical skills, during adolescence, 507–508
  during elementary school years, 391–398
Piaget, Jean, 8, 25, 28, 270–274, 276, 278
Piagetian concepts, 79–87, 269–273, 514–516
  criticisms of, 86–87
pivot- and open-class words, 287–288, 291
Placenta, 139–140
Plasticity, of behavior, 69
Play, in infancy, 202, 216–218
  observations of, in research and therapy, 57
  during preschool years, 380
"Plaza Sesamo," 301–303
Plutarch, 137
Popularity, and intelligence, 415–416
"Popularity cult," during adolescence, 545–549
Pornography, adolescents' attitudes toward, 566–567
Postnatal care, and brain damage, 146
Praise, effects on behavior, 42–43
  effects of teacher's, 490–492
Precocity, verbal, 304
Pregnancy, 138–154
  fear of, 151–154
  length of, 154
  and maternal nutrition, 145–147
  and the mother, 149–154
  among unmarried teenagers, 563–564
  women's attitudes toward, 149–154
Prejudice, 479–484
  toward obese children, 480–481
  toward opposite-sex children, 480–482
  toward other ethnic groups, 481–484
Premature infants. See low-birth-weight infants
Prenatal care, and brain damage, 146
Prenatal development, 138–154
Preoperational stage, 83

Preschool years, aggressiveness during, 317–323
  anger responses during, 317–323
  anxiety during, 312–316
  cognitive development during, 268–278
  development of independence in, 330–333
  emotional development in, 310–327
  family influences during, 344–379
  fantasy violence in, 316–317
  fear during, 312–316
  health problems in, 261–262
  intellectual development during, 298–307
  interest in violence during, 316
  language development in, 281–298
  motor development in, 264–268
  parental control during, 349–352
  peer relationships during, 379–384
  personality development in, 327–341
  physical growth in, 260
  play patterns in, 380
  prosocial behavior in, 383–384
  self-concept development during, 333–334
  sensorimotor development in, 263–268
  sex-typing in, 336–341
  sharing behavior during, 383–384
  social behavior during, 382–384
  social environment during, 344–379
Preyer, William T., 10
Progressive Eduation, 21
Projection, 122
Projective tests, 55–57
Prosocial behavior, and social learning, 109–110, 112
Proximodistal development, 73
Psychoanalysis, 17–19
Psychoanalytic theory, and breast feeding, 236
Psycholinguistics, 283–288
Psychosexual development, Freudian stages in, 122–125
Psychosocial stages, 127
Psychosomatic symptoms, during pregnancy, 150
Punishment, 105, 116
Punitivity of parents, and children's self-esteem, 435, 436–437, 444
Purdue Opinion Poll, 529, 538–539
"Pygmalion" study, 416

Questionnaires, invention of, 12
  use of in research, 52

Race prejudice, 481-484
Racial differences, in neonate size, 160
  and social class, 373
Radiation, and fetal stress, 148
Rapid-eye-movement (REM) sleep, 161-162, 164
  and tumescence, 165
Rapists, early family experiences of, 435-436
Rationalization, 429
Raven's Progressive Matrices, 419-420
Reading, and effects of anxiety, teachers' praise or criticism, and social class, 490-492
  effects of interest and revelance on, 427-429
  learning of, 404-408
Reality principle, in psychoanalysis, 121
Reasoning, in preschool children, 275-278
Recapitulation, theory of, 10
Reference group, and peer group, 462
Reflex, Darwinian or grasping, 74-75, 171-172
Reflexes, in neonates, 169-172
Regression, and frustration, 319-320
Reinforcement, and aggression, 322-323
  in behavior modification, 488-492
  and language learning, 286-287
  learning to delay, 114-116
  negative, 105
  positive, 103
  by teachers, 488-492
Rejection, as resulting from nonconformity, 114
Reliability, in research, 35-37
Replicability, in research, 39
Repression, 122, 429
Reproductive system, female, 138
Respiratory infections, 261
Response-response (R-R) research, 43-49, 219
Responses, hierarchy of, 103
Reversal shift, in problem solving, 306-307
Reversibility, and conservation, 399
  in school years, 404
Rh blood factors, 148-149
Rheingold, Harriet L., 248
Ribonucleic acid (RNA), 66
Right- and left-handedness, 68
Ritalin, as prescribed for hyperactivity, 397
Role-playing, 477, 479
Romans, attitude toward children, 4
Rooming-in, after childbirth, 154
Rooting reflex, 170-171

Rorschach test, 56-57
"Rosenthal effect," 55, 144
Rousseau, Jean-Jacques, 6-8
Russian children, 462-464, 546

Samoan adolescents, 23
Schaffer, H. L., 248
Schemas, 81
  development of, during infancy, 192-193, 198-201
Scholastic Aptitude Test (SAT) scores, recent declines in, 521-524
School, and behavior modification, 488-492
  children's attitudes toward, 494-497
  and developmental tasks, 485
  and peer group, 459-499
  praise and criticism in, 490-492
  teachers' role in, 485-494
School achievement. See achievement
School attendance, compulsory, 9
Scientific method, 33-46
Scott, Walter, 503
Sears, Robert R., 26, 53
Secular trend, in height, 509
  in sexual maturity, 508-510
Security, need for, 344-345
Seguin, Edouard, 14
Self, psychology of the, 28
Self-assertion, appearance of, 331
Self-awareness, 331
  development of during school years, 442-448
  and the ego, 121
Self-concept, and independence in infants, 249
  origins of, 334-335
  during preschool years, 333-341
Self-demand, in feeding neonates, 160-161
Self-esteem, 55
  in preschool years, 334
  studies in 443-445
Self-reinforcement, in social learning, 106-107
Self-rejection, and prejudice, 483
Self-restraint, learning of, 114-116
Semantics, and language development, 291-292
Sensorimotor development, in elementary school years, 392-398
  during preschool years, 263-268
Sensorimotor stage, 82
Sensory adaptation, in neonates, 157-158
Separation anxiety, 312
  in infants, 239

Sephardic culture, 371-372
"Sesame Street," 301-303, 484
Sex differences, and age at puberty, 506, 508-510
   and aggressiveness, 467-471
   and attitudes toward sex, 566-567
   controversies about, 189-191
   in empathy, 167
   and fear of success, 552-557
   in health problems during adolescence, 513
   in height and weight, 178-179
   in infants, 41
   in language development, 294
   in physical skills during adolescence, 507-508
   prejudices based on, 480-482
   in preschoolers' responses to tickling and cuddling, 326
   in reading ability, 427-429
   in sensorimotor development, 189-191
   in sensorimotor skills, 394-395
   and social distance in children, 480-482
   in willingness to help others, 324
Sex stereotypes, emergence of, 339
Sex-typing, origins of, 336-341
   and social learning, 337-341
Sexual adjustment, in deprived monkeys, 76
   during adolescence, 561-568
Sexual maturity, secular trend in, 508-510
Share, learning to, 109-110
Sharing, in preschool children, 383-384
Shyness, and father absence, 360
   during preschool years, 312-313
Sibling rivalry, 125
Siblings, as caregivers, 223
Simon, Theodore, 13, 79, 410
Skinner, B. F., 103
Sleep pattern, from birth through old age, 162
Smiling response, 157-158, 312, 324-327
Smith, Logan Pearsall, 533
Smoking, mothers', effects on infant birth weight, 148
"Sobering," in infants, 312
Social attraction, 474-484
   and friendship, 478-479
   and similarity, 475-477
   sociometric studies of, 474-479
Social awareness, and empathy, 477-479
Social deprivation, effects on behavior, 44-46
Social development, and child-rearing practices, 356-357

Social distance, 480-481
Social ecology, of small town, 460
Social isolation, of rhesus monkeys, 227
Social learning, 105-109
   and aggression, 320-323, 472-474
   and aggressiveness, 435, 437-438
   and helping others, 384
   in infants, 236
   and moral development, 453-454
Social learning theory, 86-87
Social norms, cross-cultural differences in, 462-464
   and peer group, 461-462
Social psychology, and child psychology, 27-28
Social responsibility, in parents and children, 352
Social roles, and empathy, 477
Social sensitivity, 477
Social skills, 479
Social-class differences, and adolescent roles, 505
   and attitudes of mothers toward pregnancy, 151-152
   and attitudes toward school, 495-496
   and child-rearing patterns, 362-368, 436-437
   and children's problem-solving ability, 364-365
   and conservation ability, 273
   and crowding in home, 368-371
   and effects of malnutrition, 180-182
   and ethnicity, 372-373
   and intelligence, 415, 418-422
   and language development, 295-298
   and mothers' vocal interaction with infants, 213
   and neonate size, 160
   and occupational choice, 558-559
   and parental harshness, 363-365
   and prenatal and postnatal care, 146
   and reaction toward rewards, 491-492
   and reactions to teachers' praise or criticism, 490-491
Social-class research, criticisms of, 373-374
Socialization, 95-97
   and altruistic or prosocial behavior, 109-110, 112
   and anxiety, 314
   and avoidance of misbehavior, 116
   and classical conditioning, 100-102
   and identification, 105-109
   and imitation, 105-109
   and instrumental or operant condition-

ing, 102–105
and learning, 97
and modeling, 105–109
and need for arousal, 111–113
and needs and drives, 110–111
Neo-Freudian theories of, 125–128
and observation, 105–109
and parental control, 116
and parental warmth, 116
and personality development, 95–134
psychoanalytic theories, of, 118–129
and punishment, 105, 116
reward value of, 113–114
Socioeconomic status (SES). See social-class differences
Sociogram, 476
Sociolinguistic theory, 292–294
Sociometry, 474–479
Space, preschoolers' understanding of, 276
Sperm, 138
S-R. See stimulus-response
Stanford-Binet Scale, 13–14, 410–412
Startle reflex, 170
Stillborn infants, 146
Stimulation, early, 226–240
Stimulus-response (S-R) research, 25–29, 39–43
Strong Vocational Interest Blank, 558
Sublimation, 122
Sucking, of fingers and hands by neonates, 167
Sucking reflex, 170–171
Sudden infant death syndrome (SIDS), 163
Suicide, adolescent, 534
Superego, 120–125
Superego rewards, 371
Surrogate mothers, 245–246, 249–253
Swimming reflex, 172
Symbolization, in infants, 211
Synesthesia, 275

Tactile contact, in infants monkeys, 244–245
Tape-recorded interviews, in research, 52
Teacher-expectancy effects, and students' performance, 416
Teachers, attitudes of, toward children's misbehavior, 492–494
as models, 109
praise or criticism by, 490–492
Teachers' values, effect of, 485–488
Television, and children's behavior, 50
effect on children's aggressiveness, 474
influence on children's emotions, 316

Temperament, 327–330
Temptation, resistance to, 449, 465–466
Terman, Lewis Madison, 11, 13–14, 410
Testing, psychological, 20
Thalidomide, and fetal abnormalities, 148
Thematic Apperception Test (TAT), 56–57, 150
Thinking, as "subvocal speech," 282
Thorndike, Edward L., 21–22, 292–293
Time, preschoolers' concepts of, 276–278
Toilet training, 123
and children's personality development, 236
Transactional psychology, 119
Tremulousness, in neonates, 157
Trophoblast, 139
Tuareg adolescents, 504
Tumescence, of neonates genitals, 165
Twins, study of, 70–72
maturation and learning in, 185
verbal development of, 370

Umbilical cord, 139, 142
Unconditioned response (UCR), 100–102
Unconditioned stimulus (UCS), 100–102
Unconscious, the, 19
Unconscious motivation, in Freudian theory, 120–121
Underachievers, 445, 470
Unobtrusive methods, 55–57
Unwed mothers, adolescent, 563–564
Urbanized societies, and adolescents, 533–534
Uterus, 138
Uzgiris-Hunt Ordinal Scales for Infant Development, 193, 195, 214–215

Validity, of psychological measures, 37
of projective tests, 56
Variables, in research, 37
Videotaped behavior, 50
Villi, 139–140
Visual cliff apparatus, 203–205
Vitamin deficiencies, 181–182
Vocabulary, growth of, 291, 292–294
Vocational aspirations, reality of, 558–559
Vulnerability, during critical periods, 77

Walking, development of, 187–188
Walking reflex, 172
Wariness, among infants, 239
Watson, J. D., 66
Watson, John B., 16–17
Weaning, and Children's personality development, 236

Wechsler Intelligence Scale for Children (WISC), changes in scores from ages 6 to 18, 517
Wechsler intelligence scales, 411–412
Weight, changes in, during adolescence, 509–510
  of preschool children, 260
Weight gain, during infancy, 180
Werther, Sorrows of, 534
Wilkins, M., 66

Withdrawing behavior, seriousness of, 493–494
Womb, 138
X-rays, and fetal stress, 148
XYY chromosomes, 68–69
Yolk sac, 139
Zambia, breast-feeding campaign in, 234
Zuñi infants, 69
Zygote, 66, 138–139, 141, 147